HANDBOOK OF MIDDLE AMERICAN INDIANS

EDITED AT MIDDLE AMERICAN RESEARCH INSTITUTE, TULANE UNIVERSITY

ROBERT WAUCHOPE, *General Editor*

MARGARET A. L. HARRISON, *Associate Editor*

INIS PICKETT, *Administrative Assistant*

DAVID S. PHELPS, THOMAS S. SCHORR, KENNETH E. OWEN, *Art Staff*

LORENE GREGG CAMPBELL, *Indexer*

ASSEMBLED WITH THE AID OF A GRANT FROM THE NATIONAL SCIENCE FOUNDATION, AND UNDER THE SPONSORSHIP OF THE NATIONAL RESEARCH COUNCIL COMMITTEE ON LATIN AMERICAN ANTHROPOLOGY

Editorial Advisory Board

IGNACIO BERNAL, HOWARD F. CLINE, GORDON F. EKHOLM, NORMAN A. MCQUOWN, MANNING NASH, T. DALE STEWART, EVON Z. VOGT, ROBERT C. WEST, GORDON R. WILLEY

HANDBOOK OF MIDDLE AMERICAN INDIANS

ROBERT WAUCHOPE, General Editor

VOLUME TWO

Archaeology of Southern Mesoamerica

PART ONE

GORDON R. WILLEY, Volume Editor

UNIVERSITY OF TEXAS PRESS ✦ AUSTIN

Published in Great Britain by the
University of Texas Press, Ltd., London

Library of Congress Catalog Card No. 65–10316
Copyright © 1965 by the University of Texas Press
All rights reserved.

The preparation and publication of the
Handbook of Middle American Indians
has been assisted by grants from
the National Science Foundation.

Typesetting by G&S Typesetters, Austin, Texas
Printing by Meriden Gravure Company, Meriden, Connecticut
Binding by Universal Bookbindery, Inc., San Antonio, Texas

CONTENTS

vii

(Continued in Vol. 3)

HANDBOOK OF MIDDLE AMERICAN INDIANS, VOLUME 2

Archaeology of Southern Mesoamerica, Part 1

GENERAL EDITOR'S NOTE

The manuscripts for the following articles were submitted at various dates over a period of two and one-half years. Because of revisions and minor updatings made from time to time, it is difficult to assign a date to each article. In some cases, an indication of when an article was completed can be had by noting the latest dates in the list of references at the end of each contribution.

1. Archaeological Synthesis of the Guatemalan Highlands

STEPHAN F. DE BORHEGYI

THE HIGHLAND MAYA culture area, here defined as those parts of central Guatemala and eastern Chiapas having an altitude of over 2000 feet, can be divided into five geographical and cultural units: (1) the *Hilly Middle Country* of Guatemala (Departments of El Quiche, Alta Verapaz, and Baja Verapaz); (2) the *Western Highlands* of Guatemala (Departments of Huehuetenango, San Marcos, Quezaltenango, Totonicapan, and Solola) and eastern Chiapas, Mexico; (3) the *Central Highlands* of Guatemala (Departments of Chimaltenango, Sacatepequez, and Guatemala; (4) the *Semiarid Eastern Lowlands* of Guatemala (Departments of El Progreso, Zacapa, Jalapa, and Chiquimula; and (5) the *Pacific Coastal Plains and Piedmont* of Guatemala (Departments of Retalhuleu, San Marcos, Suchitepequez, Quezaltenango, Escuintla, Santa Rosa, and Jutiapa) and western Salvador (Departments of Santa Ana, Ahuachapan, and Sonsonate). (Cf. Borhegyi, 1956b, p. 345, and fig. 107.)[1]

In this synthesis we are concerned primarily with the archaeology of the Western and Central Highlands of Guatemala (fig. 1, C, D) although occasional references will be made to the Hilly Middle Country (fig. 1, B). The archaeology of the Chiapas highlands (Lowe and Mason, Article 9), the Eastern Lowlands of Guatemala (fig. 1, E), and the Coastal Plains and Piedmont of Guatemala and Chiapas (fig. 1, F) will be dealt with elsewhere in this volume (Lowe and Mason, Article 9; Shook, Article 8).

The Western and Central Highlands of Guatemala are part of the long, rugged volcanic ranges of the Sierra Madre and con-

[1] I wish to express my thanks to Richard B. Woodbury, A. Ledyard Smith, Sue W. Miles, Robert L. Rands, and particularly to A. V. Kidder for their comments and for allowing me to read their contributions to this *Handbook* in advance of publication; to Michael D. Coe and Lee Parsons for their many helpful ideas; to Gordon R. Willey for useful suggestions; to Lee Tishler, Milwaukee Public Museum artist, for his art work on the charts and maps.

3

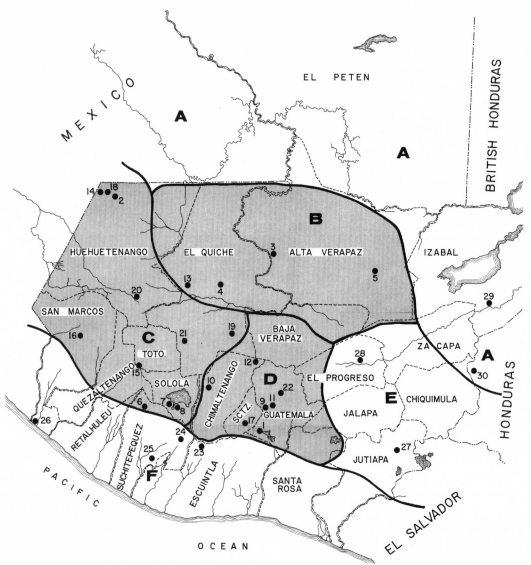

Fɪɢ. 1—MAP OF THE SOUTHERN MAYA AREA

Culture areas (after Borhegyi, 1956a): A, Tropical Rain Forest. B, Hilly Middle Country. C, Western Highlands. D, Central Highlands. E, Semiarid Eastern Lowlands. F, Pacific Coastal Plains and Piedmont.

Archaeological sites (capital letters in parentheses indicate location in culture areas; asterisks represent major excavations):

1. Amatitlan (D), Dept. Guatemala (Borhegyi, 1958b, 1959b, 1960a, 1961d).
2. Chacula (C), Dept. Huehuetenango (Seler, 1901).
3. Chama (B), Dept. Alta Verapaz (Dieseldorff, 1904; Butler, 1940).
4. Chipal (B), Dept. El Quiche (Burkitt, 1930a; Butler, 1940, 1959).
5. Chipoc (B), Dept. Alta Verapaz (R. E. Smith, 1952).

6. Chocola (C), Dept. Suchitepequez (Burkitt, 1930a).
7. Chuitinamit (C), Dept. Solola (Lothrop, 1933).
8. Chukumuk (C), Dept. Solola (Lothrop, 1933).
9. Cotio (D), Dept. Guatemala (Shook, 1952a).
10. *Iximche (D), Dept. Chimaltenango (Guillemín, 1959).
11. *Kaminaljuyu (D), Dept. Guatemala (Gamio, 1926–27; Lothrop, 1926a; Kidder, 1945, 1948; Kidder, Jennings, and Shook, 1946; Shook and Kidder, 1952; Shook, 1951a; Berlin, 1952).
12. *Mixco Viejo (D), Dept. Chimaltenango (A. L. Smith, 1955; Guillemín, 1958).
13. *Nebaj (B), Dept. El Quiche (Burkitt, 1930b; Smith and Kidder, 1951).
14. Quen Santo (C), Dept. Huehuetenango (Seler, 1901).

(Continued on facing page)

4

stitute the most spectacular feature of the country. They parallel the narrow Pacific Coastal Plain, from which they rise abruptly, and are edged on the south by a line of lofty, geologically young and active volcanoes, many of which reach altitudes of 12,000–13,000 feet. Behind these young volcanic peaks to the north there is a time-smoothed older volcanic complex, its valleys and plateaus deeply covered with volcanic ash. Farther to the north and northwest (Departments of Huehuetenango, El Quiche, and Baja Verapaz) the highlands culminate in the still more ancient crystalline metamorphic massif of the Cuchumatanes and Chuacus Mountains.

The cool, inner highland region, commonly referred to as Los Altos or Tierra Fria, consists of high and fertile valleys and pine- and oak-fringed plateaus enclosed by rugged mountain chains at elevations of 5000–8000 feet (fig. 1, C, D). To the north and south are rolling cypress-covered, subtropical foothills known as Tierra Templada. The land in the highlands is well drained by swift rivers flowing south to the Pacific Ocean from the volcanic rampart (Suchiate, Samala, Nahualate, Coyolate, Michatoya, Naranjo, Maria Linda Rivers); northeast to the Gulf of Honduras (the drainage systems of the Motagua and Polochic Rivers); and northwest to the Gulf of Campeche (Grijalva, Chixoy, Negro, Salinas, and Usumacinta Rivers).

The soil, largely of volcanic origin, is fertile; in some areas rainfall is adequate for two planting seasons. The fact that this area contained the wild forebears of such potentially domesticable food plants as maize, common bean (Phaseolus vulgaris), chili, tomatoes, squash, sweet potatoes, sweet manioc, and avocados provided man with the means to produce his own food and ultimately develop a complex civilization. Besides good soil, temperate to cool climate, and ample arable land, the highlands had many other advantages:

A. Mineral resources

1. Volcanic stone (lava) for grinding stones (metates and manos) and other artifacts, religious sculptures, and construction in the later periods.
2. Lime for mortar, corn-gruel preparation.
3. Obsidian for projectile points, weapons, cutting implements, inlays, ornaments.
4. Good clay for pottery making, wall plastering.
5. Volcanic ash (tuff) and mica for temper in pottery.
6. Iron pyrite for mosaic mirrors, inlays.
7. Specular hematite and cinnabar for red paint.
8. Copper and some gold (washed from streams) for ornaments and utensils in later periods.
9. Jade and albite for ornaments, inlays, currency (along the Motagua River valley, Departments of El Progreso and Zacapa).
10. Salt (in the Sacapulas area and along

---

the Chixoy or Salinas River, Department of El Quiche).

B. Streams and lakes
   1. Irrigation.
   2. Fresh-water fish and shellfish.
C. Forests
   1. Fuel, tools, containers, weapons, musical instruments, construction.
   2. Bark (principally from *Ficus*) for clothing, bed covers, buckets, paper making, ritual use.
   3. Aromatic pine resins for incense (*pom*) in magical and religious rituals.
   4. Pitch pine (*ocote*) sticks for outdoor illumination.
   5. Silk cotton (*kapok*) for quilted armor.
D. Useful plants
   1. Cotton.
   2. Agave, maguey, and rushes for fiber cords, rope, carrying bags, mats, woven baskets, garments, fermented drinks such as *pulque*.
   3. Calabashes, gourds, and reeds for containers, musical instruments.
   4. Medicinal herbs and dyes.
   5. Tobacco for medicinal use (along the Motagua River valley).
   6. Edible fruits such as passion fruit, pitaya, papaya, jocote, and avocado.
E. Useful animals
   1. Bees for honey and wax, for ceremonial use and fermented drinks.
   2. Birds (quetzal, cotinga, parrot) for feathers, headdresses, and cloaks (especially in the Cuchumatanes Mountains in Huehuetenango and in the Sierra de las Minas range in the Alta Verapaz).
   3. Turtles, iguanas, lizards, and armadillos for eggs, meat, and carapace.
   4. Semi-domesticated animals (turkey, quail) for eggs, meat, and ceremonial offerings.
   5. Game animals (white-tailed deer, rabbit, peccary, monkey, turkey, quail, duck, and other waterfowl) for meat, hides, furs, feathers, teeth, and claws.
F. Accessibility to Pacific coastal area.
   1. Cacao beans for ceremonial drink (*Chacau-haa*) and currency.
   2. Sea salt and various nutritious seafoods.
   3. Sea shells for ornaments and currency.
   4. Fruits and vegetables growing at lower altitudes.
   5. Palm leaves for raincoats, fire fans, thatching, and ceremonial use.
G. Accessibility to major trade routes (both land and sea) north and south from Mexico to South America.

PALEO-INDIAN OR PRECERAMIC PERIOD (EARLY HUNTERS AND FOOD COLLECTORS) 15,000 (OR EARLIER)–1,500 B.C.

The Highlands and the Pacific Coast of Guatemala were, like the rest of Central America, part of a land bridge over which early man made his way from North to South America. Although traces have been found of these early hunting bands in North America, Mexico, and even in South America, almost nothing is known of their journey through Central America. Until recently the only evidence of Upper Pleistocene fauna in Highland and Eastern Guatemala consisted of a few fossilized glyptodon, *elephas*, and mastodon bones found by paleontologists in the Departments of Guatemala, Quezaltenango, Huehuetenango, Zacapa, and Santa Rosa (Shook, 1951a, pp. 93–96). However, in 1960 M. D. Coe called attention to a black-gray obsidian fluted point in the private collection of Carlos Nottebohm in Guatemala City. This "Clovis-like" point (57 mm. long) with "fish-tail" ear protrusions at the bottom, was discovered by Nottebohm's son in 1956 a few miles west of the valley of Guatemala above the town of Mixco. Known as the San Rafael fluted point, it represents the first Paleo-Indian artifact found in Guatemala. According to M. D. Coe (1960b, p. 413), the San Rafael point is similar to other points reported from Durango, Mexico, and Costa Rica and seems to fit into the eastern Clovis series of fluted points known from Vermont to Alabama in the United States. As such, it may indicate that some of the earliest Paleo-Indian groups in Central America had predominantly east coast North American ori-

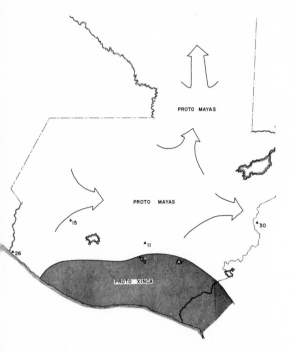

FIG. 2—EARLY PRECLASSIC PERIOD (1500–600
B.C.). Guatemalan highlands are inhabited by Pre- and
Proto-Maya groups; the Pacific Coastal area is occupied
by Proto-Xincas. Agricultural or fishing settlements, simple haphazardly arranged villages, are scattered throughout the valleys near rivers or lakes or on the ocean shore.

gins rather than west coast. Unfortunately,
we have no exact date for this early migration (Williams, 1952); we can only surmise
that early man entered the Guatemalan
highlands sometime between 15,000 and
6000 B.C. and that some of these hunting
groups later settled down to a sedentary
existence (cf. MacNeish, 1954, 1961, 1964).

Undoubtedly the economy of these early
Paleo-Indians was based on gathering wild
seeds, grains, nuts, berries and roots, and
hunting. They eventually learned to domes-
ticate food plants and to make simple
shelters which paved the way for village
life. Nothing is known of their physical
appearance since no skeletons belonging to
this early period have been found so far in
Guatemala. However, like Tepexpan "Man"
in Mexico, they were probably not unlike
recent Indians (cf. Aveleyra, 1959, fig. 2).

EARLY PRECLASSIC PERIOD (EARLY OR VIL-LAGE FORMATIVE PERIOD, EARLY FARMERS AND SEED PLANTERS) 1500–600 B.C.

The archaeological phases associated with
this period are: Arevalo (1500–1000 B.C.),
Las Charcas A (1000–600 B.C.), Valley of
Guatemala; Chiapa I-II, Chiapas.[2] (See
Table 1, p. 57.)

Modes of Subsistence

The first successful experiment in plant
domestication and food production in Guatemala probably took place at the end of the
preceding period somewhere in the Western

[2] Since recent radiocarbon dates are still tentative (Wauchope, 1954; Flint and Deevey, 1959),
the dates and names assigned to each developmental stage follow, with some modifications
(based on Warren, 1961), the chronological sequence presented by Shook (1952b, p. 4).
Shook's chronology has been recently challenged
by M. D. Coe (1961, p. 128, fig. 12), who believes that the highland Maya Preclassic, beginning with the Arevalo phase, is no older than 1200
B.C. Coe's data, combined with new findings from
Kaminaljuyu, suggest that the Las Charcas phase
should be divided into at least two components
(Las Charcas A, 1000–600 B.C. and Las Charcas
B, 600–500 B.C.) Moreover, Las Charcas B and
the Majadas phases (characterized by labial and
other lateral flanges) are not part of the Early
Preclassic, but are contemporaneous with the Middle Preclassic Providencia and Sacatepequez
phases. Since Shook's Majadas phase is based on
material found by him in a low platform mound
(C-III-6) at Kaminaljuyu in what appeared to be
a ceremonial cache, it may represent not a separate phase but simply intrusive material, most
probably from the Salcaja region of the Western
Highlands. For this reason I propose that the Majadas phase either be dropped from the Kaminaljuyu chronological sequence or be combined with
the Providencia phase (Table 1). On the other
hand, the Arevalo and Las Charcas A phases are
Early Formative in the Central Highlands and not
Middle Formative as Coe suggests. The Middle
Formative in the highlands is marked by the appearance of sizable burial mounds, basalt columnar stelae, carved jade, and labial or lateral
flanged pottery, such as found in the Las Charcas
B, Providencia and Sacatepequez phases. Since
many of these traits seem to represent La Venta
(Olmec) cultural influence, it is clear that these
periods should be set apart from those preceding
them, when La Venta influence was either nonexistent or negligible.

7

Highlands or on the hilly flanks of the Pacific Coastal Piedmont.[2a]

Stone metates and manos (as well as other milling and pounding instruments), found on the bottom of deep man-made storage pits in the archaeological zone of Las Charcas in the Valley of Guatemala and other places in the highlands, indicate that the Early Preclassic people who made these pits must have learned to reap and grind wild cereals and other plant foods. An intensified form of seed collection was made possible by the fact that these early food-gathering groups had learned to "live into" their environment. Later they acquired the intimate acquaintance with their habitat necessary for them to assume a manipulative role in the planting and reaping of certain edible wild plants, which in turn enabled and even required them to live in semipermanent communities.

There is every indication that by 1500 B.C. a sedentary way of life had come into being in the Guatemalan highlands based on a primitive method of agriculture. Gourds and food plants, primarily maize (in a small-eared form), squash (Cucurbita pepo), avocado, possibly some manioc, and later beans and chili peppers, were cultivated (Sauer, 1950, p. 508). Although we have no authentic knowledge of how these earliest farmers grew their crops, it was probably by slash-and-burn milpa farming, the planting done with the pointed wooden digging stick still used in most of Middle America. As today, the cultivation of a field was probably temporary. After the initial high yield, productivity decreased sharply and forced the farmer to move to new land to maintain his yield and support his family. A family or kin group therefore must have required a rather large

area to insure a productivity year after year.[3]

In the Guatemalan highlands during early Preclassic times maize was probably eaten much as it is today: in the immature form it is boiled and eaten from the cob, or made into a drink (atole); taken dried, it is parched, ground into meal, and cooked as flat, round cakes (tortillas) or boiled in a leaf-covering with a meat or other filling (tamales). The pre-Columbian diet was based on maize and supplemented with vitamin-rich chili peppers, squash, and pumpkin; protein- and fat-rich beans; lizard, especially iguana; turtle, iguana, and turkey eggs; turkey meat; various rodents, insects and seafood; and salt and honey. It was as healthful and well balanced as one based on meat and dairy products. At any rate, by 1500 B.C. corn, chili, and bean agriculture in the Guatemalan highlands permitted the support of a sizable population and the accumulation of sufficient food to encourage nonagricultural pursuits (cf. Termer, 1951, pp. 106–07).

Settlement Pattern and Architecture

From the scarce archaeological evidence, the settlement pattern of this formative period was probably the unplanned year-round farming village consisting of small clusters of mud-walled houses (two or three dozen) scattered over the landscape. Sites were apparently dictated primarily by agricultural needs and nearness of water. Located on level land near rivers and lakes or in the intermountain valleys and high plateaus, the sites were small, open, and undefended.[4]

[2a] Ed. note: No evidence has yet been adduced for this although possibly such will some day come to light. The most complete sequence for the development of Mesoamerican agriculture is that revealed in Puebla, Mexico (see Mangelsdorf, MacNeish, and Willey, Article 13, volume 1).

[3] According to Wolf (1959, pp. 58–59), an average Totonac family on the east coast of Mexico needs 30 acres to feed itself from field-forest rotation without declining yields. Among the Maya of Yucatan and the highlands, a family may have needed as much as 72–100 acres (see note 10). For a study of the milpa system at La Venta, and its archaeological implications, see Drucker and Heizer (1960).

[4] For a statistical point of view I have here

Evidence shows that in these open villages concentrations of conical or bottle-shaped pits, 3–4 m. deep with circular orifices, were dug through the sterile surface soil into the underlying volcanic ash (Shook, Kidder, 1952, fig. 1,b; Borhegyi, 1956b, p. 346). Some of these pits may have served the villagers as sweat baths for ritual purification and as a source of clay and ash; more were probably food storage chambers. When mold growth ended their usefulness for storing food, they were filled sometimes with sterile soil, sometimes with household debris, and occasionally even with simple burials.[5]

depended on Shook's (1952b) archaeological site survey of the Departments of Guatemala, Chimaltenango, and Sacatepequez. His is the most comprehensive of all the Guatemalan highland surveys and covers substantially one single culture area designated here as the Central Highlands (fig. 1, D.). In his survey of the Central Guatemalan Highlands Shook lists 38 potential Early Preclassic sites, in open valleys and on flat plateaus. Their distribution is as follows:

Departments	Sites surveyed	Sites Excavated and Reported
Guatemala	24	2 (Kaminaljuyu, Las Charcas)
Chimaltenango	5	. . .
Sacatepequez	9	2 (Zakat, Xaraxong)
TOTAL	38	4

It must be kept in mind that Shook's assignment of a site to a cultural period is based principally on the analysis of pottery collected from the surface, and only in a few cases on actual excavations.

[5] At Las Charcas a skeleton of a young adult, found on the floor of a pit, lay extended, face up, without ornaments or formal grave furniture (Shook, 1950a, pp. 198–99). Over the body had been dumped an incredibly rich midden of ashes, carbonized wood, corncobs, fruit seeds, animal bones and disarticulated human bones, fragments of metates, manos, bone tools, pottery vessels, figurines, and incensarios. For the presence of similar bottle-shaped storage pits in the Salcaja area (Western Highlands) see Gamio, 1926–27, pp. 212–14. Early and Middle Preclassic bottle-shaped pits are reported from the Valley of Mexico (Tlatilco: Porter, 1953, p. 19, pl. 1,b; Piña Chan, 1958, pp. 28–29, figs. 17, 18), from the Yestla-Naranjo zone of Guerrero (Lister, 1955, p. 49, map 59), and from Chiapa de Corzo in Chiapas (Period III, Escalera phase; Warren, 1962, personal communication).

No habitation mounds have yet been excavated, but many burned adobe fragments unearthed during the excavations of storage pits at Las Charcas, Kaminaljuyu, Amatitlan, Salcaja, and at pits in the Departments of Guatemala, Chimaltenango, Sacatepequez, and Quezaltenango bear impressions of poles, leaves, and corncobs. They suggest that, at least in the Central Highlands, dwellings were made much like those of today with pole-and-thatch walls partially daubed and covered with palm-leaf-thatch roofs (Shook, 1951a, p. 97). The huts were probably set up at random throughout the village; there are no signs of plazas, avenues, or other village planning (Borhegyi, 1956b, p. 346).

Generally, temple or burial mounds were not constructed during the period although some of the low, rectangular, earthern structures at Kaminaljuyu (Mounds C-111-6 and C-111-10; Shook, 1951b, pp. 240–41) could have been built by the end of the Las Charcas A phase (1000–600 B.C.), to support shrines for minor public or family (clan) ceremonies.

Arts and Crafts

POTTERY. The earliest ceramic horizon so far discovered in the Guatemalan highlands contains pottery unsurpassed in excellence. Storage pits contained monochrome (red, black, gray-brown, buff, white) and bichrome (red-on-white, red-on-buff) pottery. Vessel forms are simple, including incurved and wide-everted rims on flat-based simple- and composite-silhouette bowls; effigy, spouted (unbridged spout variety), and shoe-shaped vessels; large storage jars and some specialized forms such as miniature vessels, clay rattles, tall-footed tripod "libation" cups (the only leg form of this stage), and three-pronged incense burners (20–30 cm. high) with effigy prongs and deeply scored inverted bowl-shaped covers. Fluted, grooved, and incised geometrical decoration (including punctate incision) is common; conventionalized animal forms (monkeys) are occasionally depicted on interiors of vases or exteriors of jars. (For pottery see Shook, 1951a, pp. 96–97 and fig. 1; for incense burners, Borhegyi, 1950b, figs. 5–7; for clay rattles, Borhegyi, 1957a, fig. 1.)

FIGURINES, EFFIGY HEADS, WHISTLES, STAMPS. The period is marked by abundance of clay stamps (cylindrical and flat), small anthropomorphic clay masks (Borhegyi, 1955a), hollow effigy whistles representing standing or seated nude males and females (Borhegyi and Scrimshaw, 1957, fig. 1,a), birds and animals (mostly monkeys), and solid hand-modeled "naturalistic" clay figurines with central punched eyes. Some of the figurines depict nude, flat-chested females, frequently pregnant and seated Turkish-fashion. Many figurines have a remarkable portrait-like realism, but their stumplike hands and feet are nothing more than crude incisions (Kidder II and Samayoa, 1959, fig. 2).[6]

WEAVING, BASKETRY, MATS, ORNAMENTS. No textiles have survived from this early period except the ashy remains of a woven fibrous material discovered by Shook (1949a, p. 221) in an ancient pit at Las Charcas. Because the Early Preclassic figurines are nude except for sculptured headdresses (representing bird-skin caps?), it is questionable if cotton clothing was worn.[7]

On the other hand, basket, mat, and rope impressions occur on burned adobe fragments excavated from storage pits. Aside from a few jade ornaments (beads and earspools), very little could have been worn for personal adornment. It is likely, however, that the cylindrical and flat-stemmed pottery stamps made during this period were used to paint the nude body with red, black, or yellow designs.

STONE SCULPTURES AND ARTIFACTS. Storage pits have produced numerous chipped stone and obsidian fragments, broken metates (legless variety) and manos of igneous rock, stone celts, ungrooved axes (for clearing land?), and pestles. None of the monumental stone sculptures or larger carved jades can safely be assigned to this period except possibly some plain basalt columns (proto-stelae?) that may once have stood before now destroyed, low platform mounds at Kaminaljuyu (Shook 1951b, p. 240).

Inferences of Social and Religious Structure

It is probably safe to assume that, through the ritual use of the many clay figurines and incense burners, the individual farmer, kin-group head, or community shaman hoped to promote success and avert evil, to contact, conciliate, or even control the supernatural. This was probably more often done for individual than for communal ends. In other words, the food producers and seed planters of the Early Preclassic were primarily self-sufficient primitive farmers, and not yet true peasants.[8]

[6] Although most of the Early Preclassic figurines doubtless depict females (sometimes pregnant, sometimes holding nursing babies), probably some of the solid, flat-chested and "sexless" (micaceous, buff, chocolate-brown or red ware) figurines of the Arevalo and Las Charcas A phases actually represent males (Kidder II and Samayoa, 1959, fig. 2), especially since a few of them have what appears to be a goatee (*ibid*, fig. 1). The fact that they are not endowed with genital organs, as are the pregnant female figurines (and some of the male and female animal figurines and effigy whistles representing *pisotes* and spider monkeys), may be due to some religious prohibition among the Preclassic Maya (Borhegyi, 1958a, p. 14; Warren, 1959, p. 104). Significantly, most Preclassic Olmec figurines are also depicted devoid of sex.

[7] For the historic use of bird-skin caps in Siberia, Scandinavia, and other circumpolar areas, see

Granlund, 1953. For a nonstylized bird-skin cap representation on a Las Charcas A figurine, see Kidder II, and Samayoa, 1959, fig. 1.

[8] Peasantry in this paper is considered as a functional part of a larger social whole rather than an isolated, self-sufficient segment of society. A peasant society is composed of at least two interdependent units: a specialized central power (an administrative or control unit located in a nucleated settlement), and a large rural hinterland of peasants (living in scattered nearby hamlets). The peasantry supports the nucleated administra-

During the Early Preclassic, the struggle to eke out a livelihood permitted little if any social stratification, a necessary requirement for the existence and creation of a symbiotic town and village life. On the other hand, the diverse Early Preclassic archaeological inventory of clay and stone artifacts, along with traces of basketry, mats, ropes and the presence of extensive obsidian workshops (flake-blade and scraper instruments), suggests the gradual emergence of a group of part-time specialists. These part-time craft specialists, along with kin-group heads and/or shamans ("controllers" and/or manipulators of earthquakes, rain, weather, health, and reproduction), were probably the first men in Middle America to be supported out of an economic surplus. By 600 B.C. the gradually increasing stylistic similarity and uniformity of pottery styles, figurines, stamps, and incense burners utilized by these independent highland village farming communities indicate growing specialization and some trade and suggest that the pooling of human experience has been acclerated by intercommunication.

It is interesting to speculate on the identity and linguistic affiliation of these first sedentary occupants of the Guatemalan highlands. Most likely they belonged to a general and as yet unspecified Macro-Mayan, Macro-Penutian or Macro-Chibchan linguistic stock represented today in Guatemala by such groups as the Chorti, and the Xinca (the Ikomagi people of the Quiche and Cakchiquel chronicles?) and in Salvador and Honduras by the Lenca, Jicaque, and Paya Indians (see Thompson,

1948, Map 1). This would explain the general uniformity of the material culture (shoe-shaped jars, "archaic" figurines, tall-footed tripod censers, monochrome and bichrome pottery) which underlies Middle and Late Preclassic remains throughout most of the western and central regions of Mexico, Central America, and northwestern South America (cf. von Weber, 1922). (See fig. 2.)

MIDDLE (600–300 B.C.) AND LATE PRECLASSIC (300 B.C.–A.D. 200) OR URBAN FORMATIVE PERIOD; PROTOCLASSIC (A.D. 200–300)

The archaeological phases associated with these periods are: Las Charcas B (600–500 B.C.), Providencia-Majadas (500–300 B.C.), Miraflores-Arenal (300 B.C.–A.D. 200), Santa Clara (A.D. 200–300), (Valley of Guatemala); Sacatepequez (Zakat-Xaraxong), (Almolonga Valley); Contreras (Lake Amatitlan); Chukumuk 1 (Lake Atitlan); Salcaja 1-2 (Western Highlands); Early Balam (Zacualpa); Chama 1 A (Chixoy drainage west); Chiapa III-VII (Chiapas).[9] See Table 1.

Modes of Subsistence

The growth of the Early Preclassic highland Maya food-producing communities was eventually limited by their economy. Since it is unlikely that agricultural methods not known during the earlier period

___

tive or control units both morally and probably physically, by corvée labor, and in turn depends on it for religious and civic leadership and for a supply of specialized tools, crafts, and food items otherwise unobtainable in the individual villages. The archaeological record of the Early Preclassic period does not support such a dichotomy in the Guatemalan highlands, at least not until the beginning of the Middle and Late Preclassic periods (600 B.C.).

[9] Although Miraflores and Arenal are usually listed as Late Preclassic ceramic sequent phases, I believe that Miraflores is roughly contemporaneous with Arenal and represents an elite ceremonial version of the latter. For this reason I have combined the two phases (Table 1). An analogous case can be brought forward for the Early Classic period. The Esperanza phase (based solely on burial contents), I am convinced, represents the ceremonial grave goods of the elite Teotihuacan group, and Amatle is its provincial Maya counterpart. The Santa Clara phase (A.D. 200–300) with its diagnostic ceramic feature, the mammiform-vessel support, is considered in Table 1 as Protoclassic, corresponding in time with the Holmul I and Matzanel phases of the Tropical Rain Forest area, and with the Istmo phase (Period VII) in highland Chiapas.

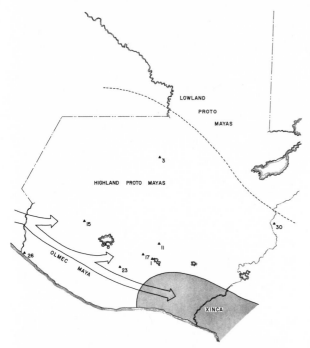

FIG. 3—MIDDLE AND LATE PRECLASSIC (600 B.C.–A.D. 200) AND PROTOCLASSIC (A.D. 200–300) PERIODS. La Venta or Olmec-Maya influences reach the Guatemalan highlands from Chiapas and Pacific coastal Mexico, dividing the Proto-Mayas into lowland and highland groups and pushing the Xincas east toward El Salvador. Large burial mounds forming parallel plazas or avenues are characteristic of the period. Beginnings of the lapidary arts (stone stelae and calendric markers) become evident.

numerous satellite villages grew up on the fringes of the primary settlement. Undoubtedly many of these new villages, although economically self-sufficient, retained a considerable degree of dependence on the growing numbers of religious and craft specialists in the primary settlement.

Settlement Pattern and Architecture

SETTLEMENTS AND SITES. The most outstanding feature of the Middle and Late Preclassic period is the beginning of religious architecture in the form of pyramidal burial mounds aligned along parallel avenues or elongated plazas. These ceremonial settlements were in open, undefended valleys and plateaus. In contrast to the probably haphazardly laid out domestic hamlets of the Early Preclassic period, the orderly arrangement of the burial mounds shows the definite concept of a ceremonial precinct, a sacred enclosure for the departed from which the village life was undoubtedly excluded. Although the primary settlement was soon overshadowed by the growth and expansion of the necropoli, the life and upkeep of these ceremonial and burial centers depended on the loyalty and participation of the farmers residing in the nearby villages.[11]

had been added to the farmers' storehouse of knowledge, expansion in numbers still required expansion in space. The necessary land could be found only by moving ever farther from the original community.[10] When communication became a problem,

[10] The average size of the milpa in Yucatan today is 10–12 acres. It is not planted for more than two years in succession; the third year a new site is selected and the old milpa is allowed to lie fallow for about 10 years. In the Guatemalan highlands, in forested regions with only occasional fertile valleys, 100 acres of land are required to maintain an average Maya family (Morley, 1956, p. 137). Even if during the height of Maya civilization land may have produced double its present yield, it is obvious why the rapidly multiplying Preclassic highland population was forced to occupy new cornfields in the peripheries (see also Hester, 1952, pp. 266–70; Palerm, 1957).

[11] Shook's survey (1952b) lists 38 Middle and Late Preclassic settlements in the Central Highland area (fig. 1, D): Department of Guatemala, 24; Department of Chimaltenango, 3; Department of Sacatepequez, 11. Most of them are classified as ceremonial centers, some with large, others with small, mound assemblages. Possible village sites (sites without mounds) are not reported by Shook. It is interesting to note that there are numerically the same number of Middle and Late Preclassic ceremonial centers in these departments as there are potential Early Preclassic village sites (see note 4). This may support the thesis that many of the earlier village settlements developed their own nucleated burial and ceremonial centers during the Middle and Late Preclassic. We must remember, however, that in most cases these sites came to Shook's attention because of the presence of mounds. Only when an analysis of the surface collections revealed the presence of Early Preclassic sherds was it evident that many of these sites had been occupied during the preceding period. The sites of the undoubtedly numerous Middle

At Kaminaljuyu, within an area of about 5 sq. km., there are more than a hundred Preclassic mounds, some of them 20 m. in height, with a base of 70–90 m., and containing 75,000 cu. m. of adobe (for a sketch-map of the site, see Lothrop, 1926a, fig. 45; Villacorta and Villacorta, 1927, p. 50). Some mounds contain as many as seven superimposed structures. To build them it must have been necessary to marshall as many as 10,000–12,000 laborers from the estimated 25,000–50,000 Middle and Late Preclassic population of the Valley of Guatemala.[12] A regular "public works" program, probably in the form of corvée labor, must have been in effect among the residents of the satellite villages, who probably commuted daily or weekly to their worship center to perform the many tasks required of them.

Very likely the superimposed temple structures and tombs represent periodic renewals accompanying the interment of a deceased (or sacrificed?) priest-leader or followed a pattern based on the annual agricultural cycle. In fact, the development of an agricultural calendar, along with intensified local food production and better methods of preservation and storage of surplus food, may have laid the basis for the cultural achievements that characterized the period.

An interesting and lesser known aspect of Middle and Late Preclassic times is the association of mounds with uncarved, usually plain columnar basalt stelae. Of the 38 Preclassic Central Highland sites listed by Shook (1952b), at least 13 have yielded such stelae. Some sites have only one or few; others like Naranjo (Department of Guatemala) probably had as many as 35 (Shook, 1952b, p. 22).[13] They range from slender shafts of columnar basalt to large, roughly shaped stelae. They stood in front of low platform mounds, erected in parallel north-south rows (see map in Villacorta and Villacorta, 1927, pp. 62–63). It appears now that the many elaborately carved stelae and stelae fragments (as well as the "silhouetted sculptures" found at Kaminaljuyu

---

and Late Preclassic villages (without large mounds and public buildings) as well as the cemeteries for the common people are still unknown.

[12] Shook and Kidder (1952, p. 46) found during the excavation of a Late Preclassic Miraflores burial mound (E-III-3) at Kaminaljuyu an average of 200 sherds per cubic meter. The great mound (20 m. high) contained the astounding total of about 15,000,000 sherds. If 30 sherds represent one vessel, it can be seen that at least 500,000 complete vessels were used, broken, and their fragments incidentally incorporated in the fill of this one mound. Multiplying this figure by the 100 or more Middle and Late Preclassic mounds at Kaminaljuyu, we reach a approximate of 50 million vessels produced over a span of 1000 years —an average production and consumption of 50,000 vessels a year. Assuming accidental and ceremonial breakage of 10 vessels a year for an average family of five persons, we reach a minimum population estimate of 25,000. We can assume that women and children were probably also enlisted in the building and rebuilding activities and probably carried many basketfuls of earth necessary for building the pyramids.

For a comparative estimate of Late Preclassic population at the site of Teotihuacan, Mexico, see Brainerd (1954, pp. 18–19); for that of Classic period Yucatan, Brainerd (1956); and for one of the "Classic" period (A.D. 802–1431) Khmer Empire in southeast Asia, M. D. Coe (1957c).

[13] According to the archaeological survey made by Shook (1952b), variously shaped, plain columnar basalt shafts or stelae were noted at the following 13 Central Highland (D) sites, all but one of which is in the Department of Guatemala: Las Charcas, Kaminaljuyu (Guatemala City area); Piedra Parada, Santa Isabel, Virginia, Cieneguilla (Canchon plateau area); Brigada, Bran, Naranjo, Pelikan (Lake Naranjo area); Cerrito, Amatitlan (Lake Amatitlan area); and Chacaya (Dept. Sacatepequez). The ceremonial use of these plain stelae may have begun at the end of Early Preclassic times or more probably during the Middle Preclassic Providencia (Majadas) phase (600–300 B.C.). (For map and photos of stelae at the site of Naranjo, see Villacorta and Villacorta, 1927, pp. 62–63.)

Late Preclassic types of plain columnar basalt shafts or stelae are known only sporadically outside the Central Highlands from such sites as Cambote (Dept. Huehuetenango), Rio Blanco (Dept. El Quiche), and Chichen (Dept. Alta Verapaz) [A. L. Smith, 1955]. They are frequent in the La Venta zone in Veracruz, and are also known from various sites in southern Chiapas (cf. Izapa: Stirling, 1943, p. 72, pl. 62; Tonala: Ferdon, 1953, pp. 92–94, pl. 19).

and other sites) were made in the Late Preclassic (Miraflores-Arenal, 300 B.C.–A.D. 200) rather than during the Classic period as previously supposed (Kidder, 1948, pp. 227–28). (For illustrations see Kidder II and Samayoa, 1959, figs. 7, 8, 91; Lothrop, 1926a, figs. 46–48.)

By Middle Preclassic times there were many ceremonial and burial centers of varying size scattered through the highlands. On the central plateau alone (fig. 1, D) 38 of the 102 archaeological sites reported by Shook (1952b) were occupied. Centrally located Kaminaljuyu was probably the seat of civic, cultural, and political power; and although there may have been a change in rulers in the Early Classic, it probably remained so until the end of the Late Classic period.

ARCHITECTURE AND BURIALS. The huge earthen mounds of the Middle and Late Preclassic ceremonial centers varied from 5 to 20 m. in height. They were faced with puddled adobe and brightly painted. Anywhere from two to eight steep balustraded stairways led to shrines of perishable materials at the summit. The orientation of the long, parallel plazas or processional "avenues" was roughly northeast by southwest. Within the mounds the richly furnished tombs, sometimes superimposed one upon another, were roofed and supported by wooden posts and crossbeams and covered with rush mats. Each tomb contained the body of some illustrious personage laid out at length on a special scaffold or wooden litter. The corpse, often covered with red paint, usually faced south and was accompanied by lavish offerings of food, jewelry, and in some instances as many as 300 pottery vessels. Some tombs contained in addition the extended bodies of sacrificed male and female retainers, including both children and adults (Shook and Kidder, 1952).

Arts and Crafts

POTTERY. In general, the ceramic art of the period, although similar in technique to that produced earlier, is considerably more varied in design, shape, and color.

Our information concerning household and ceremonial paraphernalia comes from the excavation of storage pits similar in shape to those of the previous period and from the excavation of burial mounds. There are several ceramic innovations. Labial and lateral flange decoration appears on some vessels; bichrome pottery comes into greater use in the Providencia phase (500–300 B.C.). A second color (mostly specular hematite red) is painted in bands over the white, red, or buff slip, or in simple, broadly drawn geometric or abstract designs, often depicting monkeys. The painting is frequently outlined by an incised line (Brainerd, 1954, fig. 3). Also by the Middle Preclassic at many Central and Western Highland sites a new decorative technique commonly referred to as "Usulutan" is popular, consisting of reverse or negative wavelike or cloudlike designs; it was used to decorate plates and tripod, tetrapod vessels, whistling jars, and effigy vessels (Shook, 1951a, fig. 2; Shook and Kidder, 1952, pp. 97-106). Secondary supports on pottery vessels are still rare but some appear in the form of small solid nubbins and solid conical feet. Hollow feet come in toward the end of the period in the Miraflores-Arenal phase (300 B.C.–A.D. 200) and the diagnostic feature of the Santa Clara phase (A.D. 200–300) is the hollow, bulbous or mammiform support. All leg forms appear in both tripodal and tetrapodal combinations (Gamio, 1926–27, p. 210).

The incensario cult which had its beginning during the Early Preclassic flourished and became much more elaborate during the Middle and Late Preclassic. Although the cult still centered around three-pronged censers, the censers differ from those of the earlier period in that they now have both upper and lower chamber. There is no spiked decoration on the body; the prongs, both hollow and solid, instead of representing bearded old men (rain gods)

14

are completely plain. On the other hand, the delicate geometrical openwork designs on the censer walls (Borhegyi, 1950b, fig. 7) are replaced by the addition of vertical side flanges and representations of conventionalized grotesque and even monstrous forms with thick upper lips and overhanging fangs, believed to represent feline (jaguar) or ophidian deities (Borhegyi, 1951a, figs. 1–3).[14] A curious form of censer with three top "loop handles" occurs in the Miraflores-Arenal phase (Borhegyi, 1956d).

A first cousin to the three-pronged incensario, the rimhead vessel, makes its appearance during the Late Preclassic Miraflores-Arenal phase. Typically the rimhead vessel consists of a coarse, reddish-brown ware tripod flaring-sided bowl with three projecting hollow or solid heads on the rim. The heads represent curious, highly conventionalized individuals with bald heads and pouting lower lips. They are strikingly La Venta (Olmec) in character (Borhegyi, 1950b, figs. 1–4; Gamio, 1926–27, p. 219).

FIGURINES, EFFIGY HEADS, WHISTLES, STAMPS. Solid (and occasionally hollow), hand-modeled male and female figurines in the so-called "archaic" style are especially abundant during the Middle and Late Pre-

classic. Although more conventionalized than those of the previous period, they often show such abnormalities as goiter, harelip, hunchback, and pop-eyes (Kidder and Shook, 1961, figs. 1–3). Others have jointed, movable arms.[15] The Middle and Late Preclassic human and animal figurines are made of white or reddish-brown paste covered with a well-polished white or red slip. The animal figurines, usually small and simple, represent birds, monkeys, pisotes, and dogs. Most of the anthropomorphic figurines wear elaborate, turban-like headdresses or hairdos, but some, usually females, are bald or with right side shorn (Lothrop, 1926a, fig. 56; Gamio, 1926–27, pp. 202, 218–19; Kidder II and Samayoa, 1959, fig. 6). Curiously enough, figurines and effigy whistles are almost nonexistent in the Protoclassic Santa Clara phase (A.D. 200–300). Flat-stemmed and roller stamps, which continued in use throughout most of the Middle and Late Preclassic, were abandoned by the end of the period (Shook and Kidder, 1952, p. 108). With the increasing use of cotton clothing they may no longer have been needed to decorate the body.

WEAVING, BASKETRY, MATS, ORNAMENTS. No specimens have survived from this period. However, mat impressions have been found in some Miraflores tombs in the harder-packed parts of the fill. In every case the elements were about 5 mm. wide, the weave an over-two–under-two right-angled twill.

Information about the clothing of the period can be deduced from study of the many (though badly battered and frag-

---

[14] According to Middle American religious tradition both the jaguar and the serpent are associated with the god of rain and fertility. This god was called Chac among the Maya and Tlaloc ("He who makes the plants grow") among the Nahuat- and Nahuatl-speakers of Mexico. Tlaloc frequently is depicted in the guise of the jaguar earth god who dwells in caves and mountains, and as the atlantean god of earthquakes who supports the world on his shoulders. He was considered to possess both the "heart of the mountain" and the "heart of the land." The jaguar therefore is a symbol of great power and represents dominion over human beings. For this reason the jaguar (and to lesser degree the serpent) became the symbol of priestly power vested in the earthly representatives of the powerful rain god. Although jaguar symbolism (teeth filing?) and worship were probably strongest in the La Venta zone in Veracruz, the worship center of Tlaloc was probably in Teotihuacan itself.

[15] For a possible explanation of the use of jointed-arm figurines with ventriloquism see Borhegyi (1950d, 1954a). For figurines showing enlarged goiters see Borhegyi and Scrimshaw (1957, fig. 1,*b*). The badly battered Preclassic figurines depicting pathological abnormalities may have been used in ceremonial curing rituals (cf. Reichel-Dolmatoff, 1961). They were probably broken and thrown away after they had served their purpose.

mentary) figurines and some of the stone stelae carvings. Turban-like headdresses worn over elaborately braided hairdos (much like those at Tlatilco) were apparently fashionable with both sexes. Women did not cover their breasts but wrapped short, knee-length cotton *sarongs* about their waists. That some were decorated, probably with woven patterns, is shown by incised, grooved, and punctate decoration on the figurines. Men wore short loincloths (*ex* in Maya). Cotton cloth was probably woven on hand looms similar to those used today. In light of the various cloth items worn by the figurines it is likely that cotton, which grows in the tropical lowlands of the Gulf coast of Mexico, was probably introduced to the Guatemalan highlands during this period, along with many other La Venta–like cultural traits from that area. Accordingly, spindle whorls are found for the first time in Providencia (500–300 B.C.) deposits.

In contrast to the Tropical Rain Forest area, sandals were apparently not worn. The highland figurines substantiate the evidence already provided by the tomb excavations: that there was a lavish use of jade and bone ear-, lip-, and noseplugs as well as necklaces (frequently with jade or pink *Spondylus* shell breast pendants), bracelets and anklets (of stone, shell, jade, and rope). Again, from study of the figurines, facial and body painting in yellow, black, red, and white was a common practice. Whether body painting was an everyday procedure or reserved for such occasions as funerals and penitential rites is not clear.

The use of quetzal, toucan, parrot, and cotinga feathers for adornment was probably restricted to privileged individuals. The Guatemala Museum (no. 3093) contains a good illustration of the use of feather ornaments: a Miraflores-Arenal phase (300 B.C.–A.D. 200) carved stone stela from Kaminaljuyu represents a priest with elaborate headdress and mask, holding a baton and a hafted eccentric flint (Kidder II and

Samayoa, 1959, fig. 7; for a close stylistic similarity cf. Stela 4, Izapa, Chiapas; Proskouriakoff, 1950, fig. 110,*b*).

STONE SCULPTURES AND ARTIFACTS. The stone sculpture of this period is without question the finest ever produced in the highlands. Among the monumental sculptures of the Central Highlands are the numerous plain and carved columnar basalt shafts and stone stelae discussed in the previous section. At Kaminaljuyu there are also some massive three-pronged stone censers (85 cm. high), counterparts of the more common three-pronged pottery incense burners. They are made of volcanic tuff and were probably once painted red. They represent, as do many of the pottery censers, grotesque, snarling jaguar faces with elaborate headdresses terminating in a knotted band ("bow tie") at the back (Borhegyi, 1950b, pp. 63–65, fig. 6,*a*). These impressive stone censers are a further indication that the simple, individualistic family incensario cult of the Early Preclassic had taken on a more formal, public-worship character.

Other monumental stone sculptures of this period represent large human or jaguar heads and potbellied individuals with short, thick necks (Gamio, 1926–27, p. 213; Lothrop, 1926a, figs. 53–55; Villacorta and Villacorta, 1927, pp. 39–40, 46–47; Richardson, 1940, pl. 18, figs. 33, 34), which may have served as "chac mool"-like altars in front of the temple pyramids (see map in Lothrop, 1926a, fig. 57). They show a close stylistic similarity to the colossal La Venta-style boulder heads of coastal Veracruz. Stone boulder sculptures of huge squatting toads may also have been used as altars, possibly even as sacrificial platforms (Lothrop, 1926a, fig. 47,*a*). The fact that human and probably animal (jaguar, puma, turkey) sacrifice was practiced during this period is known from the presence of the skeletal remains of animals and human retainers in the tombs (one young adult male retainer skeleton, extended and prone, in

Mound D-IV-2 at Kaminaljuyu with a sharp-edged obsidian knife embedded between the neck vertebrae; Borhegyi, 1956c, pp. 286–87). The presence of sculptured male figures kneeling on four-legged or scroll-decorated benchlike platforms (ending in long vertical, squared tenons) with ropes about their necks and their hands and ankles bound together behind their backs (Kidder II and Samayoa, 1959, fig. 9) suggests that at least some of the sacrificial victims were not altogether willing to face their impending death. Other vertically tenoned stone sculptures from the Guatemalan highlands represent pisotes, monkeys, crouching jaguars, or feline monsters seated on top of the square shafts (Richardson, 1940, fig. 36; Kidder II and Samayoa, 1959, fig. 10). The exact significance of these sculptures is unknown. They, like the exquisitely carved, tenoned "silhouette sculptures" of the same period (Kidder II and Samayoa, 1959, fig. 8; Kidder, Jennings, and Shook, 1946, fig. 141), may have served as portable markers during ceremonies or games.

Lapidary work in volcanic and basaltic stone, in addition to metates, manos, mortars, and pestles, includes obsidian blades and spools of superlative technique; well-ground axes and chisels; exquisite stone vessels of chlorite schist, marble, soapstone, and fuchsite; fine, highly polished light-green jade and jadeite carvings (including full-size jade mosaic masks, smaller figurines, pendants, earspools, and miniature vessels); and strange, mushroom-shaped effigy sculptures (Shook and Kidder, 1952; Borhegyi, 1961a, figs. 1, 2, Types A-C).

Inference of Social and Religious Structure

The rise of monumental architecture and the corresponding emergence of sacrificial and burial cults as socially sanctioned customs bespeaks a high degree of social stratification and the accumulation of wealth, power, and prestige in the hands of select individuals. The presence of elaborate burials with sacrificial retainers suggests the concept of a life after death, if not for the common people, at least for the priestly guardians of the ceremonial and burial centers.

As already noted for the figurines and incense burners, there is a decided trend toward standardization and conventionalization of all ritual material, and duplicates are frequently encountered. The changed appearance of the cult objects and ritual vessels suggests a corresponding standardization of religious ideas and ceremonies. Very likely the individualistic approach to the supernatural (via figurines and three-pronged censers), at least within the sacred burial enclosures, was replaced by a more rigid, formalized ceremonial discipline.

The presence of mushroom stones (both miniature and full size) during Middle and Late Preclassic times in the highlands and their association with metates and manos opens up intriguing speculation (Kidder, Jennings, and Shook, 1946, p. 142; Kidder and Shook, 1952, p. 112; Borhegyi, 1961a). It has recently been suggested that they were part of a magico-religious cult still surviving in parts of Mesoamerica in which the ritual consumption of hallucinogenic mushrooms (*Psilocybe mexicana* Heim), known among the Aztecs as *teonanacatl*, "divine mushroom," plays an important, if not central, role (Wasson and Wasson, 1957; Borhegyi, 1961a). Although mushroom stones have not been found in the areas where the modern cult is reported, and the hallucinogenic mushroom is unknown in the regions where mushroom stones are found archaeologically, the situation may have been different in earlier times.[16] The Mixtecs of Oaxaca today grind

[16] In Mexico hallucinogenic mushrooms are (and probably were in pre-Columbian times) used in divinatory rituals by the Nahua and Otomi peoples of central Mexico, by the Mazatecs, Mixtecs, Zapotecs, and Mixe of Oaxaca, and perhaps also by the Tarascans and a few other tribes (Wasson and Wasson, 1957; Ravicz, 1961, fig. 1). There is no evidence of their use in western and

the sacred mushroom on a metate, add water, and drink the mixture during special divinatory ceremonies (Borhegyi, 1961a, p. 503). According to 16th-century Spanish historians, the Aztecs also ate or drank the mushrooms to induce hallucinatory trances and dreams during which they saw colored visions of jaguars, birds, snakes, and little gnomelike creatures. It is very likely, then, that the presence of mushroom stones and associated manos and metates in Middle and Late Preclassic caches and tombs indicates the existence of a widespread mushroom ritual and cult similar in concept, but not necessarily in performance, to that known among the Mixtecs, Zapotecs, and Mixes of Oaxaca, Mexico. (For a detailed description of the mushroom ceremony, see Wasson and Wasson, 1957, pp. 287-321; Ravicz, 1961.)

The highland Maya stelae, unlike the Classic period lowland Maya stelae from the Tropical Rain Forest area, rarely bear glyphic inscriptions, and their use, more or less restricted to the Central Highlands, came to an abrupt end by Classic times, probably as a result of a Mexican invasion from Teotihuacan.[17] However, like their

more elaborately carved counterparts from the Tropical Rain Forest sites, these columnar shafts were probably painted and used to mark the passing of time, most likely the sacred 260-day year of the Maya. Their presence in the highlands argues for the corresponding existence of calendar priests.

As far as we know, the earliest use of plain columnar basalt shafts occurred in coastal Veracruz and Tabasco, Mexico, the area which at a later date is known to have been the heartland of the "Olmecs." Very likely the use of plain and carved stelae, large boulder sculptures, grotesque jaguar and ophidian symbolism on stone and jade objects and on pottery and stone incense burners, the custom of shaving the heads of some individuals, the use of rubber, cotton, and cotton clothing, and even the concept of monumental temple and tomb building (along with the use of red ocher paint in funerary ceremonies) was introduced to the Guatemalan highlands sometime during Middle Preclassic times from this area. There is no way of knowing whether this invasion came in the form of peoples or simply as ideas, whether it was peaceful or accompanied by warfare and conquest. However, the cultural simplicity of the Early Preclassic probably offered few barriers to the reception of such magicoreligious ideas as infant sacrifice to agricultural deities, calendric rituals, and the cult of jaguar rain monsters from the linguistically related Olmec-Maya culture. As evidenced by the rapid acceptance of jaguar symbolism on the three-pronged ceremonial censers and the number of sacrificial retainers in Late Preclassic tombs, the innovations may even have been received with enthusiasm.[18] (See fig. 3.)

---

northern Mexico, where the use of *peyote* (*Lophophora Williamsii*) served as a functional equivalent. On the other hand, mushroom stones and similar pottery "mushrooms" are known only from the states of Oaxaca, Tabasco, Chiapas, Guerrero, and Veracruz in Mexico; from the Western (C), and Central Highlands (D), the Pacific Coastal Piedmont (F), and the Eastern Lowlands (E) of Guatemala; and from El Salvador. (For a distribution of mushroom stones and pottery "mushrooms," see Borhegyi, 1957b; 1961a, Table 1; 1963, fig. 8.)

[17] At Kaminaljuyu a glyph-bearing stela fragment, discovered in 1958 and dating to the Miraflores-Arenal phase (300 B.C.–A.D. 200) represents an aged priest with an elaborate headdress holding a baton and a hafted eccentric flint. (Cf. stela in Guatemala National Museum, no. 3093; Kidder II and Samayoa, 1959, fig. 7, also of Miraflores date.) The glyph carved in the left corner of the stela expresses in the familiar Maya dot-and-bar numerical system what was probably the name of the individual, "Eight Jaguar." Stylistically, the intricate carving of the curvilinear and guilloche

design on the stela indicates La Venta, coastal Veracruz, influence (Girard, 1962, fig. 242).

[18] The route through which the postulated La Venta (Olmec or Olmec-Maya?) cultural influence reached the Central Guatemalan Highlands is, I

EARLY CLASSIC PERIOD (A.D. 300–700)

The archaeological phases associated with this period are: Aurora (A.D. 300–400), Esperanza (400–700) (Valley of Guatemala); Terrenos Bajos (Almolonga Valley); Chukumuk 2 (Lake Atitlan); Lavaderos (Lake Amatitlan); Chama 1B–2 (Chixoy drainage); Atzan (Zaculeu); Late Balam (Zacualpa); Chiapa VIII-IX (Chiapas). (See note 9; Table 1.)

Modes of Subsistence

It seems that for a while the Early Classic period followed the cultural and economic trends established during the Late Preclassic and Protoclassic. By the middle of the period, however, new agricultural techniques made their appearance: curious doughnut-shaped stones possibly used as digging-stick weights, agricultural terracing, and perhaps irrigation. The gradual migration of the farming settlements to the peripheries of the valleys and to the edges of the plateaus that began during Late Preclassic times apparently continued. It seems likely that the use of hillslopes for

agricultural pursuits necessitated the invention of agricultural terraces to keep the much needed water from running off and to preserve the equally important topsoil.[19] In turn, such terraces may have brought about the idea of irrigation. Water that gathered behind the low stone retainer walls after heavy rains was probably collected in pools and distributed through ditches over the fields. This may have led to the discovery and ultimately to the use of irrigation channels, water conduits, and reservoirs.[20]

Settlement Pattern and Architecture

SETTLEMENTS AND SITES. Sites during the Early Classic period were still undefended and situated on the open valley floors, gentle hillslopes and plateaus. For some reason, in the Central Highland area fewer sites seem to be assignable to the Early Classic occupation than to either the Preclassic or Late Classic. Many flourishing and important Preclassic sites on the Canchon plateau southeast of Kaminaljuyu in the Department of Guatemala were permanently

---

believe, the same as that suggested by Seler (1904b, p. 112), J. E. S. Thompson (1941a), Stirling (1943, pp. 72–74), Kidder, Jennings, and Shook (1946, p. 257), Ferdon (1953, p. 112); and Jiménez Moreno (1959, p. 1088, Maps 1–8). It is the route of later Teotihuacan and Pipil Mexican (Nahuat) migratory groups.

It now appears that the Preclassic builders of La Venta were actually a Maya- (or proto-Maya-) speaking group, living among such other Maya-speakers as the Huaxtecs, the "proto-Totonacs," and the Maya of Tabasco, Campeche, and Chiapas (cf. Jiménez Moreno, 1959, pp. 1021–27). The wide acceptance of the so-called La Venta artistic (and religious) style over Mesoamerica can be attributed to the fact that it spread to peoples of a similar linguistic and cultural background (see J. E. S. Thompson, 1954a, pp. 49–53; Jiménez Moreno, 1959, Map 1; Piña Chan, 1960a, Maps 8, 9). Continuous southward thrusts by Nahuat-speaking peoples at the end of the Late Preclassic period brought Teotihuacan culture into this once solidly "proto-Maya" area and interrupted the Maya cultural flow (cf. note 13 and Jiménez Moreno, 1942, Maps 1–3). (See fig. 4.)

[19] Mejicanos, an Early Classic settlement of eight mounds on the south shore of Lake Amatitlan (Dept. Guatemala), occupies a small inlet valley hemmed in on three sides by steep mountains. Everywhere on the slopes are signs of ancient agricultural terracing. Since the site of Mejicanos seems to have been occupied only during the Early Classic, this may strengthen the hypothesis that the use of agricultural terraces in highland Guatemala began at this period. (For a description of the site see Shook, 1952b, pp. 19, 20; and Borhegyi, 1959b, p. 105.)

[20] The use of prehistoric irrigation canals in the valleys of Mexico and Teotihuacan dates back to the Early Postclassic Tula-Toltec period (A.D. 900–1200) or even earlier to Classic Teotihuacan times (Millon, 1954, 1957; Wolf and Palerm, 1955; Armillas, Palerm, and Wolf, 1956). At Zacualpa, a site in the Western Highlands of Guatemala, the use of stone and clay gutters has been reported during the late Tohil phase (Postclassic, about A.D. 1200) and the Late Classic Pokom phase preceding it (Wauchope, 1948a, p. 88). For Classic period stone-lined and stone-roofed drains on the Coastal Piedmont at El Baul, Guatemala, see J. E. S. Thompson (1948, p. 38, fig. 22,c,g).

abandoned by the beginning of the Early Classic period. On the other hand, there was a mushrooming of new ceremonial sites in the Western Highlands and in the Hilly Middle Country.[21] It may be that many highland Maya farmers in the densely populated valleys and plateaus of the Central Highlands moved away in search of arable land and established new settlements in the sparsely settled intermountain valleys and plateaus of the Western Highlands and Hilly Middle Country. On the other hand, many Early Classic architectural features may simply lie buried and overlaid by assemblages of the ensuing Late Classic period. Since only a few mounds have been properly excavated, archaeological data on Early Classic sites are extremely meager.

To all appearances the bottle-shaped storage pits used so extensively during all the phases of the Preclassic throughout the Central Highlands (in the Valley of Guatemala, the Canchon Plateau, and also at sites in the Department of Sacatepequez) and at Salcaja (Department of Quezaltenango) in the Western Highlands disappear completely and permanently by the beginning of the Early Classic. None contain-

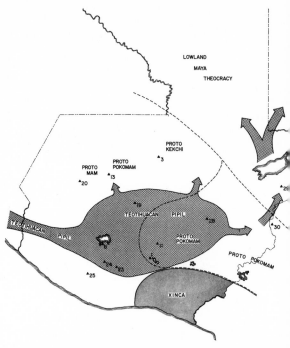

FIG. 4—EARLY CLASSIC PERIOD (A.D. 300–700) Teotihuacan-Pipil influences from Mexico establish a theocratic-oriented society in the Guatemalan highlands marked by temple mounds grouped around ceremonial plazas to form acropolis-like structures. The highland Maya divide into Proto-Mam, Proto-Kekchi, and Proto-Pokomam groups. Close commercial and economic ties exist with Mexico, particularly with Teotihuacan, Tajin, and Monte Alban.

[21] Shook's survey (1952b) of the *Central Highlands* lists only 23 sites occupied during the Early Classic, 15 sites fewer than during the Late Preclassic: Department of Guatemala, 12 sites (12 less than in Late Preclassic); Department of Chimaltenango, 5 sites (3 less than in Late Preclassic); Department of Sacatepequez, 6 sites (5 less than in Late Preclassic). A. L. Smith's survey (1955) of four departments in the *Western Highlands* and the Hilly Middle Country (El Quiche, Huehuetenango, Alta Verapaz, Baja Verapaz) reveals that of 66 sites, only 8 were occupied during Middle and Late Preclassic times. During Early Classic times 13 sites were occupied and during the Late Classic the number of sites increased to 20.

Department	Number of Sites	Late Pre-classic	Early Classic	Late Classic
Huehuetenango	11	3	5	4
El Quiche	36	1	4	8
Baja Verapaz	6	1	0	0
Alta Verapaz	13	3	4	8
TOTAL	66	8	13	20

ing Early Classic or later midden have been found either within or outside the ceremonial precincts. However, the habitation sites of this period must have been at a considerable distance from the ceremonial centers; none so far have been located. It may be that when such sites are eventually discovered they will reveal a continuation of this pattern of subterranean food preservation. On the other hand, it is quite possible that by Early Classic times large earthenware urns or baskets were preferred for storing foodstuffs. It is interesting to note that similarly constructed bottle-shaped Preclassic pits in the Valley of Mexico at Tlatilco and the ones reported from Guerrero and Chiapas also disappeared with the onset of the Classic period (see note 5).

ARCHITECTURE AND BURIALS. In general the Early Classic highland ceremonial centers tend more toward closely knit court arrangements for religious and secular observances than to the parallel plaza or processional "avenue" pattern of the Middle and Late Preclassic. In the Early Classic settlement one can even differentiate several tightly enclosed rectangular paved inner and outer courts, with terraces on alternating levels leading to acropolis-like temple arrangements. The earthen mounds are smaller (generally 5–8 m. high) than previously, and as the period progresses they seem to diminish in size and elaboration.[22] All this suggests that during the Early Classic the courts were used more and more for assemblies and market gatherings.

In the Central Highlands a new masonry technique during this period was the facing of the earthen pyramids with neatly cut volcanic pumice blocks set in adobe. In turn these blocks were covered with clay, faced with white plaster, and probably coated with some sort of vegetable shellac to protect the walls from the erosion of tropical downpours (Kidder, Jennings, and Shook, 1946, p. 17). As in the earlier phases the mounds contained as many as eight superimposed structures erected over the deep burial chambers. Narrow stairways flanked by balustrades led to the summits of these mounds where stood shrines of perishable materials. The shrines consisted of one rectangular room with a single door-

way toward the head of the stairway (*ibid.*, figs. 107–09).

Little is known about either the exterior or interior decoration of these buildings. The walls were probably painted; the framed, vertical wall zones which also appear on many substructures at Teotihuacan and are called *tableros* by Mexican archaeologists, were decorated with painted stucco designs in plano-relief. The almost identical construction of these tableros, as well as that of the sloping element at the base of the walls (called *talud* by Mexicanists), at Kaminaljuyu and at Teotihuacan certainly suggests close architectural connections between the two sites and is indicative of Teotihuacan influence or occupation of the former during Early Classic times (cf. *ibid.*, figs. 10, 11).

Although more common during Late Classic times (A.D. 700–1000), ball courts make their first appearance in the Early Classic period. The game, played in paved courts with a solid but vigorously bouncing rubber ball 6–8 inches in diameter, consisted of two competing teams varying from 1 to 15 players each.[23] The Early Classic paved ball courts of the highlands were either open-ended (especially in the Western Highlands and Hilly Middle Country) or resembled a wash basin (*palangana*) in shape. At Kaminaljuyu the sloping walls of some of the ball courts were faced with evenly cut volcanic pumice blocks, set in adobe, a characteristic feature of Early Classic architecture (see ball court str.

---

[22] The earliest known Classic period (Aurora phase, A.D. 300–400) mound at Kaminaljuyu (D-III-13) is fairly sizable (13 m. high) but such fully Classic mounds as A and B were considerably smaller (6 and 9 m. high and 20–35 m. in diameter, respectively). Mound D-III-13 in many respects represents an architectural transition between the Late Preclassic and Classic periods. In front of this mound once stood a Late Preclassic type of plain columnar basalt shaft stela. In addition the vertical platform walls of the mound were decorated with gaudily painted plano-relief motifs, and the skeletons in the tombs were extended (see Berlin, 1952, figs. 6, 9, 10).

[23] The rules and history of the Middle American competitive rubber ball game have been described elsewhere in detail (Stern, 1950; Borhegyi, 1960b). Although the appearance of ball courts in Middle America is generally considered to be a Classic period trait, it is possible that some form of rubber ball game existed during Mid-Preclassic times in the Valley of Mexico (Tlatilco). The game was probably played without the use of formal courts, but the players wore protective padding and gloves similar to those known later during Classic times (Covarrubias, 1957, p. 26, pl. 5; Piña Chan, 1958, vol. 2, pl. 18; see also note 46 and Borhegyi, 1961b).

C-II-7, Borhegyi, notes, 1958.) By the end of the Early Classic period ball courts were so popular in the highlands that every major ceremonial center boasted at least one court, and large centers such as Kaminaljuyu may have had as many as 12.[24]

The funerary architecture of the Central Highlands during the Early Classic period was essentially the same as that of the preceding period. Within the mounds the deep, roughly rectangular burial chambers were still roofed with logs; the floors, surfaced with mats, were literally covered with rich offerings and sacrificial retainers (Kidder, Jennings, and Shook, 1946). In the Hilly Middle Country at sites like Nebaj and Tzicuay (Department of El Quiche) narrow, stone-capped access passages led to large tombs frequently lined and blocked at the exit with stone slabs. The rectangular burial chambers were often also roofed with stone slabs laid flat or to form corbeled vaults (A. L. Smith and Kidder, 1951, fig. 38). At Zaculeu in the Western Highlands large circular tombs were fashionable during this period. The walls of the chamber were painted red; a stairway led down to the burial which lay under the main temple, carefully sealed

with a gigantic stone slab (Woodbury and Trik, 1953, figs. 40, 41).[25]

The burial customs of the period, including the manner of interment, the type of burial offerings and the number of sacrificial retainers, are extremely varied and, to say the least, confusing. The extended position seems to have been preferred for the principal occupant of the tomb in the Hilly Middle Country and Western Highlands. In the Central Highlands, specifically at Kaminaljuyu, the principal body was extended in Tombs A-I and A-II but in later times was wrapped in a "mummy" bundle, seated upright tailor-fashion, with the hands between the spread thighs (Kidder, Jennings, and Shook, 1946, pp. 88, 89).[26] The use of the seated position for burials and "mummy" bundles was probably introduced to the Guatemalan highlands from Teotihuacan during Early Classic times.

Retainers, sacrificed for the occasion, were numerous and included children and adults of both sexes.[27] A curious new cus-

---

[24] Shook's survey (1952b) of the 103 archaeological sites in the Central Guatemalan Highlands lists 36 sites with one or more ball courts. This number leaves no doubt as to the great popularity of the game. Ball courts reported by Shook arranged by department are:

Department	Number of Sites	Sites with Ball Courts
Guatemala	73	29
Chimaltenango .	11	2
Sacatepequez ..	19	5
TOTAL	103	36

A. L. Smith's 1955 report of four Western Highlands and Hilly Middle Country departments (El Quiche, Huetuetenango, Alta Verapaz, Baja Verapaz) notes the existence of 40 sites with ball courts out of a total of 66 Classic and Postclassic sites. Of the 13 Early Classic sites, about 8 had ball courts of the Early Classic open-end variety with no clearly defined end zones. For a detailed summary and distribution study of highland Maya ball courts see A. L. Smith (1961).

[25] Early and Late Classic stone-lined, stone-paved, stone-covered or -vaulted (corbeled arch) burial chambers and cists are reported from Xolchun, Tzicuay, Nebaj (A. L. Smith, 1955, p. 75), and Zacualpa (Lothrop, 1936; Wauchope, 1948a) in the Department of El Quiche; from Chalchitan and Tajumulco in the Department of Huehuetenango (A. L. Smith, 1955; Dutton and Hobbs, 1943); from Chama in the Department of Alta Verapaz (Butler, 1940); and from Chukumuk in the Department of Solola (Lothrop, 1933).

[26] The interment of the principal tomb occupant in an extended position has been noted at Kaminaljuyu (although only at the beginning of the Early Classic), Zaculeu, Nebaj, Zacualpa, and Chama. The interment of bodies seated in flexed position has been reported from Kaminaljuyu, Chukumuk, and Nebaj. At Kaminaljuyu it was the principal tomb occupant that was seated; at Nebaj the seated skeletons were those of sacrificed retainers. In this connection it should be noted that, at least in the Hilly Middle Country, the number of sacrificial victims per tomb increased considerably from Late Preclassic to Early Classic times, with as many as 10 in an Early Classic tomb in Mound I at Nebaj (A. L. Smith and Kidder, 1953, pp. 22, 28).

[27] Sacrificial retainers of both sexes and all ages have been reported from Kaminaljuyu, Nebaj, Zacualpa, and Zaculeu. Child sacrifices, however,

tom is represented by headless burials as well as caches of severed heads. Some of the skulls in these burials were painted with red cinnabar or were elaborately carved and stuccoed. They are believed to be trophy heads of sacrificial victims or of ememies killed or captured in war (*ibid.*, pp. 153–55, figs. 165, 170,*h*).[28]

The custom of sacrificing animals during burial ceremonies and adding their bodies to the graves, which may have begun during the Middle Preclassic, became more common during Classic times. Bones of jaguars and birds (quail and parakeet) are numerous as are the skeletons of coyotes and dogs.[29] At the pelvis of the principal

skeleton were often unworked sting-ray spines in bunches of 9 or 10. The remains of turtles, crocodiles, bats, rats, mice, and peccaries scattered on the tomb floors probably represent both sacrificial offerings and food for the journey to the underworld.[30] Unfortunately, no interments of commoners are known from the Early Classic or preceding periods. If they were buried, it must have been with little ceremony and in unimpressive graves.

Arts and Crafts

POTTERY. All our knowledge of the pottery of the period comes from the excavation of tombs and offertory caches. The two main ceramic diagnostics—the basal-flanged or basal-angled ring-stand-based bowl and the cylindrical tripod with slab legs and apron cover—interestingly enough represent the two main sources of foreign influence felt in the highlands during Early Classic times. The former is characteristic of the lowland Maya of the Tropical Rain Forest; the latter of the Valley of Mexico and in particular Teotihuacan. Along with these new pottery forms came a host of other foreign ceramic shapes and wares. Indicative of Teotihuacan influence are the round-sided bowls (with ring-stand or annular base) and effigy vessels of men and dogs made of Thin Orange ware, a fine, hard, pinkish-orange clay so named because it is often as thin as eggshell; black-brown ware ring-stand-based "cream pitchers" (usually with twisted handles); and an-

---

seem to be most frequent during Early Classic times.

[28] The custom of severing the heads of both infants and adults and burying them apart from the body between two bowls placed lip to lip may have originated on the Gulf coast of Mexico or among the Lowland Maya. In the Tropical Rain Forest the trait first appears during Chicanel (Late Preclassic) times at Uaxactun and other sites, and it became increasingly common during the Classic period. The trophy-head cult must at one time have been widespread through pre-Columbian Mesoamerica and South America. (See severed heads on the El Baul monuments, J. E. S. Thompson, 1948, figs. 2,*d,g*; 6,*d*; and on the stone stelae and panels at Izapa, Bonampak, and Chichen Itza, Orellana, 1955. For possible representations of pre-Columbian severed and shrunken heads in Mexico see Leigh, 1961.) Burials of decapitated bodies or skull burials are reported from Chukumuk, Kaminaljuyu, and Nebaj. In one instance 12 skulls were placed in a single burial (Burial 4, Late Classic or Early Postclassic at Nebaj; A. L. Smith and Kidder, 1951, fig. 46,*a*). That the persons in question had been decapitated is proven by the fact that in some instances two or three of the upper vertebrae were present with the skull. (For a relationship between the pre-Columbian ball game and sacrifice by decapitation see Knauth, 1961.)

[29] The presence of dog skeletons in some Early Classic tombs, usually at the foot of the principal occupant (Kidder, Jennings, and Shook, 1946, p. 155, fig. 138,*b*), indicates acceptance among the highland Maya of the apparently Mexican concept of burying a dog with its master to aid him in his journey to the underworld. Charnay (1887, p. 148) reports dog bones in a tomb at Teotihuacan; Covarrubias (1943) and Piña Chan (1960a, pp. 130–31) note their presence in Middle Preclassic burials at Tlatilco and Chupicuaro.

[30] The presence of sting ray spines in Early Classic tombs at Nebaj and Kaminaljuyu (A. L. Smith and Kidder, 1951, p. 57; Kidder, Jennings, and Shook, 1946, p. 156) suggests their use in penitential rites (piercing the tongue, ears, or foreskin with the spines) to atone for the "sins" of the deceased. They may also have been included so that the deceased could perform the rites and thereby purify himself before making the journey. Sting-ray spines near the pelvis have been found, though sparingly, in Late Preclassic burials at Kaminaljuyu (Shook and Kidder, 1952, p. 117). (For a distribution study of pre-Columbian sting-ray spine mortuary offerings, see Borhegyi, 1961c.)

thropomorphic jars, bowls and pottery boxes representing the Teotihuacan manifestation of the "goggle-eyed" rain god, Tlaloc. The same can be said for the elaborate two-part human effigy urns; unslipped or polished black-ware "floreros," and small, rather crudely manufactured one- or two-holed vessels (used probably to burn incense or to collect blood), commonly known as "candeleros" (Kidder, Jennings, and Shook, 1946, p. 216, fig. 93; Lothrop, 1936, p. 43, fig. 39; Linné, 1942, pp. 121–22, 161; Bernal, 1949, p. 113, fig. 182).

A detailed ceramic analysis made by Anna O. Shepard revealed that most, if not all, of new ceramic forms and wares of the period were manufactured locally in the highlands (Kidder, Jennings, and Shook, 1946, p. 269). Whether these vessels were made from copies of foreign models by native highland potters conversant with the religion of Teotihuacan as well as that of their own culture, or were made by the womenfolk of migratory Mexican groups is not clear. However, the themes and designs depicted on the cylindrical tripod vessels and on many of the incense burners are certainly more characteristic of the Teotihuacan pantheon and its religious symbolism (water, raindrop, trilobal drop element, butterfly, owl, shell and marine life, "reptile's eye" glyph, treble scroll, flower, cacao pods, human skull, various Tlaloc (rain god) representations, and tri-mountain symbols) than that of the Maya (*ibid.*, pp. 218–39; von Winning, 1961). For these and other reasons explained in a later section it seems rational to accept the theory developed by A. V. Kidder and his associates (Kidder, Jennings, Shook, 1946) that an invasion from the west put Mexican priest-rulers into the saddle at Kaminaljuyu and at other highland Maya ceremonial centers. On the other hand, the relatively unchanged appearance of Early Classic culinary vessels, similar if not identical to the earlier "Arenal," and the later Amatle and Pamplona phase

water and cooking jars, roasting plates, "frying pans" (*sartenes*), cylindrical vases, round-sided bowls, and simple ceremonial objects, suggests that the outlying satellite villages were left undisturbed by the invaders and everyday life probably continued much the same as in Late Preclassic and Protoclassic times.

A revolutionary ceramic innovation, the ceramic mold process, was most likely introduced to the Guatemalan highlands along with other Teotihuacan products and ideas during the Early Classic period. The presence of moldmade "adornos" and moldmade faces on many of the incense burners of this period leaves no doubt that the process was known in the highlands by Esperanza times.

FIGURINES, EFFIGY HEADS, WHISTLES, STAMPS. With two notable exceptions, figurines and effigy whistles are absent from the Early Classic period in the Guatemalan highlands. At Kaminaljuyu one beautifully modeled hollow figurine was found in an Esperanza tomb (Mound A, Tomb III).[31] The figurine, a squatting individual, is 5.8 cm. in height without the missing head. The delicate body is painted black, the hands yellow, the necklace green, and the head apparently red (Kidder, Jennings, and Shook, 1946, p. 214, fig. 168,*a*). A hand-modeled effigy whistle representing a seated individual with moldmade head and headdress and the body plainted black was found in an Early Classic burial at Nebaj (Burial 1, Mound 2; A. L. Smith and Kidder, 1951, p. 76, fig. 87,*a*). The appearance of these two isolated specimens in Early

---

[31] Two effigy-whistle fragments, one representing a frog and the other a monkey, found at Kaminaljuyu in the fill of Strs. B-4 and B-5 during the excavation of the Esperanza Mound B, cannot be assigned with certainty to the Early Classic period (Kidder, Jennings, and Shook, 1946, p. 214, fig. 166,*c,d*). Two small figurine fragments from Zaculeu (Dept. Huehuetenango) possibly date from the Early Classic Atzan phase but their assignment to that period is again uncertain (Woodbury and Trik, 1953, p. 215, figs. 277,*c*; 273,*b,5*).

Classic burials is somewhat surprising especially since none have ever been found in the tombs or burials of the Preclassic period when clay figurines and effigy whistles were turned out in great quantities. The custom apparently reflects Mexican influence. In the Valley of Mexico and at Teotihuacan figurines were customarily included among the mortuary offerings during most periods.[32]

Data on roller stamps and flat stamps during this period are sadly lacking. Although some have been reported from Kaminaljuyu (Kidder, Jennings, and Shook, 1946, p. 214, figs. 92,*b*; 187,*m,o*), they cannot be assigned with certainty to the period.[33]

WEAVING, BASKETRY, MATS, ORNAMENTS. The richly furnished Esperanza tombs

at Kaminaljuyu contained many impressions of the twilled mats probably used to wrap the corpse and cover the walls and floors of the tombs. Traces of basketry (coiled bundle-foundation tray-basket, sewn mat) are also reported from Kaminaljuyu along with several textile-impressed sherds and vessels (*ibid.*, pp. 98, 99). The textiles are comparable to our cheesecloth or loosely woven crash and were most likely produced, as today in the highlands, by stick looms of the backstrap type. Many of the vertical side flanges on incense burners bear textile impressions indicating that some sort of a matting or cloth was used to hold the soft clay while the censers were being made.

Although almost nothing is known of the clothing of the common people, the polychrome stuccoed vessels (*ibid.*, figs. 204, 205, 207), some of the effigy pots (*ibid.*, fig. 206,*b,c*), and the incense burners (*ibid.*, fig. 207,*g*) found at Kaminaljuyu tell us much about the ceremonial and upper-class attire of the Early Classic. On many of the vessels elaborately clothed individuals are depicted in ritual performances. Other individuals are shown with rich and elaborate green and red feather headdresses, cloaks and wings (probably made of quetzal and parrot feathers) or with fantastic masks, jade or shell earplugs, noseplugs, necklaces and bracelets (*ibid.*, figs. 206,*c*; 207,*h*; 207,*e,g*). Some of the individuals are shown barefooted (*ibid.*, figs. 205,*c,d*; 206,*c,f*), others in fringed or "tasseled" sandals (*ibid.*, figs. 204,*a*; 207,*a,h*). With few exceptions they seem to represent officiating priests similar in style and attire to those depicted on pottery vessels, incense burners, and fresco murals at Teotihuacan. However, since the pottery was locally manufactured at Kaminaljuyu there seems little doubt that the individuals on the Esperanza pottery vessels represent members of the new Teotihuacan priestly ruling class of the Central Highlands, who apparently continued to dress much the same as they

[32] It appears that in Mesoamerica clay figurines were made and used for different purposes at different times and places. They apparently served for magical healing ceremonies throughout both the highland and lowland Maya areas during the Preclassic (cf. Reichel-Dolmatoff, 1961). In the Valley of Mexico and in Guanajuato (Chupicuaro) they were made to represent deceased individuals and were included (as soul substances?) in tombs of the Preclassic and Classic periods. During the Late Classic and Postclassic this type of "funerary (or soul?) figurine" was in use on the Pacific Coast and Piedmont of Guatemala while still another type, used probably for offertory and decorative (or narrative?) purposes, was in vogue in the Hilly Middle Country and on both the east and west coasts of Mexico (Remojadas and Tarascan cultures). It is likely that the modern *nacimiento* (Nativity) figurines throughout Central America derive from this "decorative" or "narrative" type. For a different interpretation of the "archaic" and "classic" figurines, see Séjourné (1952b) and Wicke (1956). For the use of figurines with "jointed limbs" in connection with ventriloquism see Borhegyi (1954a) and Von Winning (1958).

[33] The roller and flat stamps found at Kaminaljuyu during the excavation of the Early Classic Esperanza Mounds A and B are actually of Late Preclassic date (Kidder, Jennings, and Shook, 1946, pp. 214–15, figs. 92,*b*; 187,*n,o*). The manufacture and use of roller stamps, at least in the highland Maya area, was apparently discontinued after Late Preclassic times, whereas flat (stemless or stemmed) stamps continued in use until the end of the Protohistoric period (Borhegyi, 1950e, pp. 23–24).

had in their homeland. We may assume that their elaborate clothing and ceremonial attire was accepted and worn by the local Maya upper class as well.

STONE SCULPTURES AND ARTIFACTS. Monumental stone sculptures, with the exception of a stone altar at Kaminaljuyu (Kidder, Jennings, and Shook, 1946, fig. 133,d,e), and a few horizontally tenoned stone jaguar, parrot, and serpent heads found in association with ball courts, were not produced during the Early Classic and succeeding periods. Excepting one single plain stela which stood in front of the Early Classic Aurora phase (A.D. 300–400) Mound D-III-13 at Kaminaljuyu (see note 22) and a few archaeological sites in the Hilly Middle Country, the stela cult, so fashionable during Middle and Late Preclassic times, seems to disappear completely. Even the few roughly carved stone stelae in the Hilly Middle Country (at such sites as Xolchun, Huil, Tzicuay, Nebaj, Department El Quiche) may represent lowland Maya influence in this area during the Classic period rather than a continuation of the Preclassic highland Maya stela cult (A. L. Smith, 1955, p. 72). The other monumental stone sculptures, stelae (excepting Stelae 15, 13, and 2 at Kaminaljuyu; see Miles, this volume, Article 10), and mushroom stones from the Central and Western Highlands previously thought to be Early Classic, have in the light of later evidence, turned out to be of Middle or Late Preclassic date.[34] Most were found at Kaminaljuyu in the fill or during general excavation around the Early Classic mounds and some were even re-used with unworked stone slabs in the foundations of Esperanza mound structures (Kidder, Jennings, and Shook, 1946, pp. 102–04). The apparent absence of mushroom stones in Early Classic tombs (or at least within the ceremonial precincts) suggests that the sacred mushroom cult, along with the equally popular calendric-stela, figurine, and three-pronged incense burner cults of

Preclassic origin, were banished from the Teotihuacan-occupied and/or -influenced highland Maya ceremonial centers. It is even likely that many of the Preclassic highland Maya stone monuments were intentionally smashed, scattered, and thrown into dumps or irreverently re-used as building foundations or pavings by the Teotihuacan overlords.

Among the lesser stone objects and artifacts of the Early Classic period are round, perforated "doughnut stones" (ibid., fig. 159,a; Smith and Kidder, 1951, p. 51) which were probably utilized as digging-stick weights.[35] Small, tripod metates and manos of dark igneous rock seem to be standard articles of tomb furniture and were prob-

---

[34] The list includes several stone stelae fragments (Kidder, Jennings, and Shook, 1946, figs. 167,b; 133,f), and the puff-cheeked human head from Kaminaljuyu (fig. 133,a-c); the "silhouetted relief" sculptures from the Western Highlands, Santa Cruz, Quiche (figs. 141,a,c; 141,b; 142,b) and from Kaminaljuyu (fig. 142,a,c,d); the stone prognathic human head (fig. 170,i), the squat stone effigy frog (figs. 40, 41) and various plain and effigy mushroom stone fragments from Kaminaljuyu (figs. 42; 58,c; 160,d,h). On the other hand, the three tripod mushroom stones illustrated by Kidder, Jennings, and Shook (1946, fig. 160,c,e,g) are of Classic date (see Type D mushrooms in Borhegyi, 1961a, p. 500, fig. 2).

Kidder in his "Addenda and Corrigenda" of Kaminaljuyu (1948, pp. 227–28) has already recognized the fact that some of the mushroom stones and the "silhouetted relief" sculptures, mentioned in this footnote, are of Late Preclassic, not Early Classic, date (cf. Kidder, Jennings, and Shook, 1946, p. 103).

[35] The so-called "doughnut stones" are most frequently found on the Pacific Coastal Plain and Piedmont areas (Shook, 1949b, pp. 20-21; Borhegyi notes, 1950-52). Of the 27 sites surveyed in this area, 10 had doughnut stones. They are rare among the lowland Maya and in the Hilly Middle Country. In the Central Highlands some of the doughnut stones may date from the end of the Late Preclassic. Berlin (1952, fig. 17,g) illustrates a carved Aurora phase (A.D. 300–400) specimen. Because they were frequently carved with elaborate designs (representing monkey, jaguar, or human faces) and were occasionally found within the boundaries of ceremonial centers they may have been used for ceremonial planting. However, their alternate function as batons and maceheads or symbols of power is also a possibility (Woodbury and Trik, 1953, p. 224).

ably used to grind meal for sacred purposes (Kidder, Jennings, and Shook, 1946, fig. 158; Woodbury and Trik, 1953, p. 221). Also present are green obsidian sequins (also known from Teotihuacan), obsidian points and flakes (Kidder, Jennings, and Shook, 1946, p. 159), alabaster double cups (*ibid.*, figs. 59; 154,*a,b*; Woodbury and Trik, 1953, fig. 137), celts, bark beaters, pot polishers, hammerstones, and curious fine-grained "sounding" stones (*ibid.*, p. 144). The presence of grooved, edged bark beaters with scored or corrugated faces indicates that cloth or paper was made in Early Classic times from agave fibers or the bark of certain trees, especially the Amatle tree (*Ficus* sp. *moraceae*). Although none have survived in the highlands, bark papers were probably painted as early as the Classic period with pictures, glyphs, and symbols of religious or calendric significance.[36]

Pyrite-incrusted mosaic plaques which may have been worn on state occasions as breast pendants as symbols of wealth and power or, less likely, used as mirrors, are frequently encountered in Early Classic highland tombs. Some of these plaques at Kaminaljuyu and Zaculeu have elaborately carved designs on the back surface representing priests making offerings or dancing with "wings" (*ibid.*, fig. 156; Woodbury and Trik, 1953, fig. 131).[37]

Lapidary art during the Early Classic period is characterized by fine quality of workmanship. Jade earplugs—hemispherical, tubular, and discoidal—plain or carved beads, and effigy pendants (representing monkeys, fishes, parrots, jaguars, serpents, Tlaloc heads, death's-heads, and human beings), U-shaped nose ornaments, spangles, and mosaics are frequently found among the tomb furnishings and offerings (Kaminaljuyu: Kidder, Jennings, and Shook, 1946, figs. 143–54; Nebaj: A. L. Smith and Kidder, 1951, figs. 52–63; Zaculeu: Woodbury and Trik, figs. 139, 146, 280, 281; Zacualpa: Lothrop, 1936, figs. 61, 63).

Inferences of Social and Religious Structure

As far as the lowland Maya are concerned, the term "Classic" fits perfectly, for in the Tropical Rain Forest it was the Classic period that saw the greatest architectural, engineering, artistic, and intellectual achievement. In the highlands, however, this was apparently not the case. Compared to the cultural achievements of the Middle and Late Preclassic, especially those of the Providencia (500–300 B.C.) and Miraflores-Arenal phases (300 B.C.–A.D. 200), the highland "Classic" is anticlimatic. The only artistic and cultural bright spots are those which show outside influences from Mexico, in particular from Teotihuacan and

[36] According to native tradition, the area around Lake Amatitlan where the Amatle tree grows in great abundance was one of the pre-Columbian centers of paper making in the Guatemalan highlands. Classic period bark beaters for making bark paper and bark cloth have been reported from such highland sites as Amatitlan (Borhegyi notes, 1960); Zacualpa (Lothrop, 1936, pp. 52, 53, fig. 56; Wauchope, 1948a, p. 162, fig. 178); Kaminaljuyu (Kidder, Jennings, and Shook, 1946, pp. 142, 143, fig. 61); Chama (Butler, 1940, p. 258); Chocola (Burkitt, 1924, p. 144); and Tajumulco (Dutton and Hobbs, 1943, p. 50, fig. 30). There is a possibility, however, that grooved stone bark beaters are as early as Middle Preclassic. One was found at Las Majadas (near Kaminaljuyu); two others at the site of El Trapiche in El Salvador in what appears to be Middle or Late Preclassic context (cf. also M. D. Coe, 1961, p. 110, figs. 41,*c*; 42,*b*). (For the distribution of stone bark beaters and paper manufacture throughout Mesoamerica see Linné, 1934, pp. 197–204, Map 5.)

[37] Although the first pyrite-incrusted plaques appear during the Late Preclassic at Kaminaljuyu (in Tombs I and II, Mound E-III-3; Shook and Kidder, 1952, p. 116, fig. 52), they are extremely rare (only two or three undecorated fragments are known) and do not seem to have become fashionable until the Classic and Postclassic periods.

Pyrite-incrusted plaques have been reported from Early Classic tombs at such Hilly Middle Country sites as Chama, San Jeronimo, Nebaj, Kixpek, and Chipal; and in the Western Highlands from Finca El Paraiso, Chalchitan, Quen Santo, Zaculeu, Zacualpa, and Tajumulco. In the Central Highlands they have been found only at Kaminaljuyu and Lake Amatitlan.

Tajin. Public architectural activities slow down; the temple and burial mounds grow smaller and less elaborate; the stela cult comes to an abrupt end; the sacred mushroom cult, along with the figurine and three-pronged incensario cults, disappears (at least within the ceremonial precincts); and the pottery of the Early Classic period, although superficially elegant in a Victorian sense, is far inferior in finish and quality to that of the Middle or Late Preclassic.[38]

The so-called highland "Classic" was heralded by a sharp and sudden change in the religious structure. This change, which brought an end to the individualistic approach to the supernatural so characteristic of the Preclassic, is most clearly evidenced by the disappearance of the time-honored figurine cult, not only in the highlands but simultaneously over a wide area in the Maya- and La Venta ("Olmec")-influenced or occupied territories of Mesoamerica (Sorenson, 1955). Abandoned within the ceremonial precincts were such traditional ritual items as three-pronged incense burners, rimhead vessels, mushroom stones, and plain columnar basalt stelae, presumably along with the particular religious, curing, and calendric ceremonies and gods with which they were associated. With the changes in highland Maya religion came new trends in architecture, burial customs, and art forms, all reflecting foreign influence from Mexico and, to a lesser degree, from the Maya lowlands.

To explain this drastic change in highland Maya culture, A. V. Kidder postulated

(1945, p. 74) an invasion from Mexico, particularly from Teotihuacan, which may have put a completely new and foreign group of priest-rulers into power in the Maya ceremonial centers. The accumulation of evidence since this was written has only served to strengthen Kidder's theory. There is now little doubt that around A.D. 400 the Maya highlands were invaded and occupied by a group of people who brought with them Teotihuacan patterns of life so faithful and complete that one must assume they came directly from the metropolis of Teotihuacan itself, or from one of the more important satellite colonies such as Tajin in northern Veracruz. (see fig. 4).

The newcomers to the highlands built strongly nucleated ceremonial centers in Teotihuacan style to which in most instances ball courts were added in an acropolis-like arrangement of terraces. In all probability they controlled and carried on extensive trade relations with the Tropical Rain Forest area which explains the presence of Teotihuacan-type pottery at such sites as Uaxactun and Tikal as well as the presence of numerous lowland traits among the Maya highlanders. Their widespread religious, economic, and political control over the highland Maya ceremonial centers succeeded, to a considerable degree, in eliminating or driving underground the previously popular and time-honored magico-religious and calendric cults. However, even though the more sophisticated Maya upper classes seem to have accepted readily, if not eagerly, the new and fashionable Teotihuacan religion and political dominion, the conversion may have been far less successful among the village folk.

In this connection it is important to note that during some stratigraphic excavations at Kaminaljuyu, "Late Classic" Amatle pottery was frequently found directly overlying Late Preclassic Miraflores-Arenal deposits; sometimes the upper zones of the test excavations even yielded a mixture of

---

[38] These points notwithstanding, I do not propose to rename the period. Not only is the term "Highland Classic" thoroughly entrenched in the literature, but also the use of an unfamiliar new name or phrase in a general synthesis of this type would confuse readers who wished to correlate and compare this period with other "Classic" period cultures in Mesoamerica.

A similar concern about the misuse of the term "Classic" in Mesoamerica has been expressed by Proskouriakoff (1954, pp. 65, 66) and by Wolf (1959, p. 270). For an opposite point of view see Roys (1958).

Miraflores-Arenal and Amatle wares. The apparent lack of Esperanza sherds or other Early Classic pottery diagnostics was considered somewhat of a mystery (Kidder, Jennings, and Shook, 1946, p. 103). More recently, a similar lack of Early Classic pottery was reported from the archaeological village site of La Victoria near Ocos where M. D. Coe (1959b, p. 9; 1961, pp. 86–87) postulated a hiatus in the occupation of La Victoria lasting through the Early Classic. He indicated, however, that pottery of the Early Classic period was present at the presumably "ceremonial" site of Santa Clara, 12 km. north of La Victoria. I believe this is an indication that the Teotihuacan religious ideas and architectural innovations were accepted only by the sophisticated priests and artisans of the larger ceremonial centers and were never incorporated into the life of the highland Maya villages (Borhegyi, 1960a, p. 236).

The most important change in the religious structure of highland Maya upper-class society during the Early Classic period was an all-out effort to systematize the universe and make it predictable. Heading the new Teotihuacan-derived pantheon was Tlaloc—"He who makes the plants grow"— the god of rain and fertility. His face was masked, his eyes covered with round goggles; the quetzal bird, symbol of power, spread its wings above his head. As the maker of thunder his voice was like that of the jaguar. For this reason he was often depicted as a jaguar or as a human being with jaguar paws (Borhegyi, 1959b; see also note 14). He was associated with the serpents, toads, and frogs who come out of hiding after a heavy rain. At other times he was surrounded by butterflies (the souls of the departed) or by the owls of darkness (messengers of death) (Caso, 1949b; von Winning, 1948).

Other gods who followed Tlaloc from Teotihuacan to the Guatemalan highlands were Xipe Totec, "Our Lord the Flayed One," an early form of this nature and

fertility god; the butterfly goddess; the four little hunchbacked and sometimes bearded helpers of Tlaloc (the *Tlaloques*) who resided in the Tlalocan; and Ehecatl, god of the winds (an early form of Quetzalcoatl, the Precious Serpent, with shell, serpent, and quetzal attributes and a curious snouted nose). There were also Xolotl, the Evening Star, and twin brother of Quetzalcoatl; Tepeyolotl, the jaguar god, with twisted "motion" (*ollin*) signs on his body signifying earthquake (Piña Chan, 1960a, fig. 22); Tlalchitonatiuh, the Earth's Sun, the Jaguar Sun, or Falling Sun; and last, but not least, Mictlantecuhtli, the fearsome ruler of the underworld, the Land of the Dead, represented as a skeleton or a skull with gaping jaws. Other Mexican gods may have been introduced to the Guatemalan highlands such as Huehueteotl, the old wrinkled-faced sunken-eyed fire god, but they have not been clearly substantiated through the archaeological data (cf. Borhegyi, 1959b, illustration on p. 110).

Apparently the Teotihuacan religion was peaceful rather than militant and demanding of excessive human sacrifices (Séjourné, 1960). The Teotihuacan theologists were probably the first in Mesoamerica to conceive of the universe as a series of worlds each with an allotted time span and an inevitable end in catastrophe. When one world collapsed in flood, fire, or earthquake, they believed another was born only to come, in its turn, to a violent end (Wolf, 1959, p. 88). This philosophy probably led the Teotihuacan religious specialists to divine by magical computations the sacred cycle of 52 years, at the end of which cosmic crisis threatened the survival of mankind and the universe.[39] They further be-

[39] This hypothesis is presented on the basis of admittedly weak archaeological evidence. The first representations of year bundles or so-called Teotihuacan year symbols appear on Teotihuacan pottery of the Early Classic period. It has been suggested that a year bundle represents 52 years bound together (Caso, 1959; Linné, 1941). It is possible, however, that the knowledge and use of

lieved that in order to avoid catastrophe at the end of each 52-year period man, through his priestly intermediaries, was required to enter into a new covenant with the supernatural. In the meantime, he atoned for his sins and kept the precarious balance of the universe by offering uninterrupted sacrifices to the gods.

How the Teotihuacan invaders succeeded in "selling" these new religious ideas to the highland Maya we may never know. Surely, such esoteric concepts would have been little understood and appreciated by the simple Maya farmers, who probably felt much closer to the gods of the earth and nature than to a far removed and abstract heavenly pantheon. Since the type of Preclassic face-to-face individualistic and personal covenant between man and the supernatural had changed in the Teotihuacan-oriented worship centers to a formalized and abstract religion, the priestly leaders must have been forced to seek a simpler, more direct, means of maintaining the support of the satellite villagers.

They solved this problem, I believe, in three ways. First, they introduced the ball game as a "side show" to the ceremonial activities; second, they correlated the ceremonial activities of the worship centers with regularized and controlled open-air markets; third, they instituted pilgrimages to sacred places in order to stimulate commerce and economic exchange with other areas.

When the barter exchange of the Preclassic period proved inadequate for the expanded trading activities, they adopted an interculturally accepted commodity—cacao beans—as currency (J. E. S. Thompson, 1956). Political control of the cacao-producing Atlantic and Pacific coasts thus became a vital necessity and probably explains why Teotihuacan influence was invariably directed toward the occupation of these areas. (See fig. 4.)

We can guess that the Teotihuacan priests were also supported by the military might of the Teotihuacan Eagle and Jaguar warrior knights, a pre-Columbian counterpart of the Christian crusaders (Piña Chan, 1960a, fig. 22). So by force and guile the Teotihuacan invaders succeeded in changing the highland Maya burial and worship compounds of the Middle and Late Preclassic period into metropolitan and cosmopolitan pilgrim and market centers. And by so doing they inadvertently sowed the seeds of secularization that ultimately destroyed their theocracy.

LATE CLASSIC PERIOD (A.D. 700–1000)

The archaeological phases associated with this period are: Amatle, Pamplona (Valley of Guatemala); Pompeya (Almolonga Valley); Zarzal (Lake Amatitlan); Chama 3–4, Chipal 1 (Chixoy Drainage); Chipoc, Seacal (Coban Drainage); Chinaq (Zaculeu); Pokom (Zacualpa); Chiapa X, A-B (Chiapas). (See note 9, and Table 1.)

Modes of Subsistence

This period in general seems to have been one of regional specialization. While many of the older valley sites continued to be inhabited, new sites were founded, usually on the hillslopes. On these hillslopes terrace agriculture and irrigation were probably practiced extensively. It seems that the increasing demand for luxury objects and certain food specialties (cacao?) may have induced the Maya farmers to produce more than was required by their subsistence needs. The surplus, finding its way to the regional markets, was offered in exchange for products of other areas and stimulated, to an even greater degree than in the Early Classic, regional craft and crop specialization. This in time became the basis of the tribute requirements of Protohistoric and postconquest days.

---

the 52-year cycle and the 365-day calendar preceded the Classic Teotihuacan culture (Lizardi Ramos, 1955).

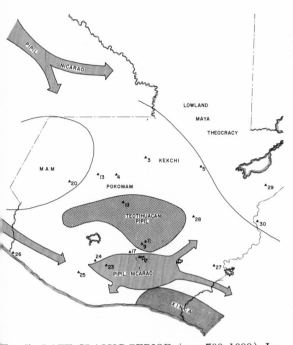

Fɪɢ. 5—LATE CLASSIC PERIOD (ᴀ.ᴅ. 700–1000). Influences from Teotihuacan diminish, although a theocratic form of society (under Teotihuacan leadership?) continues in parts of the Western Highlands and the Hilly Middle Country. Warlike groups from the Gulf coast of Mexico reach the highlands via the Usumacinta River and the Pacific coast of Mexico. Some move on to Costa Rica and Panama. Others, such as the "Tajinized-Teotihuacan-Pipil" or Pipil-Nicarao, establish themselves on the Coastal Piedmont of Guatemala and, through warlike incursions into the Central and Western Highlands, bring an end to the Teotihuacan-oriented theocracy. At the end of the period most of the valley sites are abandoned and new settlements are established on the hillslopes and hilltops.

Settlement Pattern and Architecture

SETTLEMENT AND SITES. The majority of the Late Classic ceremonial settlements still lay in the valleys and in open country close to arable land. The settlement pattern, radically different in concept from that of Preclassic times, consisted of small compact groups of pyramidal structures. Low and elongated platform mounds were arranged around tightly enclosed plazas and rectangular ball courts, the latter usually walled on all four sides. Although settlements varied considerably in size, small ceremonial centers with a single ball

court were the rule not only in the Central and Western Highlands but also in the Hilly Middle Country (Shook and Proskouriakoff, 1956, p. 98).[40] The ruins of Cotio, a site a few kilometers west of Kaminaljuyu, is representative of the smaller Late Classic ceremonial center. In an open valley near the head of a deep ravine, with a spring providing a year-round supply of water, it consists of three low (2 m. high) squarish, flat-topped mounds and one rectangular ball court. Stones were not used in the construction of the mounds, which were filled with rubbishy topsoil and brown clay and faced with adobe plaster. Lumps of burned adobe bearing imprints of small poles found on the surface of the mounds prove that they once supported buildings made of thin poles daubed with mud (Shook, 1952a). Unfortunately, as in previous periods, practically nothing is known about the habitation sites and cemeteries of the common people.

Perhaps the most puzzling aspect of the Late Classic is the deliberate abandonment of most of the highland valley sites shortly before the close of the period. Site after site was deserted, never to be reoccupied, in spite of the fact that many have been in use for more than two millennia.

[40] The sizable increase in the number of Late Classic sites in the Central Highlands is readily discernible from Shook's survey (1952b):

Departments	Total No. of Sites	Early Classic	Late Classic
Guatemala	73	12	37
Chimaltenango .	11	5	7
Sacatepequez ..	19	6	13
TOTAL	103	23	57

A relatively smaller increase in Late Classic sites is apparent in A. L. Smith's (1955) archaeological survey of the Western Highlands and Hilly Middle Country:

Departments	Total No. of Sites	Early Classic	Late Classic
Huehuetenango .	11	5	4
El Quiche	36	4	8
Baja Verapaz ..	6	—	—
Alta Verapaz ..	13	4	8
TOTAL	66	13	20

31

ARCHITECTURE AND BURIALS. Aside from the meager information on the adobe-plaster-faced mounds of Cotio, which supported thatch-roofed buildings, little is known of the public architecture at Kaminaljuyu and, in general, of the Central Highlands. It seems significant, however, that many Teotihuacan-inspired architectural innovations, such as terraced substructures made of cut pumice blocks set in adobe and faced with plaster, pebbles, and lime, and the use of the talud and tablero, were permanently discontinued at the end of the Early Classic. In the succeeding period A. V. Kidder believes (1948, p. 232) that adobe, as in Preclassic times, was again the exclusive material for mound building.

In the Hilly Middle Country, at Nebaj, mounds and floor surfaces were plastered with a mixture of ash and talpetate with little or no lime (Smith and Kidder, 1951, pp. 20–21). The plaster on the steps was apparently painted red, and the stairways were not as steep as in the preceding period. Well-cut rectangular stone blocks or slabs laid in mud were occasionally employed in the constructions. At Zaculeu in the Western Highlands Late Classic structures were too few and too incomplete to indicate any significant architectural change. It would seem, however, that such architectural features as split upper stairways, divided by rectangular blocks or by medial battered balustrades, appeared for the first time in the Guatemalan highlands toward the end of the Late Classic. The facing was either thick lime plaster or adobe with a thin coating of lime. Fragments of plaster with polychrome painting suggest that this decorative technique, better known during later periods, may have been in use at Zaculeu as early as the Late Classic (Woodbury and Trik, 1953, p. 285, fig. 39,e,g,k,m).

Based on the associated pottery, it is very likely that the use of community- and family-owned sweathouses for ritual cleans-ing and curative magico-religious rites began during Late Classic times in the Guatemalan highlands. They were probably near springs or streams on the outskirts of settlements. A community sweathouse discovered by Kidder and Shook (1959) at La Gruta on Finca El Paraiso (Department of Quezaltenango) in the Western Highlands consisted of a circular subterranean structure made of roughly cut stones. A long entrance passageway covered by stone slabs led to what had once been a beehive-shaped chamber. Three concentric benches surrounded a deep, circular central firepit containing fragments of manos and metates showing ample signs of exposure to intense heat. Although no other prehistoric sweathouses have so far been discovered in the Guatemalan highlands, their use is believed to be an ancient trait.[41]

There seems to have been considerable variety in the burial customs of the Late Classic. Cists and slab-lined crypts, similar to those of Early Classic times, continued in use at Zaculeu while narrow, rectangular, stone-lined and roofed chambers (or cists) remained the fashion for burials at Nebaj (Woodbury and Trik, 1953, p. 285; A. L. Smith and Kidder, 1951, pp. 28–30). In addition, large (3 feet high), lidded globular pottery urns with restricted orifices were used to receive the dead at Nebaj and Zaculeu.[42] This necessarily re-

[41] Sweat houses occur at Chiapa de Corzo, Chiapas, Mexico, as early as Period VIII (Jiquipilas phase), at the beginning of the Early Classic period, known in the Guatemalan highlands as the Aurora phase (A.D. 300–400) (Borhegyi notes).

[42] The orifice of these burial urns, which were probably used originally as storage jars, was so restricted it was too small to admit even a tightly flexed corpse. In the Western Highlands at Zaculeu it was the custom to cut off the top of the urn about one quarter of the way below the rim. When the body and its furnishings were in place the cut-off portion was replaced, possibly lashed into position, and occasionally the orifice was covered with a large inverted bowl. After the urn was placed in position it was reinforced about

quired a tightly contracted, seated position for the body. Although not infrequently handsome pottery vessels were placed with these burial urns, at Nebaj none were accompanied with jade or pyrite-incrusted plaques as were the bodies of important persons buried in the tombs. Urn burials were also discovered in the streets of the modern town of Nebaj and in the surrounding cornfields but never in ceremonial structures. For this reason they are considered by some archaeologists to have been the funeral form employed among the common people during Late Classic times (A. L. Smith and Kidder, 1951, p. 28). At Zaculeu and Chipal, however, urn burials were often found in temple substructures, indicating that at these sites persons buried in this fashion may have been of considerable social importance (Butler, 1940, p. 258, fig. 23,*b*). It is quite possible that the custom of urn burials derived from the Gulf Coast of Mexico, where they apparently were a popular form of interment during Early and Late Classic times (Drucker, 1943b, p. 148).

At Cotio, Zaculeu, and Chama skeletal remains of the principal tomb occupants were often extended, but by the end of the period at Zaculeu the flexed position seems to have prevailed. At Chipal, Kixpek, Chihuatal, and Ratinlixul seated burials in round or oblong vaulted chambers with side doors became popular. At Nebaj secondary persons were buried in flexed position. The custom of burying decapitated bodies and bodyless skulls continued at Nebaj; skeletal dedication offerings in pyramid piers were in vogue at Chipal. At Chama, as during the Early Classic period, the principal tomb occupants lay extended on their backs with a jade bead in the mouth (Butler, 1940, p. 258–60). At Zaculeu jade offerings in tombs diminished in quantity as well as in quality.

_____
the round bottom with earth fill (Woodbury and Trik, 1953, p. 78, figs. 42,*a*; and 179,*c,e*).

Arts and Crafts

POTTERY. In the *Central Highlands* the Amatle and Pamplona pottery of the Late Classic gives the superficial impression of degeneracy when compared with Esperanza tomb materials. It must be remembered, however, that we know only what seem to be culinary wares used probably exclusively by the common people who lived at some distance from the ceremonial precincts. Future archaeological work may prove the Amatle-Pamplona phase to have been much richer, both in handicrafts and in architecture, than is now evident (see note 9; Kidder, Jennings, and Shook, 1946, p. 258).

Kidder's studies at Kaminaljuyu led him to believe that Amatle was older than Pamplona (*ibid.*, pp. 39–41). For a while it was postulated that Kaminaljuyu was unoccupied during Late Classic times and that the Amatle and Pamplona sherds represented an Early Postclassic reoccupation of the site. This supposition was based on the discovery of a few plain Plumbate sherds in the preponderantly Amatle deposits. Subsequent discoveries of the same plain, pre-effigy-type, San Juan Plumbate in Late Classic deposits on the Pacific Coastal Piedmont of Guatemala enabled A. V. Kidder (1948, pp. 229–32) to reconsider the supposed Late Classic hiatus at Kaminaljuyu and assign Amatle and Pamplona as sequent phases to this period. There still remains the possibility that some Amatle material is of Early rather than Late Classic date. Deposits found during stratigraphic excavations 1 Kaminaljuyu of mixed Miraflores and Amatle sherds directly overlaid deposits of pure Miraflores pottery (Kidder, Jennings, and Shook, 1946, p. 103).[43]

_____
[43] It is my belief that the preponderantly culinary nature of the Amatle material suggests that this phase represents a less sophisticated indigenous Maya aspect of the Early Classic and, unlike the Esperanza tomb vessels, shows little if any Teotihuacan influence (see also note 9).

Pottery of the Amatle and Pamplona phases is characterized by a decided rarity of painted wares. A thin, hard-fired plain reddish-brown ware called Amatle Hard ware, much of it showing incipient vitrification, predominates. Forms include thin-walled, flaring-sided or straight-walled bowls with flat bottoms; tall cylindrical vases, bowls, and jars decorated with incised wavy or squiggle lines, or with a row of small circular appliqué buttons of clay, each of which was punched with the end of a reed or a small hollow bone. Bowls and jars decorated with these appliqué buttons are referred to in the literature as "Tejar ware" (*ibid.*, p. 41). Among the few painted wares are Black ware, Red ware, and Red-and White-on-Orange ware (Amatle-polychrome) cylindrical vases, round-sided ring or pedestal-based bowls, and the so-called spiked incense burners (flat-bottomed bowls ornamented with concentric rows of conical protuberances). The white paint on these vessels provides outlines and wavy lines. The red paint frequently contains specular hematite particles.

Associated with Amatle and Pamplona material throughout the Central and Western Highlands are Tiquisate cream-colored (ranging from ivory to reddish-orange) round-sided bowls, cylindrical vases, cylindrical tripods with mold-decorated slab feet, and bowls and vases decorated with figures (mostly spider monkeys) in relief, Z and Y Fine Orange jars, round-sided and pedestal-based bowls, cylindrical vases (R. E. Smith, 1958); Red-on-Buff (or Red-on-Orange) "lacquer" ware bowls; and plain orange to gray Plumbate (lustrous) cylindrical vases, jars, and shallow bowls of the San Juan and Robles types (Shepard, 1948, pp. 133–41). According to Kidder (Kidder, Jennings, and Shook, 1946, p. 41) San Juan Plumbate and Tiquisate wares seem to be more common in the Amatle phase, whereas Z and Y Fine Orange, Red-on-Buff (or Red-on-Orange) "lacquer" ware and Ro-

bles Plumbate are more diagnostic of the presumably later Pamplona phase.

In the Western Highlands (especially in the northern part of the Department of El Quiche) and in the Hilly Middle Country, fine thin-walled cylindrical or barrel-shaped, well-polished, and often polychrome (red-and-black-and-white-on-orange) vessels seem to predominate. Similar vessels have been reported from Zacualpa (Lothrop, 1936) and Zaculeu (Woodbury and Trik, 1953, fig. 265). Many of the cylindrical and globular vessels with high straight necks have magnificent designs painted against a rich orange (or dull ivory) background. A band of decorative glyphs or black and white chevrons (herringbone border) appears just below the rim (Kidder II and Samayoa, 1959, figs. 78–81). The anthropomorphic and zoomorphic paintings (in black and red) on the bodies of these vessels are superb examples of the best Maya figure painting and indicate a strong influence from the Tropical Rain Forest area.

The prevailing form of incense burner in the Central Highlands is the double-chambered, mold-decorated human effigy censer with two vertical side flanges. The human face on the censer is depicted naturalistically, usually with closed eyes (dead?), large earspools and nose bars. Sometimes human skulls are modeled or molded on the vessel walls. Among the various moldmade adornos which once must have decorated these vessels one can often find representations of ears of maize (Kidder, 1949b, fig. 6,*f-h*, pp. 16–17). At Lake Amatitlan flat-bottomed, flaring-sided vases (occasionally with two finger-punched handles) decorated with two or four concentric rows of spikes and sometimes with four agave leaves at the rim are the most common. They have been found by the hundreds at various depths on the lake floor (Borhegyi, 1958b, p. 125; cf. 1950a, pl. 1, no. 17; Kidder, 1950, fig. 2,*f*).

Also present throughout the Central Highlands are hollow, tubular censers shaped as grotesque jaguars or human beings seated cross-legged and holding bowls in their laps (Kidder, Jennings, and Shook, 1946, fig. 202,*b,d*), and stylized human effigy censers representing winged (or diving) individuals (or deities) with enormous noseplugs and earrings. This latter type of censer is frequently supported by three hollow tubular (cylindrical) legs open at the bottom (cf, *ibid.*, fig. 202,*a*; Kidder II and Samayoa, 1959, fig. 16). Large two-part vessels (50–80 cm. high) are occasionally made in the form of hollow pottery jaguars and human beings or priests dressed as the god Xipe (Borhegyi, 1958b, p. 124; cf. Kidder II and Samayoa, 1959, fig. 17).[44] Ladle censers with solid (plain, twisted, or effigy) handles are also common at Amatitlan, in the Antigua-Agua area, and at Kaminaljuyu (Borhegyi, 1950a, pl. 1, no. 14); hollow tubular-handled ladle-censers with closed pinched ends seem to replace the open-ended, Early Classic variety at Zaculeu (Woodbury and Trik, 1953, p. 191).

FIGURINES, EFFIGY WHISTLES, POTTERY, STAMPS. Pottery figurines and effigy whistles reappear in the highlands during Late Classic times and, as might be expected, are mostly moldmade. They differ greatly from their Preclassic counterparts in appearance and apparently also in function. Instead of representing pregnancy or some abnormality, most of the Late Classic specimens are so refined as to suggest their primary use as offertory or decorative objects. They are never found broken and battered. Whatever their purpose, it is quite certain that they were not intended, as were the figurines of the Preclassic, for use in magical curing or fertility ceremonies (see note 32).

Slender pottery drums (open at both ends, the upper end covered with hide) similar to Late Classic specimens from the Rain Forest area have been reported at Nebaj (A. L. Smith and Kidder, 1951, p. 72, fig. 83,*d*) and at Finca El Paraiso (Department of Quezaltenango). Other musical instruments of the Late Classic period include pottery bells and rattles from Finca El Paraiso and pottery flageolets, flutes, ocarinas (some plain, others zoomorphic) from Finca El Paraiso, El Sitio (San Marcos), Aguacatan, Xolchun (Huehuetenango) and Kaminaljuyu. Some of the instruments are made of Tiquisate or Robles Plumbate ware.

Pottery stamps are extremely rare during this period; the few pieces assignable to the Late Classic are of the flat, stemmed variety.

WEAVING, BASKETRY, MATS, FEATHERWORK, ORNAMENTS. A few textile-impressed sherds from Zaculeu and other sites are indicative of the use during the Late Classic of plain-weave fabrics (Woodbury and Trik, 1953, p. 279). That more intricate weaving patterns and methods (including even the possibility of *ikat* weaving) were known is evident from the many items of clothing depicted on the figurines, effigy whistles, and painted polychrome pottery. Articles of dress that can be identified include: loincloths; fringed (or ruffled) belts; waist- and full-length shoulder capes (often worn only over the right shoulder); *huipiles* or blouses of netlike material (cf. modern Maya huipiles of the Coban, Alta Verapaz area), leather sandals held by a

---

[44] Although the use of Teotihuacan-influenced ceramic wares and forms among the highland Maya died out by Late Classic times, some of the Late Classic moldmade (and adorno-decorated) incense burners, rimhead vessels and figurine fragments found in the Central Highlands at Kaminaljuyu and Lake Amatitlan recall Azcapotzalco (Teotihuacan IV, Late Classic) models (Tozzer, 1921, pls. 14, 16, 17; Linné, 1934, figs. 149, 150, 165, 166, 185–98). It can be postulated that Teotihuacan influence (via Azcapotzalco, Cholula, Xochicalco, and/or Tajin) continued to be felt in the highland Maya area during Late Classic times although possibly to a much lesser degree than during the preceding Early Classic period (see also note 49).

double cord passing between the first and second toes and between the third and fourth; heavy quilted cotton (or kapok) armor; and leather pads to protect the hands, elbows, and waists of ball-game players. Featherwork basketry and mats were probably in general use although the elaborate turban-like headdresses, round fans (of basket weave) and basket litters were restricted to the privileged classes (see Kidder II and Samayoa, 1959, figs. 78, 80).

STONE SCULPTURES, STONE ARTIFACTS, OTHER LAPIDARY ARTS. This period, like the preceding one, is characterized by an absence of monumental stone sculpture. The general lack of stone stelae with calendric inscriptions is particularly puzzling in the Hilly Middle Country since, as attested by the similarities in figurines and effigy whistles, this region must have been in close contact with the Tropical Rain Forest area throughout the Late Classic period. Notable exceptions are some of the unusual and beautifully carved stone monuments concentrated in the Pacific Coastal and Piedmont area around Santa Lucia Cotzumalhuapa and in southeastern Quetzaltenango (J. E. S. Thompson, 1943c, 1948).[45]

In the Central and Western Highlands the manufacture of horizontally tenoned stone heads (human, jaguar, and serpent) serving as ball-court markers continued through the Late Classic period. Similarly, the stone yokes and elaborately carved "thin (or flat) stone" heads (called *hachas* or "axe-heads" in Mexico) found in the same area are probably also of Late as well

as Early Classic date. The original use of hachas, stone yokes, and the so-called "palmate stones" or palmas of Mexico has long been a subject of speculation. Gann (1932) suggested that yokes were employed in connection with human sacrifice. Genin (1928) thought they were used as burial furniture and that hachas were sacrificial axes. Lothrop (1923), J. E. S. Thompson (1941c, 1943b), and Ekholm (1946, 1949) have presented convincing arguments that these items were either worn by ball-game players or were stone replicas of lighter-weight game accoutrement used in pre- or post-game ceremonies. Most recently, Proskouriakoff (1954) has called attention to the possibility that the stone yokes, hachas, and palmas (especially those with short horizontal and vertical tenons or sockets) could have served as hazards or portable goals for the ball game in much the same way as the stone rings of Postclassic times. Yokes, hachas, and palmas undoubtedly originated on the Gulf coast of Mexico, where they have been found in the greatest number and variety. While palmas have seldom been reported outside this area, yokes (mostly of the open end, U-shaped type) and hachas have been found throughout the highland Maya area.[46]

[45] J. E. S. Thompson (1948) considers most of the so-called Cotzumalhuapa-style stone sculptures of Late Classic date. His findings are based largely on stylistic grounds rather than on stratigraphic evidence. On the basis of recent field work it was found that many of the stone sculptures at El Baul and Bilbao were in direct association with Late Preclassic and Early Classic period ceramics. (Parsons, Borhegyi, Jenson, and Ritzenthaler, 1963.)

[46] Elaborately carved Early and Late Classic "thin stone" heads have been found in the Central and Western Highlands at Kaminaljuyu and in the Department of Sacatepequez (Borhegyi notes) at San Cristobal Totonicapan (J. E. S. Thompson, 1941a, p. 60; 1943a, pl. 10,*e*), in the Antigua-Agua and Amatitlan areas (Borhegyi field notes); in northern El Quiche (Proskouriakoff, 1954, fig. 11,*k,m*); in the Chimaltenango, Quezaltenango, Salcaja, Solola areas (Borhegyi notes); in eastern Guatemala in the Departments of Progreso, Jutiapa, Santa Rosa, Izabal (Kidder II and Samayoa, 1959, fig. 39; Proskouriakoff, 1954, fig. 11,*n*; Borhegyi notes); and in Honduras and El Salvador (J. E. S. Thompson, 1941a, pp. 60–67; Proskouriakoff, 1954, fig. 11,*l*). They are also numerous on the Pacific Coast and Piedmont of Guatemala (J. E. S. Thompson, 1948, figs. 19, 20,*g,h*: Kidder II and Samayoa, 1959, figs. 92–94).

Stone yokes in the Guatemalan highlands have been reported from about the same areas as the thin stone heads. They are mostly plain although some have been painted (or stuccoed) in red,

Mushroom stones reappear in the highland Maya area during Late Classic times (J. E. S. Thompson, 1943a, p. 121). They are mostly of the plain and/or tripod variety (Type D, Borhegyi, 1961a, p. 500, fig. 2, nos. 38–40). The tripod legs are chubby or sharp-angled; the stems occasionally bear conventionalized and stylized carved human, monkey, and bird (owls?) faces. In the Central and Western Highlands tripod mushroom stones have been reported from Kaminaljuyu, the Antigua-Agua area, Amatitlan, Mixco Viejo, Tecpan, Zacualpa, and San Martin Jilotepeque (Kidder, Jennings, and Shook, 1946, fig. 160c,e,g; Borhegyi, 1961a, p. 500).[47]

Although no mushroom stones have been found in stratigraphic excavations, the possibility exists that, like the figurines, rimheads, and three-pronged censers, they were manufactured and used throughout the Early Classic. That they have never been found in Esperanza tombs may simply indicate that, because of their religious significance, they were banned from the Teotihuacan-influenced or -occupied Maya ceremonial centers. Quite possibly their connection with the cult of the hallucinogenic mushroom was repugnant or barbaric to the Teotihuacan priest-rulers.

Among the lesser lapidary arts, the manufacture of obsidian points, lancets and tools, stone bark beaters, celts, hammerstones, polishing stones, "doughnut stones," mortars and pestles, as well as manos and metates, continued without interruption and with little change in form from Early Classic times. Tripod metates apparently became more popular as the period wore on. A few carved metates with human or animal legs have been reported from the Western Highlands (J. E. S. Thompson, 1943a, pl. 10,c; Woodbury and Trik, 1953; fig. 279o; Lothrop, 1936, figs. 55, 106).

Although not known from the Central Highlands, pyrite-incrusted plaques (or mirrors) similar to those of the Early Classic continued to be made in the Western Highlands and in the Hilly Middle Country (Nebaj and Chama; A. L. Smith and Kidder, 1951, pp. 44–50, figs. 64, 65a,c). Instead of the two suspension holes found on Early Classic specimens, one suspension hole was the custom during Late Classic times. The importance of these mirror-plaques, probably worn as pectorals, is attested by their frequent inclusion with their owner in his grave.[48]

Jadeworking continued without interruption during the Late Classic period. In the Hilly Middle Country (especially at Nebaj) Late Classic jade ornaments were fewer in number but more varied in style than those of the Early Classic. Some of the jade plaques discovered in caches at Nebaj (Cache 14 and Tomb IV, both in Mound 2) represent the finest jade work-

---

blue, and white. Carved yokes occur only rarely in Guatemala. Those found depict serpent heads and death's-heads (Lake Amatitlan, Guatemala National Museum 2200; from Asuncion Mita, Borhegyi, notes) or are decorated with human footprints (El Baul, J. E. S. Thompson, 1948, p. 24, figs. 20,b; 22,f).

To my knowledge, no "palmate stone" has ever been found in the Guatemalan highlands, a fact which undoubtedly reflects a regional difference in the ball game. The only "palmate stone"-like object in Guatemala comes from the site of La Concepcion in the Piedmont area of southeastern Quezaltenango (J. E. S. Thompson, 1943c, p. 112,g,i).

For the widespread distribution of stone yokes, thin stone heads, and palmate stones in Mesoamerica see Proskouriakoff (1954) and Jiménez Moreno (1959, Map 5). For the corresponding distribution of ball-game handstones see Borhegyi (1961b, distribution map, fig. 6).

[47] Type D tripod mushroom stones (plain and effigy) are frequent in the Pacific Coast and Piedmont as well as in western El Salvador. For their distribution by archaeological sites see Borhegyi, 1961a, p. 500. (For the Cotzumalhuapa area see J. E. S. Thompson, 1948, figs. 19,f; 20,b; Gann, 1939, p. 204.)

[48] Small commercial mirrors are often sewn on the modern highland Maya ceremonial dance costumes. These mirrors are supposed to deflect the "evil eye" of jealous spectators and safeguard the dancers (Borhegyi notes, 1950–51). It is quite possible that the prehistoric pyrite mirrors served a similar purpose.

manship ever found in Mesoamerica (*ibid.*, fig. 59*a,b*; Kidder II and Samayoa, 1959, fig. 90).

It may be significant that by Late Classic times the center of artistic jade carving had shifted from the Central and Western Highlands to the Hilly Middle Country, close to the Rain Forest area. This shift may represent the exhaustion of the highland "jade mines" or the cutting off of the Motagua River jade-bearing areas due to warfare with hostile groups from Mexico. The darker green of the Late Classic jade suggests a different source for the mineral, possibly one known only to the inhabitants of the Hilly Middle Country.

Inferences of Social and Religious Structure

During the Early Classic the Teotihuacan theocracy dominated the ceremonial centers and controlled the satellite villages throughout the Maya hinterlands. Although the esoteric Teotihuacan religion was probably readily accepted by an urban minority, it seems to have been quietly and persistently opposed by the Maya farmer, who preferred the simple folk cult of earlier times. The beginning of the Late Classic is marked in Mexico by the abandonment and burning of Teotihuacan about A.D. 650 and in Guatemala by the resulting break in the cultural and economic supply line to the Maya highlands.[49] In the years that followed there was a gradual resurgence of native Maya culture. Religious and artistic ideas and elements of the Preclassic came out of hiding, and once again ritual paraphernalia associated with the Preclassic highland Maya folk cult—rimhead vessels, three-pronged incense burners, and mushroom stones—were widespread. There is every indication that the religious beliefs and cults associated with these objects regained their popularity at the expense of the Teotihuacan religion for simultaneously Teotihuacan-type ceremonial vessels (floreros, candeleros, Tlaloc jars, and cylindrical tripods) and architectural forms (use

of tablero and talud) disappeared from the archaeological horizon (Borhegyi, 1956b, pp. 349–50). (See fig. 5.)

THE PIPIL QUESTION. In 1941 Thompson advanced the hypothesis that a group or groups of Nahuat-speaking peoples from Mexico invaded the Pacific Coast and Piedmont of Guatemala during Postclassic times (J. E. S. Thompson, 1941a, pp. 38, 39). On later evidence (1943a, pp. 118–21) he reassigned this migration to the Late Classic period. Thompson believed (1948, pp. 11–15) that the holdings of these groups once extended far to the south and that they were the ancestors of several surviving Nahuat enclaves on the Pacific coasts and Piedmonts of Guatemala, El Salvador, Nicaragua, Costa Rica, and Panama and were called "Pipiles" by the Spanish chroniclers of the 16th and 17th centuries.[50]

---

[49] The best-documented explanation of the destruction and burning of the great theocratic center of Teotihuacan is given by Jiménez Moreno (1959, pp. 1063–73, Maps 3, 4). He suggests that Teotihuacan was burned around A.D. 650 by warlike Otomi (Mazahua) groups and that Teotihuacan culture and tradition, as represented by some of the refugee groups settled near San Miguel Amantla at Azcapotzalco, continued until about A.D. 900 (Coyotlatelco phase) or even possibly up to colonial times. At Cholula, Teotihuacan tradition continued uninterrupted until about A.D. 800. This theory helps to explain the much debated existence of a Teotihuacan IV phase in the valley of Mexico (approximately A.D. 600–900) during which the manufacture and use of Teotihuacan-style moldmade adorno-decorated incense burners and moldmade figurines with elaborate headdresses continued relatively unchanged (see note 49; Tozzer, 1921, pls. 14, 16, 17).

[50] The term "Pipil" is employed rather loosely in historical and archaeological literature to describe the speech and culture of migratory Mexican- (Nahuat-) speaking groups in Central America. According to W. Lehmann (1920, 2: 978–1075), their language was an archaic form of the Nahuatlan stock known as "Nahuat (Pipiles used *t* in their speech where the Chichimecs used *tl*). Lehmann holds that some form of Nahuat was also spoken in ancient Teotihuacan.

The name Pipil translates literally as "children" though probably, as later among the Colhua-Mexica, it carried the symbolic meaning of "nobles" or "princes" (Wolf, 1959, p. 121; Termer, 1936, p.

38

He further associated these Nahuat groups (1943a, p. 119; 1948, pp. 51, 52) with the spread and manufacture of the so-called Cotzumalhuapa-style stone sculptures (ball-court panels, stelae, monuments, stone heads) with stone yokes, thin stone heads, and also with San Juan Plumbate and Tiquisate ware pottery. It is not within the scope of this synthesis to discuss the confusing history and amazingly widespread distribution of these "Pipil" groups through Mesoamerica, but new archaeological data reveal that the Cotzumalhuapa sculptures actually represent three distinct chronological periods, only the last of which can be associated with the Late Classic Pipil migration (see note 45). Also linguistic and glottochronological evidence (Swadesh, personal correspondence, 1961; W. Lehmann, 1920, 2: 978–1075; Linné, 1942, pp. 195–97) tends to favor the theory that the Early Classic Teotihuacan and the Postclassic Toltec migrants to the Guatemalan highlands were also Nahuat-speakers. From the linguistic data one would assume that for varied and yet unknown reasons (overpopulation, drought, famine, political or economic pressures, missionary zeal) not one but several waves of Nahuat-speaking migrants invaded the Guatemalan highlands between the 5th and 12th centuries. Some of the migrants established vigorous colonies in alien domains, others became the ruling upper class in otherwise non-Nahuat-speaking Maya cultures. To have exercised such a profound and lasting influence on Maya culture they must have been well organized and the cultural equal,

if not in some cases, superior, of the groups with which they came in contact.

On the basis of such archaeological horizon-markers as (1) Teotihuacan III style pottery (Thin Orange ware vessels, cylindrical tripods, Tlaloc jars, floreros, candeleros), (2) San Juan and Robles Plumbate, Tiquisate ware, Z and Y Fine Orange, stone yokes, thin stone heads, various forms of stone ball-court markers, and (3) Effigy or Tohil Plumbate, Nicoya polychrome, X Fine Orange, moldmade effigy head supports and Mixteca-Puebla-type censers, it would seem that there were at least three large-scale Nahuat migrations to the south, each on a different time level.

A.D. *400–500 First Nahuat (Teotihuacan-"Pipil") Migration.* This migration, which seems to have been primarily religious and commercial, came directly from the sacred city of Teotihuacan. Various colonies were probably established along the Veracruz and Tabasco gulf coasts (especially at Tajin and Cerro de Las Mesas), the Pacific coast of Guerrero and Oaxaca, and in the uplands of the modern states of Morelos, Puebla, and Oaxaca. Other migrants continued via the Isthmus of Tehuantepec to the Pacific Coast and Piedmont of Guatemala, and from thence to the Central and Western Highlands and the Hilly Middle Country. They influenced but apparently did not migrate to the Tropical Rain Forest area (cf. Jiménez Moreno, 1959, Map 3). (See fig. 4.)

To all appearances the Teotihuacan-"Pipil" migration left Teotihuacan when this famous religious metropolis was at its apex (between A.D. 300 and 600) and the migrants retained contact with their native city until its destruction about 650. Settling in Guatemala, in most cases in or near the rich cotton- and cacao-bearing areas, they managed to control (or even monopolize) the market economy of their new homeland. This enabled them to bring vast new areas into the economic and religious sphere of Teotihuacan, the "City of the Gods," whose

---

110; Jiménez Moreno, 1959, p. 1077). The vast volume of historical and documentary literature written about the "Pipiles" has been well summarized by Linné (1942, pp. 195–97), Termer (1936), J. E. S. Thompson (1941a; 1948, pp. 11–15), and more recently by Miles (1957b, pp. 739–42) and Jiménez Moreno (1959, pp. 1075–91, Map 5). However, there is a great diversity of opinion among scholars concerning the date and nature of the various Pipil-Nahuat migrations. Proposed dates range from as early as A.D. 300 to as late as 1511.

high priests wielded authority through Mexico and Guatemala much as the Popes from the Eternal City of Rome controlled the lives and souls of the people of medieval Europe (Jiménez Moreno, 1959, pp. 1063–69).

After the burning of Teotihuacan in 650 the various Teotihuacan-Pipil colonies in Mesoamerica either were absorbed by the native population over which they had achieved religious and economic control during the Early Classic or were pushed by other migratory groups into marginal areas.

A.D. *700–900 Second Nahuat or "Tajinized-Teotihuacan-Pipil" (Pipil-Nicarao) Migration.* After the fall of Teotihuacan in 650, its people dispersed throughout Mexico. Those groups who moved to nearby Azcapotzalco, Cholula, and Xochicalco retained, relatively unchanged, the basic structure of Teotihuacan culture and in particular the cults of Tlaloc, Quetzalcoatl, and Xipe. On the other hand, those who joined colonies from earlier Teotihuacan migrations in Veracruz, Tabasco, and Campeche (more specifically in the Cerro de Las Mesas, Los Tu las, Potonchan, Xicalango, and Laguna de Terminos regions) were brought under the strong influence of Tajin (Totonac?) and Maya (Classic Olmec?) peoples of the Gulf coast. In time they absorbed many elements of the tropical lowland Gulf coast culture, among which was the unsavory trophy-head cult and decapitation sacrifice connected with the ball game (Stirling, 1943, pp. 72–74).

In contrast to the earlier Teotihuacan migration, the "Tajinized-Teotihuacan-Pipils" were an aggressive, warlike group that may have caused widespread population displacement wherever they moved. Very possibly they contributed to the final abandonment of the Teotihuacan-influenced or -dominated highland Maya ceremonial centers causing a general withdrawal of the local population to defensible hilltop sites and a northward migration to the Hilly

Middle Country. If, as has been suggested, their arrival in the Highland Maya Area brought on the downfall of the Teotihuacan-oriented theocratic social structure, then we may say that whereas the first Nahuat migration established the "Classic World," the second Nahuat migration brought it to an end. (See fig. 5.)

A.D. *1000–1200 Third Nahuat and Nahuatl or Nonoalca-Pipil-Toltec-Chichimec Migration.* The peoples involved in the third migration were made up of Nahuatl-speaking Toltec-Chichimecs from the northern part of the Valley of Mexico and a group identified in some of the Spanish chronicles as the "Nonoalcas." These "Nonoalcas" were apparently, in themselves, a composite group. They seem to have derived from a mixture of Nahuat-speaking "Tajinized-Teotihuacan-Pipils" (Pipil-Nicarao) who remained in the Laguna de Terminos region after their brethren moved south between A.D. 700 and 800, and a new refugee group of Teotihuacan people from the great ceremonial center of Cholula. The latter group, which left Cholula sometime after 800, had before their departure been subjected for some years to the tyrannical overlordship of the "Historic Olmecs," the "Olmec-Xicalanca" or the "Tapeu (Tepeu) Oliman" of the chronicles, who were probably Nahua-Mixtec- and Chocho-Popoloca-speakers.

To complicate matters, as a result of internal dissension a large faction of Nahuatl-speaking Toltec-Chichimecs, under the leadership of their priest-ruler, Ce-Acatl-Topiltzin-Quetzalcoatl (Kukulcan in Maya) left the Toltec capital, Tula or Tollan (in the present state of Hidalgo, Mexico), and migrated via Cholula to the Gulf coast of Veracruz, Tabasco (Potonchan) and Campeche (Chacanputun), sometime around A.D. 1000. After a few skirmishes they too settled down at the mouth of the Usumacinta River in the Laguna de Terminos region (Tlapallan, Acallan or Onohualco of the chronicles). After a period

40

(according to the chronicles Quetzalcoatl lived in Tlapallan for 30 years before his death around 1030) during which the Toltec-Chichimecs presumably intermarried with the resident Nonoalca-Pipil and Chontal Maya, some of these people proceeded toward Yucatan to Chichen Itza, Uxmal, and Mayapan and became the ruling families of Yucatan, known as the Xius, the Cocoms, and the Itzas (the Ah-Tza or Ah-Xulpiti of the *Annals of the Cakchiquels*). Others, among which were the "Yaquis" or "sacrificers" mentioned in the native annals, followed the Usumacinta River and its tributaries the Pasion and Chixoy to highland Guatemala and the Alta Verapaz. (See fig. 6.)

ABANDONMENT OF CEREMONIAL CENTERS. Probably related to and as confusing as the "Pipil migration" is the abandonment of the highland and lowland Maya ceremonial centers at the end of the Late Classic period. Many reasons have been brought forward to explain the mysterious abandonment of these centers, but a satisfactory solution has yet to be found. Such factors as internal revolts, soil exhaustion, erosion, climatic change, and failure of water supply have been cited (Cooke, 1931; Sears, 1951). Any or all of these factors may have contributed to the abandonment of the Rain Forest sites, but it is hard to imagine them as important factors in the abandonment of the highland sites where arable land, good soil, and ample water were constantly available. More than likely the primary cause for the breakdown in both regions lay in the inherent weakness of the Maya and Teotihuacan theocratic social structure which, like a card castle, began to crumble at the first outward threat.

The moment fresh impulses from Teotihuacan itself were no longer felt in the highland Maya area the power of the Teotihuacan theocracy began to wane. More and more the Maya reasserted themselves putting their faith once more in their own uncomplicated animistic folk cult and losing respect for the gods of the elaborate and esoteric Teotihuacan pantheon. There had been from the beginning a precarious balance, both religious and economic between the ceremonial centers and the hinterland. It took very little to upset the entire system. This added factor, I believe, was the arrival of warlike head-hunting groups of "Tajinized-Teotihuacan-Pipils," the Pipil-Nicarao.

At the same time that the "Tajinized-Teotihuacan-Pipil" were making raids in the Maya highlands (between A.D. 800 and 1000) their equally warlike relatives in the Laguna de Terminos region may have ransacked the Puuc area in Yucatan, and traveled up the Usumacinta River to raid the Tropical Rain Forest sites of Palenque, Yaxchilan, and Piedras Negras. Frescoes and stone monuments from this region depict raids, prisoners, trophy heads, and sacrificial victims, albeit all with definite Maya countenances. If these are representations of "Tajinized-Teotihuacan-Pipil" captives, one is reminded of the elaborately carved Roman victory columns, where are depicted the very same "barbarians" who ultimately sacked and captured the imperial city of Rome.

EARLY POSTCLASSIC (A.D. 1000–1200) AND PROTOHISTORIC PERIODS (A.D. 1200–1524)

The archaeological phases associated with these periods are: Ayampuc, Chinautla (Valley of Guatemala); Primavera and Medina (Almolonga Valley); Chipal 2–3 (Chixoy drainage, west); Samac (Chixoy drainage, east); Quankyak and Xinabahul (Zaculeu); Tohil and Yaqui (Zacualpa) Chuitinamit (Lake Atitlan); Contreras Alto and Los Jicaques (Amatitlan); Chiapa XI-XII (Chiapas). (See Table 1.)

Modes of Subsistence

The abandonment of the large ceremonial centers of the *Central Highlands* at the end of the Late Classic period left many

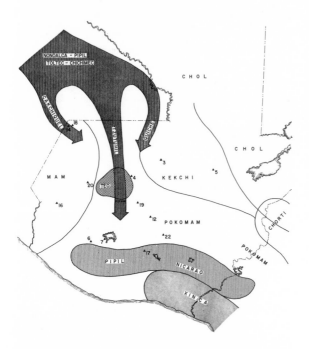

FIG. 6—EARLY POSTCLASSIC PERIOD (A.D. 1000–1200). Pipil-Nicarao groups settled on the Coastal Piedmont establish commercial and economic relationships with the highland Maya Pokomam and Mam groups and gradually extend their influence over the Central Highlands. Their expansion is interrupted by the arrival of new warlike groups from Mexico. These Nonoalca-Pipil or "backwash" Cholultec-Toltec-Chichimec groups (the ancestors of the Cakchiquel, Quiche, and Tzutuhil Maya elite) move into Guatemala from highland Chiapas and via the Usumacinta River. They drive a wedge between the Mam, Kekchi, Pokomchi, and Pokomam groups and extend their influence to the Coastal Piedmont. The hilltop settlements gradually assume urban characteristics.

Settlement Pattern and Architecture

SETTLEMENTS AND SITES. Early Postclassic (A.D. 1000–1200): At the end of the Late Classic and early in the Postclassic period the settlement pattern changed from open land or valley sites to easily defended hilltop sites, many of which were surrounded by deep ravines and occasionally protected with military outpost constructions (A. L. Smith, 1955, p. 48). As I have mentioned elsewhere in this volume (Art. 2), this change was not quite so general or abrupt as had previously been supposed by many archaeologists. In the Hilly Middle Country several valley sites were still occupied during the Late Classic (*ibid.*, pp. 78–80, fig. 42, Table 1). A major site in the Western Highlands, Zaculeu, situated on a defensible plateau surrounded by deep ravines, was continuously occupied from Early Classic times to its conquest by the Spaniards in 1525 (Woodbury and Trik, 1953). The same is true for Chinautla, a fortress site in the Central Highlands, a few miles north of Kaminaljuyu and contiguous with it across a narrow neck of land. Chinautla is certainly no older than the Late Classic period and possibly was established, although not fortified, during the Early Classic.

It is possible that the gradual occupation of hillslopes and high plateau areas began some time before the collapse of the theocratic world in Late Classic times. In the Central Highlands the centrifugal expansion of the satellite villages left the ceremonial centers with little economic and military support. This made them an easy prey to the harassments and inroads of the Pipil-Nicarao ("Tajinized-Teotihuacan-Pipils"), and at the end of the period they were completely abandoned by the Maya farmers who had formerly supported them. On the other hand, in the Western Highlands and in the Hilly Middle Country, where neither the "Tajinized-Teotihuacan Pipil" (Pipil-Nicarao) nor the Toltec-Chi-

of the intermountain valleys unoccupied. The move away from the valley sites and onto the mountain slopes and hilltops, which may have begun in the Early Classic as a search for better lands, gained momentum in the Late Classic and Early Postclassic periods as the result of internal strife and internecine warfare. Throughout the peripheral uplands the independent and culturally isolated villages returned to a Preclassic mode of subsistence. The spotty distribution of three-pronged censers tends to confirm this hypothesis (Borhegyi, 1951b, p. 176, map).

42

chimec (Nonoalca-Pipil) ever gained a foothold, many open valley sites were continuously occupied even into protohistoric times. It is likely that in certain of these areas vestiges of the Maya and Teotihuacan theocracy retained power up to the time of the Spanish conquest because some Early Classic religious practices, such as the use of seated burials, were reported as late as the end of the 16th century (A. L. Smith and Kidder, 1951, pp. 21, 28; Miles, 1957b, pp. 749–50). In other areas, however, the appearance of the Pipil-Nicarao and Toltec-Chichimec warrior groups forced the population into fortified and closely nucleated settlements. Most of these Early Postclassic (A.D. 1000–1200) defensive sites, ranging from a single group of structures to as many as eight groups, were situated on artificially leveled hilltops or tongues of land surrounded by deep ravines (cf. Mixco Viejo in Smith, 1955, fig. 137). In contrast to the Classic period the public buildings were not used exclusively for religious purposes, and for this reason were often not oriented to one another, but simply followed the irregularities of the terrain. Also the domestic structures or hamlets of the farming population were on the nearby slopes close enough to the hilltop site to use it as a refuge in time of warfare or other emergency (Miles, 1957b, pp. 768–71).

Compared to the Postclassic, the settlement pattern of the Protohistoric period reveals few, if any, structural changes. The greatest change appears to be less in the general defensive layout than in the emphasis and function of the settlement. The Toltec-Chichimecs (Nonoalca-Pipil), who according to tradition became the ancestors of the present day Central Highland Maya-Quiche, Cakchiquel, and Zutuhil tribes, brought with them from Mexico a greatly secularized concept of social organization, which was reflected in the settlement pattern of the Protohistoric sites occupied by these groups. During this period many

highland sites took on the character of medieval European castles and fortress towns. Strategically located, they were used in time of peace as temporary residences, for festival, political, and market activities. In time of war they served as fortresses for the warrior classes and as a refuge for the outlying population of the satellite villages (A. L. Smith, 1955, p. 77). With the growth of nationalism and emphasis on urban living, many hilltop fortress towns like Zaculeu, Utatlan, Iximche, Chuitinamit, Mixco Viejo, and Chinautla, in time took on a dual function and became not only places of refuge and festive gatherings but also the administrative and commercial capitals of the warring highland Maya nationality groups, the Mam, Quiche, Cakchiquel, Zutughil, and Pokomam nations.

ARCHITECTURE AND BURIALS. Due to the few marked changes in architecture of the Early Postclassic and Protohistoric, these periods will be discussed together.

To date about 20 major sites have been assigned to either or both the Early Postclassic or Protohistoric periods (Shook, 1952b; A. L. Smith, 1955, 1961). Of these, three are located in the Central Highlands (Iximche, Mixco Viejo, Chinautla); five in the Western Highlands (Tajumulco, Zaculeu, Chuitinamit, Zacualpa, and Utatlan); and 12 in the Hilly Middle Country (Chalchitan, Chutinamit, Xolchun, Xolpacol, Huil, Vicaveval, Nebaj, Chipal, Cahyup, Chichen, and Chijolom (cf. fig. 1).

The numerous architectural innovations which appear during this period at highland Guatemalan sites have been generally ascribed to foreign Mexican influences. In contrast to the adobe constructions of earlier periods, there is an increased and almost exclusive use of plaster (made of burned limestone) and stone as building materials (cf. Goetz and Morley, 1950, p. 219). Other new architectural features of the period are:

a. Square-based pyramidal structures with

43

vertically rising terraces and wide stairways divided by a plain ramp and often flanked by heavily proportioned outer balustrades. The medial ramp usually has the distinctly Mexican feature of changing from a fairly sharp incline to the vertical a brief distance short of the summit (J. E. S. Thompson, 1943a, fig. 16,e). Mexican-type twin temples built on a single pyramid platform are particularly common at Protohistoric sites.[51]

b. Rectangular-based one- or two-room superstructures (temples) usually with two rectangular piers or round columns set in a wide doorway so as to provide a temple entrance. Against the center of the wall opposite the entrance there is generally a plain, rectangular, masonry altar (Woodbury and Trik, 1953, fig. 198). Although no temple roofs have remained intact from this period, there is little doubt that, as in Mexico, they were either of thatch or beam-and-mortar construction (J. E. S. Thompson, 1943a, fig. 16,a,d; Woodbury and Trik, 1953, figs. 187–89).

c. Long, rectangular buildings with three or more extensions set on low platform mounds are more common during Protohistoric times than at the beginning of the period. There is rarely more than one room, which is furnished with benches along three of the inner walls. Doorways, as a rule of uneven numbers (ranging from 3 to 11), are separated by masonry piers or round columns and face toward the plaza (J. E. S. Thompson, 1943a, fig. 16,c; Woodbury and Trik, 1953, figs. 15, 216; A. L. Smith, 1955, fig. 27,c).

d. Small (3–6 m. diameter, 2 m. high) platforms, used as dance platforms or altars for offertory or sacrificial purposes, are particularly common during the Protohistoric period. The stairways on one or more sides are usually flanked with balustrades with vertical upper zones. Many of the platforms must have held small altar shrines, which were constructed of perishable materials or of masonry with beam-and-mortar roofs. These platform altars and shrines resemble in size, and probably also in function, the Postclassic Mexican offertory shrines known as *momoztlis* (J. E. S. Thompson, 1943a, fig. 16,b). They are usually located in the center of plazas, frequently in front of a major structure (Woodbury and Trik, 1953, figs. 187, 210–15; A. L. Smith, 1955, fig. 1,a).

e. Masonry colonnades as adjuncts of buildings are especially common at the end of the Early Postclassic and during the ensuing Protohistoric period. In layout they are strongly reminiscent of the colonnaded structures of the Toltec period in Tula and of the Mexican-influenced Yucatan Postclassic (cf. J. E. S. Thompson, 1945, pl. 2,d; Woodbury and Trik, 1953, figs. 7, 9, 187–89).

f. Round temple structures of masonry similar in style if not in function to those reported from Early Postclassic sites in eastern Mexico and Yucatan (cf. J. E. S. Thompson, 1945, pl. 2,c).[52]

g. Open-ended or enclosed "sunken" ball courts with high walls and stairways leading out at either end of the court are new features, common during both the Early Postclassic and Protohistoric periods. The vertical benches, the steeply sloping, almost vertical (85 degrees) playing walls with vertical moldings on the tops, and the long and narrow playing alleys have many Mexican counterparts. Some of the enclosed or "sunken" ball courts, as in Mexico, have well-constructed drains and water outlets (Woodbury and Trik, 1953, figs. 231–33; A. L. Smith, 1961, figs. 5–7).

---

[51] Twin temple mounds on single platforms, usually dedicated to the rain god, Tlaloc, are known in the highland Maya area at: Mixco Viejo (Dept. Chimaltenango); Cahyup, Chuitinamit (Dept. Baja Verapaz); Chinautla, Cimientos (Dept. Guatemala); and Xolpacol (Dept. El Quiche) (see A. L. Smith, 1955, pp. 75, 81–83, figs. 40, 99, 104, 112, 122, 137; and Borhegyi notes).

[52] Round temple structures are not common in the highlands, but archaeological remains of such buildings have been found at Xolpacol, Xolchun, Pacot (?) Rio Blanco, Utatlan (Dept. El Quiche); Zaculeu (Dept. Huehuetenango), Xaltenamit (Dept. Alta Verapaz); Cahyup (Dept. Baja Verapaz); Iximche (?) (Dept. Chimaltenango); and Chocola (Dept. Suchitepequez). (See Burkitt, 1930a, p. 6; Lothrop, 1933, p. 109, fig. 70,b; Pollock, 1936, pp. 124–26; Woodbury and Trik, 1953, figs. 7–9, 188,b; A. L. Smith, 1955, p. 76, figs. 17; 18,e; 28,f; 70; 71; 74; 76,a; 108.) As in Mexico, the round temple structures were probably dedicated to the cult of Quetzalcoatl as the wind god, where they appeared first in the Huaxtec area of northern Veracruz (see Pollock, 1936; Shook, 1954b, 1955b; Chowning, 1956).

As in earlier periods, little is known about the exterior and interior decoration of the Early Postclassic and Protohistoric highland temple structures. From traces of remaining pigments and stucco fragments we can assume that both the interior and exterior walls, as in Mexico and Yucatan, were painted with a variety of colors and designs. Red, green, yellow, blue, gray, and black seem to have been the most common. Some of the temple pyramids, like those at Comitancillo (Department of El Quiche) may have been painted completely red (A. L. Smith, 1955, pp. 74–75). Stucco reliefs representing human heads and animals (Chutixtiox, *ibid.*, fig. 13,*a-e*) and stucco balls containing human skulls (see Chipal ball court, Burkitt, 1930b, p. 56) were occasionally used as exterior decoration.

Common architectural features of the period which were not inspired by Mexican models are clay- or stone-lined drainage canals and ditches (Dutton and Hobbs, 1943, p. 107, fig.. 8,*f*) and "fire or censer boxes" on the summits of temple platforms (*ibid.*, fig. 8,*e,h*; Woodbury and Trik, 1953, figs. 174,*b*; 209,*b*).

Burial customs during the period vary from one region to another. Rectangular stone-lined cist tombs roofed with flat stones were apparently used during the Early Postclassic and Protohistoric times in the Western Highlands and the Hilly Middle Country. In the former area, Zaculeu, cist tombs seem not to have had doorways (Woodbury and Trik, 1953, figs. 47, 49, 51, 52). In the latter, Nebaj (A. L. Smith and Kidder, 1951, pp. 25–26), the tombs were frequently roofed with wooden beams and their entrances sealed with large stone slabs. Most of the tombs have only one chamber but in some instances, as at Tajumulco, Chutixtiox, Xolpacol, and Chipal (A. L. Smith, 1955, figs. 64,*b*; 76,*c*) there are two adjoining chambers, one circular, the other rectangular. Early Postclassic stone or adobe boxes that may have served as sarcophagi have been reported from the Western Highlands and the Hilly Middle Country, from such sites as Zaculeu (Woodbury and Trik, 1953, fig. 227,*b*), Chalchitan, Nebaj, and La Iglesia (A. L. Smith, 1955, p. 75, fig. 9,*b*). The seated (contracted) burial position was preferred throughout most of the period (Butler, 1940, pp. 262–65; Woodbury and Trik, 1953, p. 286), but by Protohistoric times a new funerary custom, cremation, became popular at some sites. Introduced from Mexico, toward the end of the Early Postclassic, cremations have been found at Zaculeu, Zacualpa, and Mixco Viejo in the Western and Central Highlands (Woodbury and Trik, 1953, pp. 78–79, figs. 138; 180,*c-e*; 197,*a-c*; 200,*f*; 212,*b,c*; 243,*r*) but never in the Hilly Middle Country, where seated burials were the mode even during Spanish colonial times. These cremations were usually placed in large Protohistoric White-on-red and Chinautla or Yaqui polychrome (Red-and-black-on-white ware) or three-handled Hilltop Cinnamon (orange ware) jars. Some of the jars were covered with lids, others with stucco-coated hide or cloth (*ibid.*, pp. 96, 283).[53] At Zaculeu, however, two Early Postclassic cremations were found, one in a Tohil-type Plumbate jar and the other in a Mexican-style tripod onyx jar. Apparently persons of both sexes and all ages, including children, were cremated. Funeral furniture consists of small objects (gold, silver, copper, shell, bone, and jade ornaments) that could be easily placed in the jars with the cremated bones and ashes (Wauchope, 1942b; 1942a; 1948a, pp. 24, 84–87; Woodbury and Trik, 1953, p. 96).

The customs of human and animal sacrifice and skull burial also seem to have continued during the period but were ap-

---

[53] The custom of cremating the deceased and placing the ashes first in burial urns and then in caves was also in vogue during and shortly after the Spanish conquest in 1530 at numerous places in highland Chiapas (see Wauchope, 1942a; Blom, 1954).

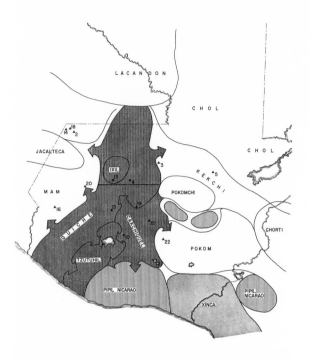

FIG. 7—PROTOHISTORIC PERIOD (A.D. 1200–1530). The territorial expansion of the Quiche, Cakchiquel, and Tzutuhil groups extends over most of the Central and Western Highlands at the expense of the Pipil-Nicarao, Mam, Pokomam, and Kekchi. The resulting intertribal warfare breaks the Pipil-Nicarao into isolated pockets and drives some of them to El Salvador, Nicaragua, and Costa Rica. Regionalism develops and leads to nationalism. Hilltop settlements are fortified and used as retreats during warfare and administrative seats for the various nationality governments during peace time. The period ends with the arrival of the Spanish conquistadors in A.D. 1524.

parently not as common as during the preceding Classic and Preclassic. Child sacrifice has been reported at Nebaj and Tajumulco (?) (Dutton and Hobbs, 1943, pp. 111–14). Bird bones, jaguar (?) claws and severed human skulls have been noted at Nebaj (A. L. Smith and Kidder, 1951, pp. 26–30).

Arts and Crafts

POTTERY (EARLY POSTCLASSIC) A.D. 1000–1200. Tohil Plumbate is by far the most important pottery diagnostic of the period. The varied and numerous anthropomorphic and zoomorphic representations found on

Tohil Plumbate vessels in highland Guatemala include headless persons, bearded men, eagle warriors, Tlaloc heads, and individuals with long upturned noses; also dogs, jaguars, pisotes, *tepiscuintles*, turkeys, birds, toads, and serpents (Butler, 1940, pl. 9,*a-d*; Shepard, 1948; Kidder II and Samayoa, 1959, fig. 85). Vessel shapes are jars, barrel-shaped vases, tripod vessels (often with hollow bulbous rattle feet; A. L. Smith and Kidder, 1951, fig. 83,*e*), tapered or recurved-lip cylindrical vases, composite-silhouette bowls, and pedestal-based bowls. Vessels frequently are decorated with intricate, incised, carved, grooved and gadrooned, geometrical and curvilinear designs (Lothrop, 1936, figs. 33–37; Woodbury and Trik, 1953, figs. 243–44; Kidder II and Samayoa, 1959, fig. 84). The color of plumbate vessels varies from lustrous pale gray to various shades of orange and reddish brown (Dutton, 1943; Wauchope, 1948a, p. 143–45; Shepard, 1948).

X Fine Orange ware, next in importance to Tohil Plumbate as a pottery diagnostic, occurs in the same vessel shapes and bearing similar incised, carved, grooved or gadrooned, and mold-impressed designs (scroll, braid, palmate, and radial motifs) (Shepard, 1948, pp. 133–37). The intricate scroll designs on both Tohil Plumbate and X Fine Orange ware are reminiscent of Tajin (Totonac) scrolls, and there is, as well, a close similarity between these wares and the various fine-textured, orange-colored paste wares of the Mexican Gulf coast. While X Fine Orange seems to be of Mexican Gulf coast (southern Veracruz or western Tabasco) origin, the place of manufacture of Tohil Plumbate is as yet unknown. This mystery will be solved once the relationship (if any) between presumably Late Classic San Juan Plumbate and Robles Plumbate and Early Postclassic Tohil Plumbate is worked out. If, as I suspect, Tohil Plumbate is a direct descendant of San Juan Plumbate, it would be safe to assume that Tohil Plumbate is also of highland Guatemalan (in particular Western Highland) derivation. Whatever its place of manufacture, Tohil Plumbate became extremely popular, and vessels of this ware were traded, along with X Fine Orange ware vessels to many parts of Mesoamerica (for their geographic distribution see Shepard, 1948, pp. 105–14 and map).[54]

The sudden extinction of plumbate ware at the beginning of the Protohistoric period is as much of a mystery as its origin. It is hard to imagine why such a popular and valuable trade item would be so abruptly discontinued. It is possible that the deposit of plumbate clay was exhausted. More likely, the plumbate-producing people may have been displaced by newcomers with no knowledge of plumbate pottery making. In this case the plumbate ceramic tradition would have died out among the dispossessed potters because of the disruption in their culture or because the clay necessary to produce plumbate ware was unavailable in their new homeland.

Just as X Fine Orange ware represents a Mexican Gulf coast influence in the Highland Maya Area, the presence of Mixteca-Puebla-type perforated bulbous vessel supports, moldmade effigy-head supports and Mixteca-Puebla-type tripod censers at vari-

ous Early Postclassic highland Maya sites suggests central Mexican and, more particularly, Mixteca-Puebla influences (Wauchope, 1948a, pp. 137–39, 148–50; Woodbury and Trik, 1953, pp. 155–59). Quite possibly the center from which this pottery style diffused was the great mercantile religious metropolis of Cholula. After the fall of Teotihuacan around A.D. 650 Cholula gained considerable religious and economic importance. A meeting ground for pilgrims and merchants from all over central and southern Mexico, it was primarily responsible for the widespread merchandising of the elaborately decorated Cholulteca polychrome ware and, no doubt, the various other Mixteca-Puebla decorative styles and vessel forms as well (Nicholson, 1961).

POTTERY (PROTOHISTORIC) A.D. 1200–1530. With the possible exception of Tohil Plumbate ware, the pottery diagnostics of the Early Postclassic are foreign and indicate in particular Gulf coast Mexican influence. In the Protohistoric period, however, the characteristic pottery types seem to be of a local and regionalized nature.

Vessel shapes include small, medium, or large, tall-necked, globular-bodied jars with two or three loop handles; flaring-sided tripod bowls with bulbous or effigy leg supports (Lothrop, 1933, fig. 61,d); round-sided hemispherical bowls, pedestal-based bowls, and Mixteca-Puebla-style tripod censers with bulbous or effigy leg supports. Sometimes the tall-necked jars (especially those of Chinautla polychrome ware) are decorated at the neck or on the handles with small, crudely moldmade, appliqué jaguar heads or with human heads with long upturned noses (Lothrop, 1933, fig. 59,k; A. L. Smith and Kidder, 1951, fig. 90; Butler, 1959, fig. 3,b). The appearance of flaring-sided tripod grater bowls during the Early Postclassic period and their continued use during the Protohistoric may indicate the introduction of new eating habits from Mexico or new methods of food preparation.

[54] Fine Orange pottery has been reported from highland Guatemala at the following sites: Zacualpa (Lothrop, 1936, pp. 26–28, figs. 22–24, 31, 44); Utatlan (Lothrop, 1936, figs. 75–78); Chipal, Pantzac, Rio Blanco, Tzicuay, Xolja Bajo, Nebaj (El Quiche; Butler, 1940, fig. 22,o, pl. 9,h,i,k,m; Borhegyi notes): Zaculeu (Woodbury and Trik, 1953, pp. 159–62, figs. 82, 83, 269); and Chichen (Alta Verapaz; Borhegyi notes). Similar but not quite identical Hard Orange vessels have been noted from several sites in highland Guatemala (Lothrop, 1933, p. 23; Dutton and Hobbs, 1943, pp. 85–88, figs. 78, 79; Wauchope, 1948a, pp. 136–37, fig. 56).

The distribution of Early Postclassic tripod vessels with hollow moldmade, carved, or incised effigy-head supports in highland Guatemala follows closely that of the Fine Orange and Hard Orange wares. For their distribution in Mexico and Central America see Wauchope (1941; 1948a, pp. 137–39, pl. 202,c, figs. 24, 57; Woodbury and Trik, 1953, pp. 155–59, figs. 81, 245).

INCENSE BURNERS (EARLY POSTCLASSIC AND PROTOHISTORIC). During Early Postclassic and Protohistoric times there was a drastic change in pottery censers. Three-pronged censers and rimhead vessels were no longer produced (Borhegyi, 1956,b, p. 351). Among the new varieties in the Central and Western Highlands are the small spike- (or stud-) decorated censers (sometimes with cross-shaped perforations; Seler, 1901, figs. 35, 36, 165, 232; Lothrop, 1933, fig. 56; Wauchope, 1948a, p. 147, fig. 65) and the effigy censers which during this period are also frequently spike decorated. These latter censers are often sizable and represent various conventionalized forms of Quetzalcoatl, Tlaloc, or Xipe (Seler, 1901, figs. 247, 248, 258–62; Villacorta and Villacorta, 1927, pp. 147, 154; A. L. Smith and Kidder, 1951, figs. 79a, 80; Dutton, 1955, p. 243; cf. Acosta, 1956–57, figs. 17, 19).

In the Hilly Middle Country during the early Postclassic elaborate anthropomorphic or zoomorphic incense burners with appliqué and mold-impressed decoration were in favor (Dieseldorff, 1926–33, 1: figs. 11–13, 18, 19, 183–204; 1936, fig. 24). The censers retain, in general, stylistic similarities with their Late Classic counterparts and frequently represent the Jaguar Lord of the interior of the earth (Kidder II and Samayoa, 1959, figs. 86, 87). Many have been found in caves where they are still objects of veneration by the present-day Maya Indians (cf. quetzal-bird-shaped censer from a cave near Purulha, Baja Verapaz, Borhegyi, 1957c, fig. 1,a,b).

During the Protohistoric period a new form of anthropomorphic censer became popular in the Western Highlands and Hilly Middle Country. The censer, which takes the form of a hollow, squatting or seated human figure with tubular arms and legs, may vary in height from 40 to 50 cm. and usually represents a Mexican god such as Xipe, Mictlantecuhtli (represented as a skeleton) or Quetzalcoatl. In most respects

the censers show stylistic similarities with their Mexican (mostly Gulf coast) prototype (Stephens, 1841, 2: 185; Burkitt, 1924, pp. 142–43; Villacorta and Villacorta, 1927, pp. 84, 152–53, 234–35; Lothrop, 1936, fig. 40; Woodbury and Trik, 1953, fig. 258,f). Unquestionably they, and the cults for which they were produced, were introduced into the highlands of Guatemala from Mexico during the latter part of the Early Postclassic.

Ladle censers (of buff-brown, orange-cinnamon, pinkish-cinnamon and micaceous wares or of incised, groove-outlined and mold-impressed red-on-white ware) continued to be popular throughout both Early Postclassic and Protohistoric (Woodbury and Trik, 1953, fig. 250). The main difference between the ladle censers of these periods and the censers of the Late Classic is a change from the earlier trough-shaped or solid handle to a hollow, plain or effigy handle. In addition, the censer dish often has numerous perforations (Wauchope, 1948a, pp. 150–51, fig. 68; Woodbury and Trik, 1953, fig. 258,c; cf. Acosta, 1956–57, fig. 19, no. 4). Occasionally the hollow censer handle terminates in a moldmade jaguar head or in a human face, usually depicted with a beard or a long, upturned nose (Dieseldorff, 1926–33, 1: figs. 113, 114, 142; A. L. Smith and Kidder, 1951, fig. 90; Woodbury and Trik, 1953, fig. 253,m-o; Guillemín, 1959, pp. 57–59).

The appearance of Mixteca-Puebla style of globular tripod censers (with perforated body and hollow, bulbous rattle legs, one of which frequently terminates in effigy form) at many highland Maya sites indicates new religious influence from Mexico. The censers are similar in shape and decorative treatment to the Protohistoric Mixteca-Puebla tripod censers of central Mexico and to those from the Toltec capital at Tula, Hidalgo (Dutton and Hobbs, 1943, figs. 82,m; 95; Wauchope, 1948a, pp. 148–49, figs. 66, 67; Woodbury and Trik, 1953, fig. 246,m,o; cf. Acosta, 1956–57, fig. 19, no. 1).

FIGURINES, EFFIGY WHISTLES, STAMPS. Figurines and effigy whistles are rare in both Early Postclassic and Protohistoric periods. The few examples reported from highland sites are of crude workmanship and can hardly be compared with the elegant moldmade figurines and effigy whistles of the Late Classic. This is somewhat surprising since the effigy plumbate vessels of the period are of exquisite workmanship and depict in artistic detail many human and animal forms. The solid or hollow modeled or moldmade figurines and effigy whistle fragments are crude representations of seated females, sometimes holding children (or dogs) in their laps, and distorted human and animal heads and body parts. Some of these clay fragments are of red, brown, or buff ware; others of Red-on-white, and Red-and-black-on-white ware (Dieseldorff, 1926–33, 1: figs. 4, 5, 32–34, 37, 42, 44, 65, 111, 112; Lothrop, 1933, p. 97, fig. 61,g-j; Butler, 1935a, fig. 4,h; Wauchope, 1948a, pp. 152–53, fig. 69; Woodbury and Trik, 1953, fig. 272; R. E. Smith, 1954b, figs. 1,j; 4,b-d). In the Hilly Middle Country a few figurines from this period are moldmade or modeled in the Classic tradition, such as two from Chipal representing a seated Xipe, or a priest wearing a Xipe mask, and a warrior slaying an enemy whom he holds by his hair (Butler, 1940, pl. 10,i,j).

Among the very few musical instruments reported from this period are an effigy drum with matting imprint on the base, from a Protohistoric cache at Zaculeu (Woodbury and Trik, 1953, p. 177, fig. 251,i); and a pottery flute, depicting Quetzalcoatl (?), at Salama, Baja Verapaz (Dieseldorff, 1926–33, 3: fig. 146).

The pottery (cameo type) stamps of the period are the flat, stemmed variety; they bear geometrical designs and, not infrequently, serpents or double-headed birds (eagles?) that remind one of the Hapsburg family crest (Butler, 1940, p. 265, pl. 10,k; 1959, fig. 3,a; Borhegyi, 1950e, figs. 8–10).

They are rectangular, square, or occasionally triangular. Some may have been used to stamp-decorate the walls of pottery vessels; others to mark patterns on bark-paper "books" or cloth items (Woodbury and Trik, 1953, pp. 209–12, fig. 117).

WEAVING, BASKETRY, MATS, FEATHERWORK, ORNAMENTS. The scant figure design on pottery and the few crudely executed figurines provide little information on textiles, featherwork, or basketry of the period. A few re-used disc-shaped sherds and some small conical or biconical plain, incised, or mold-impressed spindle whorls indicate that spinning and weaving continued to be an important part of the life of highland Guatemalan communities (Dutton and Hobbs, 1943, p. 109, figs. 37, 38; Wauchope, 1948a, pp. 153–54; Woodbury and Trik, 1953, pp. 169–72, 212, fig. 87). Fabric or mat impressions on the bottoms of some of the coarse or micaceous ware jars indicate that some of the potters put their unfired jars on fiber mats (petates) to dry, as they do today (Woodbury and Trik, 1953, fig. 286).[55] The only highland specimens of cloth come from caves just across the Guatemalan border in Chiapas (Wauchope, 1942; Blom, 1954). These fragments were associated with cremation jars of Protohistoric type. They are all plain weaves but include a few pieces painted or resist-dyed in the ikat technique, a process that survives today in highland Guatemala.

STONE ARTIFACTS, OTHER LAPIDARY ARTS. The general and most obvious characteristic of Postclassic and Protohistoric monumental stone sculpture is its crudity and lack of artistic merit. At Tajumulco in the Western Highlands (Dutton and Hobbs,

[55] Textile-marked Chinautla polychrome and Micaceous ware pottery fragments have been reported at five highland Maya sites (Zaculeu, Zacualpa, Cahyup, Chinautla, and Chutinamit (Woodbury and Trik, 1953, pp. 278–80; Borhegyi notes). They are also present at sites on the Pacific Coast and Piedmont of Guatemala (Fincas Pradera, Panama, and Variedades, all in the Department of Suchitepequez).

1943, figs. 15–23; Tejeda, 1947) some of the round stone altars and monuments bear rather crudely executed human figures, jaguars, eagles, and what appear to be sun discs. Also in the Western Highlands at Quen Santo, Uaxac Canal, Tecpan Cuapan, Jotona, Chacula, and Tres Lagunas, Seler reported many crudely manufactured stone statues, some of which he found in natural caves (Seler, 1901, figs. 80, 81, 84, 167, 171, 172, 237, 241, and plates 8,a,b; 30, 34; Burkitt, 1924, pp. 138–40; Villacorta and Villacorta, 1927, pp. 132, 141, 143, 144, 146). Several of these statues are vertically tenoned and represent human beings with arms folded across their chests and occasionally wearing "coolie" hats. They recall similar stone carvings from Las Vacas, San Cristobal el Alto, and Zacualpa (Wauchope, 1948a, p. 62, pl. 4,b); from Chichicastenango (Lothrop, 1936, fig. 103); from the Cotzumalhuapa region on the Pacific Coastal Piedmont of Guatemala (J. E. S. Thompson, 1948, figs. 4,d; 8,a,e; 16,c-e,g; 18,l-n; 62,f); and from various parts of Mexico such as Tula, Hidalgo (Seler, 1902–23, fig. 68), Tututepec and Rio Grande, Oaxaca (Piña Chan, 1960b, figs. 4, 8), Tonina and Comitan, Chiapas (with missing head, Blom and La Farge, 1926–27, 2: 269, fig. 212), and from Los Idolos, Misantla, and Tuzapan, on the Gulf coast of Mexico (Borhegyi notes, 1961, in the Jalapa and Tuxtla Gutierrez Museums).

Other stone statues and carved altars at Quen Santo in the Western Highlands, represent sun discs (Seler, 1901, fig. 190; Villacorta and Villacorta, 1927, pp. 138, 149) and crude human figures and jaguars (Villacorta and Villacorta, 1927, pp. 138, 142, 145, 149). The carved human heads suspended from the necks and waists of these statues possibly represent severed and shrunken (?) trophy heads, indicative of Mexican—more specifically, Gulf coast and Isthmus of Tehuantepec—derived religious and sacrificial cults (cf. Leigh, 1961). Probably belonging to the same cat-

egory are the many crude anthropomorphic statues with empty eye-sockets or puffy and swollen eyes reported from the same area in the Western Highlands (Seler, 1901, fig. 82, pl. 9; cf. Woodbury and Trik, 1953, fig. 244,j).

Vertically or horizontally tenoned stone ball-court markers appear only sporadically at Early Postclassic and Protohistoric sites. A handsomely executed serpent head with a human face within its jaw has been reported from Mixco Viejo (Guillemín, 1958, p. 22). Similar "Toltec-style" ball-court markers are known from Joyabaj and Zacualpa (Lothrop, 1936, fig. 49).

Absent during this period are the handsomely carved stone yokes, thin stone heads, and ball-game handstones. Since Early Postclassic and Protohistoric sites with ball courts are numerous (about 30) in the Guatemalan highlands (for their distribution see A. L. Smith, 1961, pp. 121–25), the newly arrived Mexican groups must have introduced new rules and ball-game paraphernalia. Horizontally tenoned stone ball-court rings such as those from Toltec period sites in Mexico and Yucatan have never turned up in highland Guatemala although they may have been present at some Coastal Piedmont ball courts such as El Baul (Termer, 1930b; J. E. S. Thompson, 1948, pp. 37–38). In spite of their absence at highland archaeological sites they are frequently referred to in the native annals (Popol Vuh: Goetz and Morley, 1950, pp. 134, 135, 145, 152).

According to these native chronicles the Postclassic Mexican migratory groups also brought with them to the highlands the cult of "idolatry" and other "unnatural customs" (phallic cults, adultery, homosexuality, heart sacrifice; see Goetz and Morley, 1950, p. 158). The small to medium-sized, carved stone boxes and stone incense burners or receptacles representing the wrinkled-faced old fire god and phallic human and animal sculptures reminiscent of the Mexican rain god, Tlaloc, are further indications of such Mexican affiliations (Lothrop, 1936, figs. 50–53, 89). It is surprising to note, however, the almost total absence in the Guatemalan highlands of chac mool statues, serpent columns, and representations of prowling jaguars and coyotes generally indicative of Early Postclassic, Toltec-Chichimec influence.[56]

Mushroom stones are absent in both Early Postclassic and Protohistoric times. The only exception is a plain atypical tripod stone, with round base, from the predominantly Protohistoric site of Mixco Viejo in the Central Highlands. It may, however, represent a (Late Classic?) heirloom at this site (H. Lehmann, personal communication).

"Luxury" vessels of Mexican onyx (travertine or "alabaster" *tecali* vases) of excellent workmanship have been reported from the Western Highlands and the Hilly Middle Country from such sites as Zaculeu (Woodbury and Trik, 1953, pp. 242–43, fig. 139), Tajumulco (Dutton and Hobbs, 1943, p. 51), Nebaj (A. L. Smith and Kidder, 1951, fig. 83,*b*), Chipal (Butler, 1940, p. 262, pl. 9,*o*), Kixpek, and Coban (Borhegyi, 1952b). Vessel shapes include small barrel- or pear-shaped jars; plain, ring-stand-based, tripod or cylindrical vases; and crouching spider monkey effigy vessels, the latter reminiscent of the beautiful obsidian and rock crystal monkey effigy vases of the Aztec period in Mexico (cf. Bernal, 1950). The Early Postclassic Mexican onyx vessels may have been imported to the Guatemalan highlands from highland Chiapas, perhaps directly from the famed "alabaster" quarries near the present-day Maya-Tzotzil town of Zinacantan (Berlin, 1946, pp. 26–27, pl. 4,*f*).

Other luxury objects and ornaments such as shell (mostly of red *Spondylus* variety), bone, or jade beads, spangles, armlets and pendants; gray-black obsidian earspools and tubes (Butler, 1940, pl. 11,*a,h,k,l;* 1959, fig. 405); and iron pyrite mosaic plaques are known from several sites in the Western Highlands and Hilly Middle Country (Chipal, Kixpek, Nebaj, Tajumulco, Quen Santo), but they are fewer in number and cannot be compared in artistry with specimens from the Classic period (Butler, 1940, p. 262; Dutton and Hobbs, 1943, figs. 31, 33; A. L. Smith and Kidder, 1951, fig. 67,*a*; Woodbury and Trik, 1953, pp. 236–38. fig. 281,*q*; Kidder II and Samayoa, 1959, fig. 88). Turquoise ornaments and mosaics, previously unknown in the highland Maya area, appear for the first time during this period but they are not as handsomely executed as those from Mexico and Yucatan (Woodbury and Trik, 1953, pp. 239–401, fig. 136). Small, perforated, anthropomorphic stone masks of jadeite or soapstone in the form of scepter heads or wands are frequently found at such Hilly Middle Country and Western Highlands sites as Nebaj, Chipal, Oncap, and Zacualpa (Lothrop, 1936, fig. 62; A. L. Smith and Kidder, 1951, figs. 89; 90,*c*). They often are depicted with long, upturned noses, somewhat reminiscent of the manikin scepter heads shown on many lowland Maya Classic period stelae of the Huaxtec upturned-nose sculptures of the Mexican Gulf coast (cf. note 59; Kidder II and Samayoa, 1959, fig. 89).

Among the ordinary household objects, metates of vesicular igneous rock are primarily of the tripod variety, occasionally with animal effigy legs (Villacorta and Villacorta, 1927, p. 158; Dutton and Hobbs, 1943, fig. 26; Woodbury and Trik, 1953, pp. 221–23, fig. 279); manos are usually square or elongated rollers. Stone mortars and pestles, hammerstones, grooved bark beaters (from Chacula, Tajumulco, and Zacualpa) (Wauchope, 1948a, p. 162, fig. 78), biconically perforated "doughnut"

---

[56] Stone sculptures depicting prowling jaguars in Tula-Toltec style have been reported from Finca El Portal in the Central Highlands (J. E. S. Thompson, 1943a, pl. 10,*g,h*). Similar carvings are known from such Pacific Coastal Piedmont sites as Sabanas Grandes (Shook, personal information) and Finca El Salto (Borhegyi notes).

stones, green stone celts, flakers, chisels, drills, obsidian flake-blades, and scrapers are common at many highland sites (Dutton and Hobbs, 1943, figs. 24–30; A. L. Smith and Kidder, 1951, fig. 84,g; Butler, 1959, fig. 5). The few paint palettes known are from Zaculeu, Nebaj, and San Agustin Acasaguastlan (A. L. Smith and Kidder, 1951, fig. 84,d; Woodbury and Trik, 1953, pp. 150, 259–60, fig. 279,f-h).

One of the interesting features of the period and especially of the Protohistoric is the appearance and relative abundance of stemless or straight-stemmed bifacially chipped, leaf-shaped, obsidian and chert (chalcedony) points, with expanding or tapering triangular butts (Dutton and Hobbs, 1943, fig. 25; Wauchope, 1948a, pp. 158–60 pls. 23, 24; A. L. Smith and Kidder, 1951, fig. 88,a; Woodbury and Trik, 1953, pp. 225–29; Butler, 1959, fig. 5,d). Their presence on the surface at many fortified hilltop sites seems to indicate increased military activities and warfare during the period and suggests that at least some of the points may have been used as spearthrower darts or as arrow points for bows, a weapon previously unknown in the highlands.

METALLURGY. Metalworking in copper, gold, silver, zinc, and tin (and their alloys) was not practiced in the highlands until the beginning of the Early Postclassic period. Although known from earlier periods in Central America and northwestern South America (and probably also in central Mexico) metalworking (by means of repoussé, mise-en-couleur plating, filigree, and lost wax–cire perdue casting) was introduced to the Guatemalan highlands only around A.D. 1000 and can be ascribed to Mexican and southern Central American influences. Small, spherical or pear-shaped bells (occasionally decorated with wirework), finger rings, hair ornaments, earplugs, beads, axes, repoussé discs, animal figurines (frog, jaguar), tweezers, pins, needles, thin tubes, lip plugs (of Mexican style), and coiled strips of wire have been noted from various Western Highlands and Hilly Middle Country sites, such as Tajumulco (Dutton and Hobbs, 1943, p. 57, 115–16, fig. 34) Zaculeu (Woodbury and Trik, 1953, pp. 263–65, figs. 152–54); Chutixtiox (A. L. Smith and Kidder, 1951, fig. 88,f); Nebaj (A. L. Smith and Kidder, 1951, p. 59, fig. 88,f); Chipal (Butler, 1940, p. 265, pl. 11,b,e,f,i,j; 1959, figs. 4, 5); Zacualpa (Lothrop, 1936, pp. 75–76, figs. 72, 73); Xikomuk (Borhegyi notes); and Kaminaljuyu (two engraved copper discs of doubtful authenticity; Kidder, Jennings, and Shook, 1946, p. 145).

Gold objects of tumbaga (gold-copper) and of silver-copper alloy, some with elaborate repoussé decoration in the forms of discs, pendants, paper-thin sheets or oblong strips, small human and animal figurines, beads, earplugs, necklaces, hair ornaments, headbands, and small spherical cups have been reported from Tajumulco (Dutton and Hobbs, 1943, p. 57, fig. 34,u); Zaculeu (Woodbury and Trik, 1953, p. 263, fig. 285); Nebaj (A. L. Smith and Kidder, 1951, pp. 58, 59, figs. 20; 88,e); Chipal (Butler, 1940, p. 265, pl. 11,c,d,g); Zacualpa (Lothrop, 1936, pp. 62–75, figs. 67, 68; J. E. S. Thompson, 1943a, p. 124, pl. 12,g; Nottebohm, 1945); Finca El Paraiso (Shook, 1947, pp. 179–84); Utatlan (Stephens, 1841, 2: 187); Iximche (Guillemín, paper in preparation, see IDAEH, vol. 12, no. 1, 1960, p. 129 for illustration); and from Kaminaljuyu (Kidder, Jennings, and Shook, 1946, p. 145; fig. 166,a,b).

Since both gold and copper ornaments have been found in association with plumbate vessels (Tohil and Robles types) there can be little doubt that the introduction of metallurgy to the Guatemalan highlands occurred at the beginning of the Early Postclassic period and that it was introduced from Mexico via the Nonoalca-Pipil-Toltec-Chichimec migrants, whose mastery of metalworking is frequently mentioned in the native annals. The use of metals during Early Postclassic times was sporadic, but by the Protohistoric, probably due to intensified trade relationships with Mexico, it had increased to such an extent that such utilitarian objects as axes, pins, and needles were often made of copper rather than stone or bone (Lothrop, 1936, fig. 73).

Inferences of Social and Religious Structure

The Early Postclassic period in the Guatemalan highlands is heralded by the arrival of the third Nahuat and Nahuatl migration from Mexico, designated earlier in this paper as the Nonoalca-Pipil-Toltec-Chichimec people. These "Nonoalcas" of the chronicles lived near the Laguna de Terminos region in Campeche on the Mexican Gulf coast (Annals of the Cakchiquels, 1953, p. 57) and were a highly composite ethnic group consisting of a mixture of Gulf coast Huaxtec-Mayas, Totonacs (?), "Tajinized-Teotihuacan-Pipils" (the Pipil-Nicarao), and a group of Nahuat-speaking Teotihuacan migrants who were forced out of Cholula sometime after A.D. 800. Around A.D. 1000 these "Nonoalcas" were joined by a group of Nahuatl-speaking refugee Toltecs largely of Chichimec derivation who, according to native legends, were led by their priest-ruler Ce-Acatl-Topiltzin-Quetzalcoatl (Kukulcan-Gucumatz).[57] Apparently these Toltec-Chichimec groups intermarried freely with the "Nonoalcas" and Chontal-speaking Mayas of the Laguna de Terminos region (cf. J. E. S. Thompson, 1945, pp. 12–13). As a result, the inhabitants of the Gulf coast of Mexico living near the mouth of the Usumacinta River and westward along the coast of Tabasco, although apparently retaining their native Chontal-Maya speech, acquired many "Toltec-Chichimec" cultural traits.

Around A.D. 1100, for some reason yet unknown, these various linguistically and culturally mixed groups began to expand northward to Yucatan and southward to the Guatemalan highlands. Some (the "Yaquis" or "sacrificers," the ancestors of

the modern Quiche-Maya) followed southward the Usumacinta River and its tributaries, the Pasion, Chixoy, and Lacantun. Others (the ancestors of the modern Cakchiquel and Tzutuhil-Mayas) followed the Grijalva and Jatate Rivers through Chiapas and entered the Guatemalan highlands somewhere in the northwestern part of the present Department of Huehuetenango. The former group displaced (or subjugated?) the native inhabitants of the Hilly Middle Country (the Xibalba of the native chronicles?), among whom were the ancestors of the present-day Chol-Maya, Kekchi, Pokomchi, Cholti, and northern-Pokomam Mayas (Goetz and Morley, 1950, pp. 159–69). The second group coming from Chiapas met resistance from the original inhabitants of the Western and Central Highlands, the ancestors of the present-day Mam-Maya, Jacalteca, Chuh, and southern-Pokomam (see fig. 6; also map in Miles, 1957b, fig. 1; Recinos and Goetz, 1953, pp. 66–67).

The appearance of these migratory groups from the Laguna de Terminos region in the Guatemalan highlands coincides with numerous drastic changes in the highland archaeological picture occurring soon after A.D. 1100. Although open to some

[57] The term "Toltec," like "Pipil," has been used in various periods and by different writers in many confusing connotations. One use of "Toltec" was in reference to a "citizen of Tollan" (Tulan), i.e. an urbanite or city-dweller. When, by the middle of the 10th century (or according to other authors, about A.D. 850), Toltec culture reached a high level of complexity, the term "Toltec" was applied to well-made, artistic things and came to be regarded as a title of distinction. To be a "Toltec" indicated that the person was a metropolitan city-dweller and implied that he was a "cultured" person, a "wise man" such as an artist, scientist, master weaver, or architect. This honorary use of the word "Toltec" continued even after the fall of the Toltec capital, Tula, sometime around A.D. 1116 (or 1168?). Many ruling families of Mexico and the Maya area claimed descent from the "Toltecs" just as many rulers of medieval Europe claimed succession from the Roman Caesars. (For good summaries of Toltec cultural and artistic characteristics see Jiménez Moreno, 1941; Dutton, 1955, 1956.)

question, it appears that these people represented a "backwash" Mixteca-Puebla and Toltec influence responsible for the introduction to the Guatemalan highlands of the following customs:

1. Custom of cremation instead of inhumation and the use of various types of crematory jars (Wauchope, 1942, 1945).
2. Cults of the war and solar gods, along with the cults of crude stone, clay, or wooden idols (among which may have figured vertically tenoned, cross-armed anthropomorphic stone statues and temple images and phallic statues in both human and animal forms), accompanied by "idolatry" (the feeding of idols with food, incense, and blood) and "heart-sacrifices" previously foreign to the highland Maya population (Goetz and Morley, 1950, pp. 180–81, 188, 190–92; Recinos and Goetz, pp. 48, 52–53, 82–84; McDougall, 1946).
3. Cult of "sacred bundles" such as the *Pizom Gagal* or *Giron-Gagal* ("Bundles of Greatness") mentioned in the Popol Vuh and The Lords of Totonicapan (see Goetz and Morley, 1950, pp. 205–06; and Recinos and Goetz, 1953, p. 170), a cult which with some modifications seems to survive today in the "cristo-pagan" cult of "bundles" and *cofradía-cajas* among some highland Guatemalan Quiche, Cakchiquel, and Tzutuhil groups (cf. Mendelson, 1958).
4. Caves as places of idol worship. These caves may also have been connected with the collecting and veneration (and shrinking?) of human trophy heads (cf. Seler, 1901, figs. 140, 141, 172, 218, 219, pls. 8,*b*; 30; Leigh, 1961). For descriptions in the native annals of cave cults with idols and the decapitation of prisoners see Goetz and Morley (1950, pp. 174–76, 184; Recinos and Goetz, 1953, pp. 73–76, 178–80).
5. Knowledge of metallurgy (gold, copper, tin, silver, and their alloys) and the use of malleable metal ornaments, weapons and tools (Goetz and Morley, 1950, pp. 200–01).
6. Form of dual rulership (the joint rulers coming from two different families) similar to that found among contemporary Nahuatl groups in Mexico (Chichimecs, Tenochcas) in which one of the pair had a slightly junior position. Among the Quiche and Cakchiquel, two chiefs from two different families served as co-rulers (see J. E. S. Thompson, 1943a, pp. 130–31; Goetz and Morley, 1950, pp. 228–35). This form of dual rulership may reflect the Quiche and Cakchiquel veneration of legendary twin heroes and twin gods (see Popol Vuh; Goetz and Morley, 1950, pp. 94–95, 107–08, 126; see also use of twin temples (item 10).
7. Proud memory that their ancestors came from the great city of Tollan (Tula, or Tulan). The loyalty of these groups to their "hometown" of Tula is evident in the native legends relating to various long trips taken by the Quiche and Cakchiquel royal princes to receive the insignia of royalty and the picture writings or "paintings of Tulan" from the court of Nacxit (Kukulkan, Quetzalcoatl) the Lord King of the East (Wauchope, 1948a, pp. 38–39; Goetz and Morley, 1950, pp. 206–10; Recinos and Goetz, 1953, pp. 64–65, 172, 176–77).
8. Basic change in the social structure from a primarily theocratic society to a more secular, militaristic, urban middle-class-dominated society where the power structure lay in the hands of warrior-rulers and wealthy (slave-holding?) merchant farmers.
9. Change from the open land and valley settlements to fortified hilltop towns (*tenamit, tinamitl, tecpán*), many of which were surrounded by deep ravines and protected by military outposts (see J. E. S. Thompson, 1948, p. 128; Miles, 1957b, pp. 768–71; Goetz and Morley, 1950, p. 219).
10. Changes in architectural features and forms which include round temple structures, twin temples (for twin gods?) colonnades, and small altar structures (*momoztlis*) in the center of plazas; all in the specialized service and honor of such Mexican-derived deities as Quetzalcoatl (see Goetz and Morley, 1950, p. 189) in his form as the Feathered Serpent, Kukulkan, Gucumatz, or Tepeu, and his twin brother Xolotl; Tohil-Tlaloc (in his bearded form and/or

with a long upturned nose); Tlalchitonatiuh (in the form of the rising and/or falling sun god); Xipe Totec and the triplet gods or rain, thunder, and storm, Tohil-Huracán, Avilix, and Hacavitz (Goetz and Morley, 1950, pp. 175–76).

11. New religious paraphernalia such as Mixteca-Puebla type of tripod censers, copper bells (worn about the ankles for ceremonial dances?), and ladle censers (with perforated bottoms and covers).

12. New and more secularized forms of the rubber ball-game played in enclosed "sunken" courts with more or less vertical side walls. New ball-game rules and paraphernalia including stone rings and stuccoed clay (and stone?) heads or balls (with horizontal tenons) which occasionally contained (severed?) human skulls (see Burkitt, 1930b, p. 56; cf. also Goetz and Morley, 1950, pp. 111–15, 145, 152–53, 163).

13. New food habits and methods of food preparation involving *molcajetes* (tripod pottery bowls with sharp grooves on the interior of the vessel bottom) to grind chili or fruit (see Goetz and Morley, 1950, p. 135); perforated jars called variously "steaming vessels," colanders or *pichachas* in which corn was probably washed after being boiled in lye (Lothrop, 1933, pp. 70, 88, figs. 42; 56,b; Dutton and Hobbs, 1943, fig. 82,a; Wauchope, 1948a, p. 151); clay mixing bowls (or clay-lined pits) sunk into the house floor for use in making hominy (*nixtamal*), (Wauchope, 1948a, pp. 87–88, pls. 9,b,c,d; 13,a,a'); and *comales* or clay griddles (flat round dishes mostly of micaceous ware) for roasting seeds, chilis, and the flat corn cakes called *tortillas*.[58]

14. Regularized trade relations with Mexico on established inland and waterway trade routes, and the import of luxury objects such as turquoise, gold and copper ornaments, and metal tools. This regularized trade with Mexico was probably carried out by traveling members of various specialized and organized merchant guilds (*pochtecas*) which made use of protected trading posts, rest stations, and regional markets, and were under the tutelage of the god Ek-Ahau, or Ek-Chu-Ah, the Black Lord (cf. Mendez, 1959; J. E. S. Thompson, 1956).[59]

15. Intensified warfare and territorial expansion for primarily economic motives made possible by the use of such new weapons as pottery jars filled with hornets and wasps, and bows and arrows (Goetz and Morley, 1950, pp. 201–03, 221–23; Recinos and Goetz, 1953, pp. 66–67, 73–74, 173–74).

16. Torturing and decapitation of prisoners captured in warfare, and the ritual of arrow-sacrifice in which prisoners were tied to a tree (or a rack), arms extended, and shot with arrows much as in the "Morning Star" sacrifice of the Pawnee of North America (Recinos and Goetz, 1953, pp. 73–76; Goetz and Morley, 1950, p. 221; cf. Linton, 1922).

17. Possible introduction of syphilis, which may have had a disastrous epidemic effect on the native highland Maya population and contributed to their drastic decrease in number prior to the Spanish conquest.[60]

---

[58] The use of comales and tortillas was presumably unknown among the highland and lowland Maya until as late as the Protohistoric or Spanish colonial period (J. E. S. Thompson, 1930, pp. 95–96; Borhegyi, 1959a, p. 56–57).

It is still not quite clear whether comales are of pre- or post-Columbian origin in southern Mesoamerica and whether or not they were used in the Guatemalan highlands before the Spanish conquest. However, it is certain that they were not native to the Maya Indians (who preferred to eat corn in the form of tamales) and represent a Mexican innovation introduced probably no earlier than the Protohistoric period by traders or by migratory groups from Mexico.

[59] Ek-Chu-Ah (Schellhas' God M) was intimately connected with cacao and therefore particularly close to the merchants, who used cacao as their chief currency. God M is frequently represented with a long pointed nose. The cult of this merchant god (along with the salt and amber trade) still survives along the same ancient trade routes throughout Central America, Mexico, and even New Mexico in the United States. It is accompanied by salt and clay or earth-eating (geophagy) and the veneration of the miraculous image of the Black Christ (El Cristo Negro) of Esquipulas (cf. Borhegyi, 1953, 1954b).

[60] Human bones and crania showing evidence of osteitis with destructive syphilitic lesions were encountered at Zaculeu only in the last levels of occupation (Quankyak and Xinabahul phases) during which the indigenous Mam-Maya population was, according to native annals, subject to

18. Intensified use of a bark paper (*amatle*) and animal skins for painted divinatory and genealogical "books," folded drawings (the "paintings of Tulan"), and for bark-paper flags used in various religious and secular ceremonies (cf. Goetz and Morley, 1950, pp. 209–10).[61]

The general impression of the Early Postclassic and Protohistoric periods is that all art forms show signs of artistic retrogression and that the occupants of the highlands during these times were too busy with other, primarily military, affairs to take the time necessary to develop skill and artistry in stone, wood, and clay. Although not wholly lacking in artistic skill, design and form, Early Postclassic and Protohistoric period lapidary work and pottery making cannot compare with the skillfully carved jade ornaments, beautiful figure painted (and carved) vases, and moldmade figurines of the Hilly Middle Country during Late Classic times, nor with the Teotihuacan-inspired arts of the Early Classic.

The tribal aim of the newly arrived Mexican groups seems to have been the acquisition of the best agricultural lands, markets and such industrially important regions as the salt-, cotton-, and cacao-producing Pacific Coastal Piedmont and the flint, volcanic stone, obsidian, jade, and copper-rich Western and Central Highlands. The militant Quiche, Cakchiquel, and Tzutuhil sought to expand at the expense of the Mam-Maya, Pipil-Nicarao, and Pokomam tribes (see Woodbury and Trik, 1953, pp. 9–11; map in Miles, 1957b, fig. 1, p. 737) who controlled most of the finest cotton- and cacao-producing lands. Following this was a bitter economic and military struggle between the various Mexican tribes themselves for political hegemony. Confederacies were forged one after the other, only to be broken at opportune times (see fig. 7).

In summing up, we may say that the intensive intertribal warfare, large-scale territorial expansion and Mexican colonization of the Guatemalan highlands during the Early Postclassic and Protohistoric periods led towards social heterogeneity and away from the highland Maya homogeneous folk-type society of the Preclassic and Late Classic periods. Increased political consciousness gradually broke down and superseded the "village-mindedness" and economic self-sufficiency of the satellite villages and forged the various highland Guatemalan Indian groups into nations, each with its own "king" (or kings), "capital," and major religious center.

There is no question that by the end of the 16th century these competing nations, weakened as they were by internal and external conflicts, would have fallen victim to the rapidly expanding and militant Aztec (Mexica) confederation. Instead, fate decreed that Spain, itself a newly born and militant empire of Europe, should conquer and subjugate both the Mexica and the Maya population of the New World.

"Quiché" overlordship (Goetz and Morley, 1950, pp. 228–30; Woodbury and Trik, 1953, pp. 312–19, figs. 292–94; Borhegyi, a review of Woodbury and Trik, 1953, in *Revista Interamericana de Bibliografía*, 1954, 4: 310–12).

[61] The reappearance of stemmed, flat clay stamps during the Early Postclassic and Protohistoric period may be ascribed to their possible use for stamping designs on bark paper (Borhegyi, 1950e, p. 24).

CHRONOLOGICAL HORIZONS	APPROXIMATE DATES	CENTRAL HIGHLANDS KAMINALJUYU		WESTERN HIGHLANDS		HILLY MIDDLE COUNTRY CHIXOY DRAINAGE		CHIAPAS (MEXICO)		MIGRATIONS OR INFLUENCES FROM MEXICO
		CEREMONIAL ELITE	PROVINCIAL RURAL	ZACULEU	ZACUALPA	WEST	EAST	CHIAPA DE CORZO		
SPANISH COLONIAL	A.D. 1530									SPANISH
PROTOHISTORIC	1200	CHINAUTLA		XINABAHUL	YAQUI	CHIPAL 3	SAMAC	TUXTLA	XII	AZTEC (MEXICA)
EARLY POSTCLASSIC	1000	?	AYAMPUC	QUANKYAK	TOHIL	CHIPAL 2		RUIZ	XI	QUICHE – CAKCHIQUEL TOLTEC – CHICHIMEC (NONOALCA – PIPIL)
LATE CLASSIC	800	?	PAMPLONA	CHINAQ	POKOM	CHIPAL 1	SEACAL	PAREDON	X-B	"TAJINIZED TEOTIHUACAN– PIPILES" (PIPIL– NICARAO)
	700					CHAMA 3-4	CHIPOK	MARAVILLAS	X-A	
EARLY CLASSIC	400	ESPERANZA	AMATLE	ATZAN	BALAM	CHAMA 2	?	LAGUNA	IX	TEOTIHUACAN (III)
	300	AURORA				CHAMA 1-B		JIQUIPILAS	VIII	
PROTOCLASSIC	200	SANTA CLARA	?			CHAMA 1-A	?	ISTHMO	VII	
								HORCONES	VI	
LATE PRECLASSIC	0	MIRAFLORES	ARENAL					GUANACASTE	V	LA VENTA (OLMEC)
	300			SALCAJA	SAN CRISTOBAL					
MIDDLE PRECLASSIC	500	PROVIDENCIA (MAJADAS)	SACATEPEQUEZ (ZAKAT) ?	?	?	?	?	FRANCESA	IV	
	600	LAS CHARCAS B						ESCALERA	III	
	1000	LAS CHARCAS A		?	?	?	?	DILI	II	?
EARLY PRECLASSIC	1500	AREVALO						COTORRA	I	
	B.C.	?								

TABLE 1.

REFERENCES

Acosta, 1956–57
Armillas, Palerm, and Wolf, 1956
Aveleyra, 1959
Barbour, 1957
Berlin, 1946, 1950, 1952
Bernal, 1949, 1950
Blom, 1954
—— and LaFarge, 1926–27
Boggs, 1950
Borhegyi, 1950a, 1950b, 1950c, 1950d, 1950e, 1951a, 1951b, 1951c, 1952b, 1953, 1954a, 1954b, 1955a, 1956b, 1956c, 1956d, 1957a, 1957c, 1958a, 1958b, 1959a, 1959b, 1960a, 1960b, 1961a, 1961b, 1961c, 1961d, 1963
—— and Scrimshaw, 1957
Brainerd, 1954, 1956
Burkitt, 1924, 1930a, 1930b
Butler, 1935a, 1940, 1959

Caso, 1949b, 1959
Charnay, 1887
Chowning, 1956
Coe, M. D., 1956, 1957b, 1957c, 1959b, 1960b, 1961
Cooke, 1931
Covarrubias, 1943, 1957
Dieseldorff, 1904, 1926–33
Drucker, 1943a, 1943b
—— and Heizer, 1960
——, ——, and Squier, 1959
Dutton, 1943, 1955, 1956
—— and Hobbs, 1943
Ekholm, 1946, 1949
Ferdon, 1953
Flint and Deevey, 1959
Foshag and Leslie, 1955
Gamio, 1922, 1926–27

Gann, 1925b, 1932, 1939
Genin, 1928
Girard, 1962
Goetz and Morley, 1950
Goubaud, 1949
Granlund, 1953
Guillemín, 1958, 1959
Hester, 1952
Jiménez Moreno, 1941, 1942, 1959
Kidder and Samayoa, 1959
Kidder, 1945, 1948, 1949b, 1950
——, Jennings, and Shook, 1946
—— and Shook, 1959, 1961
Knauth, 1961
Kubler, 1961
Lehmann, W., 1920
Leigh, 1961
Linné, 1934, 1941, 1942, 1947
Linton, 1922
Lister, 1955
Lizardi Ramos, 1955
Longyear, 1952
Lothrop, 1923, 1926a, 1933, 1936, 1961
Lowe, 1959b
McDougall, 1946
MacNeish, 1954, 1961, 1964
Maudslay, 1889–1902
Memorial de Solola, 1950
Mendelson, 1958
Mendez, 1959
Miles, 1957b
Millon, 1954, 1957
Morley, 1935, 1956
Nicholson, 1961
Nottebohm, 1945
Orellana Tapia, 1955
Palerm, 1957
Parsons, Borhegyi, Jenson, and Ritzenthaler, 1963
Piña Chan, 1958, 1960a, 1960b
Pollock, 1936
Porter, 1948, 1953
Proskouriakoff, 1950, 1951, 1954
Rands, 1954
Ravicz, 1961
Recinos and Goetz, 1953
Reichel-Dolmatoff, 1961
Richardson, 1940

Roys, L., 1958
Ruz, L., 1945c, 1959
Satterthwaite, 1952
Sauer, 1936, 1950
Saville, 1899, 1909
Sears, 1951
Séjourné, 1952b, 1959, 1960
Seler, 1901, 1904b
Shepard, 1948
Shook, 1949a, 1949b, 1950a, 1950c, 1951a, 1951b, 1952a, 1952b, 1954b, 1955b
—— and Kidder, 1952
—— and Proskouriakoff, 1956
Smith, A. L., 1955, 1961
—— and Kidder, 1943, 1951
Smith, R. E., 1952, 1954b, 1958
Sorenson, 1955
Starr, 1897
Stephens, 1841
Stern, 1950
Stirling, 1943, 1957
Stone, 1949
Stromsvik, 1950, 1956
Strong, 1947
Swadesh, 1953
Tax, 1951
Tejeda, 1947
Termer, 1930b, 1936, 1951
Thompson, J. E. S., 1930, 1941a, 1941c, 1943a, 1943b, 1943c, 1945, 1948, 1950, 1954a, 1956, 1959b
Torquemada, 1723
Tozzer, 1921
Villacorta and Villacorta, 1927
Von Weber, 1922
Von Winning, 1948, 1958, 1961
Warren, 1959, 1961
Wasson and Wasson, 1957
Wauchope, 1941, 1942a, 1942b, 1948a, 1949, 1954
Weitlaner, 1948
Wicke, 1956
Willey, 1956b, 1956c
Williams, 1952
Wolf, 1959
—— and Palerm, 1955
Woodbury and Trik, 1953

2. Settlement Patterns of the Guatemalan Highlands

STEPHAN F. DE BORHEGYI

M AN HAS SHAPED his environment to his needs in spite of geographical and climatic limitations of landscape. With dwellings and temporary or permanent settlements, he has gradually changed and controlled his surroundings. Through a study or survey of the nature, size, extent, and limitations of ancient dwellings and settlements unearthed in excavations, archaeologists can reconstruct with reasonable accuracy something of the type and complexity of the cultural institutions which once governed the lives of these communities. The settlements reflect such things as social distinctions, means of social control, and relative size and density of population. They also indicate subsistence activities, availability of food supply, and degree of economic specialization.

With these factors in mind, let us survey the changes in settlement pattern in the Guatemalan highlands during a span of more than two millennia. Factual data concerning settlement patterns in each period will be presented first, followed by inferences relative to the social structure and cultural change of the communities which built the settlements.

THE GEOGRAPHICAL SETTING

The territory of the Maya in southeastern Mexico, Guatemala, British Honduras, and parts of El Salvador and Honduras, can conveniently be divided into six geographical and cultural units:

(A) Tropical Rain Forest Area, (B) Hilly Middle Country, (C) Western Volcanic Highlands, (D) Central Volcanic Highlands, (E) Semiarid Eastern Lowlands, and (F) Pacific Coastal Plains and Piedmont (see also Borhegyi, 1956b, p. 345). For the purpose of this study we are concerned only with the settlement patterns of the region of the Maya highlands, in effect the Western and Central Highlands (shown in fig. 1 as *C* and *D*) and with occasional references to the Hilly Middle Country (*B*).

The Highlands and the Hilly Middle Country of Guatemala include a region of sharply contrasting climate, topography,

59

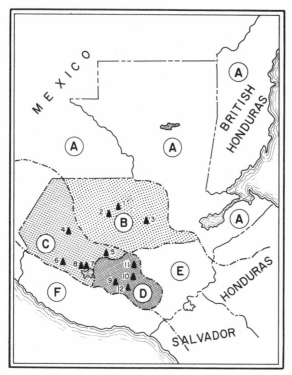

Fig. 1—MAP OF THE SOUTHERN MAYA AREA. *Culture areas:* A, Tropical Rain Forest. B, Hilly Middle Country. C, Western Highlands. D, Central Highlands. E, Semiarid Eastern Lowlands. F, Pacific Coastal Plains and Piedmont. *Archaeological sites:* 1, Chama. 2, Chipal. 3, Chipoc. 4, Zaculeu. 5, Zacualpa. 6, Salcaja. 7, Chuitinamit. 8, Chukumuk. 9, Terrenos. 10, Kaminaljuyu. 11, Chinautla. 12, Amatitlan. (After Borhegyi, 1956a, fig. 107.)

and agricultural potential. The high basins and fertile valleys that have been formed between the various mountain ranges offer almost ideal conditions for human settlement. In the highlands a cool climate prevails the year around; the volcanic-ash–covered soil, watered by an abundance of streams, fed by heavy rains from mid-April through November, produces more than sufficient food supply. Oak and pine woods which provide fuel and building material are scattered throughout the mountain ranges. The great canyons (*barrancas*) were and still are the major obstacle to communication and to the development of large settlements.

The gently rounded, misty mountain-

tops to the north in the Hilly Middle Country are covered with cypress groves and tropical vegetation, whereas the sharp and more recent volcanic cones to the south are topped with pine and crowned most of the day in fog. The interior valleys in both the Highland and Hilly Middle Country regions are drained by rivers flowing northward to the Rio Negro or Chixoy systems and the Motagua River. On the south side of the Cordillera the rivers rush down to the Pacific Ocean through the fertile piedmont, once a rich cotton- and cacao-bearing country.

According to the 1950 Guatemalan population census figures, of the total of 2,788,-122 inhabitants of Guatemala, 1,491,725 (53.5%) are Indians. Of this population, a total of 1,848,244 (66.3%) live in the Highland area (comprising about 11 departments, including those of Alta and Baja Verapaz in the Hilly Middle Country). Of these 1,178,510 (63.8%) are Indians. In other words, the Indians far outnumber the non-Indians in the Highlands and Hilly Middle Country. All of this indicates that today, and most probably also in pre-Columbian times, the Highlands and the Hilly Middle Country attract and support a more concentrated population than any of the other sections of Guatemala.[1] One does not have to be an environmental determinist to detect that in this area there was and is an unusually close relationship between culture and nature. The fact that this area contained the wild forebears of such domesticable food plants as maize, black beans, avocado, and squash gave it the necessary potential for man to control his food production and ultimately to develop a great civilization.

Today the Maya Indian population of the Highlands and Hilly Middle Country lives in compound, clustered, or dispersed

[1] Excluding the Preclassic and Classic occupation of the Peten Rain Forest area, which has been variously estimated from 300,000 to several million (Termer, 1951).

villages, with more or less well-defined, centrally located plazas. In addition, there also exist some so-called concourse centers (or "vacant towns," like Chichicastenango) where the plaza is of considerable regional importance for markets and for periodic religious communal gatherings although with the exception of the transitory Indian officials (*encargados*), the majority of the population permanently resides in distant hamlets, or *caserias*. Each of these villages, whether compound, clustered, dispersed, or concourse, today represents a self-sufficient agricultural, social, religious, and political entity. In a previous paper (Borhegyi, 1956a) I have suggested that the types of present-day settlements of Highland Guatemala closely parallel the basic pre-Columbian patterns and that these settlement forms have remained more or less unchanged despite 16th-century Spanish efforts of *reducción* and the coming of the machine age.

The pre-Columbian Settlement Pattern

Early Preclassic Period (Early or "Village" Formative Period) 1500–600 B.C.

The archaeological phases associated with this period are Arevalo and Las Charcas A (Valley of Guatemala).[2]

Site Features (Early Preclassic). The choice of location of Preclassic sites seems to have been dictated primarily by agricultural needs. Land was needed in the immediate vicinity of the settlement to raise the recently domesticated food plants, maize, squash, and avocado. The sites, on level land in the valleys and on the plateaus, were small, open, and undefended.

From the scanty archaeological material at hand, it appears that the basic settlement pattern of this Formative Period was the unplanned year-round farming-village consisting of small clusters of mud-walled

houses scattered over the landscape. Each cluster may have represented an autonomous, self-sufficient, agricultural, social, religious, and political entity. Although no habitation mounds have yet been excavated, we know from the many burned adobe fragments bearing impressions of poles, leaves, corncobs, and other vegetable materials found in excavations of large refuse pits in the Central Highlands (as at the sites of Las Charcas, Sacatepequez, Xaraxong), that dwellings were made of pole and thatch with walls partially daubed with adobe. Such houses must have been repaired and rebuilt frequently (Shook, 1949, p. 221; 1951a, p. 97). Apparently these huts were arranged at random throughout the village area, probably on low earthen foundations. There are no signs of plazas, or other indications of village planning. Scattered within the village area, 2–4-m.-deep conical or bottle-shaped pits with circular orifices were dug through the frequently sterile surface soil into the underlying volcanic ash. Some may have served the villagers as sweat baths for ritual purification, but more probably they were food storage chambers, sealed with stone slabs, to safeguard the growing larder of agricultural products. When mold growth ended their usefulness as food storage chambers, many were left empty. Others were filled with household debris (ashes, corncobs, fruit seeds, animal bones, disarticulated human bones, broken *manos* and *metates*, cooking vessels). A few even contained simple burials sparsely furnished with food containers and personal ornaments (Shook, 1950a).

Apparently no temple or burial mounds were constructed during this period. It is possible, however, that some of the low, rectangular, earthen structures at Kaminaljuyu (Mounds C-III-6 and C-III-10; Shook, 1951b, pp. 240–41) were built during the end of this period. They may have served for minor public or family ceremonial functions, thus heralding the beginning of the

[2] For an explanation of the Las Charcas A period and its chronological rendering, see Borhegyi, Article 1, note 2, and Table 1.

monumental temple and burial architecture of the following period.

INFERENCES (Early Preclassic). Although there has been insufficient excavation of Preclassic sites, to determine their precise extent, we can assume that the "farming villages" covered at most a few acres, and that the principal nucleating forces were: (1) availability of arable lands, (2) soil and climatic conditions favorable for small-scale *milpa* agriculture, (3) availability of a permanent supply of water and fuel, (4) availability of game, fish, and fruit, (5) proximity to such sacred localities or cult objects as mountains, hills, hot or cold springs, caves, lakes, water holes, woods, boulders, or trees.

Middle and Late Preclassic and Protoclassic Periods, 600 B.C. to A.D. 300.[3]

The archaeological phases associated with this period are: Las Charcas B, Providencia-Majadas, Miraflores-Arenal, Santa Clara (Valley of Guatemala); Terrenos Altos, Zakat-Xaraxong (Almolonga Valley); Chukumuk 1 (Lake Atitlan); Salcaja 1-2 (Western Highlands).

SITE FEATURES (Middle and Late Preclassic). The period is characterized by the continued use of open, undefended valley and plateau sites, and the appearance of huge earthen mounds, as much as 20 m. in height. These mounds were laid out to define long, narrow, parallel plazas or avenues which were separated by a single row of buildings oriented roughly northeast-southwest (fig. 2). The truncated pyramidal earthen mounds with steep, open stairways were built without the use of stone or lime mortar and were faced with puddled adobe. They were covered with brightly painted (red, green or black) adobe plaster and on the summits supported perishable thatch-roofed, mud-and-pole–walled structures which probably served as temple or altar shrines. Sometimes these mounds contained

several elaborate tombs (Shook and Kidder, 1952).

In contrast to the haphazardly laid out hamlets of the earlier period, the organized planning of the plazas and surrounding mounds shows the definite concept of a ceremonial precinct, a sacred burial enclosure, from which the village life was apparently excluded. One may surmise that in plan and function the scattered house clusters or "farming villages" in the open valleys remained much the same as in the former period but gradually the previously autonomous village clusters may have become subsidiary to a major ceremonial or "worship" center. It can be assumed that each major worship and burial center was built, supported, and maintained by the communal efforts of several dispersed type of satellite farming villages and hamlets. In other words, the villagers remained rural residents although they became participants in the life of the ceremonial centers. We can therefore see in this period the beginnings of the agglutinated, concentrated, or clustered types of settlement pattern, with the burial center and its plaza serving as the functional nucleus or "worship center" for the several outlying farming villages.[4]

By the end of the Late Preclassic period there is evidence of a steady growth and elaboration of settlements of the Guatemalan highlands. Apparently they reached their population and prosperity peak during Late Preclassic times (300 B.C. to 300 A.D.). There was a great growth in size of certain important ceremonial centers, open and undefended as before, in the Valley of Guatemala; on the Canchon plateau (Shook, 1952b; Shook and Proskouriakoff, 1956, fig. 1) in the Salcaja Valley; around Lakes Amatitlan (Contreras, Borhegyi, 1959b) and Atitlan (Chukumuk); in the

---

[3] For an explanation of the chronology see Borhegyi, Article 1, note 2, and Table 1.

[4] For a similar type of village concentration around major and minor ceremonial centers in the Tropical Rain Forest areas of Peten and British Honduras, see the *"zones"* and "districts" of Bullard, 1960b.

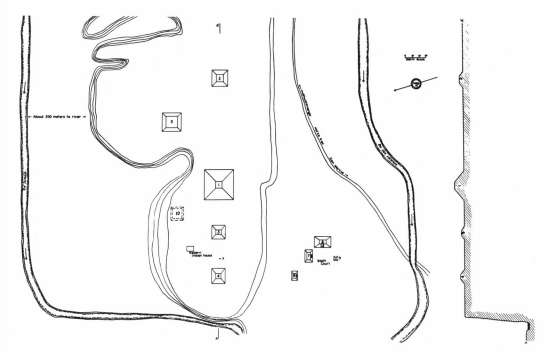

F<small>IG</small>. 2—CAMBOTE, DEPT. OF HUEHUETENANGO. A Late Preclassic site, undefended on a tongue of land formed by the convergence of two rivers, with large mounds (13 m. high) laid out to define long, narrow, parallel plazas or avenues oriented roughly NE-SW. (After A. L. Smith, 1955, p. 7, fig. 47.)

Aguacatan Valley (Chalchitan, A. L. Smith, 1955, fig. 51); in the Sacapulas area of the Rio Negro river valley (Rio Blanco, *ibid.*, fig. 59); in the Salama region (El Porton, *ibid.*); and in the Rio Coban Valley in the Alta Verapaz (Chichen, Santa Elena, Chinchilla, *ibid.*, fig. 42).

C<small>ONCEPT</small> <small>OF</small> "U<small>RBANISM</small>." Recently there has been some contention that the prehistoric Maya ceremonial centers were actual cities with a rather high degree of "urbanism." Certain characteristic features of these centers tend to support this claim, but any final decision must depend greatly on the definition of "city" and "urbanism." Both concepts, notoriously hard to define, have been employed rather loosely by archaeologists. In order to differentiate the forms of permanent settlements, we need also to define "village" and "town." Utilizing the definitions proposed by Sanders for Central Mexico (1956, p. 117) based on the

mode of life of the inhabitants, we have: *a village*—a nucleated or scattered, self-sustaining, socially homogeneous community or center for aggregation of hamlets, with population running at least into the hundreds and in which at least 75 per cent of the population spends at least 75 per cent of their time in agricultural pursuits; *a town*—a socially homogeneous rural community or center for aggregation of villagers in which the bulk of the population is still dedicated to agricultural pursuits but in which trade and craft specialization are added as secondary activities, reducing the percentage of population devoted to agriculture to below 75 per cent; *a city*—a socially heterogeneous, economically interdependent community in which over 75 per cent of the population spends over 75 per cent of its time in nonagricultural pursuits.

These definitions conflict with those of

63

other archaeologists, who consider the development of urbanism a prerequisite of
civilization and define cities not according
to the mode of life of the inhabitants but
by: (1) size and extent of the settlement,
(2) size and density of the population, (3)
level of technological and economic advance of its inhabitants, (4) size and number of public buildings, and (5) level of
the intellectual arts employed by its inhabitants.

Although these factors are all part of
urban development, I cannot agree that
they alone are sufficient to create metropolitan centers. An increase in the density
of population may be necessary to bring
about the social stimuli for urbanization,
but mere increase in size does not always
imply technological or economic advance.
"Urbanism," as I view it, is a social process
by which man redefines his ways of interaction with his fellow man, rather than
increasing his interaction with his environment. It implies a high degree of impersonal
interaction between socially heterogeneous
individuals of cosmopolitan attitudes and
religious beliefs.

The Maya ceremonial centers with their
encircling farming settlements were more
than just large farming communities since,
in addition to a sizable population (50,000
estimated for Kaminaljuyu), they: (1)
were well-advanced technologically and
economically (signs of many localized industries at Kaminaljuyu such as obsidian,
jade, pottery and shell workshops), (2)
possessed many monumental public buildings (more than 100 Preclassic mounds at
Kaminaljuyu, some of them 20 m. in height,
with a base of 70 by 90 m.), and (3) had
reached a relatively high level of esthetics
(monumental stone sculptures, decorated
building façades, sophisticated pottery
decoration).

Nevertheless, in spite of their size and
technological complexity, they were but
sacred burial precincts or worship centers.
A so-called urban "elite" may have resided

temporarily or permanently in these centers
but there can be little doubt that the majority of the inhabitants were socially and
ethnically homogeneous, and that the monumental temple and mortuary structures
were built and maintained not by their
dwellers, but by the common religious and
economic support of the subsidiary farming
villages. A close symbiosis between the
ceremonial center and its satellite villages
was a vital necessity to the very existence
of the center. The constant human interaction based on the well-defined ceremonial
movements from the villages to the worship
center apparently created sufficient social
incentive to accelerate technological progress and cultural complexity. The estimated
50,000 inhabitants of Kaminaljuyu in Late
Preclassic times that lived scattered over the
valley floor in small dispersed hamlets made
up a socially homogeneous rural community.
The bulk of the population was dedicated to
agricultural pursuits and only about 25 per
cent were engaged in trade, craft, and religious specialization. Therefore, considering
the mode of life and the degree of homogeneous interaction, Kaminaljuyu and other
Preclassic and Classic highland Maya (and
Mexican) ceremonial centers were not true
cities, but *sacred towns*. They were the
worship centers for several farming villages
and were dedicated to the gods. In bringing about their existence, the Preclassic
Maya farmer had redefined his ways of
interaction, not with his fellow man, but
with his gods.

The Maya settlements of the highlands
were, more specifically, extended-boundary
towns, much like 6th century Athens with
its loosely federated Attic villages (Miles,
1957a, 1958). The Attic town, like the
typical settlement of the Guatemalan highlands, was based on closely knit kin relationships, a common form of worship, and
homogeneous religious beliefs, all under
the same tutelary gods. In both areas the
ceremonial movements from the hamlets to
the "worship" centers were well defined

and regulated by calendric events. The new roles and obligations assumed by some of the farmers in their dual capacity as tillers of the soil and as priests or craftsmen were defined primarily to suit the gods. Without any drastic change in residence pattern, both Attic and highland Maya society acquired an "urban" outlook which set the stage for true urbanization in a later period. Athens eventually became a truly heterogeneous metropolis; the Maya ceremonial centers, on the other hand, were abandoned by the end of the Classic period, and only the newly established settlements of the greatly secularized Postclassic period acquired an urban character.

INFERENCES (Middle and Late Preclassic). One may wonder just what caused the sudden upsurge of monumental architectural activities, the building of large and tall pyramidal temple and burial mounds, during this period. No doubt, sedentary life gave opportunities for improved housing accommodation and paved the way for architecture. But monumental architecture and engineering also requires technical sophistication, inventiveness, and a solid economic base. It can be assumed that the Preclassic farmers must have found new ways to intensify their food collecting and production, probably by introducing crop rotation, irrigation, or terrace agriculture. They must also have found better ways to preserve and store surplus food and other commodities. It may be that the domestication of new food plants produced a better protein diet, and thus contributed to the increase in population. These innovations, in turn, permitted the redistribution of human energy and the withdrawal of certain individuals from direct food-producing activities, making possible the existence of part- and full-time nonagricultural specialists. Simultaneously, village specialization in certain crafts and crops, created a need for organized trade relationships with neighboring settlements. The exchange of commodities was accompanied by an exchange of ideas. Eventually the newly found bonds were expressed at common places of worship and market activities which were probably located in most cases within easy reach of the supporting villages, near sacred places or objects.

The monumental building activities were probably carried out in the service of the supernatural and the dead. Unquestionably these enormous cooperative tasks were a long time in completion and several thousands of people must have participated in the activities. Pilgrims from the satellite villages who flocked to these centers may have been turned into temporary labor battalions, efficiently marshalled and directed by their leaders. Clearly, the participants must have been well organized, and motivated by religious zeal or by a promised reward in the afterlife.

We can postulate that the principal nucleating forces in the Late Preclassic, in addition to those of earlier periods, were: (1) population increase and the rise of part-time specialists, (2) concentration of wealth and power in certain settlements, and in the hands of certain able individuals, (3) localization of religious and burial rituals in a ceremonial precinct, (4) availability of mass labor forces motivated by religious zeal, (5) growth of the market pattern in the ceremonial precinct for the distribution of surplus food and other commodities, (6) nearness to major ceremonial centers and established trade routes, and (7) nearness to the burial places of deified (?) priest-rulers. It is obvious from this list that the nucleating forces which created the ceremonial centers of the Late Preclassic were predominantly cultural rather than physical.

Early and Late Classic Periods (Rise, Culmination, and Fall of the Theocracy) A.D. 300–1000.

The archaeological phases associated with these periods are: Aurora, Esperanza, and Amatle-Pamplona (Valley of Guate-

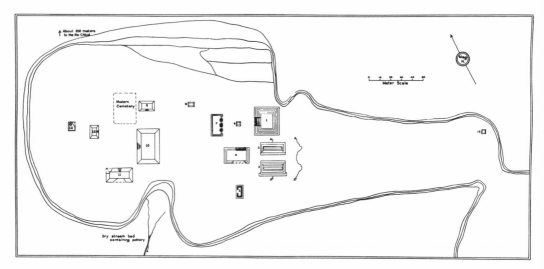

Fɪɢ. 3—CHICOL, DEPT. OF HUEHUETENANGO. An Early Classic site, undefended near the River Chicol, with closely knit court arrangements and sloping-sided ball court. (After A. L. Smith, 1955, p. 8, fig. 48.)

mala); Terrenos Bajos, Pompeya, and Portal (Almolonga Valley); Chukumuk 2 (Lake Atitlan); Mejicanos and Amatitlan (Lake Amatitlan); Chama 1B-2 and Chama 3-4, Chipal 1 (Chixoy drainage, west); Atzan and Chinaq (Zaculeu); Balam and Pokom (Zacualpa).

Sɪᴛᴇ Fᴇᴀᴛᴜʀᴇs (Early Classic, ᴀ.ᴅ. 300–700). For a while, at least, the Classic period seems to have followed the cultural and settlement pattern trends established during the Late Preclassic. Sites seem to have multiplied steadily (Shook, 1952b; Shook and Proskouriakoff, 1956, fig. 1; A. L. Smith, 1955) throughout the highlands as well as in the Hilly Middle Country. Generally they were still undefended and spread out on the open valley floors and plateaus and near river beds. The earthen mounds, however, were much smaller than their Preclassic counterparts and the ceremonial centers show a closely knit court arrangement rather than the parallel plaza pattern of the Late Preclassic. One can even differentiate several tightly enclosed paved inner and outer courts with acropolis-like mound arrangements on alternating levels (see fig. 3). There seems to have

been a growing tendency toward the establishment of more centralized locations and court assemblages for ceremonial observances, market gatherings, and perhaps for the first time, for ritual ball games in courts open at both ends and generally with sloping side walls.

A new masonry technique of this period was the facing of the earthen pyramids with neatly cut volcanic pumice blocks set in adobe. They were sometimes faced with white plaster, and occasionally contained as many as eight superimposed structures (Mounds A and B at Kaminaljuyu; Kidder, Jennings, and Shook, 1946). Narrow stairways with balustrades led to the summits of these mounds where stood shrines and altars of perishable materials. Within these mounds the deep burial chambers were roofed with logs and lined with mats, and were filled with rich offerings and sacrificed retainers.

Many of the new ideas of this period may have been the result of foreign religious, architectural, and artistic concepts emanating in all probability from Teotihuacan, Mexico. These ideas apparently spread throughout Mesoamerica and were felt

66

everywhere with varying degrees of intensity. Some of them were probably carried by itinerant merchants who dispersed them along with trade goods. Others may have been the result of actual foreign domination.

INFERENCES (Early Classic). During this period, even more than in the Late Preclassic, there must have been a constant need for a supply of free laborers to build and rebuild the many shrines and temples. As before, one source of laborers may have been pilgrims; others may have been recruited from the satellite villages. Very likely the participants came from far and near to offer their devotions to the images of the gods, and to their priestly representatives. As in present-day Guatemala, thousands probably flocked to the major ceremonial centers to participate in feast days, market days, and special rites or ritual games.

Whether the priests of the ceremonial centers actually formed a class and resided, along with their families and attendants, in the ceremonial centers, or continued to live as "commuters" in one of the nearby satellite villages cannot be determined. It is possible, however, that as today in the so-called "vacant towns" in Guatemala, and Chiapas, Mexico (Chichicastenango, Bunzel, 1952, p. 187, and Borhegyi, 1956a, p. 104; Santa Eulalia, La Farge, 1947, p. 4; and Zinacantan, Chiapas, Vogt, 1959) the individual, during his tenure of religious or political office, was expected to move into the ceremonial center with his family in order to participate in the complex and taxing annual round of ceremonies. At the end of the ritual year (or years) he probably turned the office over to the incumbent and moved back to his village home to resume his activities as a corn farmer until such time as he was called to assume another and higher office. Although such an office or "burden" may have resulted in personal economic loss, it was balanced by the prestige gained as a representative of the people.[5]

The extended-boundary type of settlement pattern with its "vacant town"-like ceremonial center would have been ideally suited to such a system of rotating or "commuting" "urban" residents (Miles, 1957a, 1958). If such were the case, it would mean that, at least in the Maya highlands, excepting the Teotihuacan intruders, there was no permanent, aristocratic priestly class assigned to the major ceremonial centers and that there was no dynastic succession, as apparently was the case among the Maya of the Tropical Rain Forest. It would also indicate that in the Maya highlands there was in existence a social system with considerable vertical mobility in which selected priests proceeded from lesser to higher offices based on services performed rather than by virtue of birth. In such a situation the gulf separating the priestly "intellectuals" from the farmers would not have been as wide as previously supposed.

SITE FEATURES (Late Classic A.D. 700–1000). Toward the end of the period in the Central and Western Highlands and in the Hilly Middle Country rebuilding activities seem to have slowed down. Instead of the burial and temple mounds, low elongated platform mounds were arranged around smaller tightly enclosed plazas and rectangular ball courts. By this time, however, the ball courts were closed at both ends (Shook, 1952b; Shook and Proskouriakoff, 1956; A. L. Smith, 1955). The majority of the settlements, although smaller in size, were still in open country close to arable

[5] As late as 1932, some of the *alcaldes rezadores* (chief prayermakers) at the town of Santa Eulalia in the Western Highlands of Guatemala were still drawn from the nearby (10 miles east) townships of Santa Cruz Barillas and Quetzal. Santa Eulalia is regarded by these townships as the ceremonial capital of the region. The prayermakers from Barillas and Quetzal resided with their families in Santa Eulalia during the term of their office. (La Farge, 1947, pp. 4, 131.)

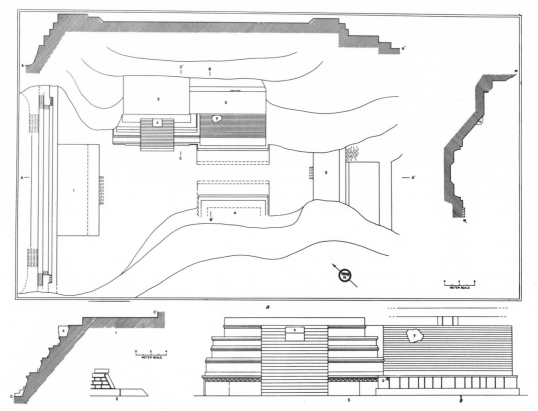

FIG. 4—CHIJOLOM, DEPT. OF ALTA VERAPAZ. A Late Classic site, potentially defensive on the hilltop, with mounds arranged around a small tightly enclosed plaza and rectangular sloping-sided ball court with closed ends. (After A. L. Smith, 1955, p. 57, fig. 130.)

land. However, since the extent of the agricultural exploitation zone was determined by the gradual exhaustion of the soil, and by the distance to which a farmer could travel, work in the fields, and return on the same day, some of the Late Classic valley settlements now had to be moved to the nearby hillslopes. By this time many of the valley floors were literally covered with Preclassic and Early Classic structures (fig. 4).

INFERENCES (Late Classic). The Late Classic period must have been an era of close regional integration and prosperity, as attested by the numerous archaeological remains. A reorientation of cultural goals also seems obvious from these changed cultural inventories. It is quite possible that by the end of this period some of the minor ceremonial centers (especially those

of the hillslopes) were used more and more for habitation, localized market gatherings, and for secularized ball-game activities, rather than for burial and ceremonial purposes. The Preclassic "grave-oriented" *necrotropic* society became by Late Classic times more and more secularized, and the recently emerged warrior, merchant, and artisan elements became increasingly powerful. Mass-produced moldmade pottery vessels and figurines were turned out in ever-increasing numbers to meet the needs of a growing population. It would almost seem that the major ceremonial centers lost out in prosperity and popularity to the mushrooming localized minor centers and that the large extended-boundary towns began to break down in favor of many smaller extended-boundary towns. This change may reflect a weakening of the divine power of the major gods and a growing pantheon with many newly emerged but powerful lesser gods. However, I believe it is more likely that the constant building activities forced the expanding population to move farther and farther from the valley sites in search of unoccupied farmlands. Eventually these farm plots became so far distant from the original settlement that commuting became impractical and new centers were established locally. A modern counterpart of this type of "suburbanization" was reported by Redfield in Yucatan (1950, pp. 2–8). Chan Kom, a daughter settlement, wished to break with its "mother-town" Ebtun 30 miles distant. Chan Kom and several other villages originated when Ebtun became overpopulated and land became scarce. The country to the south promised a better harvest of corn and beans. However, once Chan Kom had been established, the settlers found it a heavy and unwelcome burden to return the long way to Ebtun to perform the traditionally imposed labor for the mother community which no longer held their loyalty. The struggle continued for nearly 50 years, the Chan Kom settlers resenting the authority of the distant mother village, the Ebtun people resenting the disobedient and thriving daughter settlement. In 1926 Chan Kom finally achieved independence from its "mother" town.

It is easy to visualize a similar type of situation brewing during Late Classic times and resulting in the "split-up" of many major ceremonial centers. This would have weakened the power of the central authorities, if such power ever existed in the major ceremonial centers. The smaller settlements would unquestionably have desired independent ceremonial and political status. The persons whose duty it was to move into the major ceremonial center and assume offices (*cargo*) on their own time and expense were probably happier to assume similar offices in a nearby smaller center where they were closer to their kin groups and, therefore, better known and respected.

This same theory may also help to clarify the most startling settlement phenomenon of Middle American prehistory: the apparent abandonment of the Maya ceremonial centers by the end of the Late Classic period. Although in the Guatemalan highlands and in Chiapas the relinquishing of the ceremonial centers could have been influenced by such factors as soil exhaustion, climatic change, epidemic, contact with hostile migratory groups from Mexico, and/or periodic revolts of the food-producing classes against the abuses of their theocratic rulers, these factors were very likely secondary in importance to a growth of nationalism, self-dependence, and self-support on the part of the minor centers and satellite villages. The move away from the valley sites and onto the hilltops may have been further accelerated by reasons of self-defense against hostile Mexican and greedy neighboring groups. Once the people found themselves located at an inconvenient distance from the old ceremonial centers, they weakened and at last severed their support. By the end of this period the ceremonial centers were totally abandoned and left to decay, evidence of a singular lack of respect for the previous world order. Not even the burial mounds remained immune, and many of them were desecrated and looted by greedy tomb-robbers (Mound E-III-3, Shook and Kidder, 1952).

Postclassic and Protohistoric Period (Rise of the Militaristic Society) A.D. 1000–1524.

The archaeological phases associated with this period are: Ayampuc, Chinautla (Valley of Guatemala); Primavera and Medina (Almolonga Valley); Chipal 2–3 (Chixoy drainage, west); Samac (Chixoy drainage, east); Quankyak and Xinabahul (Zaculeu); Tohil and Yaqui (Zacualpa); Chuitinamit (Lake Atitlan); Contreras Alto and Los Jicaques (Amatitlan).

SITE FEATURES (Early Postclassic, A.D.

69

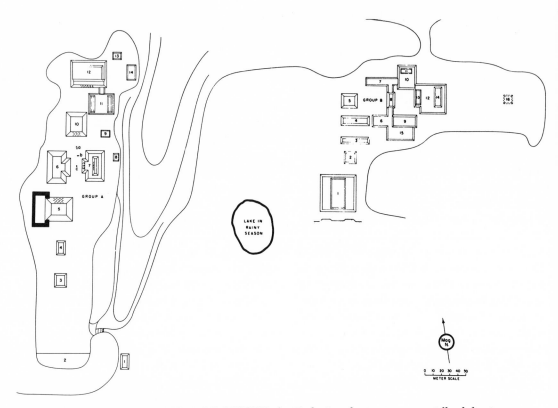

F<small>IG</small>. 5—LA LAGUNITA, DEPT. OF QUICHE. An Early Postclassic site, potentially defensive, consisting of two groups surrounded by deep ravines with a narrow causeway leading up to Group A. (After A. L. Smith, 1955, pp. 36, 37, fig. 90.)

1000–1200). By the Early Postclassic period the open and undefended valley and plateau sites and centers were almost totally abandoned. Most settlements were moved or newly established on more easily defensible and strategically located hilltops, or isolated mountaintops. Many of the sites were surrounded by deep ravines and protected by military outpost constructions (fig. 5). This change from the undefended open valley sites to the hilltops was not so abrupt, however, as was previously thought by many archaeologists. The excellent site survey of the Western Highlands and the Hilly Middle Country conducted by A. L. Smith (1955, Table 1, fig. 42, pp. 78–80) clearly indicated that several valley sites such as Chalchitan (Aguacatan region), Caquixay (Nebaj area), Chichen and Chicuxab (Coban area in the Alta Verapaz)

continued to be occupied during Postclassic (A.D. 1000–1200) and even Protohistoric times (A.D. 1200–1524). On the other hand, some of the characteristic hilltop sites such as Huitchun (Aguacatan region), Xolja Alto (San Andres Sajcabaja region), Esperancita, Seacal, Chijolom (Alta Verapaz), and Mixco Viejo (Chimaltenango) were apparently established during the Late Classic. One major Western Highland site, Zaculeu (Huehuetenango), a defensive plateau site, was continuously occupied from Early Classic times to the Spanish conquest in 1525. Smith also lists several potentially defensive sites located at intermediate elevations on the hillsides, such as Chicol (Huehuetenango region), Xolchun (Sacapulas region), Tzicuay (Quiche), Patzac (San Andres Sajcabaja region), and Chinchilla (Alta Verapaz)

70

which, in some cases, were continuously occupied from Late Preclassic to Postclassic times. Similar situations have been recorded by Shook (1952b) in the Central Highlands. Surface collections made at Chinautla (Shook, 1952b, p. 12), a typical inaccessible hilltop site a few miles north of Kaminaljuyu, yielded a considerable amount of Early Classic (Esperanza), and Late Classic (Amatle, Pamplona, and San Juan Plumbate) sherds and even one early Preclassic (Las Charcas) figurine fragment in addition to characteristic Postclassic material. While the Preclassic specimen may have been an heirloom brought from an earlier site, there can be no doubt that the fortress site of Chinautla was certainly established during the Late Classic period, and possibly even as early as the Early Classic. It is therefore quite clear that not all hilltop sites can arbitrarily be assigned to the Postclassic and Protohistoric periods. Neither can it be said that all Early and Late Classic sites were located in the open valleys.[6]

INFERENCES (Early Postclassic). The Early Postclassic period was characterized by a marked shift from priestly to secular authority, complicated by the arrival of foreign (Mexican) migratory groups and by the growing importance of warrior and merchant classes. Some of these migratory groups claimed Tula or Toltec origin, and brought with them many new architectural, religious and socio-political innovations. The shift from the undefended valley sites to defensive hilltop positions can probably be explained as a breakdown of the former "sacred" society into smaller, warring "nationality" groups, each craving independence and self-government. We may safely assume that the formation of the Quiche, Cakchiquel, Zutuhil, and Mam national

"kingdoms" dates to this period. From the archaeological data, we can also infer that hilltop settlements were used more and more as administrative centers for the nationality groups and as places of refuge for the villager in time of danger.

Nucleating forces new to this period were: (1) need for easily defensible and strategically located intermediate and hilltop locations, (2) nearness to trade and pilgrimage routes ("roadside hamlets" and centers), (3) development of a secular administrative and military bureaucracy, (4) nearness, in some cases, to cacao- (used as unit of currency) producing areas, (5) dependable water supply in case of prolonged warfare and hilltop isolation, and (6) migration and peregrinations of militant foreign groups (Toltecs, Nahuas, Pipils). Other forces which may have been responsible for some of the changes in the settlement patterns of this period were: (1) gradual replacement of the atlatl and other weapons by the bow and arrow, which may have made living in the open valley sites hazardous, (2) change from inhumation to cremation (less need for impressive and large burial mounds), (3) increased secularization of games, dances, and market activities, (4) growing importance of the warrior class and mercenary soldiers (the warrior orders of "eagle" and "jaguar," seclusion of young warriors in bachelor houses, military outposts), (5) growing importance of an itinerant and wealthy merchant class (rest stations near established roads), and (6) increasing administrative separation of "church and state" due to the newly assumed strength of the warrior and merchant classes.

SITE FEATURES (Protohistoric, A.D. 1200–1524).[7] The Protohistoric defensive sites, ranging from a single group to as many as eight groups, were situated on artificially leveled hilltops or tongues of land sur-

---

[6] As in the Guatemalan highlands, in Chiapas, Mexico, many Late Classic sites were already located on hillsides, and continued to be occupied during the Postclassic period. (Lowe, 1959b, pp. 15–18.)

[7] Ed. note: Corresponds to Late Postclassic in other terminologies.

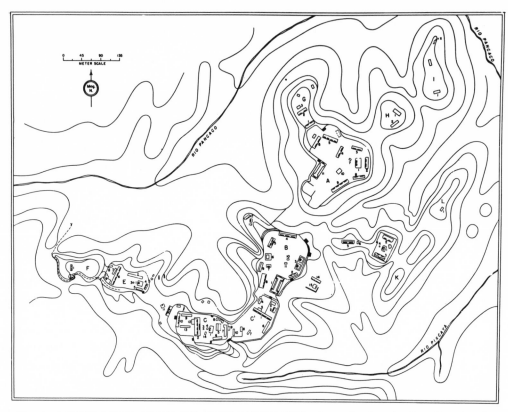

Fig. 6—MIXCO VIEJO, DEPT. OF CHIMALTENANGO. A predominantly Protohistoric site, defensive, located on a hilltop surrounded by deep ravines and accessible only by a narrow trail. Consists of at least 12 groups containing many multichambered "palace structures," twin temples, grouped around large, well-paved courts, with altar platforms at their centers. Enclosed "sunken" ball courts built with side benches. (After A. L. Smith, 1955, pp. 63–68, fig. 137.)

rounded by deep ravines. The buildings were often not oriented to one another, but simply followed the irregularities of the terrain. Such Mexican architectural features as "twin temples" placed on a single substructure, and multichambered, spacious dwellings or "palaces," some supported by massive columns, were grouped around large, well-paved courts. These courts, much like those of Mexico, had at their center a temple structure with several altar platforms. Skillfully constructed drainage systems at the corners of the courts suggest that the new settlements were designed for more or less permanent habitation, unlike the "vacant" or concourse "worship" centers of previous periods. These and other signs indicate a growing empha-

sis on city living and secularization. The formerly sacred ball courts were built with side benches and in the shape of the letter I (sunken courts) and may have been used to a great extent for entertainment, while the sacred enclosures or plazas frequently became the scene of secular market gatherings and dance fiestas (fig. 6). As might be expected, trade and specialization were extensive and widespread. During this period a prosperous class or guild of merchants and artisans came into being, enjoying the benefits of a concentrated surplus of wealth and social standing. It must be understood, however, that these hilltop settlements could never have accommodated large aggregations of people for any extended period. The bulk of the population, as in

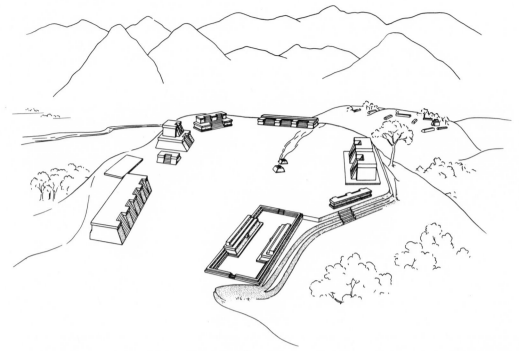

Fig. 7—MIXCO VIEJO, DEPT. OF CHIMALTENANGO. Restoration sketch of Group B by S. F. Borhegyi. (After A. L. Smith, 1955, fig. 40.)

former times, probably continued to live in nearby hamlets or satellite farming villages (fig. 7).

INFERENCES (Protohistoric). The greatest change in the settlement pattern of this period was not so much in its layout as in its emphasis and function. Whereas in earlier periods the ceremonial centers served as a focus for pilgrimage and religious activities, during the Protohistoric period it is probable that the sites took on more and more the character of medieval European fortress towns.[8] Used in time of peace for festival, political, and market activities, much as in Europe, the Maya hilltop settlement became in time of war a refuge for the neighboring farmers and merchants and served as a fortress for the militant warrior class and their lords. Excellent examples of such defensive hilltop

sites are Chuitinamit (meaning "fortress above the village") in the Rabinal valley (A. L. Smith, 1955, pp. 48–53) and Chinautla on the Guatemalan plateau (Shook, 1952b, p. 12). Towns like these were also protected by several small outlying military outposts. Many, like Zaculeu, Utatlan, Iximche, Chuitinamit, and Mixco Viejo, may even have become provincial administrative and commercial capitals as well as fortress strongholds for the warring nationality groups (Mam, Quiche, Cakchiquel, Zutuhil, and Pokomam nations). Like the Aztecs of Mexico, the Quiche and Cakchiquel Maya nations of highland Guatemala became in Protohistoric times sizable militant empires with expansionistic tendencies, by means of military conquests, religious evangelization, economic penetration, and colonization. Their expansion was cut short only by conquerers from Spain, another militant nation which had only recently achieved the status of an empire.

[8] For similar Protohistoric fortress settlements in Mexico see Armillas, 1951.

73

DISCUSSION AND SUMMARY

Highland Maya Settlement Types

Throughout the course of history in the Guatemalan highlands and in the Hilly Middle Country of the Alta and Baja Verapaz, there have been two main types of settlement. One is the settlement with the primary purpose of providing shelter and habitation and which consisted of perishable domestic architectural forms (sometimes making use of low platform mounds) and built near arable lands with sufficient fuel and water resources. The nucleating forces for these settlements were primarily physical. Based on their size, extent, and mode of life, we may differentiate three subtypes of settlements: (1) *hamlets* or *"small clusters"* with local orientation and food supply (5–20 houses), (2) scattered, dispersed *farming villages* or *minor aggregate clusters* (50–100 or more houses) with local orientation and food supply, and (3) *satellite farming villages* or *major aggregate clusters* (100 or more houses) with regional orientation and food supply and allegiance to a minor or major ceremonial center or "national capital."

The settlements in this first category were probably composed of roughly rectangular (or apsidal) thatch-roofed huts with wattle-and-daub or stone walls. Occasionally these huts may have had a covered porch, and they were built not infrequently on low platform mounds made of earth or stone. Some of them may have contained family altars and shrines. Even as early as Early Preclassic times these structures were probably much like the hamlets of the present-day Maya Indians of the highlands (Wauchope, 1938).

The second main type of settlement is that with the primary purpose of providing religious and civic administration and which consisted of permanent, monumental edifices and truncated pyramids, built near sacred places, or in defensible locations. The principal nucleating forces for these settlements were primarily cultural: (1) *minor ceremonial and administrative centers* or compound, agglutinated villages with small central plazas used as focal points of village activities, with regional orientation and food supply (10–30 structures); (2) *major ceremonial or concourse centers* (vacant towns) with well-defined central plazas of considerable regional or national importance for religious (pilgrimage centers, secular (defensive sites) and communal gatherings (30 or more structures). This same settlement form can also be regarded as an extended-boundary type of town resulting from the aggregation of several dispersed farming villages with religious and economic and nationalistic goals. Such centers were occasionally supported by an entire area or nation and in the case of a few major pilgrimage centers, the area of influence may even have crosscut ethnic and linguistic boundaries (cf. Copan, Kaminaljuyu).

The settlements in this second category were built during the late Preclassic and Classic periods primarily for religious and burial purposes. Beginning in Late Classic times they became increasingly secularized and took on civic, defensive, and administrative functions as well.

REFERENCES

Armillas, 1951
Borhegyi, 1956a, 1956b, 1959b
Bullard, 1960b
Bunzel, 1952
Kidder, Jennings, and Shook, 1946
La Farge, 1947
Lowe, 1959b
Miles, 1957a, 1958
Redfield, 1950
Sanders, 1956

Shook, 1949a, 1950a, 1951a, 1951b, 1952b
—— and Kidder, 1952
—— and Proskouriakoff, 1956
Smith, A. L., 1955
Termer, 1951
Tax, 1951
Vogt, 1959
Wauchope, 1938
Willey, 1956c

3. Architecture of the Guatemalan Highlands

A. LEDYARD SMITH

THE HIGHLANDS of Guatemala as defined here include all those parts of the republic that have an altitude of over 500 m. as well as the Motagua Valley between Progreso, Department of Progreso, and Zacapa, Department of Zacapa. The focus of this paper is on ceremonial centers and the public buildings that form them rather than on dwellings. Tombs are also discussed but only from an architectural point of view and when forming parts of a ceremonial structure. The archaeology of the area under consideration is divided into three major cultural periods, Preclassic, Classic, and Postclassic. These three periods are subdivided into an Early Preclassic (before 1000 B.C.), a Middle Preclassic (1000–300 B.C.), a Late Preclassic (300 B.C.–A.D. 300), an Early Classic (A.D. 300–600), a Late Classic (A.D. 600–900), an Early Postclassic (A.D. 900–1200),[1] and a Late Postclassic (A.D. 1200–1500).[1]

In general, the archaeology of the Maya highlands is less well known than that of the neighboring lowlands to the north, and this is true specifically of architecture.[2] The first notices of pre-Columbian buildings in the Maya highlands were given by 16th-century writers, of whom Fuentes y Guzmán (1882–83) is the best source although Alvarado (1924) and Bernal Díaz del Castillo (1908–16) referred to the subject. Fuentes y Guzmán, although far from accurate, describes and illustrates some of the ancient sites. There are no 18th-century accounts, but at the beginning of the 19th-century Domingo Juarros (1823), who relied upon Fuentes y Guzmán for much of his information, takes up the topic again. Later, Stephens (1841) and Catherwood (1844) took a firsthand interest in the native architecture of the Guatemalan highlands. Brasseur de Bourbourg (1857–59) gives some descriptive material and ideas on the function of buildings, Bancroft's writings (1882) contain general information on the subject. Toward the end of the century both Maudslay (1899, 1889–1902)

---

[1] Ed. note: This chronology follows the Goodman-Martínez-Thompson correlation for the Classic and Postclassic periods.

[2] See Pollock, 1940, for a survey of sources on Maya lowland archaeology and architecture. See also Pollock, Article 15.

FIG. 1—XOLCHUN, PACOT, AND ZACULEU. *a (above)*, Xolchun, Dept. of Quiche, Early and Late Postclassic site; Pacot, a Late Postclassic site, on hill beyond. (Restoration drawing by Tatiana Proskouriakoff.) *b (below)*, Zaculeu, Dept. of Huehuetenango, Str. 1, Period 1-G, an Early Postclassic temple. (After Woodbury and Trik, 1953.)

FIG. 2—CHUTIXTIOX AND CAHYUP. *a (above)*, Chutixtiox, Dept. of Quiche, a Late Postclassic site. *b (below)*, Cahyup, Dept. of Baja Verapaz, Group A, a Late Postclassic site. (Both restoration drawings by Tatiana Proskouriakoff.)

and Sapper (1895, 1897, 1898) give excellent descriptions of a few ruins as well as accurate plans of sites and individual buildings.

Field excavations in Guatemalan highland architecture began, on a large scale, with the work of Kidder and his associates in 1936. These were started at the great site of Kaminaljuyu near Guatemala City, and this work continued for many years. Other major excavations in the highlands are those of A. L. Smith at Nebaj, Guaytan, and Chutixtiox, of Wauchope at Zacualpa, of Woodbury and Trik at Zaculeu, and Lehmann at Mixco Viejo.[3] More recently, the Guatemalan government has supported archaeological programs at the ruins of Iximche, under the direction of Guillemín, and again at Kaminaljuyu, by Espinosa.

ARCHITECTURAL ASSEMBLAGES

The Guatemala highlands is an area of sharply contrasting topography, a factor that played an important part not only in the size and extent of ancient sites but also in the disposition of buildings. In the present report we are interested only in the ceremonial centers of these towns or cities, centers composed of civic and religious buildings. It may be said in a broad way that where the terrain permitted, buildings were usually arranged in orderly fashion and oriented with reference to each other. In a few sites the orientation conforms roughly to the cardinal points, but this is more likely due to accident than design.

[3] References to these and other studies are: Berlin (1952), Blom (1932a), Borhegyi (1950a), Burkitt (1930b), Dutton and Hobbs (1943), Gann (1939), Guillemín (1959), Kidder (1935), Kidder, Jennings, and Shook (1946), La Farge and Byers (1931), Lothrop (1926a, 1933, 1936), Recinos (1913), Seler (1901), Shook (1947, 1952a, 1952b), Shook and Kidder (1952), Shook and Proskouriakoff (1956), A. L. Smith (1940, 1955), A. L. Smith and Kidder (1943, 1951), Stromsvik (1952), Termer (1931), Thompson (1943), Villacorta and Villacorta (1930), Wauchope (1948a), Woodbury and Trik (1953).

There are several definite types of architectural assemblages. These will be taken up under the cultural periods in which they occur. In many if not most cases it is difficult to know just what mounds belong in a given period when a site has been occupied during more than one cultural period. When this is the case, and it usually is, the terminal period is used. Where possible this has been determined by the pottery recovered. In all periods there is a considerable difference in the size of the ceremonial centers. They vary from a few mounds to the very large assemblages of important cities.

There is little doubt that in Preclassic times the highlands were well populated and that settlements with their civic and religious centers were distributed throughout the area. The Preclassic sites are located in open, undefended positions. Unfortunately, many mounds and, undoubtedly in a good many cases, entire towns have been leveled by modern agriculture and settlements. The best-known sites of this period, abandoned before the beginning of the Classic period, lie on the Canchon plateau southeast of Guatemala City. Although it is possible that mounds were being constructed as far back as the Arevalo and Las Charcas phases of Kaminaljuyu (1500–1000 B.C.), one of the earliest clear associations is with the Majadas phase (ca. 500 B.C.). The characteristic Preclassic mound assemblage is a long narrow plaza bordered by the large ceremonial structures. In some cases two parallel plazas are separated by a single row of mounds as at the ruins of Santa Izabel (fig. 7b). The plazas are oriented slightly east of north, and in a number of cases the principal pyramid, which faces east on the plaza, looks across to a small structure with an erect plain monument in front of it. During the last phase (Santa Clara) of the Preclassic period in the valley of Guatemala, which more or less corresponds to the Late Preclassic period, there

79

FIG. 3—CHUITINAMIT, DEPT. OF BAJA VERAPAZ, A LATE POSTCLASSIC SITE. *a* (*above*), Group D. *b* (*below*), Group C. (Both restoration drawings by Tatiana Proskouriakoff.)

is a decline of Preclassic architectural traditions that precedes radical cultural changes (Shook and Proskouriakoff, 1956, p. 97).

Our knowledge of Early Classic centers is unfortunately meager. In many cases the mounds are overlaid by assemblages of the Late Classic period. San Antonio Frutal, in the Guatemala valley, is an example of an Early Classic site. Here we have a closely knit arrangement of earth mounds forming plaza groups. This type of assemblage becomes typical in the Late Classic period. Structures are oriented to one another and face on three or four sides of one or more courts or plazas. These sites now have stone-faced buildings and, whether large or small, usually have a ball court. During the Classic period towns and cities continued to be built in open country without regard for defense. Some examples of Late Classic sites are Eucaliptus in the Guatemala valley (fig. 7,b), Esperancita, Seacal, and Santa Elena in the Department of Alta Verapaz (A. L. Smith, 1955, figs. 128; 129; 135,a), and Chicol and Llano Grande in the Department of Quiche (Smith, 1955, figs. 48; 92,a).

During the Early Postclassic period two principal types of assemblages occur. Both types usually are in valleys or on the slopes of hills close to valleys. One, except for the introduction of small platforms possibly used as altars or dance platforms, is not unlike the centers of the Late Classic period. These small platforms usually occur in the centers of courts. Examples of some of these sites are Chichen near Coban, Alta Verapaz (fig. 5,a), Chalchitan near Aguacatan, Huehuetenango (Burkitt, 1930b, pl. 30), La Lagunita and Pantzac in the San Andres Sajcabaja region (Smith, 1955, figs. 90, 93), and Tzicuay in the Nebaj-Cotzal-Chajul region of Quiche (Smith, 1955, fig. 86). The other type of assemblage, which continued on into Late Postclassic times, consists of a compact group of buildings bordering one or two

plazas and an open-end ball court leading into one of these plazas. The plazas normally have a small platform in the center. The land surrounding the plazas is usually higher and supports structures on three sides. This type of grouping is found mostly in the Nebaj-Cotzal-Chajul area but occurs also at Huitchun and Chalchitan in the vicinity of Aguacatan (fig. 4,a) and at Pantzac near San Andres Sajcabaja. Other good examples are Huil (fig. 4,b), Oncap (Smith, 1955, fig. 21), and Chipal, San Francisco, and Chichel (Burkitt, 1930b, pls. 27–29). Of the above-mentioned sites Huitchun and Chipal were still occupied in Late Postclassic times, and only pottery of this period was recovered from Oncap.

The Late Postclassic period saw a great change in the choice of site locations undoubtedly due to military activities of the time. Ceremonial centers were now well fortified, being protected by defense walls and situated on the crests of hills or tongues of land surrounded by deep ravines. These defense sites, which are composed of a single building group or as many as eight groups, are formed by long single-room structures with three or more doorways facing on a plaza. In the center of the plaza is generally a temple structure with one or more altar platforms associated with it. The sites are also distinguished by long, open multi-doored buildings, "twin temples" resting on a single substructure, and usually by at least one ball court of the enclosed type. Although this kind of assemblage is found throughout most of the highland area, it seems to be missing in the Nebaj-Cotzal-Chajul region and in the Alta Verapaz. Some good examples of defense sites are Pacot, Chuitixtiox, Quiche (figs. 1,a; 2,a), Cahyup, Chuitinamit, Baja Verapaz (figs. 2,b; 3), Mixco Viejo (fig. 5,a). There are also the well-known defense sites of Utatlan, Iximche, and Zaculeu, which are often mentioned in the accounts of the conquest of Guatemala by Alverado.

The ruins of Vicaveval form a unique

Fig. 4—CHALCHITAN AND HUIL. *a (above)*, Chalchitan, Dept. of Huehuetenango, ball-court group. Its latest ceramic period is Early Postclassic. *b (below)*, Huil, Dept. of Quiche, an Early or Late Postclassic site. (Both restoration drawings by Tatiana Proskouriakoff.)

assemblage in Late Postclassic times. This site, situated on a high hill northwest of Cotzal, Quiche, consists of an enclosed ball court and a small plaza with an altar in the center. The site is placed in a semicircle of terraces forming an amphitheater (Smith, 1955, figs. 22, 85).

MATERIALS

During the Preclassic period the fill of mounds was composed of surface soil, clay, sand, and talpetate. Grass was often added as a binder. Unworked stones were sometimes included in the fill, but as far as we know stone was not used for masonry. In Classic and Postclassic times stone appeared in the construction of buildings both in the fill and as masonry facing.

In almost all cases the builders in the highlands made use of materials found in the vicinity of the town or city they were constructing. For example, at Nebaj soft *sarro*, a water-laid lime deposit, was obtained from the nearby river and nicely cut and shaped; or, at Cahyup, outcrops of schistose, which readily splits into slabs, provided a source of construction material. Lime, obtained by burning limestone and utilized for the making of mortar and plaster for floors and for surfacing walls, was an extremely important material at almost every site. It served also for stucco decoration. Wood, too, must have played an important role in the construction of walls of buildings, lintels, beam-and-mortar and grass-thatched roofs, corner posts, and coverings of tombs.

MASONRY

In the Preclassic period mounds were built of puddled adobe with no use of stone or lime plaster. Mound E-III-3 at Kaminaljuyu is the best-known structure of this period. Here black soil, clay, and small amounts of sand and talpetate mixed with chopped grass were thoroughly puddled and spread as fill while still malleable. The fill was built up evenly, and terrace walls and stairs were roughly modeled from the base up. In all but the two earliest structures of Mound E-III-3, which were wet-troweled to smooth their surfaces, the entire surface was finished with a thin coat of fine-textured, chocolate-brown adobe (Shook and Kidder, 1952, p. 66).

By the end of the Early Classic period masonry as a surfacing of buildings had come into use. Good examples of this are Strs. A-7 and A-8, Mound A, Kaminaljuyu (Kidder, Jennings, and Shook, 1946). Here lumps of waterworn pumice laid in clay made up the mass of the constructions. This was coated with a hard concrete-like mixture of lime and small pebbles, which in turn was surfaced with pure lime. Moldings, made of neatly squared pieces of pumice, were supported by thin slabs of rock nicely worked and evenly aligned.

There is considerable variety in masonry during the Late Classic and Postclassic periods. At Nebaj they used a mixture of well-cut sarro and rough limestone; at Pantzac, in the San Andres Sajcabaja region of Quiche, nicely faced tufa blocks; at Cahyup in the Baja Verapaz, schistose slabs; and at Chijolom and Seacal in the Alta Verapaz, beautifully cut limestone. In most cases the stones were laid in mud mortar, and the surface of the wall was covered with a thick layer of plaster which ran back a few centimeters into the cracks between the stones, helping to bind them. In a few instances wall stones were laid in adobe and then covered with a thin layer of adobe, which in turn was covered with a thin layer of plaster. At Chijolom, Alta Verapaz, no plaster was used to surface the walls. Here, the fine-grained limestone was nicely finished and cut to fit so well that it was laid without mortar. This is the best stonework so far found in the highlands (fig. 7,a).

TYPES OF BUILDINGS

Temples (long open single-room buildings with three or more entrances), altar plat-

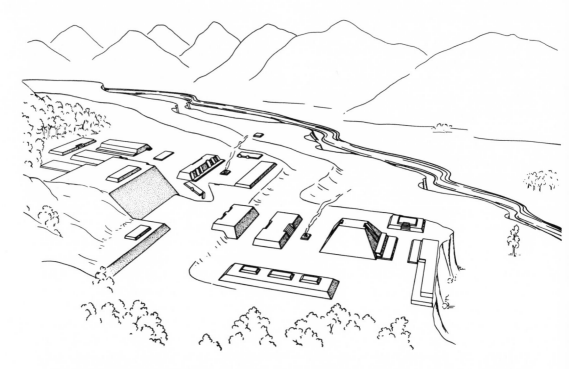

FIG. 5—CHICHEN AND MIXCO VIEJO. *a (above),* Chichen, Dept. of Alta Verapaz. Final period
Early Postclassic. *b (below),* Mixco Viejo, Dept. of Chimaltenango, Group B, a Late Postclassic
site. (Both renderings by Kisa Noguchi Sasaki of sketch by S. F. Borhegyi.)

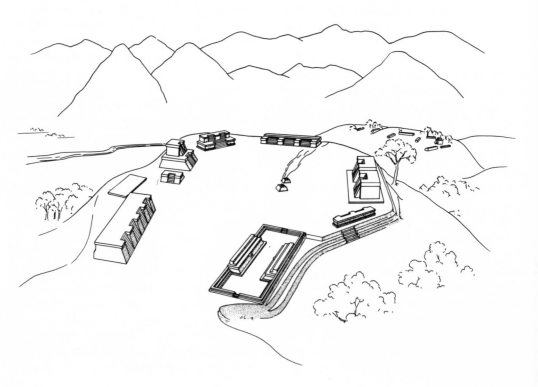

forms, altar shrines, and ball courts are the more common structures associated with highland sites. With the exception of Mound E-III-3 at Kaminaljuyu (Shook and Kidder, 1952) we have little information on the architectural details of buildings during Preclassic times and not much more in the succeeding Classic period. It is not until the Postclassic, especially the Late Postclassic, that we have substantial detail. Except for vaults at Papalgualpa and Asuncion Mita no corbeled vaults have been found in the highlands (A. L. Smith, 1940, fig. 11). In buildings where lintels were used they were usually of wood.

Temples

The high pyramidal substructures constructed in the Preclassic period occasionally have on their summits large post holes and impressions of wooden wall poles on fragments of hardened adobe, indicating they once supported temple buildings of perishable materials. In the case of Mound E-III-3, Kaminaljuyu (which gives us our only knowledge of the details of this period) Str. 4a and possibly others supported several platforms that once carried small temples or shrines (Shook and Kidder, 1952, pp. 52, 54). Each one of the superimposed substructures enclosed in this mound was terraced and had a broad, partially inset and partially projecting stairway leading to its summit. Stairways were plain, having no central blocks or balustrades.

Of the few mounds excavated of the Early Classic period, Mounds A and B, Kaminaljuyu, give us the most details in temple construction (Kidder, Jennings, and Shook, 1946). From wall-prints on the surface of the summit platform of Mound A, Str. 5, and post holes in this and in other substructures, it was possible to determine that the temples had consisted of one rectangular room with a single doorway opening toward the head of the stairway (fig. 6). Roofs were probably beam-and-mortar

or thatch. The eight superimposed substructures of Mound A vary greatly from early to late (Kidder, Jennings, and Shook, 1946, figs. 106–109). The three earliest are simple blocks of earth. These are followed by single-slope pyramids with heavy superior cornices resting on the projecting ends of thin stone slabs. Later pyramids had a plinthlike basal step, frontal platforms, and sloping terraces topped by vertical moldings. In the last two phases the summit platforms had sloping walls. All substructures had a balustraded stairway on one side.

Excavation of Late Classic buildings has given us no information as to what the plans of temples were like. It is possible that they did not vary much from the Early Classic ones. The little information we have about substructures during the Late Classic period comes from Zaculeu, where split stairways came into use at this time (Woodbury and Trik, 1953, p. 285).

In Early Postclassic times temples were built of stone. The best-known temple of this period is Str. 1 at Zaculeu (fig. 1,b). It is a single-rectangular-room building with a large opening in one of the long sides. The opening is divided into three entrances by two square columns. Against the center of the wall opposite the entrances was a plain rectangular altar. The lower part of the exterior faces of the walls is sloping, forming a batter.

During the Late Postclassic period temples are for the most part simple in plan. With few exceptions, they are one-room buildings often with an altar built against the center of the back wall. Temples of more than one room occur at Chuitinamit, Str. 2, in Group B (A. L. Smith, 1955, fig. 122,a) and at Zaculeu, Strs. 17, 37, and 4 (Woodbury and Trik, 1953, figs. 25, 37, 7, 9, 187, 188). The first three are two-room buildings; the latter, Str. 4 at Zaculeu, has three rooms, two rectangular front rooms and a circular rear room. Entrance to temples was almost always through three door-

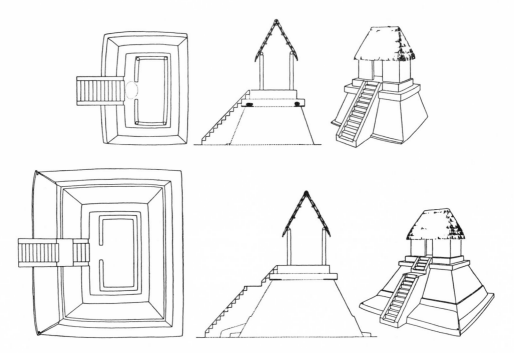

FIG. 6—KAMINALJUYU, DEPT. OF GUATEMALA. *a (above)*, Strs. A-5, A-6, Early Classic period. (After Kidder, Jennings, and Shook, 1946.) *b (below)*, Str. A-7, Early Classic period. (After *idem*.)

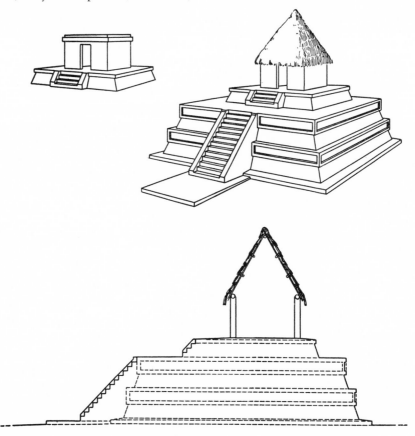

ways created by two rectangular, or some-times round, columns in a wide opening in one of the long sides.

Although no roofs remained in the high-lands, there is little doubt that they were either of thatch or beam-and-mortar. The high roofs that have been restored by ar-chaeologists on some of the temples in the Late Postclassic period may be questioned (figs. 2, 3). They are of Mexican design and were suggested by the presence of twin temples on a single substructure, one of the many Mexican architectural features of the period. The twin temples in the great plaza of Tenochitlan, as shown by Sahagun, have roofs of this type (fig. 8).

During the Postclassic period, both Early and Late, substructures supporting temples are usually nearly square and al-most always rise in vertical terraces. Stair-ways occur on one, three, or four sides and normally project from them. They are flanked by balustrades with a vertical up-per zone. At Xolchun, Quiche, Str. 2 has an oval substructure, which is most un-usual (fig. 1,a).

Long Buildings

Although we know that there were long mounds that undoubtedly supported super-structures of perishable materials in both Preclassic and Classic times, we do not know what type of buildings they were.

Long buildings with three or more en-trances were built in Early Postclassic times at Chalchitan in Huehuetenango, Xolchun in Quiche, and at Tzicuay in the Nebaj-Cotzal-Chajul region; but it was not until the Late Postclassic period that they be-came one of the typical structures.

These long constructions, usually on low platforms, rarely have more than a single room. Doorways are along one side. As in temples, the molding at the base of the exterior faces of the walls often is sloping, forming a batter. Doorways, as a rule of uneven number, range from three to eleven and are separated by masonry piers or rectangular or round columns. In a few cases long buildings have doorways at either end of the room. A common feature is benches around three sides. There often is a recess or small altar in the center of the bench against the back wall. Some build-ings, however, have a single bench extend-ing the length of the back wall, especially if there are doorways in the end walls. Long buildings have a wide distribution throughout the highlands. They occur at almost all Late Postclassic sites. It has been suggested that the larger of these structures may have been *tecpans* or administrative buildings and that the smaller ones may have housed the temple staffs during festi-vals. Those supported by the ranges of ball courts, of course, were for the spectators. Examples of this type building may be seen at Chutixtiox, Cahyup, Chuitinamit, Chalchitan, and Huil (figs. 2–4) and at Zaculeu (Woodbury and Trik, 1953, fig. 9).

The substructures that supported long buildings are normally low in comparison to temple pyramids and rise in one or several vertical terraces. They may have stairways on one, two, three, or four sides. As a rule stairways project and are flanked by sloping balustrades with vertical upper zones. Depending on their length, stairways may be divided by ramps into as many as six stairways (fig. 3,b). These ramps are similar in form to the balustrades.

Altar Platforms

These small platforms, probably used for offertory purposes, do not occur until the Classic period and are most common in Late Postclassic times. They range, rough-ly, from 3 to 6 m. across, from 0.60 to 2 m. high, and are nearly square. They may have stairways on one, two, three, or four sides; when on two sides they are opposite each other. In almost all instances the stair-ways are flanked by balustrades with ver-tical upper zones. Altar platforms are placed in plazas and courts, frequently in

FIG. 7—CHIJOLOM, SANTA ISABEL, EUCALIPTUS, AND CHUITINAMIT. *a (above),* Chijolom, Dept. of Alta Verapaz. Final period Early Postclassic. (Rendering by Kisa Noguchi Sasaki of sketch by S. F. Borhegyi.) *b (below),* Type sites, left to right: Santa Isabel, Dept. of Guatemala, Preclassic; Eucaliptus, Dept. of Guatemala, Late Classic; Chuitinamit, Dept. of Baja Verapaz, Group C, Late Postclassic. (After Shook and Proskouriakoff, 1956.)

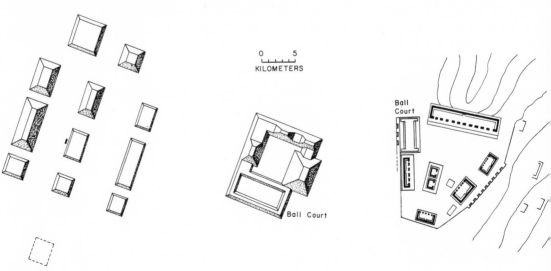

front of a temple structure (figs. 2; 3,*b*; 5).
Two good examples are in Plaza 1 at Zaculeu, Strs. 11 and 12 (Woodbury and Trik,
1953, figs. 213,*b*; 215). The open-end *a*
type of ball court almost always has an
altar platform in the center of its adjoining
court. Huil and Oncap in the Nebaj-Cotzal-
Chajul region are examples of this. (A. L.
Smith, 1955, figs. 19, 21). In cases where
these platforms are extra large they may
have been used for ceremonial dances or
other such purposes. A large platform is
seen in Str. 16 at Zaculeu (Woodbury and
Trik, 1953, fig. 24).

Altar Shrines

There is little doubt that many of the
altar platforms carried small buildings
made of perishable materials as well as of
masonry. Whenever these little structures
have been found they have been called
altar shrines. As in the case of altar platforms, they do not occur until the Classic
period and are most common in the Late
Postclassic. In most instances the tops of
altar platforms are in very poor condition,
but occasionally remains of the low walls
of altar shrines have been found. These
little single-room structures may have a
doorway in only one side as at Xolchun,
Chutixtiox, and Chalchitan (figs. 1,*a*; 2,*a*;
4,*a*). Str. 12 at Chutixtiox, a small building
with doorways in all four sides (Smith,
1955, p. 19, fig. 61,*e*), and Str. 6 at Xolpacol
in Huehuetenango, a small circular building with four doorways (Smith, 1955, p.
26, fig. 76,*a*), are two altar shrines that
differ from the normal type. From evidence
in the debris there is little doubt that the
latter supported a beam-and-mortar roof.

Ball Courts

There is no evidence of ball courts having been built before the Late Classic
period, but from that time on the game
must have been very popular in the highlands, for almost every site of any size had
its court. The 130 or more ball courts

found in this area fall with few exceptions
into one of the following five categories:
open-end, open-end *a*, enclosed, enclosed *a*,
"palangana" (Smith, in press).

The *open end* court has no end zones
defined by masonry walls. The profile has
a sloping bench face, a level bench top, and
a sloping playing wall which sometimes
has a vertical molding at the top (fig. 5,*a*).
In some cases the benches extend around
the ends of the playing walls. Where details have been found, the backs of the
ranges were terraced. These courts, probably constructed in Late Classic times, usually occur in valleys. They have a wide
distribution, being found in the Departments of Huehuetenango, Alta Verapaz,
Progreso, and the Sacapulas, Nebaj-Cotzal-
Chajul, and San Andres Sajcabaja regions
of the Department of Quiche.

The *open-end a* court has open ends and
one end leads into an adjoining plaza. This
plaza normally has an altar platform in its
center. The profile of the court has a vertical
bench face, an almost level to slightly sloping bench top, and a sloping playing wall
with a vertical upper molding (fig. 4). An
exception to this is the court at Chalchitan,
where the bench face is sloping. Benches
sometimes extend around the ends of the
playing walls; stairways may occur on the
ends and backs of ranges. In several instances ranges support long single-room
structures overlooking the playing alley.
With few exceptions open-end *a* ball courts
are located in valleys or on the slopes of
hills close to the valleys. From the ceramic
evidence, they were constructed in Early
and Late Postclassic times. Most of these
ball courts are in the Nebaj-Cotzal-Chajul
region, but several occur in the Department
of Huehuetenango and in the San Andres
Sajcabaja region of Quiche.

The *enclosed* court has high walls which
define end zones, and stairways lead out
at either end. The profile has a vertical
bench face, a level bench top and a steeply
sloping playing wall with a vertical mold-

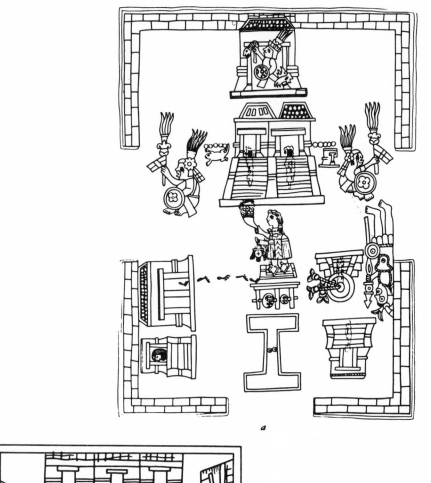

a

b

c

FIG. 8—DRAWINGS FROM SAHAGUN. *a*, Plan of Tenochtitlan, Codex Matritense, Primeros Memoriales, cap. 1, pl. 11. *b*, Group showing long houses, two temples on a single substructure, altar shrine, Codex Florentino, vol. 4, bk. 12, pl. 158, no. 159. *c*, Two temples on a single substructure, Codex Florentino, vol. 4, bk. 12, pl. 150, no. 88.

90

ing at the top (figs. 2,a; 5,b). The plan of the court with its long narrow playing alley and expanded end zones takes the form of a capital I. Benches may or may not extend around the ends of the playing walls. The backs of ranges were usually terraced. In most cases these terraces could have been used to ascend to the top. In some instances long single-room buildings, open on one side and facing the playing alley, were constructed on the top. Enclosed courts are found only in defense sites and usually on hilltops. They are associated with the Late Postclassic period.

The *enclosed a* court has walls which define end zones, and, like the enclosed type, it has the shape of a capital I. The profile has a vertical bench face, a sloping bench top, and a vertical playing wall (Smith and Kidder, 1943, fig. 3; Stromsvik, 1952, fig. 15). These courts, probably constructed in Late Classic times, are located in valleys near San Pedro Pinula in Jalapa, at Asuncion Mita in Jutiapa, and in the Motagua valley in Progreso.

The "*palangana*" court is a rectangular enclosure with surrounding walls of even height and with no end zones. A typical ball court of this type is the one at Cotio in the Guatemala valley (Shook, 1952a, p. 182, fig. 1,b). There are no details of the profile of these courts. In several cases "palangana" courts have a mound on one of the long sides. Located in valleys, the "palangana" courts were constructed during the Late Classic period. There are 52 courts of this type recorded, two-thirds of which are in the Guatemala valley. The rest are located in the Departments of Sacatepequez, Chimaltenango, Jalapa, Santa Rosa, and in Quiche in the Zacualpa and San Andres Sajcabaja regions.

In general it may be said that the slope of the playing walls of ball courts, which varies from 45 to 85 degrees, becomes steeper from early to late. Also it can be assumed that all courts that were complete-ly enclosed had drains. In several such courts, where there has been sufficient excavation, water outlets were uncovered.

Markers occur in ball courts in the highlands in the form of stone tenoned heads. These represent jaguars, parrots, and serpents, the latter occasionally with a human face in the open mouth. Such markers are found in all except open-end and enclosed types. They are usually set horizontally in the center of the playing walls near the top. In some instances there were three markers on a side, one in the center and one at each end of the playing walls. In open-end *a* type courts elaborate stucco heads were sometimes attached to the center of the playing walls where the upper molding begins. Although no markers were found in the enclosed courts they had mortises in the center of the playing walls near the top. It is possible that portable markers were used in these. No stone rings or alley markers have been found in the highlands.

DECORATION

Unfortunately we know little about the exterior, and nothing of the interior, decoration of buildings in the highlands. As for the interiors, we can assume that the walls were painted with a variety of colors and scenes. On the exterior, besides stairways, balustrades, and moldings, which form a great deal of the decoration, little remains beyond occasional carved stones or traces of paint or stucco.

Moldings are usually vertical, arranged horizontally on the outside of structures. They are commonly found on substructures either as a basal molding or as a cornice on the upper edge of a terrace. At Kaminaljuyu molding-framed vertical zones occur on Strs. A-7 and B-4 (Kidder, Jennings, and Shook, 1946, figs. 108, 113). These appear on many substructures at Teotihuacan and are called *tableros* by Mexican archaeologists. The only traces of upper moldings found on superstructures were parts of a vertical molding at Cahyup and the cornice of Str. 4-L at Zaculeu (Woodbury and Trik, 1953, fig. 187,*b*, p. 42).

Other than the stone heads recovered from ball courts, little stone carving associated with buildings has been found. A beautiful example of stone cutting and fitting is on the bottom terrace of Str. 2 at Chijolom, Alta Verapaz. Here the stones just below the cornice form a line of inset T's (fig. 7,*a*).

Stucco decoration must have been used extensively on the outsides of structures. The projecting stones along the terrace walls of Strs. 1 and 6 at Zaculeu indicate this. At Chipal stucco balls containing human skulls were found on the exterior of one of the buildings (Burkitt, 1930b, p. 56). Traces of stucco decoration, of human heads with elaborate headdresses, occur on the playing walls of ball courts. One of the best-preserved stucco decorations was a life-size jaguar at the base of the steps of Str. 3 at Chutixtiox (A. L. Smith, 1955, fig. 13,*a-c*).

Traces of paint have been found on the outside of buildings in all periods. There is little doubt that paint played an important part in the exterior decoration of structures. Of the colors found on the walls of buildings—red, yellow, green, blue, gray, and black—red was the most common. At Comitancillo, not far from Sacapulas, Quiche, Strs. 5 and 6, twin pyramids, have traces of red paint everywhere on their plaster surfaces.

TOMBS

Tombs occur in special burial structures, as at Guaytan in the Motagua valley, in and under temple substructures, in the platforms supporting long buildings, and in altar platforms.

The earliest tombs in the highlands were found in Mound E-III-3, Kaminaljuyu. These date from the Middle Preclassic period (Shook and Kidder, 1952, pp. 56–65). It was the custom at this time to bury

important people in prominent buildings. The tombs, rectangular in shape, were cut into the mounds and were above ground level. The roofs, which were made of timbers, were supported by two heavy beams resting on four large posts placed in the corners of the chambers.

During the Early Classic period rectangular tombs were roofed with wooden cross-beams supported by wooden posts. These were sunk below ground level under the main structures of Mounds A and B at Kaminaljuyu as well as under the platforms projecting out in front of these mounds (Kidder, Jennings, and Shook, 1946). At Zaculeu a large circular burial chamber was cut out of the natural deposit under the main temple pyramid, Str. 1. This tomb was approached by a rough stairway leading down into a rectangular antechamber. From the antechamber a passageway leading into the burial chamber was blocked by a large stone slab (Woodbury and Trik, 1953, figs. 3, 40). The most elaborate Early Classic tombs were stone-lined chambers with corbeled vaults and long masonry passageway entrances blocked by stone slabs. Tombs such as this were found at Nebaj (Smith and Kidder, 1951), Chalchitan, and Tzicuay (A. L. Smith, 1955, pp. 13, 34), and they were apparently constructed during the latter part of the Early Classic and the early part of the Late Classic periods. At Guaytan, 14 burial mounds contain similar tombs constructed in Late Classic times (Smith and Kidder, 1943). In some instances these tombs have benches along both sides and the back wall.

Rectangular stone-lined cists roofed with flat stones occur at Zaculeu, Zacualpa, Nebaj, Xolchun, and Tajumulco. In most cases this type of tomb, which was constructed in Classic and Early Postclassic times, was sealed by the roof and had no other entrance. At Nebaj, however, Tomb VIII, an Early Postclassic stone-lined cist, roofed with wooden beams supporting thin stone slabs, was closed by two large slabs placed against the open end (Smith and Kidder, 1951, pp. 25–26).

Three Late Postclassic tombs have been found at Chutixtiox and Xolpacol. Two have two chambers, an inner circular vault and an outer rectangular anteroom. The two parts are joined by a narrow entrance (Smith, 1955, figs. 65,*b*; 76,*c*). The third tomb, Str. 10, Chutixtiox, had a single rectangular stone-lined chamber with a doorway sealed with a stone slab (Smith, 1955, fig. 64).

Stone boxes that undoubtedly served as sarcophagi were used at Chalchitan (Str. 27), Nebaj (Mound 2), and La Iglesia (Str. 1), probably during the Early Postclassic period (Smith, 1955).

Discussion

There is strong evidence that the Preclassic and Classic periods, and the earlier part of the Postclassic period, was a time of relative peace in the Guatemala highlands. This contrasts with the warlike conditions that followed and continued until the Spanish conquest. This is seen in the differences between the nondefensive valley sites of the early periods and the later hilltop defensive sites. The former are open to attack from all sides; the latter are not only located in easily defensible positions but have the added protection of high walls and terraces. The latter are also strategically placed so as to protect valleys, where the people undoubtedly still lived and grew their crops. The fortified sites were surely used for religious and governmental purposes as well as places of refuge in time of enemy attack. The many house sites found closely associated with these fortified centers were probably used as temporary residences during festivals.

Architectural evidence from the Guatemalan highlands indicates strong and continued contacts with central Mexico. These contacts began in the Early Classic period

and continued through into Late Postclassic times. The direction of influence seems to have been from Mexico to Guatemala. For example, in the Early Classic period at Kaminaljuyu, Kidder mentions new architectural ideas that point toward Teotihuacan. He says: "Almost every feature of the new style is duplicated at that site; the sloping zones, the carefully aligned molding slabs, the profile of the molding-framed vertical zones . . ., and particularly the peculiar compositions of the outer layer, which at Teotihuacan is also composed of small bits of stone (*tezontle molido*) and lime, with a thin finish of pure lime . . ." (Kidder, Jennings, and Shook, 1953, p. 45). Later, especially during the Late Postclassic period, such features as twin temples on a single platform, altar platforms, altar shrines, double stairways, the batter at the base of superstructure walls, enclosed ball courts, round structures, and balustrades with nearly vertical upper zones are all shared by both the Guatemalan highlands and central Mexico. Another possible tie with Mexico is the long structures at such sites as Cahyup and Chuitinamit (figs. 2,*b*; 3). Sahagún (1905) illustrates Mexican buildings that have all these features (fig. 8). This figure shows a plan of Tenochtitlan that has an assemblage much like the groups at Chuitinamit and Cahyup, long structures on three sides of a court, with an altar shrine and a pyramid supporting two temples.

By contrast, architectural links between the Guatemalan highlands and the Maya lowlands are less pronounced. The basic lowland feature of the corbeled vault, as used in the roofing of superstructures, is missing in the highlands although corbeled vaults do occur in some highland tombs. Aside from the feature of the central masonry block in the upper parts of stairways and, possibly, the open-end ball court, there is little in the highlands that one can recognize as typical of Peten architecture.

REFERENCES

Alvarado, 1924
Bancroft, 1882
Berlin, 1952
Blom, 1932a
Borhegyi, 1950a
Brasseur de Bourbourg, 1857–59
Burkitt, 1930b
Catherwood, 1844
Díaz del Castillo, 1908–16
Dutton and Hobbs, 1943
Fuentes y Guzmán, 1882–83
Gann, 1939
Guillemín, 1959
Juarros, 1823
Kidder, 1935
——, Jennings, and Shook, 1946
La Farge and Byers, 1931
Lothrop, 1926a, 1933, 1936
Maudslay, A. C. and A. P., 1899

Maudslay, A. P., 1889–1902
Pollock, 1940a
Recinos, 1913
Sahagún, 1905
Sapper, 1895, 1897, 1898
Seler, 1901
Shook, 1947, 1952a, 1952b
—— and Kidder, 1952
—— and Proskouriakoff, 1956
Smith, A. L., 1940, 1955, 1961
—— and Kidder, 1943, 1951
Stephens, 1841
Stromsvik, 1952
Termer, 1931
Thompson, J. E. S., 1943a
Villacorta and Villacorta, 1930
Wauchope, 1948a
Woodbury and Trik, 1953

4. Pottery of the Guatemalan Highlands

ROBERT L. RANDS and
ROBERT E. SMITH

THE CERAMICS of the Guatemalan high-lands have great time depth and regional variation. In this portion of the Maya Area (fig. 1) the pottery is of special interest because, as compared to the Maya lowlands, the highlands appear to be more directly located on major north-south routes of diffusion or migration. Moreover, there are indications that an advanced development of Preclassic culture occurred in the highlands; on a later level furnishings in the tombs of Kaminaljuyu have provided some of the closest ties between the Classic period cultures of central Mexico and the Maya. Again, intimate connections with alien peoples are suggested by the well-known Postclassic occurrence of Mexican deities on Tohil Plumbate pottery, which must have been manufactured in or near the highlands of Guatemala. A detailed knowledge of ceramic developments is necessary for a proper evaluation of such phenomena and their place in the broader outlines of Mesoamerican prehistory. Too often, however, the plotting of

highland pottery sequences and intraregional relationships is on unsure footing.

Several factors are responsible for our inadequate understanding of highland pottery. The absence of a series of dated monuments, with which the pottery might be correlated, has tended to prevent the refinement of Classic period chronologies within the highland region. In addition, Kidder has expressed the belief that during the Classic period greater cultural diversity, hence a more complex archaeological situation, existed in the highlands than in the Maya lowlands (Smith and Kidder, 1951, p. 79). For the most part such a conclusion appears to be well founded, although it has become increasingly clear, in the western lowlands, that localized ceramic styles crowd in on one another, in this respect being fully comparable to the highland situation.

The most telling reason for the retarded state of knowledge about highland pottery, however, is simply the paucity of intensive field investigations. Stratigraphic excava-

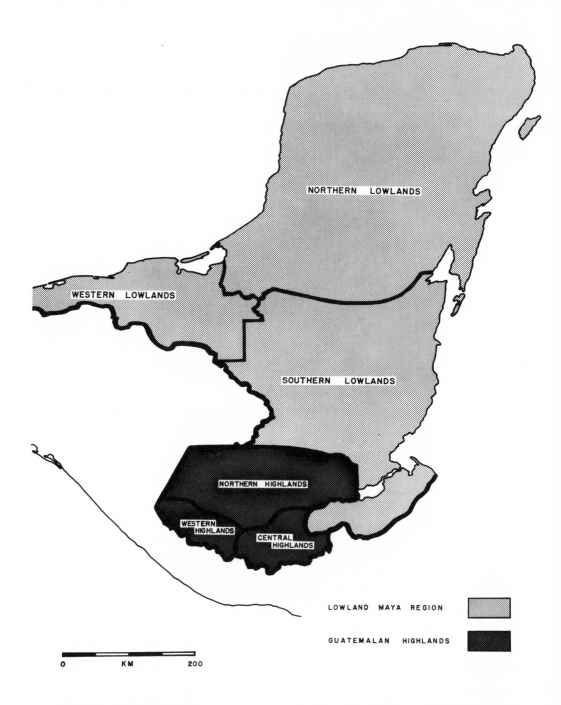

Fɪɢ. 1—MAPS OF THE MAYA AREA, SHOWING CERAMIC ZONES. Ceramic zone boundaries drawn arbitrarily to follow political boundaries. *a (above)*, Entire Maya area. *b (opposite)*, Highland Maya region.

96

NORTHERN ZONE

WESTERN ZONE

CENTRAL ZONE

• CHACULA

• FLOJERA

• ILOM

• RATINLIXUL

• KIXPEK

• CHAMA

• TZICUAY
• CHIPAL

• CARCHA
• CHIPOC

• SAMAC

• SEACAL
• CHAJCAR

CHICHEN

• COBAN
CAHABON •

RIO

• NEBAJ
• CHALCHITAN

• ZACULEU

• ZACAPULAS

RIO   POLOCHIC

• SAJCABAJA

• TAJUMULCO
• MOMOSTENANGO

• UTATLAN

• CHICHE

• ZACUALPA

RIO

MOTAGUA

• SALCAJA

TZANJUYU
PARAISO •

PANAJACHEL
• IXIMCHE

CHINAUTLA •

CHUITINAMIT •
• CHUKUMUK

ZACAT
CAUQUE

COTIO •
• KAMINALJUYU

• ANTIGUA

PIEDRA PARADA •
• CANCHON

AMATITLAN
CONTRERAS •

• VIRGINIA

0   50
KILOMETERS

97

tion has been rare, reports detailing ceramic sequences being published only for Zacualpa[1u] and Zaculeu.[1v] Tajumulco[1cc] and Chipoc,[1j] which appear essentially to be single-period sites, have been reported on; exca-

vations at Nebaj[1n] have yielded information on certain ceramic complexes without giving a complete picture of the pottery of the site as a whole. Although two admirably detailed descriptions of pottery from tombs

[1] Site references are indicated by a footnote number (1) plus a lowercase italic letter. Sites are listed alphabetically by ceramic zone. Important unpublished materials in the photographic files of the Peabody Museum of Archaeology and Ethnology, Harvard University, are abbreviated as PM-Files.

Northern Zone

[1a] Cahabon, Alta Verapaz (R. E. Smith, 1952)

[1b] Carcha (San Pedro), Alta Verapaz (R. E. Smith, 1955b)

[1c] Chacula, Huehuetenango, including the site of Uaxac Canal (Seler, 1901)

[1d] Chajcar, Alta Verapaz (Dieseldorff, 1926–33)

[1e] Chalchitan, Huehuetenango (A. L. Smith, 1955)

[1f] Chama, Alta Verapaz (Butler, 1940; Dieseldorff, 1926–33; Vaillant, 1927)

[1g] Chiche, Quiche (Wauchope, 1948b; Lothrop, 1933)

[1h] Chichen, Alta Verapaz (A. L. Smith, 1955)

[1i] Chipal, Quiche (Butler, 1940, 1959)

[1j] Chipoc, Alta Verapaz (R. E. Smith, 1952)

[1k] Flojera (La), Alta Verapaz (R. E. Smith, 1955d)

[1l] Ilom, Quiche (Termer, 1931; R. E. Smith, 1955d)

[1m] Kixpek, Alta Verapaz (Butler, 1940)

[1n] Nebaj, Quiche (Smith and Kidder, 1951)

[1o] Ratinlixul, Alta Verapaz (Butler, 1940)

[1p] Sajcabaja (San Andres), Quiche (Lothrop, 1936)

[1q] Samac, Alta Verapaz (R. E. Smith, 1952)

[1r] Seacal, Alta Verapaz (R. E. Smith, 1949b, 1952)

[1s] Tzicuay, Quiche (A. L. Smith, 1955; PM-Files)

[1t] Zacapulas, Quiche (Lothrop, 1936)

[1u] Zacualpa, Quiche (Wauchope, 1948a, 1950; Lothrop, 1936)

[1v] Zaculeu, Huehuetenango (Woodbury and Trik, 1953)

Western Zone

[1w] Chuitinamit, Solola (Lothrop, 1933)

[1x] Chukumuk, Solola (Lothrop, 1933)

[1y] Momostenango, Totonicapan (Lothrop, 1936)

[1z] Panajachel, Solola (Lothrop, 1933; R. E. Smith, 1955d)

[1aa] Paraiso (Finca), Quezaltenango (Shook,

1947; Shepard, 1948; Kidder and Shook, 1959)

[1bb] Salcaja, Quezaltenango (Gamio, 1926–27; Vaillant, 1927; Lothrop, 1933, 1936; Porter, 1953; Kidder, 1954; PM-Files)

[1cc] Tajumulco, San Marcos (Dutton and Hobbs, 1943; Shepard, 1948)

[1dd] Tzanjuyu, Solola (PM-Files)

[1ee] Utatlan, Quiche (Lothrop, 1933, 1936; Wauchope, 1949)

Central Zone

[1ff] Amatitlan (Lake), Guatemala, including the site of Zarzal (Shook, 1952b; Borhegyi, 1958b, 1961d)

[1gg] Antigua, Sacatepequez, including the sites of Medina, Pompeya, Primavera, Terrenos and Xaraxong (Borhegyi, 1950a; Shook, 1952b)

[1hh] Canchon, Guatemala (Shook, 1952b)

[1ii] Cauque (Santa Maria), Sacatepequez (Shook, 1948, 1952b)

[1jj] Chinautla, Guatemala (Shook, 1952b)

[1kk] Contreras, Guatemala (Shook, 1952b)

[1ll] Cotio, Guatemala (Shook, 1952a, 1952b)

[1mm] Iximche, Chimaltenango (Wauchope, 1949)

[1nn] Kaminaljuyu, Guatemala. (Publications include Kidder, Jennings, and Shook, 1946; Kidder, 1945, 1948, 1961; Shook, 1951a; Shook and Kidder, 1952; Kidder and Shepard, 1944; Berlin, 1952. Ceramic data on Kaminaljuyu and adjacent sites, including some otherwise unpublished information, appear in the Year Books of the Carnegie Institution of Washington, Nos. 34–37, 47–50, and in Shook, 1952b.)

[1oo] Piedra Parada, Guatemala (Shook, 1952b)

[1pp] Virginia, Guatemala (Shook, 1952b)

[1qq] Zacat, Sacatepequez (Shook, 1952b)

Of these sources, Vaillant (1927), Lothrop (1933, 1936) and Shepard (1948) present pottery from various parts of the Guatemala highlands; Dieseldorff (1926–33) illustrates numerous specimens from the Alta Verapaz. Additional publications, important for the illustration of highland pottery, are Gordon and Mason (1925–43); Kidder and Samayoa Chinchilla (1959); Villacorta C. (1938); Villacorta and Villacorta (1927); Seler (1904b, 1902–23, especially vol. 3, pt. 4); Kidder (1949b, 1950); R. E. Smith (1944); and, for incensarios, Borhegyi, 1950b, 1951a-c, 1952a, 1958b). A useful summary of highland Guatemalan ceramic history is included in Thompson (1943a).

at Kaminaljuyu have appeared (Kidder, Jennings, and Shook, 1946; Shook and Kidder, 1952), the long sequence of named phases at the site has been barely outlined in print.[1nn] The analysis of highland pottery leaves much to be desired, even where intensive digging has been done. At only two highland sites, Zacualpa and Chipoc, has unslipped utilitarian pottery been adequately described, and it is therefore impossible to determine its differences, temporally and regionally. Studies of pottery at Kaminaljuyu and Zaculeu, two of the most thoroughly excavated sites, deal primarily with tomb offerings, although abundant stratified sherd material was unearthed in the general digging. The one highland site where ceramic history is carefully documented is Zacualpa, showing a Late Preclassic through Late Postclassic occupation. However, the total count is but slightly over 2500 sherds and a small number of vessels, 73 per cent of the specimens occurring in the Early Postclassic period (Wauchope, 1948a).[2] Surface reconnais-

sance, by Shook (1952b) in the Central Altiplano and by A. L. Smith (1955) in the Departments of Huehuetenango, Quiche, Baja Verapaz, Alta Verapaz, and Chimaltenango, has greatly increased information about site occupations according to period, although detailed ceramic descriptions from these surveys have not been published. Butler's investigations in the Alta Verapaz, including field work and the analysis of Burkitt's earlier excavations, provide a useful if somewhat sketchy chronological framework for this strategically located zone; important sites include Chama,[1f] Ratinlixul,[1o] Chipal,[1i] and Kixpek[1m] (Butler, 1940, 1959; Burkitt, 1930b). Uncontrolled digging, resulting in extensive museum and private collections, is the basis for an important segment of our knowledge of highland Guatemalan pottery. Of special importance are the Dieseldorff and Rossbach Collections and the extensive holdings of the Museo Nacional de Arqueología e Etnología of Guatemala. Problems involved in establishing the provenience of unrecorded specimens, and the archaeological significance to be gleaned from these pieces, are discussed by Kidder (1954).

Ultimately, it would be desirable to extend to the Guatemala highlands the type-variety system recently employed in the descriptive analysis of pottery from the Lowland Maya Region.[3] At the present time, this is impossible for the great bulk of highland ceramics. Certain types, which appear to be shared with the lowlands, will, however, be referred to by designations used in the lowlands. This practice, in itself, implies nothing as to the origin of the pottery although, parenthetically, we believe that in most of these cases the evidence favors a derivation of the style in question from the Maya lowlands. Possibilities of the occasional trade of actual specimens cannot be evaluated in the absence of comparative technological analy-

---

[2] Quantification in published studies of highland pottery is further illustrated by the fact that the most thoroughly investigated ceramic complexes of Kaminaljuyu, dating from the Late Preclassic and Early Classic periods, are based on totals of approximately 450 and 375 whole vessels, respectively (Shook and Kidder, 1952; Kidder, Jennings, and Shook, 1946). The four ceramic phases of Zaculeu rest largely on some 530 vessels, more than 200 of which relate to the Early Classic period (Woodbury and Trik, 1953). The Chixoy sequence in the Alta Verapaz was worked out on the basis of approximately 240 vessels, 145 of which date from the Late Classic (Butler, 1940), while 136 specimens, approximately half of Early Classic origin, comprise the published vessels from Nebaj (Smith and Kidder, 1951). Pottery from Chipoc, which in many respects forms the best rounded ceramic complex described for the Guatemala highlands, totals slightly more than 3700 sherds (R. E. Smith, 1952).

[3] Smith and Gifford, 1959; Smith, Willey, and Gifford, 1960. See also Smith and Gifford, Article 19, where lowland Maya pottery is summarized in the framework of the type-variety system and, in note 3, the units of ceramic description and analysis are defined (type, variety, mode, group, complex, and ware).

(Text continued on p. 107)

FIG. 2—CORRELATION OF LOCAL CERAMIC SEQUENCES IN THE GUATEMALAN HIGHLANDS

Zone / Site	MIDDLE PRECLASSIC (early aspect)	MIDDLE PRECLASSIC (late aspect)	LATE PRE-CLASSIC, PROTO-CLASSIC	EARLY CLASSIC	LATE CLASSIC	EARLY POST-CLASSIC	LATE POST-CLASSIC
NORTHERN ZONE — Zaculeu			Atzan		Chinaq	Qankyak	Xinabahul
Zacualpa		Balam (early aspect)	Balam (late aspect)		Pokom	Tohil	Yaqui
Chixoy Drainage		Ia (Chama 1)	Ib (Chama 2)		II (Chama 3, 4; Chipal 1); Chipoc	III (Chipal 2)	IV (Chipal 3)
WESTERN ZONE — San Marcos					Tajumulco		
Quezaltenango Valley			Salcaja				
Atitlan Basin			Chukumuk			Chuitinamit	
CENTRAL ZONE — Valley of Almolonga		Zacat	Xaraxong	Terrenos	Pompeya / Pamplona	Primavera	Medina
Valley of Guatemala	Arevalo / Las Charcas	Providencia / Sacatepequez / Majadas	Santa Clara / Arenal / Miraflores	Esperanza / Aurora	Amatle	Ayampuc	Chinautla

Fig. 3—SELECTED CERAMIC UNITS: CENTRAL HIGHLANDS. For significance of symbols see note 9.

PERIOD AND PHASE	Ware group	Ceramic unit	Chinautla	Ayampuc	Amatle-Pamplona	Aurora-Esperanza	Miraflores-Arenal-Santa Clara	Majadas-Providencia; Sacatepequez	Las Charcas-Arevalo
			Late Postclassic	Early Postclassic	Late Classic	Early Classic	Late Preclassic-Protoclassic	Middle Preclassic: late aspect	Middle Preclassic: early aspect
	BROWN WARES	Streaky Gray-brown							X
		Glossy Gray-brown						X	X
		Coarse Incised Black-brown					•	X	
		Fine Incised Black-brown					X		
		Crude Black-brown				X			
	WHITE WARES Monochrome–Dichrome	White (paste and surface)						X	•
		White (yellowish paste)						X	X
		Verbena White (incised; red-brown paste)					X		
		Red-on-white							X
		Purple-on-white						X	X
		Red-on-cream			•	X			
	RED WARES	Pallid Red						X	X
		Purple-on-fine red						X	
		Incised Fine Red					X	X	
	USU-LU-TAN	Usulutan					X	•	
		Red-painted Usulutan				•	X		
	FINE PASTE	Fine Ivory					•	X	
		Fine Polished Black						X	
	MISCELLANEOUS	Utatlan Incised-dichrome						X	
		Incised Zinc Orange						X	
		Thin Orange				X			
		Esperanza Flesh-color				X			
		Tiquisate			X	?			
		"Hard ware" (Tejar, "Squiggle")			X	X			
		San Juan Plumbate		?	X				
		Tohil Plumbate		X					
		"Tile ware"		X					
		"Micaceous ware"	X						
		White-on-red	?			?			
	POLY-CHROME	Dos Arroyos Orange-polychrome				X			
		Amatle Polychrome			X				
		Chinautla Polychrome	X						

Form mode	MIDDLE PRECLASSIC: early aspect (Las Charcas-Arevalo)	MIDDLE PRECLASSIC: late aspect (Majadas-Providencia; Sacatepequez)	LATE PRECLASSIC-PROTOCLASSIC (Miraflores-Arenal-Santa Clara)	EARLY CLASSIC (Aurora-Esperanza)	LATE CLASSIC (Amatle-Pamplona)	EARLY POSTCLASSIC (Ayampuc)	LATE POSTCLASSIC (Chinautla)
Squat jars with sharply-angled shoulders (Fig. 13,a)	X	X					
Incurved-rim bowls (Fig. 13,b)	X	X					
Faceted-shoulder bowls and jars		X	X				
Labial-flange bowls		X	X				
"Flowerpots" (outcurved footless vases)			X	•			
Small solid tripod supports (nubbin, conical) (Fig. 9,e)		•	X	•			•
Small solid tetrapod supports (nubbin, conical)			X	•			•
Bowls with grooved everted rims (Fig. 9,e)			X				
Lateral-flange bowls			X				
Lateral Z-angle bowls			X				
Shallow bowls with standing walls			X				
Shallow, gutter-spout trays			X				
Low neck, wide-mouth jars with high shoulders (Fig. 9,c)			X				
Deep bowls ("Goblets") (Fig. 14,b)			X				
Cylinders with horizontal moldings (tripod, footless)			X				
Covers: strap handles (Fig. 9,c)			X				
Hollow mammiform supports			•	X			
Pedestal base				X	X		
Ring-stand base				X	X		
Scutate covers: knob handle (Fig. 15,c)				X	X		
Floreros				X	X	•	•
Miniatures				X	X		
Hemispherical bowls, with or without secondary supports				X	X	•	•
Outturned-rim bowls, basins (Fig. 10,h)				•	X	X	X
Tall footless cylinders, outcurved at top					X	X	X
High neck, globular jars (cf. Fig. 19,e)					X	X	?

102

FIG. 5—SPECIAL VESSEL FORMS. *Provenience given as Zacualpa (Lothrop, 1936). N, W, C, northern, western, and central ceramic zones, respectively. For references see appropriate sites in note 1. For significance of symbols see note 9.

	PRE-CLASSIC					EARLY CLASSIC							LATE CLASSIC					EARLY POST-CLASSIC					LATE POST-CLASSIC	
	Balam (early aspect) (Zacualpa) (N)	Chixoy Ia (Chama) (N)	"Salcaja Preclassic" (W)	Kaminaljuyu, Late Preclassic (C)	Kaminaljuyu, Middle Preclassic (C)	Nebaj Early Classic (N)	Atzan (Zaculeu) (N)	Balam (late aspect) (Zacualpa) (N)	Chixoy Ib (Chama) (N)	"Zacapulas Early Classic" (N)	"Salcaja Early Classic" (W)	Aurora-Esperanza (Kaminaljuyu) (C)	Nebaj Late Classic (N)	Chinaq (Zaculeu) (N)	Pokom (Zacualpa) (N)	Chixoy II-Chipoc-Cahabon (N)	Amatle-Pamplona (Kaminaljuyu) (C)	Nebaj Postclassic (N)	Qankyak (Zaculeu) (N)	Tohil (Zacualpa) (N)	Chixoy III-Samac (N)	Tajumulco (W)	Xinabahul (Zaculeu) (N)	Chinautla Phase (C)
Shoe-shaped vessels (Fig. 15,g)						X	X																	?
Tall-footed tripods (Fig. 10,a)	X	?		X	X	X	X	?			?													
Cups	X	X	X	X	X																			
Pitchers		X	X	X		X	X						X											
Effigy whistling vessels (Fig. 15,d)			X	X	X																			
Usulutan effigies		X	X	X	X																			
Pot stands		X		X		X	X						X			X								
Rim-head vessels (Fig. 21,b)						X							X									?		
Two-part effigies divided at the waist (Fig. 15,e)									X				X			X								
Thin Orange effigies													X			X								
Floreros						X	X						X			X								
"Cream pitchers" (Fig. 10,g)						X	X						X			X								
Standard cylindrical tripods (Fig. 15,a–c)						X	X						X	X										
Basal-flange bowls and dishes						X	X						X	X		X	X	X						
Ring base (Fig. 10,b,c)						X	X					X	X	X				X						
Tetrapod						X	X						X	X										
Tripod (Figs. 10,a, 15,f)						X	X						X	?		X	X	X						
Standard cylindrical vases (Fig. 16,e,f)																X	X	X		*				
San Juan Plumbate cylindrical vases																X								
Double-bottomed pedestal vases (Fig. 11,f)																		X	X	*	X			
Pyriform vases (Fig. 18,e)																?		X	X	X	X			
Tohil Plumbate effigies (Fig. 18,c,g,h)																		X	X	X	X			
Tripod bowls with effigy-head supports (Fig. 11,e)																?		X	X	X	X		?	X

FIG. 6—INCENSARIOS AND CEREMONIAL CONTAINERS: SELECTED FORMS. N, W, C, northern, western, and central ceramic zones, respectively. For references see appropriate sites and comparative studies of incense burners in note 1. For significance of symbols see note 9.

Form	PRE-CLASSIC: Balam (early aspect?) (Zacualpa) (N)	"Salcaja Preclassic" (W)	Kaminaljuyu district, Late Preclassic (C)	Kaminaljuyu district, Middle Preclassic (C)	EARLY CLASSIC: Nebaj Early Classic (N)	Atzan (Zaculeu) (N)	Balam (late aspect?) (Zacualpa) (N)	"Sajcabaja Early Classic" (N)	Tzicuay Early Classic (?) (N)	Aurora-Esperanza (Kaminaljuyu) (C)	LATE CLASSIC: Nebaj Late Classic (N)	Chinaq (Zaculeu) (N)	Pokom (Zacualpa) (N)	Chixoy II-Chipoc (N)	"Salcaja Late Classic" (W)	Amatle-Pamplona (Kaminaljuyu district) (C)	EARLY POST-CLASSIC: Nebaj Postclassic (N)	Qankyak (Zaculeu) (N)	Tohil (Zacualpa) (N)	Chixoy III-Samac (N)	Tajumulco (W)	LATE POST-CLASSIC: Xinabahul (Zaculeu) (N)	Chinautla Phase (C)
Cylinders (non-effigy) (Fig. 12,a)			X	X						X						X							
Effigy cylinders (Fig. 12,f)			X	X								X						X					
Three prongs																							
Modeled effigy prongs (Figs. 12,a, 21,a)			X	X						X						X			X				
Plain			X	X												X							
Moldmade effigy prongs (Fig. 12,g)																	X	X					
Vertical side flanges																							
Long, uninterrupted (Fig. 12,b,c)			X	X						X						X			X				
Short, interrupted (Fig. 20,a,f)																	X	X					
Anthropomorphic seated figures																							
Bowl on head (Fig. 12d)										X						X							
Bowl in lap								X	X	X													
Tripod bowls with basal molding (Fig. 20,c)						X					X	X				X							
Jars (non-effigy)													X										
Two chambers (hour glass, pedestal base) (Fig. 20,a)			X									X		X		X	X	X	X			X	
Ladle censers			X	X		X	X	X	X		X	X	X	X	X	X	X	X	X			X	X
Plain handle			X	X			X	X	X		X	X	X	X	X	X	X	X	X				
Effigy handle (Fig. 20,b)													?	?	X	X	X	X					X
Solid handle																							
Trough												?	?	X	X	X	X						
Twisted ropelike															?	X							
Hollow handle																							
Open-ended																	X	X					
Closed end, pinched and flattened																							
Closed end, upturned																	X	X					
Closed end, miscellaneous																		X	X				
Perforated base										X									X			X	X
Moldmade decoration on bowl exterior (Fig. 21,g)																						X	X
"Mixtec-type" tripod censers (Fig. 12,h)																			X	X		X	X

FIG. 7—INCENSARIOS AND CEREMONIAL CONTAINERS: SELECTED FEATURES. N, W, C, northern, western, and central ceramic zones, respectively. For references see appropriate sites and comparative studies of incense burners in note 1. For significance of symbols see note 9.

PERIOD AND PHASE	SPECIAL FEATURES						FEET				HANDLES			COVERS								SURFACE & DECORATION					
	"Fishtail" protuberance (Fig. 12,d)	Miscellaneous effigy	Tlaloc effigy jar	"Loop-nose" effigy	Pellet in lips, beak	Twisted eye-nose loop (Fig. 12,f)	Tetrapod	Tripod (Fig. 20,c)	Spiked, filleted (Fig. 20,c)	Effigy (Fig. 20,f)	Plain (Fig. 20,d)	Effigy	Twisted ropelike	Scored	Loop handle, ring	Gramophone-shaped	Tall "smokestack"	Anthropomorphic (full-figure)	Wide-brimmed with central handle	"Duck pots," "duck-bill covers" (Fig. 12,e)	Miscellaneous effigy covers	Openwork (Fig. 12,a,h)	Spikes, studs (Fig. 20,a,d)	Indented or impressed fillets (Fig. 20,a)	White coating	Red coating	Blue paint
LATE POST-CLASSIC																											
Xinabahul (Zaculeu) (N)											X											X	X		X	X	
Chinautla Phase (C)																						X	X		X	X	X
EARLY POST-CLASSIC																											
Nebaj Postclassic (N)		X						X													X	X	X	X	X	X	
Qankyak (Zaculeu) (N)								X													X	X	X	X	X	X	
Tohil (Zacualpa) (N)			X						X			X							X	X	X	X	X	X	X	X	
Chixoy III (N)		X							X	X												X		X	X	X	
Tajumulco (W)				X						X																	
LATE CLASSIC																											
Nebaj Late Classic (N)		X						X			X			X	X						X	X	X	X	X	X	
Chinaq (Zaculeu) (N)								X			X			X													X
Pokom (Zacualpa) (N)					X				X			X				X											
Chixoy II-Chipoc (N)				X		X			X			X				X				X							
"Salcaja Late Classic" (W)					X	X																					
Amatle-Pamplona (Kaminaljuyu district) (C)									X	X			X									X					
EARLY CLASSIC																											
Nebaj Early Classic (N)		X					X	X			X										X				X	X	
Atzan (Zaculeu) (N)			X				X	X			X				X				X		X				X	X	
Balam (late aspect?) (Zacualpa) (N)			X									X							X		X						
"Sajcabaja Early Classic" (N)																	X	X				X	X	X			
Tzicuay Early Classic (?) (N)																	X	X				X	X	X			
Aurora-Esperanza (Kaminaljuyu) (C)		X																X	X			X	X	X	X	X	X
PRE-CLASSIC																											
Balam (early aspect?) (Zacualpa) (N)		X												X	X										X	X	
"Salcaja Preclassic" (W)		X												X	X												
Kaminaljuyu district, Late Preclassic (C)	X	X												X	X										X	X	
Kaminaljuyu district, Middle Preclassic (C)	X	X																							X	X	

FIG. 8—TECHNIQUES OF DECORATION. °Provenience given as Zacualpa (Lothrop, 1936). N, W, C, northern, western, and central ceramic zones, respectively. For references see appropriate sites in note 1. For significance of symbols see note 9. For supplementary data on incensarios and ceremonial containers see figs. 6, 7.

PERIOD AND PHASE		Chamfering	Usulutan resist (cf. Fig. 14,d)	Punctating (Figs. 9,a, 14,e)	Modeling, often appliquéd (Figs. 14,a,f, 17,a)	Incising (Figs. 9,d–f, 11,b, 17,f,g)	Groove-incising (Figs. 9,b,c, 18,d)	Fluting	Plano-relief (Figs. 14,a, 17,a)	Stuccoed-and-painted (Fig. 15,c)	Notching (cf. Fig. 20,c)	Polychrome painting (Fig. 16,a, c–f)	Classic resist (Figs. 10,c,d, 17,b)	Impressing (Fig. 15,e)	Gadrooning (Fig. 17,e)	Gouged-and-incised (Figs. 10,e, 21,f)	Reserve space (Fig. 16,e,f)	Modeled-carving (Fig. 17,e)
LATE POST-CLASSIC	Xinabahul (Zaculeu) (N)											X				X	X	
	Yaqui (Zacualpa) (N)										•	•		X			•	
	Chuitinamit (W)				•		X					•	X					
	Chinautla (C)			•			•		•		•	•			•	•	•	
EARLY POST-CLASSIC	Nebaj Postclassic (N)		•			•				•					•			•
	Qankyak (Zaculeu) (N)			•	X	•	X	•		•	•	•	X		•			
	Tohil (Zacualpa) (N)		°		?	•	X	•	•	°	•	•	X			•		
	Chixoy III-Samac (N)				?	•	•	•		•					•			
	Tajumulco (W)			X	X	X	X								•	•	•	
LATE CLASSIC	Nebaj Late Classic (N)					•	•			°		X	X		•			
	Chinaq (Zaculeu) (N)			•	?	•	?	?		°		X	•					
	Pokom (Zacualpa) (N)			X	?	•	?	•		X	•	°	°		•		°	•
	Chixoy II-Chipoc-Cahabon (N)				?	•	X	•	•	X	•	•	X		•	•	X	•
	Amaté-Pamplona (Kaminaljuyu) (C)				X	X	•		•			•			•	•	•	•
EARLY CLASSIC	Nebaj Early Classic (N)				?	•	•	?				•						
	Atzan (Zaculeu) (N)			•	?	•	X			X		•	X		•	•		
	Balam (late aspect) (Zacualpa) (N)			•	?	X	•		•	°		°	X		•		°	
	Chixoy Ib (Chama) (N)			X	•	•	•											
	Aurora-Esperanza (Kaminaljuyu) (C)				X	•												
PRE-CLASSIC	Balam (early aspect) (Zacualpa) (N)	•	•	•	X	•	•											
	Chixoy Ia (Chama) (N)	•	X	X	•	X	X											
	Chukumuk Preclassic (W)		X	X	•	X	•											
	Kaminaljuyu district, Late Preclassic (C)			•	X	•	•	X										
	Kaminaljuyu district, Middle Preclassic (C)				X	•	•											

106

sis. In the past, locus or binominal names have sometimes been given for ceramic materials in the highlands (e.g. "Utatlan ware," "Chinautla Polychrome"). More commonly, descriptive terms have been employed ("black-on-red incised ware"). Such designations were not, of course, made in accordance with the then unformulated type-variety system. To designate certain ceramic units by one naming system and others by a different set of names is inconsistent, but no alternative appears practical at the present time. We are hopeful that many of the terms utilized in the present summary article will be replaced by more standardized names in the not too distant future.

CHARACTERISTICS OF HIGHLAND GUATEMALAN POTTERY

Several distinctive aspects help to set apart the pottery of the uplands of Guatemala from that of one or more neighboring regions. Only a few of these traits can be suggested here. Some ceramic features show significant time depth and occur frequently, often being subject to intensive elaboration. These may be recognized as pottery traditions. Negative traits, poorly represented in the highlands, are also mentioned. The various features are distinctive not because they are found exclusively in a single area but because of pronounced differences in duration or frequency of occurrence. Some pottery types showing highland-like characteristics were actually diffused or traded into the highlands, indicating the extended distribution of ceramic features which seem "at home" in that region. In some cases, too, pottery from outside sources may have won ready acceptance in the highlands because it gave a novel expression to familiar, basically satisfying forms (compare Linton, 1936, on the diffusion of "compatible" traits). Contrasts to lowland Maya ceramics are especially noted.

Technology

Little can be said about technological features which might characterize highland pottery, for the necessary analyses have not been made on wide enough a scale. Important differences may well be present from one part of the highlands to another. It is not surprising, in view of intensive volcanism in parts of the highlands, that tempering materials of volcanic origin (ash, volcanic sand, basalt) were commonly found in the best-studied assemblage of pottery, that from Kaminaljuyu (Shepard in Kidder, Jennings, and Shook, 1946, pp. 261–69). Volcanic ash temper, however, likewise appears in pottery from limestone regions in the Maya lowlands. The presence in part of the Guatemala highlands of hard, semivitrified to vitrified wares is possibly more significant culturally. Extending in time from at least the Early Classic through Early Postclassic periods, this technologically excellent, often thin-walled pottery included ceramics which were both oxidized (Esperanza Flesh-color, Amatle and Pamplona "hard ware") and reduced (Plumbate) (Shepard in Kidder, Jennings, and Shook, 1946, p. 269). Other pottery from the Guatemala highlands shows indications of incipient vitrification (Shepard, 1948, p. 126; Woodbury and Trik, 1953, p. 118; Wauchope, 1948a, p. 137)—a feature which, to be sure, is not totally lacking in the Maya lowlands (R. E. Smith, 1955b, p. 27). However close their cultural connections may prove to be, these wares stand apart from the bulk of soft-paste Maya and Mesoamerican pottery.

Surface Treatment

Slipped pottery, black to brown-black in color, is widespread in the highlands, occurring more abundantly in the Preclassic and Early Classic than in later horizons. This does not constitute a single, homogeneous ware, and relationships within and outside the highlands can only be conjectured. Dull red pottery was also in common use (Vaillant, 1927, p. 27). Differences from the Waxy, Gloss, and Slate Wares of the lowland Maya Region are generally marked (R. E. Smith, 1955b; Brainerd, 1958); waxy and lustrous slips, although present in the highlands, are decidedly less frequent than in the Maya lowlands.

Decoration

For the most part, painting was of secondary importance in the Guatemala highlands. It is true that polychrome pottery attained a high development in the Alta Verapaz–northern Quiche–Huehuetenango zone (fig. 16), which has strong Peten affiliations. Figure-painted vases from Chama[1f] are justly famed for their artistry. Nevertheless, compared to the southern Maya lowlands, highlanders outside the Northern Zone depended little on color as a means of ceramic embellishment. When painting was practiced, this was often done on a stuccoed surface or by resist techniques—specialized approaches which in certain periods loom comparatively large considering the general unimportance of painting. Also, occasional use was made of simple linear designs on dichrome pottery, and shortly before the Spanish conquest White-on-red pottery, although carelessly painted, was both abundant and fairly elaborate (fig. 19,c). Of greater importance during most of the sequence, however, was alteration of the surface through incising, stamping, texturing, and appliquéing with spikes, fillets or life forms. Esthetic effects were frequently achieved by combining such techniques with modeling—an alternative, quite different in orientation, to the lowland Maya polychrome tradition.

Shape

From earliest times in the archaeological record (fig. 13,c) to the Spanish conquest, whole vessels or their appendages were modeled in the shape of the bodies or faces of humans, animals and grotesques. The treatment of handles and tripod feet as effigies was of increased importance in late horizons (figs. 11,e; 19,d; 21,j), although modeled effigy handles on scutate covers constitute an Early Classic diagnostic. Sustained interest in effigy modeling is indicated both by local ceramic production and by the importation of new effigy forms. In addition to appearing in many local types, effigy vessels occurred frequently in pottery of Usulutan decorative technique, which was apparently produced in a number of centers, both within and outside the Guatemalan highlands (Shepard, 1947, p. 192). Effigies were also prominent in Thin Orange pottery (clearly imported from south-central Mexico), Nicoya Polychrome (of Central American derivation), Tiquisate Ware (from the Pacific coast), and Tohil Plumbate (manufactured in or near the highlands but perhaps made or influenced by people of non-Maya origin).

Handles are a common feature on highland pottery. These are normally vertical, generally used on jars, and often placed so that one end springs directly from the lip (fig. 13,a). Considerable variation on this pattern exists, however. Handles occur frequently in a lower position on the neck or body, even toward the base. Especially in the later horizons, three or four handles would be placed at different heights on the vessel (fig. 19,e). Handles are present on pitchers, cups, wide-mouth bowls, and other forms. Strap handles were popular, loop handles, twin loops fused together, and twisted ropelike handles also being well represented. Horizontal "comal"-like handles are also known. Ladles comprise a specialized form, apparently earlier here than in the Maya lowlands. A general interest in handles, stronger than in the southern Maya lowlands or even northern Yucatan, is indicated.

On the other hand, a series of forms which were strongly developed over much

108

of the Lowland Maya Region during the Classic period was only weakly to moderately represented in the highlands. Included are such related vessel shapes as composite silhouette ring-stand bowls, basal-flange bowls, and basal-or-lateral-ridge tripod plates. In comparison to the basal-flange vessels of the lowlands, those of the highlands were more likely to be wide-mouthed dishes, comparatively flat based, and tripodal (fig. 11,*a*); they also appear to have persisted in relatively greater strength into Late Classic or Early Postclassic times. Cultural lag at the margins of a zone of diffusion, which appears to have centered in the Peten lowlands, is indicated.

Function

An outstanding feature of highland pottery was the intensive production and elaboration of incense burners (figs. 12, 20). Many of these ceremonial objects were apparently used as stands or covers rather than as receptacles for the incense, whereas vessels having stylistic characteristics similar to incensarios were occasionally used to hold caches (Borhegyi, 1959a; Smith and Kidder, 1951, pp. 29–31). Regardless of their precise functions, incensario-like vessels from the highlands were more numerous and diversified than comparable forms over most of the Lowland Maya Region. The relative importance of the incensario tradition in the highlands was especially pronounced during the Preclassic and Early Classic periods. Afterwards, western and northern lowland forms became increasingly abundant and ornate, incense burners in the highland region continuing to be made in great quantity though with lessened elaboration. Effigy forms, often depicting grotesque supernaturals, were commonly employed, especially during the earlier periods. Incensarios with three plain or effigy prongs, "loop noses," vertical side-flanges, elaborate anthropomorphic covers or other chimneys, and tri-

podal supports are among the forms which appear to center in the highlands. On the other hand, an ornament looping under the eyes and twisting over the nose, found on incense burners from the northern part of the highlands (fig. 12,*f*), may have been of lowland Maya origin. The so-called "Mixtec" type of ladle censer (fig. 12,*h*) may, as the name suggests, have been derived from as far away as south-central Mexico.[4]

Comales (clay griddles for making tortillas) have been cited as a highland characteristic, occurring there abundantly in one form or another from Preclassic times, yet largely lacking from the Maya lowlands (Kidder, Jennings, and Shook, 1946, p. 208; Brainerd, 1958, p. 55).[5] So sharply contrasting a distribution would suggest fundamental differences in food preparation between highland and lowland Maya cultures. Borhegyi, however, has identified various so-called comales as incensario covers, suggesting that most if not all preconquest examples from the Guatemala highlands were actually used in the burning of incense (Borhegyi, 1959a, pp. 56–57). Whatever the function of these objects, their predominantly highland locus presents another contrast with lowland Maya ceramics.

CERAMIC ZONES

Within the somewhat arbitrarily defined limits of the Guatemalan highlands, it is

_____

[4] In a different context, Nicholson (1961) has stressed the danger of using the ethnic and linguistic term "Mixtec" instead of the geographic-stylistic name, "Mixteca-Puebla." However, the term "Mixtec-type" censer is well enough established to continue its provisional use here. As indicated above, it is hoped that the unsystematic terminology now prevailing in highland ceramic studies will soon be replaced by a more rigorous naming system.

[5] Comal-like objects, when occurring in the Lowland Maya Region, seem mostly to have been distributed close to the highlands. These objects occur in Preclassic through Late Classic periods at Copan (Longyear, 1952, p. 91) and are described as abundant in all deposits at Guaytan (Smith and Kidder, 1943, p. 140).

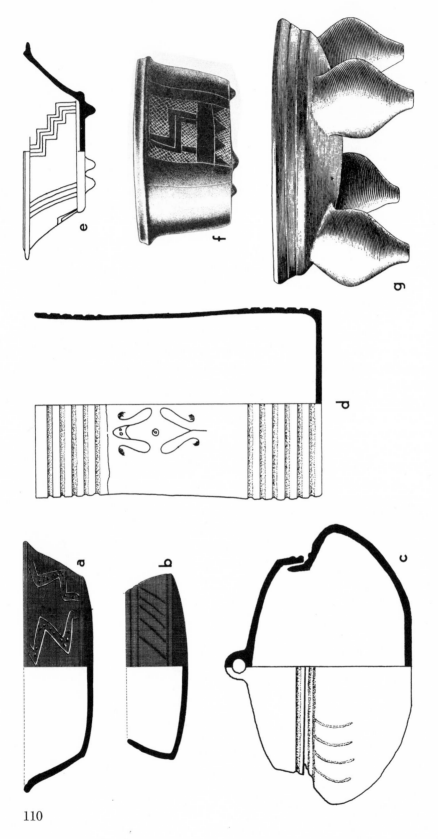

FIG. 9—SELECTED EXAMPLES OF POTTERY FROM THE PRECLASSIC AND PROTOCLASSIC PERIODS

a–f, Preclassic. *g*, Protoclassic. *a,b*, Zacualpa (Balam phase, early aspect). *c–e*, Kaminaljuyu (Miraflores phase). *f,g*, Salcaja district. *a*, Punctate-incised brown bowl (after Wauchope, 1948a, fig. 27,*a*). *b*, Groove-incised brown-black bowl with insloping walls (after *idem*, fig. 28,*e*). *c*, Groove-incised Usulutan resist vessel with restricted orifice; cover has centrally placed strap handle (after Shook and Kidder, 1952, fig. 45,*h*). *d*, Fine In-

cised Black-brown cylinder (after *idem*, fig. 22). *e*, Incised Fine Red tripod bowl (after *idem*, fig. 34,*b*). *f*, Incised black tripod bowl (after Lothrop, 1936, fig. 97,*b*). *g*, Red tetrapod dish (after Lothrop, 1936, fig. 90,*b*). Diameters at rim: *a*, 27 cm.; *b*, 16 cm.; *c*, 16 cm.; *d*, 23 cm.; *e*, 27 cm.; *f*, 21 cm.; *g*, 30 cm.

possible to recognize three major ceramic zones. These are the *Northern* (comprising the Departments of Alta Verapaz, El Quiche, and Huehuetenango), *Western* (Solola, Totonicapan, and portions of Quezaltenango and San Marcos), and *Central* (Chimaltenango, Sacatepequez, Guatemala, Baja Verapaz, and parts of El Progreso and Jalapa). Little can as yet be said about the eastern part of the Central Zone. Huehuetenango might be considered apart from the Quiche and Alta Verapaz, although a close ceramic relationship existed during the Classic period. To indicate this, a broken line, running along the eastern foothills of the Cuchumatanes range, is used to subdivide the Northern Zone (fig. 1,*b*).

Northern Zone

Major sequences known at the present time within the northern highlands are from Zacualpa[1u] in the south, Zaculeu[1v] in the west, and the centrally located Chixoy drainage. Named phases have been given for these developments only at Zacualpa (Balam, Pokom, Tohil, and Yaqui Phases, early to late) and Zaculeu (Atzan, Chinaq, Qankyak, Xinabahul). Phases at the two sites are approximately coeval, covering the Classic and Postclassic periods, although Balam beginnings clearly pertain to a Late Preclassic horizon. Approximate correlation of these and other highland chronologies is given in figure 2. Zacualpa and Zaculeu, unlike many other highland communities, were not abandoned at the close of the Classic or Early Postclassic periods. These centers do not, therefore, reflect the characteristic shift from open sites to easily defensible, hilltop locations which is so striking a phenomenon over much of the Guatemala highlands. On the other hand, the earlier part of the Chixoy sequence is based primarily on stratified tomb materials at Chama[1f] (Chama 1–4) and for later horizons on typological differences in pottery excavated at Chipal[1i] (Chipal 1–3). The two sites, Chama and Chipal, lie at markedly different elevations and are separated by a distance of almost 50 km., but their developments have been combined into a single ceramic column, known as Chixoy I–IV (Butler, 1940). Published collections of pottery from Chipoc,[1j] Seacal,[1r] and Samac,[1q] in the more easterly Coban district, have been correlated with the later parts of this sequence, which apparently extends from the Late Preclassic or Protoclassic through Late Postclassic periods.

Additional sites have provided useful ceramic data. Outstanding among these is Nebaj,[1n] with a rich, well-documented series of sequent tombs and caches. Pottery, apparently from tombs but with specific assemblages unknown, comes from Chajcar,[1d] Tzicuay,[1s] and Ilom.[1l] Seler's early investigations in the environs of Chacula[1c] provide data about the ceremonial pottery of extreme northwestern Huehuetenango. Extended surface reconnaissance, supplemented by limited test-pitting, has provided another dimension to ceramic studies in the Northern Zone, some 41 sites yielding pottery assignable as to period (A. L. Smith, 1955; R. E. Smith, 1949b). Among these sites, Chalchitan[1e] and Chichen[1h] have unusually long occupations. Approximately 15 per cent of the survey sites were occupied in the Late Preclassic period; 24 per cent in the Early Classic; 39 per cent in the Late Classic; 37 per cent in the Early Postclassic; and 41 per cent in the Late Postclassic.

Cultural differences within the northern highlands must have been conditioned by typography. The Chixoy and Chajul Rivers flow northward to the Maya lowlands, and at sites within this drainage system, such as Chama,[1f] Ilom,[1l] and Nebaj,[1n] polychrome pottery with Peten affiliations is more strongly represented than at such sites as Zaculeu,[1v] which lies across the Cuchumatanes range to the southwest, or Zacualpa,[1u] south of the Sierra de Chuacus.

111

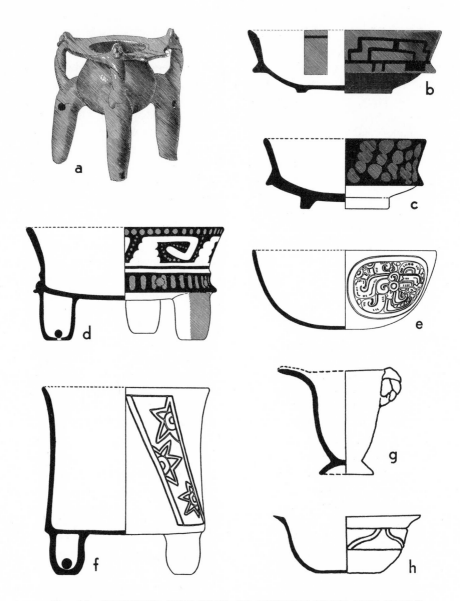

FIG. 10—SELECTED EXAMPLES OF POTTERY FROM THE EARLY
CLASSIC PERIOD (*a*, POSSIBLY PRECLASSIC)

a,b, Zacualpa (Balam phase, undetermined aspect and late aspect, respectively). *c–f,* Zaculeu (Atzan phase). *g, h,* Kaminaljuyu (Esperanza phase).
a, Tall-footed tripod cup (after Wauchope, 1948a, fig. 30,*c*). *b,* Black-on-red
basal-flange bowl (after *idem,* fig. 34,*b*). *c,* Classic resist basal-flange bowl
(after Woodbury and Trik, 1953, fig. 112). *d,* Classic resist tripod bowl
(after *idem,* fig. 109). *e,* Gouged-and-incised brown hemispherical bowl
(after *idem,* fig. 71). *f,* Incised Red-and-buff cylindrical tripod vase (after
idem, fig. 64). *g,* Black "cream pitcher" (after Kidder, Jennings, and Shook,
1946, fig. 69,*f*). *h,* Incised Thin Orange bowl (after *idem,* fig. 68,*p*).
Diameters: *a,* 13 cm.; *b,* 20 cm.; *c,* 16 cm.; *d,* 20 cm.; *e,* 19.2 cm.; *f,* 16.5
cm.; *g,* 13.5 cm.; *h,* 16 cm.

112

The relative importance of rivers, as a factor channeling cultural contact, and mountain ranges, as a barrier to such contact, remains unknown. In general, localized differences within north highland pottery are not expressed in differing techniques of decoration or other isolated, sharply defined traits but result from combinations of techniques on certain vessel forms. To be sure, as Zaculeu is compared with Zacualpa on the basis of individual traits, one is struck by the importance of resist painting at the former site and by its insignificance, according to norms of the northern highlands, in materials excavated at the latter. While of interest, this apparent difference may be grossly exaggerated by the nature of the material, the Zaculeu pottery coming largely from tombs, the Zacualpa from stratified digging. As yet, little can be said about dominant, possibly indigenous types or wares at the various sites.

Nowhere in the northern highlands has Early or Middle Preclassic pottery been recognized, at least in any definable context. This is in contrast both to the Maya lowlands (Ecab, Capul, and Mamom phases) and to the southern rim of the highlands (Las Charcas through Providencia phases at Kaminaljuyu).[1nn] A peripheral ceramic position, with attendant cultural lag, has been suggested for the northern highlands in Classic times (Smith and Kidder, 1951, p. 77; A. L. Smith, 1955, p. 69). Nevertheless, contacts between the Guatemala highlands and the Lowland Maya Region, where ceramic chronology is anchored to calendrical inscriptions, were closer in the north than in other upland zones, and these contacts were maintained throughout the Classic period. Accordingly, chronological refinement is better in the Northern Zone than for the highlands as a whole.

Western Zone

Three districts have contributed most to our knowledge of western highland ceramics. From east to west these are the Lake Atitlan basin, the Quezaltenango valley, and the rugged Tajumulco–San Marcos locale. Unfortunately, none of these has provided a finely seriated chronology. Lothrop's pioneer studies on the margins of Lake Atitlan (Lothrop, 1933) produced essential criteria for an apparently interrupted Middle or Late Preclassic-Postclassic sequence (Chukumuk 1–2, Chuitinamit) (fig. 2). A clear-cut Late Classic ceramic complex was not defined. Other sites near Atitlan include Panajachel[1z] and Tzanjuyu.[1dd] Best known Quezaltenango valley sites are in the vicinity of Salcaja[1bb] and Momostenango,[1y] abundant Late Preclassic pottery having been taken from numerous small cemeteries in the locality. Sites in the Tajumulco–San Marcos district are generally small and scattered, in contrast to those on the nearby Pacific coast (Shook, 1947, p. 179). Tajumulco[1cc] itself dates from the Early Postclassic period. Also, sites of ceramic importance lie on the fringes of the western highlands. To the north, the well-known Quiche Indian capital of Utatlan[1ee] has yielded Late Postclassic pottery, in keeping with the site's protohistoric position. From the Finca Paraiso,[1aa] at an elevation of 1000 m. on the Pacific slope, has come pottery suggesting a significant Late Classic–Early Postclassic transition.

Pottery from the western highlands gives the impression of strongly localized differences. In part, this may reflect unequal occupation of a given district through time. Thus, collections of pottery from Salcaja-Momostenango[1bb, y] are largely Preclassic in date, whereas ceramics from the Tajumulco district, as now known, indicate a significant Postclassic occupation. It is problematical to what extent this picture will be changed by more intensive field work. Of possible importance is the exceptionally heavy concentration of Tohil Plumbate in pottery excavated at Tajumulco[1cc] and gathered from nearby highland and coastal sites (Shepard, 1948). The abun-

113

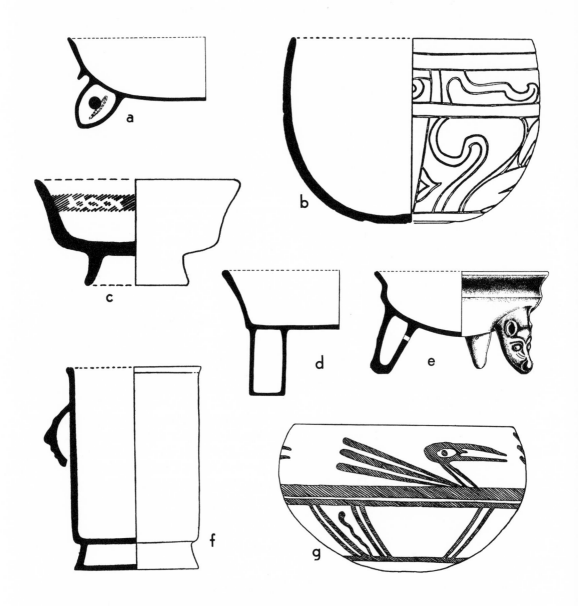

Fig. 11—SELECTED EXAMPLES OF POTTERY FROM THE LATE CLASSIC
AND EARLY POSTCLASSIC PERIODS

a–c, Late Classic. *d–g*, Early Postclassic. *a*, Chipoc (Tepeu 2 equivalent). *b*,
Zaculeu (Chinaq phase). *c*, Kaminaljuyu (Amatle phase). *d–f*, Zaculeu (Qankyak
phase). *g*, Zacualpa (?). *a*, Tripod basal-flange dish (Incised Orange-on-cream)
(after R. E. Smith, 1952, fig. 17,*a*). *b*, Incised Light Brown bowl (after Woodbury and Trik, 1953, fig. 78). *c*, Amatle Polychrome ring-stand bowl (after Shook,
1952a, fig. 2,*e*). *d*, Cylindrical-footed tripod bowl (red-and-buff) (after Woodbury
and Trik, 1953, fig. 85). *e*, Tripod bowl with effigy-head feet (after *idem*, fig.
81,*e*). *f*, Stuccoed-and-painted double-bottomed cylindrical red vase (after *idem*,
fig. 84). *g*, Red-on-orange bowl (after Lothrop, 1936, pl. 2,*f*). Diameters: *a*, 25.2
cm.; *b*, 14 cm.; *c*, 14 cm.; *d*, 24.4 cm.; *e*, 19 cm.; *f*, 17.5 cm.; *g*, 15 cm.

dance of this pottery—the prime diagnostic of the Early Postclassic period throughout highland Guatemala—has led to the suggestion that its center of manufacture was close to Tajumulco. Robles Plumbate, a possible precursor of Tohil, is up to the present time known almost exclusively from Finca Paraiso,[1aa] a scant 50 km. to the southeast.

Central Zone

Ceramic sequences in the central highlands are keyed to excavations at the great site of Kaminaljuyu,[1nn] supplemented by fairly intensive reconnaissance (Borhegyi, 1950a, 1961d; Shook, 1952b). The Kaminaljuyu sequence is based primarily on tomb furnishings, on the seriation of fill from mounds, and on refuse from underground, single-phase pits. The occupation of the site, which apparently lasted from early in the Middle Preclassic through the Late Classic periods, has been divided into a series of 11 phases (Shook, 1951a; Shook and Kidder, 1952; Kidder, 1961); two additional phases, scarcely represented at Kaminaljuyu itself, carry the sequence up to the Spanish conquest (Shook, 1952b). When published in detail, this chronology should prove of exceptional importance to highland studies. At the present time, however, the ceramic composition of most phases has not been thoroughly documented. The possibility must be left open that, rather than comprising sequent divisions within a chronological continuum, some of the named phases will prove to be approximately contemporaneous, reflecting intrusion or functionally differentiated ceramic complexes. For purposes of the present summary, it appears useful to lump phases rather grossly, according to period, as follows:

Middle Preclassic (early aspect): Las Charcas, Arevalo.
Middle Preclassic (late aspect): Majadas, Providencia. (Sacatepequez, a nearby western

development, apparently is not strongly represented at Kaminaljuyu.)
Late Preclassic-Protoclassic: Miraflores, Arenal, Santa Clara.
Early Classic: Aurora, Esperanza.
Late Classic: Amatle, Pamplona.
Early Postclassic: Ayampuc (barely represented at Kaminaljuyu).
Late Postclassic: Chinautla (barely represented at Kaminaljuyu).

Unexcavated sites, or those subject only to minor testing, contribute to the ceramic picture of the central highlands. Borhegyi (1950a, 1956b) has suggested a sequence in the Valley of Almolonga, near Antigua (fig. 2). Elsewhere, especially promising Preclassic occupations are indicated by pottery at Canchon,[1hh] Contreras,[1kk] Piedra Parada, [1oo] and Virginia,[1pp] all located somewhat south of Kaminaljuyu. Survey sites giving ceramic evidence of occupations extending from Preclassic into the Postclassic periods are Chinautla,[1jj] Antigua,[1gg] and Santa Maria Cauque.[1ii] Of 76 ceramically datable sites (including Kaminaljuyu) reported on by Shook (1952b), approximately 64 per cent were occupied in the Preclassic; 24 per cent in the Early Classic; 57 per cent in the Late Classic; 1 per cent in the Early Postclassic; and 13 per cent in the Late Postclassic. Not all Preclassic sites were assignable as to phase, but of 37 sites which could be placed with reasonable assurance, 41 per cent dated from Las Charcas-Arevalo, 54 per cent from Majadas-Providencia-Sacatepequez, and 57 per cent from Miraflores–Arenal–Santa Clara. These figures take on special interest when compared with site occupations from the Northern Highlands (A. L. Smith, 1955). Middle Preclassic pottery appears to have been much more strongly entrenched in the central highlands than in the Northern Zone where, indeed, it is yet to be located. A peripheral ceramic position for the north highlands is again suggested, as seen from the south as well as from the Maya lowlands. Whereas the number of sites occu-

FIG. 12—SELECTED EXAMPLES OF INCENSE BURNERS, VARIOUS PERIODS

a,b, Preclassic. *c–e,* Early Classic. *f,g*(?), Late Classic. *h,* Early Postclassic. *a,* Chiquimulilla district. *b,* Kaminaljuyu (Miraflores style). *c,d,* Kaminaljuyu (Esperanza phase). *e,* Zacualpa (Balam phase). *f,* Chama (Chixoy II). *g,* Salcaja. *h,* Zaculeu (Qankyak phase). *a,* Three-pronged cylindrical incensario with modeled effigy prongs of Las Charcas type (after Borhegyi, 1950b, fig. 7,*a*). *b,c,* Three-pronged flanged cylindrical effigy incensarios (after Borhegyi, 1951a, fig. 1,*d*, and 1950b, fig. 8,*h*, respectively). *d,* Anthropomorphic seated incense burner (after Kidder, Jennings, and Shook, 1946, fig. 89). *e,* "Duck-pot" or "duck-bill" censer (?) cover (after Wauchope, 1948a, fig. 37,*c*). *f,* Cylindrical effigy incensario with interrupted side flanges (after Butler, 1940, fig. 23,*a*). *g,* Three-pronged incensario fragment with mold-made effigies on prongs (after Borhegyi, 1951b, fig. 1,*d*). *h,* "Mixtec-type" tripod censer (after Woodbury and Trik, 1953, fig. 79,*a*). Total heights: *a,* 37.5 cm.; *b,* (without prongs), 38 cm.; *c,* 50 cm.; *e,* 23 cm.; *f,* 38 cm.; *g* (prongs only), 24 cm. Diameters of orifice: *d,* 23 cm.; *h,* 6.2 cm.

116

pied in later periods fluctuated wildly in the Central Zone, there is evidence of steady increase in the north after the Middle Preclassic. Particularly striking is the near-absence of Early Postclassic (Ayampuc, or Tohil Plumbate horizon) pottery from sites which up to now have been discovered in the central highlands. In both the North and Central Zones, however, pottery reveals a Late Postclassic shift of population to new, easily defensible locations.

CERAMIC CHARACTERISTICS BY PERIOD

In the Guatemala highlands, comparisons of pottery through time and space cannot yet be made systematically or with desirable precision. Shared features of pottery must therefore be presented in various ways, sometimes by mode, in other cases on the basis of ware, ceramic group, or type. General characteristics of the pottery will be pointed out, according to ceramic zone, for each of five periods (Preclassic-Protoclassic, Early Classic, Late Classic, Early Postclassic, Late Postclassic). The development of certain specialized forms and decorative techniques in the highlands as a whole will then be examined (see also figs. 3–8).

Preclassic and Protoclassic Periods

Well-slipped monochrome and dichrome pottery, with dull to lustrous finish, was characteristic throughout the Preclassic. Many additional features which typify Preclassic horizons over Mesoamerica as a whole are to be found in the highlands, in one phase or another. This is illustrated by a comparative survey (Wauchope, 1950), which showed that of the 21 ceramic traits charted in the Mesoamerican Preclassic, all but two were present in the Guatemala highlands. A typical inventory for Middle and Late Preclassic-Protoclassic pottery results. Certain apparent absences may also be significant. Rocker-stamping, cord-marking, shell-stamping and iridescent painting, diagnostics of the Ocos phase on the Pacific

coast of Guatemala (M. D. Coe, 1961), have not been reported from the highlands. Likewise, the narrow-mouth, pointed-bottomed bottle characteristic of the Mani Cenote (Ecab phase of Yucatan) has not been described for the highlands, although a similar pattern-burnished monochrome is said to occur (see below under Central Zone). Such negative traits support our inclination to place the known beginnings of ceramics in the Guatemala highlands in a Middle Preclassic horizon, early aspect (fig. 2).

NORTHERN ZONE. As currently understood, the north highland ceramic sequence commences with Late Preclassic shapes and decorative features. Traits are present which in other localities characterize the Protoclassic horizon, but up to now in this zone they have not been segregated as a distinct complex. Among these traits, polychrome decoration is largely absent except perhaps at the site of Tzicuay.[1s] Best known Preclassic-Protoclassic materials are Chama 1 and in part 1–2 transition —collectively designated Chixoy Ia (Butler, 1940)—and the earlier part of the Balam phase at Zacualpa (Wauchope, 1950, p. 242). If specimens purportedly from Zacualpa actually come from the northern highlands, an additional body of Preclassic pottery is available (Lothrop, 1936).

Surface finish and decoration are moderately standardized. Slips occasionally have a soapy or waxy feel, although this tactile quality is less pronounced than in most Preclassic pottery from the Lowland Maya Region. Both the Sierra Red and Flor Cream Ceramic Groups appear to be represented at San Pedro Carcha.[1b] Dominant surface colors in the northern highlands, however, range from black to brown, frequencies at Chama[1f] suggesting a shift from black to "Smoked" black-brown. Zoned decoration appears in the form of punctate or crosshachured areas outlined by incising (fig. 9,a). Broad-line geometric incising,

117

Fig. 13—SELECTED EXAMPLES OF POTTERY FROM THE PRECLASSIC PERIOD

a,b, Kaminaljuyu (Las Charcas phase). *c,* Unknown provenience (Las Charcas phase). *d,* Unknown provenience (Sacatepequez phase). *e,* Salcaja district. *f,* Unknown provenience. *a,* Incised Pallid Red jar. *b,* Red-on-buff incurved bowl. *c,* Pallid Red (?) effigy bowl, heavily fire-clouded. *d,* Purplish-red-on-white cylindrical bowl. *e,* Glossy black rim-flange bowl. *f,* Utatlan Incised-dichrome tetrapod bowl. (*a–e,* courtesy, Peabody Museum, Harvard; *f,* after Lothrop, 1936, fig. 74,*b'.*) Maximum diameter: *a,* 47.5 cm. Diameters at orifice: *b,* 16 cm.; *c,* 17.4 cm.; *d,* 18.5 cm.; *e,* 12.5 cm.; *f,* 19.3 cm.

vertical short slashed lines, and horizontal preslip grooving appear on other Preclassic pottery. Although resist-decorated Usulutan pottery is absent from controlled excavations (Wauchope, 1950), examples are reported from Zacualpa[1u] and La Flojera[1k] (fig. 14,d). Characterizing this widespread pottery are light-colored parallel lines, executed with a multiple-point applicator, appearing in negative style against the red or orange slip. Among the most distinctive pottery is "Utatlan ware" (Utatlan Incised-dichrome), up to now best known in collections reportedly from Zacualpa. Black-painted areas appear on a specular hematite red slip and are edged by wide lines incised, after drying or firing, into the brown paste (cf. fig. 13,f). Designs on Utatlan Incised-dichrome are generally rectilinear although cursive elements and stylized naturalistic forms are present; motifs include the step-and-angular scroll and monkeys. Incised three-color polychrome is rare.

Shapes include a significant range of diagnostics. Late Preclassic vessel forms, corresponding to those of the Chicanel phase in the southern lowlands and essentially free of Protoclassic influences, are especially well represented at San Pedro Carcha.[1b] Included are plain and grooved wide-everted rim plates, lateral-flange-or-ridge bowls, and small-mouthed jars. A lateral-flange dish (Flor Cream Type?) reportedly comes from Zacualpa (Lothrop, 1936, fig. 17,d). Examples of Utatlan Incised-dichrome consist mostly of flaring-walled, flat-based bowls, footless or with hollow tripod supports. Also known from the northern highlands are basal-angle bowls with insloping walls (fig. 9,b). Mammiform tetrapods, the hallmark of the Protoclassic horizon in southern Mesoamerica, were present on bowls, plates, and vases (fig. 14,c). These supports are known in forms both large and small, hollow and solid, symmetrically breast shaped and irregularly humped, although the number

which have been recovered from any one site is not great. Of these related forms, the solid mammiform foot may be of relatively late occurrence (Wauchope, 1948a, p. 97). Other Protoclassic shapes, including pot stands, pedestal-base bowls, and jars with bridged spouts, appear sporadically over the Northern Highland Zone.

Occasionally vessel shapes and designs, singly or in combination, indicate specific relationships to other parts of the Guatemala highlands. At Chama,[1f] a "Smoked" flat-based bowl with tripod nubbin feet, flaring wall, and paneled crosshatched decoration corresponds to pottery at Salcaja and is regarded as an import from that locality by Butler (1940, fig. 21,g). At Tzicuay,[1s] tetrapod bowls supported on swollen, slightly humped mammiform feet or tall, cylindrical legs, once again, are strongly reminiscent of pottery that occurs frequently in the Salcaja district (cf. fig. 9,g). An Utatlan Incised-dichrome vessel, reportedly from Zacualpa, depicts a curious quadruped, shown in bilateral symmetry, similar to those found commonly on Fine Incised Black-brown pottery of the Late Preclassic period at Kaminaljuyu[1nn] (fig. 9,d). The quadruped reappears on tetrapod polychrome vessels from Tzicuay.[6]

WESTERN ZONE. Protoclassic features are abundant in collections of funeral pottery from the Quezaltenango valley and in sherds from early levels on the shores of Lake Atitlan. Little controlled excavation, however, has been done in the western highlands, and it is difficult even to suggest when the earliest significant Preclassic occupation may have commenced; Tlatilco-

[6] These designs are examples of the so-called "hocker" motif, which is widely distributed in the New and Old Worlds (Schuster, 1951; Covarrubias, 1954, pp. 34–40). Similar designs appear on Tzakol 3 pottery at Uaxactun (R. E. Smith, 1955b, p. 71). Such considerations decrease the reliability of the quadruped as a horizon-marker, although specific similarities at Kaminaljuyu and in the northern highlands, together with associated Late Preclassic ceramic features, may be significant.

119

FIG. 14—SELECTED EXAMPLES OF POTTERY FROM THE PRECLASSIC AND PROTOCLASSIC PERIODS

a,b,d–f, Preclassic. *c*, Protoclassic. *a,b*, Kaminaljuyu (Miraflores phase). *c*, Zacualpa (Balam phase, early aspect). *d*, La Flojera. *e*, Chukumuk. *f*, Salcaja district. *a*, Plano-relief Coarse Incised Black-brown bowl (after Shook and Kidder, 1952, fig. 68,*d*). *b*, Fine Incised Black-brown deep bowl (goblet) (after *idem*, fig. 64,*e*). *c*, Groove-incised tetrapod black vase (after Wauchope, 1948a, pl. 19,*d*). *d*, Usulutan resist tripod bowl (courtesy, Peabody Museum, Harvard). *e*, Punctate-incised red-on-orange bowl) (after Lothrop, 1933, fig. 36,*a*). *f*, Red spouted effigy (after Lothrop, 1936, fig. 91,*a*). Heights: *b*, 13 cm.; *c*, 17 cm.; *f*, 19.6 cm. Diameters: *a*, 27 cm.; *d*, 15 cm.; *e*, 25.4 cm.

like traits cited by Porter (1953) could prove helpful in providing a minimal dating. Within the western highlands differing interpretations of the local chronology have been published. Borhegyi (1956b) has listed sequent Salcaja 1, 2 phases, the latter, dating from the Late or Urban Formative, being coeval with Chukumuk 1. On the other hand, Wauchope (1950) recognized a single phase at Salcaja[1bb] (Urban Formative or Protoclassic) but distinguished two Preclassic phases at Chukumuk,[1x] Salcaja equating with Chukumuk 2. Stratigraphic excavations, particularly in the Quezaltenango valley, are clearly requisite to a solution of these chronological problems.

Highly polished, glossy-surfaced pottery is more commonly found in the Quezaltenango valley tombs than in the Atitlan basin. Black to black-brown bowls occur in this ware, a frequently encountered form having flat base, three nubbin feet, flaring sides, and labial molding. Postfiring cross-hachured panels further distinguish this pottery, red pigment sometimes being rubbed into the incised lines (fig. 9,f). Grooved or incised wide-everted rims, in some cases taking the shape of effigies, also appear on glossy black bowls. Dull-surfaced pottery, red or black in color, is also abundant in the Salcaja-Momostenango district. Typologically the lustrous black vessels with flangelike everted rims (fig. 13,e) should antedate the numerous dull-surfaced tetrapods with their typically Protoclassic mammiform or tall cylindrical legs (fig. 9,g).

In addition to the differing importance of polished black pottery, distinctive emphases are present in the ceramic patterns of Lake Atitlan and the Quezaltenango valley. This may in part be due to the coexistence of local traditions, in part to disconformities in the Chukumuk-Salcaja sequences as they are at present understood. Usulutan pottery, in any case, appears to be more strongly represented in the Atitlan basin, the Salcaja-Momostenango district being reminiscent of the northern highlands in the general unimportance of this technique. Also, to judge from extant examples, preslip incising, orange-surfaced pottery, which Lothrop (1933, p. 37) believes was locally made, and zoned punctation occur more frequently at Chukumuk (fig. 14,e). On the other hand, shoe-shaped vessels, bottles, and other spouted forms may have a greater frequency in the Quezaltenango valley (fig. 14,f). Needless to say, uncertainties in determining relative abundance make all such observations highly tenuous when one is comparing partially illustrated grave goods with materials obtained in controlled digging.

Relationships occur both with the Northern Zone (see above) and the central highlands. From the Salcaja district comes pottery resembling the well-described Fine Incised Black-brown of the Late Preclassic period at Kaminaljuyu. Shared traits include: cylinders with horizontal moldings, goblets, modeled faces, incised scrolls with triangular hachured bases, and incised arcs with pendant vertical lines (cf. fig. 14,b; Shook and Kidder, 1952, fig. 66,a; Gamio, 1926–27, p. 217). Slipped surfaces of Kaminaljuyu Fine Incised Black-brown, however, have a velvety finish with low-to-medium luster, in contrast to the high shiny gloss of comparable black pottery at Salcaja.

CENTRAL ZONE. Pottery with white (cream), red, and gray-brown to black-brown surfaces underwent a number of typological changes during the Preclassic period. Although information about quantification and interfingering of these types is lacking, figure 3 is an attempt to indicate the general succession and diagnostic importance of these and other ceramic units. Omitted from the chart are red-on-buff pottery, which apparently occurred abundantly throughout the sequence at Kaminaljuyu,[1nn] other long-lived ceramics for which diagnostic changes from one period

121

FIG. 15—SELECTED EXAMPLES OF POTTERY FROM THE EARLY CLASSIC PERIOD (a, POSSIBLY PROTOCLASSIC)

a, Unknown provenience, probably Salcaja district. b, Panajachel. c–e, Kaminaljuyu (Esperanza phase). f,g, Nebaj. a, Incised red cylinder tripod (after Kidder, 1954, fig. 3,b). b, Incised Classic resist squat cylinder tripod (after R. E. Smith, 1955b, fig. 1,h). c, Stuccoed-and-painted cylinder tripod, "Teotihuacanoid" style (after Kidder, Jennings, and Shook, 1946, fig. 204,a). d, Red-on-cream pisote effigy whistling vessel (after idem, fig. 179,h). e, Two-part effigy, textile-impressed and incised (after idem, fig. 190,d). f, Caldero Buff-polychrome tripod basal-flange bowl (after A. L. Smith and Kidder, 1951, fig. 83,c). g, Shoe-shaped effigy vessel (after idem, fig. 74,q). Heights: a, 16.3 cm.; e, 28.5 cm. Lengths: d, 28.5 cm.; g, 14.5 cm. Diameters: b, 18 cm.; c, 15.5 cm.; f, 38.5 cm.

to another are unknown, and minor types. Series of developments are suggested: from Streaky to Glossy Gray-brown; Coarse Incised to Fine Incised Black-brown (figs. 21,c; 14,b); white paste to red-brown paste in white-surfaced pottery; Red-on-white to Purple-on-white (fig. 13,d); Pallid Red to Purple-on-fine red to Incised Fine Red (fig. 9,e). Usulutan resist, perhaps present throughout the Preclassic sequence, was most abundant in the Late Preclassic. Utatlan Incised-dichrome and Incised Zinc Orange were probably diagnostic of Middle Preclassic pottery in its late aspect.

Changes in surface finish and decoration were accompanied by shifts in vessel shape and other form modes. Uncertainty exists as to the degree to which the developments were synchronous or proceeded at varying rates, perhaps cross-cutting different types. It appears that pottery decorated with Usulutan technique underwent a series of changes in shape while remaining relatively constant in surface finish and decoration, although even in this case resist "clouding" may have had a slightly different temporal position than the sharper, more distinctly patterned wavy lines. A provisional sequence of selected diagnostic shapes, both whole vessels and other features, is given in figure 4. Omitted from the chart are forms of great duration, such as comales. Patterned changes are indicated in basic categories of vessel forms. *Jars* first appear as wide mouthed and squat, maximum diameter occurring in a medial position on the vessel wall (fig. 13,a). Wide orifices were retained on Late Preclassic jars, but shoulders had shifted to a notably higher position. Slipped jars often are found in red, red-on-buff, red-and-white-on-buff, and Purple-on-fine red pottery. At the beginning of the Kaminaljuyu sequence, *low bowls and dishes* were flat based with outflared sides. Incurved rims were sometimes present on these vessels (fig. 13,b), but feet, ridges, and the composite silhouette in its varied aspects were wholly or largely

absent. Outflared flat-based bowls continued in the following phases but with the addition of the labial flange and, in small numbers, small solid tripod or tetrapod supports. In the Late Preclassic period, convex-based bowls, lateral-flange and Z-angle bowls, bowls with grooved everted rims, shallow bowls with standing walls, and abundant conical tripod and tetrapod feet gave a new variety and elaborative treatment to the bowl as a vessel form. On the other hand, a great deal of standardization was present in the often graceful yet "astonishingly unimaginative" decoration characteristic of each type (see Shook and Kidder, 1952, p. 68). Low bowls and dishes occurred in many types, including most if not all of those given for the Preclassic in figure 3. Notable during the Late Preclassic were similarities in shape of the abundant Usulutan and Fine Red bowls. Another basic shape, the *cylinder or subcylindrical vase*, had apparently appeared fairly early at Kaminaljuyu in the form of slightly outcurved, footless "flowerpots." The Late Preclassic period saw the further development of the vase as a cylinder (fig. 9,d), normally bearing one or more pronounced horizontal moldings. Characteristically, cylinders and goblets occurred in Fine Incised and undecorated Black-brown pottery. *Special forms*, including shoe-shaped vessels, cups with tall slender tripod feet, effigies, and a wide variety of incensarios, had early occurrences and, in some cases, continued to be important throughout the Preclassic period (figs. 4–7).

Fitting the Preclassic sequence of Kaminaljuyu into a broader framework poses certain problems. We believe that the Las Charcas phase, traditionally regarded as the beginning of the central highland sequence, is approximately contemporaneous with the lowland Maya Mamom phase of Uaxactun (R. E. Smith, 1955b), i.e., falling in the early part of the Middle Preclassic period. The unusually early and distinctive Ocos

123

d

a

b

e

c

f

phase diagnostics from the Pacific coast of Guatemala are absent from both Kaminaljuyu and Uaxactun, and although pattern-burnished monochrome is reported from the central highlands in the Las Charcas and Sacatepequez phases (Brainerd, 1951, p. 77), the other characteristic of the Ecab phase in northern Yucatan—a distinctive pointed-bottomed bottle with thickened rim—is unknown. Beyond this, Las Charcas and Mamom share closely corresponding types of fired clay figurines (see Articles 5 and 20 in this volume). In form and color, Las Charcas Red-on-white closely resembles Muxanal Red-on-cream Type of the Mamom phase, whereas on the Pacific coast Conchas Fine Red-on-cream follows shortly after the Ocos phase in the La Victoria sequence and is regarded by M. D. Coe (1961, p. 81) as an import, probably from the Kaminaljuyu district. Vessel shapes shared by Las Charcas and Mamom are cuspidor-like bowls and nearly cylindrical bowls and dishes. Chicanel, the following phase of Uaxactun, shows another set of resemblances with later materials in the central highlands: labial-flanged, flaring-sided dishes (Providencia and Sacatepequez phases), and vessels with labial flange, lateral flange, lateral Z-angle, basal angle, round sides, recurving sides, outsloping sides with thickened rim, and incurving rim (Miraflores). Wares at Uaxactun and Kaminaljuyu usually differ, but the similarities in shape and occasionally combinations of attributes are impressive. M. D. Coe (1961, p. 128) presents other arguments against the exceptionally early dating

for Las Charcas which has sometimes been advanced.

Early Classic Period

In the Guatemala highlands a strong continuity existed in Preclassic-Protoclassic and Early Classic pottery. This is illustrated by difficulties experienced by earlier workers in the region. In ceramic sequences for the Alta Verapaz and Zacualpa, differences were more or less explicitly recognized between pottery having Preclassic and Early Classic characteristics, but such contrasts as did exist were felt to be outweighed by basic similarities. Accordingly, the Chama 1 and 2 "sub-periods" were grouped into a single period, "Chixoy I" (Butler, 1940). The earlier, Preclassic-like part of this we refer to in figure 2 as "Chixoy Ia." Similarly, Wauchope originally felt that the coexistence of Preclassic and Classic features at Zacualpa raised doubt as to whether the former traits should be considered holdovers or as truly contemporaneous with the typologically later ones, and a single "Balam" phase was recognized (Wauchope, 1948a, p. 29). Subsequently, however, conviction was expressed that a clear-cut Preclassic occupation must exist at Zacualpa (Wauchope, 1950, p. 242), and in figure 2 we refer to "early" (Preclassic) and "late" (Early Classic) aspects of the Balam phase. Whereas abundant horizon-markers—generally associated with the Teotihuacan culture of central Mexico—help to give the Esperanza phase of Kaminaljuyu a different cast from the Preclassic pottery complexes, the intermediate Aurora phase (Berlin,

FIG. 16—SELECTED EXAMPLES OF POTTERY, ASSIGNABLE TYPOLOGICALLY TO THE LATE CLASSIC PERIOD (TEPEU 1 EQUIVALENT)

Early Classic datings have previously been given the vessels in a–c. a,b, Nebaj. c, Zaculeu. d, Ilom. e, Chama district. f, Ratinlixul. a, Saxche Orange-polychrome tripod basal-flange bowl (after A. L. Smith, 1955d, respectively). e,f, Juleki Cream-Black-on-orange deep bowl (after *idem*, fig. 81,f). c,d, Saxche Orange-polychrome deep bowls (after Woodbury and Trik, 1953, fig. 265,s, and R. E. Smith, 1955d, respectively). e,f, Juleki Cream-polychrome cylindrical vases (courtesy, Peabody Museum, Harvard, and after Kelemen, 1943, pl. 130,b, respectively). Diameters: a, 19.2 cm.; d, 13.6 cm. Heights: b, 12.5 cm.; c, 19 cm.; e, 19 cm.; f, 21 cm.

125

1952) serves to establish a partial continuity in ceramic patterns. However, no clear-cut Protoclassic horizon, comparable to that of Holmul I in the Maya lowlands, has been isolated in the central highlands, and Aurora is grouped with Esperanza in the Early Classic period (fig. 2).

NORTHERN ZONE. Considerable homogeneity exists in Early Classic materials from Zaculeu (Atzan phase),[1v] Zacualpa (Balam),[1u] Chiche,[1g] Nebaj,[1n] and other sites. It is possible, however, that the Nebaj Early Classic should be dated relatively late in the period, as it exhibits a number of Late Classic features. As a matter of fact, cultural lag in Peten-oriented traits may be present, in varying degree, at all these sites. A soapy feel to the slip, present also in some Preclassic pottery, is noted during the Classic period in the Quiche for red, orange-red, chocolate-brown, and brown-black pottery (Wauchope, 1948b, p. 146; 1950, p. 224).

Black to black-brown pottery continued from Preclassic horizons throughout the Early Classic period. It is generally well smoothed, ranging from occasional high luster (some examples of Polished Black at Zaculeu)[1v] to velvety, medium gloss (Nebaj[1n] Fine Black). Lustrous and micaceous tendencies are noted at Zacualpa.[1u] At Chama[1f] a trend is observable from "Black" (Chixoy Ia) to "Smoked" black-brown (Chixoy Ib). Polished Brown, while well represented in the Atzan phase of Zaculeu, tended to replace Polished Black in the subsequent Chinaq materials. It would be premature, however, to suggest a general drift throughout the northern highlands from black- to brown-surfaced pottery. Black bowls, rounding to an almost vertical rim, occur in Early and Late Classic pottery, decorated with finger-dimpling below the rim or with similar decorations over the entire vessel wall (Nebaj, Zaculeu). Cylindrical tripods and other distinctive shapes also appear in the black-brown pottery. Additional slipped monochromes, varying in frequency according to site but of some importance in the Early Classic period, include red (Zacualpa, Zaculeu), orange (Zaculeu), and cream (Zacualpa).

Resist decoration was important during the Early Classic period in parts of the northern highlands. At the present time two distinctive styles may be recognized, best known from Zaculeu[1v] and Nebaj.[1n] Zaculeu Resist Painted, believed to be a local product (Woodbury and Trik, 1953, p. 197), occurs mostly on shallow bowls similar to Polished Black shapes. Tripod cylinders, one with slab feet, are among the numerous Atzan phase vessels bearing resist painting. Designs, which are boldly ornate, include: the step-and-angular scroll, generally edged by dots; stylized birds; bars; and rows of small circles, often in parallel horizontal and diagonal arrangements (fig. 10,d). Resist-painted pottery typical of the Early Classic at Nebaj is simpler; the negative design may consist entirely of irregularly scattered circles, although simple linear patterns also occur. The Nebaj type of decoration appears most frequently on basal-flange ring-stand bowls (cf. fig. 10,c).

In general, painted decoration was sporadic. Simple bands and other linear arrangements, often abrupt and angular, occur in black-on-red (Chiche,[1g] Zacualpa)[1u] (fig. 10,b). The best-represented polychrome type during the Early Classic period was, apparently, Dos Arroyos Polychrome (red-and-black-on-orange). As in the Lowland Maya Region, the basal-flange bowl was a favored Dos Arroyos form, with its variations in style including floor decoration. Occupying this position are deer, stylized fish—a popular subject at Nebaj[1n]—and, at Zaculeu,[1v] a strange dragon-like creature. Painting the interior wall of the bowl with bird and conventionalized human face (Nebaj) differs somewhat from the lowland use of rim banding, including simple line and geometric elements. Early

Classic stuccoed-and-painted pottery in the northern highlands is best known from Zaculeu. There it occurs mostly on Polished Black but was also used as a secondary coating for other wares, including polychrome and resist-decorated pottery. In contrast to the well-known patterns of Teotihuacan and Kaminaljuyu,[1nn] stucco painting from Zaculeu is not known to occur on cylindrical tripods, and motifs obviously of central Mexican inspiration were not employed.

Certain shapes have value as horizon-markers or are so distinctive that, whatever their range in time, specific cultural continuity is indicated. Comparison of these forms throughout the Guatemalan highlands as a whole is postponed until a later section (pp. 142–144, below, and figs. 5–7). For now, traits may simply be enumerated: shoe-shaped vessels (fig. 15,g); tall-footed tripod pitchers and cups (fig. 10,a); "cream pitchers" with handle, pedestal base and gutter spout; pot stands; floreros; cylindrical tripods (fig. 10,f), often with slab feet; basal-flange bowls, with ring-stand or tripod supports (figs. 10,b; 15,f); tripod censers, often with a rudimentary flange or basal molding (fig. 20,c); "duck pot" covers, probably for censers (fig. 12,e); and two-part effigies.

WESTERN ZONE. Early Classic materials, while not fixed stratigraphically, are occasionally reported from the western highlands. Cylindrical tripods are especially diagnostic. Slab-leg cylinders with stamped panels supposedly come from Utatlan,[1ee] as well as a typically Esperanza-like pitcher, although this provenience may be seriously questioned. Tripod cylinders with squat bodies but notably tall supports are said to be from Panajachel,[1z] decorative features including vertical fluting, resist painting, incised braid band, and basal freize of appliquéd death's-heads (fig. 15,b). Another group of cylindrical tripod vessels is believed to come from Salcaja and to date from the early part of the Early Classic

period (Kidder, 1954). These have dark red to brown slip with low-to-medium gloss and are characterized by relatively large, often open-bottomed feet; double moldings below rim and sometimes at base; sharp basal molding; and post-finish incising repeated on opposite sides of the vessel in a complex, often curvilinear style (fig. 15,a). One of this group of five tripod cylinders has mammiform feet. A typically highland form of basal-flange bowl, with flaring sides, tripod supports and only vaguely convex base, also occurs in collections from the Salcaja district. [1bb]

CENTRAL ZONE. Two Early Classic phases, Aurora and Esperanza, are recognized at Kaminaljuyu.[1nn] The earlier ceramic complex, Aurora, is distinguished by the following elements: abundant stuccoed tetrapods; abundant Crude Black-brown bowls (present in Esperanza but with the greatest frequency in early tombs); stuccoed Usulutan (also present in the early Esperanza tomb, B-I); tetrapod incensarios, again apparently more frequent in Aurora; and tetrapod basal-flange bowls (Berlin, 1952). Largely or entirely absent from Aurora are important Esperanza traits—Thin Orange, cylindrical tripods, and Peten-like polychrome. The following discussion relates specifically to the much better known Esperanza phase (Kidder, Jennings, and Shook, 1946).

Esperanza pottery taken as a whole shows a marked decline from Late Preclassic wares of Kaminaljuyu in excellence of finish and variety of form. This was accompanied, however, by a shift to technologically superior pastes, which were harder and more durable. Incipient vitrification is indicated in the abundant, cleanly fracturing Esperanza Flesh-color ware. Coarse brown pottery was also frequent, but it is in the presence of numerous vessels, imported or showing the impact of foreign styles, that the ceramic assemblage of Esperanza takes on particular chronological significance. For, as revealed by the

127

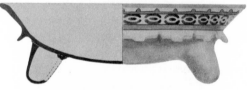

128

contents of several tombs, two sets of influences impinged simultaneously on Kaminaljuyu, one from Peten-like cultures in the Lowland Maya Region and the other from Teotihuacan and ceramically related cultures of central Mexico. A third set of influences, of unknown origin, is suggested by a group of fine-paste black and ivory bowls.

Aside from a red-painted Usulutan tetrapod bowl, which may relate to the Aurora phase, known examples of polychrome are restricted to basal-flange bowls. Two types, "Polychrome A" and "B," are recognized (Kidder, Jennings, and Shook, 1946), there being six vessels of the former and a single specimen of the latter. Both types have ring-bases, but Polychrome B is considerably more shallow and also differs in the presence of a short, thin flange and squared lip (flanges in Polychrome A are broad and downslanting, lips being rounded). In these respects, as in color combination and dot outlining, Polychrome A resembles Actuncan Orange-polychrome Type in the Lowland Maya Region (a Tzakol 1 diagnostic at Uaxactun), the only attribute suggesting lateness being a cream underslip. Polychrome B, on the other hand, corresponds precisely to Dos Arroyos Orange-polychrome Type (Tzakol 2–3). It is believed that Mound A, which contained most of the orange-polychrome basal-flange bowls with Actuncan affinities, was started earlier than Mound B, which yielded one Actuncan-like and one Dos Arroyos vessel, and that interments at Mound B continued later than at Mound A (Kidder, Jennings, and Shook, 1946, pp. 93, 94). The relative

sequence of the mounds as a whole, therefore, is consistent with the temporal position of the two polychrome types in the Peten. Moreover, the Actuncan Orange-polychrome-like bowl from Tomb B-I is stratigraphically earlier than the Dos Arroyos specimen from the Tomb B-II. However, because of the over-all ceramic uniformity, the opinion is voiced that the life of the two mounds covered "no more than a century, perhaps as little as fifty years" (Kidder, Jennings, and Shook, 1946, p. 94).[7]

Stuccoed-and-painted pottery from the Esperanza tombs was abundant and often elaborately executed. Radically different styles, decorative techniques and shapes are present. Within the large group of stucco-painted tripod cylinders, "Mayoid" and "Teotihuacanoid" examples have been recognized, as well as a few suspected imports from Teotihuacan (Kidder, Jennings, and Shook, 1946, pp. 228–29). A number of black and ivory carved hemispherical bowls were also stuccoed, in addition to one of the Actuncan-like Orange-polychrome basal-flange bowls. The latter is a particularly significant piece, for the style and motifs of the painting on the secondary stucco coat

---

[7] Complexities in the dating of "Polychrome A" and "B" are further indicated by the temporal position of the two types at Copan. At the latter site, the Actuncan-like form, "A," existed side by side with Dos Arroyos Orange-polychrome ("B") in the beginning of the Early Classic period but considerably outnumbered Dos Arroyos in the second part of the Early Classic (Longyear, 1952, pp. 26, 29). Chronologically, this relative frequency is the reverse of that indicated in the tombs of Kaminaljuyu and at Uaxactun.

FIG. 17—SELECTED EXAMPLES OF POTTERY FROM THE LATE CLASSIC PERIOD

a–f, Tepeu 2 equivalent. a,b, Chipoc. c, Unknown provenience. d, Nebaj. e, Chajcar. f, Zacualpa (?). g, Antigua district. a, Black deep bowl with monkey-face frieze and plano-relief medallions (after R. E. Smith, 1952, fig. 11,g). b, Classic resist tripod dish (after idem, fig. 17,h). c, Brown-on-cream cylindrical bowl (after idem, fig. 14,j). d, Sacatel Cream-polychrome terraced basal-flange bowl (after A. L. Smith and Kidder, 1951, fig. 82,b,c). e, Modeled-carved high-necked vase (after Dieseldorff, 1926–33, vol. 1, fig. 180). f, Incised cream vase (after Kelemen, 1943, pl. 135,b). g, Incised black cylindrical vase (after A. Kidder and Samayoa Chinchilla, 1959, pl. 22). Diameters: a, 16.8 cm.; b, 23.2 cm.; c, 13.6 cm.; d, 32.5 cm. Heights: f, 12 cm.; g, 20 cm.

are clearly in the tradition of Teotihuacan, whereas the vessel shape and original polychrome decoration were both in the lowland Maya tradition (Kidder, Jennings, and Shook, 1946, p. 236, fig. 207,*a*). Motifs of the "Mayoid" group include the Serpent X and shell symbols, bare feet, rounded nose ornaments, and pendant napkin-like objects held in the hand. The style is essentially that of the Maya lowlands; the cylinders are tall and provided with covers. Among the "Teotihuacanoid" motifs are butterfly deities, flowered or noded speech-scrolls, droplets, the tri-mountain and serpent-eye symbols, sandals, and large covering capes. A horizontal row of nucleated discs appears in the costume; the featherwork is flat and symmetrically massed. Notwithstanding the impressive differences in decoration, the "Teotihuacanoid" cylindrical tripod vessels are, once again, tall and provided with covers (fig. 15,c). In contrast, the cylinders suspected to be of Teotihuacan origin are squat with openwork slab or round-bottomed feet and are without covers. A basal band of appliquéd heads, comb-and-bar elements, or repeated triangles is a regular feature. Designs include serpent-eye medallions, cheek-painting, droplets, bands of pendant hooks, and the face of the god Tlaloc. Plano-relief cylinders, as well as those with painted stucco decoration, comprise this presumedly imported group. Another group of stuccoed pottery consists of carved vessels, usually hemispherical bowls but including a cylinder tripod, with beautifully smoothed ivory or black surfaces and apparently untempered paste. These were normally given a thin maroon hematite undercoat and either stuccoed and painted in pastel colors or covered with green stucco. A similar maroon sizing was placed on several effigies prior to stuccoing. It is of no little interest that, in the Late Preclassic period, a similarly colored undercoat was used prior to stuccoing and that the Miraflores stucco was argillaceous, as

was that of at least some of the Esperanza black and ivory vessels. This is apparently in contrast to the majority of Esperanza stuccoes, which seem to have been calcareous in nature rather than of clay composition (Kidder and Shepard, 1944; Shepard *in* Kidder, Jennings, and Shook, 1946).

Selected pottery types and vessel shapes of the Esperanza phase are given in figures 3–7. Of those not already discussed, Thin Orange (fig. 10,*h*) is of special importance, for this ware was abundant in the tomb furnishings and, because of its distinctive technological and stylistic attributes, can be assigned a single center of manufacture, presumably somewhere in Puebla. Effigy vessels and simple-silhouette ring-base bowls were common, the latter closely resembling a frequent Esperanza Flesh-color shape. Specialized forms in other wares, in addition to those previously mentioned, include miniature vessels; "cream pitchers" —almost universally present in the important tombs (fig. 10,*g*); a pot stand; floreros, one modeled into an anthropomorphic Tlaloc with incensario characteristics; other Tlaloc effigy jars; a wide variety of incense-burner forms, with anthropomorphic figures sometimes serving as stand or cover, with gramophone-shaped covers, and with other flamboyant elaborations; two-part human effigies divided at the waist (fig. 15,*e*); and an effigy whistling vessel (fig. 15,*d*). Subspherical black vessels bore distinctive, post-finish incised designs, but decoration of the Esperanza pottery was largely achieved by effigy modeling or painting on stuccoed surfaces. Only a handful of polychrome vessels have been found, although these have proved to be exceptionally important for cross-dating. Significantly, in view of the abundance of resist-painting elsewhere in the highlands, this negative technique is almost completely unknown at Kaminaljuyu in the Esperanza and subsequent phases (Smith and Kidder, 1951, p. 67).

Late Classic Period

In the better-surveyed portions of the highlands, lying in the Northern and Central Zones, Late Classic sites were abundant, indicating the existence of a large population. Yet over the southern portions of the highlands the pottery of this period lacked strongly marked characteristics. In part this may reflect a reduction in elaboration such as might be brought about by increased standardization or "mass production" on a local level. Also partially responsible for this situation may be a lessened importance of the burial cult, with diminished interest in providing the dead with numerous grave furnishings, including luxury items which may have been imported from over a wide area. Perhaps a general slackening of trade was involved. In the northern highlands, contacts were maintained with the Lowland Maya Region, but elsewhere the cultures appear to have become relatively isolated, free at least of influences stemming from this source.

NORTHERN ZONE. Ceramic patterns in the northern highlands provide important exceptions to the general reconstruction which has just been advanced. Not only did this zone remain within the Peten diffusion sphere but burials continued to be well stocked, and in the Chama[1f] district one of the great polychrome styles of all Mesoamerica emerged. This is best known on footless cylindrical vases, although polychrome globular vessels with high straight necks were also frequent. A variety of the Juleki Cream-polychrome Type, which at Uaxactun is an element of the Tepeu 1 ceramic complex, is present in the Chama 3 climax of naturalistic figure painting. Features include framing bands of alternating black and white chevrons, careful brushwork with accurate anatomical detail, richly costumed human figures in vivid scenic compositions, and grotesque mythological beings such as the bat god

(fig. 16,e,f). Sites other than Chama showing much the same complex of stylistic traits occur along the Chixoy drainage.

The Chipoc phase, identified farther to the east in the Alta Verapaz, perhaps dates from slightly later in the Late Classic period. A number of types are shared with the Chixoy drainage, but a more complete ceramic assemblage is known at Chipoc,[1j] utilitarian as well as decorated pottery being abundant. Sherds from strap-handled jars and plain red vessels are numerous. Incised pottery is well represented, especially on orange-on-cream cylinders and cream (or cream-and-black)-on-Mikado brown cylinders (fig. 21,d). Resist painting was popular, usually appearing in simple geometric arrangements, and occurred mostly on tripod basal-flange bowls but also on cylinders and tripod dishes (fig. 17,b). Modeling, used mostly in connection with other decorative techniques, especially took the form of a monkey-face frieze (fig. 17,a), while the monkey also appeared in incised and painted decoration. Important Chipoc motifs included bending-forward seated personages with exaggerated, gesturing hands (cf. fig. 17,c), a thick double scroll, and the conch shell.

In the later Seacal tomb,[1r] Tepeu 3–like pottery included a flaring-sided tripod plate with notched sharp Z-angle, which occurred with a resist-painted cylinder, barrel-shaped vase, and ring-stand cylindrical vases. An incised cylindrical vase from the tomb depicts dancing individuals, a late pose in Classic sculpture from the Lowland Maya Region. Excellent examples of modeled-carving occur at Chajcar[1d] (fig. 17,e), and back in the Chixoy drainage, Chama 4 developments also witnessed the rise of fine naturalistic carving, often in panels on cylindrical vases, in the modeled-carved technique (Pabellon Modeled-carved Type of Altar Fine-orange Group).

Outside the Alta Verapaz, north highland sites remained in contact with the

132

Maya lowlands but without achieving vigorous climax styles. Saxche Orange-polychrome (fig. 16,c) and Uacho Black-on-Orange cylinders and deep bowls (fig. 16,b), types with a Tepeu 1 dating at Uaxactun, appear occasionally at Zaculeu[1v] and Nebaj;[1n] also at the latter site occurs a red-and-black-on-orange tripod bowl, bearing glyph banding on the inner wall, which is similar to the Tepeu 1 Saxche Orange-polychrome Type (fig. 16,a). At both of these highland sites, the types are known to occur in tombs containing other ceramic materials distinguished by strongly Early Classic features; datings in the Early Classic period have, therefore, traditionally been given. We believe, however, that the Nebaj pieces, which are found in the sealed-off entrance to the tomb rather than in the tomb itself, may be considered Late rather than Early Classic in date as well as type (Smith and Kidder, 1951, fig. 36). The evidence for late deposition is less clear-cut for the cylindrical vase from Zaculeu (Woodbury and Trik, 1953, fig. 41; Lathrap, 1957, p. 43). Even if the burials are considered to be terminal Early Classic, cultural lag, one way or the other, may be involved. Woodbury argues for cultural precocity in the northern part of the highlands, although Kidder, whose view we share, rejects the idea of the development of red-and-black-on-orange polychrome in the highlands because this color combination is much more typical of lowland Maya ceramics and because polychrome decoration of any sort was little practiced in the highlands during Early Classic times

(Woodbury and Trik, 1953, p. 193; Smith and Kidder, 1951, pp. 63–64). Should Late Classic polychrome styles in this color combination have first developed in the northern highlands, the subsequent diffusion must have been strangely selective, for very few of these and other abundant Peten-like pieces appear to have penetrated much south of Coban, Joyabaj, Zacualpa and Zaculeu, or the general region of the Sierra de las Minas and Chuacus range (R. E. Smith, 1955b, p. 8).

A number of traits, established in the northern highlands during Early Classic times, continued in modified form into the Late Classic period. Among these were black to black-brown pottery (declining at Zaculeu,[1v] Nebaj[1n] and Chama),[1f] stucco decoration (declining at Zaculeu), resist painting (declining at Zaculeu but making its appearance at Chama), and the basal-flange bowl. In the latter, a slight shift from ring-base to hollow tripod supports seems to be indicated over the northern highlands, although early tripod examples and late ring-base forms do occur. A sequence within the basal-flange bowls from ring-base polychromes to resist-painted tripods is pronounced in the Alta Verapaz.

WESTERN ZONE. Little can be said about ceramic developments in the western highlands during the Late Classic period. However, from Finca El Paraiso,[1aa] at the southern margin of the highlands, comes Robles Plumbate, vitrified pottery which may be transitional to the San Juan and Tohil Plumbate Groups (Shepard, 1948, pp. 125–26). Squat, collared jars and modified

FIG. 18—SELECTED EXAMPLES OF PLUMBATE WARE

a,b, Robles Plumbate Group (Late Classic–Early Postclassic transition). c–h, Tohil Plumbate Group (Early Postclassic). a, Paraiso. b, Tajumulco. c, Chipal. d, Samac. e, Zacualpa (?). f, San Andres Sajcabaja. g,h, Unknown provenience (Alta Verapaz). a, Miniature effigy vessel (courtesy, Peabody Museum, Harvard). b, Stamped jar (after Shepard, 1948, fig. 12,n). c, Anthropomorphic effigy (after A. Kidder and Samayoa Chinchilla, 1959, pl. 85). d, Groove-incised tripod dish (after R. E. Smith, 1952, fig. 26,b). e, Grooved-and-incised pyriform tripod (after Shepard, 1948, fig. 11,j). f, Lamp chimney (after Shepard, 1948, fig. 8,h). g, Bearded-man head effigy (after Dieseldorff, 1926–33, vol. 3, fig. 32). h, Pedestal-base bust effigy (after idem, fig. 33). Diameter: d, 24 cm. Heights: b, 12.8 cm.; c, 18 cm.; e, 18.4 cm.; f, 19.9 cm.; g, about 15 cm.

cylinders diverge from the earlier San Juan Plumbate, while effigies modeled in low relief, band-incising employing conventionalized animal heads, and shoulder-stamping (fig. 21,e) differ from the distinctive Tohil approach to effigy modeling and incising. Specialized effigy forms occur, including miniatures (fig. 18,a) and bells in the shape of a human head. Robles Plumbate apparently occurs on a horizon equivalent to Tepeu 3, at the close of the Late Classic period.

CENTRAL ZONE. San Juan Plumbate, although extremely rare, is the "index fossil" for the Amatle ceramic complex, relating it to the Magdalena phase of San Agustin Acasaguastlan and to the San Juan phase of El Baul (Smith and Kidder, 1943; Thompson, 1948; Kidder, 1948). Differences from the better-known Tohil Plumbate exist in paste, shape, and decoration, although the characteristic slip and surface treatment are the same. San Juan pastes are distinguished by their ferruginous nature and contain sparse flakes of volcanic ash (not noted in Tohil Plumbate) as well as a greater amount of minute opaline inclusions (Shepard, 1948, pp. 93, 123–25). In striking contrast to Tohil, effigy vessels are absent, the tall cylinder with direct or slightly outcurving rim being the dominant form. Spiral or horizontal grooving, incised curvilinear patterns, and appliquéd buttons constitute a fundamentally different approach to decoration. Another important trade ware is Tiquisate, from the Pacific coast. Tiquisate pottery, which had Early Classic beginnings, is cream to beige in color; a wide range of shapes and decorative techniques occur, the latter including incising, modeling, grooving, and stamping.

The Amatle and Pamplona ceramic complexes, undifferentiated stratigraphically but apparently sequent, are characterized by the abundance of "hard ware"—thin and semivitrified, seemingly the successor to Esperanza Flesh-color. The pottery is well made but simple, slip and painting being uncommon. The most frequent decorated types are Tejar, ornamented with appliquéd and reed-impressed buttons, and "Squiggle," with incised wavy lines beneath the rim. Tejar may largely be restricted to Amatle. Large basins with outward-turning rims are numerous, small flaring-sided bowls seem best represented in Amatle, and spiked incense burners are abundant in Pamplona deposits. Other common forms are tall-necked jars, two-handled "comales," and cylindrical vases (fig. 17,g). An unevenly applied, thin white slip is sometimes present, permitting the brick red color of the paste to show through as a faint flush. Amatle Polychrome bears simple rectilinear elements, such as bands and triangles, in white and red designs on orange or buff; shapes consist of tripod or pedestal-base bowls (fig. 11,c).

Early Postclassic Period

One of the most important horizon-markers in all of Mesoamerican prehistory, Tohil Plumbate, was extensively traded over much of the Guatemala highlands and penetrated far beyond the Maya Area. Yet this pottery has rarely been found in the Central Zone, in spite of the comparatively intensive work done there and the fact that it lies between the two major centers from which the Plumbate has been recovered, southwestern Guatemala and El Salvador. The Early Postclassic was ushered in on the heels of profound changes. The period seems to have begun with or soon after the abandonment of Kaminaljuyu, and to judge from the result of Shook's survey (1952b) a population decrease took place over the entire Central Altiplano, only 1 per cent of the known datable sites being occupied in the Early Postclassic. The collapse of the great Classic centers of the Peten and Usumacinta had also taken place, and the northern highlands, in particular, must have been affected by this upheaval. Although the population seems to have remained stable in the north—39 per cent of the ceramically datable sites having been occupied in the Late Classic compared to 37 per cent in the Early Postclassic (A. L. Smith, 1955)—polychrome pottery of lowland Maya affiliation no longer formed part of the ceramic complex. Instead, to judge by the popularity of Tohil Plumbate, the north highlanders looked south and west for major ceramic imports and inspiration.

NORTHERN ZONE. Tohil Plumbate (fig. 18,c-h) takes its name from the Tohil phase of Zacualpa.[1u] The pottery is also well represented in the Qankyak phase of Zaculeu,[1v] Chixoy III at Chipal,[1i] and, indeed, throughout the Northern Zone. Features have been detailed in Shepard's (1948) great study. Characteristics of the various Plumbate groups, including Tohil, are single or double slips with high iron content, fired under reducing conditions at unusually high temperatures (ca. 950°C.) to produce a hard, lustrous, vitrified surface, dominated by pale and olive-gray colors but with softer oxidized areas of orange or reddish-brown. A metallic iridescence is not uncommon. Tohil pastes, nonferruginous and tempered with fine feldspar, differ from those of the earlier San Juan Plumbate. Vessel shapes are dominated by the jar and pyriform vase, tripod bowls being a much more rarely encountered form. Effigies are very frequent, including animals, birds, and anthropomorphic subjects, the latter occurring as head vessels, bust effigies, and entire figures. Among the anthropomorphic figures, the occurrence of Mexican deities—including Tlaloc, Xipe Totec, and perhaps such gods as Xochipilli, Xiuhtecutli, and Ehecatl—is of great interest, suggesting a non-Maya origin for the potters. Sketchily incised abstract design is based on the simplified scroll and, like a number of other Tohil Plumbate features, shows affiliations with the Silho Fine-orange Group (Shepard, 1948, pp. 133–37; R. E. Smith, 1957,

pp. 137–38). Resemblances of a more generalized nature extend to Nicoya Polychrome (Lothrop, 1926b, p. 115; Shepard, 1948, pp. 137–39).

Fine Orange Ware (fig. 19,a) was of less frequent occurrence. Pedestal-base and tripod pyriform vessels at Zaculeu, bearing plano-relief decoration, have been identified as "Z" Fine Orange, i.e. of the Balancan Fine-orange Group (Woodbury and Trik, 1953, figs. 82, 83) but may belong to a transitional type, between Balancan and the later Silho ("X") Group (R. E. Smith, 1958, pp. 155, 157). Fine Orange of Chixoy III occurs chiefly at Kixpek, in both the Altar (Cedro Gadrooned, Pabellon Modeled-carved) and Silho (Pocboc Gouged-incised) Ceramic Groups. A transitional date (Tepeu 3), between the Late Classic and Postclassic, would be given for Altar ("Y") Fine-orange in the Maya lowlands, although at Kixpek an association with Tohil Plumbate is indicated (Butler, 1940, p. 264). The Kixpek association of Silho Fine-orange with Plumbate is, however, a common one. Virtual identity not only in design but in paste, as determined by neutron activation of elements in the clay, has been found to occur in shallow, round-sided Pabellon Modeled-carved bowls from Kixpek and Piedras Negras (Sayre, Murrenhoff, and Weick, 1958). These vessels were clearly intrusive at the latter site, where they appear to be restricted to the Tamay Ceramic Complex, more or less coetaneous with the cessation of organized hierarchal activities. Fine Orange is also reported for Zacualpa, although one specimen is actually of Tiquisate Ware and the other definitely not Fine Orange (Lothrop, 1936, figs. 77 and 76, respectively).

Additional trade pieces and diagnostics occur, although in some cases dating is not completely clear cut. "Mixtec-type" tripod censers, with perforated walls and one leg serving as a long handle, appear in Early Postclassic contexts in the Alta Verapaz,

FIG. 19—SELECTED EXAMPLES OF POTTERY FROM THE EARLY POSTCLASSIC AND LATE POSTCLASSIC PERIODS

a,b, Early Postclassic. *c–e,* Late Postclassic. *a,* Uaxac Canal. *b,* Tzanjuyu (?) or Zacualpa (?) districts. *c–e,* Zaculeu (Xinabahul phase). *a,* Kilikan Composite Type, Silho Fine-orange Group (after Seler, 1901, fig. 23). *b,* Nicoya Polychrome (?) effigy tripod (after Kelemen, 1943, pl. 145,*d*).

c, White-on-red jar (after Woodbury and Trik, 1953, fig. 248,*e*). *d,* White-on-red tripod bowl with effigy-head feet (after *idem,* fig. 248,*g*). *e,* Cinnamon globular jar (after *idem,* fig. 249,*l*). Heights: *a,* 25 cm.; *b,* 20 cm.; *c,* 28 cm. Diameters: *d,* 28 cm.; *e,* (including handles), 28 cm.

Zacualpa,[1u] and Zaculeu[1v] (fig. 12,*h*). A Nicoya Polychrome tripod bowl, presumably of Nicaraguan or Costa Rican origin, was associated in a Zaculeu grave with two Tohil Plumbate jars and two tripod bowls having effigy-head supports. Another possible Nicoya Polychrome vessel, an effigy jar, was present with Tohil Plumbate in a Samac tomb.[1q] Tripod bowls with effigy-head supports were widespread and abundant, the hollow, usually moldmade feet occurring in the shape of grotesque alligator and other animal heads, or rarely those of humans. Although it is true that the form appears to have been introduced prior to Tohil Plumbate in the Alta Verapaz, Zacualpa, and perhaps Zaculeu, and to have survived into the Late Postclassic at various hilltop sites, the effigy-head tripods were, predominantly, an Early Postclassic trait. Cylindrical-footed tripod plates, with flaring walls and flat base, are associated with a number of Qankyak diagnostics at Zaculeu (fig. 11,*d*). This form occurs on the same time level at Tajumulco,[1cc] outside the Northern Zone. In the Peten, however, the cylindrical-footed tripod plate is diagnostic of Tepeu 2, and in the Alta Verapaz this shape, like the effigy-head tripod, is present in Chipal 1 materials, perhaps datable as Late Classic.[8]

Although horizon-markers were numerous in the northern highlands during the Early Postclassic period, additional wares and decorative devices were not strongly or distinctively elaborated. Several sherds of Brown-and-black-on-cream Polychrome were recovered at Zaculeu,[1v] apparently from Qankyak deposits, whereas other polychrome types occurred rarely at Zacualpa[1u] and in the Chixoy. Simple linear designs and occasional stylized life forms appear in red on an orange, cream, or buff slip at Zaculeu and Zacualpa (fig. 11,*g*). Resist

[8] Butler's revised Chixoy chronology would move Chipal 1 materials upward in time, although a Late Classic dating for the forms in question is apparently still favored (Butler, 1959, pp. 28, 31).

painting continued in the Alta Verapaz but was absent from Zaculeu and, perhaps effectively, from Zacualpa. Stucco decoration, however, continued in use at Zaculeu, where it is present on four Qankyak phase pedestal vases, three of them with double bottoms (fig. 11,*f*). At Zacualpa, heavy-walled miniatures were a Tohil phase diagnostic, as was "tile ware"—a dense, porous paste comparable to that of a modern flowerpot, usually occurring in unslipped bowls and jars.

WESTERN ZONE. It is an open question if Tohil Plumbate had its origin in the western highlands, but such a possibility is consistent with several lines of evidence, which have been discussed at greater length by Shepard (1948, pp. 115–22). Plumbate was unusually abundant at Tajumulco, 41 vessels, more than that of all other wares combined, being excavated by Dutton and Hobbs (1943). Pottery was found in 19 of 21 graves at Tajumulco, Plumbate occurring in 15 of these. Plumbate sherds were also frequent at the site. Compared to Tohil Plumbate in other collections, an unusually large number of the Tajumulco finds were bowls. Perhaps effigy jars, as a favored form, were more likely to be traded in quantity from their source than were bowls, the latter serving for comparatively localized consumption. Moreover, Plumbate at Tajumulco appears often to have been of inferior workmanship, and as Shepard (1948, p. 121) points out, "a disproportionately high percentage of poor vessels having little trade value . . . would be expected in the region of manufacture." Tempering materials of common wares at Tamjumulco are different from the temper of Tohil Plumbate—evidence that Tajumulco itself was not the center of manufacture. However, two sherds of thick-walled red ware from the site bear a rock temper which cannot be distinguished from the tempering material of Plumbate (Shepard, 1948, p. 122). Among other possibilities, this might suggest that Tajumulco was

138

close enough to the source of Tohil Plumbate to have received both Plumbate and utilitarian pottery in trade. Surface samples and private collections examined by Shook have shown Plumbate to be abundant in the greater Tajumulco district, apparently concentrated in the Cutzulchima and Naranjo valleys and fanning out from these drainage systems over the Pacific slope and coastal plain (Shook, 1947, p. 180; Shepard, 1948, p. 112). Not far to the southeast, Finca Paraiso[1aa] has yielded Robles Plumbate, which is probably ancestral to Tohil, and a few Plumbate specimens from Tajumulco itself show Robles and San Juan characteristics (fig. 18,b; Shepard, 1948, pp. 117–20).

In addition to Tohil Plumbate, Tajumulco[1cc] shared numerous features with various sites in the northern highlands during the Early Postclassic period. Among these were linear painting in red on a surface ranging from orange to buff; black, red, and red-on-buff effigy-head tripod bowls with convex base; red-and-buff cylindrical-footed flat-base tripod bowls; "Mixtec-type" perforated-walled censers with a well-modeled effigy forming the long leg; red cylindrical pedestal vases with double bottom and a hollow human head modeled a short distance below the rim; and Pocboc Gouged-incised Type, Silho Fine-orange Group. Comparisons were close with many sites, all of the above traits, with the possible exception of Silho Fine-orange, being known from the Qankyak phase of Zaculeu.[1v]

Several sites in the Atitlan basin, including Chuitinamit[1w] and Tzanjuyu,[1dd] have yielded Early Postclassic materials. Present are Tohil Plumbate, possible Nicoya Polychrome (fig. 19,b), effigy-head tripod redware (Tzanjuyu), linear painting in red, and perforated censer or "steaming" vessels. Incised Red-on-white, a common type at Chuitinamit which Lothrop (1933, p. 95) did not find elsewhere in the Atitlan district, occurs in the form of flat-based tripod bowls with cylindrical legs—a horizon diagnostic—and bears gouged-and-incised panels of interlocking frets and other devices (fig. 21,f). A similar style was found on a Qankyak phase bowl from Zaculeu (Woodbury and Trik, 1953, fig. 81,b).

CENTRAL ZONE. As previously indicated, the Early Postclassic (Ayampuc) horizon is poorly represented in the central highlands. Tohil Plumbate is recorded at perhaps a half-dozen locations in the zone (Shepard, 1948, p. 108; Wauchope, 1948a, pp. 144–45; Shook, 1952b, p. 36; Kidder, 1961, p. 569). Associated ceramic materials are, by and large, unknown.

Late Postclassic Period

Although distinctive horizon-markers exist, the major criterion for Late Postclassic pottery is its post-Plumbate temporal position. The term "Protohistoric" has sometimes been used for this period (e.g., A. L. Smith, 1955), but with only partial justification, for over the highlands as a whole the detailed analyses have not been made which would permit associations of specific pottery complexes with particular ethnic groups. The Guatemala highlands offer an

FIG. 20—SELECTED EXAMPLES OF INCENSE BURNERS, VARIOUS PERIODS

a–c, Early Classic. d,e, Late Classic. f, Postclassic. a,b, Zaculeu (Atzan phase). c,d,f, Nebaj. e, Zarzal. a, Effigy pedestal incensario with modified hourglass shape (after Woodbury and Trik, 1953, fig. 256,d). b, Ladle censer with effigy handle (after idem, fig. 258,l,l'). c, Tripod incense burner with basal molding (after A. L. Smith and Kidder, 1951, fig. 77,e). d, Flat-sided, flat-bottomed effigy censer (after idem, fig. 80,d). e, Double-chambered effigy incensario (photo, Milwaukee Public Museum). f, Tripod effigy censer with vertical side flanges (after A. L. Smith and Kidder, 1951, fig. 79,a). Diameters: a, 29 cm.; b, (bowl only), 22 cm.; c, 33.7 cm.; e, (top), 30 cm. Heights: d, 30.5 cm.; f, 24.5 cm.

139

FIG. 21—SELECTED POTSHERDS, VARIOUS PERIODS

a–c, Preclassic. *d,* Late Classic. *e,* Late Classic–Early Postclassic transition. *f–j,* Postclassic. *a,* Kaminaljuyu (Las Charcas style). *b,* Kaminaljuyu (Miraflores style). *c,* Kaminaljuyu (Providencia or Miraflores phase). *d,* Chipoc (Tepeu 2 equivalent). *e,* Paraiso. *f,* Chuitinamit. *g–i,* Zaculeu (Xinabahul phase). *j,* Unknown provenience (Late Postclassic). *a,* Modeled effigy incensario prong (after Borhegyi, 1950b, fig. 5,*f*). *b,* Rim-head effigy (after Borhegyi, 1950b, fig. 4,*h*). *c,* Coarse Incised Black-brown sherd. *d,* Incised Cream-on-Mikado brown sherd (after R. E. Smith, 1952, fig. 15,*v*). *e,* Stamped jar shoulder, Robles Plumbate Group. *f,* Gouged-and-incised dichrome tripod dish fragment (red and white) (after Lothrop, 1933, fig. 60,*d*). *g,* Mold-impressed ladle fragment (after Woodbury and Trik, 1953, fig. 250,*g*). *h,i,* Chinautla Polychrome sherds (after *idem,* fig. 249,*d,e,* respectively). *j,* Chinautla Polychrome effigy handle. (*c,e,j,* courtesy, Peabody Museum, Harvard.)

140

exceptionally fertile field for the direct historical approach; and when centers of manufacture, regional varieties, and the relative frequency of certain widespread ceramic types are better understood, it should be possible to relate a number of ceramic assemblages to definite socio-cultural groups.

NORTHERN ZONE. White-on-red pottery has been found repeatedly in Late Postclassic fortified hilltop sites, and in recognition of this association the name Fortress White-on-red has been adopted (Woodbury and Trik, 1953, p. 173). Tripod bowls, some with effigy-head supports, and tall-necked jars are the principal vessel forms (fig. 19,d,c). Broad-line and fine-line styles, the latter characterized by curvilinear designs, radiating lines and the frequent use of dots, have been recognized at Zaculeu,[1v] the conquest period capital of the Mam, where the type is a Xinabahul phase diagnostic. In the Alta Verapaz, however, Butler (1940) reports "White Line on Red" from the Late Classic through Late Postclassic periods (Chixoy II–IV). A Chixoy III (Early Postclassic) pedestal-base bowl differs from standard White-on-red shapes known to the west and south, although tightly coiled scrolls springing from a field of concentric circles constitute a typical design (Butler, 1940, fig. 24,f).

Chinautla Polychrome, the second major diagnostic of Late Postclassic pottery in the Guatemala highlands, was apparently less well represented in the Northern Zone than to the south, although some of the Yaqui phase polychrome jars from Zacualpa[1u] appear to be affiliated. One of the jars, reportedly from Zacualpa, depicts skulls, crossbones, and celestial eyes in a manner strongly reminiscent of the Mexican codices (Lothrop, 1936, fig. 30). Late Postclassic jars, polychrome and unslipped, were often used to hold cremations.

WESTERN ZONE. Diagnostics are in part similar to those already mentioned for the northern highlands. White-on-red occurred abundantly at Utatlan,[1ee] stronghold of the Quiche Indians at the time of the conquest, and at Chuitinamit,[1w] 16th-century capital of the Tzutuhil. Also present at Chuitinamit and Utatlan, though apparently in smaller quantities, was Chinautla Polychrome or a closely related red-and-black-on-white type. Wauchope's excavations at Utatlan suggest that White-on-red may have slightly preceded the polychrome. Moldmade ladle censers were well represented at Utatlan, apparently extending, on the Late Postclassic horizon, to Zacualpa[1u] and Zaculeu[1v] in the north (fig. 21,g) and eastward into the Central Zone. Utatlan's resemblances to central highlands ceramics is strengthened by the presence of "micaceous ware," which occurred in the form of strap-handled jars and flat, shallow plates or dishes.

CENTRAL ZONE. White-on-red was apparently less abundant in the central highlands than to the north and west. Wauchope (1949) found this type less common at the Cakchiquel capital of Iximche than at the Quiche center, Utatlan, whereas Shook's ceramic diagnostics for the Chinautla phase of the Central Altiplano appear not to include the type (Shook, 1952b). White and red designs painted on a buff ground were, however, present. Especially abundant and diagnostic was Chinautla Polychrome, with red and black decoration on a white surface, which ranges to gray or buff—a pottery that constituted the greatest percentage of sherds obtained at the type site of Chinautla.[1ii] At the Spanish conquest, this site lay in Pokoman territory. Chinautla Polychrome was well-represented in other Late Postclassic sites of the Central Zone. The type has been found in a burial associated with the bones of a horse, leading to the nickname "Horse Polychrome" and indicating its survival into the Spanish period (Kidder, 1961, p. 569). Somewhat similar red-on-buff and white-on-red jars are produced today in the modern pottery-making center of Chinautla, close to the aboriginal ruins, and are widely traded in the Guatemala highlands (R. E. Smith, 1949a; McBryde, 1947). Jars with strap handles were common in the aboriginal pottery, these appendages sometimes being modeled to represent jaguar heads (fig. 21,*j*). Parallel linear designs in red and black were characteristic, often appearing in a triangular arrangement (fig. 21,*h,i*); rows of triangles, solid or filled with dots, formed other frequently employed designs.

DEVELOPMENTAL PATTERNS IN VESSEL FORMS AND DECORATIVE TECHNIQUES

Different patterns of development are to be observed in Guatemala highland pottery. Certain modes of form or decoration are sufficiently restricted in time to be diagnostic of phase or period, while other features, of greater duration, derive cultural significance from their traditional usage. Among the trait occurrences charted in figures 3–8, some show short, intensive histories in the highlands and others reveal notable longevity. Additional traits suggest moderate or intermittent occurrences, the latter perhaps being partially due to the smallness of the archaeological samples.[9]

As would be expected, more regular development is discernible at a single locality (figs. 3, 4) than over an extended region (figs. 5–8). Among other factors, this is probably due to a tendency for traits to diffuse at differing rates from site to site, experiencing slightly different growths in each location. To illustrate this well-known aspect of culture history, the geratest popularity of Classic resist decoration was attained at Zaculeu[1v] and Nebaj[1n] during the Early Classic period but not until the Late Classic in the Chixoy drainage (fig. 8). Again, although ladle censers had a long occurrence at both Zaculeu and Zacualpa,[1u] the tubular-handled variety was present throughout the sequence at the former site but did not appear at the latter until possibly the Early Postclassic period (fig. 6).

On the other hand, a number of widely distributed ceramic features were largely if not entirely restricted to a single horizon. With some significant exceptions, these traits tend to be found in figure 5 (Special Vessel Forms) rather than in 6 and 7 (Incensarios and Ceremonial Containers) or 8 (Techniques of Decoration). The vessel forms in question rarely occur abundantly and are perhaps never well represented in general digging, although they may sometimes constitute a significant segment of the funeral pottery from a site. For such reasons they have often been regarded as trade pieces, an hypothesis which only occasionally has been tested through technological analysis. These, in any case, are the horizon diagnostics which up to now loom so large in our understanding of highland chronology. Conversely, there is little knowledge of the unfolding and development of Guatemalan highland culture as revealed by the great body of indigeneous utilitarian ceramics.[10]

The horizon-markers which we have

---

[9] It should constantly be borne in mind that the accuracy of the charts has been adversely affected by limited archaeological sampling and, often, by incomplete publication. Comparative quantification has therefore been impossible, either from one period to another at a single locality (figs. 3, 4) or at various sites (figs. 5–8). Nevertheless, in several of the charts we have suggested relative differences in abundance or nature of occurrence, "X" being used to indicate strongly diagnostic traits unrelated to precise quantitative representation and the dot (•) to indicate traits of seemingly lesser importance. Relative abundance is perhaps most systematically shown in figure 8, Techniques of Decoration. In this chart the dot is employed most frequently, for traits of varying importance at different sites are being compared, whereas in figures 3 and 4 a screening process has eliminated traits which are of little diagnostic importance in the Kaminaljuyu district. In figures 5–7 the small number of extant specimens has made inadvisable any attempt to record more than mere presence of the trait. The question mark (?) is used rather sparingly, considering the lacunae in the data.

[10] Even utilitarian pottery may have been extensively traded, if one may infer from modern highland Maya practices. Contributing to such trade, perhaps, was the difficulty of locating suit-

142

charted are most numerous in the Early Classic and Early Postclassic periods. Of these, Thin Orange and Tohil Plumbate have been demonstrated by technological analysis to be trade wares, having exceptionally broad distributions in Mesoamerica. Other forms, appearing on an Early Classic level in different highland zones and extending outside the region, are two-part effigies, "cream pitchers," floreros, and cylindrical tripods (fig. 5). The cylindrical tripod forms a fairly closely knit trait complex, often having slab, openwork, or gashed feet, a basal frieze, and decoration in one or more panels. However, certain tripod cylinders from Kaminaljuyu are unusually tall and provided with scutate covers, a rare feature in other parts of the highlands, whereas cylinder tripods from Zaculeu differ in the presence of resist decoration and the absence of stucco painting. Pottery apparently restricted to the Early Postclassic, in addition to the various forms of Tohil Plumbate, includes highly standardized double-bottomed pedestal vases and "Mixtec-type" tripod censers (figs. 5, 6). Modes of shape, however, seem to constitute somewhat less sensitive criteria for Late Classic pottery. The footless cylindrical vase, it is true, occurred largely in the Late Classic but not exclusively so (fig. 5); certain specialized form modes, such as the terraced basal flange (fig. 17,d) probably were limited to this period. Late Classic polychrome types, of the Saxche and Palmar Groups, were present in north highland sites and the Maya lowlands, but unlike the Early Classic polychromes of lowland derivation (Dos Arroyos and perhaps Actuncan Ceramic Groups) apparently did not penetrate into the southern part of the Guatemala highlands. Certain Postclassic polychromes suggest either a completely different source (Nicoya Poly-

chrome, rare but present in the Early Postclassic) or localized developments (Chinautla Polychrome of the Late Postclassic).

A number of vessel forms had a long history in the highlands. These were often incensarios or ceremonial containers bearing resemblances to known incense burners (figs. 6, 7) but included shoe-shaped vessels, rim-head vessels, and tall-footed tripods (fig. 5). Partly, no doubt, as a result of limited sampling, these forms sometimes give the impression of an irregular occurrence through time; if a trait disappears from the materials obtained from one site, it is likely to reappear in another locality, perhaps at a considerably later period. Borhegyi has called attention to the erratic temporal distribution of certain incensario forms in the Guatemala highlands, postulating the existence of a conservative folk cult which "went underground" and perpetuated the traits, although they had disappeared from the formalized hierarchal religion of the ceremonial centers (Borhegyi, 1951b, pp. 170–71; 1956b). Three-pronged incensarios, often cylindrical in shape, modeled with grotesque faces and bearing vertical side flanges, were prominent in the Kaminaljuyu district during the Middle and Late Preclassic periods (figs. 12,a,b; 21,a). Bifurcated "fishtail" protuberances on the incensario tops were also known, as well as similarly placed loop handles or rings. All these traits formed a well-knit complex during the Preclassic of Kaminaljuyu, several of the features often occurring on a single specimen. Following the Preclassic, however, the traits became disassociated, no longer clustering in a single incensario form. Perhaps this regrouping of attributes, in varying combinations at different times and places, may help to explain the situation observed by Borhegyi; for, although incensarios having three prongs are unknown from the Early Classic period, most of the features with which the prongs had formerly been associated continued without

------

able clay in the young volcanic region mantled with lava and ash, which forms the southern rim of the highlands (McBryde, 1947, p. 54).

interruption. This may constitute a less drastic disruption of the incensario tradition than Borhegyi has suggested.

In any case, the Early Classic period did witness the appearance of new incensario forms: hourglass-shaped with two chambers, often modeled as a grotesque face with a looping nose; anthropomorphic seated figures; the Tlaloc jar; a wide variety of flamboyant covers and chimneys; and ladle censers. Spiked incensarios, although reported as occurring in the Kaminaljuyu Preclassic, seem first to have appeared in quantity in the Northern Zone, during the Early Classic period. Few if any basic innovations took place in the Late Classic, although there was a general decline in elaboration; spiked censers of simple shape spread into the central highlands, and effigy prongs, now moldmade, reappeared (fig. 12,*g*). In spite of the widespread artistic decline, outstanding examples of ceramic modeling are known on Late Classic incensarios from Lake Amatitlan[1ff] and in the Chama[1f] district (figs. 20,*e*; 12,*f*). "Mixtec-type" tripod censers, with one leg serving as a handle, were an Early Postclassic introduction, and ladle censers with moldmade decoration on the bowl exterior were a Late Postclassic feature.

CONCLUSIONS

During certain periods of Guatemalan highland ceramic history, important differences set apart the Northern Ceramic Zone from those lying to the south. Middle Preclassic pottery, although well established at Kaminaljuyu and known to a lesser degree at other southern centers, has yet to be identified in the northern highlands. A greater uniformity was present over the entire region in Late Preclassic times. Although Protoclassic traits such as mammiform feet are represented in all zones, a well-defined complex comparable to Holmul I (Merwin and Vaillant, 1932) or Floral Park at Barton Ramie (Willey and Gifford, 1961) has not been located. Poly-

chrome pottery, notably, is absent from Protoclassic materials known in the highlands, except at Tzicuay. During the Early and Late Classic periods, north highland ceramics were subject to strong influences from the Maya lowlands. These extended southward to Kaminaljuyu on an Early Classic level, perhaps largely in the form of trade, where they coincided with another set of stimuli from central Mexico. However, with the beginning of the Late Classic period, the southern portions of the highlands appear to have been effectively sealed off from trade with the Lowland Maya Area. Interestingly, the increased ceramic regionalism, which characterizes the Late Classic in the Guatemala highlands, is also to be found at this time in the Maya lowlands. However, with the collapse of Classic centers in the greater Peten, the northern highlands seem to have turned southward for ceramic inspiration. This was also the period of Tohil Plumbate, which, traded widely, may have promoted the exchange of other goods and concepts. In spite of late disturbances, the various parts of the highlands appear to have maintained fairly close ceramic contacts throughout the Postclassic periods.

Clearly, it would be a mistake to conceive of ceramic history in the highlands simply in these terms, as a pulsation which brought the Northern Zone alternately into closer or more remote contact with the south. Significant differences existed within the north, and along the southern belt of the highlands there were complex and little understood relationships which can as of now be only the subject of speculation. Unsolved ceramic problems revolve around: (1) the nature of contacts between the Western and Central Zones on all time levels; (2) affiliations among the Atitlan, Quezaltenango, and San Marcos districts in the west; (3) the blank spot which at present characterizes our knowledge of the eastern portion of the Central Zone; (4) gaps or partial gaps in available sequences, such as paucity of Classic materials in the west and of Early Postclassic pottery in the central highlands. In addition, there is need for publication and verification of the longest sequence of phases yet named from the Guatemala highlands, that from Kaminaljuyu; systematic study of contacts outside the region, particularly with the Pacific coast and toward Mexico; and ethnic identifications on all fronts, including the intrusive Mexican elements that are suggested by pottery at Kaminaljuyu, by Tohil Plumbate, and by such forms as "Mixtectype" incensarios. Work in the Quezaltenango valley seems particularly pressing, stratigraphic excavations throughout the highlands being necessary in the solution of the problems outlined above and others equally significant.

REFERENCES

Berlin, 1952
Bierhenke, Haberland, Johansen, and Zimmermann, 1959
Borhegyi, 1950a, 1950b, 1951a, 1951b, 1951c, 1952a, 1956b, 1958b, 1959a, 1961d
Bowditch, 1904
Brainerd, 1951, 1958
Burkitt, 1930b
Butler, 1940, 1959
Coe, M. D., 1961
Covarrubias, 1954
Dieseldorff, 1926–33
Dutton and Hobbs, 1943
Gamio, 1926–27
Gordon and Mason, 1925–43
Hay, 1940
Kelemen, 1943
Kidder, A., and Samayoa Chinchilla, 1959
Kidder, A. V., 1945, 1948, 1949b, 1950, 1954, 1961
——, Jennings, and Shook, 1946
—— and Shepard, 1944
—— and Shook, 1959
Lathrap, 1957
Linton, 1936
Longyear, 1952
Lothrop, 1926b, 1933, 1936

—— and others, 1961
McBryde, 1947
Merwin and Vaillant, 1932
Nicholson, 1961
Porter, 1953
Sayre, Murrenhoff, and Weick, 1958
Schuster, 1951
Seler, 1901, 1902–23, 1904b
Shepard, 1947, 1948
Shook, 1947, 1948, 1951a, 1952a, 1952b
—— and Kidder, 1952
Smith, A. L., 1955
—— and Kidder, 1943, 1951
Smith, R. E., 1944, 1949a, 1949b, 1952, 1955b, 1955d, 1957, 1958
—— and Gifford, 1959
——, Willey, and Gifford, 1960
Tax, 1951
Termer, 1931
Thompson, J. E. S., 1943a, 1948
Vaillant, 1927
Villacorta, C., 1938
—— and Villacorta, 1927
Wauchope, 1948a, 1948b, 1949, 1950
Willey and Gifford, 1961
Woodbury and Trik, 1953

5. Preclassic Pottery Figurines of the Guatemalan Highlands

ALFRED V. KIDDER

LITTLE IS KNOWN regarding the Preclassic figurines for the Guatemalan highlands, our information to date being limited almost entirely to the single site of Kaminaljuyu.[1] Few other upland ruins have been more than superficially examined, with publication of the results (for Kaminaljuyu and lesser sites in the neighborhood, see: Gamio, 1926–27; Lothrop, 1927a; Kidder, Jennings, and Shook, 1946, and bibliography; Kidder, 1948; Shook, 1952b; Shook and Kidder, 1952; Carnegie Institution of Washington, Year Books 35–45).

Kaminaljuyu, in what are now the western outskirts of Guatemala City (elevation about 1550 m.), was a large, obviously important ceremonial as well as domiciliary center, occupied, perhaps continuously, from the earliest now known local Preclassic cultures through the Late Classic, a span of something like a thousand years. No substantial evidence has yet been found there of a preceramic stage nor at Kaminaljuyu or elsewhere in Guatemala of a Paleo-Indian culture, although eventual discovery of both is certainly to be expected.

At Kaminaljuyu all structures, except wattle-and-daub dwellings, built directly on the ground or on low adobe platforms were earthen mounds protectively surfaced in various ways against rain erosion. Most were shrine or temple substructures, or the sides and ends of ball courts. Some mounds were only briefly used, others longer; in such cases they usually were enlarged by burial under new construction. Extensive terracing or leveling of the originally somewhat irregular terrain was also done at certain times. Altogether, an enormous amount of earth was handled and rehandled. And from first to last, household refuse was continuously and heavily deposited, thrown about at random or dumped into pits dug through the surface humus to recover the underlying clay and volcanic ash for various uses. Accordingly, sheet-refuse or refuse from pits transected in leveling operations went into the earth scraped up for erection or enlargement of

---

[1] The Department of Alta Verapaz, although part of highland Guatemala, is omitted from the present paper because archaeologically it seems to have been more closely allied to the Maya lowlands (see Rands and Rands, Article 20).

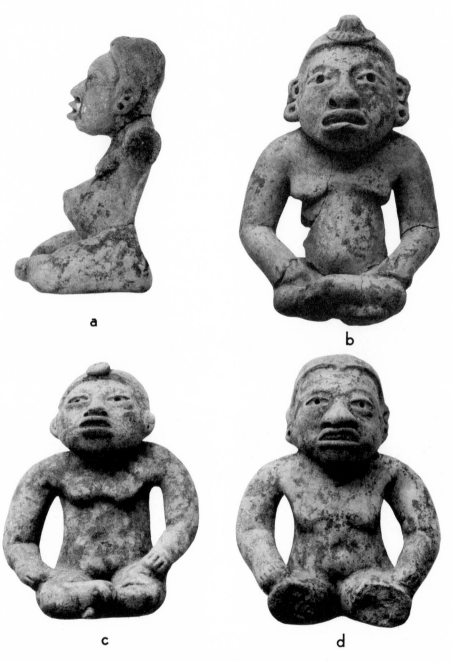

Fig. 1—COPALCHE, GUATEMALA (LAS CHARCAS PHASE). *a*, Height 15 cm.,
white slip. *b*, White slip, red headdress. Moreno Coll.

Fig. 2—COPALCHE, GUATEMALA (LAS CHARCAS [?] PHASE). Height 17.6 cm., chocolate-brown slip. Moreno Coll.

mounds. Thus, contemporary cultural material or material of any older Preclassic or Classic phase might be included, rendering accurate chronological ranking of structures usually difficult, sometimes impossible, as often was confident assignment to phase of specimens recovered in the small amount of controlled mound excavation by E. M. Shook and myself. Excavation, indeed, or at least careful test-pitting and trenching, of all Kaminaljuyu's 200 or so

remaining tumuli would be necessary to establish the exact sequence of their construction or the order of succession of the site's many ceramic and figurine types. We erred seriously in failing to clear and fully to record the contents of a much greater number of pits because, along with the numerous sherds always in them, there very often was a figurine head or two. The pits, on accomplishment of whatever purpose for which they were dug, seem quickly to have been filled. Thus, most hold refuse recently thrown from nearby buildings. A pit's contents, therefore, normally represent no more than one of the site's several ceramic phases. As after the first couple of seasons we had become reasonably sure of the sequence of the phases, we could date, so to speak, with considerable confidence all major figurine and pottery types. Had we emptied more pits, we would doubtless have been able to answer a number of still open questions as to minor varieties and the nature of intertype relationships.

Many hundred figurines from Kaminaljuyu, mostly Preclassic, are in the Guatemala National Museum. Others were available to me in several large private collections. The majority, aside from the relatively few found in our excavations, had been bought from farmers, from workmen making bricks and adobes or engaged in the recent wholesale razing of mounds for real estate developments. Small boys keep a keen eye on such operations and on ditching for pipelines. Thus, assignment of a figurine to any part of the site, or to any given mound, is almost never possible.

Research is further handicapped by the fact that the collections usually consist only of heads, as local people do not bother to save the less salable arms, legs, or bodies. So figurines cannot often even partially be reconstructed. Complete examples are of the utmost rarity, because at Kaminaljuyu they were not buried with the dead, as they often were, for example, at Tlatilco and Chupicuaro in Mexico; nor did they any-

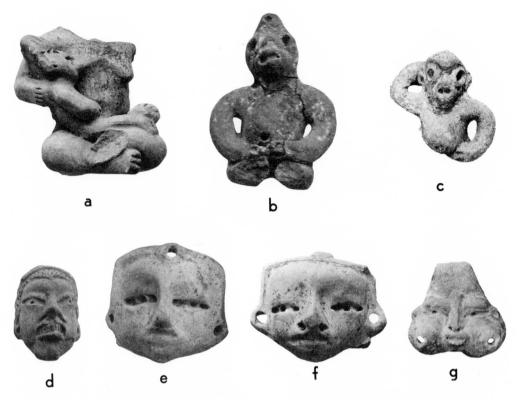

Fig. 3—LAS CHARCAS (?) PHASE, GUATEMALA. *a,f*, Copalche, Moreno Coll. Heights: *a*, 9.3 cm.; *b*, 5.4 cm.; *c*, 6.0 cm.; *e*, 5.5 cm.; *g*, 5.5 cm.

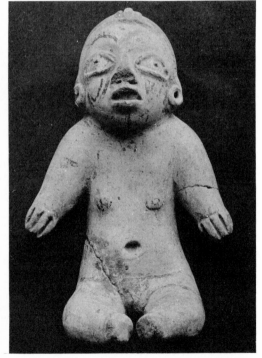

Fig. 4—DEPARTMENT OF SAN MARCOS, GUATEMALA (LAS CHARCAS [?] PHASE). Cream-white slip, black-paint lines.

Fig. 5—SALCAJA, GUATEMALA (LAS CHARCAS [?] PHASE). Height 13.5 cm., unslipped. Garavito Coll.

149

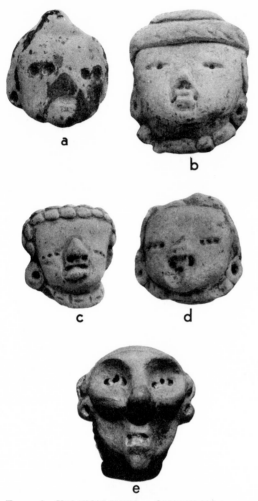

a

b

c

d

e

Fig. 6—KAMINALJUYU, GUATEMALA. *c,* Mound E-II-3 (Providencia phase). Provenience of others unknown. *e,* Height 6.7 cm., red-brown slip with white paint in punches. Nottebohm Coll., Sacatepequez phase.

where at the site, so far as is known, form part of ceremonial caches. Even the heads are often badly battered, sometimes to such an extent that one or another feature of classificational value is missing or damaged beyond usefulness.

Figurines of the sort here considered were modeled by hand rather than cast in molds. In Mesoamerica they were thus made, so far as we know, almost exclusively during Preclassic times. Practically all are of human beings, shown standing or, less

commonly, seated. The former seem seldom to have stood more than 15 cm. high; the latter were apparently a little smaller. The entire body was represented, the head disproportionately large. Inability to give exact measurements, or even average dimensions, of the several recognizable types is due to their shockingly bad condition. Hardly a single specimen except some of the earliest even approaches completeness. Never at Kaminaljuyu, nor I think elsewhere, has clear evidence been found that figurines were deliberately broken, as the edges of the fragments are seldom sharp, and many are badly battered. Furthermore, the fragments were almost always single finds. I cannot recall our ever recovering the whole or even most parts of any one figurine, always excepting the earliest sort. Pieces of broken ones seem simply to have been thrown on the rubbish that accumulated from day to day at so populous a site as Kaminaljuyu.

Why figurines normally occur in such a sad state is not understood. It is generally and probably correctly believed that they played a part in some cult, presumably of fertility, as they so often depict females, generally pregnant. Further to explain the battering of these figurines, it may well be that after they had served whatever purpose for which they were made, they perhaps ended up as often do the wooden *kachinas* of certain Pueblo Indians. These are handsomely painted and garbed effigies of supernatural beings, which play a ceremonial role, after which they may be turned over to the children. Writing of effigies from Jarmo in Iran, Vivian Broman (1958, p. 23) suggests that "these animal figurines represent human wishes or desires." She further suggests that "the magic of the wish lay in the actual manufacture." Magic, she feels, may have been retained until the wish was fulfilled and the effigies then have been discarded, or given to the children for playthings.

Nearly all Preclassic Kaminaljuyu figu-

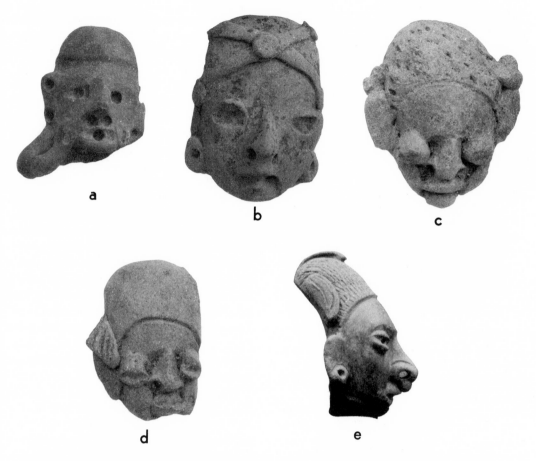

FIG. 7—KAMINALJUYU, GUATEMALA (ARENAL [?] PHASE). *e*, Height 11 cm., orange-red slip, Moreno Coll.

rines represent females, as is indicated by the high percentage of specimens with obviously pregnant abdomen (fig. 1,*a*). Unmistakable breasts also generally prove this (fig. 1,*b*,*c*), although some without could be thought male; but there occur a few flat-chested Preclassic figurines that possess the vulva, which, however, was rarely represented. I know of none from Kaminaljuyu endowed with corresponding male parts. This was not due to inability to model them, for on animal figurines (dogs, pisotes, monkeys) they apparently are always present.

No unfired specimen, if ever any was in that condition, has survived. Without technological studies, one cannot be sure that significant subtypes may not exist. The following principal classes are recognizable: (1) light-colored paste, unslipped; (2) red-brown paste, unslipped; (3) red-brown paste, white slip; (4) red-brown paste, red slip. Within these categories, classification might well be based primarily on head form and shape of face; secondarily on the depiction of eye, nose, mouth, ears, and on hair-do, headdress, ornaments. So very few heads are accompanied by any considerable part of the body that this important element of the figurines could not adequately be treated, although in some cases it is possible to

151

Fig. 8—KAMINALJUYU, GUATEMALA (ARENAL PHASE). Height 19 cm.

hazard a guess as to head-body relationship. There are three principal positions: standing (fig. 2), seated with legs extended (fig. 1,d), seated Turkish-fashion (figs. 1,b,c; 3,a). Arms may be held stiffly outward, or bent down at the elbow; often they are close to or actually touching the body, with a hand on each side of the abdomen (fig. 1,b,d). Hands are usually no more than a slight terminal flattening of the arms (fig. 2), the fingers indicated by three or four parallel longitudinal incisions (figs. 1,b-d; 3,a). Feet are seldom represented at all, the legs normally tapering rather abruptly to rounded ends (fig. 1,a-c).

Classification is rendered difficult by the great number of variant specimens. Some seem to fall between two recognizable types and might represent evolutionary stages; others may have been traded from

areas at present little or not at all known to us; still others were perhaps local inventions or aberrant products of individual fancy.

In nomenclature, I have felt it unnecessary to follow closely the trail blazed at the American Museum of National History by G. C. Vaillant, who profited by the inspiring leadership and close cooperation of C. L. Hay. Together they pioneered Mexican and, in fact, all Mesoamerican archaeological taxonomy, producing a series of brilliant monographs (Vaillant, 1930 to 1935). In them they assembled the Mexican Preclassic figurines in lettered groups with numbered subgroups. This system has been used by most Mexican students, including Miguel Covarrubias, that uniquely gifted judge of every form of aesthetic expression. The figurines of Kaminaljuyu, however, show considerable divergence from these Mexican norms and can best be treated differently.

The writing of this paper has been somewhat more than mere fulfillment of the archaeologist's unavoidable task of recording the results of his delvings, because I have also felt a duty to express my admiration for and gratitude to the long-vanished modelers of these little effigies that have given me so many happy hours. I have wished I might confidently credit them and their Preclassic Middle American congeners with the important role I think it probable they played among the layers of foundations for New World artistic and spiritual advancement. Just appraisal of their contribution, however, is not possible at present, because adequate data are still lacking. I must, therefore, limit myself at this time to summarizing such few data as were gathered during an investigation which both Shook and I regret we were unable to carry beyond the veriest beginnings.

REFERENCES

Borhegyi, 1950b, 1954c
Broman, 1958
Carnegie Institution, 1936–46
Coe, M. D., 1961
Gamio, 1926–27
Kidder, 1948
——, Jennings, and Shook, 1946

—— and Shook, 1961
Lothrop, 1927a, 1961
Ricketson and Ricketson, 1937
Shook, 1952b
—— and Kidder, 1952
Vaillant, 1930, 1931, 1935a, 1935b

APPENDIX

OUTLINE OF GUATEMALAN HIGHLAND PRECLASSIC FIGURINE TRAITS BY PHASE

Robert L. Rands

LAS CHARCAS PHASE (MIDDLE PRECLASSIC, EARLY ASPECT)

Fig. 1. Copalche, Guatemala.

Figs. 2, 3. Kaminaljuyu and Copalche. Las Charcas in date or affiliations.

Fig. 4. Department of San Marcos. Las Charcas?

Fig. 5. Salcaja. Las Charcas?

Paste: often reddish.

Slip: mostly white.

Frequently seated.

Standing, often with rocker feet (deeply concave at instep) (fig. 2).

Back: slightly concave, sometimes markedly so (fig. 1,*a*).

Subjects:

Females (modeled breasts; swollen abdomen, i.e. pregnant; vulva occasionally indicated (figs. 1, 4).

Mother-and-child (infant seated on mother's lap or, more rarely, suckling at her breast (figs. 3,*a*; 5).

Males (bearded). Relatively infrequent, except on the effigy three-pronged incensarios (Borhegyi, 1950b).

Animal figurines, especially monkeys (fig. 3,*c*).

Human-head effigy whistles, especially puffed-cheek variety (fig. 3,*g*).

Effigy rings (face on finger ring). Rare.

Human-head types:

1. *Naturalistic* [cf. Mamom (Ricketson and Ricketson, 1937, pls. 73, 74) and Vaillant's Type A (Vaillant, 1930, pp. 120–22)]. (figs. 1; 3,*d*; 4.)

Rounded heads.

Eyes: grooved-and-punctate. Groove is characteristically well defined, deep and elliptical. Punctation: usually a single central punch for pupil. Occasionally slight modeling to emphasize the outline of the groove.

Nose: typically broad and wedge-shaped, with punctate nostrils.

Mouth: teeth occasionally indicated (fig. 1,*d*).

Head and headdress: Details only occasionally shown, but may be indicated by: (a) incising; (b) punctating (fig. 3,*d*); (c) hair or headdress generally emphasized at center of head (figs. 1,*c*; 2; 5); (d) minute conical cap, sometimes worn atop head (fig. 1,*b*).

2. *Square-headed* (figs. 3,*e,f*; 5).

Wide-faced. Flat. Less marked modeling of eyelids and lips than in Naturalistic type. Hairline, extending from ear to ear, closely parallels outline of the head.

Projecting ears, often rounded, with circular perforation.

Otherwise, generally similar to Naturalistic type, including central emphasis of hair or headdress at top of head.

3. *Crude* (figs. 2; 3,*b*).

General crudity. Absence or de-emphasis of grooved-and-punctate eyes.

Occasional traits:

Addition of fugitive red and yellow paint to white slip.

Hand raised to head or cheek (both human and monkey figurines).

PROVIDENCIA AND SACATEPEQUEZ PHASES
(MIDDLE PRECLASSIC, LATE ASPECT)

Fig. 6,*a,b*. Providencia phase, Kaminaljuyu.

Fig. 6,*c,d*. Typological associations with Providencia, Kaminaljuyu.

Fig. 6,*e*. Sacatepequez phase, Department of Sacatepequez.

Paste: characteristically white.

White slip continues.

Tendencies for Providencia eyes to have double punctate pupils (fig. 6,*a*) or for eye grooves to be more shallow and less elliptical than in Las Charcas. Straight narrow grooves, sometimes blurred when punched (fig. 6,*b-d*).

Grotesque exaggeration of bony structure (Sacatepequez) (fig. 6,*e*).

Wasp-waist torsos occur in Providencia fill, in a more pronounced form than on definite Las Charcas examples.

Jointed figurines (Borhegyi, 1954c).

Chubby-cheeked heads:

Often with appliquéd elements around top of head, extending from ear to ear, indicating the hair or headdress (fig. 6,*c,d*).

Necklace of corresponding elements is sometimes shown under the chin (fig. 6,*b-d*).

MIRAFLORES AND ARENAL PHASES (LATE PRECLASSIC)

Figs. 7, 8. Miraflores-Arenal phases, Kaminaljuyu. (Fig. 7,*a* shows Miraflores features, others predominantly Arenal.)

Red slip: important in Miraflores. Some have black slip.

Unslipped red-brown paste, plus slipped examples: Arenal.

Deep punctation (eyes, nostrils, mouth, top and bottom of rectangular ears): Miraflores (cf. fig. 7,*a*).

Faces: long and narrow, as compared to earlier figurines (figs. 7,*e*; 8).

Heads: some with markedly sloping forehead (fig. 7,*e*).

Hair, headdress: increasing elaboration, especially in Arenal: Considerable use of punctation to indicate hair or headdress (fig. 7,*c,e*). Hairline (or beginning of headdress) frequently indicated by an arched incised line or fillet (fig. 7,*c,d*); appliquéd bands may also cut across the upper part of the head to lend variety and sophistication to the coiffure (fig. 7,*b*).

Nose: prominent nose and nostrils, the latter deeply punctate (fig. 8) or with a hole passing completely through the septum (fig. 7,*e*).

Eyes: Miraflores: grooved-and-punched eyes continue (cf. fig. 7,*a*). However, groove consists of a straight, narrow, sharply defined slit (thereby differing from the ellipsoidal tendency of Las Charcas eye grooves or the less clean-cut groove of Providencia).

Arenal: deeply gouged eyes, sometimes modeled, with less frequent use of punctation to indicate pupil. Some eyes approach the well-known coffee-bean type (fig. 8). Use of modeling to indicate brow ridges. *Heavy-eyed* type (Kidder and Shook, 1961): modeled-and-gouged but lack central pupil punch; eyes appear to be distended from their sockets (fig. 7,*c,d*).

Note: eyes on effigy rim-head vessels consist of protruding, rounded to ellipsoidal fillets, without interior modification (Borhegyi, 1950b).

COMMENTS:

In the Preclassic figurine sequence at Kaminaljuyu, the "Naturalistic" Las Charcas figurines provide the most abundant basic connection with the Mamom phase at Uaxactun. Correspondences extend to Vaillant's Type A.

The puffed-cheek human-head effigy whistles of Las Charcas also bear close Mamom similarities.

The chubby-cheeked figurine, which apparently relates to the upper Middle Preclassic at Kaminaljuyu, is characterized by appliquéd elements framing its head from ear to ear. Similar forms occur as a minority type in Uaxactun Mamom, are abundant at Coban, and are also represented at Topoxte (Rands and Rands, Article 20).

The Las Charcas–Mamom correspondences would appear to support an equivalent temporal position for these phases, for the Las Charcas figurines more closely resemble Mamom than do those of the Middle and Late Preclassic at Kaminaljuyu. A partial exception may be provided by the chubby-cheeked (Providencia?) figurines.

Figurines from the later Kaminaljuyu phases are not represented at Uaxactun. They would presumably equate in time with Chicanel, which is largely or entirely without figurines.

Las Charcas–Mamom stylistic correspondences appear stronger than those between Kaminaljuyu and the La Victoria Preclassic on the Pacific coast, where Type A figurines also occur. However, Conchas phase "Man from Mars" headdress and effigy ring from the latter site provide specific correspond-ences to Las Charcas materials (M. D. Coe, 1961, pl. 54,a, fig. 42,a).

The big break in the Kaminaljuyu Preclassic figurine sequence apparently separates Miraflores-Arenal from Las Charcas–Providencia. However, Las Charcas materials are easiest to recognize as a distinct complex, because they are sometimes found in unmixed lots and are more likely to be represented by complete figurines.

In general, it is not yet clear how much overlapping and interfingering exists from one phase to another.

6. Classic and Postclassic Pottery Figurines of the Guatemalan Highlands

ROBERT L. RANDS

IN THE Guatemala highlands, the intensive development of Preclassic figurines at Kaminaljuyu, and probably at other sites yet to be excavated, was followed by a significant reduction in the figurine tradition.[1] This class of ceramic objects became few in number and, for the most part, unelaborated in treatment. Such a situation contrasts sharply with the pattern of fluctuation in lowland Maya figurines, where there is an Early Classic lull, pronounced Late Classic peak, and Postclassic decline. Differences from the flourishing figurine industry on the Pacific coast are also marked. The minor role accorded highland figurines following the Preclassic is of added interest because, throughout the ceramic history of the region, effigy modeling on pottery containers constituted a major focus of attention. Various appendages to vessels, such as handles and rim-heads, were frequently modeled in the shape of humans and animals (fig. 1). In style and general artistic concept, although not necessarily in specific form, a close relationship exists between these abundant miniatures and the comparatively scanty figurines. In the present state of knowledge, it is sometimes impossible to determine if a fragmentary modeled head originally adorned a vessel or was joined to a body as a separate figurine.

Because of absence of controlled excavations in most parts of the Guatemalan highlands, a firm sequence of figurine types has not been established for the Classic and Postclassic periods. Regional distinctions are likewise vague. Even at Zaculeu, a well-worked site yielding an unusually large number of figurine fragments, the great majority of specimens cannot be assigned to definite phases (Woodbury and Trik, 1953). As Kidder has described for Kaminaljuyu, there was a constant mixing and redeposition of material, making it difficult to ascertain whether the occasional figurine found under stratigraphic conditions is representative of its level or intrusive. In discussing individual specimens or groups of figurines from the highlands, therefore, we cannot give equal weighting to consid

[1] This article has profited from suggestions by Robert E. Smith and Stephan F. Borhegyi.

156

FIG. 2—KAMINALJUYU. (Courtesy, Peabody Museum, Harvard.)

FIG. 1—KAMINALJUYU, FRAGMENT OF RIM-HEAD VESSEL. (Courtesy, Peabody Museum, Harvard.)

erations of time, space, and style. In a few instances, properties of paste, slip, or painted design prove most useful in relating the figurines to a pottery type or group and thereby establishing their temporal and cultural position. Again, resemblances to figurine materials outside the Guatemalan highlands provide suggestions of time, although the comparisons vary in specificity and reliability. Finally, certain stylistic features, shared by figurines and better-dated objects from the highlands, offer hints for periodization.

EARLY AND LATE CLASSIC

The near-absence of figurines at Kaminaljuyu during the Esperanza (Early Classic) phase has been contrasted with their importance at contemporaneous and culturally related Teotihuacan. This striking difference, it is held, suggests either that persons from Teotihuacan did not actually reach Kaminaljuyu or that figurines formed part of a folk cult not practiced by these upper-class migrants (Kidder, Jennings,

and Shook, 1946, pp. 214, 256). It is interesting, therefore, that a single weathered, wide-faced figurine head from Kaminaljuyu, probably moldmade (fig. 2), shows possible Teotihuacan affiliations. Resemblances also exist to flattish figurine heads from the Maya lowlands, which Butler (1935a) has designated "Style Y" (Rands and Rands, Article 20, figs. 46, 47). An Early Classic dating is indicated for the latter type at Piedras Negras; the Kaminaljuyu specimen may belong to the same horizon.

Such a cultural and chronological placement, however tentative, underscores the paucity of figurines at Kaminaljuyu during the Early Classic period. The single surely established Esperanza figurine from the site consists of a well-fired hollow body, with head, necklace, and breechcloth added of a yellowish, apparently unfired substance (Kidder, Jennings, and Shook, 1946, p. 214, fig. 168,a). The presence of the figurine as tomb furniture is reminiscent of Teotihuacan practices rather than of basic patterns in the Guatemala highlands.

Although lacking definitely established chronological position, a number of figurines recovered from highland Guatemalan sites probably pertain to Early or Late Classic horizons. Wauchope (1948a, p.

157

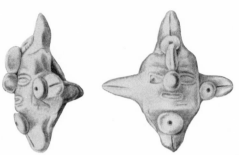

FIG. 3—RABINAL DISTRICT. Height 5.8 cm. (Courtesy, Peabody Museum, Harvard.)

FIG. 4—ZACULEU. Height 7.5 cm. (After Woodbury and Trik, 1953, fig. 277,*c.*)

127) has voiced the possibility that crudely modeled clay figures at Zacualpa were actually coeval with the Pokom phase deposits in which they occurred, rather than being of Preclassic origin, and in this connection has cited the crude execution of relatively late stone sculptures in the highlands. A separate group of stylistic attributes are shared by figurines, apparently both moldmade and hand-modeled, from various parts of the highlands. Whether these date from a common horizon or reflect the retention of traits over a large time span is problematic. These features, which contrast strongly with the style of lowland Maya figurines, include staring, oval eyes, produced by double outlining so that the lids stand out sharply; wide straight mouths, often with a double outline to the lips; and, of less constant association, circular earplugs without central perforations (fig. 3). At Zaculeu, figurines showing these features occur in Early Classic (Atzan) and Postclassic (late Qankyak or early Xinabahul) deposits (figs. 4, 5). Although these traits may prove to be concentrated in the northern highlands, clay heads showing some of the characteristics are known from as far away as San Agustin Acasaguastlan in the Motagua Valley (A. L. Smith and Kidder, 1943, fig. 53). On the Pacific slope, prominent eyelids of similar type are diagnostic of Cotzumalhuapan-style stone sculpture, provisionally dated as Late Clas-

sic but with the "possibility that its start may have to be moved back to the Tzakol-Esperanza horizon" (J. E. S. Thompson, 1948, p. 51). A characteristic of Early Classic carved jades from the northern highlands and elsewhere is a square-cornered bar mouth, in which a single line indicates the division of the lips; it may be significant that this feature is closely duplicated on a clay head obtained at Rabinal, Baja Verapaz (fig. 3; compare jades in Rands, Article 21, figs. 34, 41). A general similarity is also to be seen in the mouth treatment on Early and Late Classic pottery incense burners from the northern highlands (Rands and R. E. Smith, Article 4, fig. 20,*a,d*).

FIG. 5—ZACULEU. Width (at earplugs) 18.2 cm. (After Woodbury and Trik, 1953, fig. 276,*d.*)

FIG. 6—ZACULEU, WHISTLE. Length 11 cm. (After Woodbury and Trik, 1953, fig. 115,*a*.)

Additional figurine-like objects may be attributed to the Classic horizon. A specimen of typical Late Classic lowland Maya style is reported from Panajachel, on Lake Atitlan (R. E. Smith, 1955d, fig. 1,*g*). The single Early Classic (Atzan phase) whistle from Zaculeu is elongated, has a side mouthpiece, contains clay pellets, and is decorated with a pattern of grooves (fig. 6). The only other figurine-like specimen definitely assigned to the Atzan horizon at Zaculeu is a flat, "star-shaped" head, representing a type that occurs more commonly in Qankyak phase (Postclassic) deposits at the site (fig. 4; Woodbury and Trik, 1953, pp. 214, 215). Resemblances exist to "star-shaped" heads on Early Classic miniature mushroom stones from Kaminaljuyu (Borhegyi *in* Wasson and Wasson, 1957, fig. 2, nos. 19, 41, 42). Specimens have four to eight projecting points, radiating out from the face; loop handles were sometimes added on the backs. It is uncertain if this peculiar type had the long history at Zaculeu suggested by its occurrence in presumedly unmixed deposits, or if its temporal position was more restricted. Figurines of any sort have not definitely been found in the intervening Late Classic (Chinaq) de-

posits at Zaculeu, being regarded as "probably present but very rare" (Woodbury and Trik, 1953, p. 285). Large modeled feline heads of fired clay, some with finished back and base, are found in the northern highlands (fig. 7). Certain of these have been described as possible plaza monuments, architectural ornaments, or altarpieces (Wauchope, 1948a, pp. 14, 62, pl. 4,*c*; A. L. Smith and Kidder, 1951, fig. 86,*q*). Multiple functions are possible, some being large, two-part hollow figurines or urns (Kelemen, 1943, pl. 141,*d*). A late Pokom or Tohil dating is indicated at Zacualpa.

Although localized figurines styles appeared during the Classic period, the Guatemala highlands were not completely isolated from neighboring areas. Moldmade figurines of Tiquisate ware—concentrated on the Pacific slope, as were other objects of this pottery—occasionally found their way into the highlands, especially in the Quezaltenango, Amatitlan, and Antigua districts. The prominent lidded eye and bar mouth, seen to advantage on the Tiquisate figurine in figure 8, is not always associated with this southern type. However, comparisons to figures 3–5, from the northern highlands, indicate the existence of shared stylistic concepts, contrasting with the eye-

FIG. 7—CHALCHITAN DISTRICT. Maximum width 14 cm. (Courtesy, Peabody Museum, Harvard.)

159

FIG. 8—ANTIGUA DISTRICT. Height 18 cm. (Courtesy, Peabody Museum, Harvard.) Tiquisate ware.

and-mouth treatment found on figurines from the Lowland Maya Area. Influences reaching the highlands, apparently stemming from the Maya lowlands and rare to absent in Tiquisate figurines, include the well-known forehead ridge, rising vertically above the nose (figs. 3–5). The site of Nebaj appears, in several respects, to have been on a stylistic frontier. A human-effigy whistle from a Late Classic Nebaj tomb is of unmistakable Alta Verapaz style, with basic lowland affiliations (Rands and Rands, Article 20, fig. 16). Yet the majority of pottery heads found at or near the site are representative of highland modeling, or at least that of the northern highlands (A. L. Smith and Kidder, 1951, fig. 86).

POSTCLASSIC

Modeling of anthropomorphic and animal effigies was an outstanding characteristic of Tohil Plumbate pottery. The great majority of pieces, whether heads, busts, or full figures, served as containers. In addition, Plumbate figurines, consisting of hollow images open at the bottom, occur in the Quezaltenango Valley (fig. 9; Shepard, 1948, p. 34, fig. 21,k,l). Figurines in Plum-

bate style are also known from Coban, in the Alta Verapaz (fig. 10; Dieseldorff, 1926–33, vol. 1, figs. 32–34, 44). Characteristics include seated female figures, with long hair framing the face, and lips drawn back to reveal prominent teeth (compare Tohil Plumbate effigy vessels in Shepard, 1948, fig. 20,b,d,g,j). On the same Early Postclassic horizon but differing in ware, animal figurines and whistles were recovered at Tajumulco (Dutton and Hobbs, 1943, pp. 59–62). Tohil levels at Zacualpa yielded a fine-featured head as well as cruder examples, of generalized "Archaic" style (Wauchope, 1948a, p. 152). At Zaculeu, the only group of figurines found in situ is from a Postclassic cache; the specimens are considered to be contemporaneous (Woodbury and Trik, 1953, p. 214). The cache is dated at the close of the Qankyak (Tohil Plumbate) phase or at the beginning of the Xinabahul. It is believed that the majority of figurines at Zaculeu date from approximately this time, yet it is difficult to recognize diagnostic features.

FIG. 9—QUEZALTENANGO VALLEY. Height 18 cm. (After Shepard, 1948, fig. 29,g.) Tohil Plumbate.

FIG. 10—COBAN. (After Dieseldorff, 1926–33, vol. 1, fig. 65.) Tohil Plumbate style.

Characteristics of the horizon may, however, include kneeling, moldmade female figures, to which heads, made in separate molds, were joined. A clearly kneeling female is also represented by one of the Tohil Plumbate figurines (fig. 9), whereas on the somewhat analogous figurines of the earlier Tiquisate horizon the knees of seated or kneeling female figures seem more consistently to be reduced to a basal platform.

Chinautla Polychrome and red-on-buff figurines mark the end of the pre-Spanish sequence in the Guatemala highlands. Again, modeling appears commonly on vessels in the ware, as well as on the figurines, although the latter represent humans whereas effigy handles on pots characteristically take the form of jaguar heads (fig. 11; Rands and Smith, Article 4, fig. 21,j). To judge from the few recovered examples, figurines bear simple linear designs, often employing parallel lines and triangles; are sometimes slightly restricted at the sides,

expanding to flat base and head; and bear impressed or serrated head crests (Dieseldorff, 1926–33, vol. 1, fig. 37; R. E. Smith, 1954b, figs. 1,j; 4,b-d). As with other types, the details of distribution within the highlands is a matter of conjecture.

In summary, little is known about figurines in the Guatemala highlands during the Classic and Postclassic periods. The decline of figurines from their Preclassic importance, as seen at Kaminaljuyu, is striking. Teotihuacan influences, although perhaps discernible in Early Classic figurines, are extremely rare. Localized styles seem eventually to have emerged, relatively free of outside influence yet perhaps closer to so-called "Pipil" developments along the Pacific slope than to the Classic Maya efflorescence in the north. It is possible that with the apparent Late Classic cessation of commerce between the lowland Maya area–north highlands and the southern highlands (R. E. Smith, 1955b, pp. 7–8), the inhabitants of the latter zone turned to the Pacific slope for their ceramic inspiration. With the subsequent collapse of Classic Maya civilization in the Peten, peoples of the Alta Verapaz, whose figurine production had previously been in the lowland tradition, also became oriented toward the

FIG. 11—ANTIGUA DISTRICT. Height 16 cm. (Courtesy, Peabody Museum, Harvard.) Chinautla Polychrome.

161

south, if we may judge from the handful of extant figurines in Plumbate style. This is a marginal situation, and the possibility of cultural lag, perhaps over sizable spans of time, increases the difficulty of determining chronological changes on the basis of typology. The need, as so often, is for the establishment of stratigraphic sequences through intensive and widespread excavation.

REFERENCES

Borhegyi, 1957b
Butler, 1935a
Dieseldorff, 1926–33
Dutton and Hobbs, 1943
Kelemen, 1943
Kidder, Jennings, and Shook, 1946
Shepard, 1948

Smith and Kidder, 1943, 1951
Smith, R. E., 1954b, 1955b, 1955d
Thompson, J. E. S., 1948
Wasson and Wasson, 1957
Wauchope, 1948a
Woodbury and Trik, 1953

7. Artifacts of the Guatemalan Highlands

RICHARD B. WOODBURY

T HE NONCERAMIC ARTIFACTS of highland Guatemala are neither its most
impressive nor best recorded evidence from the past. They have considerable importance, nevertheless, as they indicate a broad range of prehistoric activities,
including economic and technological, for
which neither pottery nor ceremonial architecture can be expected to furnish satisfactory evidence. As in much of Mesoamerica, objects of perishable material are
rarely found, although originally they probably made up a major portion of the artifact inventory. Also, archaeological interest
in ceremonial sites and in richly furnished
graves has meant that few everyday objects
have come to light. Thus the following
survey cannot be a fully rounded account
of the prehistoric material culture of the
region, but is a summary of our present
knowledge.[1]

The nonceramic artifacts of highland
Guatemala can be divided into those serving utilitarian, commonplace purposes and
those whose function was mainly ritual or
symbolic. The first class includes metates
and manos, bark beaters, pounding and
abrading stones, some but not all of the
chipped flint and obsidian, bone tools, cloth,
and matting. Most of these are poorly represented in archaeological collections, since
practically no village or city sites have been
dug, and everyday objects are rare in the
grave furnishings of the important personages, the source of most of our data. Nevertheless, since the characteristics of many of
these types of artifacts changed little
through the centuries, our small sample
provides a fairly good picture of the less
perishable equipment of the general pop-

[1] Most of our data come from the long series
of careful excavations and comprehensive reports
by the Department of Archaeology of the Carnegie
Institution of Washington, which halted its work
in the highlands in 1950. In these reports the
artifact descriptions and comparative notes by A.
V. Kidder have furnished the basis of much of this
survey. To avoid burdening the text with numerous
references, the following titles can be cited as the
source of most of the specimens mentioned: for
the Formative or Preclassic, Shook, 1951a; Shook
and Kidder, 1952; for the Classic, Berlin, 1952;
Kidder, Jennings, and Shook, 1946; Smith and
Kidder, 1943; Smith and Kidder, 1951; for the
Postclassic, Dutton and Hobbs, 1943; for both the
Classic and Postclassic, Butler, 1940; Wauchope,
1948a; Woodbury and Trik, 1953.

163

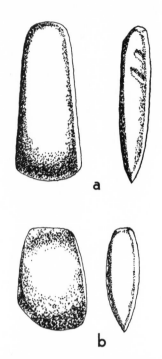

FIG. 1—CELTS. *a*, Postclassic (Qankyak phase, Zaculeu), length 8.6 cm. *b*, Early Classic (Atzan phase, Zaculeu), length 5.4 cm. (scale 1/2). (From Woodbury and Trik, 1953, fig. 120,*a,b*.)

ulation. The second class of artifacts includes stone vessels, some of the chipped stone objects, the pyrite-incrusted plaques, jade jewelry, metal, shell, stuccoed objects, and some of the cloth and other perishable products. Some of these things have been studied and published in great detail, both for clues to cross-dating and to trade and other inter-areal relationships, and for information on the techniques and skills of the ancient craftsmen.

It should also be pointed out that the preponderance of Early Classic data probably obscures the variety and richness of the material culture of the later centuries of the Formative,[2] still relatively poorly known. Also, a similar paucity of data makes evaluation of the Postclassic difficult. However, the widely held impression

[2] Ed. note: Also referred to as the Preclassic period.

164

that the Postclassic saw a waning of artistic achievement (see, for example, Holden, 1957) is borne out for the Guatemalan highlands by the gradual disappearance of pyrite-incrusted plaques and stucco decoration.

CELTS (fig. 1)

Enormous amounts of wood must have been needed for burning the lime used in large quantities by Postclassic builders; beams and poles were required for roofs and walls from Formative times onward; and clearing farm land was probably an important annual activity. Nevertheless, celts (ungrooved axes) are scarce at sites of all phases. They may have been more important tools than this scarcity suggests, however, being used and worn out or lost far from settlements and ceremonial centers. It is also possible that celts were not needed for some of these activities, as experiments in Yucatan (Hester, 1953, p. 288) have shown that land can be cleared "with bare hands, unworked stone tools, and fire" about half as fast as with steel tools.

In highland Guatemala celts are usually found much worn or fragmentary, but occasionally in perfect condition and used as grave furnishings. The oldest known are from the Las Charcas phase of the Formative, currently dated at about the 4th century B.C. Other celts come from the Formative site of Cambote; from the Early Classic at Kaminaljuyu, Zacualpa, and Zaculeu; from the Late Classic at Cotio (Shook, 1952a) and San Augustin Acasaguastlan; and from the Postclassic at Tajumulco and Zacualpa.

Throughout this time celts show only slight variations. They were made of various hard, fine-grained igneous rocks, shaped by pecking followed by careful grinding and polishing. The faces are slightly convex and cross sections range from rectangular to nearly circular. They are usually small, 5–12 cm. long, but occasionally much larger. No grooving or notching for the handle occurs; they were probably hafted by insertion in a slotted or perforated wooden handle, a technique shown in several Classic sculptures at lowland sites (Proskouriakoff, 1950, p. 96, fig. 34,*w-a'*). Grooved axes are extremely rare (Kidder, 1943) and can be accounted for either by trade from northern Mexico or by independent invention. Adzes are unreported from highland Guatemala.

BARK BEATERS (fig. 2)

At many sites from Veracruz to Costa Rica there have been found thick discoidal or rectangular tools with the edge grooved for hafting and one or both faces scored or corrugated. They are identified from ethnographic parallels as bark beaters, used to make cloth or paper from fibers of the agave or the bark of various trees (Linné, 1934, pp. 197–204). They were probably hafted with a withe looped around the stone and tightly bound. In the Guatemalan highlands they have been found mainly in the Late Classic and Postclassic, but at least one fragment comes from the Early Classic. The paper made with these beaters was, of course, extremely perishable, even though its white plaster sizing and the painting it bore have sometimes been detected by careful excavation. It seems certain that from Early Classic times onward paper was made, perhaps chiefly to be painted with portrayals and symbols of religious or calendrical significance.

PERFORATED STONES

"Doughnut stones" occur at many sites in the central highlands and more rarely in the northern highlands and on the Pacific slope. A few have come from adjacent regions of El Salvador and Honduras. Their distribution and probable function are discussed by Shook (1949b, pp. 14, 20–21) and Kidder, Jennings, and Shook (1946, pp. 141–42). They occur from the Formative through the Late Classic, and possibly

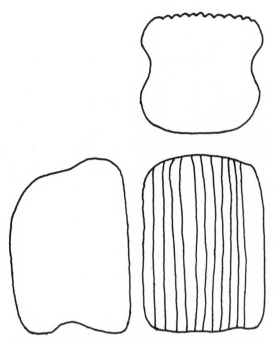

FIG. 2—BARK BEATER. Postclassic, Zacualpa, length 9.2 cm. (scale 1/2). (From Wauchope, 1948a, fig. 78.)

into the Postclassic. They are generally of vesicular lava, sometimes of limestone or harder stone, and are shaped by pecking with little subsequent smoothing. The outer diameter is about 10–17 cm. and the biconical perforation is usually about 3.5 cm. in diameter. Many specimens show wear in this perforation and it is generally supposed that they were digging-stick weights. Since firm attachment to a straight stick would be difficult, the weight may have rested above a knob or short branch.

METATES AND MANOS (fig. 3)

Equipment for corn grinding was an essential part of the furnishings of every Indian house from early times, and possibly grinding slabs of a simple type were used even before maize agriculture began, but few metates and manos have been found in datable contexts. From Formative times onward metates were carefully shaped, rounded or rectangular slabs of hard igneous rock,

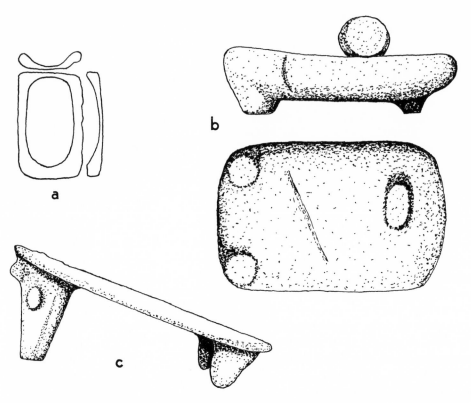

FIG. 3—METATES. *a,* For domestic use, from Zacualpa, length about 60 cm. (scale 1/20) (from Wauchope, 1948a, fig. 75). *b,* From Early Classic tomb, Zaculeu, length 37 cm. (scale 1/6) (from Woodbury and Trik, 1953, fig. 279, *q,q'*). *c,* From Postclassic tomb, Zaculeu, length 45 cm. (scale 1/6) (from *idem,* fig. 279,*p*).

the grinding surface gradually wearing deeply at the center, leaving the ends thicker and sometimes leaving an unworn ridge along each side. The mano was usually elliptical to rectangular, shorter than the metate's width, and used on one or both faces. The tripodal metate characteristic of modern Guatemala replaced the legless type for everyday use at a time not yet determined, probably late in the Postclassic. However, the tripodal metate was used, at least for special purposes, as early as the Early Classic. In tombs at Kaminaljuyu and Zaculeu miniature and normal-sized metates were included with the elaborate burial offerings. They have rounded corners, nearly horizontal (little used?) grinding surfaces, and three short knoblike legs. Their manos

are nearly cylindrical, thickened toward the center, but were pushed rather than rolled. Similar tripodal metates are not recorded for everyday use, so these were probably made to grind corn for sacred purposes. Also of probable ritual function are the finely made tripodal metates found in Postclassic graves and caches; the slab is thin and steeply sloping, worn very smooth but still flat, and the single leg supporting the high end is sometimes carved as an animal head. (This may be a local echo of the elaborate effigy metates characteristic of Costa Rica at this time and sometimes traded as far as Santa Lucia Cotzumalhuapa, on the Guatemalan Pacific slope [Mason, 1943, fig. 31; J. E. S. Thompson, 1948, p. 41].) Long cylindrical manos were used with these metates. The modern Guatemalan metate is similar but much heavier, less carefully shaped, and undecorated.

Mortars and Pestles

Unless the mortars and pestles were wooden, this technique of preparing food or pigments was little used. Deep, bowl-shaped tetrapod stone mortars occur in the Kaminaljuyu Formative, and small shallow mortars, though rare, come from Kaminaljuyu in the Formative and Early Classic, and at Tajumulco in the Postclassic. Three of the Formative examples are frog effigies, a shallow depression in the back serving for grinding. The pestles of these and most other mortars are plain, elongated stones, although a bell-shaped pestle was found at Tajumulco. The small size and shallowness of most of these mortars suggest use for special foods, such as seasonings, or for pigments, but residues of any kind have not been reported.

Paint Palettes

Slabs or dishes clearly used for grinding and mixing pigments are as rare as mortars and pestles. At San Agustin Acasaguastlan and Zaculeu small, oval or rectangular dishes were found, a low rim bordering the working surface, which was stained with red pigment in two out of three examples. One of these palettes, Postclassic in age, was supported on three small feet. Several kinds of pigment have been found in small pottery vessels or in circumstances suggesting a wrapping of cloth or leather, but these containers would not have served for grinding and mixing.

Hammerstones

The quarrying and shaping of building stone undoubtedly required the work of many laborers. We can assume on the basis of practices elsewhere that irregular pieces of hard rock were used in quarrying and shaping, held in the hand and used to peck or crumble the softer stone. The

shapes of the tools would be fortuitous at the start; with use they would approach the spherical. Such tools have only rarely been noticed and reported: from the Early Classic, at Kaminaljuyu; Early or Late Classic, at San Agustin Acasaguastlan; Classic or Postclassic, at Zaculeu.

Rubbing and Polishing Stones

Few tools have been found which can be identified as used for abrading, smoothing, or polishing. Archaeological attention has focused on the products of these processes —the sculpture, pottery, jewelry, polished plaster walls and floors—and not the means by which they were achieved. The few small irregular pieces of pumice and other abrasive materials reported indicate the kind of simple tools that were needed in large numbers of craftsmen. Such tools would have been worn to mere scraps and

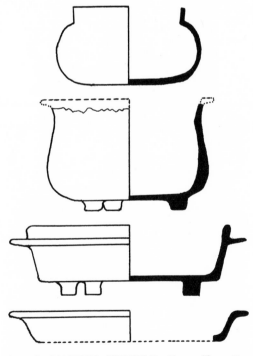

Fig. 4—MARBLE VESSELS. From Formative tomb (Miraflores phase, Kaminaljuyu), diameters about 15–24 cm. (scale 3/11). (From Shook and Kidder, 1952, fig. 50,*a,b,c,e*.)

FIG. 5—CARVED AND STUCCOED STONE VASE. Formative (Miraflores phase, Kaminaljuyu), height 9.5 cm. (scale about 1/2). (From Shook and Kidder, 1952, fig. 51.)

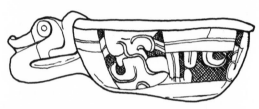

FIG. 6—INCISED STONE VASE. Formative (Miraflores phase, Kaminaljuyu), length 21 cm. (scale about 3/7). (From Shook and Kidder, 1952, fig. 77,a.)

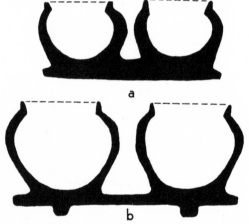

FIG. 7—DOUBLE CUPS. Early Classic (Esperanza phase, Kaminaljuyu), length 15 and 19 cm. (scale about 2/5). (From Kidder, Jennings, and Shook, 1946, fig. 59,a,b.)

discarded and their shapes would rarely have been distinctive enough for the manner of use to be inferred. However, at Kaminaljuyu there was found in an Early

Classic context a tool used to smooth and polish the face and upper part of the throat of jade earplug flares; it is of hard stone, irregular except for the conical working surface, and shows by its wear that it had long use, probably with a fine abrasive.

Stones of convenient size, often river cobbles, were used for a variety of rubbing and smoothing processes. At Zaculeu, for example, two plaster smoothers were found, their edges still incrusted with plaster showing marks of workmen's fingers. Small pebbles and small greenstone celts have been identified as pottery polishers, their faceting the result of use, but their rarity suggests that most pottery polishing was done with other tools, perhaps of hard wood.

STONE VESSELS (figs. 4–8)

Although never plentiful, vessels of stone occur in graves from the Formative onward, usually of relatively soft materials but carved with care in a variety of shapes and sometimes decorated with incision or relief. The largest group from a single locality is also the oldest, 16 vessels from the Miraflores phase tombs at Kaminaljuyu; they are mostly small, and are of schist, marble, soapstone, and other materials. There are globular and cylindrical jars, and flat-bottomed bowls with or without

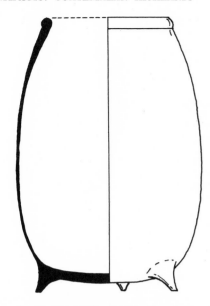

FIG. 8—ALABASTER VASE. Postclassic (Qankyak phase, Zaculeu), diameter 12 cm. (scale 1/2). (From Woodbury and Trik, 1953, fig. 138.)

FIG. 9—MUSHROOM STONE. Formative (Miraflores phase, Kaminaljuyu), height 37 cm. (scale about 1/4). (From Shook and Kidder, 1952, fig. 78,*f*, left-hand panel only.)

a broad flange below the rim; several are tripodal. One is decorated with a pair of faces (Tlalocs?) in relief; another has an animal head and basketry pattern in relief and also polychrome stucco decoration. The Early Classic is represented by three vessels, from Kaminaljuyu and Zaculeu, double cups of alabaster—a pair of small cups on a rectangular base with or without four small feet. A single Late Classic alabaster vessel is of quite different shape, flat-bottomed with outward-sloping walls and truncated conical cover. In the Late Classic alabaster vessels, both ring-based and tripodal, occur in several sites, usually associated with plumbate pottery or metal: Chipal, Tajumulco, Zacualpa, and Zaculeu. They are globular or pear-shaped, quite different from the marble vases of the Ulua area; they may be inspired by vessels made in central Mexico of *tecali*, a banded calcite sometimes mistaken for onyx.

MUSHROOM STONES (fig. 9)

These carved stone objects, about 20–30 cm. high, have been found at a few high-

land Guatemala sites, and also in Chiapas and on the Pacific slope of Guatemala. Minor differences in form distinguish the specimens of the Formative from those of the Classic (Borhegyi, 1957b), the earliest examples having a groove around the top, an effigy stem, and a square or tripod base. Later forms often have a plain stem instead of an animal form and lack the groove on the top. Some mushrooms, of undetermined age, have a seated human figure forming the stem. None has been found in unquestionable Postclassic association. Their function has long been a matter of speculation and it has recently been suggested that they were part of a cult still surviving in parts of Mesoamerica in which hallucinogenic mushrooms played a central role (Wasson and Wasson, 1957; Borhegyi, 1961a), although the stone mushrooms have not been found in the areas where the modern cult is reported. An as-

169

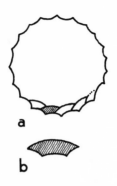

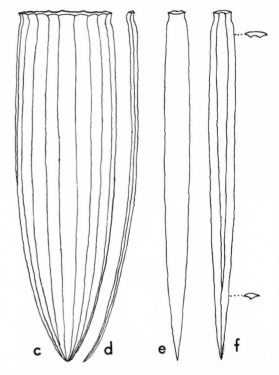

FIG. 10—OBSIDIAN BLADES. *a,* Diagrammatic section of core, showing amount of core removed in striking several blades. *b,* Enlarged cross section of one of blades from core, showing single convex surface of inner face and three convex surfaces comprising outer face. *c,* Side view of typical core. *d–f,* Views of edge, inner face, and outer face of typical blade (scale 1/2). (From Kidder, Jennings and Shook, 1946, fig. 55,*a–f.*)

sociation of these stones with the Maya nine lords of the night is suggested by the finding, in a Miraflores phase deposit at Kaminaljuyu, of nine miniature mushroom stones (14–18 cm. high) associated with nine miniature metates and manos (Borhegyi, 1961a). Caches of objects in groups of nine have occasionally been found in various parts of the Maya area, but not previously including mushroom stones; if other such assemblages are found in controlled excavations, this proposed interpretation will be strengthened. Pottery objects representing mushrooms, found in El Salvador, may possibly be similarly associated with the use of narcotic mushrooms.

CHIPPED STONE OBJECTS (figs. 10, 11)

"Unaltered obsidian flake-blades were by far the most common stone implements of the Guatemalan highlands" (Kidder, Jennings, and Shook, 1946, p. 135). They occur at virtually all sites, beginning in the highlands with the Las Charcas phase of the Formative. On the Pacific Coast they

appear in the Conchas phase (M. D. Coe, 1961, p. 107), although they are absent in the preceding Ocos phase. It is probable that they were in use at least as early in the highlands as on the coast as the coastal obsidian came from upland sources. Not only are other stone artifacts less numerous than unaltered obsidian blades, but of chipped stone objects the great majority is of obsidian and only rarely in the form of tools with additional shaping. This is doubtless due in part to the effectiveness of the unaltered obsidian blades with their razorsharp edges, in part to the abundance of obsidian in the volcanic highlands, and in part to the remarkable skill developed by the ancient craftsmen who made these blades. The technique was probably similar to that observed in Mexico in the 16th century (see new translations of the relevant passages of Torquemada and Motolinia by J. E. S. Thompson *in* Kidder, Jennings, and Shook, 1946, pp. 135–36). The obsidian blades are slender, slightly curving, with a triangular or trapezoidal cross

170

section. The larger end preserves a small area of the striking platform of the core, and the other end tapers to a sharp, delicate point. When new, the edges are extremely sharp. Long, "unused" blades found in caches and graves are often as long as 18–20 cm. and only 1–2 cm. wide. But the majority of blades are found broken into short pieces, their edges dulled and nicked by use; such blades tend to be wider and thicker than the "unused" blades, as befits their role as everyday tools.

The slender obsidian blades from graves and caches frequently occur in groups of almost identical specimens, the Miraflores phase tombs at Kaminaljuyu, for example, having sets of 15, 8, and 3. Most of the Esperanza phase tombs at the same site had sets of 2–10 blades, many with the outer surface of the butt rounded by fine chipping. Large groups of blades were found at San Agustin Acasaguastlan in a Late Classic or early Postclassic tomb, and out of 382 blades in a group 225 had shallow notches near the butt, as though they had been suspended to form a necklace or the

fringe of a garment. The use made of most of these delicate blades was probably not ornamental, however. Ceremonial bloodletting, as shown in various works of art from lowland Maya centers and as reported in the 16th century, was probably practiced extensively in the highlands. These undulled blades, their sharp tips and edges appearing unused, would have been excellent for the purpose, and would show no dulling from such a use. These blades are discussed further by Kidder (1947, pp. 4–32) in an extensive study of the typology, distribution, and use of obsidian and flint in Mesoamerica. One particularly interesting find in Alta Verapaz is cited, three flake-blades each in a jar with the bones of a human finger, suggestive of personal sacrifice going beyond bloodletting.

Obsidian and occasionally chert or flint were fashioned into several shapes of bifacial tools which would have served as knives hafted on short, stout handles and as lances or spears on long shafts. Pictorial evidence from Mexico and the lowlands of Guatemala indicates both uses. Many

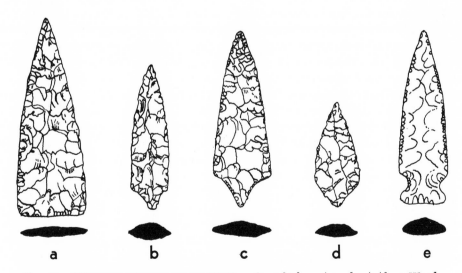

FIG. 11—CHIPPED POINTS OR BLADES. *a*, Straight base (stemless) (from Woodbury and Trik, 1953, fig. 122). *b–d*, Contracting or tapering stem (from *idem*, fig. 123,*a–c*). *e*, Expanding stem (from *idem*, fig. 124,*a*). All from Zaculeu, Postclassic (*a–d*, Qankyak phase; *e*, Qankyak or Xinabahul phase). Length of *a* 10.4 cm. (scale 1/2).

171

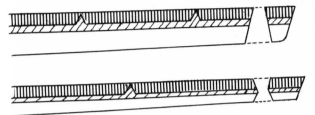

FIG. 12—CROSS SECTIONS OF PYRITE-INCRUSTED PLAQUES. Early Classic. Pyrite polygons shown by vertical hatching, cement by oblique hatching, and stone disk plain. Conical and biconical perforations shown at right (scale, actual size). (From Woodbury and Trik, 1953, fig. 129.)

ot these points or knives have tapering or contracting stems; this shape occurs in the Early Classic and in the earlier part of the Postclassic. There are also a few chipped points with rounded or straight bases. Even rarer are points with notches which form an expanding stem; they are relatively late, probably all Postclassic, as is generally true for notched points throughout Mesoamerica. Neither the large "chopping" or general utility tools of flint nor the eccentrics of obsidian that occur in the lowlands are found in the highlands, except on the Pacific slope.

Although they are not numerous, interest attaches to a few large, exquisitely chipped knives (or points) with both ends pointed or with one rounded or squared end (Kaminaljuyu, Early Classic; San Agustin Acasaguastlan, Late Classic; Nebaj and Zaculeu, Postclassic). These tools, of both flint and obsidian, are widely distributed in Mesoamerica (Kidder, 1947, pp. 18–19, 24–25). Since they are found in ritual deposits and seldom show dulling from use, the belief that they served as knives for human sacrifice is not unreasonable.

Mention should be made of the occasional use of fortuitously shaped flakes or other fragments of obsidian (rarely flint) for scrapers; these are sometimes carefully sharpened by chipping along a convenient edge. Also, obsidian served for rare special uses, where its high luster was effective. A

stuccoed deer or rabbit head in the Early Classic tomb at Zaculeu had an eye made of a short section of obsidian flake-blade. Two tombs of the same age at Kaminaljuyu contained groups of tiny perforated obsidian flakes, which may have been sewn on garments as sequins.

PYRITE-INCRUSTED PLAQUES (figs. 12–14)

Some of the most remarkable products of prehistoric American craftsmen are seldom seen in museum collections or found by archaeologists in an even moderately good state of preservation. These are stone disks on which polygons of iron pyrite were precisely fitted to form a mosaic, polished to a mirror brightness. Pyrite decomposes easily in dampness, so that these plaques are often found rotted and barely recognizable. Nevertheless, they were masterpieces of the stoneworker's craft and when new must have been dazzlingly beautiful. The disks, of slate or sometimes shale or fine sandstone, range from 8 to 25 cm. in diameter and are generally perfect circles. They are 0.4–0.7 cm. thick, sometimes thinner toward the edge. Early Classic disks were beveled toward the rear and had two pairs of suspension holes (rarely, two single holes) near opposite edges. This type of plaque persists in the Late Classic, but began to be replaced by plaques perforated by a single central pair of holes which were connected by a groove running beneath the pyrite mosaic, so that a suspension cord would not show on the front. These plaques, continuing into the Postclassic, were sometimes beveled toward the front and the bevel sometimes carried stucco decoration. Pyrite has a hardness of 6.0 to 6.5 (Mohs' scale), about the same as glass, but on the few undecayed plaques found the pieces of pyrite are so perfectly shaped and fitted that the joints are almost invisible, a result of long and careful grinding of each bit of pyrite. The polygons are usually about 2–4 cm. across, rarely as much as 10 cm. Their edges are beveled

Fig. 13—CARVED BACK OF PYRITE-INCRUSTED PLAQUE. Early Classic (Atzan phase, Zaculeu), diameter 23 cm. (scale 3/4). (From Woodbury and Trik, 1953, fig. 131.)

so that they could be held more firmly by the adhesive, which was apparently a very fine clay mixed with an organic glue.

Besides the circular plaques just described there are a few square plaques, circular plaques with atypical arrangements of suspension holes, and mosaics combining pyrite, jade, and other materials. Plaques became increasingly rare in the later Postclassic and their manufacture probably ended before the 16th century.

The backs of the stone disks forming foundations for plaques were usually plain, but several finely carved or stuccoed backs have been found. At Kaminaljuyu three Early Classic plaques had elaborate polychrome stucco decoration in the same Teotihuacan style that appears on some of the

173

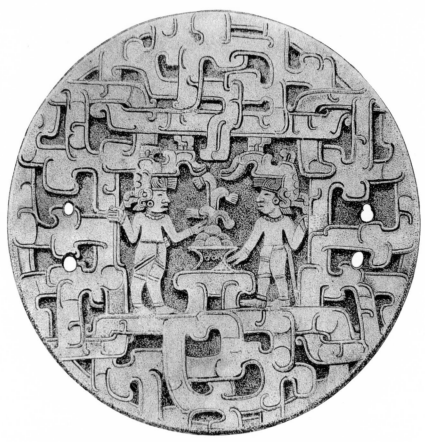

F<small>IG</small>. 14—CARVED BACK OF PYRITE-INCRUSTED PLAQUE. Early Classic (Esperanza phase, Kaminaljuyu), diameter 19 cm. (scale 3/5). (From Kidder, Jennings, and Shook, 1946, fig. 156, upper.)

stuccoed tripodal jars associated with them. The elaborate carved back of another Early Classic plaque at Kaminaljuyu is in the Tajin style of Veracruz, and two of the same age from Zaculeu, unfortunately fragmentary, have scenes in a style perhaps related to the Pacific slope.

The prototype for these remarkable mosaics has apparently been found in the Miraflores phase of the Formative, in the form of rectangular plaques made by grinding down large sherds and mounting small rectangles of pyrite on the concave surface.

Pyrite plaques are not only one of the most remarkable of Middle American minor works of art, but one of the most widely distributed, attesting to the interest and value accorded them. They have been found from Pueblo Bonito in northern New Mexico to Cocle in Panama (finds at 27 locations are reported in Kidder, Jennings, and Shook, 1946, pp. 132–33), and their regional and temporal variations have significance as clues to trade relations and to the contemporaneity of widely separated cultural assemblages. Because of their great numbers in the Guatemalan highlands (35 from Mounds A and B at Kaminaljuyu, 33 in the large tomb at Zaculeu, caches at Chama of 29 and 37, over 200 at Nebaj, and about 15 from Lake Amatitlan at a depth of 40 feet) this may prove to be the

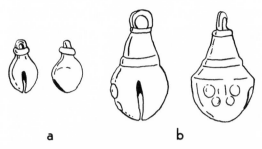

a   b

FIG. 15—COPPER BELLS. Postclassic (Qankyak phase, Zaculeu), lengths 1.7 and 3.4 cm. (scale, actual size). (From Woodbury and Trik, 1953, fig. 152,a,b.)

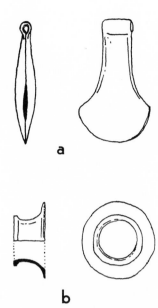

a

b

FIG. 16—COPPER TWEEZERS AND EAR SPOOL. Postclassic (Xinabahul phase, Zaculeu), length of a, 6.4 cm., diameter of b, 3.9 cm. (scale 1/2). (From Woodbury and Trik, 1953, fig. 154,a,c.)

major source of their production and spread.

The purpose served by these plaques is uncertain. They were greatly treasured; most of them are from graves and caches, although sometimes intentionally destroyed; some lay with skeletons, as though originally worn or carried on the chest; a few at Nebaj lay in bowls apparently specially made for them. They would not have been effective mirrors, since the separate reflections from the pyrite polygons would have produced a distorted image. Nevertheless, they would have a blinding, yellow brightness, making them conspicuous and impressive objects visible from a great distance. Their role, then, was probably symbolic, part of the infinitely elaborate ritual paraphernalia used by the priests or leaders in whose graves they have been found.

METAL (figs. 15–17)

Although objects of gold, tumbaga (a copper-gold alloy), and copper have been found only in very small numbers, many can be approximately dated and have been analyzed by W. C. Root of Bowdoin College, so that they contribute significantly to our knowledge of New World metallurgy. Within Guatemala the oldest specimen is from San Agustin Acasaguastlan, a scrap of tumbaga gilded by the *mise-en-couleur* process (sufficient surface copper

removed with acid to produce a nearly pure gold surface when burnished); its association with San Juan plumbate places it at the close of the Late Classic. A short distance to the east, at Copan, Honduras, two leg fragments from a tumbaga figurine, possibly of Panamanian origin, were found in a Late Classic cache, but are apparently a redeposit of later date (Longyear, 1952, p. 112). At Tazumal in western El Salvador copper has been reported in a Late Classic context (Kidder, 1948, p. 229) but no details have been published. Other presumed Classic or Formative metal objects in the Maya area are of doubtful association, or are actually Postclassic (Lothrop, 1952, pp. 22–23; R. E. Smith, 1955c).

The earlier (Tohil Plumbate) horizon of the Postclassic is represented by finds from Nebaj, Tajumulco, and Zaculeu. They include about 30 copper bells, mostly pear-shaped, a few pieces of gold foil, one with repoussé decoration, and several forming

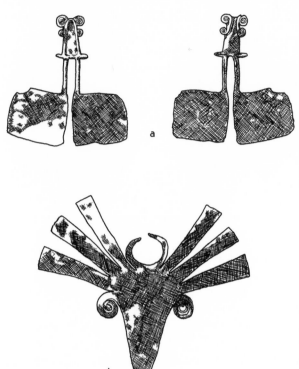

FIG. 17—TUMBAGA ORNAMENTS. Gilded by *mise-en-couleur* technique. Postclassic (*a*, Qankyak phase; *b*, Xinabahul phase; both from Zaculeu). Length of *a*, 5.0 cm.; width of *b*, 11.2 cm. (From Woodbury and Trik, 1953, fig. 285,*a,a,'b*.)

coverings for small flat or tubular wooden objects; a painted copper bird head originally mounted, with a bell inside, on a turquoise-decorated stone disk; and a tumbaga pendant gilded by the *mise-en-couleur* technique, a frog with exaggeratedly flattened feet in a style common in Panama but also copied in Oaxaca. The gold, tumbaga, and copper bird head came from Mexico in all probability, but most of the bells are believed to be local Guatemalan products, as *cire-perdue* casting was known in Guatemala at least by late prehistoric times (Lothrop, 1952, p. 25).

Documented metal for the later (post-plumbate) horizon of the Postclassic is scarce; at Chipal were found a gold ring, copper bells, and a gilded tumbaga frag-

176

ment. At Zaculeu there were a rectangular plaque and four convex disks of a unique silver-copper alloy, perforated as though for sewing on a garment; a gilded tumbaga "butterfly" pendant in a style native to Oaxaca; and tweezers, ear spools, and a ring of copper. The age and place of origin are unknown for three gold disks with repoussé decoration (Lothrop, 1936, pp. 61–75; Nottebohm, 1945), although they are probably Postclassic Mexican imports. At the time of the conquest of Guatemala little metal of any sort was reported, in contrast with Mexico.

BONE OBJECTS

Few bone artifacts have survived decay in the damp earth of the highlands, but enough has been found to indicate that a considerable variety of everyday tools was made, as well as finely decorated objects of symbolic significance. No difference from Early Classic to Postclassic can yet be defined, and the Formative is barely represented. Utilitarian objects include awls, needles with both drilled and gouged eyes, and antler tines used as flakers for shaping flint or obsidian. Some of these tools come from graves and caches and may have served in the making of ritual equipment which thus gave them an aura of sanctity which their form alone would not suggest.

Jaguar jaws were cut away from the skull and almost certainly made into masks or headdresses with part or all of the skin attached. The spine of the sting ray was apparently used to draw blood from the body for religious reasons (see Tozzer, 1941a, pp. 113–14, for the observations of Landa and others on this practice). In Kaminaljuyu's Formative tombs they were found in a cluster beside a skeleton as though thrust in the belt, and similar clusters have been found in Early Classic tombs. A few elaborately carved bone objects have been found, such as fragmentary tubes and an elegantly incised human skull from the Early Classic. Human bone seems to have been rather extensively used for ceremonial objects (see Kidder, Jennings, and Shook, 1946, pp. 153–55, for discussion and examples). The probable antiquity and artistic virtuosity of bone carving in the Guatemalan highlands is best suggested by the remarkable decorated human femurs from a late Formative tomb at Chiapa del Corzo in neighboring Chiapas (Agrinier, 1960).

SHELL OBJECTS

Because of the attractive luster of its surface, the handsome color and interesting shape of some species, and the ease with which it can be carved, incised, cut, and ground, shell was used in large amounts for a great variety of nonutilitarian objects, even though it had to be imported from the Pacific Ocean, the Gulf of Campeche, or the Gulf of Honduras. About 20 species have been identified, the majority from the Pacific. Unfortunately, shell rots easily in damp ground and many of the finest pieces found are fragmentary and discolored. The largest amounts of shell have been found in Early Classic graves at Kaminaljuyu (see Kidder, Jennings, and Shook, 1946, pp. 145–52 for extensive comparative notes) and at Zaculeu, but shell continued in use through the later periods as well. Less excavation has been done in Formative graves, but those of the Miraflores phase contained among their rich furnishings only a few small disk beads and a pendant, suggesting that shell was less popular or less available then than later.

Discoidal beads are the most numerous type of shell ornament; an Early Classic burial at Zaculeu had some 5000 small disk beads used to decorate a belt, anklets, and possibly wristlets of perishable material, and with another burial were about 2000 disk beads scattered over the chest and hips as though fallen from a garment. Disk beads were also strung as necklaces, often with beads of other shapes and materials, or with pendants. Tubular beads,

sometimes of large size, were made in lesser numbers. *Spondylus* was probably the most popular genus, because of its handsome red color; besides being used for beads and pendants, these shells were sometimes made into small dishes to hold cinnabar, jade, or other precious substances. Univalve shells, especially *Oliva*, were often prepared for suspension by merely cutting the tip; sets of a few to about 400 were found in the Early Classic tombs of Kaminaljuyu, probably hung on ceremonial costumes as tinklers.

A few small figurines and heads of shell have been found, mostly inferior to those of pottery or jade, and several disks with elaborate cut-out, inlaid, or painted decoration. Shell trumpets were made by cutting off the tip of the spire of a large conch (*Fasciolaria*); these were sometimes painted or incised, and military and ceremonial uses are presumed. The extensive prehistoric use of shell may be related to the mythologic and religious importance the Maya attached to water and water-dwelling creatures, particularly the conch (J. E. S. Thompson, 1950, pp. 173–74).

CLOTH

For the highland Maya there is available neither the abundant and sometimes detailed representation of textiles that occurs on lowland sculpture (d'Harcourt, 1958; Proskouriakoff, 1950) and painting (Ruppert, Thompson, and Proskouriakoff, 1955), nor any such quantity of textile fragments as was dredged from the Cenote at Chichen Itza (Tozzer, 1957, p. 198). Nevertheless, from early Formative times onward cloth was probably woven in quantity and with great skill. Our scanty evidence is mostly impressions on pottery, and therefore it can only be assumed that cotton was the major material. Early Classic to Postclassic sherds at Kaminaljuyu and Zaculeu show the imprints of hard-twisted yarns used in open plain weaves, some of which would have had about the texture of modern cheesecloth. Closer weaves also occur, but less commonly. Thread counts for warps and wefts range from about 10 to 36 per 2.5 cm. In one instance the textile impression was intentionally used on the surface of an effigy vessel, and in other cases it resulted from cloth being used against the inner wall of a vessel during its manufacture. A few sherds have been found (Kidder, 1949b) in which a plain weave of single threads was modified by pairing some of the warps to give a striped or ribbed effect. The only specimens of cloth itself from the highlands come from caves just across the Guatemalan border in Chiapas (O'Neale, 1942; Wauchope, 1942; Blom, 1954; I. W. Johnson, 1954). These were associated with cremation jars of late Postclassic type. The fragments are all plain weaves with single and with triple wefts, and include pieces decorated by painting in several colors and by resist-painting in the batik technique. The variety and complexity of modern Guatemalan Indian weaving suggests that most of the techniques and some of the decorative motifs had a long pre-Columbian history (O'Neale, 1945, p. 1), although the extent of introductions in colonial times from both Europe and Southeast Asia has never actually been determined.

BASKETRY AND OTHER PERISHABLE OBJECTS

In spite of unfavorable conditions for preservation, traces of a few perishable objects have been found. From the Formative (Las Charcas phase) there have been reported, but not described, impressions of baskets, mats, and rope, and also (Miraflores phase) evidence that twilled mats were used in large numbers in tombs. The richly furnished Early Classic tombs of Kaminaljuyu contained only one uncertain trace of basketry, but they revealed extensive impressions of twilled mats used to cover walls and floors and to wrap corpses. At San Agustin Acasaguastlan a Late Classic tomb also contained impressions of mats, the

largest about 2.40 by 1.60 m. The imprints of such mats have also been found on pottery, where griddles were rested on them during the shaping of the soft clay. The mats appear to have been much like the *petates* made in Guatemala today.

Of the feathers that were doubtless used extensively in headdresses, traces have been found in only three Early Classic tombs. Copal has also occasionally been found, both as lumps and made into beads and ear ornaments.

STUCCOED OBJECTS

A common method of decorating objects of many kinds was the use of a coat of white or light gray stucco on which paint was applied, often in elaborate polychrome designs. Pottery decorated in this manner makes up an important part of the more elaborate furnishings of many Early Classic tombs; the numerous other traces of stucco found in these tombs indicates that its most lavish use, however, was on objects of perishable materials. Since most of these would at best have been extremely fragile, they may have been made specially for the burial rites. At Kaminaljuyu traces of stucco-decorated gourds were found in Formative tombs. Early Classic tombs at the same site contained several kinds of stuccoed nonceramic objects (see Kidder, Jennings, Shook, 1946, pp. 274–77, for Shepard's technical analyses of stucco): a dozen "trays," oval with vertical sides; "sheets" a meter or more across, perhaps of both hide and bark cloth; and on one of the mortuary "litters" (itself only a trace on the tomb floor) traces of round or oval fan. At Zaculeu similar sheets were found in an Early Classic tomb, and also stuccoed wooden (?) bowls and a stucco-decorated deer or rabbit head, originally a profile (of wood?) with the same portrayal on both surfaces. At Nebaj a plaque of perishable material carried stucco decoration which included a human figure and glyphs. The most interesting stuccoed object yet found is a mass of flakes in a Late Classic grave at San Agustin Acasaguastlan (Kidder, 1935, p. 112), which suggested by their arrangement that they were the sizing for the pages of a codex. The quality and abundance of stucco decoration, and the occurrence of bark beaters in Classic times makes this a reasonable possibility, but the decay of the foundation material precluded any separation or identification of the stucco fragments.

REFERENCES

Agrinier, 1960
Berlin, 1952
Blom, 1954
Borhegyi, 1957b, 1961a
Butler, 1940
Coe, M. D., 1960a
d'Harcourt, 1958
Dutton and Hobbs, 1943
Hester, 1953
Holden, 1957
Johnson, I. W., 1954
Kidder, 1935, 1943, 1947, 1948, 1949b
——, Jennings, and Shook, 1946
Linné, 1934
Longyear, 1952
Lothrop, 1933, 1936, 1952

Mason, J. A., 1943
Nottebohm, 1945
O'Neale, 1942, 1945
Proskouriakoff, 1950
Ruppert, Thompson, and Proskouriakoff, 1955
Shook, 1949b, 1951a, 1952a
—— and Kidder, 1952
Smith, A. L., and Kidder, 1943, 1951
Smith, R. E., 1955c
Tax, 1951
Thompson, J. E. S., 1948, 1950
Tozzer, 1941a, 1957
Wasson and Wasson, 1957
Wauchope, 1942, 1948a
Woodbury and Trik, 1953

8. Archaeological Survey of the Pacific Coast of Guatemala

EDWIN M. SHOOK

THE AREA discussed here includes the coastal plain and the southern slopes of the barrier range of geologically recent volcanoes paralleling the Pacific coast. The line of volcanic peaks varies from 20 km. inland at the Guatemala–El Salvador border to a maximum of 70 km. just south of Lake Atitlan. This fringe of land between the mountain range and the Pacific coast runs west-northwest from the El Salvador to the Mexico border at the Rio Suchiate. It has an astounding range of altitude, climate, and vegetation. The land begins to rise immediately at sea level and reaches over 4000 m. at Volcan Tajumulco near the frontier of Mexico. The elevation above sea level markedly affects the climate and vegetation. Locally, the area is defined as *tierra caliente* from 0 to 1000 m., *tierra templada* from 1000 to 1900 m., and *tierra fría* above 1900 m. Average annual temperature for tierra caliente is above 23°C., for tierra templada 17–23°C., and for tierra fría below 17°C. The annual rainfall and its distribution throughout the year also varies significantly with land height above the

sea. The lowest area along the coast averages 1400 mm. of rainfall yearly, increasing inland to 3000 mm. at 200 m. elevation, and 5000 mm. in the belt between 200 and 1500 m. Above this to the volcanic peaks a very wet cloud belt exists although the total precipitation amounts to slightly less than the 200–1500 m. zone. The natural flora and fauna, as might be expected, are affected by the temperature and rainfall.

Innumerable small rills and streams originate on the steep wet slopes of the volcanoes, join and rush in torrents towards the coastal plain. These cut deep, narrow ravines in the mountain slopes. Many of the streams flow across the coastal plain, others join larger rivers which originate in the Guatemala highlands to the north and have cut outlets to the Pacific between the volcanoes. The result is a narrow coastal plain exceedingly well watered by a multitude of streams flowing from north to south. These, heavily laden with soil and detritus eroded from the highlands and the volcanic slopes, annually flood the lower areas. Thus the coastal plain is mostly alluvial, rejuve-

FIG. 1—PRECLASSIC STAGE

From ——— B.C. to approx. A.D. 200. *a,* Distant view
of principal mound at archaeological site of Santo
Domingo, elev. 630 m., above town of San Pablo,
Dept. of San Marcos. *b,* Excavation of Late Preclassic urn burial showing pottery vessels and
stone artifacts surrounding large urn containing
skeleton. El Jobo, elev. 20 m., 2 km. east of Ayutla, Dept. of San Marcos. *c,* Jaguar pedestal sculpture from vicinity of El Sitio, elev. 140 m., 11 km.
south of Malacatan, Dept. of San Marcos. Robles

Coll., Quezaltenango. *d,* Stone scepter found with
urn burial at El Sitio. Length 32 cm. *e,* Redstone
serpent, ornament or fetish, from fill of structure
at El Sitio. Max. length 7.4 cm. *f,* Stela, carved in
Izapa style from base of mound at El Jobo. Width
60 cm., depth 52 cm., max. height of assembled
fragments 1.5 m.

nated and incremented by soil deposited through frequent floods, and fertile for agriculture.

The natural environmental conditions of the south coast of Guatemala have been advantageous to man from early times. Ready access to marine food and products, a rich fauna and flora, fertile soil (M. D. Coe, 1961), and an abundance of fresh water are prime factors bearing directly on the occupation and utilization of this area by man from the earliest settlers to the present-day population. It may be reasonably assumed that the availability of wild game, edible tropical vegetation, salt, fish, crustaceans and shellfish sufficed even pre-agriculturalists who undoubtedly penetrated the south coast.

Although no positive evidence of pre-agriculturalists or preceramic cultures has yet been found on the south coast of Guatemala, this lack may be attributed to the paucity of investigation in the area, particularly along the lower reaches of rivers and estuaries near the coast. A few small shell middens have been cursively examined at Ocos, Champerico, Tiquisate,

Puerto San Jose, and Iztapa. Those tested may have been seasonal campsites of agriculturalists. The middens quite likely resulted from small groups living temporarily on the coast for salt making during the dry season and for fishing. There are still over 200 km. of coastal plain between the Rio Suchiate and Rio de Paz from the beach inland for 20 km. which is archaeologically virtually unknown. The shores of the estuaries paralleling the coast and the lower riverbanks offer an excellent opportunity for the discovery of shell mounds and other cultural evidence of preceramic inhabitants and of early sedentary peoples. (See map and list of sites.)

The present knowledge of the distribution of over 200 known archaeological sites on the south coast of Guatemala indicates that the heaviest concentration of ruins occurs on the lower plain from just behind the estuaries and frequently flooded zone several meters above sea level to approximately 300 m. elevation. The volcanic foothills between 300 and 1000 m. elevation also have small sites, some medium-sized, and an occasional major one (fig. 1,a), but

Fig. 2—EARLY CLASSIC STAGE

Approximately A.D. 200–550. All from burials in a single mound, O-17, Toliman Farm in Tiquisate area. Site 9 km. inland from the Pacific Ocean on west bank of dry streambed, 2 km. east of Rio Nagualate. Elev. 13 m. (scale 1/4) 2,c,f,h–k,n represent part of mortuary furniture of Burial 1; l,m from Burial 2; a,b,d,e,g,o from other interments in Mound O-17. a, Tiquisate ware cylinder on pedestal base. Two opposite carved panels. b, Brown cylindrical tripod. Feet hollow, closed, cylindrical without vents or pellet rattles; two opposite carved diagonal panels with cinnabar rubbed into the carving. c, Plain brown cylindrical tripod. Feet solid conical. d, Tiquisate ware cylindrical tripod. Plain hollow slab feet with single slot vent at rear. Decoration in black resist painting with large circular element repeated four times. e, One of a pair of Tiquisate ware cylindrical tripods, each with four nearly identical carved, possibly moldmade, panels on exterior wall and band of 12 knobs around wall base. Five of the six hollow slab feet on the two vessels have a

single round perforation in back. All bear mold-stamped decoration on the front. f, Brown cylindrical tripod with two identical opposite panels on exterior wall. These evidently were moldmade as were designs on front of closed hollow slab feet without vents. g, Tiquisate ware monkey-effigy jar with bridged spout. h, Specular hematite red bowl. i, Black vessel with two horizontal encircling incised lines. j, Highly polished brown vessel decorated with preslip vertical grooves. k, Unslipped bowl. Postfiring, fugitive white paint thinly applied as band on rim and on exterior of pedestal base. l, Esperanza Flesh ware jar. Human face appliquéd and incised on neck. m, Incised and polished black vessel. n, Side and bottom views of a pair of stones showing wear on slightly concave underside. Dense, gray volcanic stone. Both may be reused tops of mushroom stones. o, Two-legged metate with mano. Medium texture, gray volcanic lava stone.

182

altogether fewer in number and more widely separated one from the other than in the lower zone. Above 1000 m. archaeological sites with mounds are rare. Those encountered are normally village sites of a few low structures arranged around a plaza. They are located along modern and, very likely, ancient trade routes, which parallel the courses of rivers draining from the highlands to the coast through passes between volcanoes. Also, on the steep mountain slopes above 1000 m. elevation up to the volcanic peaks are remains of pre-Columbian, colonial, and modern Indian shrines. The pre-Columbian shrines are evident from rock carvings and deposits of pottery. Colonial or modern shrines may easily be recognized by heavily burned fireplaces, quantities of broken pottery, Christian crosses, and sometimes by a thatch roof. Occasionally, a pre-Columbian stone sculpture may be re-used as an idol in a modern shrine (fig. 4,g). Shrine sites often are on prominent hilltops, mountain peaks, promontories, or at the bases of spectacular rock cliffs or rock formations, at springs, heads of streams, on top of ancient mounds or beneath giant kapok trees in densely forested areas.

Most of the cultural material recovered above 300 m. pertains to the Late Classic and Early and Late Postclassic periods. Rarely does material of earlier cultures appear. One example may be cited: a complete human figurine of Early Preclassic type (Shook, 1949c, fig. 3) unearthed during farming operations at Chanchicupe, Department of San Marcos. This modern village, at the west base of the Volcan Tajumulco and near the Rio Cutzulchima, is on the trail from the south coast to the Highlands via the towns of San Pablo and Tajumulco (Dutton and Hobbs, 1943, pp. 13, 14, and Map II). The few Preclassic objects are offset by hundreds of finds, again incidental to general farming, of plumbate and other pottery vessels, moldmade figurines, spindle whorls, ladle-type

censers, whistles, flageolets, stone sculpture, and artifacts belonging to Late Classic and Postclassic periods.

I have investigated several narrow, north-south segments of the Pacific coastal plain between the borders of Mexico and El Salvador more thoroughly than much of the intervening areas. Brief surveys were made in 1942 and 1948 along the course of the Rio Los Esclavos. Sites were located, surface collections obtained, and private archaeological collections recorded. The greater part of the cultural material pertains to a heavy Late Classic occupation. Some stone sculpture from the region of Pasaco may belong to a later period, perhaps the Early Postclassic. A more intensive reconnaissance, accomplished at various times between 1942 and 1952, covered the important coast-to-highland segment between Puerto San Jose and Kaminaljuyu. The sites and the known cultural material from the immediate vicinity of Puerto San Jose have been reported (Shook, 1945, 1949b). The coastal part of this region contains a long Preclassic occupation (Shook, 1949b, p. 16), in contrast to the remarkably little evidence of activity during Early Classic times (ibid., p. 17). However, the majority of the archaeological sites from the beach to the volcanic rampart demonstrate widespread habitation in the Late Classic period (ibid., pp. 17, 18). Distinctive features of this cultural stage will be treated later in more detail. Cultural material and sites of the Early and Late Postclassic are virtually unknown in the Puerto San Jose–Escuintla segment. This state of knowledge is due partly to lack of field research. Historically, a considerable population of Pipil centered around Escuintla at the time of the Spanish conquest in A.D. 1524.

Reconnaissance and test excavations were carried out in 1946 and 1947, from the foothills of the volcanoes to the beach in the narrow, north-south segments in the Tiquisate area between the Madre Vieja

184

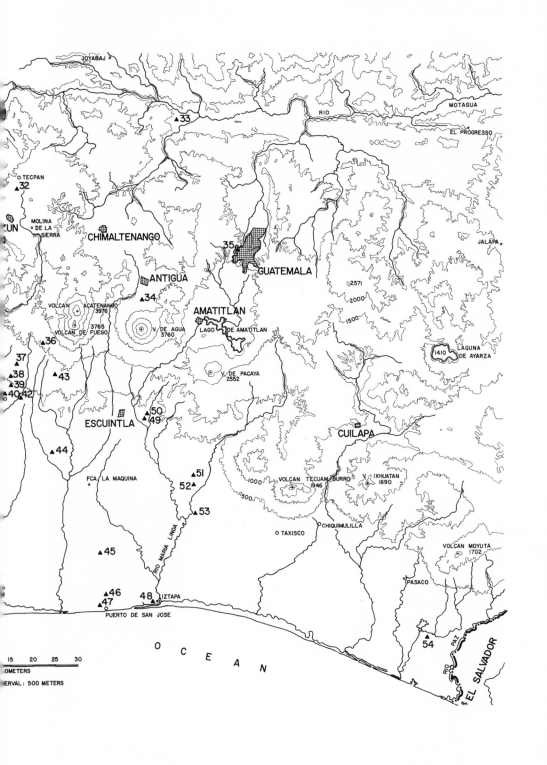

JOYABAJ

▲33

RIO

MOTAGUA

EL PROGRESSO

O TECPAN
32

MOLINA
DE LA
SIERRA

CHIMALTENANGO

JALAPA

ZUN

35

GUATEMALA

2571

2000

▲ANTIGUA

▲34

1500

VOLCAN ACATENANGO
3976

AMATITLAN

3765
VOLCAN DE FUEGO

▲ V. DE AGUA
3760

LAGO DE AMATITLAN

1410

LAGUNA
DE AYARZA

36

37
▲

▲38
▲39
40 42

▲43

V. DE PACAYA
2552

50
ESCUINTLA ▲49

CUILAPA

▲44

FCA. LA MAQUINA

▲51

1000

VOLCAN TECUAM BURRO
1946

V. IXHUATAN
1690

52 ▲

500

▲53

▲45

O TAXISCO

CHIQUIMULILLA

VOLCAN MOYUTA
1702

PASACO

RIO MARIA LINDA

▲46
47

48 IZTAPA

PUERTO DE SAN JOSE

54

RIO PAZ

EL SALVADOR

O C E A N

15   20   25   30
OMETERS
ERVAL: 500 METERS

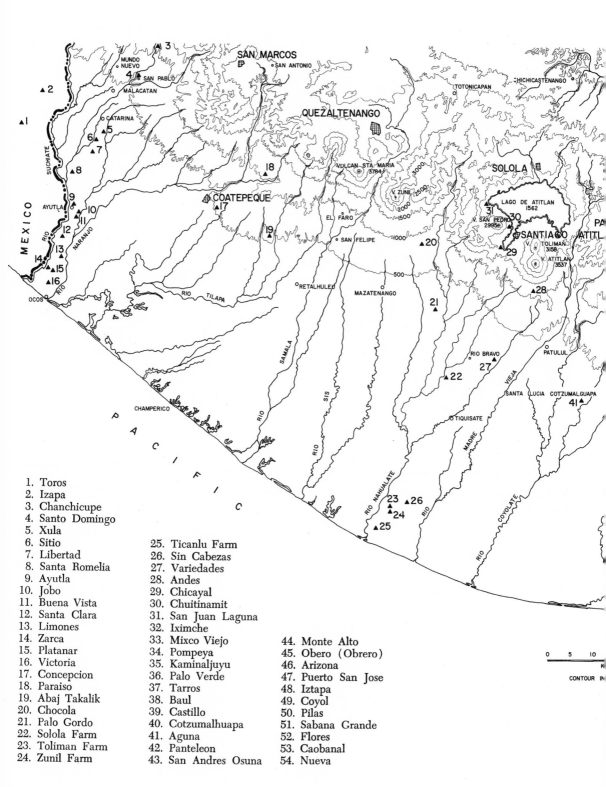

1. Toros
2. Izapa
3. Chanchicupe
4. Santo Domingo
5. Xula
6. Sitio
7. Libertad
8. Santa Romelia
9. Ayutla
10. Jobo
11. Buena Vista
12. Santa Clara
13. Limones
14. Zarca
15. Platanar
16. Victoria
17. Concepcion
18. Paraiso
19. Abaj Takalik
20. Chocola
21. Palo Gordo
22. Solola Farm
23. Toliman Farm
24. Zunil Farm
25. Ticanlu Farm
26. Sin Cabezas
27. Variedades
28. Andes
29. Chicayal
30. Chuitinamit
31. San Juan Laguna
32. Iximche
33. Mixco Viejo
34. Pompeya
35. Kaminaljuyu
36. Palo Verde
37. Tarros
38. Baul
39. Castillo
40. Cotzumalhuapa
41. Aguna
42. Panteleon
43. San Andres Osuna
44. Monte Alto
45. Obero (Obrero)
46. Arizona
47. Puerto San Jose
48. Iztapa
49. Coyol
50. Pilas
51. Sabana Grande
52. Flores
53. Caobanal
54. Nueva

0   5   10
K

CONTOUR IN

and the Nahualate Rivers and in the Ocos-Ayutla-Malacatan region between the Melendrez-Naranjo and Suchiate rivers. These two segments of coastal plain will be described below in some detail as examples of the archaeological problems and potentials of the south coast of Guatemala.

The lower zone of the hot coastal plain from near sea level at Ocos to 300 m. elevation at Malacatan between the drainages of the Melendrez-Naranjo and Suchiate rivers contains an abundance of Preclassic sites. These are located within a few kilometers of the beach to approximately 40 km. inland and generally along small tributary streams of the larger rivers. The sites range in size from a cluster of several low mounds to enormous groups of structures formally arranged around plazas and courts (fig. 1,a). La Victoria is typical of the small sites, El Jobo and El Sitio of the large ones. Others, as Izapa and Los Toros, also are numerous just across the Rio Suchiate in Chiapas, where identical environmental and ecological conditions exist.

Excavations by M. D. Coe (1961) at La Victoria disclosed a long Preclassic occupation; and those by Shook (1947, pp. 179–81) at El Jobo and El Sitio provided evidence that large ceremonial structures had been erected as early as what may be termed Middle Preclassic times. At the latter sites, burials had been cut into the existing structures in Late Preclassic times. These burials were contained in large, especially made, pottery urns, the lower containing the tightly flexed body in seated position and the upper urn inverted as a cover over the lower. Ornaments which may have adorned the deceased were found inside the lower burial urn, while pottery and other furniture lay close around its perimeter (fig. 1,b). One example of this type of burial at El Sitio had beads and carved ornaments of jade with the skeleton, and outside the urn several pottery vessels and a carved stone scepter (fig. 1,d). Two of the vessels, both tripod bowls—one with

solid nubbin, the other with hollow, mammiform feet—have a primary decoration in Usulutan technique and a secondary decoration of polychrome-painted clay stucco. These, and a third vessel—a Fine Incised Black-Brown bowl—were certainly trade items and serve to place the El Sitio burial firmly in the Preclassic Arenal phase of Kaminaljuyu. The carved stone scepter (fig. 1,d), the only example I know from Mesoamerica, lay in an east-west line outside the urn. The skeleton faced west, towards the scepter. The latter, evidently a symbol of authority comparable to the manikin scepter so frequently depicted in Lowland Classic art, suggests that the deceased had been a man of importance.

Similar Preclassic urn burials were excavated at El Jobo (Shook, 1947, p. 181), a major site on the west bank of the Rio Melendrez just east of Ayutla. The burials came from a single mound which in late 1946 was being cut away by the landowner to level his backyard. It could not be ascertained if the urn burials were contemporary with construction or intrusively buried in the earth-filled mound. These burials were lavishly furnished (fig. 1,b), one with about 30 pottery vessels and stone artifacts.

El Sitio, El Jobo, Izapa, and several other Preclassic sites in the area have large stone monuments and occasionally pedestal sculptures. Most of the stelae, except at Izapa, are plain and frequently are of columnar basalt. El Jobo has a finely carved stela in the Izapa sculptural style (fig. 1,f). Pedestal sculptures often depict jaguars, carved in full round, seated on their haunches atop a tall vertical shaft (fig. 1,c).[1]

All the Preclassic sites examined in the Mexico-Guatemala border area seemingly were abandoned at some time during or at at the end of the Preclassic period. I, from

---

[1] Ed. note: These sculptural styles are treated in detail by Miles, Article 10.

my earlier excavations and surface collections, and Coe at the more thoroughly investigated site of La Victoria, found no recognizable Early Classic cultural material. This may be due to insufficient knowledge of the local ceramic types or to insufficient exploration. However, all documented material from excavations and from a considerable amount of pottery and artifacts in private collections lacked Early Classic specimens. This statement pertains only to the limited area surveyed between the Melendrez-Naranjo and Suchiate rivers. Farther east, in the vicinity of Tiquisate between the Madre Vieja and Nahualate rivers, I excavated and recorded quantities of Early Classic material (fig. 2).

Returning again to the Ocos-Ayutla-Malacatan zone, we know that the entire region was intensively occupied during the Late Classic period. Many new settlements were established. Most of the long-abandoned Preclassic sites were reoccupied. Communities ranged in size from a few houses, as indicated by barely perceptible low platform mounds, to major centers. The frequency of Late Classic sites on the coastal plain left only small land areas without mounds. Generally, large centers

are approximately 10 km. apart with small to medium sites between. The major ruins, such as Santa Clara, Los Limones, and La Zarca—6, 10, and 13 km. south of Ayutla— show a formal pattern of structure arrangement around plazas and courts. This formality is less conspicuous in sites with only low platform mounds.

Construction normally consists of an earth fill without stones or of earth with river boulders. Structure surfaces bear a thin finishing coat of brown clay or adobe. One example of construction unique for the south coast of Guatemala was observed at Los Limones (Shook, 1947, p. 181; M. D. Coe, 1961, p. 147). Here the earth cores of the structures were retained by walls built of water-rolled stones, carefully selected for size from the nearby riverbed, laid in lime mortar. Terraces and walls were surfaced with a lime plaster. The lime for the mortar and plaster, both of excellent quality, had been obtained by burning quantities of seashells. Many incompletely burned fragments of shell, together with river sand, served as the aggregate in the mortar and plaster.

Surface recognition of Late Classic sites is possible in many instances from the ar-

FIG. 3—LATE CLASSIC STAGE

Approx. A.D. 550–900. (Scale of *d,g–k*, 1/4.) *a,b*, thin stone heads or "hachas" found together at Caobanal. Elev. 50 m., 1 km. east of Rio Maria Linda, Dept. of Escuintla. *a*, max. height 22.5, width 21.5 cm. *b*, max. height 24.5, width 20.5 cm. Roberto Berger Coll., Guatemala. *c*, Plain stone yoke from Pacific coast of Guatemala. Site unknown. Max. height 39.5 cm. Frederico Pasch Coll., Guatemala. *d*, Mushroom stone from Solola Farm, elev. 100 m., in Tiquisate region. Porous gray volcanic stone. Max. height 27.5 cm. C. L. Watson Coll., Guatemala. *e*, Decorated, soft red jar with open spout. San Juan Plumbate from El Sitio, Dept. of San Marcos. *f*, Typical urn burial, the lower vessel containing tightly flexed body and the inverted upper one serving as cover. Height of lower urn 55 cm., max. interior diameter 71 cm. Restored height of both vessels approx. 1.15 m. Ticanlu Farm. Elev. 6 m., 2 km. east of Rio Nagualate, 3 km. inland from the Pacific. *g*, Tiquisate ware bowl with preslip grooved decoration

found with *h* in fill of mound at Zunil Farm, elev. 11 m., 3 km. east of Rio Nagualate and 8 km. inland. These bowls, *g* and *h*, formed a cache, with *h* inverted as cover over *g*, containing a fetal human skeleton. Outside the bowls was a pottery spindle whorl. *h*, Tiquisate ware, tripod bowl with basal molding and hollow mold-stamped slab feet. One large circular vent in back wall. Found inverted over *g*. *i,j*, Seated female figurine whistles; only faces made in mold, all else hand-modeled. Whistle mouthpiece in left shoulder. Traces of unfired red, yellow, white, and black paints. From urn burial in Mound O-17, Toliman Farm. This type of figurine apparently predates the developed Late Classic type in which entire front half of figurine was moldmade. *k*, Gray ware cylinder with incised and grooved decoration. Luis Larranaga Coll., Tiquisate. *l*, Ruins of Sin Cabezas, elev. 17 m., 4 km. east of Rio Nagualate, 11 km. inland from the sea. Acropolis-type mound at south end of Main Plaza.

186

a   b   c

d   e   f

g   i   j

h

k   l

chitectural forms present. Diagnostic features are large, acropolis-type structures placed at the south ends of plazas (fig. 3,*l*), and at least one enormously long mound. These long mounds may measure up to 100 m. and more in length and range in height from 1 to 10 m. They often occupy the entire long side of a plaza. Ball courts, also a Late Classic feature, are far less common on the south coast than in the Guatemalan highlands. Only six ball courts are known on the Pacific coast, one each at: Santa Clara, Palo Gordo, Solola (near Tiquisate), El Baul, Flores, and Sabana Grande.

Cultural debris of the Late Classic occupation in the Ocos-Ayutla-Malacatan region thinly covered the surface of the old Preclassic structures but extended to greater depth on the level courts and plazas near these structures. A few sites, wholly occupied in Late Classic times, had cultural refuse to a depth of 1.1 m. where tested by excavation in open, level areas near low platform mounds.

One strati-test was dug on the northern outskirts of Santa Romelia, just above Ayutla, in an attempt to obtain household refuse from a typical small rural community. The several dozens of rectangular platform mounds at Santa Romelia ranged in height from those barely discernible above ground level to a maximum of 1.5 m. for a few structures near the site's center. The strati-test, 4 m. from the nearest mound and covering a space 1 by 2 m., produced what logically should be the household refuse of the common people. The surface layer to 30 cm. had been churned by modern cultivation, roots, and burrowing animals. It contained, however, weathered Late Classic pottery types and obsidian lancets and chips, with only a minor admixture of later material. Below, apparently undisturbed deposits continued to 1.1 m. depth from the surface without discernible change in Late Classic ceramic types. Of the potsherds recovered from the test, the Late Classic pottery types and obsidian counted for a third of the total. These were evenly distributed from surface to bottom in the strati-test. Essentially, plumbate here at Santa Romelia formed a heavy percentage of the total pottery used. Similar results were obtained at the nearby site of La Libertad and at Ayutla, where low archaeological mounds are scattered throughout the modern town.

Fig. 4—POSTCLASSIC STAGE

Approx. A.D. 900–1525, and modern. *a–c*, Early Postclassic (A.D. 900–1200) Tohil plumbate. *a*, Hollow, female figurine, height 14.8 cm. from Tiquisate region. Raul Moreno Coll., Guatemala. *b,c*, Jar forms, height of animal effigy 14 cm., gadrooned jar 15.5 cm. From El Faro, elev. 800 m., Dept. of Quezaltenango, 6 km. north of San Felipe, or from Mundo Nuevo, elev. 800 m., 4 km. north of Malacatan, Dept. of San Marcos. Alfredo Toepke Coll., Guatemala. *d*, Late Postclassic (A.D. 1200–1525) textile-marked sherds, max. length of upper left fragment 9 cm., from Los Andes, elev. 1200 m. on Finca Panama, south slope of Volcan Atitlan, Dept. of Suchitepequez. All sherds are from flat, unslipped *comales* (tortilla griddles) identical to those from Variedades and other sites near Finca Panama. Textile impressions occur only on exterior or underside of comal. *e*, Pacific coastal plain, looking north to Volcan Atitlan. Late Postclassic archaeological site of Variedades covers open field in foreground. Elevations at far edge of cultivated field are natural hillocks. *f*, Late Postclassic bird-head effigy supports for Red-on-White tripod vessels. Latter often are grater bowls (*molcajetes*) with floor incised or scored. Effigy feet bear an all-over white to cream slip on which red decoration has been painted in horizontal stripes. Bird eyes and beak also may be painted red. Examples illustrated from surface at Platanar–La Zarca, elev. 7 m., 12 km. north of Ocos, Dept. of San Marcos. Length of center specimen 9 cm. *g*, Modern Mam Indian shrine at Paraiso, elev. 1100 m., 5 km. north of Colomba, Dept. of Quezaltenango. Copal incense is burned on raised stone slab before pile of stone and broken pottery surmounted by pre-Columbian stone sculpture. Wood post and cross timber are remains of thatched hut which formerly sheltered the shrine.

a

b

c

d

e

f

g

Common forms in San Juan Plumbate are tall cylinders, small jars (fig. 3,e), bowls, and burial urns. The quantity of each under conditions as described suggests that here plumbate served utilitarian purposes. The bowls are suitable for both cooking and serving food. Burials of children in plumbate urns were excavated at Santa Clara and Buena Vista near Ayutla (Shook, 1947, p. 181). The frequency of rim sherds of these characteristic vessels in most ceramic collections from the Ocos-Ayutla-Malacatan region indicates that this type of burial urn predominated during the Late Classic period. Elsewhere on the south coast at this time, the majority of burial urns were of unslipped pottery (fig. 3,f). Less common forms in San Juan Plumbate pottery are moldmade human figurines, drums, bells, and quite small effigy jars with or without basket handles. Most of the forms and decorative motifs differ from the widely traded Postclassic Tohil Plumbate (fig. 4,a-c).

The known distribution of Late Classic San Juan Plumbate extends to the northwest in the Rio Grijalva drainage of central Chiapas (Sorenson, 1956, p. 14; Shook, 1956b, p. 25) through the southern highlands and south coast of Guatemala as far east as the middle Motagua Valley (Smith and Kidder, 1943, pp. 161–62). From my field surveys, the heaviest concentration of sites with this pottery type occurs on the Pacific coastal plain and foothills between the drainage of the Rio Tilapa in Guatemala and the Rio Coatan in Chiapas. This area coincides with the heart of the historic Soconusco Region, a rich cacao-producing area at the time of the Spanish conquest and continuing well into colonial times. Quantitatively, the largest amount and greatest variety of forms of San Juan Plumbate are found in the region between the upper reaches of the Naranjo and Suchiate rivers. The actual source of San Juan Plumbate may never be pinned down to a specific archaeological site. However, it is worth noting that excellent clays exist and today are utilized for the manufacture of brick, floor tile, and roof tile at Santa Romelia and Xula near the town of Catarina between Ayutla and Malacatan. It is not known if these clays are suitable for pottery. The immediate area, possibly within a radius of 20 km. of Santa Romelia, presents the most likely source of Late Classic San Juan Plumbate.

It appears from the evidence that this region and most of the Pacific coastal plain underwent a drastic population shift at the end of the Late Classic. Scores of known major Late Classic centers down to the smallest rural village seemingly were abandoned. There is no certain record to date of an Early Postclassic site in the 0–300-m. elevation zone of the south coast. Sporadic finds of Tohil Plumbate sherds on the surface and a few other diagnostics of the period do occur (Shook, 1949b, p. 18), but are conspicuous by their rarity. In the volcanic foothills, above 300 m. elevation, Early Postclassic finds increase in frequency (fig. 4,a-c); from 1000 m. up the volcanic slopes and the river drainages between volcanoes, sites of this period increase markedly in number. Small Early Postclassic sites are a particular feature of southwest Guatemala, of which the ruins of Tajumulco are typical. One might postulate from the observable lack of population on the lower plain that the area became untenable around A.D. 900–1000, possibly due to movement into or through it by the Pipil or other expansionist groups out of Mexico. It is noteworthy that the plumbate ceramic tradition continued vigorously with a new type, Tohil, in the foothills and upper slopes in southwest Guatemala during Early Postclassic times (fig. 4,a-c). Basic changes were made in paste and style (Shepard, 1948) from Late Classic San Juan Plumbate. Effigy styles are strongly Mexicanized. Trade in Tohil Plumbate extended throughout and even beyond Meso-america. The time synchronizes with the dominance of the Toltec in highland Mexico and their far-flung influence.

The Late Postclassic period, incredible as it may seem, is even less known archaeologically on the south coast of Guatemala. A few surface finds of typologically late ceramic fragments at La Zarca (Shook, 1947, p. 182) represent tripod grater bowls (*molcajetes*) with elongated, bird-head effigy feet (fig. 4,*f*). Similar pottery feet were collected on the surface in the Tiquisate area. One definite Late Preclassic habitation site was discovered on the Pacific coastal plain at Variedades near the Rio Bravo (Kidder, 1949b, p. 13). Here a field clearing exposed a level area of several acres littered with cultural refuse: pottery, manos and metates, obsidian, and other stone artifacts. Although there were no mounds or slight undulations in the level terrain to indicate where houses of perishable material once stood (fig. 4,*e*), burned adobe fragments bearing impressions of small poles did indicate house construction. The amount of refuse suggested a village of some time depth. Diagnostic of the Late Postclassic period were fragments of flat comales, some with textile marks on the undersurface (*ibid.*, fig. 3). These represent the only flat type of comal known to occur on the south coast of Guatemala prior to the Spanish conquest (fig. 4,*d*).

To return to the Classic stage, one region tested by survey and excavations demonstrated intensive occupation during Early Classic times. This was the general region of Tiquisate between the Madre Vieja on the east and the Nahualate River on the west. Here no cultural boundary is implied. Many unstudied archaeological sites are reported, and similar ecological conditions exist beyond these rivers. However, test excavations between Tiquisate and the sea disclosed Early Classic remains underlying much of the heavy Late Classic overbur-

den. The latter obscures the architectural arrangement and composition of the Early Classic ruins. These, when encountered, were identical in construction to the overlying Late Classic structures—an earth fill surfaced with adobe floors and plaster, often bearing an over-all red paint. Distinction could be made only from cultural contents. Burial customs, pottery, and certain artifacts sharply distinguish the Early from the Late Classic period (figs. 2, 3). All Early Classic burials recovered in the Tiquisate region had been deeply interred in the fill of pyramidal structures and platforms, or in open areas away from structures. Normally the bodies were buried in a fully extended position with grave furnishings placed around the head and shoulders. Charcoal and marks of fire surrounding the skeletons indicate mortuary rites involving the burning of small fires. In one grave the body lay flexed on its side; in two others the individuals had been seated crosslegged. Multiple burials in a single grave evidently were not uncommon. One excavated on Toliman Farm below Tiquisate contained three skeletons, one seated and two extended. These may have been sacrificed attendants of the seated individual. Eight pottery vessels and two hemispherical stone objects accompanied this interment (fig. 2,*e*,*f*,*h-k*,*n*).

Ceramic forms diagnostic of the Early Classic period in the Tiquisate region are tripod cylinders (fig. 2,*b-f*), some with scutate covers; shallow to deep bowls and cylinders with pedestal or annular bases (fig. 2,*a*,*k*); and jars with bridge-spouts (fig. 2,*g*). The tripod cylinders may have hollow slab feet or cylindrical, round-bottomed feet. There are examples also of solid conical feet and solid slab feet. Some of the hollow and solid slab feet are moldmade.

The pottery is predominantly monochrome. Specular hematite is employed often as an over-all red slip, sometimes in combination with a light-colored slip, and occasionally as solid, broad, horizontal bands of red. Polychrome decoration is exceedingly rare and such vessels, usually Peten-type, basal flange, polychrome bowls, obviously are imported. The most common methods of ornamentation are incising (the incision frequently filled with red or white paint), grooving, plano-relief, modeling, molding, and appliqué (fig. 2). Also found sporadically are vessels decorated with negative painting of black on a light-colored background (fig. 2,d).

Knowledge of Early Classic artifacts is limited. Pottery candeleros, both single- and two-holed ones, occur as do the "napkin-ring" type of earplug. Stone artifacts include obsidian flake-blades and chips; plain and carved jade beads, pendants, and earplugs; plain amazonite beads; polished greenstone celts; hemispherical stones (fig. 2,n); and manos and metates. The latter have only two short legs which elevate one end of the metate (fig. 2,o). Manos are as long as the metate widths, wearing the metate almost evenly in cross section. Monumental stone sculpture assuredly assignable to the Early Classic period is unknown on the south coast of Guatemala.

The Late Classic remains, in contrast to the preceding, are abundantly represented throughout the Pacific coastal plain and volcanic foothills. The density of sites ranging from village size to major centers has been mentioned previously. A heavy Late Classic population also lived in the Tiquisate region (Shook, 1950b, p. 63) and the remains stratigraphically overlie and deeply bury those of the Early Classic. Innovations are best depicted in the material culture and burial customs.

The dead, as in Late Preclassic times around Ayutla, were tightly flexed and seated in large, especially made, pottery urns (fig. 3,f). Lack of preservation prevented determining whether the bodies had been wrapped or bundled. The size of the human body apparently governed the size of the burial urn. Infants, children, and adults were placed in urns of appropriate size. Invariably, a second urn of equal or a shade smaller dimensions was inverted as a cover over the lower containing the body. Small mortuary offerings accompanied the body in some instances, but offerings customarily lay close around the outside of the urn. Interments in the Tiquisate area were found in all types of religious and civic structures tested, below courts and plazas, under house floors, and in cemeteries on the peripheries of the sites. One cemetery was investigated adjacent and pertaining to the site of Solola 9 km. north of Tiquisate, a second at Ticanlu 17 km. southwest of Tiquisate, and a third at Puerto San Jose (Shook, 1949b, p. 18). Cemeteries probably were more common on the south coast than the present archaeological record indicates. The three mentioned, accidentally discovered during modern construction activities, had nothing on the level ground surface to indicate an ancient cemetery. The urn burials lay from 0.9 to 1.0 m. below the surface and were irregularly spaced from 2 to 3 m. apart.

Of the scores of Late Classic burials recorded from the south coast of Guatemala, only one was not of the urn type. This, a rock-lined chamber containing two adult skeletons, was excavated by A. V. Kidder and me (Shook, 1947, p. 182) below a mound at El Paraiso. The stone floor and walls of the tomb had been painted red. The principal skeleton sat cross-legged facing south with his back against the north wall. A second skeleton lay extended across the feet of the seated person. The high status of the principal occupant was evident by the lavish stock of grave furniture. This included 67 pottery vessels; nine bells, three drums, one flageolet, one whistle, three figurines, and nine spindle whorls of pottery; many jade and shell ornaments; one pyrite mosaic plaque; obsidian flake-blades;

192

and several types of paint pigment. The contemporaneity of the tomb with the prevalent Late Classic urn-burial type was proved by the discovery of two urn burials under identical stratigraphic conditions in the same Paraiso mound.

The Late Classic occupation is further attested by distinctive vessel forms and pottery objects appearing for the first time on the south coast. Abundant are mold-made figurines (fig. 3,*i,j*), spindle whorls, and a variety of musical instruments of pottery. These include drums, bells, ocarinas, flageolets, and figurine whistles.

The dominant fine pottery throughout most of the coastal area during Late Classic times is Tiquisate ware (fig. 3,*g,h*) (J. E. S. Thompson, 1948, pp. 45–48; Shepard, 1948, pp. 139–41). Only in the Ocos-Ayutla-Malacatan region is Tiquisate ware heavily superseded by San Juan Plumbate. The latter's distribution thins out southeastward toward the El Salvador border.

Polychrome decoration remains a rarity on the south coast. A few trade sherds of Copador ware were recovered in Late Classic deposits in the Tiquisate region. Decoration in bichrome is moderately well represented, as is negative painting, although monochrome wares remain predominant. The use of specular hematite red on pottery appears more common on the Guatemala Pacific coast than elsewhere in Mesoamerica. Incising, grooving, carving, modeling, and appliqué continue as decorative techniques (fig. 3). Increasingly common are pottery vessels with mold-made decoration in relief.

A variety of ceremonial objects of stone occur in the Late Classic period (Thompson, 1948, figs. 18–23). Among these are mushroom stones, flat or thin stone heads (*hachas*) and yokes (fig. 3,*a-d*). Thin stone heads and yokes occasionally are found together (Gann, 1932). Caches of nine thin stone heads have been discovered at Aguna and Tiquisate.

Monumental sculpture is highly developed in certain regions, particularly at Santa Lucia Cotzumalhuapa (Thompson, 1948), but many sectors of the south coast entirely lack carved stone monuments.[2]

Objects of metal rarely are found. One recent find of gold discs, purportedly with San Juan Plumbate, was made at Santa Clara below Ayutla. Should this association be correct, it represents the only occurrence on the south coast of metal in a Late Classic context. The few other known finds, of copper and gold objects at Tajumulco (Dutton and Hobbs, 1943, p. 57) and of gold at El Paraiso (Shook, 1947, p. 182), pertain to the Early Postclassic period.

The material culture of the south coast differs more in Late Classic times from that of the southern highlands of Guatemala than might be expected from the geographic proximity of the two areas. Several differences may be cited. The coastal region has a preponderance of burial urns which occur only sporadically in the highlands. Tiquisate ware, rim-head vessels, the use of specular hematite red, moldmade figurines, pottery musical instruments, and spindle whorls are features particularly abundant on the coast and relatively scarce in the highlands. Flat comales which are so prevalent in the uplands are absent from all periods on the coast except in Late Preclassic times. These are but a few of the outstanding differences in cultural material between the two areas.

Thompson (1948) exhaustively treats the historical sources for the south coast of Guatemala, and M. D. Coe (1961) those for the Soconusco region. Historically the sources imply, and the archaeological data at present suggest, that the area was a crossroads of cultural influence and subjected to repeated movements of different ethnic groups. Coe (1960a) deals with the important possibility of linkage between

[2] Ed. note: See Miles, Article 10.

the early cultures of this region and those of Ecuador and Peru.

In this report, the sketchiness of our knowledge of the total cultural story of the Guatemala coast region is only too appar- ent. Yet, geographically this is obviously a key area, not just for the local archaeology but for hemispheric problems relating to the diffusion and development of man in the New World.

REFERENCES

Coe, M. D., 1960a, 1961
Dutton and Hobbs, 1943
Gann, 1932
Kidder, 1949b
Melhus, 1949
Shepard, 1948

Shook, 1945, 1947, 1949b, 1949c, 1950b, 1956b
Smith, A. L., and Kidder, 1943
Sorenson, 1956
Thompson, J. E. S., 1948
Tozzer, 1957

9. Archaeological Survey of the Chiapas Coast, Highlands, and Upper Grijalva Basin

GARETH W. LOWE and
J. ALDEN MASON

Though an area central to the Meso-american high cultures, the state of Chiapas has been largely neglected by archaeologists until recent years. As a result, its wider cultural relationships have been poorly known. The northeastern section of Chiapas, a relatively uniform region of low mountains, narrow valleys, and tall tropical forests, has been logically considered a western extension of the Lowland Maya subarea in consequence of the presence there of the Classic Maya ruins of Tonina, Palenque, Bonampak, Yaxchilan, and dozens of others of lesser stature. On the other hand, the larger southwestern portion of the state, which includes the Pacific coast and two highland provinces separated by the upper Grijalva basin, has not lent itself so well to inclusion in any one of the usual Mesoamerican culture areas, though it has in part been broadly labeled as belonging to the Highland Maya territory.

The difficulty in classifying the pre-Hispanic cultural relationships of southwestern Chiapas arises partly from lack of investigation. To a greater extent, however, it re-sults from the distinctiveness of the several topographic regions comprising this part of the state and of the varying cultural influences which affected one or the other but not all of them through the passage of time. An understanding of its physiographic regions is therefore essential to formulation of the culture history of southwestern Chiapas. These regions are: (1) the Pacific Coastal Plain, (2) the Sierra Madre de Chiapas, (3) the Central Depression or Upper Grijalva Basin, and (4) the Central or Chiapas Plateau (see fig. 2). Though archaeological investigation of these regions has been uneven and inadequate, it has been sufficient to indicate that they have experienced somewhat distinct regional developments. Accordingly, they each may be considered valid archaeological regions and will be described as such here. The discussion of each region will be preceded by a brief summary of the environmental setting. Unless otherwise noted, the sources used for the geographical data are Müllerried (1957) and Waibel (1946). The map in figure 1 shows sites or place names mentioned in the text.

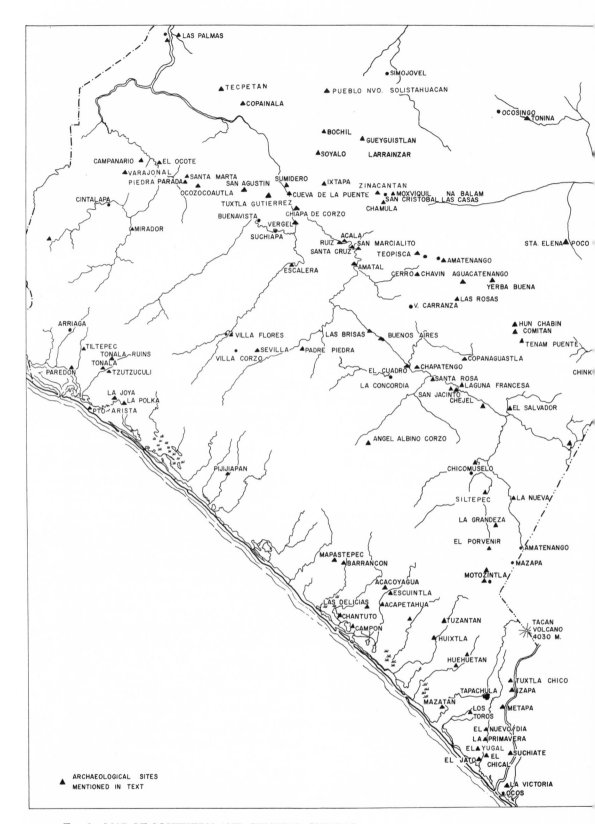

Fig. 1—MAP OF SOUTHERN AND CENTRAL CHIAPAS

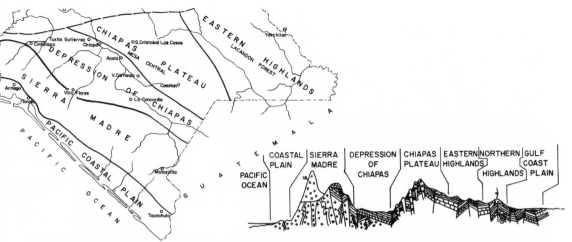

FIG. 2—PHYSIOGRAPHIC REGIONS OF SOUTHERN AND CENTRAL CHIAPAS
(After Müllerried, 1957.)

The most adequate archaeological sequence for Chiapas is that established by the New World Archaeological Foundation for the locality of Chiapa de Corzo in the Central Depression (fig. 3). This sequence includes a revision of data presented by Warren (1959), to whom acknowledgement is made for help in re-aligning the sequence (personal communications). Conformation of the Chiapa ceramic periods to subdivisions of the standard Preclassic, Classic, and Postclassic periods of Mesoamerican prehistory enables their use in the following discussions as chronological divisions for correlating developments in those parts of Chiapas lacking a specific regional chronology.

PACIFIC COASTAL PLAIN

Environment

The Pacific Coastal Plain has a northern point of origin at the Isthmus of Tehuantepec in Oaxaca and extends through Chiapas to Guatemala. Extending northwest to southeast, the Chiapas sector of the coastal plain (fig. 2) is 280 km. in length, varying in width from only 15 km. on the northwest to 35 km. on the southeast. This narrow plain is primarily composed of clays, sands, and gravels, the detritus deposited in the alluvial fans of the many swift streams draining the adjacent Sierra Madre. The largest of the Pacific-slope rivers is the Suchiate which, descending from the 4030 m. high Tacana volcano, serves as the boundary here between Chiapas and Guatemala.

The Pacific Coastal Plain has been the principal overland route for travel between Mexico and Central America during most of pre- and post-Hispanic times. Also the richness of the southeastern section made it the outstanding area for cacao production in Mesoamerica, a circumstance which attracted the attention of both the Aztec and Spanish conquerors. This is the ancient province of Soconusco which figured in the Aztec trade lists (see Thompson, 1956, for a discussion of the role of cacao in Mesoamerican commerce and ritual and of the importance of the Soconusco district in the cacao trade).

Archaeology

No adequate survey or major excavation in any of the archaeological sites in the Pacific Coastal Plain has ever been made. In 1947 Drucker was able to test 14 sites, visit as many more, and note reports of perhaps 30 additional ones, most of which were concentrated on the southeast. He concluded, "Few regions can compare with

197

| EXTERNAL CORRELATION | | Chiapa de Corzo Phases | Chiapa Ceramic Periods | Generalized Cultural Periods | Estimated Absolute Dates | EXTERNAL CORRELATION | |
| North | West | | | | | East | South |
Gulf Coast (Olmec-La Venta) Equivalents	Oaxaca (Monte Alban) Equivalents					Lowland Maya (Uaxactun) Equivalents	Highland Ma (Kaminaljuy Equivalent
		Zapotal	XIV	Modern	A.D. 1824		Modern
		Villa Flores	XIII	Colonial	1524		Colonial
	M.A. V	Urbina		Protohistoric	1480		Chinautla
Soncautla		Tuxtla	XII	Late Postclassic	1350		
		Suchiapa	XI-B	Middle Postclassic	1200		
	M.A. IV	Ruiz	XI-A	Early Postclassic	950		Ayumpuc
	M.A. III-B	Paredon	X-B		800	Tepeu 3	Pamplona
		Maravillas	X-A	Late Classic	550	Tepeu 1,2	Amatle
Upper Tres Zapotes	M.A. III-A	Laguna	IX	Early Classic B	350	Tzakol	Esperanza
	II-III Transición	Jiquipilas	VIII	Early Classic A	200	1,2,3	Aurora
						Matzanel	
Middle Tres Zapotes	M.A. II	Istmo	VII	Late Protoclassic			Santa Clara
		Horcones	VI	Early Protoclassic	100 B.C.		Arenal
Lower Tres Zapotes		Guanacaste	V		250	Chicanel	Miraflores
	M.A. I	Francesa	IV	Late Preclassic	450		Providencia
La Venta Complex A		Escalera	III		550	Mamom	Majadas
		Dili	II	Middle Preclassic	1000		Las Charcas
La Venta Pre-Complex A		Cotorra	I	Early Preclassic	1500		Arevelo
		Santa Marta		Preceramic	7000 (?)		

FIG. 3—CHRONOLOGICAL TABLE FOR SOUTHWESTERN CHIAPAS

Ed. note: In general, this chart coincides with Mesoamerican culture periods as defined by Willey, Ekholm, and Millon, Article 14, Volume 1. The principal differences are the setting of the Middle–Late Preclassic line at 450 B.C. in the present chart instead of at 300 B.C., the use of the term "Protoclassic" here for the latter part of the chronological range of the Late Preclassic, and the division of the Postclassic period into Early, Middle, and Late rather than Early and Late.

the Chiapas coast in the abundance of archaeological remains" (1948, p. 143). Numerous individuals have alluded to particular artifacts, monuments, or ruins in the coastal region, primarily to those found in the localities of Tonala and Tuxtla Chico-Izapa. These have been brief descriptive observations unaccompanied by excavations (Bancroft, 1882; Brinton, 1897; Burkitt, 1924; Gamio, 1946; Hewett, 1936; Marquina, 1939; Palacios, 1928a; Pineda, 1845; Sapper, 1897; Satterthwaite, 1943a; Seler-Sachs, 1900).

C. A. Culebro (1939) has described the Chiapas coastal sites under the headings of the Tonala and Soconusco districts, valid subdivisions which will be used here.

Tonala District

Except for the ruins in the vicinity of Tonala little is known of the archaeology of the coastal section of this district which extends from the Oaxaca border to beyond Mapastepec. Culebro (1939) lists a number of sites in or near the coastal plain, including La Polka, Arista, La Permuta, Pijijiapan, Chalatenco, Novillero, Zapotal, and Mapastepec. A recently reported site near Mapastepec is Barrancon, a Late Preclassic and Protoclassic mound group on the highway presently under construction to Tapachula.

A brief survey of the Tonala vicinity by Navarrete (1959b) confirmed the late Postclassic date for the ruin of Paredon (Drucker, 1948) on the edge of the lagoon or Mar Muerto southwest of Tonala. The mound group consists of six tamped-earth platforms arranged about a plaza with two smaller platforms in its center. Five plain stelae of granitic stone are aligned on the north-south axis of the plaza. It seems possible that Bancroft (1883) was correct in terming this the aboriginal Tonala captured by Pedro de Alvarado, as suggested by Ferdon (1953, p. 3).

Sherds collected by Navarrete (1959b) from Tiltepec and from Tzutzuculi on the outskirts of the town of Tonala suggest both Preclassic and Late Postclassic or historic period occupations for these earthen-mound sites. Failure to find ceramics of the Classic period at the sites on the plain suggests that occupation at that time was centered in the foothills to the north.

The ruins of Tonala, located on the mountain side about 13 km. northwest of the railroad town of Tonala, were mentioned in numerous earlier accounts, but they were not carefully mapped and described until the last decade (Ferdon, 1953). This truly impressive site is characterized by massive stone-faced primary platforms built on the top slopes of four spurs jutting out from a high granite ridge (the ruin is about 600 m. above the level of Tonala town, itself only some 50 m. above sea level). The architecture is typified by the use of dressed block-and-slab masonry, with individual units often of enormous size (fig. 4). The major substructural forms are basal platforms serving as leveling terraces, and primary platforms ranging from 1 to 3.5 m. in height, usually with sloping sides, which support lower supplementary and building platforms. Stairways are centrally located on the front of the structures. They may be either projecting or partially inset, but never have stairside extensions (balustrades). Many of the platforms have batter-notched corners and apron moldings (Ferdon, 1953).

There seems little doubt that Tonala was a religious center and that the one- to three-roomed buildings on the platform summits served as temples. Nothing about the site other than its elevated location suggests fortification. Particular religious structures seem to be the three precincts in which masonry walls enclose three sides of a rectangular area with a single temple in its center. The numerous stone monuments which also suggest that Tonala was a religious shrine have been discussed in a separate article.

Stone-paved ramps connect various levels and components of the Tonala ruin. In addition, two paved causeways appear to lead from the ruin down toward the coastal plain, the eastern one apparently terminating at a smaller ruin, La Tortuga (Ferdon, 1953, pp. 9, 119). No other ruins in Chiapas have been definitely related to Tonala, but the presence of stone causeways at a number of sites in the Sierra Madre described by Culebro (1939) suggests possible affiliations in that direction.

The cultural relationships and chronological placement of the Tonala ruin have not been resolved satisfactorily. On the basis of architectural and sculptural comparisons Ferdon saw a beginning occupation in the Late Preclassic and a major occupation during the latter part of the Early Classic and beginning of the Late Classic periods (1953, pp. 106–13). This is as close an estimate as can be made without excavation. Ceramics obtained by Drucker from a series of test pits dug in 1947 have not been studied. It is noteworthy, however, that Drucker recognized in his material no resemblances to other pottery from the coast. He suggested that study might show it to be an extrusion from the Chiapas highlands (1948, pp. 167–68).

Nothing about the observed pottery or architecture of Tonala is suggestive of the Preclassic dating implied by the presence of Olmec-style stelae at the site (Ferdon, 1953, pp. 110–12), and it is possible that

199

Fɪɢ. 4—PACIFIC COAST REGION. Masonry wall of Precinct B-1, Tonala, Chiapas. (After Drucker, 1948.)

these monuments were moved there from elsewhere. In this regard it is worth noting that the pottery recovered from Tzutzuculi by Navarrete and assigned by him to Chiapa II phase (1959b, p. 6) is of the Middle Preclassic period and contemporaneous with the Olmec occupation of La Venta (see below). Tzutzuculi, only about 14 km. from the Tonala ruin, conceivably could be the home of the Olmec-style stelae now at that site.

Soconusco District

The only well-known archaeological site in this district is Izapa-Tuxtla Chico, a zone of earthen-mound groups northwest of Tapachula now famous for its associated sculptured stone monuments. The first serious archaeological excavation in the Soco-

nusco seems to have been that of Stirling, who in 1941 uncovered the monuments of Izapa sufficiently to permit their photography and description (1943, pp. 61–74; pls. 49–62). A few of the earthen pyramids and elongated platforms arranged about the half-dozen plazas at Izapa are covered with boulders, apparently the eroded remains of former structural walls (Stirling, 1943, p. 62). No significant excavations have been made in the mounds of this zone. (A five-year program of investigations at Izapa was commenced by the BYU–New World Archaeological Foundation in the fall of 1961, after this article was written.)

Stirling was unable to determine the date or cultural affiliations of the Izapa zone beyond those suggested by the monuments which seemed to him to be related both to

200

the early stone art of the southwestern Gulf coast of Mexico (primarily Olmec) and to early Maya art, yet with a distinctive local style (1943, p. 73). Few sherds were noted by Stirling and none diagnostic. The paucity of sherds was again noted by Drucker when in 1947 he dug a series of 12 test trenches within the confines of the site and recovered only a few thousand sherds worth keeping. San Juan Plumbate, a Late Classic ware, was found by Drucker in all trenches dug by him in Izapa, leading him to postulate that the principal occupation of the site should be equated with the "San Juan horizon" defined by J. E. S. Thompson (1948) at Cotzumalhuapa in Guatemala. Examination of Drucker's notes shows also a Late Preclassic occupation at Izapa, and a small pottery sample recovered by Lowe from a drainage canal in the southern sector of Izapa apparently represents an undisturbed Late Preclassic refuse deposit (Lowe, 1959b, p. 68; fig. 59,c). A larger sample recently collected from the same trench has a small percentage of Early Protoclassic sherds as well (Warren, personal communication); and Piña Chan, on the basis of his limited survey material, shows an occupation for Izapa from Late Preclassic through Early Classic (1960c, Cuadro 2).

The foregoing observations indicate two major periods of occupation for Izapa, the earlier one during the Late Preclassic to Protoclassic periods and the later during the San Juan or Late Classic period. Whether there was an actual break in the occupation of the site between these periods only further investigation can determine, but the undisturbed situation of the stone monuments and wide distribution of the San Juan Plumbate sherds indicate that the older ceremonial centers at Izapa continued to function, their altars and stelae still revered.

The archaeology of the Soconusco district as a whole, though still lacking adequate investigation, is better known than that of the Tonala district as a result of the recent surveys in this part of the coast (Drucker, 1948; Dutton, 1958; Lorenzo, 1955; Piña Chan, 1960c). Detailed studies of the artifacts recovered from these surveys remain unpublished and no independent cultural sequence for the district has been established. The available information can be ordered by cultural periods as follows.

PRECERAMIC (?). Drucker found the lower levels of a shell midden on the edge of the Pampa de Chantuto, a shallow lagoon of brackish water south of Mapastepec, to be without ceramics although containing other artifacts and food remains (1948, p. 165). This discovery of a possibly preceramic level was followed by Lorenzo, who excavated, again, at Chantuto and at another nearby shell midden at Campon (1955). The results of these investigations remain inconclusive with respect to chronology or to the implications of an early developmental phase despite the persistence of stone artifacts and food remains to lower levels than those at which ceramics were found. The materials recovered did not permit determination of wider cultural relationships. Lorenzo concluded that the site may represent merely a nonceramic camp utilized by segments of higher culture groups for securing marine food or that, as a remote possibility, it may have been a preceramic establishment which later came into contact with contemporary ceramic-using peoples (1955, p. 49).

EARLY AND MIDDLE PRECLASSIC. The recent work of M. D. Coe at La Victoria, a beach site near Ocos, Guatemala, just over the frontier from Chiapas, has established for the general Soconusco region one of the earliest culture phases in Mesoamerica, that of Ocos (1959a, 1959b, 1960a). Ceramics comparable with this and its sequent phase of Conchas have been found in the Chiapas district of Soconusco at Mazatan, a site west of Tapachula on the Coatan river (Piña Chan, 1960c). Striking counterparts of the Ocos and Conchas pottery wares are found in Ecuador (Coe, 1960a; Evans and Meggers, 1960) and are thought to have arrived there via sea travel. It also appears possible that influences moving north from this early cultural hearth in the Coatan-Suchiate zone underlay the Central Depression (Chiapa I and II) and Gulf coast Olmec developments, or, more likely, that each of these groups arose from a common ancestral culture. The suggestion that temple mounds are associated with the Ocos phase, despite its early date (to ca. 1500 B.C.) and its lack of determined predecessors, points up the unique and important position of the Rio Suchiate locality (Coe, 1959a,b; see also Willey, 1960, p. 15, n. 66).

LATE PRECLASSIC. Sites in the Soconusco with a determined occupation during the Late Preclassic period (Chiapa III, IV, V) are Los Toros, a large mound site on the east bank of the Los Toros arroyo southwest of Tapachula; El Nuevo Dia and adjacent mound groups near the Rio Cahuacan crossing of the Pan American railroad (El Manzano) south of Tapachula; Acacoyagua and Escuintla in the Cintalapa-Cacaluta drainage (Drucker, 1948, pp. 156–63), and Mazatan and Izapa (see above).

PROTOCLASSIC. There are few significant data for the Protoclassic (Chiapa VI and VII) developments in the Soconusco, although a few Protoclassic sherds have been noted at Izapa (see above). Certain of the Izapa stelae also suggest a Protoclassic date (Coe, 1957b, p. 608). The "archaistic" figurines described by Drucker (1948, p. 159; figs. 7, 8), which he characterizes as having flat, triangular faces, rather crude bodies, and nearly all serving as whistles, are very likely of Protoclassic date. Kidder (1940) has illustrated similar examples from Escuintla (fig. 5; the vertical holes running through the figurine heads are whistle ducts rather than cord channels). These Chiapas examples resemble very closely the typical figurines of eastern El Salvador in that they are usually upright with thickened spread legs and cleft feet

for support, have fingers and toes indicated by incisions, have hands on the hips or at the waist, and have similar facial features including coffee-bean eyes (private collections, El Salvador; also Longyear, 1944, pls. IX: 23, 31, 32; XII: 5, 6). According to Haberland (personal communication), this figurine type definitely occurs later than the Formative types of El Salvador and pertains to a "Classic" stage. Also, Lothrop as early as 1927 assigned figurines of this general type (1927b, figs. 11, 17) to the upper part of the "archaic" in El Salvador and even indicated that they were found with later material including polychrome pottery of Mayan inspiration (pp. 182–84).

The Usulutan ware stated by Drucker to be abundant in the Los Toros zone, associated with an archaistic figurine (1948, p. 147), may in part pertain to the Protoclassic period since Usulutan ceramics are known to continue into the Classic stage at Copan and elsewhere; and in El Salvador a later variety of the pottery is associated with the archaistic figurines (Haberland, personal communication). At Chiapa de Corzo, Usulutan trade ware appears only during the Early Protoclassic period (Chiapa VI).

EARLY CLASSIC. There are almost no data for the Early Classic (Chiapa VIII and IX) periods in the Soconusco, other than that Piña Chan indicates a Classic period occupation for his surveyed sites on the basis of two or three poorly diagnostic wares (1960c, Cuadros 1, 2). It seems quite probable that the local variant of the Protoclassic continued here until disrupted by the early Mexican migrations or cultural influences which made their impact on coastal and highland Guatemala at the beginning of the Esperanza or closing Early Classic phase about A.D. 350.

LATE CLASSIC. Horizon markers for the Late Classic period (Chiapa X-A, B) on the Pacific coast are the San Juan and Robles Plumbate wares (Smith and Gifford, 1959, p. 20). As indicated earlier, San Juan Plumbate is a dominant ware at Izapa. At La

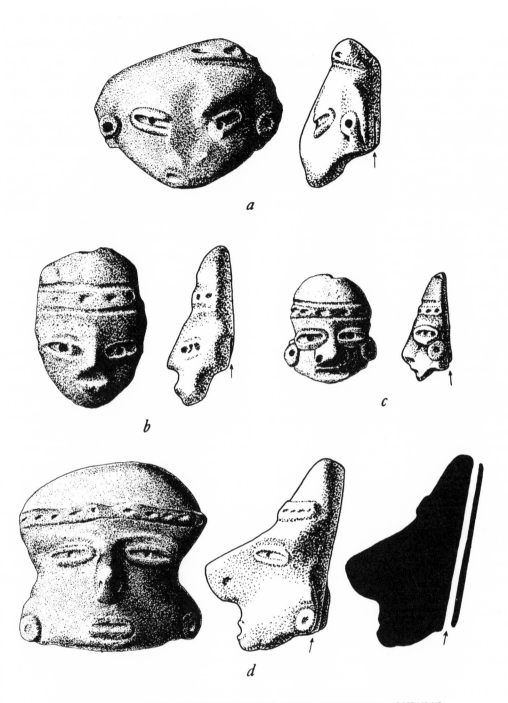

Fig. 5—ARCHAISTIC FIGURINE HEADS FROM ESCUINTLA, CHIAPAS
(After Kidder, 1940.)

Primavera, south of Tapachula, Drucker noted that perhaps a third to a half of the sherds recovered were of plumbate, mostly of the unelaborated San Juan forms (1948, p. 159). His drawings of the profiles and grooved decoration (n.d.) indicate a very close correspondence to the Velasquez Incised type of San Juan Plumbate (Smith and Gifford, 1959, p. 127; Thompson, 1948, fig. 55). San Juan Plumbate was also found in the zone between La Primavera and the Pacific, at the sites of El Jato, El Chical, and El Yugual (Drucker, 1948, p. 158; Piña Chan, 1960c).

The only site shown to have had a Late Classic occupation on the basis of a presence of Robles Plumbate is that of Metapa, a cluster of 14 earthen mounds on the Suchiate River south of Tapachula (Dutton, 1958, p. 54). This recently defined ware is undoubtedly present at other sites in the Tapachula vicinity.

On the basis of abundant Fine Orange and related ceramic wares having close counterparts at certain Tabasco sites, Piña Chan (1960c) believes a site at Huehuetan to be an important Late Classic center.

POSTCLASSIC. According to the presence of the diagnostic Tohil Plumbate there are a number of sites in the Soconusco district datable to the Early Postclassic period (Chiapa XI-A), particularly in the Rio Coatan–Suchiate section and also in the Rio Cintalapa drainage. But definitive data are lacking (cf. Drucker, 1948, pp. 156–62; Dutton, 1958; Piña Chan, 1960c). A number of effigy-vessel supports, mostly from grater bowls, secured by Drucker at El Chical and El Yugual, indicate extensive Postclassic occupation of this zone (1948, p. 158; n.d.). A similar lot of Mixtec or Mexican-related material was found at Huehuetan I, a group of 20 small mounds scattered about a larger central mound near the railway station. Several objects of metal,

probably of copper and including an axe and needle, were reportedly found earlier at this site (Drucker, 1948, p. 158). It is probable that Huehuetan was occupied continuously at least from Late Classic to conquest times, though Drucker states that the colonial town, presumably the site of the Aztec garrison, lies several kilometers to the north in the edge of the foothills (1948, p. 154). In the Rio Cintalapa drainage, the vicinity of Acacoyagua west of Escuintla and extending south to Las Delicias also produced quantities of Postclassic artifacts (1948, pp. 159–65; figs. 9–11). In this same zone, the site of Xoconocho, said to be the capital of the pre-Aztec Nahuat-speaking groups of the Chiapas coast, has not been investigated.

Due to lack of exploration of contact-period sites or any adequate excavations in the Soconusco, it is impossible to make any intelligent elaboration of historical allusions to preconquest cultural patterns or historical events. The pertinent historical data have been summarized and discussed by Culebro (1937; a new treatise published in Huixtla in 1958 was not available to us), Vivó (1942, 1946b), and others.

SIERRA MADRE DE CHIAPAS

Environment

Paralleling the low, narrow Pacific coastal plain, the Sierra Madre de Chiapas mountain province rises steeply to an elevation of about 1500 m. at its northwestern limit with Oaxaca and to a general height of about 3000 m. on the southeast frontier with Guatemala. On the northeast the range descends more gradually to a mean elevation of 700–500 m. above sea level in the Central Depression. Comprising an area approximately 280 km. long, 50 km. wide on the northwest and 65 km. wide on the southeast, the Sierra Madre is a region of complex morphology having in places deep

FIG. 6—CHIAPA I CERAMIC FORMS, CHIAPA DE CORZO. (After Dixon, 1959b, figs. 2–20, *passim*.)

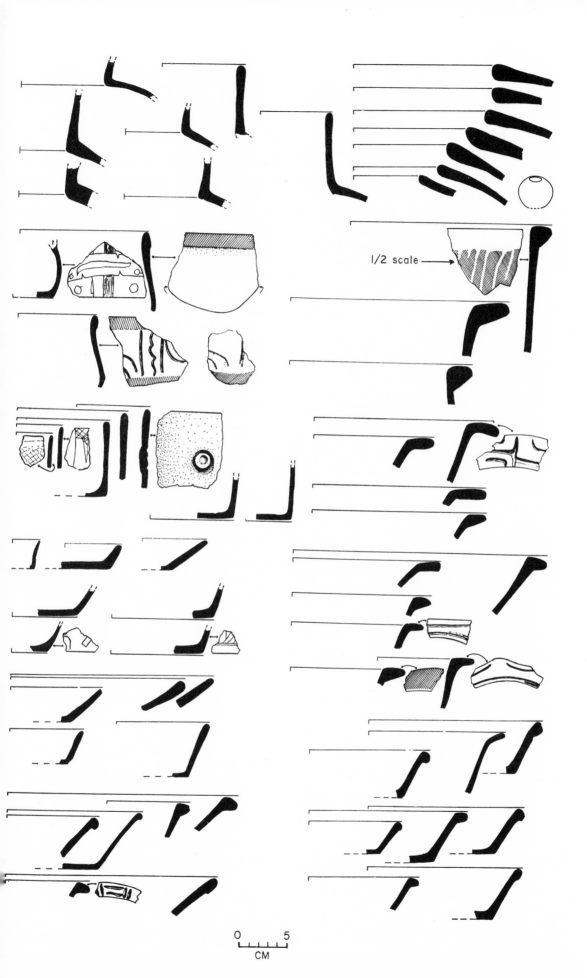

1/2 scale

0   5
CM

or broken canyons, in others ridges or peaks, and in others intermontane plains or valleys.

The Sierra Madre has always been sparsely peopled and has effectively separated the more densely populated coastal and interior regions of Chiapas. Since the conquest communications across the southeastern Sierra have been restricted to a few difficult trails, the principal one being from Huixtla over the pass of La Cruz at 1970 m. and descending to Motozintla and on through the Amatenango Valley. From there a foot or horse trail continues through the precipitous canyon of the Cuilco River (a tributary of the Grijalva) to the Central Depression at La Nueva. In the northwest sector of the Sierra Madre the terrain is less abrupt and a cart road crosses over a 1240-m. pass between Tonala and Villa Flores; the paved highway from Arriaga to Tuxla Gutierrez crosses the divide at only 630 m. following the pass which presumably has always given the most ready access to and from the Central Depression.

Only during the present century with the spread of coffee fincas has the Sierra Madre region undergone much development at human hands. Waibel describes a definite immigration of Quiche and Mam Indians from Guatemala into the region as a result of the expansion of the coffee plantations. In this movement the Indians escaped their old creditors and during the Mexican ejido allocations obtained virgin corn lands in the higher Sierra Madre pine forests not useful for coffee. Today, the indigenous inhabitants of the southeastern Sierra Madre de Chiapas rely upon subsistence digging-stick agriculture and part-time labor on the coffee fincas (1946; Gamio, 1946). Motozintla is the only substantial town in the Sierra Madre, having gained its importance from its midway position on the busy Huixtla–La Nueva cross-Sierra camino.

Archaeology

The Sierra Madre is the least well known of the archaeological regions of Chiapas. Waibel, quoting Sapper (1897, p. 367), states that in the Sierra Madre archaeological ruins had been found only in the Motozintla Valley. He cites this fact, together with the presence of small isolated linguistic groups, as evidence for the ancient importance of the valley as a migration route (1946, p. 138). Culebro, on the basis of wide personal experience in the highlands, lists about 20 sites in the Sierra Madre. Most of these cluster in the mountains close to the Motozintla Valley and may have been related to the cross-Sierra route but situated higher up with defense and/or access to moister farm lands in mind (Motozintla, in a rain-shadow zone, is the driest spot in Chiapas despite proximity to rainiest regions on the Pacific slope). Culebro (1939) indicates the presence of "fortifications" at five of the sites on peaks paralleling the valley.

A survey of the Motozintla Valley floor in 1956 by the New World Archaeological Foundation failed to find many good diagnostic ceramics at the six sites examined, but found some evidence of occupation from the Late Classic through the Postclassic periods (Lowe, 1959b, pp. 65–68). No plumbate sherds of any sort were found, suggesting that the valley is outside the plumbate-manufacturing center postulated for the Pacific sector of the Chiapas-Guatemala frontier (Dutton, 1958; see also Shepard, 1948, pp. 112, 113, 145).

In the lower and more open northwestern Sierra Madre no comprehensive survey has been made, but materials from a few known mound sites near the Pan American Highway indicate a cultural context some-

FIG. 7—CHIAPA II CERAMIC FORMS, CHIAPA DE CORZO. (After Dixon, 1959b, figs. 23–42, passim)

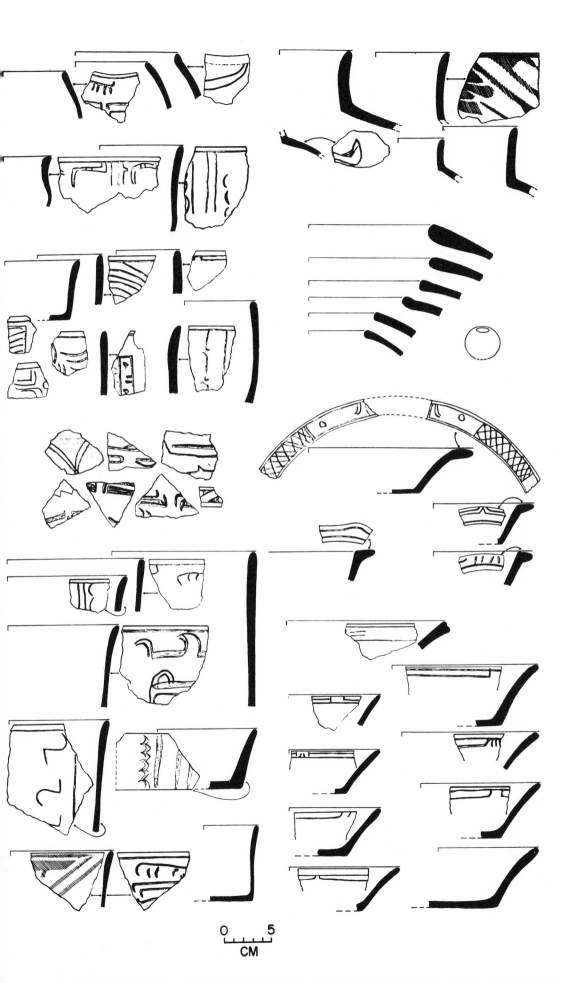

0   5
CM

what distinct from those known elsewhere in Chiapas, and a Classic period development possibly related to Tonala is suggested (F. A. Peterson Cintalapa survey, New World Archaeological Foundation collections, Museo Regional, Tuxtla Gutierrez, Chiapas).

The lower portions of the northeastern slopes of the Sierra Madre are considered a part of the Central Depression, the region to which they appear to have been most closely related in both pre- and postconquest times. Adequate surveys of the Sierra Madre, however, both of its highland and slope segments, are a prerequisite to further postulations of the historical role of this natural impediment to cultural interchange.

CENTRAL DEPRESSION (UPPER GRIJALVA BASIN)

Environment

A great block-faulted area between the Sierra Madre and Central Plateau, the Central Depression of Chiapas forms an irregular trough extending 250 km. southeast from the vicinity of Cintalapa to the Guatemala frontier (fig. 2). Its width varies between 25 and 75 km. The Grijalva River occupies a narrow trench running through the eastern segment, and several tributary rivers and smaller ridges and valleys both parallel to and opposing the river channels break up the Depression into distinctive zones. The floor of the Depression averages between 500 and 700 m. above sea level and the Grijalva in its trench leaves the basin west of Chiapa de Corzo at an elevation of only 380 m.

With a dry tropical climate, the Depression has an annual rainfall of about 1 m. in the northwest and 1.5 m. in the southeast. The area is practically rainless from November through May and as a result the vegetation is typically subdeciduous or savanna with evergreen tropical forest confined to river plains and higher slope areas of the surrounding mountains on the northwest and southwest margins of the Depression.

The western section of the Depression is now readily accessible via the paved Pan American highway, and other all-weather roads connect the principal towns. Modern economic activities are largely confined to maize agriculture and cattle grazing, with an important coffee-processing industry in Tuxtla Gutierrez, the commercial center for the region as well as capital of the state. Most maize is grown by digging-stick methods though oxen and wooden plows are used on some of the more level community lands. No Indian communities remain within the Depression except near Venustiano Carranza, a zone more closely related to the highlands than to the rest of the Depression. (For a fuller description of the upper Grijalva basin and its subregions, see Lowe, 1959b).

Archaeology

A few of the great many archaeological sites in the Central Depression have been briefly noted by travelers and scientists but no excavations were undertaken until the 1940's. Stirling at Piedra Parada (unpublished but see his 1945, 1947) and Berlin at the Sumidero, Chiapa de Corzo, and San Pedro Buenavista sites (1946a) made sufficient investigations to show evidence of Late Preclassic through Middle Postclassic occupation for the western end of the Depression. No other methodical investigation was made until 1953 when a preliminary survey by the New World Archaeological Foundation (N.W.A.F.) showed the dominance of Late Preclassic and Late Classic ceramic types in the region (Sorenson, 1956).

Results of the N.W.A.F. program to date include surface collections of ceramics from over 250 mound sites, the digging of test trenches at 12 of these sites, and architectural investigations at the sites of Chiapa de Corzo, San Agustin, and Santa Rosa.

(Shook, 1956b; Agrinier, 1960; Dixon, 1958, 1959a,b; Lowe, 1956, 1959a,b; Navarrete, 1959a,b, 1960; Warren, 1959, Hicks and Rozaire, 1960; Mason, 1960; Sanders, 1961.) The only zone of the Central Depression remaining unsurveyed is that of the savanna and foothills extending southeastward from Villa Corzo through Angel Albino Corzo (Jaltenango) and La Concordia to Chicomuselo. It is too early to draw final conclusions about the over-all pre-Hispanic cultural development of the Depression and its wider Mesoamerican relationships, but a description of the culture-historical trends so far apparent seems to be the best way of presenting the work of the N.W.A.F.

PRECERAMIC PERIOD (Santa Marta phase, ca. 7000–1500 B.C.). The earliest culture so far identified in southern Mesoamerica has been found in the dry shelter cave of Santa Marta overlooking the plain and archaeological site of Piedra Parada about 5 km. northwest of Ocozocoautla. Excavated in 1959 by MacNeish and Peterson (Art. 12, vol. 1), the 2-m. deposit of refuse in the Santa Marta shelter produced well-stratified evidence of 10 distinct occupations, divisible into four separate cultural phases covering a great span of time. The earliest five occupational levels, distinguishable by lenses of charcoal and animal bones, have been assigned to the preceramic Santa Marta phase and are discussed elsewhere in the Handbook. This debris apparently is that of a seasonal camp of incipient agriculturists. The sixth occupational level, termed the Cotorra phase, contained the first ceramics, a complex very similar to that of Chiapa I, the earliest horizon found at Chiapa de Corzo. Above this level were mixed Classic and Postclassic deposits.

EARLY PRECLASSIC PERIOD (Chiapa I, ca. 1500–1000 B.C.). The Chiapa I ceramics of Chiapa de Corzo (fig. 6), as characterized by Dixon (1959b, Pit 50 period), are typically neckless jars (*tecomates* or "seed jars"); vertical-wall bowls; flaring-wall bowls with exteriorly thickened, direct or

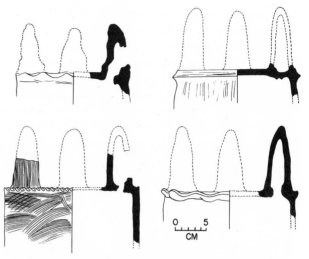

FIG. 8—CHIAPA II THREE-PRONGED INCENSE BURNERS, CHIAPA DE CORZO. (Courtesy, New World Archaeological Foundation.)

everted rim; jars with neck; and recurved bowls, in that order of diminishing frequency. Wares are described as White, Red-and-White Bichrome, and Unslipped. Decoration is usually pattern incising augmented on the unslipped neckless jars by punctation, rocker-stamping, applied fillets, raised ovals, and raking. Associated with this type sample were a stone bowl, basin metates, a mano fragment, and a sandstone reamer (*op. cit.,* p. 19). The Chiapa I ceramic and artifact inventory subsequently has been enlarged somewhat, but the only evidences of architecture so far associated with the phase are pieces of polished adobe plaster including carefully squared corner fragments.

The Cotorra ceramic sample from Santa Marta cave, though conforming closely to the Chiapa I complex as known at Chiapa de Corzo and elsewhere in the Central Depression, is characteristically composed of smaller vessels with thinner walls and rougher surface and in all is less elaborated in both form and decoration. The excavators conjecture that this situation indicates that Santa Marta was either more provin-

209

cial or earlier than other Chiapa I sites (MacNeish and Peterson, 1962). The radiocarbon date for the Santa Marta Cotorra phase differs little from that obtained for the comparable phase at Chiapa de Corzo:

Sample M-978: Charcoal from Square S1E2, Level 5 (occupation 6), Santa Marta Cave. Age 3280±200 years (1320 B.C.± 200).

Sample GRO-774: Charcoal and ashes from Pit 50, Chiapa de Corzo. Associated with sherds of earliest phase (Chiapa I). Age 3010±100 years (after correcting to 240 years earlier for Suess effect [see Dixon, 1959b, p. 41n], 1292 B.C.±100).

These individual dates are from undetermined positions within the period and should be considered only as relative indicators of its temporal position.

Chiapa I ceramics have so far been found in the Central Depression at Santa Marta, Chiapa de Corzo, Santa Cruz, Mirador, Padre Piedra, and Villa Flores; additional excavations will surely find a wider distribution since its earlier position makes it less prone to superficial recovery. On the Chiapas coast it has been found only at Mazatan. The allied pottery types of the Ocos phase at La Victoria, Guatemala, are much more sophisticated and make Chiapa I look provincial. There is reason to believe that Chiapa I is either an interior Chiapas regional outgrowth at the end of the Ocos occupation or that the two are uneven developments of a common source culture. North of Chiapas at the site of La Venta, Tabasco, Chiapa I sherds appear as rarities, possibly indicating that this ceramic complex barely reached there before it took on characteristics more similar to Chiapa II.

MIDDLE PRECLASSIC PERIOD (Chiapa II-III, ca. 1000–450 B.C.). With the exception of Santa Marta Cave, Chiapa I is everywhere followed by Chiapa II, a period with a slightly evolved ceramic inventory that has not yet been completely described (see fig. 7, a selection from Dixon, 1959b, Pit 38 period). Typical of the period are abundant hand-modeled figurines, usually with punctate eyes (fig. 9), and a three-pronged incense-burner-stand complex (fig. 8). Architectural evidences for the period are stone-faced terrace platforms and rectangular house or temple foundations of small boulders (fig. 16,d).

In addition to continuing at Chiapa de Corzo, Santa Cruz, Mirador, Padre Piedra, and Villa Flores, Chiapa II ceramics occur as the earliest phase at Tuxtla Gutierrez, Cueva de la Puente, Vergel, Escalera, Finca Amatal, Buenos Aires, El Cuadro, Santa Rosa, San Jacinto, Laguna Francesa, and Sevilla in the Central Depression. On the Pacific coast equivalent pottery has been so far found at Tzutzuculi and Mazatan. The Conchas I subphase at La Victoria has material very similar to Chiapa II though with a characteristically better polish. The presence of grater bowls and other traits distinguish this coastal Guatemala context from that of Chiapa de Corzo (M. D. Coe, 1959a,b; 1961).

The closest ceramic ties of Chiapa II on the north are with the earliest pottery of La Venta, Tabasco (cf. Drucker, 1952a, figs. 38,a,b; 39, and especially the Drucker, Heizer and Squier, 1959, illustrations of La Venta Phase I and II cache vessels, fig. 42,b,c,e,). Certainly La Venta outlasted Chiapa II, extending into Chiapa IV times before it was abandoned.

Despite the apparent cultural affiliations between the early La Venta and Chiapa II centers, a number of differences suggest a religious or cultic distinction between the Chiapas and Tabasco regions during this

FIG. 9—CHIAPA II FIGURINES
All solid except heads in right-hand file. Chiapa de Corzo. (Courtesy, N. W. A. F.)

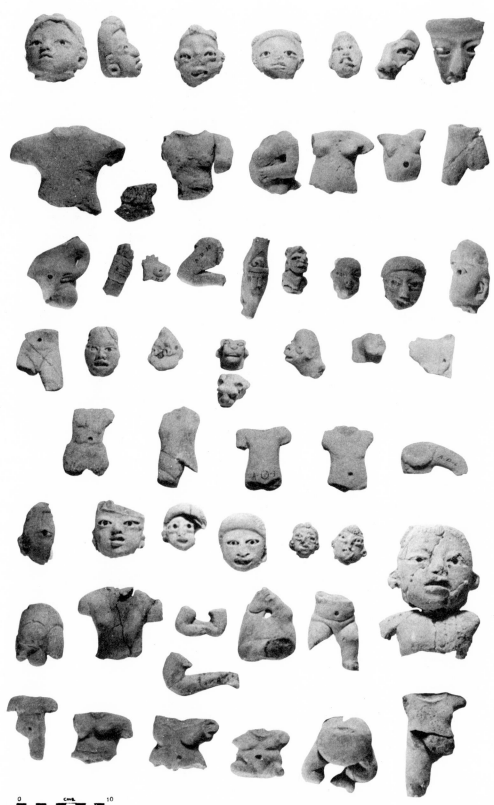

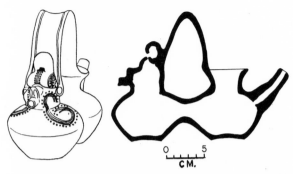

0 —— 5
C M.

FIG. 10—CHIAPA III BLACK-WARE WHISTLING VESSEL. Burial offering, Mound 7, Chiapa de Corzo. See also fig. 11. (Courtesy, N. W. A. F.)

which seem to have extended over much of the New World (M. D. Coe, 1960a).

The Chiapa III phase was apparently a period of short duration but one marking a sharp change in cultural practices at Chiapa de Corzo. The well-polished monochrome red, black, brown, and white vessels shown in figs. 10 and 11, diagnostic for the phase, are from burial caches intrusive through the clay floors of Str. 7-E, an earthen platform characteristic of the period at Chiapa de Corzo. The largest structure so far known for Chiapa III is a clay stepped platform over 6 m. high which forms the core of Mound 13 at Chiapa de Corzo (Hicks and Rozaire, 1960).

The Chiapa III occupation seems to be intrusive at Chiapa de Corzo where circumstances suggest either a greatly reduced population or the existence of a clearly defined minority group. Preliminary analysis shows that most refuse deposits sampled grade from Chiapa II into IV despite the presence of the distinct phase III burials, mound constructions, and rare rubbish pits. It is very probable that introduction of the new Chiapa III pottery techniques, including the first use at Chiapa de Corzo of highly polished "waxy" slips, was a harbinger of intensified interregional relationships which soon resulted in the further developed ceramic complex characterizing the more stable sequent Chiapa IV society. There seems to be no question that the new Chiapa III techniques came in from the south where hard, lustrous polishing was a ceramic trait throughout the Early and Middle Preclassic in Guatemala.

Chiapa III corresponds in many respects to the developed Mamom phase of the Guatemalan Peten though no mound building of this phase has been discovered there. (It apparently is present as a Mamom trait, however, in neighboring British Honduras at Nohok Ek [see M. D. Coe, 1957a, p. 25]).

early period of Mesoamerican civilization. The three-pronged incense-burner complex in Chiapas at least superficially indicates that the closest Chiapa II religious ties were with the central highlands of Guatemala where such types were a prominent feature of the coeval and apparently equally populous Las Charcas phase (Borhegyi, 1950b; 1951a,b). Related burner types have not been reported from La Venta or elsewhere in Mexico other than Chiapas during the Preclassic, and a southern Guatemala or western El Salvador point of origin is probable. Sculptured stone monuments, characteristic of the Gulf coast Olmec culture, are rare in Chiapas, and Olmec-style jade ornaments are not associated with the central Chiapas Preclassic. On the other hand, certain figurine types (fig. 9) are very similar for Chiapa II and La Venta (Drucker, 1952a, pl. 26) and some of these in turn have corresponding types in the Mamom phase of the Lowland Maya subarea. This latter phase appears to have its base in a Chiapa II-related culture, though as a whole it is more like the succeeding Chiapa III phase. It appears that the Gulf coast Olmec cult developed as one of many regional manifestations of underlying Early and Middle Preclassic cultural influences

FIG. 11—CHIAPA III POTTERY. From burial offerings in Mound 7, Chiapa de Corzo. Approx. scale 1/5. (Courtesy, N. W. A. F.)

Fig. 12—CHIAPA IV POTTERY. Vessels at left center and upper right are carryovers from Chiapa II. Burial offerings, south plaza, Chiapa de Corzo (approx. scale 1/5). (Courtesy, N. W. A. F.)

The black ware whistling vessel (fig. 10) is one of the earliest known examples and suggests diffusion from the south though it appears to be of local manufacture. Pronged incense burners are absent during this period and figurines are extremely rare, negative traits continuing in the succeeding period, at least at Chiapa de Corzo. Chiapa III pottery is present at earthen-mound sites throughout the Central Depression but always as a minor quantity.

LATE PRECLASSIC PERIOD (Chiapa IV-V, ca. 450–100 B.C.). The pottery of Chiapa IV forms the Preclassic complex most widespread in the Central Depression. Surface collections show that over 50 of the examined sites had an occupation during this period. It appears to have been a time of widened cultural interchange with the west and north, witnessing the first arrival of a few trade or tribute vessels of Monte Alban I type from Oaxaca and a greater number of fine paste gray-black ware vessels apparently from the Los Tuxtlas region of the Gulf coast (provenience in both cases supported by paste analysis).

The sophistication of this period at Chiapa de Corzo is evident not only in the great variety of monochrome pottery forms accompanying numerous burials (figs. 12, 13) but also by the abundant clay stamps, both flat and cylindrical, bearing symbolic designs (fig. 13,a). The shell earplug pendants (fig. 13,e) are the earliest known appearance of the plumed serpent at Chiapa de Corzo. It has a form very similar to that noted at La Venta (cf. Monument 19 and Stela 3 in Drucker, Heizer, and Squier, 1959, pp. 197–200, figs. 55, 67). The earliest vessel decorated with stucco painting so far found at Chiapa de Corzo accompanied the burial with the shell serpents (Burial 74).

Ceremonial architecture of this period at Chiapa de Corzo involved the enlargement of the existing Chiapa III platforms and the introduction of poor quality lime plaster floors and structural caches. The latter con-tained pottery, jade beads, and a sherd-backed pyrite mirror.

During Chiapa IV subregional specialization began to take place in the Central Depression, becoming more marked in the ensuing phases. In the Mirador zone on the Soyatenco (upper La Venta) River west of Ocozocoautla a variant of the three-pronged composite or "assemble-it-your-self" incense burner (Borhegyi, 1959a) becomes dominant, whereas at Chiapa de Corzo the principal burner at this time is an inner-handled, funnel-based cylindrical type. The composite burners are more abundant in the Mirador zone than in any other locality so far known in Mesoamerica, and, perhaps, they are earlier there as well. An elaborate and distinctive figurine complex begins at this time at Mirador also, and appears rarely as traded items elsewhere (Peterson, 1963).

Another Chiapa IV regional manifestation appears at San Agustin, a small site west of Tuxtla Gutierrez, where a lime-aggregate terraced pyramid (fig. 14) was constructed (Navarrete, 1959a). Similar use of decayed limestone as a building material has not been found at Chiapa de Corzo, and has been noted at only one other site in Chiapas, El Cielito (Navarrete, 1960). Pottery from the tomb within the San Agustin structure is also a distinctive lot, though in general suggestive only of Chiapa IV. Jade beads similar to the smaller ones from the San Agustin tomb have been found with Chiapa IV burials at Chiapa de Corzo, but the earplug flares and tubular bead are exceptional in Chiapas.

Radiocarbon dates secured from Chiapa IV material are:

Sample GRO-1056: Charred material from Chiapa IV refuse deposit beneath Mound 1, Chiapa de Corzo. Age 2130±60 years (after adding 240 years for Suess effect 424±60 B.C.).

Sample GRO-1524: Bits of charcoal in earthen matrix of Chiapa IV burial be-

a

b

c

d

e

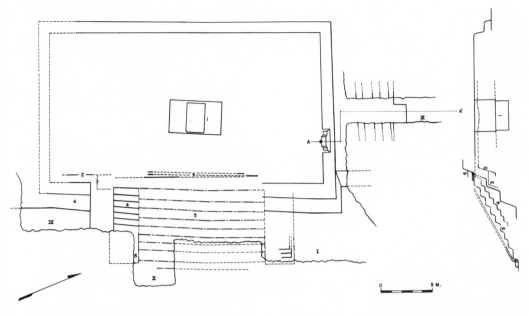

Fig. 14—CHIAPA IV ARCHITECTURE. Plan and profile of lime-aggregate platform structure at San Agustin, Chiapas. (After Navarrete, 1959a, fig. 2.)

neath Mound 1, Chiapa de Corzo. Age 2270±45 (after adding 240 years for Suess effect 564±45 B.C.).

The Chiapa V phase is characterized by a greatly modified ceramic assemblage. Clearly reflecting developments which are typical of much of southern Mesoamerica, there is an introduction and elaboration of medial and labial flanged bowls and plates, frequently with knobs or effigy elements on the flanges. An unending variety of composite-silhouette forms in polished red and black wares is diagnostic, and tetrapod vessel supports, both nubbin and hollow, occur rarely. Bichrome painting, usually red-on-cream in a great diversification of curvilinear patterns applied to either interiors or exteriors of polished red bowls, is also typical, as is the absence of figurines. The inner-horned incense-burner bowls make a rare first appearance in this period, as do white-rim black

ware bowls, both of which types become ubiquitous and undergo marked evolution during ensuing periods. The fact of the traceable evolution of the white-rim effect, at first created by painting and later by controlled firing, suggests that central Chiapas shares the origin of this vessel type which eventually became widespread over the entire Isthmus region.

There are very strong stylistic resemblances between the diagnostic Chiapa V pottery and certain Chicanel types found at sites in the Campeche, Yucatan, and Peten regions of the Maya Lowlands with which the most direct relationships of Chiapa de Corzo must have existed at this time. Other parts of the Central Depression itself, however, have produced lesser amounts of the Chicanel–Chiapa V diagnostics and seem rather to have perpetuated and further elaborated their own regional styles apparently

G. 13—CHIAPA IV CERAMIC AND SHELL ARTIFACTS. All from Chiapa de Corzo south plaza burial offerings except five small flat stamps at upper left, and incised vessels at lower left, from Mounds 7 and 33 (approx. ale: stamps 1/2, vessels 1/5, shell earspool pendants 1/3). (Courtesy, N. W. A. F.)

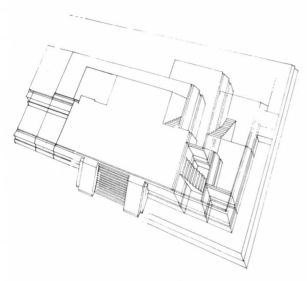

Fig. 15—CHIAPA VI ARCHITECTURE, CHIAPA DE-
CORZO. The 1-H platform structure, showing sequent
enlargements. Platform height 3.5 m. See also fig. 16,c.
(Courtesy, N.W.A.F.)

under stronger influences from the highland regions of Guatemala.

A single radiocarbon date has been secured for Chiapa V:

Sample GRO-1525: Charcoal from a fallen
structural timber lying at the base of a
Chiapa V refuse deposit under Mound
1, Chiapa de Corzo. Age 1930±30 years
(after adding 240 years for Suess effect
210±30 b.c.).

EARLY PROTOCLASSIC PERIOD (Chiapa VI,
100 b.c.–a.d. 1). The beginning of the Protoclassic development at Chiapa de Corzo is
marked by the elaboration of cut stone
architecture and, with the exception of a
few domestic forms, a completely different
assemblage of ceramics (figs. 17,b,c, 18, 19,
20). The earliest constructions are low platforms stepped up slightly from front to
rear, supporting a one- or two-room temple
apparently built of adobe bricks. Ever-

larger stone-faced temple platforms and
multiroomed "palace" structures were built
in quick succession as Chiapa VI advanced
(figs. 17,a; 15; 16,b,c) but neither the corbeled vault nor lime for bonding the well-
squared and smoothed limestone blocks
was used. Roofs appear to have been flat,
of thick clay applied over timbers and
broad leaves, and capped with a hard-finished lime plaster for impermeability.

Chiapa de Corzo was of sufficient importance at this time to receive trade or tribute
pottery from many of its major contemporary centers in Mesoamerica, but the
previously abundant Chicanel-like types
are notably absent. This pattern is characteristic for the length of the Chiapa VI
occupation during which the rudimentary
Maya modes are mostly lacking in the five
tomb offerings and many dedicatory caches
and ceremonial dumps of the period found
at Chiapa de Corzo. Chiapa VI seems to
have had its closest affiliations with the
Arenal phase of sites such as Kaminaljuyu
in the highlands of Guatemala, but both
its architecture and its ceramics show local
development or manufacture with the exception of certain finer vessels which appear to be imports from that related area.
Other vessels certainly arrived in Chiapa
de Corzo from southern Veracruz, Oaxaca,
and El Salvador. The number of mammiform tetrapod vessels in Chiapa VI collections is perhaps unequaled in any other excavated collection in Mesoamerica. Many of
them, such as those in figure 19,a, appear
to be imports from an unidentified region.
The finely carved human femurs from
Tomb 1, Chiapa de Corzo (fig. 21), may
also have been imported (Agrinier, 1960;
Dixon, 1958).

A trait seemingly peculiar to the Central
Depression of Chiapas is that of the shal-

Fig. 16—CHIAPA DE CORZO ARCHITECTURE. a, Chiapa VII structure in Mound 1 with stucco
frieze remnant. b, Str. 5-H (Chiapa VI); see plan, fig. 17,a. c, Str. 1-H (Chiapa VI). d, Chiapa II room
foundations, south plaza. (Courtesy, N. W. A. F.)

a

b

c

d

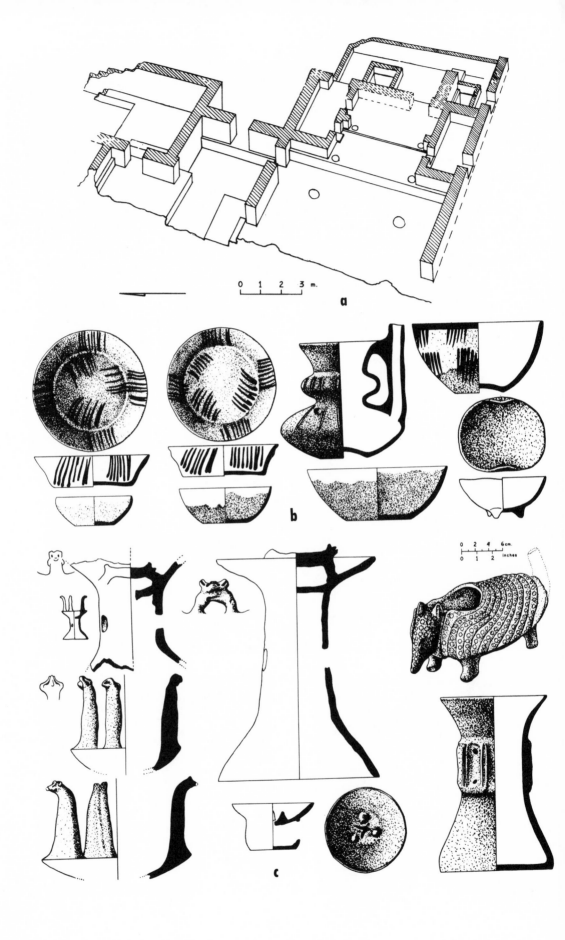

a

b

c

0 1 2 3 m.

0 2 4 6 cm.
0 1 2 inches

low ceremonial burner bowls with three inner horns clustered around a central vent (figs. 18; 19,e). This censer type, associated with the deep vertical-wall bowls of coarse ware upon which they were placed for use (fig. 18), is very common in Chiapa VI caches at Chiapa de Corzo, and examples are found occasionally at other sites in the Depression. The only other region so far known to share this general type of burner is western El Salvador, where there is a large example with a pedestal base in the Tazumal museum at Chalchuapa. Several new incense-burner types appear at Chiapa de Corzo toward the end of the Chiapa VI period. One has effigy prongs (fig. 19,f) and the others (fig. 17,c) include a combined form of the rim horn and three-pronged incense-burner complexes of the highland Guatemala Late Preclassic (Borhegyi, 1950b, 1951a,b; Kidder and Shook, 1946). Other unique items are the clay "anvils" (figs. 19,b).

The trend toward regionalism was intensified in the Central Depression during the Early Protoclassic period with a continuation of Late Preclassic assemblages and the development of specialized pottery types which were traded widely. A hard-finished orange ware with blotches or bands of metallic luster was manufactured at Mirador, where quantities of over-fired kiln rejects are found, and traded vessels are numerous in the Chiapa de Corzo caches. Sherds of this ware are found in surface collections from throughout the western end of the Depression. At Santa Rosa, in the upper end of the basin, potters emphasized a distinctive and highly polished black ware (fig. 20) with an astonishing elaboration of wide everted, modeled, and incised rim bowl and plate forms (Brockington, in preparation). Cylindrical and effigy forms also appear in this ware which is recognizable by the tendency of its makers to polish the black slip until the brown paste shows through. Traded examples of Santa Rosa black ware have been found in Chiapa de Corzo Period VI caches, and sherds are present in surface collections from throughout the eastern end of the Depression and from the Comitan and Pacific coast districts.

Radiocarbon dates secured from Chiapa VI architectural associations are:

Sample GRO-1589: Charcoal from burned roof beam, Mound 5, Chiapa de Corzo. Chiapa VI cache in association. Age 1680±45 years (after adding 240 years for Suess effect, A.D. 38±45).

Sample GRO-1932: Charcoal from ashy layer on floor of buried platform structure, Mound F, Santa Rosa, Chiapas. Early Protoclassic sherds in association. Age 1750±65 years (after adding 240 years for Suess effect, 38±65 B.C.).

LATE PROTOCLASSIC PERIOD (Chiapa VII, ca. A.D. 1–200). Climaxing a trend begun in the preceding phase, Chiapa VII maintained few relations with the Maya Lowlands and additionally seems to have severed the former close relations with highland Guatemala in the establishment of a local culture which might be defined as Isthmian. Rare Protoclassic Maya trade wares are present at Chiapa de Corzo but the dominant ceramics are, as indicated, apparently of western derivation. These emphasize vertical- and flaring-wall bowls and other forms including low-necked jars and bulbous-bottom vases in a smudged black ware typically having "white" oxidized rims, basal portions, or blotches (fig.

Fig. 17—CHIAPA VI ARCHITECTURE AND CERAMICS, CHIAPA DE CORZO. a, Plan of Str. 5-H; pottery shown below is from caches in this building. For photograph see fig. 16,b. b, Common forms of decorated vessels, including multiple-brush-striped bowls, bulbous-neck jar, oxidized-rim black ware bowls, and pinched-rim tripod bowl. c, Unusual vessels from Str. 5-H, including coarse ware three-pronged incense-burner stands, armadillo effigy, and tall vase of unique form. (Courtesy, N.W.A.F.)

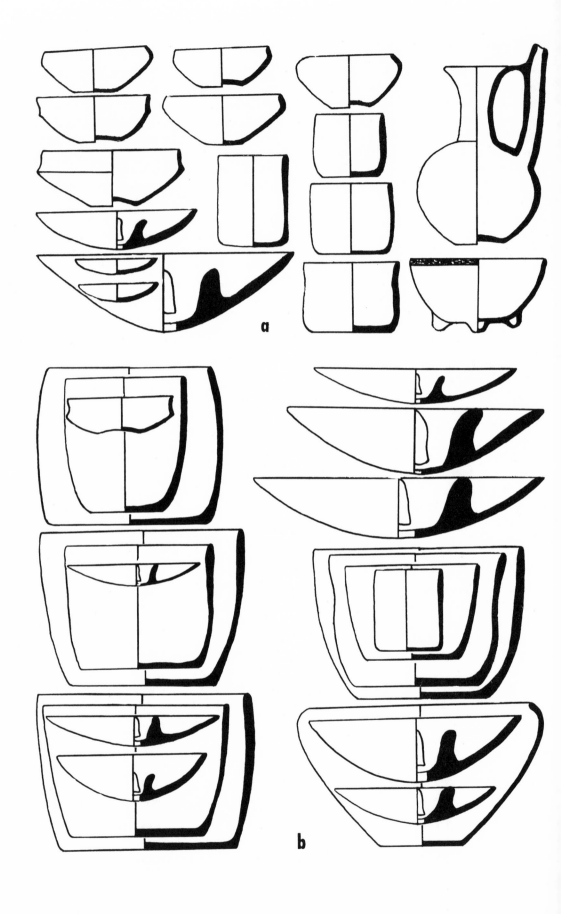

a

b

22). This smudged black pottery, in both ware and form, is distinct from the white-rim black ware of the preceding period and may be distinguished from that of the succeeding period most readily by its harder firing, usual lack of incised designs, and absence of supports or basal embellishment. The Juchitan-Tehuantepec region of the Isthmus, and to a lesser extent the Gulf coast, are seen as the major new influences in this essentially transitional period at Chiapa de Corzo.

Architectural proliferation of the period included the only example of a stucco frieze so far discovered at Chiapa de Corzo, attributed to the end of Chiapa VII (fig. 16,a). The unexplained custom of placing small basaltic pebbles in simple dedicatory cache vessels continued. The remains of feline skeletons in two caches are the first suggestion of the jaguar as a cultic element at Chiapa de Corzo (with the exception of a modeled clay head of Chiapa II affinity —see fig. 9, center).

In other zones of the Central Depression, Late Protoclassic horizon markers such as early Maya Polychrome, swollen vessel supports, ring bases, or the diagnostic hard-fired gray-to-black Isthmus ware provide evidence of Chiapa VII occupation at many sites. By and large, however, local regional styles seem to have continued.

A single radiocarbon date is available for the Late Protoclassic period in Chiapas:

Sample GRO-1916: Charcoal from stub of carbonized post *in situ* in floor at 4.10 m. depth, Mound B, Santa Rosa, Chiapas. Late cache, structure, and Protoclassic sherds in association. Age 1605±60 years (after adding 240 years for Suess effect, A.D. 113±60).

EARLY CLASSIC A PERIOD (Chiapa VIII, ca. A.D. 200–350). Concentrated in the northwestern sector of the Central Depression, the cultural elements of the Chiapa VIII period are essentially elaborations of the preceding one. Platform structures are extended and increased in height, achieving the first real stone-faced pyramid complex at Chiapa de Corzo. Caches placed above Tombs 2 and 3 in the final construction of Mound 12 at this site (Mason, 1960a) represent well the pottery of the period. The principal ceramic diagnostic continues to be the smudged black ware, with or without oxidized rims or blotches. Bowls of this ware frequently have knobs on the rim or a basal frieze or raised zone bordering the base decorated with a great variety of punctate designs. Incised hachured triangles or wave motifs placed at intervals around the outer wall surface and sometimes filled with red pigment are characteristic. Small nubbin feet and potstands also occur infrequently, as do hollow tripod supports, ring bases, and stucco painting. Inner-horn burner bowls are much in evidence in Chiapa VIII caches, and reach the end of their evolution very rudely made. Two jaguar effigies with burner bowls on their backs evidence the continuance of this suggested cultic symbol noted in the previous period.

Additional evidence for the Early Classic A ceremonial emphasis in the Central Depression are masses of Chiapa VIII pottery noted so far in over 40 caves of the Ocozo-coautla-Cintalapa subregion. First reported by Stirling (1945, 1947), the massive offerings are unassociated with occupational debris or burials and suggest consistent usage of the caves for the soliciting of the gods (of the underworld?). Most of the caves are very difficult of entry and suggest that such rites were of great importance to the participants. Apparently this ceremonial usage was almost entirely confined to

FIG. 18—CHIAPA VI RITUAL POTTERY. Partial contents of two ceremonial dumps from below floors of Str. 1-H, Chiapa de Corzo. All are coarse ware except for tetrapod, which is cream ware with red band on lip. (Courtesy, N. W. A. F.)

FIG. 19—EXCEPTIONAL CHIAPA VI POTTERY, CHIAPA DE CORZO. *a*, Polished red (at left) and polished black-brown mammiform tetrapod vessels with stuccoed design (scale 1/6). *b*, Clay "anvils" of unknown use (scale 1/4). *c*, Incised tetrapods (scale 1/4). *d*, Rare ring-base bowl with multiple-brush striping (scale 1/4). *e*, Large inner-horn burner bowls from Mound 1 caches (scale 1/5). *f*, Three-pronged incense burner from Str. 5-H cache (scale 1/5). (Courtesy, N. W. A. F.)

FIG. 20—ARTIFACTS FROM SANTA ROSA, CHIAPA VI PERIOD. *a,b,d–g,* Santa Rosa polished black pottery. *c,* Perforated stone of unknown use common at this site. *d,* Wild-pig effigy head. Scale of *c,d,* 4/5; diameters: *a,* 22 cm.; *b,* 24 cm.; *e,* 27 cm.; *f,* 21 cm.; *g,* 22 cm. (Courtesy, N. W. A. F.)

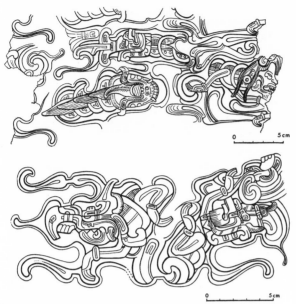

FIG. 21—CHIAPA VI BONE ARTIFACTS. Carved designs on human femurs found in Tomb 1, Str. 1-H, Chiapa de Corzo. (After Agrinier, 1960, figs. 1, 9.)

typical Chiapa VIII ceramics has also been identified in the interior region of the Isthmus of Tehuantepec (Delgado, in preparation).

The well-defined stratigraphic position, the abundance of diagnostic Chiapa VIII wares at a large number of sites, and the "purity" of their cultural context indicate that western Chiapas was a major cultural center during the Early Classic A period. This period seems to have generally preceded the arrival of Classic Teotihuacan traits in southern Mesoamerica.

EARLY CLASSIC B PERIOD (Chiapa IX, ca. A.D. 350–550). From this point on we can be less explicit about the archaeology of the Central Depression due to the lack of pertinent site excavations. The Chiapa de Corzo site seems to have been generally abandoned, with no architectural construction known to date after the preceding period. Chiapa IX is represented there by three burial offerings of Teotihuacan-like vessels, but more definite Teotihuacan evidences are lacking anywhere along the Grijalva trench. In the Mirador-Soyatenco zone, however, quantities of solid gashed and hollow fret slab legs and other Teotihuacan or Early Classic Maya types have been secured in surface or purchase collections, and a polished black cylindrical tripod with an effigy face and slab feet was recovered from the slope of the largest Mirador mound. If this evidence suggests that the Mirador locality was an important Teotihuacan-influenced (or controlled?) outpost, it is the only one so far indicated for Central Chiapas.

LATE CLASSIC PERIOD (Chiapa X, ca. A.D. 550–950). Whatever may have taken place following Chiapa VIII and during the Chiapa IX period of regional specialization, before the end of Late Classic times the Central Depression was experiencing what appears to have been its maximum pre-Hispanic occupation. Sources for this population build-up, lacking local antecedents and occupying many locations never be-

the Early Classic A period, but publication by Peterson (in preparation) of the abundant materials collected from the caves and adjacent surface sites is expected to contribute much to knowledge of the general Classic period developments in Central Chiapas and their wider relationships (N.W.A.F. collections, Museo Regional, Tuxtla Gutierrez, Chiapas). Present data indicate a general abandonment of most occupied archaeological sites at the close of this Period VIII florescence.

Rare examples of early Tzakol Maya polychrome and other Early Classic diagnostics testify to the contemporary status of Chiapa VIII, but Lowland Maya influence seems to have been minimal. What superficially seem to be Chiapa VIII trade pieces appear at Monte Alban and Zaculeu. At the latter site polished black vessels in forms identical to Chiapa VIII are the earliest and most abundant of the Atzan phase pottery types (Woodbury and Trik, 1953, p. 118, figs. 234, 236). A site with

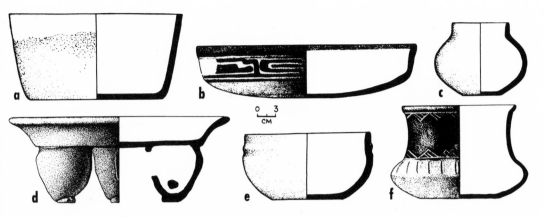

Fig. 22—CHIAPA VII POTTERY. Typical vessel forms from period at Chiapa de Corzo. *a,c,f*, Smudged black ware with oxidized portions. *b*, Red and black on buff polychrome. *d*, Cream ware. *e*, Coarse buff. (Courtesy, N. W. A. F.)

fore occupied, are still unknown. But strong ceramic relations with the Amatle phase of highland Guatemala and the San Juan phase of the Pacific coast suggest arrival of peoples from that direction. So does the use of three-pronged incense-burner stands, again popular in highland Guatemala during the Middle and Late Classic.

Sites of the Late Classic period are most abundant in the foothill and ridge regions of Central Chiapas where they usually incorporated extensive terracing of hillsides, abundant house foundations, low temple mounds, and open-end ball courts (cf. Lowe, 1959b; Navarrete, 1960). Advanced agricultural techniques are indicated for the slopes west of the Rio La Venta and for the uplands on the east of the Grijalva Valley (Guzman, 1958), where there is evidence of agricultural terracing by means of stone walls laid across the drainage pattern designed to catch and hold soil and moisture. On the La Venta Canyon rim these engineering works include check dams across arroyos and are accompanied by vast zones of stone house foundations and intermittent ceremonial precincts. Apparently population pressure rather than the need for defense was the motive behind the tendency to build many major Late Classic settlements on rocky and poorly watered sites.

The limestone ledge country above the precipitous Rio La Venta Canyon is also the location of some of the most impressive ceremonial centers in the Central Depression which apparently date to the Middle or Late Classic periods, such as Cerro del Campanario. El Ocote (Russell, 1954) is another such site, with massive platform walls of huge squared stone blocks. Pottery of various phases and organic materials in a shaman's bundle recovered from a rare dry cave in the La Venta Canyon below this general area have been described by King (1955).

Perhaps the most impressive site in the Central Depression, mainly because of its uniquely excellent architectural preservation, is Varajonal, a major ceremonial center recently discovered by Peterson in a heavily wooded section of limestone uplands on the left margin of the Rio La Venta Canyon. Only briefly visited, this as yet uninvestigated site has the only corbeled vault construction known in the Depression, apparently a tomb though now quite empty. The chamber, described as beehive-shaped, is entered by a narrow stone-lined passage roofed with slabs and is located beneath one of the many long platform mounds at the site (Peterson, personal communication). Such stone-lined chambers with corbeled vault and an en-

227

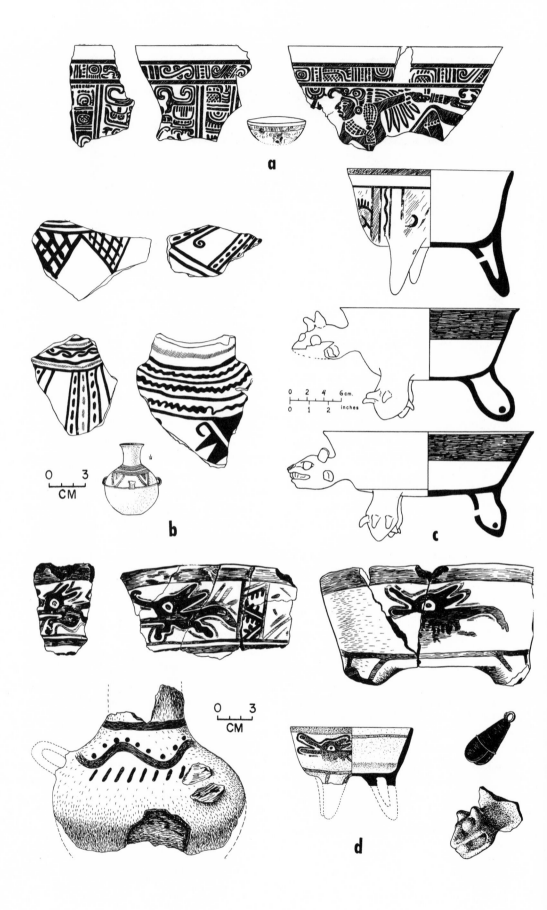

a

b

c

d

trance through a long masonry passage are most typical of Nebaj and Guaytan in highland Guatemala, where they are apparently Early Classic and "early Late Classic" in time (A. L. Smith, 1955, p. 75; see also A. L. Smith and Kidder, 1943, 1951). This is our chief reason for placing this site in the Late Classic, as the few sherds recovered were undiagnostic. The situation of the huge I-shape ball court at Varajonal, with many of its excellent masonry walls still intact, is also suggestive of the Late Classic court types of highland Guatemala. The extremely good state of preservation of these ruins suggests a later date, and it is possible that the site was occupied over considerable time, as the superimposed structures suggest. The numerous platforms are faced with block-and-slab masonry and support still-standing walls of superstructures which appear to be multiroomed.

The end of the Late Classic period seems best represented along the Grijalva trench where the occurrence of Tepeu 3–related ceramics, including carved Fine Orange ware (fig. 23,a), supports such a distinction. Large ceremonial centers in the Chapatengo-Chejel and Upper Tributary subregions of the Grijalva basin (Lowe, 1959b) appear to have been constructed during the Late Classic period though they continued in use into the Postclassic era.

The Late Classic seems to have ended in a general abandonment of most settlements in western Chiapas. On the basis of his Frailesca survey of about 60 sites, Navarrete (1960) concluded that there was a much reduced population of the southwestern sector of the Depression during the Early Postclassic which finally dwindled to nothing by the start of the Late Postclassic.

He reasoned that this depopulation resulted from the inability of the land to support longer a large population due to the great erosion of arable soils following the maximum land usage during the Late Classic. A similar abandonment of Late Classic sites has been noted in the central highlands of Chiapas by Adams (1960; see below). But the role of erosion as an original factor in this abandonment is denied by Guzman. He describes the widespread terracing of this period as capable of supporting intensive agriculture through the control of soil and moisture loss. He concluded, "Disruption of the system may have been due to one or more factors, but probably not to soil depletion" (1958).

EARLY POSTCLASSIC PERIOD (Chiapa XI-A, ca. A.D. 950–1200). Relatively little is known of the Early Postclassic occupation of the Central Depression. All survey reports refer repeatedly to "Late Classic or Postclassic" ceramic types in surface collections. The Sumidero site excavated by Berlin (1946a) contained Tohil Plumbate vases in two tombs and is therefore assignable to this period. The Sumidero platforms and main pyramid were faced with cut stone and their corners faced the cardinal points. Berlin (1946a, footnote) saw a stylistic similarity between the ceramics of Sumidero and Piedra Parada (Stirling, 1945).

The horizon-marking Tohil Plumbate has been found at other sites in the Depression including the Ruiz site excavated by Berlin in 1956 (Lowe, 1959b), which was characterized by earthen mounds with poor stucco surfaces, circular interior altars, a floor painting, and a long, narrow, multi-entrance structure with rubble pillars. This site probably dates toward the end of the

FIG. 23—LATE DECORATED WARES FROM THE CENTRAL DEPRESSION. *a*, Fine Orange, carved, Late Classic, from Finca El Salvador, Chiapas. *b*, Chinautla polychrome from Finca El Salvador. *c,d*, "Chiapanec" pottery and copper bell from town streets of Chiapa de Corzo. (After Lowe, 1959b, figs. 11, 12, 32.)

229

period. Tohil Plumbate has been found also at a few of the large ceremonial centers in the Chapatengo-Chejel section of the Grijalva River valley.

MIDDLE POSTCLASSIC PERIOD (Chiapa XI-B, ca. A.D. 1200–1350). Though not well known, the Middle Postclassic period is represented by several sites in the Central Depression. Navarrete (ms.) identified a number of V-Fine Orange sherds in the collections from trenches within the town of Chiapa de Corzo and this is a Middle Postclassic ware (R. E. Smith and Gifford, 1959, pp. 19, 144). These Tabasco imports apparently date the beginning of concentrated population in the late pre-Hispanic history of this townsite, which except for the Early Classic period has been occupied to one degree or another for 3000 years.

Berlin assigned the San Pedro Buenavista site to the post-Tula (or post-A.D. 1150) era on the basis of its architecture. The investigated structure at this site was a broad stone-faced platform with stairway approaches on three sides (1946a, p. 28). Sherds are very scarce at this and many of the other Postclassic sites.

LATE POSTCLASSIC AND PROTOHISTORIC PERIODS (Chiapa XII, ca. A.D. 1350–1524). The best-known segment of the Postclassic occupation in the Central Depression is that of the Chiapanec villages conquered by the Spanish. Chiapanec sites typically have shallow stratigraphy with no suggestion of time depth in excess of the A.D. 1350 date postulated here; the Protohistoric period corresponds to the most recent Mexican influences in the valley associated with late "Mixtec" and Aztec incursions but it is insufficiently known to justify separate treatment. The Chiapanec capital had the same site as the present Chiapa de Corzo, but subsequent colonial activities destroyed all above-ground traces of the occupation. Taking advantage of an extensive pipe-laying project through the streets of Chiapa de Corzo which occasioned the digging of deep trenches, Navarrete recently has been able to define the Chiapanec-colonial stratigraphy and on the basis of the resulting typology has determined the areal extent of the Chiapanec occupation (ms.). The diagnostic pottery, characterized by polychrome and cream-ware tripods (fig. 23,c,d), hollow-handle ladle-type incense burners, Mixtec polychromes and monochromes, and local domestic types, has been found only at sites along the Grijalva River from below Chiapa de Corzo to Santa Cruz, and in the zone south of Tuxtla Gutierrez around Suchiapa. The area encompasses the Chiapanec villages known at the time of the conquest, and there are no data to support the idea that the Chiapanec once populated any greater area of the Depression.

It is possible, of course, that the identified "Chiapanec" assemblage is a Mexican-Mixtec veneer acquired by the stylish Chiapanec in a late phase of their history which saw them confined to the smaller area, and that a different archaeological context characterized their arrival and earlier occupation in Chiapas. On the basis of traditions and linguistic studies the Chiapanec are thought to have arrived here in the latter half of the first millennium of our era, a time level which would equate approximately with the Late Classic peopling of the Central Depression.

It must be noted that a ceramic complex strikingly similar to that of the Chiapanec, including the unique "bird feet" (fig. 23,c), is found at Naco in Honduras (Strong, Kidder, and Paul, 1938, pls. 3, 4). Naco is thought to have been occupied by a Nahuatl-speaking tribe (op. cit., p. 21). As with most Chiapanec sites, Naco proved to be a shallow "one culture" site (op. cit., p. 33). Stone (1957) has reported similar pottery at sites in southeastern Honduras.

The contact-period pottery or archaeological situation for the Zoque region extending west across the Central Depression from Tuxtla Gutierrez has not been described, though the occupation area is well

F IG. 24—LATE CLASSIC CARVED DESIGN. Vessel from tomb at Ixtapa, Chiapas. (After Orellana, 1954a; drawing by Ramiro Jiménez.)

known. The contact situation in the south-eastern end of the Depression is equally unknown, though the presence of Chinautla polychrome (fig. 23,*b*) at several sites indicates expected relations with nearby highland Guatemala settlements. Some of the late ceremonial centers on the Upper Grijalva River plain have pottery similar to that of Copanaguastla, a principal pre-Hispanic center which became a colonial town of importance (Adams, 1960; see below). Failure of the Spanish accounts to make note of the Grijalva centers, however, suggests that they had passed their apogee prior to the conquest.

CHIAPAS PLATEAU

Environment

The Chiapas Plateau, also known as the *Mesa Central* or *Altiplanicie de Chiapas*, is a massive Cretaceous upland separating the Grijalva and Usumacinta drainage systems (Schuchert, 1935). Paralleling the Central Depression, the Chiapas Plateau varies greatly in altitude and area, forming a roughly triangular region with its apex reaching almost to Ocosingo on the north, according to Müllerried (see fig. 2). The

region in its northeast sector approximates 1000 m. above sea level, its southeastern sector 1000–1500 m., and its central sector up to 2000 m. The highest peaks, north of San Cristobal Las Casas, are Cerro Zontehuitz (2858 m.) and El Huitepec (2660 m.).

The surface drainage of the plateau is poorly developed as a result of numerous fault-line scarps which have divided the area into ridges and basins draining internally through sinks. As a result contemporary human settlement is dependent on the rather infrequent perennial water sources—water holes in the elevated basins and springs on the slopes below the plateau rim. The dispersed Tzeltal and Tzotzil settlements predominate in the pine-oak country at higher elevations, relying on sheep raising, wage labor, and maize from forest clearings and rented lowland milpas for subsistence. Ladino hamlets and towns, interspersed with coffee fincas on the higher slopes and cattle ranches and cane fields on the lower, characterize the marginal valleys of the plateau (Adams, 1960).

The Pan American Highway runs the length of the plateau, connecting the larg-

231

er commercial centers of San Cristobal, Teopisca, and Comitan with the Guatemala frontier.

Archaeology

The Chiapas Plateau divides readily into a number of archaeological provinces or subregions, though as yet they are poorly defined for lack of any over-all investigation of the region. On the basis of research to date, three subdivisions are suggested: (1) the western plateau margins, (2) the central highlands, and (3) the Comitan plain.

Western Plateau Margins

No archaeological survey has been made of this district, which centers on a transect through the pine-clad valleys and peaks running from Ixtapa by Soyalo and Bochil to Pueblo Nuevo Solistahuacan, route of an old trade road and of the new graveled highway to Simojovel, Pichucalco, and Tabasco. Numerous mound sites and carved stone monuments are known in the district, however, and at least at Ixtapa two such sites have been reported upon briefly by Orellana (1954a,b). Both are hill sites, with earth-filled mounds faced with either boulders, slabs, or shaped stone blocks. Clandestine digging in one of the principal mounds disclosed a slab-roofed tomb with several outstanding Maya vessels, all flat-bottom cylinders, including one with a carved scene (fig. 24) showing a "gran señor or Halach Uinic" receiving an offering (Orellana, 1954a, p. 114). A small salt industry carried on near salt springs in the canyon below Ixtapa explains the pre-Hispanic importance of the locality.

The great mountain and hill area extending northwest from the Ixtapa-Simojovel line to the Grijalva River on both the south and west is almost archaeologically unknown. Brief survey trips of the New World Archaeological Foundation in 1953, however, located a number of mound sites in the region west and east of the Grijalva in

the Las Palmas zone. Showing Late Classic Maya affiliations, these sites typically have enclosed ball courts faced with slabs. Culebro (1939) indicates ruins and monuments at Tecpetan and Copainala, both important colonial towns in isolated localities still largely occupied by Zoque Indians (Cordry and Cordry, 1941).

Central Highlands

Ruins and monuments in the central highlands of Chiapas have been noted by a number of authors, including Blom and LaFarge (1926–27), Brinton (1897), Culebro (1939), Sapper (1897), Schumann (1936), and others. The mountaintop Late Classic site of Moxviquil, above San Cristobal Las Casas, was partially investigated by Blom and Weiant in recent years. R. M. Adams and T. P. Culbert carried out a surface survey and program of stratigraphic test pitting at sites located in a 20-km.-wide transect extending through the highlands from the latitude of San Cristobal Las Casas south to the Rio San Vicente Valley in the Central Depression (McQuown, 1959). Although details of the stratigraphic sequence remain subject to modification through continuing research, Adams has formulated a sequence of changing territorial organization patterns for the central highlands based on investigation of over 40 sites (1960). His sequence can be summarized briefly here:

SAK PHASE (Late Preclassic). The highlands survey located only two sites surely dating to this period, near Teopisca and Villa Las Rosas. Both are modest valley-bottom or terrace-margin settlements consisting of a scattering of house platforms or occasional ceremonial platforms around a central pyramid. The paucity of Sak remains in the transect studied stresses the unpopularity of the highland region compared to the contemporary heavily occupied Grijalva basin, from whence these few early influences seem to have arrived. (Adams, 1960, pp. 6–7.)

232

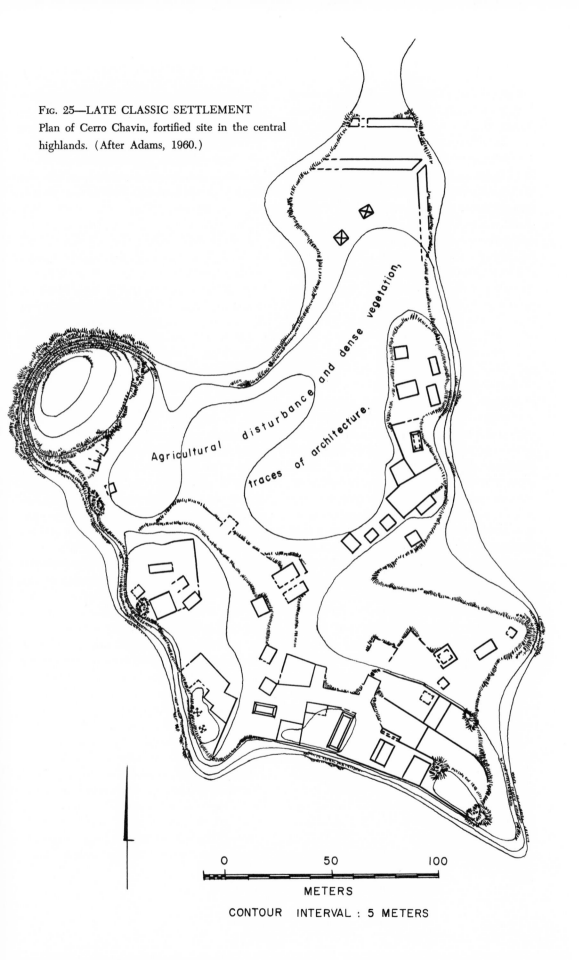

Fig. 25—LATE CLASSIC SETTLEMENT
Plan of Cerro Chavin, fortified site in the central highlands. (After Adams, 1960.)

Agricultural disturbance and dense vegetation, traces of architecture.

0   50   100

METERS

CONTOUR INTERVAL : 5 METERS

KAN PHASE (Early Classic). Beginning during the latter part of the Early Classic period, there was an influx of population into the Chiapas Plateau apparently from the east and southeast. This movement may have been associated with the separation of the Tzeltal-Tzotzil linguistic groups thought to have taken place 1000 to 1500 years ago on the basis of glottochronological data assembled by McQuown (1959). But beyond the occurrence of sparse Kan phase ceramics at many headland sites, the character of this earliest widespread occupation is poorly understood. In general, sites of this phase are in defensible positions, though it is not known if defense was the determining factor. (Adams, 1960, pp. 7–10.)

TSAH PHASE (Late Classic). On the basis of present evidence the most widespread occupation of the highland region was achieved during this period. Settlements were regularly placed in highly defensive locations on steep ridgelines, bluffs, hilltops, or even sharp pinnacles. Echelons of terraces, sometimes with retaining walls 3 or 4 m. high, composed the living areas of most sites. A definitely fortified site of this phase is Cerro Chavin, built on a promontory with a single access isthmus blocked by stone walls with offset entrance (fig. 25). There seems to have been a preference for placing a number of sites on hills clustering around the moderate-sized basins whose bottom lands were suitable for intensive agriculture, particularly those of Teopisca-Amatenango and Aguacatenango. However, Yerba Buena, one of the largest of the Late Classic highland sites and one approaching urban proportions, seems to have been the only site related to the Cruz Quemada valley below it. Adams suggests that independent communities, each with its need to maintain its own defense, were the dominant form and sociopolitical organization for this time and place. (Adams, 1960, pp. 10–17.)

The tendency toward military considera-

tions in the placement of settlement sites, which Adams believes actually started in the Chiapas highlands before the end of the Early Classic (Adams, 1960, p. 9), coincides with the warlike nature of much of the Maya representational art of the nearby Usumacinta lowlands (Rands, 1952) to modify former ideas of the Classic Maya as a peaceful society.

YASH PHASE (Early and Middle Postclassic). The rarity of the widely traded horizon-marking Fine Orange and Plumbate pottery in the central highlands, a factor adding to the difficulty of defining the Early Postclassic occupations there, suggests that this region was one of minor importance which imported few luxury items at this time. Most of the independent, defensively organized sites that were grouped around the scattered valley bottoms of the highlands during the Late Classic period were unoccupied during the ensuing centuries. Apparently most of these sites were abandoned either at or soon after the close of the period, though a few of the larger, more strategically located, settlements seem to have persisted somewhat longer. Two important new centers achieved prominence during the Yash phase. One of them is Na Balam, possibly a territorial seat commanding much of the fertile valley of the Rio Tzaconeja. This site has clearly distinguishable ceremonial and secular components, the former including an enclosed ballcourt and a spacious series of ascending plazas surmounted by pyramids and platforms. (Adams, 1960, pp. 18–19, 58–59.)

LUM PHASE (Late Postclassic). The Late Postclassic period is marked by a shift of settlements toward the larger valleys which could maintain more intensive exploitation and toward the formation of organized groups of communities centering on "capitals." There is little evidence of Mexican influence in ceramics or architecture in contradistinction to much of the neighboring highland region in Guatemala. Aztec incursions were few and short lived, the area apparently having lacked sufficient trade goods to justify expensive conquest. Major populated localities at the time of the Spanish conquest were Zinacantan, west of San Cristobal Las Casas; Chamula (Cerro de Ecatepec), south of that town; Gueyguistlan (Santiago), to the north of Larrainzar; and Copanaguastla on the Rio San Vicente. The impressive ceremonial nuclei comprised in the Copanaguastla zone are distinctive for having no defensive arrangements. A small-scale program of test soundings at these centers has shown a continuity between the pre-Hispanic and colonial occupations. The Dominican settlement, a gridiron town laid out around the imposing church convent, was abandoned about 1620. (Adams, 1960, pp. 19–22, 47–49.)

Comitan Plain

Antiquities in the Comitan plain have been described by several authors including Blom (1929), Blom and LaFarge (1926–27), Culebro (1939), Orellana (1954a,b), Seler (1901), Stephens (1841), and others. Most of these descriptions are of the relatively well known Late Classic Maya ruins such as Hun-Chabin on the edge of Comitan, Tenam Puente a few kilometers to the east, and Chinkultic on the Guatemala frontier (fig. 2). The sculptured monuments at these sites have been discussed further by Morley (1937–38, vol. 4) and Proskouriakoff (1950). Thompson (in Ruppert et al, 1955, p. 6) notes that the site of Santa Elena Poco Uinic (Palacios, 1928a), off the northern margin of the Comitan plain, is artistically and architecturally most similar to the Chinkultic and Tenam sites, all of which demonstrate exceptionally well cut masonry superior to that of Maya sites such as Bonampak in the region west of the Usumacinta River. He suggests the possibility that this Late Classic upland development may be historically related to the Tojolabales populating the district at the time of the conquest, separated from the Tzeltal and Chol groups who occupied the districts to the west and east, respectively.

Knowledge of the Comitan Valley archaeology has been broadened recently by Piña Chan (1960c) and Shook (1956b, p. 21), who report a number of small Late Preclassic mound sites on the plains between Comitan and Chinkultic. Several of the large hilltop ceremonial centers were also shown to have had occupations extending into the Postclassic period, and a few suggest beginnings in the Preclassic period (Piña Chan, 1960c, Cuadro 2).

The situation of the Comitan plain indicates the value of further research there. Forming a relatively flat and open "saddle" between the higher mountains of central Chiapas and the Cuchumatan Mountains of Guatemala, the plain would seem to have offered a natural communication route between the northern and southern sections of eastern Chiapas. This was, in fact, the route followed by the farthest southwestern extension of the Classic Maya stela cult. The only present-day road into the Selva Lacandona (eastern highlands of Chiapas) extends from Comitan to Ocosingo, skirting the western edge of the Comitan plain and passing through very rough country.

REFERENCES

Adams, R. M., 1960
Agrinier, 1960
Bancroft, 1882
Berlin, 1946a
Blom, 1929
—— and LaFarge, 1926–27
Borhegyi, 1950b, 1951a, 1951b, 1959a
Brinton, 1897
Burkitt, 1924
Coe, M. D., 1957a, 1957b, 1959a, 1959b, 1960a
Cordry and Cordry, 1941
Culebro, 1937, 1939
Dixon, 1958, 1959a, 1959b
Drucker, 1948, 1952a, n.d.
——, Heizer, and Squier, 1959
Dutton, 1958
Evans and Meggers, 1960
Ferdon, 1953
Gamio, 1946
Guzman, L. E., 1958
Hewett, 1936
Hicks and Rozaire, 1960
Kidder, 1940
—— and Shook, 1946
King, 1955
Longyear, 1944
Lorenzo, 1955
Lothrop, 1927b
Lowe, 1956, 1959a, 1959b
MacNeish and Peterson, 1962
McQuown, 1959
Marquina, 1939
Mason, J. A., 1960a, 1960b
Morley, 1937–38
Müllerried, 1957

Navarrete, 1959a, 1959b, 1960, n.d.
Orellana, 1954a, 1954b
Palacios, 1928a
Peterson, 1963
Piña Chan, 1960c
Pineda, 1845
Ponce de León, 1882
Proskouriakoff, 1950
Rands, R. L., 1952
Ruppert, Thompson, and Proskouriakoff, 1955
Russell, 1954
Sanders, 1961
Sapper, 1897
Satterthwaite, 1943a
Schuchert, 1935
Schumann, 1936
Seler, 1901
Seler-Sachs, 1900
Shepard, 1948
Shook, 1956b
Smith, A. L., 1955
—— and Kidder, 1943, 1951
Smith, R. E., 1958
—— and Gifford, 1959
Sorenson, 1956
Stephens, 1841
Stirling, 1943, 1945, 1947
Stone, 1957
Strong, Kidder, and Paul, 1938
Thompson, J. E. S., 1948, 1956
Vivó, 1942, 1946b
Waibel, 1946
Warren, 1959
Willey, 1960
Woodbury and Trik, 1953

10. Sculpture of the Guatemala-Chiapas Highlands and Pacific Slopes, and Associated Hieroglyphs

S. W. MILES

A GREAT NUMBER of new sculptures have been found over the past few years in the Guatemala-Chiapas highlands and Pacific slopes. A large proportion of the new material is from early periods, which in this analysis forces discussion and illustration to more detailed examination of early new material than of the later better-known pieces.[1]

The bulk of monuments are known from a few great sites and concentrated zones— Kaminaljuyu, Izapa, the Cotzumalhuapa zone, and the midhighland Quiche zone. Only a tiny fraction of the known sculptures was excavated under conditions which permit clear definition of associated ceramic phases. Without an entirely secure basic chronology any classification must be tentative, but, fortunately, a skeletal frame of sculptures from controlled excavation can serve as general stylistic reference for many of the "floating" monuments, particularly in the early periods when local styles were less narrowly crystallized.

There is little evidence that sculpture of the highlands and Pacific slopes was not primarily religious in function. Nearly every piece was found in a ceremonial center closely associated with religious structures; most exhibit a wealth of conventional references—realistic, fantastic, and abstract —to mythical beings, gods, animals, and places. A few stelae on the slopes may be candidates for historical notation of important events and the late Cotzumalhuapa busts appear to be individual portraits.

Although probably religious, little respect was shown monuments, particularly at Kaminaljuyu. They were smashed and

[1] This paper, originally intended as a long monograph, is here greatly condensed, and debts for aid and data are extensive. The Bollingen Foundation provided fellowship funds for two long field trips. E. M. Shook loaned me drawings and field data from his personal files. Heath-Jones gave me freely of her unpublished research on early hieroglyphic and archaeological data. Srs. Gustavo Espinosa and Carlos Samayoa y Chinchilla provided information, field notes, and the important opportunity and space to work on them and on my own material. Mr. and Mrs. Welland Gay served as field assistants in 1959, and are responsible for the extent and success of that research and photographing season. The U.S. Information Service in Guatemala placed at my disposal facilities for a coastal survey. Miss Avis Tulloch has prepared all final drawings.

237

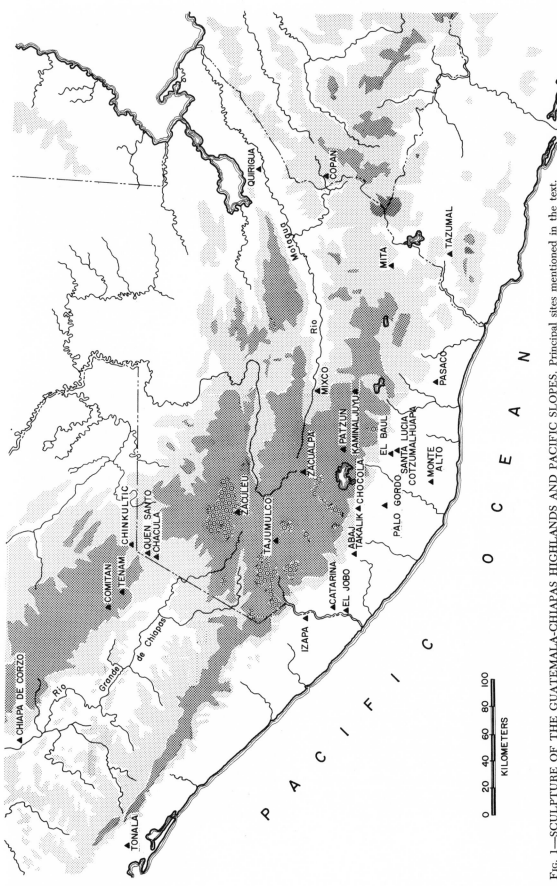

Fig. 1—SCULPTURE OF THE GUATEMALA-CHIAPAS HIGHLANDS AND PACIFIC SLOPES. Principal sites mentioned in the text.

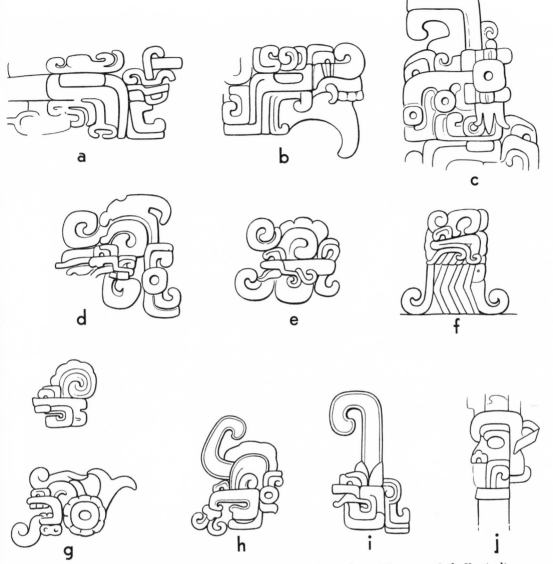

FIG. 2—DRAGON MASKS OF DIVISIONS 1 AND 2. *a,* Kaminaljuyu, Monument 2. *b,* Kaminaljuyu, Stela 5. *c,* Kaminaljuyu, Stela 5. *d,* Kaminaljuyu, Stela 4. *e,* Izapa, Stela 1. *f,* Izapa, Stela 1. *g,* Izapa, Stela 1. *h,* Izapa, Stela 3. *i,* Izapa, Stela 3. *j,* Izapa, Stela 11.

scattered, re-used as foundation or paving or thrown into dumps. Only rarely were stelae or fragments carefully buried.

The major category of architectural sculpture cannot yet be treated. There is fragmentary evidence that adobe relief on the faces of pyramids was well developed but to date the fragments known are too small and ruined to be more than suggestive. It is possible that some stone monuments were actually used as wall panels in temples and ball courts and are truly architectural, but since none have been found *in situ,* they are here classed as freestanding stelae.

A few small sculptures are included, either because they are fundamentally monumental in conception and constitute an aspect of major art, or because they are particularly relevant to large sculptures.

Style is variously defined by art historians but, practically, each style has its

239

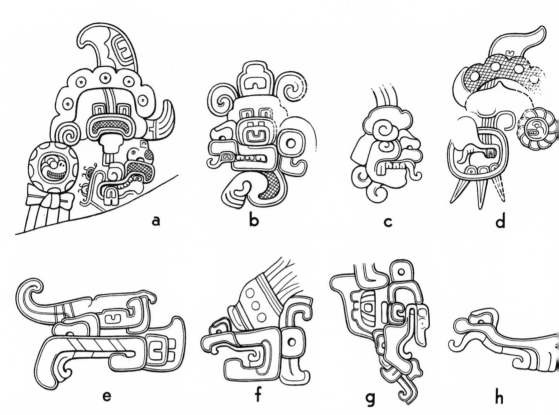

FIG. 3—MASKS OF DIVISION 3. a, Kaminaljuyu, Stela 10. b, Kaminaljuyu, Stela 10. c, Kaminaljuyu, Stela 10. d, Chocola, Stela 1. e, Kaminaljuyu, Stela 11. f, Kaminaljuyu, Stela 11. g, Kaminaljuyu, Stela 11. h, Kaminaljuyu, Stela 11.

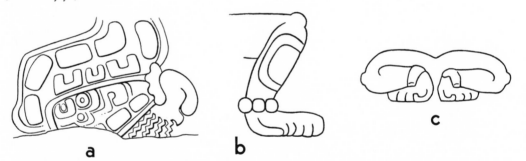

FIG. 4—KNOBBED LEGS. a, Kaminaljuyu, Monument 2. b, Kaminaljuyu, Stela 4. c, Izapa, Stela 11.

own peculiar content and criteria which can be referred to the broad categories of motifs, form relations, and qualities (Schapiro, 1953, p. 289).

A feature of all styles of the highlands and Pacific slopes, excepting some of the earliest, is wealth of symbols in complex relations. Many sculptures appear to have been intended for "reading," for they are far from presenting a simple concept or two

for rapid visual understanding. Izapa developed unusual narrative stela compositions which look like expressions of mythical episodes or occasionally whole myths. In an entirely different organization the same tradition appears in some of the Cotzumalhuapa compositions.

Unfortunately, the significance of many symbols is remote and can be grasped only in the grossest fashion, if at all. It is often

240

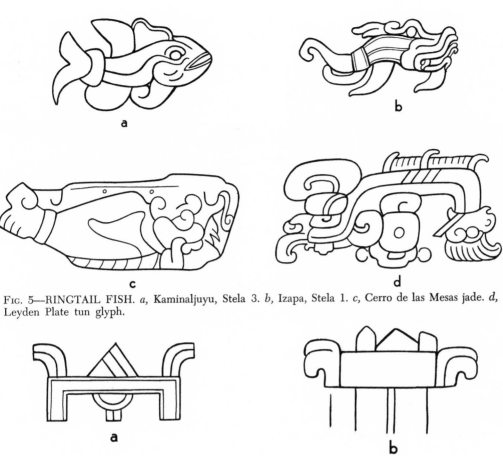

FIG. 5—RINGTAIL FISH. *a*, Kaminaljuyu, Stela 3. *b*, Izapa, Stela 1. *c*, Cerro de las Mesas jade. *d*, Leyden Plate tun glyph.

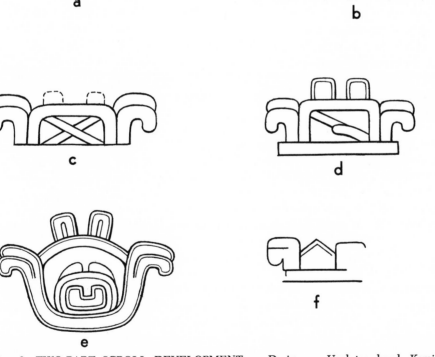

FIG. 6—TWO-PART SCROLL DEVELOPMENT. *a*, Design on Usulutan bowl, Kaminaljuyu, Providencia phase. *b*, Pectoral, Kaminaljuyu, Stela 4 (inverted). *c*, Right wing, Izapa, Stela 2. *d*, Left wing, Izapa, Stela 2. *e*, Earplug, Kaminaljuyu, Stela 10. *f*, Left wing, Izapa, Stela 4.

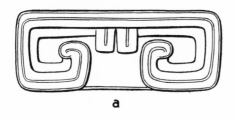

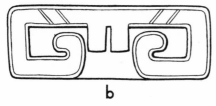

FIG. 7—PLATFORMS
a, Kaminaljuyu, Stela 11. *b*, Izapa, Stela 4.

not possible to go beyond general indications of importance in frequency of appearance, relative prominence in terms of size, placement, and elaboration in interpreting significance. When a symbol placed in a strikingly prominent position on an early sculpture becomes part of a sandal or wristlet in a later composition, its persistence is shown but its role has obviously changed. Shifting attitudes and values so expressed can be roughly outlined in early periods, and treated with more assurance for later times.

Many symbols have great longevity over wide areas; so that few are significant criteria of period or style as such. But the great differences in details of execution and the emphasis and role given them are sensitive indicators of time and style affiliations.

A favorite symbolic motif, both as single subject and as a detail in more complex compositions, is the dragon head (figs. 2, 3, 8). In the earliest forms it cannot be surely identified with any particular animal; the eye, eyebrow, and teeth are orienting features. Subsequently, it has feline, bird, fish, anthropomorphic, and distinctly reptilian features. In a few sculptures as many as three variants appear in the same composi-

tion and, often, the attributes of more than one animal are synthesized in a dragon head or mask. Ultimately, in Early Classic a serpentine form became predominant in the slopes and highlands. Covarrubias (1957, figs. 22, 36) compiled several charts showing the history of the dragon in the areas of his concern; with a full range of examples in Middle America several areal diagrams could be drawn clarifying the history of emphases placed on the related forms.

The well-known divisions of Preclassic, Classic, Late and Postclassic periods are used as major time compartments. In the first, which represents a very long time, there are four subdivisions that correspond roughly to major ceramic phases. The fourth subdivision extends into the Early Classic boundary.

Calendrical and hieroglyphic material is treated in a separate section.

PRECLASSIC SCULPTURES

Division 1: Kaminaljuyu, Izapa, Monte Alto, Pasaco, Abaj Takalik, Sin Cabezas, midhighlands

On very slim chronological indications, the large boulder sculptures of human figures and heads are placed in the first chronological division of Preclassic.

Lothrop, who first described a few examples from Kaminaljuyu (1926a, pp. 163 ff., figs. 53–55), felt they were "archaic" and noted their resemblance to similar pieces at Copan. Richardson (1940, p. 397) suggested that they showed a vague resemblance to the colossal heads of La Venta and Tres Zapotes. Drucker considered the remote possibility that they might be related to "a very early developmental [Olmec] horizon" (1952a, p. 222), but it was Covarrubias who pointed out a real basis for their antiquity, although he does not mention these sculptures specifically. Covarrubias (1957, pl. 18) pictures two small stone figures and points out their resem-

242

FIG. 8—MASKS OF DIVISION 4. *a*, Izapa, Stela 2. *b*, El Jobo, Stela 1. *c*, Late Preclassic bowl, Chiapas (after Navarrete, 1960, fig. 32,*g*). *d*, El Baul, Stela 1. *e*, Kaminaljuyu, Silhouette 2. *f*, Kaminaljuyu, Silhouette 2 (from newspaper photo). *g*, Abaj Takalik, Stela 3.

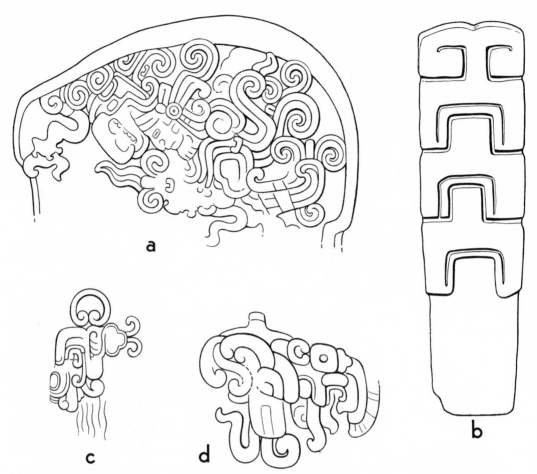

Fig. 9—MISCELLANEOUS MOTIFS. *a,* Top of Stela 3, Abaj Takalik. *b,* Kaminaljuyu, Stela 11. *c,* Head of jaguar, Izapa, Stela 12. *d,* Sky head, Tikal, Stela 4.

blance to early figurines. He suggests that their features are what one would expect for early or pre-Olmec. In addition to a resemblance to Las Charcas figurines, there is slight support for an early assignment in a small surface sherd collection made at Monte Alto, which showed extremely early types and nothing later than Middle Pre-classic.[2]

The Monte Alto figures and heads are carved in crude but decisive fashion on boulders that could not have been much

larger than the finished figures. There are three fat heavy-shouldered individuals each clasping his chest or belly, with small legs wrapped around the lower part of a sexless body. The soles of the feet face each other. The faces have heavy flat noses, fat squarish cheeks, thick lips, and long ears with small earplugs indicated. Two examples show eyes with the characteristic heavy upper lid and fatty lower lid (fig. 10,c) indicated by a groove above the cheek, so well known from "Olmec" sculptures and jades.

The third full figure and the three enormous heads are most unusual in being asleep or dead with closed eyes.

[2] Collection made by S. W. Miles, analyzed by E. M. Shook, December, 1960.

FIG. 10—*a*, Kaminaljuyu, Monument 6. *b*, Abaj Takalik, Monument 6. *c*, Monte Alto, Monument 2. *d*, Kaminaljuyu, Monument 2. *e*, Patzun.

245

At Abaj Takalik,[3] Monuments 2 and 3 (Thompson, 1943c, p. 111,*b,c*) are clearly similar sculptures. The faces are badly battered but still exhibit the same heavy cheeks and long ears; legs and feet wrap around the base on Monument 2; the lower part of Monument 3 is missing. Monument 3 also has a rounded collar about his neck and indication of heavy shelflike shoulders, closely resembling Monte Alto Monument 2 and Covarrubias' (1957) plate 18, bottom, in this respect.

There are many scattered reports of figures in this style. A huge figure exists at Palo Gordo, and several have been found in the Obrero area on the Pacific slopes and moved (information from E. M. Shook) to the fincas of Las Virginias and La Maquina (Richardson, 1940, pl. 18,*e,é*). In the vicinity of Lake Atitlan are several isolated figures. There is apparently one at Izapa (Carnegie photographic file) and one at Iximche in the midhighlands.

At Kaminaljuyu in the Guatemalan highlands portions of about a dozen large boulder figures are known (Monuments 3–9, 11, 12, 15; two fragments, fig. 10,*a*). All have suffered heavy damage. If anything, the highland figures are more generalized and crude than the slope sculptures. Although large, the highland pieces are generally smaller in size and have two distinctive characteristics: several wear round stiff fringe collars, and five carry concave discs on their chests or bellies (Lothrop, 1926a, fig. 53). The disc from one was found in Preclassic fill (Kidder, Jennings, and Shook, 1946, p. 242). A very crude similar piece was found at La Nueva, Jutiapa (Termer, 1948, pl. 24, no. 3).

One of the Kaminaljuyu figures (Monument 5)[4] has the battered features of a whiskered and snarling jaguar, and a sec-

[3] This site was originally known by the names of the two fincas into which it stretches, Santa Margarita and San Isidro Piedra Parada. A new numbering of monuments at Abaj Takalik (Standing Stones) is shown below with corresponding illustrations in Thompson, 1943c.

San Isidro Piedra Parada	Santa Margarita	Abaj Takalik
p. 110,*a*	. . . . . .	Stela 1 with Altar 1
. . . . . .	p. 110,*b*	Stela 2
p. 111,*a*	. . . . . .	Monument 1
. . . . . .	. . . . . .	Altar 2
p. 111,*f*	. . . . . .	Altar 3
p. 111,*b*	. . . . . .	Monument 2
. . . . . .	p. 111,*c*	Monument 3
p. 111,*d,e*	. . . . . .	Monument 4
p. 111,*f*	. . . . . .	Monument 5
		Monument 6
		Stela 3

[4] Previously published designations of Kaminaljuyu sculptures and their new numbers follow, together with designations of recently found sculpture:

Lothrop 1926a	Villacorta and Villacorta 1927	This Article
A	F	Stela 1
B	—	Stela 2
C	G	Monument 1
D	A	Monument 2
E	E	Altar 1
F	B	Monument 3
G	D	Monument 4
H	C	Monument 5
I	L	Monument 6
J	M	Monument 7
K	R	Monument 8
L	Q	Monument 9
M	J	Monument 10
N	I	Stela 3
O	N(?)	Monument 11
P	P(?)	Monument 12
Q	—	Monument 13
R	O	Silhouette 1
—	H	Monument 14
		Monument 15
		Monument 16
		Monument 17
		Monument 18
		Stela 4
		Stela 5
		Stela 6
		Stela 7
		Stela 8
		Stela 9
		Stela 10
		Stela 11
		Stela 12
		Stela 13
		Stela 14
		Stela 15
		Altar 2
		Monument 19
		Silhouette 2
		Altar 3

ond (Monument 15)[5] those of a bird. A related female figure was found near Santiago La Laguna.

There are six small-size portable stone counterparts of the human boulder figures in the Guatemala Museum. Four of the little rotund individuals were picked up at Kaminaljuyu. That these were widely distributed is shown by Covarrubias' illustrations and Stirling's find in the shell mound at La Ceiba, Tabasco (1957, pl. 62,c). Several of the small figures have clearly drilled mouth corners and nostrils.

A third group of human figures on large boulders was found by E. M. Shook at the coastal site of Sin Cabezas (1950b, pp. 62–63). Four handsomely carved, but now headless, figures are seated on pedestals, the unmodified lower parts of the boulders. The crossed legs and generalized treatment of feet and hands resemble the fat-faced figure at La Maquina (Richardson, 1940, pl. 18,e,é) and a small rotund headless figure from Kaminaljuyu.

The Sin Cabezas sculptures were associated with Late Classic ceramics, but the fact that no trace or fragment of the heads could be located at the site indicates that they may well have been discovered and reset by Late Classic occupants.

It is also quite possible that these highly developed figures are actually later in time, a local development of the boulder-figure tradition. Shook suggested that the sculptural handling is strongly related to that of the southern Veracruz wrestler (Covarrubias, 1957, p. 19). Two additional small examples of this type were found at Abaj Takalik (J. E. S. Thompson, 1943c, p. 112a,b). Burly shouldered headless figures clasp distended bellies (cf. Shook, 1950b, Sculpture 2).

The subject matter of other boulder sculptures is animal, realistic and fantastic.

[5] Monument 11 probably also had a bird face; it shows the peculiar claws at the sides and a large chest disc.

The last head in the north-south row at Monte Alto is an enormous fantastic jaguar (Richardson, 1940, pl. 18,c). The characteristics of this head—the high back-curved elements over the eyes, the rectangular nose, and fangs—relate it to the boulder heads of similar and smaller size from coastal Ahuachapan, Salvador (Jiménez, 1957, facing p. 16; Richardson, 1940, fig. 33, 34,a). The huge fat figure at Palo Gordo wears an extreme version with an overly large nose of this type of mask. A recently discovered head at Finca Cayagunca, near Lake Cuatepeque, combines the jaguar features with those of a bird (Jiménez, 1957, p. 13). But there is sufficient difference in the organization of the elements of nose, curled eyebrow, and mouth fangs in the Salvador heads to suggest a collateral development that extends much later in time.

Up the coast and slopes toward the northwest, at Abaj Takalik a huge boulder head (Monument 6, fig. 10,b) was removed in 1958 from the middle of a modern road running through the site. The small sample of pottery from fill over and around the head is early to middle Preclassic. The reptilian (frog or snake) head itself is sketched on an unmodified boulder in broad grooves. The eyes have small feathers above them, and the top and back are carved with very realistic feathered wings.

The frog altar at Izapa (Stirling, 1943, pl. 50,a) is both more simple and more realistic, but the curved elements over the eyes may represent feathers. Also, without feathers but perhaps related, are the sculptured jaguar and reptilian boulders on the Guerrero Slopes (Moedano, 1948, figs. 4–6).

Monument 2 from Kaminaljuyu also belongs in the first division (fig. 10,d). Broken, it now is an enormous piece of volcanic stone, triangular in cross section, carved in low flat relief on two sides as a scaled body and fantastic head. Tail, feet, and snout are missing. The bent joints of the legs are knobbed in a mode usual in

247

Division 2. The fantastic dragon head with its four-part eyebrow and long fangs divided and curved defines the monument as a member of Division 1 (fig. 10,a). The same dragon head appears on Las Charcas pottery (information from T. Proskouriakoff) and, specifically, does not recur in identical detail.

At Padre Piedra in the Frailesca, Chiapas, a very large broken sculpture is probably early Division 2 or Division 1 (Navarrete, 1960, fig. 11). Navarrete's very sparse ceramic material from the site is restricted to Cotorra and Dili phases, comparable to Chiapa I and II. The simplicity, rigidity, and pose of the standing figure and the geometric character of the clothes recall the great monument at Viejon in Veracruz found buried in the extremely early Trapiche trash (Medellin, 1960c, pl. 9).

Division 2: Kaminaljuyu, San Juan Laguna and Chicayal (on Lake Atitlan) Izapa, Tonala, Abaj Takalik, Chalchuapa, Tajumulco, Cotzumalhuapa Zone

Several members of the second division are securely placed chronologically. In Mound C-III-6 at Kaminaljuyu E. M. Shook found a finely carved small stela, Stela 9 (fig. 11,a), and the bases of two pedestal (P 1 and P 2) sculptures (Shook, 1951b, p. 240). Together with three plain shafts of basalt they were placed around a large slab of stone set into a pit. A cache of early Providencia pottery, some fine jade, and evidence of fires were above the slab.

Pedestal sculptures are figures of jaguars, pisotes (A. Kidder and Samayoa, 1959, p. 49), monkeys, and men carved in the round on the top of a carefully shaped, usually square shaft. The area of attachment of the figure to the shaft may be plain or it may have a little four-legged or scroll-ended bench. A headless jaguar seated on a scroll-ended bench (P 3) came from deep in the fill of Mound E-III-3 (information from E. M. Shook), further confirming the early occurrence of the type.

Pedestal sculptures probably had a long history; only the three noted above were found in specific archaeological contexts. The extremely wide distribution in the highlands and Honduras, on Pacific slopes and coast from Salvador to Tonala, in the Isthmus, and at Tlapacoya near Tres Zapotes, nearly always associates this form with sites showing an early occupation and frequently with boulder sculptures. The largest number by far is to be found at Kaminaljuyu, where pieces of a dozen or so are known.

One type represented in six examples from the Pacific slopes may be restricted to that area: a jaguar with stylized features, high loaf-shaped headdress, and attenuated hindquarters sits on a square shaft up to 2 m. in height (fig. 11,d). Squared fangs, an exaggerated nose, and stylized ears formed by a long back-curving element relate these figures to the Monte Alto jaguar mask-head and to the early Salvador relief heads (Richardson, 1940, fig. 33; Jiménez, 1957, facing p. 16). One of these was found at Izapa; three more were taken from sites near Malacatan and small sites in the Department of San Marcos. The head of a monkey (Thompson, 1943c, p. 112,g,i) from Concepcion, near Abaj Takalik, wears a similar headdress and is probably from a pedestal sculpture.

Another pedestal type that has a limited range on the basis of present information occurs at Tonala (Ferdon, 1953, pl. 20,f), at Tlapacoya, Veracruz (Stirling, 1943, pl. 15,b), at Catemaco, Veracruz (Blom and LaFarge, 1926–27, fig. 19), and in the park at San Antonio, Department of San Marcos. These share an undifferentiated transition of shaft to figure and raise questions of connections with the shaft sculptures of Costa Rica and Nicaragua (see Richardson, 1940, figs. 38, 39) though the styles are remote and quite possibly much later. A human figure on a decorated pedestal from near Comitan also differs quite strongly (Seler-Sachs, 1900, p. 155) although a

248

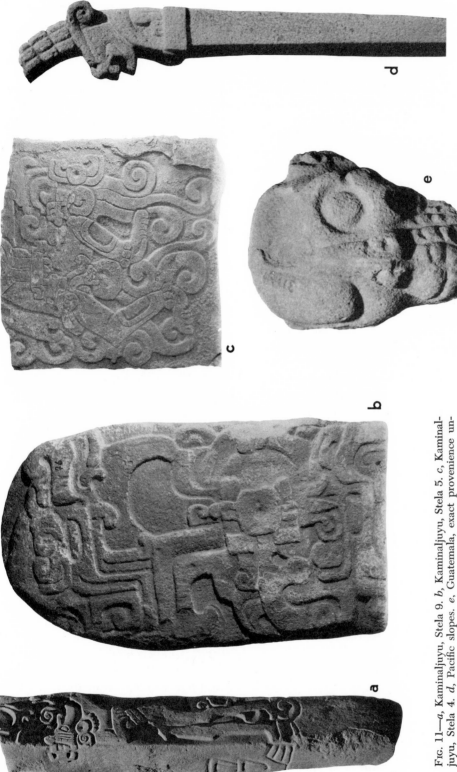

Fig. 11—a, Kaminaljuyu, Stela 9. b, Kaminaljuyu, Stela 5. c, Kaminaljuyu, Stela 4. d, Pacific slopes. e, Guatemala, exact provenience unknown.

pedestal pisote from the same area is very similar to the Kaminaljuyu pisotes (Seler, 1901, fig. 277).

Lothrop (1933, figs. 63,b,c; 64) reported sculptures on short pedestals from Lake Atitlan. And there are three from near Tajumulco as well as a monkey on a tall pedestal (Tejeda, 1947, p. 121).[6]

Dieseldorff (1926-33, Table 39) pictures a beautifully carved pedestal sculpture of a human figure kneeling on a scroll-ended bench. It is most unusual in showing the head half in flesh and half skeletal. A head apparently broken from a similar sculpture is in the Museum at Guatemala (fig. 11,e). The concept, though not the style, is the same as that in a clay mask from Tlatilco (Covarrubias, 1957, pl. 4, top).

Kidder and Samayoa (1959, p. 61, fig. 23) illustrate a very handsome small sculpture of a man seated on a bench. The ends of the bench are decorated with generalized scrolls like those of pedestal sculptures. The figure's hands and feet are small blocks, his big mouth is drooped, and his long ears lack decoration. The bench type associates him with the early Providencia pedestals, and the manner in which his bunched-muscle shoulders are carved relates him to the figure Covarrubias shows (1957, pl. 18, bottom) whose heavy shoulders, wrap around legs and head are so strongly like the boulder sculptures of Monte Alto.[7] Four bunched-muscle bench

figures are pictured by Villacorta and Villacorta (1927, p. 112; this article, fig. 10,e) from "El Molino de la Sierra," near Patzun, Chimaltenango. Another was found at Kaminaljuyu. Also related to this group is the greenstone figure of a bearded, droop-mouthed man wearing a pointed cap and carrying a baby jaguar over his shoulder (Kidder, 1954, fig. 9,b). The hands and feet, heavy shoulders and facial carving are the same as the bench figures.

Kelemen (1943, pl. 253,c) illustrates a kneeling, bearded figure from the Ulua Valley, Honduras, that also belongs with this type, though it is more sophisticated in handling and approaches a sub-Olmec category.

Stela 9 from Mound C-III-6, Kaminaljuyu, is carved with the figure of a praying man. One hand is raised and speech-scrolls rise from his mouth. The extremely long chin suggests a beard (fig. 11,a). The background is cut away, and features are indicated in the broad grooves, tilted planes, and rounding surfaces in the scrolls and earplug. The scrolls are executed in the same technique as the pedestal jaguar ears. The design wraps around three sides of the basalt shaft; on the right (not shown in fig. 11) is a grotesque animal head and a flexible hand. Although the slender physical type differs from previous pudgy human figures, the blocky hands and feet are similar.

Parts of two additional stelae at Kaminaljuyu are members of this division. Stela 4 (fig. 11,c), represented by its lower half, depicts a six-toed figure dancing amidst scrolls. The scroll form, loose with thickened terminals, is like that on Stela 9, though handled in a flat plane. The joints are knobbed; the figure has patches on his lower legs (fig. 4,b). Confirmation of a Division 2 position for this sculpture shows in the chest ornament (see fig. 6), which is a close variant of the symbol on a Providencia bowl (information from E. M. Shook). Figure 6 illustrates the develop-

[6] The long square shaft and scroll-bench-topped pedestals have a secure Division 2 context. The short, round pedestals exhibit traits otherwise occurring only in Late Classic (cf. the cross-armed figure from near Los Encuentros, Guatemala, Ricketson, 1936, fig. 4). The pedestal fragments from El Baul (J. E. S. Thompson, 1948, fig. 18,a,g) are indeterminate. Another criterion may be the proportion of the figure on top of the shaft to unbroken shaft length. The definitely early pedestals show a long shaft with a relatively small figure.

[7] Altar 6 at La Venta, in many ways the crudest at the site, shows a human figure with enormous heavy shoulders and block hands. The legs are crossed and the feet generalized. The conception and carving of the body are very similar to the bench figures (Stirling, 1943, pl. 38,a).

ment of this motif with its small two-part end scrolls.

At the dancer's left knee is the scroll-eye variant of the dragon (fig. 2,*d*). Characteristic are the human nose with a long alveolar bar and exposed teeth. The earplug with its appendages resembles that of the Monte Alto jaguar head. Attached to the front of nose, bar, and forehead is a mask-like extension which in several later examples becomes a great upturned or down-moving snout (see fig. 2).

Probably Stela 5, Kaminaljuyu (fig. 11,*b*), belongs in this division also; the scroll forms and dragon mask suggest it. A human head carved in low flat relief is surrounded by variations on the dragon mask—one with a four-part scroll eyebrow forms the headdress, another with the same type eyebrow and down-curved snout is under his chin, while the third with a small scroll eye is at the back of head, facing left (fig. 2,*b*,*c*).

Entirely on the basis of its simplicity and fluid lines, so like Stela 9, the beautiful ring-tail fish, Stela 3, found by Lothrop (1926a, fig. *a* and fig. 5,*d* in this article) is placed in this division. It is the only occurrence of the ring-tail fish at Kaminaljuyu, but this symbol had a long and very interesting history at Izapa (see below) and in Veracruz, where it became very important.[8]

[8] La Venta Stela 5 a fish (possibly a ring-tail) is the major part of the right bearded-man's head-dress (Drucker, Heizer, and Squier, 1959, fig. 67); one may also be attached to his belt (*ibid.*, fig. 69). Two ring-tail fish with noses joined form the head-dress of the principal figure on Stela 2 at La Venta (Drucker, 1952a, fig. 49). Continuing the tradition, Stela 3 at Cerro de las Mesas, the Stela of San Miguel Chapultepec, and probably Stela 6 at Cerro de las Mesas show single figures with a ring-tail fish above a local development of the dragon mask as headdress on the human figures (Stirling, 1943, figs. 10,*c*,*b*; 11,*b*). A ring-tail fish with mask is the tun sign on the Leyden plate; a jade fish in a Late Classic Cerro de las Mesas cache has a ring-tail on the reverse side (Drucker, 1955, fig. 4). Lothrop, 1926a, noted other occurrences, and it occurs in Codex Nuttall and on one of the bones from Monte Alban Tomb 7 (Covarrubias, 1957, pl. 56, top).

The only other currently known site that surely has stelae stylistically in Division 2 is Izapa. Several that are classed as Division 2 show traits common to later sculptures as well; the margin of error here is probably wide and examination with a larger series of chronologically fixed monuments may shift some Izapa sculptures into Division 3.

Izapa Stela 6 (Stirling, 1943, pl. 50,*b*), a roughly shaped stone, carries two Izapa signatures in early form—a U-shaped symbol at the top, and a straight line across the base, below which the butt is rough. A great potbellied jaguar, roaring, has monkey paws like Kaminaljuyu Stela 4, except that there are five toes, although all right feet. The earplug has Division 2 pendants. The jaguar's face was apparently purposefully battered so that the details of his up-curved muzzle are not clear. In place of a tail there is a little jaguar mask at the base of spine.

On Stela 3 (Stirling, 1943, pl. 50,*a*) a man with scroll-eyed dragon mask and scalloped hat (fig. 2,*h*) raises a hatchet-like weapon against a great dragon whose tongue and fang end in unthickened opposing scrolls. The earplugs of all heads and masks are the same type with double attached appendages. The dragon head at the lower left is a new type, the "blind" variant. No eye is indicated; the toothless lower jaw is (fig. 2,*i*). The presence of shallow incised outlining may be its earliest use or it may indicate that this stela, as well as those that follow, are placed one division too early.

The Izapa signature at the top of the stela is clearer; the U-symbol is squared and outlined with a band beneath and a broad diagonal to each side. Every carved Izapa stela, with two exceptions, having an undamaged top shows this signature or some elaboration of it. Stirling (1943, p. 62) regards this signature as a stylized jaguar. The two exceptions, Stelae 19 and 20 (*ibid.*, pl. 57,*a*,*b*) each with altar, appear to be

251

developments of the Izapa signature although neither shows an independent U. These two are probably members of Division 3, which shows considerable and similar elaboration of the signature.

Izapa Stelae 10, 11, 23, and 1 have little in common with each other beyond the signature. On Stela 10 (*ibid.*, pl. 56,*b*; fig. 12,*c* this article) a fat nude man, whose head form and fat cheeks are reminiscent of Kaminaljuyu Stela 5, is being taken to pieces by two small but equally naked men. There is probably a dragon mask in the upper scrolls, which are close to the early Division 2 type, but the eroded surface fogs definition. Probably Stela 8 (Stirling, 1943, pl. 58,*a*) belongs with Stela 10. Scrolls are similar and the signature the same. Unfortunately, available photographs and notes are inadequate to determine the other motifs.

Stela 11 (*ibid.*, pl. 53,*a*) presents two striking innovations. A two-headed serpent-dragon (Olmecoid masks on the backs of both heads, fig. 2,*j*) provides a frame for a knob-jointed beast whose open jaws are snapping at a flying bird-man. The feet of the beast are like those on Stela 6 and the knobbed joints (fig. 4,*c*) are the same as Kaminaljuyu Stela 4 and Monument 1. The convention was not used again.

The new Stela 23 (fig. 12,*d* from photograph by K. A. Dixon) and Stela 1 (Stirling, 1943, pl. 49,*a*) have an important feature in common: the scroll-eyed dragon is closely associated with water. On Stela 23 waves are depicted as pronged scrolls, similar to the speech-scrolls on Kaminaljuyu Stela 9; on Izapa Stela 1 the wavy lines have fish as if to remove all question of the scroll-eyed dragon's association. Actually, Izapa Stela 1 seems to represent a fishing god. The net he holds contains a ring-tailed fish (fig. 5,*b*); the scroll-eyed dragon with water is directly beneath. The figure wears a fishtailed scroll-eyed dragon in his headdress (fig. 2,*g*) and his feet rest on finned fish heads. Finned fish bracelets

are on his arms, fins are at his ankles. Even the basket on his shoulder shaped like a fish trap has a scroll-eyed head attached to its bottom (fig. 10,*g*).

The altar with Izapa Stela 1, Altar 1, is a magnificent boulder carving of an indeterminate animal whose limbs and feet are in the same style as the Izapa Stela 11 monster.

The motif of Izapa Stela 23, a diving or flying figure heading toward the water, is repeated later, as a secondary figure, on Izapa Stelae 2 and 4. The flyer wears a scroll headdress and a catlike face mask. The details of the signature and the double-headed sky serpent are not clear, but seem to flank the figure and rise above his feet, respectively (fig. 12,*d*).

Division 2 is characterized by highly dynamic vigorous depiction throughout; and, at Izapa, the strong impression is that each stela presents an episode in a myth. That the myths interlock is clear from the common symbols and variations on similar forms. At Kaminaljuyu single figures in active poses are accompanied by symbolic statements which are more static than the incipient narrative forms at Izapa.

Four Pacific slope boulder monuments and Izapa Monuments 2 and 3 (Stirling, 1943, pls. 53,*b*; 60,*d*) have been deliberately left unclassified. That they belong somewhere in Divisions 2 to 3 is probable, but their relationships to the sculptures discussed previously are difficult to assess. All are essentially Olmec in style.

It was implied in the description of Division 1 that the great heads and boulder figures of the highlands and slopes were pre-Olmec but related, possibly lineally, possibly collaterally, to that style. A jade pendant in the Kaminaljuyu Mound C-III-6 cache supports this idea, as do the bench figures of Division 2. The jade figurine that Shook (1951b, p. 240) defines as Olmec has drilled eyes, nostrils, long generalized ears, drooping mouth, a hat with a notch, block feet and hands. The shoulders and

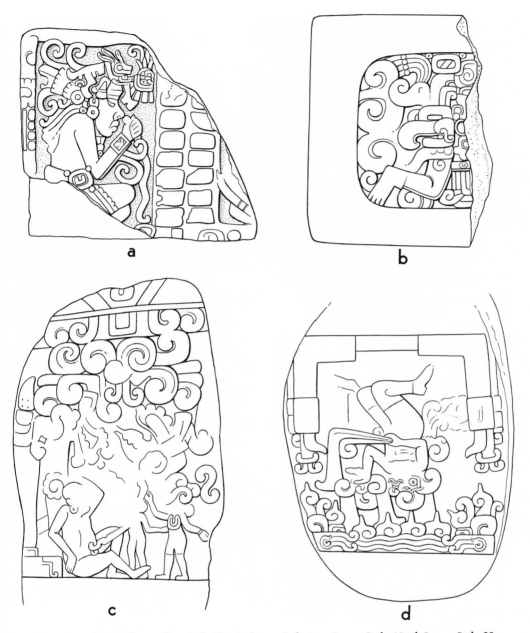

Fig. 12—*a*, Kaminaljuyu, Altar 1. *b*, Kaminaljuyu, Stela 1. *c*, Izapa, Stela 10. *d*, Izapa, Stela 23.

pectoral muscles are well developed. The C14 date of the pit fire is 1056 B.C. ±, making it older than the Offering 3 figurines at La Venta (Drucker, Heizer, and Squier 1959, pl. 26,*d-f*, p. 147; C14 date for Phase II, p. 264). This La Venta group includes an unusual Olmec figure with tabs on his belt like those of Guatemalan figures. Any or all of these figurines may, of course, have

been heirlooms for generations prior to burial.

Since there is no evidence for assigning chronological priority to the slope monuments they are, from southeast to northwest:

1. Chalchuapa: four Olmec men in pictographs on an unshaped boulder (Boggs, 1950, fig. 1).

253

Fig. 13—KAMINALJUYU, STELA 10

2. Abaj Takalik, Monument 1: running figure with wing at hips and wearing an Olmec "mask" (Thompson, 1943c, p. 111,a).

3. Izapa, Monument 2: anthropomorphic jaguar figure seated in mouth of a fantastic beast with both jaguar and reptilian characteristics (Stirling, 1943, pl. 53,a).

4. Tonala, Petroglyph 2: a jaguar face in

Olmec anthropomorphic style with round eyes, drilled nostrils and mouth corners (Ferdon, 1953, pl. 23,b). Possibly Petroglyphs 1 and 3 belong in the same group, although they are not explicitly Olmec in style.

The mask and accouterments of the Abaj Takalik figure closely resemble those of the men in the Chalcacingo, Morelos, sacrifice scene (Covarrubias, 1957, fig. 24), in which a rather fat nude man with his dragon mask shifted to the back of his head is about to be dispatched by paddle-bearing, clothed and masked individuals who have wings at their shoulders. The dragon masks combine bird and jaguar features.

The related Chalcacingo cliff relief (Covarrubias, 1957, pl. 13) has scrolls of the general type as Division 2 sculptures, and the seated personage wears sandals or shoes with differentiated heels like that on Izapa Stela 23.

The men on the Chalchuapa, Salvador, boulder have hands, feet, and faces congruent with the jade figure in the Kaminaljuyu Stela 9 cache, and one of them (a) wears a winged cloak similar to Chalacingo and Abaj Takalik.

Petroglyph 1 at Tonala with its obviously round eyes and drilled nostrils and mouth corners has an early look compared with the La Venta classic Olmec types, but it could also be a provincial or distant representation of the anthropomorphic jaguar. A small sculpture found recently in the Tonala vicinity is also Olmec. Martínez Espinosa (1959) pictures a small basalt slab carved in low relief with a helmeted figure, having a broad drooping mouth, broad nose, and ovoid slanting eyes. The hands and feet are block.

Finally, on Izapa Monument 2 the figure seated within open jaws is broken and badly eroded (Stirling, 1943, pl. 53,b), but the head shape, shoulders, and pose are unmistakably Olmec. The jaws vaguely resemble Tres Zapotes Stela D (Stirling, 1943, pl. 14). This monument and Izapa Monument 3 (Stirling, 1943, pl. 60,d) may be later than the boulder and petroglyph sculptures since the battered figure in Monument 2 approaches developed Olmec style, whereas the reliefs are good candidates for a developmental style. Also, the badly battered dragon masks on Izapa Stelae 23 and

11 are quite close to the Abaj Takalik face mask though not as fully developed.

Division 3: Kaminaljuyu, Chocola, Izapa

Division 3 represents the apogee of Preclassic sculpture. It has few members but one of the most brilliant styles developed in Middle America.

Two great sculptures recently excavated at Kaminaljuyu in secure Miraflores phase context provided the definition of the style. Stela 11 (fig. 15,a), in mint condition, shows a single standing human figure with a stiff hide cape attached to his shoulders[9] and a headdress composed of two variants of the dragon mask with a third under the chin (fig. 10,f,h). A fourth mask attached to the heavy belt (fig. 10,e) is a type that became widely popular (cf. Stela D, north side, Stirling, 1943, pl. 14,c; and El Meson Stela, Covarrubias, 1957, fig. 68). The figure stands on a platform whose design is identical to that of Izapa Stela 4 (fig. 7), and carries in his left hand a ceremonial hatchet like that on Kaminaljuyu Stela 10, and a unique "eccentric" flint found in Miraflores Tomb 1 in Mound E-III-3 (Shook and Kidder, 1952, fig. 79,c). A new concept is the sky head looking down from the top of the stela, in this case a downcurved muzzle variant of the familiar dragon (fig. 10,g).

The magnificent black basalt sculpture, Stela 10 (fig. 13)[10] was broken up and partially scaled before being buried with Stela 11. A great bearded and helmeted anthropomorphic jaguar dominates the composition from the right upper corner. The head

---

[9] The stiff shoulder cape is represented also on the figures of Stela D, Tres Zapotes (Stirling, 1943, pl. 14,a) and on minor figures 2, 4, 6, and 7, Stela 2, La Venta (Drucker, 1952a, fig. 49).

[10] Kaminaljuyu Stela 11 was discovered by E. M. Shook, who at Heath-Jones's instance re-entered the pit in which Stela 10 had been found and excavated by Gustavo Espinosa. Shook found Stela 11 a few feet from where Stela 10 had been buried at the same level and under the same 14 floors; Shook conclusively defined both as Miraflores (Heath-Jones, 1959).

wears a nose mask armed with teeth and fangs. The standing figure to the left may represent a god since his three-pronged eye and tufted beard are traits appearing usually with special masks. The third figure is that of a human being whose scaled-off lifted hands must have held an offering. Below the arms is a long hieroglyphic text.[11] An anthropomorphic version of the dragon mask is tied to his back (fig. 3,a). A duplicate of this mask with scalloped and peaked hat is worn on the belt of the figure in the Chocola monument, which in slightly different combination shows most of the features of the Kaminaljuyu sculpture including two pronged-eye heads with sparse beards (fig. 3,d). The Chocola sculpture shares the lapidary carving technique in delicacy of detail and precision that the Kaminaljuyu pieces exhibit.

At Kaminaljuyu there is a third great fragmentary stela, Stela 8, in Miraflores style, but the content is almost totally erased by careful thin scaling. Enough remains to show that a large figure stands on a platform with arm outstretched. A small man kneels to the left; both face right. The framing is like that of Stela 10.

Kaminaljuyu Stela 10 is particularly interesting for the number of small masks: one with a three-part hat on the temple of the left figure, another on the belt tab wearing a pointed cap, and a third (larger) with a pronged eye on his chest. Both small masks (fig. 3,b,c) show variation in the alveolar plate or upper lip that presages later depiction; in each, the forward-protruding lip or plate is swollen instead

of merely rounded and the front tooth is a long out-curving fang.[12]

Another feature of Stela 10 is the high number of U-symbols: the great bearded face has one in the eyebrow and another as an earplug (fig. 6,e); the small-head mask has the U as an eye, and it occurs in small details four other times. The same symbol becomes a glyph framed by an elaborate cartouche above the bearded god's head. Stela 11 has eight examples of the U-symbol, twice in cartouche and twice above the eyes in dragon masks; Chocola Stela 1 has seven. An additional point is that both Kaminaljuyu Stela 10 and Chocola Stela 1 have snake bodies supplied with bird heads and wings. In neither sculpture, due to extensive damage, is the relationship to the total composition at all clear, and, in both, this composite is in a subordinate position behind a major figure.

Two Izapa stelae are in the Miraflores style, Stelae 4 and 9. Altar 3 with its beautiful bird should probably be placed here also. The figure on Stela 4 wears a scallop-hatted anthropomorphic mask on his belt and the great feather cape or wing has outlined and tilted feathers. The flying god is winged and bears wing symbols reminiscent of the Division 2 ornaments (fig. 6,c,d).

Izapa Stela 9 is badly weathered but the handsome outline of a Miraflores figure is clear. He wears a great fluffy headdress, and the stiff leather shoulder shield is combined with a long feather cape most like Chicola. Both stelae have the Izapa signa-

---

[11] The finding that elaborate sculpture, great mounds, and sumptuous tombs were Miraflores in phase brought A. V. Kidder in 1948 (p. 228) to suggest that high development was extremely early in the highlands. The absence of evidence of calendar and writing precluded full definition by Kidder. But in 1957, on the basis of preliminary analysis of the hieroglyphic text of newly excavated Stela 10, Heath-Jones announced the necessity of redefinition of the relations between highlands and lowlands and defined a fully Maya culture in the highlands.

[12] The anteriorly swollen nose or alveolar plate is also present on the right serpent head on the Cerro de las Mesas carved turtle shell (Drucker, 1952b, fig. 1); the left head wears a nose mask. Both show the forward-curving front fangs and horn-shaped object rising from above the nose like the Kaminaljuyu Stela 10 shoulder mask and the Chocola belt mask. The three-part eyebrow on the turtle shell is like that on a Division 4 sculpture from Guatemala and strongly suggests that the turtle shell, as well as the Olmec figurines in the same cache, was an heirloom and possibly an import. The swollen noses on the serpent head and headdress mask of La Venta Monument 19 imply that this sculpture may also be closely related.

ture at the top. The figure on Izapa Stela 4 shows very thick, large thighs and relatively small feet which is an anatomical feature of several of the figures on La Venta Stela 3.

Two very small fragments of portable sculptures found at Kaminaljuyu have great implications for the areal communication so patent in Miraflores style. The first is a fragment of a slab showing a Miraflores anthropomorphic variant of the dragon with a peaker cap (fig. 16,b). The second, a slightly larger fragment of a thin slab, bears a mat sign and the Izapa signature of U and diagonals (fig. 16,e). These may have been models for larger sculptures. Or were they tiny portable stelae for migrant traders or artists of Kaminaljuyu and Izaja? In any event, they entirely confirm the connections and related sculptures noted above.

In-the-round Miraflores sculpture has as few certain members as relief. Several years ago Villacorta (information from A. V. Kidder) excavated in Kaminaljuyu Mound D-III-6 three enormous stone versions of three-pronged incensarios, Monuments 16, 17, 18 (fig. 16,a), which can now be classified. Specifically the eyes, eyebrows, and tuft beards are directly from, or associated with, Stela 10. Furthermore, these great monuments are closely related to the synthetic large muzzled masks of Uaxactun E-VIIsub (Ricketson and Ricketson, 1937, figs. on pp. 82, 83). The Kaminaljuyu monuments show the subnose-alveolar projection so prominent at Uaxactun (and perhaps incipient in the Salvador jaguar masks). In full front it is possible to see the synthesis of highland and Tabasco Olmec elements in E-VIIsub: the pronged eyebrows together with the late Preclassic scroll types and alveolar projection, which in profile and in later times is given a lowland Maya interpretation of serpent, earth monster, long-nosed Chac, et . The three great Kaminaljuyu heads are in Miraflores style, but the pyramid from which they

were excavated, D-III-6, is Arenal phase ceramically (information from A. V. Kidder and E. M. Shook).

Probably the very handsome frog altar (Altar 3) in the Guatemala Museum is Miraflores. It is merely a large version of the "toad" mortars from Mound E-III-3 (Shook and Kidder, 1952, fig. 78). Monument 8 at Tonala is in the same style (Ferdon, 1953, pl. 22,f).

Two small human bone carvings found in Tomb 1 at Chiapa de Corzo[13] (Dixon, 1958, p. 56) are also in Miraflores style, though their ceramic context is later. Both bones present variations on the dragon mask; two versions of the bare-alveolum type, and two with alveolar plates, one bearded, that wear a three-part hat and a pointed one, respectively. Attached small decorative tabs, scattered U-symbols, eyebrows, and scroll forms both single and double relate closely to Miraflores monumental sculptures.

Division 4: Kaminaljuyu, Abaj-Takalik, Izapa, El Jobo (Ayutla)

Division 4 is frankly very largely a series of hypotheses. In it are included sculptures that are, or appear to be, late Preclassic, Protoclassic, and some which undoubtedly will ultimately prove to be Early Classic. This is a mixed transition Division with many innovations and temporary peculiarities. With more controlled examples the grouping made here will certainly be revised.

There are three basic sorts of composition on stelae and altars: a narrative style, two figures facing each other with an incensario or hieroglyphic column between them, and the single standing figure. A third type of sculpture is silhouette.

The earliest signs of change toward confused composition appear at Izapa, as an aspect of their local narrative style. There

[13] For fine detailed drawings made from Keith A. Dixon's casts of the bones by Ramiro Jiménez Pozo, see Agrinier, 1960.

Fig. 14—IZAPA, STELA 5

are strong iconographic links to Division 3, but the over-all treatment is something new.

Izapa Stelae 2, 21, 22, possibly 7, 12, 18, and 5, seem to be almost a sequence, and are more late Preclassic and Protoclassic than members of Early Classic. In these sculptures narrative compositions reach a climax.

Izapa Stela 2 (Stirling, 1943, pl. 49,*b*) has a fruit tree growing out of a dragon head (fig. 8,*a*), a motif also on Stela 5 (fig. 14). The dragon variant is the long-snouted type that was widely adopted. A bird-man flies above and two tiny crudely carved human figures appeal to the flyer.

258

Izapa Stela 21 (Orellana, 1955) may depict an actual event: the defeat and decapitation of an important enemy. The rare motif of holding a trophy head is repeated on El Jobo Stela 1, where the head is carried by a strap passed through the cheeks (fig. 15,*b*); on Tres Zapotes Stela A a severed head is carried by the hair (Stirling, 1943, fig. 3). A realistic jaguar rides on the top of the roofed palanquin and the victorious killer wears a jaguar helmet. The human figures are badly proportioned and crudely handled.

Stela 22[14] shows a scroll form with an indented exterior outline that became popular and recurs on Stelae 12 and 5. (Chocola has filet scrolls that anticipate the form.) Izapa Stela 12 presents two additional innovations: the dragon mask with bared alveolum and high scroll headdress, and the motif of two seated figures in consultation with an object between them. The two-headed dragon supports a limp jaguar (for the head, see fig. 9,*c*), whose paws are like monkey hands. And the Izapa signature at the top shows U elements displaced to the sides (Stirling, 1943, pl. 54).

Stela 18 is in part scaled but the two principal figures at the bottom are involved in animated discussion, with an incense burner having a bared-alveolum mask (*ibid.*, pl. 55). Behind each is seated a secondary figure; all wear kilts. It is interesting that the two men on the right have stiff feathers in their headdresses whereas the two at left wear mask headgear. Could the feather headdress indicate foreigners? The stiff straight feathers on the right figures are similar to the feathers of Kaminaljuyu Stela 11.

Izapa Stela 5 (fig. 14) presents a fantastic visual myth. A nine-branched tree whose origins are in a subterranean dragon variant divides the scenes. On the left bottom

[14] Izapa Stela 22, fragmentary, was found in the north part of the site by A. V. Kidder, who photographed the sculpture. It is now lost. On two trips I was unable to locate any part of it.

two men, seated opposite each other over an incensario that is like Kaminaljuyu Stela 11, wear peaked caps. The larger figure has a secondary man behind him who supports a short post with a bare-alveolum dragon. At the back of the smaller figure a little man with a long lock of hair has some business with the tree roots. Directly above his head a small helmeted man seems to present two ring-tail fish to a larger figure wearing a cape and having birds on his left shoulder and on top of his head. On the right side, bottom, again two men sit in consultation, the larger having a flunky with an umbrella behind him. This large man appears to be a sculptor with a small slab at his knee and a chisel in his left hand. He gestures toward the child in front of his small companion. Above is another large man whose face is erased with an enormous headdress. At his back a smaller figure carries a child on his shoulders. The whole is framed by great dragon heads, one quite serpentine, with enormous scroll hats, set on posts. Two ring-tail fish hang from the signature at the left while at the right birds (one looks like a vulture) contemplate the tree. The signature itself has the U-element framed centrally with secondary slanted U's to the sides. The framing of the central element is also a feature of Izapa Stelae 18 and 12. Scrolls are flattened and sometimes notched except for the apparent water at the bottom and right.

The tiny amount of the subject matter of Stela 7 (Stirling, 1943, pl. 51) is insufficient for classification. A great twined coiling body appears to have a bird-head termination (possibly jaguar) and a created serpentine head at the right. It is beautifully carved similar to Stela 12, unlike the badly executed ill-proportioned Stela 5.

Very near Izapa the site El Jobo has produced one fine stela (Shook, 1947, pp. 180–81; fig. 15,b in this article). The late type Izapa signature is at the top. Though badly scaled, a large figure carries a trophy head and a femur topped with an anthropo-

morphic head (fig. 8,b) and tipped with a long knife blade. A small bound headless figure kneels at his feet and wears anklets of a soft tied material like Kaminaljuyu Stela 11. Surface sherd collections and a trench indicated the site is Late Preclassic (Shook, 1947, p. 181). From Abaj Takalik, the lower part of handsome Stela 3 (fig. 16,g),[15] shows well-proportioned feet and legs standing on a panel containing a framed U-symbol flanked by dragon heads (fig. 8,g). The feet wear "heeled" socks indicated by pecking and red paint; the scroll, probably from a loincloth apron, ends on one side in another framed U. The scrolls are very similar to "un-Maya" Uaxactun Stela 10 and tend to confirm Proskouriakoff's suggestion (1950, p. 103) of a very early date for that stela and its relations to peripheral styles.

Three important stelae on the slopes form a subdivision which is distinctly Early Classic in style although several features still tie them to Division 4. Two carry controversial bar-dot place numeration dates which are consistent with their style.

Stela 2 at Abaj Takalik, with evidence of an inscription now largely scaled, was analyzed by Proskouriakoff (1950, p. 176), and shows clear relationship to lowland Early Classic. The one important feature not discussed is the large bearded head surrounded by dragon mask and scrolls (fig. 9,a for the central head). This concept had its beginning in Division 3 on Kaminaljuyu Stelae 10 and 11 and in the flying figures at Izapa. It became a part of lowland tradition in the very early period; Tikal Stela 29 (Shook, 1960, p. 32) has a bearded sky god and Tikal Stela 4 (fig. 9,d) carries a dragon mask with a fringe beard as a downward-looking sky head.

Abaj Takalik Stela 1 (fig. 17,c) has also been discussed by both Thompson (1943c,

[15] The remainder of this stela is reported to show an elaborate body and headdress. It is currently incorporated in a large stone chimney, sculptured side turned in.

Fig. 15—*a*, Kaminaljuyu, Stela 11. *b*, El Jobo, Stela 1.

p. 103) and Proskouriakoff (1950, p. 176). The standing figure wears an unfamiliar mask over his lower face, and his necklace closely resembles El Baul Stela 1. The belt mask is a bird form; the dragon-headed snake that twists below the outstretched hand carries a little jaguar on his back. The dragon features are like those of the belt mask on Silhouette X (fig. 8,e) and very similar to the tun glyph on the Leyden Plate (fig. 5,d).

Stela 1 at El Baul also shows a number of traits with very early lowland Classic style (Proskouriakoff, 1950, p. 175), as well as specific associations with other slope sculptures. Most notable perhaps is the balance of the single human figure with the weight on the forward foot, a consistent feature of highlands and slopes in contrast with the lowland Classic more static pose with the weight solidly on the back foot. The necklace is like that on Abaj Takalik Stela 1, and Silhouette X. A fat-cheeked sky head looks down from scrolls emerging from a hand, and a dragon mask is mounted on a netted post behind the figure in a manner similar to the dragon posts on Izapa Stela 5 (fig. 8,d). Originally it had been painted red like Abaj Takalik Stela 3.

The El Baul stela is the only one of this subclass which has a ceramic context. Earlier excavations did not reach the level of installation which included Arenal sherds as the latest (Miles, in preparation).

Another probable member of this subdivision discussed above is Kaminaljuyu Altar 1.

In the highlands at Kaminaljuyu there seems no doubt that Division 4 merges into Early Classic style, a situation complicated by the fact that there are very few whole sculptures. Stelae, altars, and silhouette pieces are fragmentarily represented in sufficient number and excellence of execution to indicate that the standards achieved in Miraflores were not abandoned.

At Kaminaljuyu the Miraflores idea of framing a stela became popular. On fragmentary Altar 1 two seated men confront each other across a small stela or panel carved with eroded hieroglyphs (fig. 12,a). The left figure's face and arms are strongly reminiscent of Stela 10, and there is a large U-symbol on the heavy belt. The deer in the headdress and the symbol in front of the deer's hooves are like a small silhouette sculpture from the slopes (fig. 16,f).

Another stela fragment, Stela 6 (Kidder, Jennings and Shook, 1946, fig. 133,f), belongs to this transition period. A human figure, showing filet outlining, like Izapa, bends over a serpentine type of dragon head. Not clear in any photograph are a confused series of little masks, and symbols on the dragon head above the eye.

Four additional fragments of framed stelae appear to be transitional. The lower section of Stela 13 is a bared-alveolum serpentine head with flames before his nose (fig. 17,a). The smashed corners of two stelae and Stela 7 (ibid., fig. 167,b) exhibit nearly erased design framed with single to three lines. There is not enough content left for style or period definition.

Stela 1 (which may have been a wall panel, or an altar) is unusual in shape with a curved front surface that made a horizontal panel; the left weathered half is all that remains (fig. 12,b).[16] A human figure leaning forward with bent knee is represented. The break bisects his front-turned loincloth apron. An enormous dragon head with downcurved snout is fastened to the belt and obscures the hip. The dragon's teeth are represented by an upper-filet and a great fang at the corner of the mouth. The toothless lower jaw resembles that of earlier examples (cf. Stela 11). The human leg is fileted and carries a circle on the thigh. Either a square-toed soft moccasin is represented or the foot is turned to a top view, a characteristic of Late Classic

[16] E. M. Shook suspects that a new sculpture at Kaminaljuyu, a tenoned head, is made on the right half of Stela 1. Fragments of the same type of carving appear on one side.

Cotzumalhuapa sculpture. The scrolls with small rounded terminals are turned in opposite directions.

It is interesting to note that footgear first appears in Division 4. On Stela 3, Abaj Takalik, are ankle "socks"; Silhouette X wears platform sandals of Early Classic lowland type, Kaminaljuyu Stela 1, possibly moccasins; and Izapa Stela 5 "boots" occur on more than one figure.

Silhouetted reliefs, a class of sculpture as of the moment limited to highland Guatemala, belong primarily in Division 4, although it probably began earlier and shares features with Early Classic.

Two small fragments associated with Late Preclassic pottery at Kaminaljuyu (Kidder, 1948, pp. 227–28) provide the general context; none of the whole or fragmentary pieces exhibit traits that are definitely late.[17]

Silhouette 1 (fig. 16,c) wears a dragon belt-mask having, below, knotted cords (something like a bow-tie) and three leaf-like elements dependent below, and, at his back, a dead serpent; the partially anthropomorphic head has had flesh stripped from the jaws and the scaled body hangs limply down behind the figure's legs.

Silhouette X, exact provenience unknown (Kidder, Jennings, and Shook, 1946, fig. 141,b, discussed by Proskouriakoff, 1950, p. 178), is a human figure with a number of characteristics related to Early Classic styles in the lowlands. The belt head is human wearing a long dragon snout, having a "bow-tie" with three elements below that resemble Classic Maya "shells" (fig. 8,e). The feather headdress remotely resembles Izapa Stela 18.

The "bow-ties" on these two silhouettes help place a third piece from Kaminaljuyu, Monument 17 (fig. 16,d). This headless

and legless human figure is a stiff compromise between in-the-round sculpture and silhouette; the back is pecked like silhouettes with no carryout of the features carved on the face. Below the battered space where a face had been carved are a fine "bow-tie" and stiff bib.[18]

Two silhouette sculptures have long pedestals and technically qualify for that category. However, neither is in the round; both are carved on one side and pecked on the back. The first is reported to have come from Santa Cruz Quiche (Kidder, Jennings, and Shook, 1946, fig. 141,c) and presents a dragon head with the former three-part hat reduced to a trefoil eyebrow.[19]

Kaminaljuyu Silhouette 2 was found August 3, 1960, by Gustavo Espinosa (reported in the newspaper El Imparcial). An extraordinary stone ring, surmounted by a triangle and bearing four carved dragon heads stood vertically on a long shaft (fig. 8,f), with basal swelling like the Santa Cruz silhouette. Basalt columns flanked the ring. As Espinosa notes, this piece closely resembles four stone rings on pedestals in coastal Guerrero from sites near Petatlan and Tecpan (Hendrichs, 1943, figs. 1, 2, 3, 7, 4). Hendrichs believes the Guerrero rings, which also carry dragon heads and and in one case intertwined bodies of "serpents," are ball-court markers. They are comparable in size to Silhouette 2. None were found in situ; the Kaminaljuyu ex-

[17] The death's-head motif of the pectoral on Silhouette X which Proskouriakoff suggests as late (1950, p. 178) also occurs on the loincloth of the Chocola figure.

[18] E. M. Shook found this piece in the possession of a private collector who reported that it had been turned up in the course of water main excavation, 50 cm. below surface in the E-IV section of Kaminaljuyu.

[19] Two examples on geographically distant pots (fig. 8,c; Navarrete, 1960, fig. 32,g; Stirling, 1957, pl. 66,a) repeat this type of dragon in Late Preclassic phase ceramics. The La Isla pot, with its over-the-eye U, appears to be the prototype for Early Classic Serpent X. See Covarrubias, 1957, fig. W, while the trefoil over the eye is subsequently an attribute of Classic jaguars in the lowland Maya area.

Fig. 16—*a*, Kaminaljuyu, Monument 17. *b*, Kaminaljuyu. *c*, Kaminaljuyu, Silhouette 1. *d*, Kaminaljuyu fragment. *e*, Kaminaljuyu fragment. *f*, Abaj Takalik, Silhouette 1. *g*, Abaj Takalik, Stela 3.

ample was apparently associated with a pit containing a pottery offering, phase unreported.

It is possible that Silhouette 2 represents a ball-court marker or goal, characteristic of the game prior to the development of walled courts; the game must have had a long history prior to the actual construction of walled courts, which are Late Classic at Kaminaljuyu and as yet unreported in any phase in Guerrero.

A small silhouette (fig. 16,*f*) was found at Abaj Takalik. At the base of a stone cross a deer is carved in relief; in place of a tail is a framed U-symbol with flames similar to that on Kaminaljuyu Altar 1. A bird is perched on top of the cross.

EARLY CLASSIC SCULPTURES: Kaminaljuyu

In Esperanza Mound B at Kaminaljuyu Altar 2 shows two elaborately dressed figures kneeling beside a panel (Kidder, Jennings, and Shook, 1946, fig. 133,*d,e*). Proskouriakoff has pointed out the similarity in motif of Altars 1 and 2 to the early altar fragment at Polol (1950, p. 110). Stela 15, which is represented by a small fragment showing the feet and legs of two individuals on either side of a panel, again repeats this basic motif (fig. 17,*d*). The men's sandals are of the same type as Silhouette X.

Stela 13, a rattlesnake tail (fig. 9,*b*), duplicates the tail of a serpent carved on an Esperanza double-spout jar (Kidder, Jennings, and Shook, 1946, fig. 71,*c*).

Probably Stela 2,[20] known from two fragments, is Early Classic; the fragment showing a leg makes it clear that the knees were not in contact (fig. 17,*b*). The upper fragment has an arm and the upper part of a great stiff feathered cape, which continues

behind the leg in the lower piece. An atlatl is held at the shoulder. Nearly erased scrolls on the side of this stela indicate that it is a re-used stone.

Another nearly scaled fragment, from Esperanza Mound A, and a corner bit with border and scroll are the last of the Kaminaljuyu stelae currently known. In spite of their wretched habits of scaling and recarving or smashing their sculptures, it is obvious that the highlanders of Kaminaljuyu and the people of the slopes had an extraordinarily long history as master sculptors. That there were wide-ranging contacts with other peoples is equally clear, although at present it is not possible to be precise in terms of priority or direction.

The long development that appears to end in Early Classic with primarily Maya relations is followed by an entirely new series of styles whose external associations are with Mexico and largely distinct from the Maya tradition. It is possible that the strong Teotihuacan infusion in Esperanza was responsible for the reorientation of sculptors.

LATE CLASSIC SCULPTURES: Tonala, Cotzumalhuapa district, Pasaco, Kaminaljuyu, midhighlands; Chinkultic, Tenam, Comitan

In the high Chiapas lake district at the northwest corner of Guatemala are Chinkultic and Tenam, two very unlikely Maya sites with monuments dated in Classic style from 9.7.17.12.14 to 10.0.15.0.0. Proskouriakoff (1950, pp. 186, 187) placed the elegant Chinkultic ball-court marker and six of the 10 stelae in the Late Classic Maya style ranging from the Formative to Decadent phases. Tenam Stela 1 is stylistically dated at 9.17.0.0.0±2 katuns (*ibid.*, p. 195). Farther up in the Chiapas highlands at Comitan another single stela is a member of this intrusive tradition that must have arrived by way of the nearby rivers Zacatal and Lacantun, southwestern headwaters of the Usumacinta. At present there

---

[20] The lower part of Stela 2 was found by Lothrop (1926a). Later it was broken and built into a wall, from which A. V. Kidder retrieved it. The upper section was brought to the Guatemala Museum by a farmer.

FIG. 17—*a*, Kaminaljuyu, Stela 13. *b*, Kaminaljuyu, Stela 2 (2 parts). *c*, Abaj Takalik, Stela 1. *d*, Kaminaljuyu, Stela 15.

265

is no indication that the lowland colonies had any appreciable effect on the styles of the Pacific slopes.

There is very slight evidence of some continuity of styles in the slopes from Tonala to the great Cotzumalhuapa district and its highland extensions. The battered fragment of Tonala Stela 9 depicts standing figures on front and back. The knees are puffy, as in the Cotzumalhuapa figures; the feet are squared and fillet outlining of clothing and leg bands is deep and heavy (Ferdon, 1953, pl. 20, *a,d*). The stela that stood in Tonala village plaza (*ibid.*, pl. 24,*e,f*) lacks the puffy knees but adds a specific detail of importance: both figures wear loincloths that are looped in a peculiar double knot identical to that common in Cotzumalhuapa carving, as Ferdon noted (1953, p. 104–07). The two great altars, one jaguar with double scrolls about the eyes and the second an alligator head (*ibid.*, pls. 21,*a-d*; 22,*a-d*) have tassels in relief with the same loop and knot.

At Tonala station a fragmentary stela presents an active ball-player with square-toed moccasins and knee guard (*ibid.*, pl. 24,*d*) but no specific connections with the other monuments at Tonala or in the Cotzumalhuapa zone.

The human heads in raised relief on the sides of Altar 1 resemble three in the vicinity of Quen Santo (Seler, 1901) and an altar at San Jeronimo (Orellana, 1952, pl. 6).

The Cotzumalhuapa district is a cluster of sites on the Pacific slopes in Guatemala, which have produced an enormous amount of related sculpture that lacks definitive connections to the previous styles of the area with the tenuous exception of Tonala. Santa Lucia Cotzumalhuapa, El Baul, Los Tarros, and El Castillo form a nucleus within a few kilometers of each other. Aguna, Palo Verde, Panteleon, Osuna, and Palo Gordo are neighboring; and stretching to the east from Palo Gordo to Pasaco are many small sites that have produced single monuments either in pure Cotzumalhuapa style or closely related.

Thompson's excavation at El Baul is the only published account of ceramic phases associated with the style. A cache under Monument 7 indicates a beginning phase related to Esperanza, and, although he found San Juan Plumbate, Thompson did not locate any Postclassic Tohil Plumbate pottery in the site (1948, pp. 43–45).

Monument 7 (*ibid.*, fig. 8,*a*) pictures a human figure behind a giant crab.[21] Two small medallions in the upper corners contain human busts with arms crossed, and possibly tied, at the wrist on the chest. This motif is very widespread often in Late Classic contexts but surely extending into Postclassic.

Six whole, and one partial, stelae or ball-court panels from Cotzumalhuapa and three at Palo Verde (Thompson, 1948, figs. 2,*a-c,e-g*; 3,*a*) present a new treatment of the motif of sky god and human figure. Broken Monument 7 shows only an uplifted hand and speech-scroll with the long-haired cross-armed god emerging from a serpent's jaws above.[22] Proskouriakoff has noted technical resemblance of this monument and others to Piedras Negras and Quirigua (1950, p. 175). The six whole slabs at Cotzumalhuapa all show ball-players (Thompson, 1948, p. 19) stretching a hand and looking toward a sky deity. Five are apparently praying with Teotihuacan-type "tabbed" speech-scrolls; in the sixth a death manikin of Tajin type is linked to the main figure by a line resembling the prayer-scrolls of the others. The Palo Verde monuments differ in not showing the sky god explicitly but the ball-players holding

[21] The crab immediately brings to mind the incident in the Popol Vuh in which Zipacua, an earth giant, is killed by a giant crab (Recinos, Goetz, and Morley, 1950, pp. 102–03) built by Hunohpú and Xbalanqué.

[22] A stela with a strikingly similar sky motif is on the Oaxaca coast at Rio Grande. A cross-armed figure looks down from the jaws of a jaguar (Piña Chan, 1960b, photo 4).

FIG. 18—*a*, Chichicastenango. *b*, La Nueva. *c*, La Nueva. *d*, El Castillo, Stela 1. *e*, Chuitinamit.

"offerings" over their heads and looking skyward. These three have Xiuhcoatl borders.

The association of ball-players and death manikins, handled in the heavy fillet fashion of the Tajin death figures, reinforces the suggestion Stirling made in connecting Cotzumalhuapa Monument 9 and Cerro de Las Mesas Monument 4 (1943, p. 34). Several small additional traits, such as headdresses with vertical elements (cf. Cotzumalhuapa Monument 1 and Tajin ball-court panel in Proskouriakoff, 1960, fig. 9,*b*), the high frequency of draped, rather than straight-hemmed, kilts in both, and the tall triangular headdress of Cotzumalhuapa Monument 13 and Type II-B figurines of Xipe at Cerro de las Mesas (Drucker, 1943b, pl. 33) provide an impression that several ball teams left the southwestern Veracruz area at a time of strong Teotihuacan influence, and that they settled happily and prosperously on the rich Pacific slopes. Monuments 1 and 21, Cotzumalhuapa, and Monument 4, El Baul (Thompson, 1948, figs. 2,*d*; 5,*a*; 6,*d*) emphasize in grisly scenes the type of human sacrifice that accompanied the ball-players. The great flying sun vultures (Monuments 16, 17) are vaguely reminiscent of the Tula vultures.

Thompson (1943d, p. 120) showed that Monument 4, El Baul, depicts the sacrifice of eagle-and-jaguar warriors and demonstrated the presence of those warrior societies in the Cotzumalhuapa district. Recently discovered murals at Teotihuacan (Séjourné, 1960, figs. 30, 31) show clearly that these were ancient, and in theme, if not explicitly in style of depiction, as widespread late Late Classic phenomena, as is the Aguna Xipe sculpture (Thompson, 1948, fig. 11,*a,b*). Many torn hearts and sacrificial knives (Séjourné, 1960, figs. 39, 41, 42) appear in the hands of priests and deities in Teotihuacan murals although the painters apparently shrank from direct

presentation of sacrifice. The remote frontier was more brutal.

Monument 1 at El Castillo (Burkitt, 1933, fig. 9; fig. 18,*d* in this article) specifically affirms the Teotihuacan influence. Behind the head of the sky god is a sun disc with interlaced bands (cf. Caso, 1959, fig. 8). A human figure climbs a "rope" set with fangs as a stylized lower serpent jaw. The climber wears socks or moccasins like those on Stela 1 at Kaminaljuyu. Ceremonies, including an actual ball game, and consultations between two men, occasionally with one or more retainers, death's-heads and hieroglyphic notations further vary the subject matter in relief on stelae and great unshaped boulders.

The magnificent jaguar in the round at El Baul (fig. 19,*a*; Thompson, 1948, fig. 17,*c*) is unique but generically comparable to one at Piedra Labrada, Guerrero (Piña Chan, 1960b, photo 10), which though headless is collared and wears a Cotzumalhuapa type of loincloth.

Monumental heads in relief and in the round were also produced. Monument 29 (Thompson, 1948, fig. 9,*c*) is representative of a type found throughout the area: a face skeleton wears bark-cloth flaps in his ears, a long-haired wig retained by a headband often featuring an X cross, and deer tails sprout above the ear. (Cf. with the tail of the deer on Cotzumalhuapa Monument 14.)[23]

El Baul Monument 3 (*ibid.*, fig. 10,*d*), the in-the-round type, is a smiling fringe-bearded human head with deeply wrinkled

[23] Tenuous but important confirmation of the ritual importance of deer tails, also called "flowers," and the connection of the deer with death is in Preuss (1955, p. 379) and Kelley (1955). On Monument 14 a deer is about to perform a sacrifice. Preuss also found a close association with the deer and the god of the planet Venus (1955, p. 391) confirming Thompson's pre-Toltec proposal and indicating that Quetzalcoatl may have had a deer form in earlier days. Several of the Cotzumalhuapa death manikins also wear deer tails on the sides of their heads.

cheeks; often, as at El Baul, this type wears a Xiuhcoatl headband.

Full figures in the round include jaguars and anthropomorphic monkey-faced individuals (Thompson, 1948, figs. 17,c,i; 16,e; 15,f).

Four great portrait busts, portrait heads and heads of serpents, alligators, jaguars, and monkeys are all tenoned. Proskouriakoff relates the portrait busts to lowland Maya Classic (1950, p. 176). Several of the portrait heads wear round tams or hats that come to a low peak or a button (fig. 19,b). These hats appear also on coastal Late Classic figurines. A notable feature of the portraits is the thin long-lipped physical type represented. Nearly all have deeply furrowed brows and cheeks, and mouths with a grim sour puritanical downturn.

Two Cotzumalhuapa outlyers are particularly interesting. In the vicinity of highland Antigua several tenoned heads are such specific duplicates that the site, or sites, must have been contemporary with the slopes (Seler, 1900, Tables 37, 38, and pp. 217, 218; Thompson, 1948, fig. 15,a,b,d same as Seler, p. 218). The sites are still uninvestigated.

Several relatively small sites east of Cotzumalhuapa district have produced single pieces now in the Guatemala Museum or found by E. M. Shook in the course of a coastal survey (Shook, photographic file). Las Pilas near Escuintla is an example. A fine collared serpent head having typical double scrolls at the eyes apparently decorated a mound there.

A second concentration of sculptures, however, is in the vicinity of Pasaco. At La Nueva, Termer found part of a great relief stela whose ruined condition does not hide the fact that it is like the Cotzumalhuapa zone portrait busts with a large panache of long feathers (Termer, 1948, pl. 25, 12). At the same site is a death's-head altar with deer tails. Two fine collared snakes in the round (fig. 18,b,c) at this site are a different treatment of a familiar subject. Tenoned heads and a sun-disc altar, very similar to Cerro de las Mesas and the Quen Santo area, are also present (Stirling, 1943, fig. 13; Termer, 1948, pl. 25, 9; Seler, 1901, figs. 89, 105, 109).

None of the tenoned heads have been found in situ, except two serpents at El Baul (Thompson, 1948, p. 36, fig. 14,d) that appear to have been architectural decorations as were some of the relief cross-armed figures. Certainly, however, with the prominence of the ball game, serpents and jaguars were employed as markers on courts. The parrot with emergent human face from Los Tarros (Thompson, 1943c, fig. 17,g,h) closely resembles the cruder parrots from Asuncion Mita ball courts (Stromsvik, 1950, fig. 7,a-c). The same is true of the two matched parrots with human faces in the beaks at Finca Pompeya, Antigua (Seler, 1900, Table 38). It is possible that the human faces in serpents' jaws at Panteleon and El Castillo (Thompson, 1948, figs. 12,e; 14,a) are also ball-court markers, although walled courts have not certainly been identified as yet in the Cotzumalhuapa district.

The parrot-head court markers at Asuncion Mita are similar to those at Copan (Stromsvik, 1952, figs. 21, 23) in being provided with vertical tenons, although the Copan parrots carry no human faces. Mita is further linked with Copan by the presence of Copador pottery. A large head of the old fire god from the Pacific slopes (exact provenience unknown), very like one at Copan (fig. 19,d), suggests that much more evidence of communication may be found.

At Kaminaljuyu a large number of heads, tenoned both vertically and horizontally, are generically related to the slope types. The heads represent serpents, jaguars, birds, and men. One bird and one serpent have human faces in open beak and jaws. The elements above the eyes continue local tradition in being either trefoil or plain. One battered human head wears a head-dress made up of vertical elements. Since most were recovered in uncontrolled excavation, there is no certainty which were employed as pyramid decorations and which as ball-court markers with the exception of two beaten jaguar heads. G. Espinosa found them in place as central court markers in Mound C-III-4, together with a re-used broken jaguar-pedestal sculpture.

At Guaytan, in the Middle Motagua Valley (Smith and Kidder, 1943, p. 177, fig. 60), Zacualpa (Wauchope, 1948a, pl. 1,a,b), and Chalchitan (A. L. Smith, 1955, figs. 7, 9) Late Classic type of ball courts were equipped with tenoned serpent and jaguar markers. Perhaps the first sculpture of this type is the Patzun head (fig. 19,c), which is a great serpent with a trefoil eye-piece and a handsome human face in the open jaws. Seler reports a collared jaguar head from Quen Santo (1901, fig. 121).

Although occasional plain stelae are reported in the northern highlands, the practice of carving such monuments seems to have been abandoned in the midhighlands.

POSTCLASSIC SCULPTURES: Tajumulco, Mixco Viejo, Chuitinamit, Quen Santo district, Comitan

The three dominating features of Postclassic sculpture are its general crudity, lack of artistic merit, and continued strong foreign influence, primarily Mexican.

At the late site of Tajumulco several altars and one small stela (Dutton and Hobbs, 1943, figs. 15, 16, 20, 21; Tejeda, 1947) appear to be a degenerate extension of the Cotzumalhuapa style. Sculptures 1 and 6 have jaguars, eagles, and sun discs. Human figures are very stiff and crudely handled. Faces usually are framed in simple headdress shape like an inverted U. Below the knee garments continue this Cotzumalhuapa innovation for special individuals who may have been rulers.

Sporadic finds in coastal and midhighland sites show similar treatment (A. L. Smith, 1955, fig. 25,f; this article, fig. 19).[24] The ball-court marker at Mixco Viejo (fig. 19,e) is an exception. Although the serpent head is hurriedly carved, its proportions are good and the Toltec-style face within the jaws is very handsomely executed. A vertically tenoned Toltec head from Joyabaj is similar.

At the museum in Chichicastenango are a great many small portable and semiportable figures, stone incense burners (including the old fire god), and carved boxes from sites in the midhighlands (Lothrop, 1936, pp. 50–51, 85, 87, illustrates a few). The small sculptures occasionally have Tlaloc features (fig. 18,a) and bring to mind the Quiche legend of carrying their gods on long trips.

Entirely without archaeological context, to date, a southern tradition is involved in the late sculpture of the Pacific slopes. These are the short round pedestal sculptures of human and anthropomorphic figures which frequently show legs in low relief on the side of the pedestal in Nicaraguan style (Richardson, 1940, fig. 83). One reported to be from Tiquisate is clearly phallic (fig. 19). At Tajumulco and from other sites in the vicinity there are six examples (Tejeda, 1947, pp. 120–21). The four decorative roof slabs and the small two-part serpents from the Cakchiquel site of Chuitinamit also have strong southern affiliation (Lothrop, 1933, pp. 84–85; fig. 18,e in this article). A slow diffusion of southern ideas may have begun very early, although its major influence appears in strength only very late.

In the lake district of Chiapas and Guatemala at Quen Santo, Gracias a Dios, Tres Lagunas, and west at Comitan, altars similar to Tajumulco, round pedestals and small crude human figures hung with tro-

[24] Compare with Hendrichs, 1943, fig. 5, which is strikingly similar, though from distant coastal Guerrero.

FIG. 19—*a*, El Baul. *b*, Santa Rosa. *c*, Patzun. *d*, South coast. *e*, Ball-court marker, Mixco Viejo. *f*, South coast.

271

phy heads are reported by Seler (1901). A few continue the cross-armed tradition, and characteristic are puffy eyes with a narrow slit, or a completely round eye, or a rectangular eye with raised border and vacant socket. Most strikingly southern are two figures from Cave 1 at Quen Santo (Seler, 1901, figs. 218, 219).

The late chac-mool idea known to have been part of the Salvador development (Richardson, 1940, fig. 35; Von Weber, 1922, figs. 39–42) is only indirectly expressed at Tajumulco in the crouching figures with cavities in their backs (Tejeda, 1947, p. 113).

Two occurrences of prowling jaguars on the Pacific slope, at Coyol on Finca El Salto (Tozzer, 1957, fig. 147; Thompson, 1949, figs. 4,a,b) are not dissimilar to the jaguars on Tajumulco altars (Tejeda, 1947, pp. 114, 116) although these are not in procession.

Sporadic stucco sculptures in the mid-highlands are late but are too fragmentary for definition. The impression is that people too preoccupied with other affairs did not have the necessary long leisure for substantial sculpture in stone.

It is tempting to identify the southeastern intrusion with the Chiapaneca, but there is still serious question whether their presence in Chiapas should be attributed to a late northwestern movement, or to long-term residence of an abandoned enclave. In any event the Early Classic style in the highlands and slopes gave way to essentially foreign ideas that have demonstrable association with Mexican highlands and coastal slopes and with southeastern Central American traditions.

The correlation of sculpture divisions with highland ceramic phases is summarized in Table 1.

HIEROGLYPHS AND CALENDAR

The types of calendar in use just before the conquest can be reconstructed from ethnographic and historical sources.

A 365-day year, divided into 18 named months, each consisting of 20 named days was in general use.[25] Thirteen numbers running concurrently with the days made a virtual round of 260 days. A five-day period, following the 18th month, produced another structural feature, that of the 4 year bearers. Other units known ethnologically such as 40-day units, "feet of the year," and the 110-day Ik period of the Pokom calendar were undoubtedly elements in preconquest calendars, though their function is unknown.[26]

There is evidence in early highland native-Spanish manuscript dictionaries of a preconquest unit called *may*, which is regularly defined as an "age of 20 years." Among the Cakchiquel in the late preconquest period chronicled in the Annals, *may* referred to a strictly vigesimal count of 20 periods of 400 days each. This was probably a very late invention since it explicitly counted only from an insurrection that occurred in 1493 (Recinos and Goetz, 1953, p. 109), without evidence of prior existence. The 400-day "year" was independent of the solar approximation of 365 days. There is no evidence that *may* referred to 400-day counts among other peoples using the term, nor is it possible to determine which, either a 360- or 365-day unit, was used in the *may*; the same term was applied to both.

Of the five mechanically possible patterns of year bearers only two were in known use in the highlands: the southeastern calendars of the Quiche, Cakchiquel,

[25] Full comparative lists of day names and month names and discussion of meanings is presented in Thompson, 1950, pp. 67–121.

[26] LaFarge, 1947, pp. 176–78, reports "teams" of day lords in modern Chuj of Santa Eulalia. The senior day calls upon others of the "team" to deal with a particular situation. A possible representation of the same idea is in Ordóñez (1907, facing p. 264, written ca. 1794) for Tzeltal-Tzotzil. A double wheel carries the 20 day names in order in the exterior round; year bearers of the Akbal pattern are underlined. The internal wheel lists year bearers and day names in groups, not in normal order, possibly 4 "teams." LaFarge gives a total of 12 "teams."

Late Postclassic		Mexican "Pipil"	Highland crude small sculpture Trophy heads Tazumal
Early Postclassic	Tohil Plumbate	3rd "Pipil" (A.D. 900 ?)	Tajumulco Soconusco
Late Classic	San Juan Plumbate	2nd "Pipil" (end of Teotihuacan III 650 ?) Calendrical shift in Cakchiquel and Quiche (?)	Highland tenoned heads in jaws Cotzumalhuapa style Tonala
Full Early Classic	Esperanza Early Classic	First "Pipil" (Teotihuacan)	Kaminaljuyu, Abaj Takalik stelae altars
Division 4	Arenal	Connections with Maya lowlands (transitional and innovating)	Izapa narrative style Altars with two figures Silhouettes "Classic" single figures
Division 3	Miraflores	Peak of Preclassic: Kaminaljuyu-Izapa interconnections	Miraflores style Hieroglyphs and full calendar in highlands
Division 2	Late Providencia Early	Sporadic "Olmec" on coast	Developmental, highland and coastal styles
Division 1	Las Charcas Arevalo	Pre- or Proto-"Olmec"	Earliest dragon Boulder figures Kaminaljuyu and coast

Mam, and Ixil used the Ik group; the northwest Tzeltal and Tzotzil, Chuj, and Jacalteca the Akbal pattern, one day in advance. The others are unknown.

Except in northwestern Guatemala, information on the beginning date of the year is chaotic. However, if the difference of year-bearer pattern is acknowledged, the calendars of the Chuj, Jacalteca, Mam, and Ixil all commenced their year 40 days earlier than the Yucatec, Chol, and probably Kekchi of Alta Verapaz, and the Maya of Classic inscriptions. Since there was a strong lowland "invasion" in Chiapas at Chinkultic, Comitan, and Tenam in Late Classic times, Tzeltal-Tzotzil may well have had a lowland type of year. Berlin (1951) presents strong evidence of very close relationship to the Yucatan Maya calendar described by Landa.

The use of the name *Wotan* or *Watan* for the third day, instead of the regular Maya *akbal*, provides a special link among the Chuj, Jacalteca, Tzeltal, and Tzotzil. This group also had the name *ahau* for the 20th day, while all other calendars known in the highlands called that day *hunahpu*.

Both Quiche and Cakchiquel peoples suffered heavy Mexicanization and adopted some Nahua month names—the Cakchiquel at least four, the Quiche three. Although they were close allies for a long period, available data indicate that Quiche groups began their annual count at different times from the Cakchiquel, who commenced their year 100 days earlier than the northwestern highlanders.

Both Quiche and Cakchiquel have the month Tacaxepual in the same position relative to the European year in the Tovar calendar; although the 15th month of the year for Quiche, it is the first for both Cakchiquel and Tovar (Kubler and Gibson, 1951, pp. 19–20). Of the many lists of month names Motolinía's list most closely corresponds to the Guatemalan lists by including two Pachtli names, the 11th and 12th. The Relación de Teutilan is next with one Pachtli name (Castañeda, 1581, pp. 217–20). See Table 2.

TABLE 2—COMPARATIVE "MONTH" NAMES

Cakchiquel (1685)	Motolinía list Tlaxcala or Puebla	Teutitlan del Camino (1581)
1. Tacaxepual	1. Tlacaxipe-hualiztli	1. Tlacaxipe-hualiztli
11. Nabei Pach	11. Pachtli	11. Hecoztli
12. Rucan Pach	12. Hueypachtli	12. Paxtli
17. Izcal	17. Izcalli	17. Yzcalli

Caso (1958b, p. 77) finds seven additional names to have similar meanings and regards them as Toltec.

The absence of Nahuatl suffixes in the Guatemalan names suggests the adoption of calendrical reform brought about no later than the A.D. 900 Pipil incursions. It is also possible that the adoption was on a Late Classic level since at least one shift had separated the Quiche from the Cakchiquel counts.

There is no direct 16th-century statement about lunar and Venus counts, but modern survivals show that these were certainly important preconquest features of the calendar. The moon was counted, probably, as it is today among the Tzotzil from the first day (or night) of complete disappearance as new moon (Schulz, 1942, p. 7). There is no concrete information as to how the Venus cycle was reckoned.

Widespread highland use of hieroglyphic codices is attested by reference to them in several early reports. The codices are described as of three types: divinatory, calendrical, and historical.

The inscriptions at Chinkultic, Comitan, and Tenam are the only presently known Late Classic texts on stelae. These do not differ from Classic lowland inscriptions and demonstrate the same cycle and katun counts. At many sites are plain stelae which may have been stuccoed and painted with hieroglyphs. Short hieroglyphic texts on Late Classic pottery are frequent from Alta Verapaz and widespread in the central highlands. One bar-dot numeral on the Tonala station stela (Satterthwaite, 1943a, fig. 1,e) in front of a death-masked head

274

glyph suggests an acquaintance with hieroglyphs in the area.

On the coastal slopes hieroglyphs in an entirely different system are associated with the Cotzumalhuapa-style sculpture. Thompson (1948, pp. 32–33, fig. 62) has shown that these hieroglyphs are probably all day glyphs and their closest affiliation is with little-known types from southern Mexico. Several remain unidentified. Stela 3 at Cotzumalhuapa possibly depicts a scene of astronomical observation. The Mexican cross-stick observation glyph is at the right above the uplifted gloved hand of the central figure, while at the top a deity wearing a "Venus" hat and sun disk on his chest descends from open serpent jaws. Burland (1958) believes Stela 1, El Castillo, represents the passage of Venus.

The Cotzumalhuapan glyphs have little relation to the distorted drawings of "Pipil" glyphs made by Fuentes y Guzmán from a Sonsonate tribute roll, which shows a system of enumeration like that of the valley of Mexico. It is probable that the Sonsonate calendar was like that reported by Oviedo from the Nicarao and which was apparently counting the year in Mexico fashion using the same year bearers (Lothrop, 1926b, pp. 74–75). Swadesh (1954–55, p. 178) places the separation of Salvadoreño Pipil from Mexica at ca. A.D. 900, which is too late for the Cotzumalhuapa Pipil. Thompson (1948, pp. 49–50) found the major occupation at El Baul beginning about A.D. 650 and lasting until ca A.D. 925, ending before the manufacture of Tohil Plumbate. Jiménez Moreno (1954–55, pp. 220–22) links the end of Teotihuacan III with Pipil migration toward Guatemala ca. 750 and Sahagun's tlamatininos, "wise men," perhaps from Morelos, who fled to Guatemala.

The hieroglyphic texts that are certainly Early Classic are confined to two altars at Kaminaljuyu, which are so damaged as to be unreadable, except for some bar-dot numerals, and an earplug text for six glyphs which are early in type although they face right instead of the usual left (Kidder, Jennings, and Shook, 1946, p. 106).

Preclassic texts, with the majority of hieroglyphs eroded or chipped away, are represented on El Baul Stela 1 and on Abaj Takalik Stela 2. The style—without period or cycle identifying glyphs, but with numerals carved in columnar place-numeration-fashion—is now quite well established and an increasing frequency of discovery is to be expected. The Preclassic dates, with associated pottery phase at El Baul of Arenal, suggested a prior calendrical formulation which is confirmed in Heath-Jones' analysis of the long text on the Miraflores Monument 10 at Kaminaljuyu. The monument carries the earliest hieroglyphic text known. In a summary report (1959, p. 37) Heath-Jones defined the text as conclusively Maya, on a comparative basis, including all known archaeological Mesoamerican hieroglyphic systems. She found a highly developed writing and Maya calendar presented in the text and identified an ancestral Maya civilization in Miraflores phase at Kaminaljuyu.

No earlier evidence of hieroglyphic or calendrical material is currently known.

REFERENCES

Agrinier, 1960
Berlin, 1951
Blom and LaFarge, 1926–27
Boggs, 1950
Burkitt, 1933
Burland, 1958
Caso, 1958b, 1959
Castañeda, 1581
Covarrubias, 1957
Dieseldorff, 1926–33
Dixon, 1958
Drucker, 1943b, 1952a, 1952b, 1955
——, Heizer, and Squier, 1959
Dutton and Hobbs, 1943
Ferdon, 1953
Fuentes y Guzmán, 1932–33
Hay, 1940
Heath-Jones, 1959
Hendrichs Perez, 1943
Jiménez, 1957
Jiménez Moreno, 1954–55
Kelemen, 1943
Kelley, D. H., 1955
Kidder, A., and Samayoa, 1959
Kidder, A. V., 1948, 1954
——, Jennings, and Shook, 1946
Kroeber, 1953
Kubler and Gibson, 1951
LaFarge, 1947
Leon, 1907
Lothrop, 1926a,b, 1927a,b, 1933, 1936
Martínez Espinosa, 1959
Medellin Zenil, 1960c
Miles, 1957b

Moedano K., 1948
Navarrete, 1960
Ordóñez y Aguiar, 1907
Orellana Tapia, 1952, 1955
Paso y Troncoso, 1905
Piña Chan, 1960b
Preuss, 1955
Proskouriakoff, 1950, 1954
Recinos and Goetz, 1953
——, ——, and Morley, 1950
Richardson, 1940
Ricketson, 1936
—— and Ricketson, 1937
Satterthwaite, 1943a
Schapiro, 1953
Schulz, 1942
Séjourné, 1960
Seler, 1901
Seler-Sachs, 1900
Shook, 1947, 1950c, 1951b, 1960
—— and Kidder, 1952
Smith, A. L., 1955
—— and Kidder, 1943
Stirling, 1943, 1957
Stromsvik, 1950, 1952
Swadesh, 1954–55
Tejeda, 1947
Termer, 1948
Thompson, J. E. S., 1943c, 1943d, 1948, 1949, 1950
Villacorta and Villacorta, 1927
Wauchope, 1948a
Von Weber, 1922

11. Summary of Preconquest Ethnology of the Guatemala-Chiapas Highlands and Pacific Slopes

S. W. MILES

THE LAST FEW centuries prior to Spanish conquest in the Maya highlands were years of shifting wars and skirmishes, of changing alliances and betrayals. New types of political and military organization and heavy pressures from internal movements and foreign conquest were contributing to an emergent concept of empire, though the disparate warring groups were too small and evenly balanced to maintain major gains against each other.

Fortunately, many of the wars, claims, and counterclaims were recorded either in native chronicles or elicited in testimony presented in 16th-century Spanish courts. Land titles with genealogies and scraps of history (often reading like descriptions of Mexican title lienzos), early Spanish descriptions, and dictionaries provide information from which the structures of social and political activity may be inferred.

The linguistic map (fig. 1) presents approximate boundaries of speech areas as of the conquest period. Several areas shown as separated actually faded into each other with mutual intelligibility extending almost to the far corners of each. A few real borders, such as that separating the Mam and Aguateca from their neighbors, and the Ixil from theirs, were prominent.

Ethnographic and archaeological data are in agreement with a general lowland affiliation of the Tzeltal-Tzotzil, Tojolabal, and Chuj and support McQuown's construction of relationships (1956, pp. 191–195). Quiche, Cakchiquel, and Tzutuhil form another group, Pokom and Kekchi a third.

Motozintla[1] and Chicomulteca[2] are old enclaves about whom there is very little information. The Xinca propose a mystery of affiliation that time has not yet resolved.

The Nahua-speakers are somewhat tangled. Linguistic evidence indicates that some, at least, were rather early arrivals (ca. A.D. 1000, Swadesh, 1954–55) but the Soconusco Nahua domination appears to be later and mixed with a local population

---

[1] Ed. note: Also known as Motozintlec (F. Johnson, 1940, p. 108 and map; J. A. Mason, 1940, Table I, p. 83).

[2] Ed. note: Also known as Chicomuceltec (F. Johnson, 1940, p. 107 and map; J. A. Mason, 1940, Table I, p. 83).

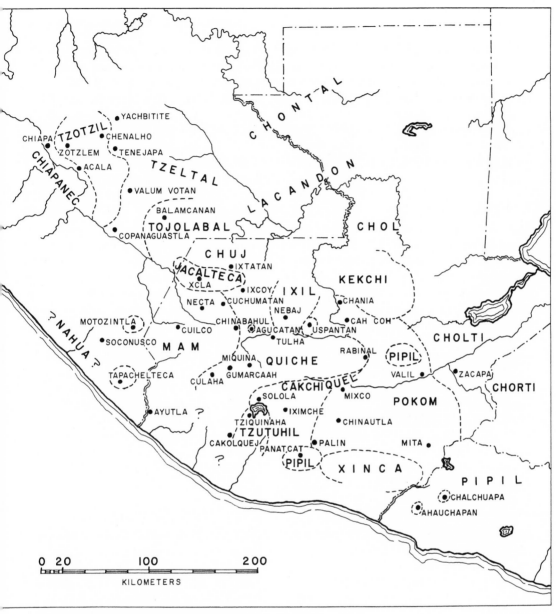

Fig. 1—APPROXIMATE 16TH-CENTURY LINGUISTIC AREAS
Names of towns are Maya as far as can be determined.

that may have been Tapachulteca, as Vivó (1942, p. 156) thinks, or may have had Motozintla affiliations. The early 16th-century demise of many thousands of the Pacific slope and coastal populations prevents easy identification.

That Nahua, or Nahuat, was understood in many urban centers is obvious from the ease with which Alvarado's auxiliary Mexicans communicated with local people in the 16th century. Occasionally, town record books were kept partly in Nahua in postconquest times (Miles, 1957b, pp. 140–42) and early records attest occasional Nahua enclaves such as Petatan in the Cuchumatanes. It appears probable that the first Nahua-speakers, who may have arrived as early as Early Classic times (ca. A.D. 300–

277

600), were reinforced by at least two or three further infusions, the last being the domination of Soconusco under Ahuitzōtl (Jiménez Moreno, 1954–55, p. 235).

Although there is greater cultural community, in general, within a speech area, the districts demarcated linguistically on the map are in no fashion tribal or political units.

SETTLEMENT PATTERN

This protohistoric era, which probably opened about A.D. 1200 (A. L. Smith, 1955, p. 69), saw sweeping change in the location of town sites. The midhighlands valley and slope sites with poor defense qualities were largely abandoned, and new centers on defensible heights or spur plateaus were constructed. In a few cases old sites, well placed for security, were rebuilt with new architectural features that accompanied the general revision in living conditions.

The areas bordering the midhighlands—the Pacific slopes, the high mountain districts of Cuchumatan and Chiapas, and Verapaz—show little variation from earlier locations and less innovation in building styles.

Historically, the new defendable locations can be attributed to the constant state of war that gripped the highlands; the new architectural features, some of which reach several hundred years back in time, are defined by A. L. Smith as Mexican (1955, pp 70–77).

Borhegyi (1956a, p. 105) has suggested that three modern types of town were characteristic of preconquest settlements: (a) dispersed villages, probably a scattered or agglutinated small-house village; (b) compound villages, having a well-defined "plaza" important in commercial life; (c) concourse centers: ceremonial or pilgrimage centers having a small permanent population connected, primarily, with the ceremonial functions of the site.

Documentary and archaeological evidence both confirms and slightly modifies Borhegyi's threefold classification. Sixteenth-century towns such as Iximche and Rabinal in the midhighlands, and Ixtatan in the Cuchumatanes, can be classed with Borhegyi's compound villages, though the term village scarcely is appropriate for the considerable populations accumulated in these locations. A large supporting population was associated with these towns in villages and hamlets and scattered dispersed villages. Small local temples and even ball courts characterize these secondary centers. A major economic difference in preconquest times undoubtedly affected the concentration of population: the steady payment of tribute, both by the immediate supporting population and by peoples under military domination. The resultant patterns for much of the highlands are best expressed by a combination of Willey's Types A and C (1956a, p. 111; Type A houses are packed in close to the ceremonial center, Type C houses are grouped in hamlet or village clusters) for major "capitals," and Types B and C (Type B houses are dotted over the landscape) for pilgrimage or concourse centers.

Features of all late period centers are recognizable temples atop pyramids, small shrines or adoratories, dance platforms for the performance of religious and historical musical dramas, and "long houses" that probably had various functions, as schools for boys sent for temple service, barracks for an elite guard, and storehouses for sacred paraphernalia, arms, and tribute. Such structures may also have served traveling merchants. Ball courts, often associated with very small assemblages, attest the high importance of the game. And, as Borhegyi points out, the plaza concept and the orderly grouping of buildings within and around open spaces is a universal preconquest feature of highland settlements.

Although religious architecture was specialized and well developed, ordinary houses were apparently very simple. None of the house platforms in the vicinity of Cahyup (A. L. Smith, 1955) show surface features and they imply relatively temporary structures.

Sites in the Cuchumatanes are smaller, on the whole, than those of the midhighlands and show a higher frequency of Willey's Type C settlements, which was apparently the prevailing contemporary pattern. The Chiapas mountains are as yet unreported, but extrapolating from modern patterns, Types B and C appear probable in preconquest times. The border marches of Tzotzil towns on the Chiapaneca frontier developed a defensive style according to early Spanish descriptions.

The slopes of Soconusco, Suchitepequez, Cuzcatlan, and Sonsonate lack topographic features for the location of easily fortified town concentrations. Little is yet known of late sites but two, late Abj Takalik and Los Limones below Ayutla, are entirely unfortified. In fact, the rich slopes were prey to any and every marching group, with towns paying tribute now to one conqueror, then another. (See below, Political Systems.)

Much ceremonial activity occurred in caves remote from the religious buildings of the towns. J. E. S. Thompson (1959b) has shown that caves were ancient sites of worship, but the accounts of images in caves by Seler (1901), Recinos (1957, p. 454), Las Casas (1909, p. 466), and Núñez de la Vega (1702) imply that there had been a late development of cave-temples in response to the constant warfare. There is also strong indication that ancestor worship was a focal point of cave ritual.

Economic Base and Trade Relations

The fundamental unit of production and consumption throughout the area was the extended family, which formed a household group. Most of the population was engaged in subsistence agriculture with small surpluses for tribute and trade, and, often, a household specialty such as pottery

production, weaving, mask carving, and weapons making. Areal resources sometimes provided household producers with materials for articles widely traded, but only a small proportion of the population lacked agricultural lands for maize, beans, chile, and turkeys. Slaves and rare artisans —featherworkers, sculptors, and metalworkers—apparently held no agricultural lands. War captains, priests, and rulers certainly depended as much on tribute income as on family lands.

Land tenure is difficult to assess but probably depended on clan and lineage holdings and distribution. Among the Pokom individual families held the same lands through several generations. Since the priesthood was lineage-linked, it is uncertain whether or not there were any lands devoted entirely to temple service. Títulos from all sources indicate the general practice of naming all parcels of land.

Human carriers handled interdistrict and international trade, and, doubtless, the modern pattern of individual householders handling their own produce was a feature of ancient commerce.

Three major products of the highlands and two of the Pacific slopes were of high importance in both local and interareal trade. In the highlands salt, jade, and quetzal feathers figured prominently; on the slopes cacao and cotton were major items. In local terms, pottery, copal production, obsidian, and grinding stones were exchanged. A major item from foreign sources was copper for axes from Mexico via Tehuantepec (Las Casas, 1909, p. 623). Woven goods were bought in Guatemala from Tentitlan (Castañeda, 1581).

The rich cacao and cotton production of the Pacific slopes figured largely in Mexican interest in Soconusco and Guatemala and in the wars for immediate domination. Quiche, Cakchiquel, Tzutuhil and Pipil groups contested tribute in cacao, and created and broke alliances with each other in apparent attempt to control the great

279

chocolate-producing areas. In the east a more quiet international trade network disposed of the cacao and cotton of the Pokom, Kekchi, and Chol (Scholes and Roys, 1948).

The big products of the Chiapas highlands were *pabuchil,* amber, and feathers which funneled through Tzotzil hands at Zotzlem (Zinacantan) to Chiapanecas and Mexica (Blom, 1959). Salt springs near Zotzlem were so valuable that the Chiapaneca were constantly fighting to retain control (Ximénez, 1929–31, 1: 360).

KINSHIP SYSTEMS

True for all societies in the area, a statement from Pokom describes the status of an orphan: "A man who is upright like a post, with no sons, nor relatives; a man alone like a dead tree without leaves or branches, who has no one" (Miles, 1957b, p. 757). The opposite is "man with many relatives and comrades with whom no one would fight" (*ibid.*).

In an important recent study Carrasco (1959) analyzed the clan-lineage structure of the closely related and often allied Quiche-Cakchiquel peoples. Carrasco drew on early Spanish reports and on the great native chronicles, the Popol Vuh, the Annals of the Cakchiquel, and the history of Don Juan Torres.

In Quiche three great groups, the Nima Quiche, the Tamub and the Ilocab, were subdivided into phratries (four in Quiche proper) and moieties (the Tamub and Ilocab), with a varying number of clans (*nimha,* great houses) in each subdivision. The system was an expanding one, easily adapted to a growing population and a program of conquest and colonization.

Territorial units prior to the expansion were apparently expressed in the word *chinamit,* which was both equated with *nimha* in several documents and defined as an actual civic-religious center, implying that each clan lived in a particular area associated with a town site which the Span-

iards described as "fortified and crowded." Carrasco points out (1959, p. 4) that in new settlements, called *calpul,* in the Juan Torres document, members of both moieties of Tamub were included, so that the territorial unity of clan groups was no longer intact.

The Annals of the Cakchiquel (Recinos and Goetz, 1953) the Historia de los Xpantzay (Berlin, 1950), and a tribute list for Solola (Carrasco, 1959, p. 5) indicate that the Cakchiquel of Iximche Solola were organized in groups similar to the Quiche. Four major groups, the Zotziles, Tukuches, Cakchiqueles, and Akajales, were subdivided into clans and lineages of unknown numbers.

In the east Rabinal was a principal town. Though their speech was a Quiche dialect, Rabinal Achi (Brasseur de Bourbourg, 1862), there was a strong Cakchiquel element, and Rabinal was at odds with the Quiche of Gumaarcah. At times, and perhaps permanently, Rabinal was allied as one related people with Iximche (Recinos, 1957, p. 147). The number of divisions and clans is uncertain but it included the Rabinaleb, the Zamaneb, the Chacachib, and the Chacahome.

The Pokom in Alta and Baja Verapaz and south were in retreat before Quiche assault. They lacked, apparently, the large phratry and moiety groups, though patriclans and lineages were characteristic of both north and south (Miles, 1957b, pp. 756–60).

Data are most scanty for Ixil, Chuj, and Jacalteca. Slight indication of clan and lineage organization suggests that there was probably general similarity of organization. Certainly all had patrilateral units. Among the Mam, a 17th-century lexicon (Reynoso, 1644) and current data (Miles, field notes, 1955–59) indicate clan-territorial units, with internal lineage structures.

In Chiapas, Guiteras Holmes' modern studies of Tzeltal (1947) and Tzotzil (1960) societies provide a basis for extrapolation. Guiteras found a strict clan exogamy and wide, nonlocal distribution of clans. The equivalent of calpul, *culibal* in Cancuc, is territorial and endemic, suggesting a situation like the new conquest settlements of the Tamub. There were, for instance, four clans in Cancuc, each with a cave association (Guiteras Holmes, 1947, p. 1), and organized as moieties, apparently (*ibid.*, p. 6). Lineages are landowning units.

In examination of Tzotzil towns, Guiteras Holmes (ca. 1960) found a similar lineage, clan, territorial arrangement with variations, and an extremely important feature —a shift from an Omaha type kinship terminology toward a strongly generational structure. In her investigation the term for mother's brother was strongest in resisting shift, where other lineage terms had yielded entirely.

Kinship terminology from much of highland Guatemala was apparently moving away from strong linear emphasis of an Omaha type in the 16th century. The fragmentary dictionary and documentary data are inadequate, at this point, for full analysis. Quiche and Cakchiquel terms may have suffered modification in the course of Mexicanization so evident in other aspects of their culture. There is a scattering of Mexican lineage and personal names with highest frequency among the Tzutuhil, who were often allied with coastal Pipil. The Pokom and Mam terms, so far as information goes, hint at linearity. If Guiteras' construction is correct (and there is no current evidence to oppose it), then a general highland Maya structure of patri-clans and lineages of Omaha type were probably widespread, with possible exception of the expansionist Quiche-Cakchiquel who had modified descriptive systems.

Further terminological features for all highland Maya were emphasis on relative age and careful sex distinction. Many of the same terms, or their linguistic cognates, were widely employed.

On a general base of Spanish complaints and extension of modern practice, plural marriage was customary whenever a man could afford it. The levirate and sororate operated; and men, generally, as a product of temple and war service, married late (after 25) and suffered institutional homosexual servitude to elder residents in both temple and warrior's establishments. In the Alta Verapaz fathers lectured their sons about avoiding such entanglements (Las Casas, 1909, p. 627), but in Tzotlem (Ximénez, 1929–31, 1: 360) fathers obtained young boys for their sons in temple houses.

Fundamental to the varied groups, however, was the extended household. With or without plural wives, this unit was the basic social and economic group. Attached people included members of two or three generations and, clearly, on occasion four. A long house or compound of several small structures housed a patriarch, his wives, male children married or unmarried, unmarried female children, grandchildren, impoverished relatives of any generation and a few slaves and/or servants (landless poor). This group supported, and were provided for by, the head of household in a self-subsistent unit which contributed tribute or tax toward the maintenance of the lineage and clan chiefs, and who participated in special crisis expenses of marriage and death. As far as evidence goes, marriage was ordinarily a clan problem, settled with lineage approval and carrying the obligation of bride-price or temporary matrilocal service.

Class lines clearly crosscut clans and, in some cases, lineages, where lineage heads, by virtue of age, prowess, and accumulated knowledge, rose above a general status. Specialized information was apparently restricted to particular upper-class groups (such as histories, knowledge of writing) and, of course, the priesthoods proper. Many ordinary men served temple needs, but few were schooled in actual detail of ritual and secret (Las Casas, 1909, p. 618). To a much lower degree, craft information was also lineage property, as it is today, metal tech-

nique, pottery making and weaving specialties, and carving.

Warfare and hunting were open to all,
but top positions were a prerogative of the
sons of the ruling families. The Quiche
captain Tecum Uman, who perished in the
Spanish conquest and who is still celebrated, is an excellent example. The con-
tending warrior princes of the Rabinal Achi
are obvious additions. The privilege of pre-
siding over one of the historical or religious
dance-dramas was probably also restricted
to members of a leading lineage, though
actual participation, like warfare, was open
to all who had skill and could afford the
expenses of sacrifices, time away from other
work, and costume preparation.

The situation on the Pacific slopes was
very fluid. Pipil groups had long established hold over some of the cacao lands,
perhaps as early as A.D. 600–650. J. E. S.
Thompson summarizes the 16th-century
sources (1948, pp. 11–15). The general clan-
barrio system of calpulli may have been a
part of the earliest emigré social organization but possibly was a modified later system (*Pipil* is a conquest-period term, and
the late rather unreliable Spanish sources
do not distinguish between early groups
and the late 15th to 13th century Mexica
who maintained communication with the
Valley of Mexico.) Hereditary offices and a
patrilateral organization are clear, however, in the early 16th-century sources.

Pipil were surely conquerors and mixed
with a varied and unknown coastal population. Their four-part ruler-captain system, calendar, and possibly kinship were
adopted by the three groups with whom
they intermarried, Quiche, Cakchiquel, and
Tzutuhil.

POLITICAL SYSTEMS AND STATES

Montezuma was so concerned about the
Spaniards in the Caribbean that he sent
urgent messages to the people of coastal
Guatemala and the Cakchiquel. The messages were acted upon by Soconusco and

Iximche. Soconusco had been sending semi-
annual tribute to Tenochtitlan for almost
40 years and the Tzutuhil and Cakchiquel
had intermarried, had treaties, and fought
with the Nahua of the Pacific slopes.

These three groups (Quiche, Cakchiquel,
and Tzutuhil) had been closely allied but
broke apart with the revolt instigated by
Quicab's sons against his tyranny. There is
some question as to which Quicab (there
were at least two) was at fault. Meanwhile,
separatist groups, such as the Rabinal,
were jealous of the territory they had won
and entirely opposed to Quiche domination
from Gumaarcah.

The marches, guarded and defended in
steady warfare by the Quiche state,
stretched from Joyabah to Quezaltenango
and the borders of Huehuetenango. Tribute
imposed after successful raids was drawn
from many coastal towns. The Tamub
branch claim credit for much of the success
against the people of the Pacific slope
(Recinos, 1957, pp. 71–94). Rabinal contested the claims of Quiche to Ixil, Nebaj,
and Chajul (Rabinal Achi). But both Pokom and Mam on the eastern and western
flanks of the Gumaarcah state yielded territory and towns.

It is clear that much of the warfare had
its roots in economic need or greed. The
land- and tribute-hungry Quiche and Cakchiquel colonized conquered territory and
subjected the former owners to adject servitude. The salt springs at Tulha (Sacapulas)
became the Quiche rulers' private property
and were operated by gangs of captive
Cakchiquel and former Mam lords.

There is some evidence that a Mam
group fought both Rabinal and Quiche interests in Ixil country, but the Pokom appear to have withdrawn with a mind to
diplomacy, intermarriage, and alliance,
where profitable, with both Cakchiquel and
potentially hostile Pipil.

Time depth is very difficult to evaluate.
Wauchope (1948a, pp. 29–40; 1949, p. 18),
working three main sites—Gumaarcah, Ix-

imche, and Zacualpa—could not find archaeological coordination earlier than ca. A.D. 1300 between ceramics and genealogical reckoning. Other evidence suggests that the innovations in midhighland culture were Toltec (perhaps A.D. 800) and part of the great dispersals which may have commenced in the Classic period (ca. A.D. 650) with continued subsequent arrivals and steady communication. Calendar and religious revisions demonstrate at least two later waves of powerful groups of Mexicans.

Mexicanization of other highland peoples is less obvious, and there is far less information to draw on.

From Pokom Chama, Memoria Título del Barrio de Santa Ana, 1565, is a statement, "we are seven groups" (clans?), which is a general confirmation that Pokom folk were truly the Vucub Amaq, who were alternately enemies and allies of the Cakchiquel and Quiche.

Pokom politics borrowed terms for war captains from Quiche-Cakchiquel, but there is little evidence that they had more than a hereditary lineage power structure, with a semifeudal granting of land and privilege to high-born and able war captains.

For Jacalteca and Chuj there is only the indication that particular towns were powerful and held surrounding districts subject. Among the Mam-speaking folk, two lineages or clans are mentioned as "chiefly," and individual towns can be singled out as prominent. But all peoples bordering on the militant, expansionist Quiche or Cakchiquel were in retreat and turning toward conservative reaction. Class and lineage prerogatives were more tightly held, and resistance to innovation was entrenched long before the Spaniards' arrival.

Chiapas, Tzentzal, and Tzotzil are very difficult to assess. At Zotzlem (Zinacantan) there was constant pressure from the warring Chiapanecas, and several Mexica attempts to dominate the area were tempo-

rarily successful or were thrown off. Rich in salt and amber and in contact with more highly developed state organizations, the men of Zotzlem kept to a clan and lineage organization through which military chiefs were selected and deposed when unsuccessful (Ximénez, 1929–31, 1: 360).

Questions of organization on a village-town level and the internal handling of regular political and administrative activities are very difficult to answer. Las Casas (1909, p. 624) describes temple service for all boys, supervised by older members and taught by the priests. Apparently, however, the children of rulers, priests, and scribes were early segregated and given special training in keeping with their station as heirs to their fathers' offices. Hereditary occupations and class-linked offices allowed for little mobility, suggesting that Carrasco's thesis (1959) of a preconquest social-political ladder may not hold for much of the highland Maya area.

Most disciplinary problems were handled within kin groups. Serious theft, murder, and adultery were brought before the lord of the town. Appointed market judges and tribute collectors acted in the name of the town lord and may have been drawn largely from his kin. (This outline is a lean and very lame construction, which surely will be revised on detailed study of the manuscript dictionaries known from the mid-highlands.)

Nearly all our information on the 16th-century Pipil of the Pacific slopes is drawn from Fuentes y Guzmán's report (1932–33) based on his knowledge of Sonsonate and its documents.

A late (Toltec?) migration brought a four-captain military system to Nahua peoples already well established on the Pacific slopes. A mild ruler was selected after slaughter of unusually harsh ones, and a different system of councils and committees of noblemen set up. Long military association and intermarriage with the Tzutuhil lasted until reverses in combat with the

Mexica – – – – – – – – – – – – – – Merchants and conquest influences
(A.D. 1300?)

Early Toltec (?) — Quetzalcoatl cult (Tohil phase in
(A.D. 800–900?)   Guatemalan highlands)

                    Quiche-Cakchiquel calendrical shifts (?)

Late Classic period — From Puebla or western Mexico:
(A.D. 600–700)   the Cotzumalhuapa "Pipil"

Early Classic period – – – – – – – – – –Teotihuacan-Esperanza movement
(A.D. 300–600)

Cakchiquel and Quiche forced them into retreat. There is considerable evidence of close association with Pokom towns as well (Miles, 1957b).

Clearly, there were three and possibly four major movements of Nahua-speaking peoples down the Pacific coast. The earliest that can be identified archaeologically is the Early Classic period Teotihuacan group, who may or may not have actually spoken Nahua. The second is close on the heels of this and is well known by a distinctive Cotzumalhuapa style of sculpture. A third movement represents probably the Toltec peoples. The fourth, probably not a movement, was perhaps a series of outthrusts of influences as a result of, or allied with, the empire builders in the valley of Mexico. These thrusts had profound influence among the midhighland Maya peoples, which still await detailed examination. (See Table 1 for suggested chronological schedule.)

GENERAL NOTES ON RELIGION

The early Spaniards in Chiapas and Guatemala were impressed by the diversity of gods and ritual invoked on every occasion of crisis or celebration, and by the rapidity with which good Catholic saints were identified with local deities, demigods, heroes, and spirits. Two special features were especially intriguing: the claimed ability of many Guatemalans to become animals, and

the religious calendar (whose structure is discussed in Article 10).

The Quiche prince-captain, Tecum Uman, died as a quetzal, or an eagle, in the battle with Alvarado. Powerful men had several *nagual* forms which they could become for special purposes. Ordinary people had merely one animal, plant, or natural counterpart whose fate and health were linked as both guardian and prophet with each individual. Among most people of the area a nagual was connected with the day of birth, and was divined by a calendar priest, always called when a child was born.

As each individual had one or more naguals, each household, lineage, and clan had a god or gods who provided particular benefices to devotees. As the prowess of an individual was dependent on his nagual, that of household to clan and town was involved with their gods.

The calendar, with its 20 day lords, or rulers of the days, and 13 numbers, is the most widespread common feature of religion. The 260-day ritual round made by the combination of numbers with day lords had a million uses. It governed divination for finding a lost turkey or commencing a major military expedition. The days and numbers ruled the success of any enterprise and foretold the outcome of plans or illness. An enormous part of religious concern had to do with health, and whether wound or illness were a result of malignant and powerful action by an enemy or were the product of unconfessed sins. Confession was rarely made to a calendar priest but normally to head of household. In the event that a sick person were of high status, slaves of the household, even own sons by slave concubines, were sacrificed to appease angry spirits.

There is strong evidence that at least some of the day lords were actually ancient men who, as legendary heroes were made members of the calendrical roster. Among the highland Maya, the Tzeltal-Tzotzil, Chuj, and Jacalteca substitute *Votan* for the regular third day, Akbal. He is explicitly stated to have been a man who measured the earth (Núñez de la Vega, 1702). He retained the earth-cave association of Akbal and may also have had jaguar attributes.

Possibly the Hunahpu, "one blow-gun hunter," in Quiche mythology and the 20th day for the midhighland peoples was also an ancient hero. At least, his namesakes figure most prominently in early myth (Recinos, Goetz, and Morley, 1950) together with "Small jaguar" (Xbalanque), whom Las Casas (1909, p. 330) reports as an unrequited adventurer in Pokom country and the introducer of human sacrifice.

Sacrifice, in general, seems to have been held to flowers, turkeys, and incense except in extremity. When a very famous opponent was captured, as in the Rabinal Achi, sacrifice was inevitable. Otherwise human sacrifice was rather rare and confined to crises believed to be vital for the health and continued existence of the land and people. The land (each small piece and each spring had its god or "owner") had to be constantly tended with offerings of incense, turkeys, and blood.

The "ancestors," "great mother" and "great father," were everywhere worshipped, although Quiche-Cakchiquel areas gave more prominence to foreign deities. Interestingly, although still inexplicably, the "ancestors" were identified with partic-

ular caves near towns. The Pokom, Quiche, Cakchiquel, and the Chiapas Maya shared an ancestral cave association which involved seven caves in which people themselves originated. In the Cuchumatanes the number was reduced to one, and at death the soul retired via the cave to live in the interior of the earth.

Las Casas (1909, p. 466) describes towns that had placed their idols in remote areas and caves, and the Popol Vuh reports the sad circumstance of having to seat their gods in ravines.

The cold windy peaks of the mountains were all sacred, but particular mountains were gods of great power and the objects of long pilgrimages. Quiche, Cakchiquel and Tzutuhil peoples awaited the dawn, each on its sacred mountain. In the Cuchumatanes each town had an especially sacred peak, one of four that supported earth and sky simultaneously (Miles, field notes). The directional color associations differed from the 16th-century Yucatec in placing green, not yellow, to the south (confirming a suggestion by J. E. S. Thompson, 1950, p. 112). Red was east; white, north; and black, west.

Rituals, as Las Casas points out (1909, pp. 465–66), were of two sorts, public and private. Public festivals were set by the calendar and varied in number and time from one area to another. The gods were dressed richly and carried in procession with trumpets and drums from the temples to the town ball court. The actual days of fiesta were preceded by a period of general fasting and continence.

Las Casas does not describe the ball game itself, nor the dance-dramas that were regular features of many celebrations. The dramas were sometimes historical, commemorating a victory, like the Rabinal Achi; frequently they were the re-enactment of an important myth such as the Deer Dance.

On at least one occasion (Recinos and Goetz, 1953, p. 102) Quiche war ritual included carrying their god into battle, and defeat led to his capture.

In some places, according to Las Casas (1909, p. 466), the high priest fasted and sacrificed his blood in a little hut remote in the mountains, praying for the town and atoning for the peoples' sins. At times of great danger the fast lasted nearly a year.

Private rituals accompanied every life crisis and each step in the practice of agriculture. Incense, birds for sacrifice, flowers, and a jug of liquor were necessary ritual equipment. Ordóñez y Aguiar (1907, note 24) reports a recipe for fermented drink of terrible strength, including a live frog to hasten the fermentation.

Religious observance of crises in the lives of the ruler and his family transformed normally private ritual into public ceremony. The most spectacular were funerals. Las Casas (1909, pp. 629–31) describes the building of the tomb and the sacrifice of slaves and dogs to accompany the dead lord. Tombs became sites of worship, especially if the dead man had been known as just and wise.

The gods were not organized into anything like a pantheon but were creators of earth-sky and life and "owners" or patrons of natural phenomena and of activities. They were roughly ranked in terms of their ascribed power and its extent. The "owner" of a small spring controlled the local flow of water, and, if he were malignant the water might sicken drinkers. The lord of the winds and rains was the special god of Gumaarcah and appealed to by all. Votan, apparently in jaguar guise, was the great lord for some of the Tzeltal.

The sun and moon, Venus, several stars, and constellations were generally known as gods. The concept of local lords of mountains and day lords capable of communicat-

ing and interceding with these celestial powers was widespread. Quiche, Cakchiquel, and Tzutuhil show strong Mexicanization in this and explicitly identify their god with Quetzalcoatl and name a class of priests, the Yaqui sacrificers and Toltecat. In fact the coastal Pipil were called "Yaqui" by the highlanders.

Probably on an earlier level the deer cult, prominent in the western mountains, is reminiscent of Cora-Huichol ideas and of the Cotzumalhuapa and Late Classic sculpture at Cotzumalhuapa.

The Pipil proper are reported to have worshipped the sun, primarily, together with Quetzalcoatl and Itzqueye and a hunting god. Sacrifice of men was apparently far more frequent than among the highlanders.

The personnel of religion were highly specialized; even the simple calendar priest, who divined and cured, needed years of study. The sons of high priests commenced education for their hereditary offices early in life, as did scribes and painters. (Las Casas, 1909, p. 618, and Núñez de la Vega, 1702, describe calendrical and historical codices.) In some areas the high priest and the ruler were one and the same individual, but usually the ruler was primarily a military leader. Since the gods' approval was essential for any public enterprise, the high priest was a man of great political power, who could well control many of the activities of the actual ruler.

The number and grades of lower-level temple personnel cannot be assessed but probably varied greatly according to the size and number of shrines. The bottom ranks were boys, resident in long houses associated with the temples, sent to be educated and to work as temple servants.

REFERENCES

Berlin, 1950
Blom, 1959
Borhegyi, 1956a
Brasseur de Bourbourg, 1862
Breton, 1917
Carrasco, 1959, 1961
Castañeda, 1581
Chonay and Goetz, 1953
Fuentes y Guzmán, 1932–33
Dieseldorff, 1903
Guiteras Holmes, 1947, 1960
Jiménez Moreno, 1954–55
Johnson, F., 1940
Las Casas, 1909
Leon, 1907
McQuown, 1956
Mason, J. A., 1940
Memoria Título de Santa Ana, 1565

Miles, 1957b
Núñez de la Vega, 1702
Ordóñez y Aguiar, 1907
Paso y Troncoso, 1905
Recinos, 1957
—— and Goetz, 1953
——, ——, and Morley, 1950
Reynosa, 1644
Scholes and Roys, 1948
Seler, 1901
Smith, A. L., 1955
Swadesh, 1954–55
Thompson, J. E. S., 1948, 1950, 1959b
Vivó, 1942
Wauchope, 1948a, 1949
Willey, 1956a
Ximénez, 1929–31

12. Archaeology and Prehistory in the Northern Maya Lowlands: an Introduction

E. WYLLYS ANDREWS

THE NORTHERN Maya lowlands are separated from the Maya lowlands of the south by a line running from the Caribbean coast of northern British Honduras, across the Crown colony, along the northern frontier of the Department of Peten in Guatemala, and then directly across to the Laguna de Terminos of the Bay of Campeche in Mexico. Although it has long been recognized that these northern lowlands contained the buried remains of all that connected Maya culture, after the south had been abandoned, with the new and overpowering culture of the invaders from Spain, the Yucatan Peninsula has remained as "'somewhat apart" to many Maya archaeologists. It was at first defined as a "New Empire," an archaeological zone colonized by refugees from the break-up of the southern cities. When this concept became untenable and evidence accumulated that people had been living on the entire peninsula for a long time, Yucatan still was denied a status comparable to the south. The word "Classic" was applied to Maya culture allegedly dominated by and ending with the collapse of the "Old Em-

pire" cities. According to these interpretations, Yucatan remained "provincial" or, at best, "peripheral." For 40 years of archaeological research this outlook prevailed, and work in the northern region was concentrated entirely on the decadent phases which led to the collapse of Maya civilization not long before the Spaniards arrived. In this view, all that was intellectually or aesthetically admirable belonged to the south, and scholars mournfully traced its degeneration in the north.[1]

As we examine the new and much longer cultural sequence which emerges, however, we find ourselves unable to express our conclusions in terms of the cultural

[1] Except for those credited elsewhere, the illustrations have been drawn from material I am now preparing for publication. The work at Mayapan, Acanceh, Yaxcopoil, and Sihunchen, and the beginning stages at Dzibilchaltun were done in 1941–42 for Carnegie Institution of Washington; the East Coast material was gathered in 1955–56 for the Middle American Research Institute at Tulane University. The data on Dzibilchaltun are drawn largely from Tulane's present program of research at the site under auspices of the National Geographic Society, the National Science Foundation, and the American Philosophical Society.

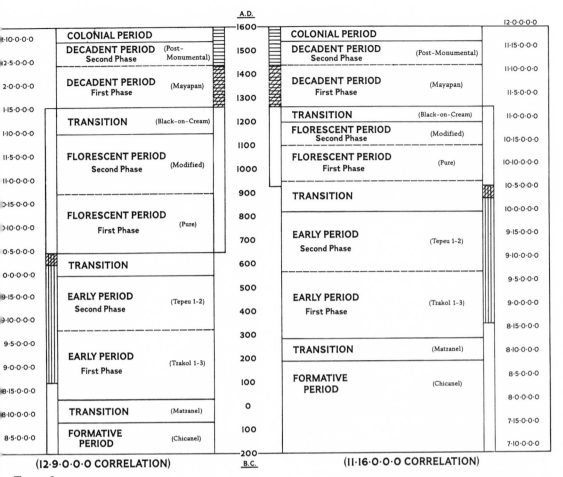

(12·9·0·0·0 CORRELATION)	A.D.		(11·16·0·0·0 CORRELATION)
13·10·0·0·0	1600	12·0·0·0·0	
	COLONIAL PERIOD	COLONIAL PERIOD	11·15·0·0·0
12·5·0·0·0	DECADENT PERIOD (Post-Monumental) — Second Phase	DECADENT PERIOD (Post-Monumental) — Second Phase	
	1500		
	1400		11·10·0·0·0
12·0·0·0·0	DECADENT PERIOD (Mayapan) First Phase	DECADENT PERIOD (Mayapan) First Phase	
	1300		11·5·0·0·0
11·15·0·0·0			
	TRANSITION (Black-on-Cream)	TRANSITION (Black-on-Cream)	11·0·0·0·0
	1200	FLORESCENT PERIOD (Modified) Second Phase	
11·10·0·0·0	FLORESCENT PERIOD (Modified) Second Phase		10·15·0·0·0
	1100		
11·5·0·0·0		FLORESCENT PERIOD (Pure) First Phase	10·10·0·0·0
	1000		
11·0·0·0·0			10·5·0·0·0
	900	TRANSITION	
10·15·0·0·0			10·0·0·0·0
	800		
10·10·0·0·0	FLORESCENT PERIOD (Pure) First Phase	EARLY PERIOD (Tepeu 1–2) Second Phase	9·15·0·0·0
	700		9·10·0·0·0
10·5·0·0·0			
	600		
10·0·0·0·0	TRANSITION		9·5·0·0·0
	500		
9·15·0·0·0	EARLY PERIOD (Tepeu 1–2) Second Phase	EARLY PERIOD (Tzakol 1–3) First Phase	9·0·0·0·0
	400		
9·10·0·0·0			8·15·0·0·0
	300		
9·5·0·0·0		TRANSITION (Matzanel)	8·10·0·0·0
	200		
9·0·0·0·0	EARLY PERIOD (Tzakol 1–3) First Phase	FORMATIVE PERIOD (Chicanel)	8·5·0·0·0
	100		
8·15·0·0·0			8·0·0·0·0
	0		
8·10·0·0·0	TRANSITION (Matzanel)		7·15·0·0·0
	100		
8·5·0·0·0	FORMATIVE PERIOD (Chicanel)		7·10·0·0·0
	200 B.C.		

TABLE 1

taxonomies of the past. We are therefore obliged to create new terms to describe cultural evolution in our area. As we see it, these neither violate nor invalidate conclusions founded on concentrated and capable research in the southern area. But we do believe they are mandatory to accommodate new and now amply documented evidence regarding evolution of human culture in the area as a whole.

These new schematics are outlined in Table 1, in which the center column gives dates in our own chronology and the columns on either side summarize the developmental periods in terms of the two most widely known and used correlations of European and Maya calendars.[2] It will be noted that the zones connected by vertical shading are fixed with reasonable certainty in the Maya Long Count; those joined by horizontal shading are fixed in our own calendar. Adjacent segments less certainly fixed in the two calendars are cross-lined with diagonal shading. The length of the completely unshaded areas between is the determinant in choice of a correlation of the two calendars. Divergences from previously used nomenclatures will be explained in the pertinent sections below.

[2] Ed. note: The 11.16.0.0.0 correlation is frequently referred to as the Goodman-Martínez-Thompson correlation; the 12.9.0.0.0 correlation is associated with the name of Spinden.

289

Geographic and Cultural Subdivisions

The Peninsula of Yucatan, lying entirely within the tropics, is a recent limestone formation stretching due north from the older geological structures of the Cordillera in Guatemala, hilly at its base, completely flat in the north. There is a gradual increase in rainfall from north to south, and also from west to east. Beyond the coast itself and the coastal fringes of partially to wholly inundated swampland, there are no ecological zones which have been demonstrated to be valid factors in human cultural development. It remains to be determined to what extent the low brush country of densely inhabited northwestern Yucatan and the higher forests of sparsely inhabited Quintana Roo and southern Campeche are the result of different climate, or of different intensity of slash-and-burn agriculture, which in the north has continuously prevented the forest from reaching climax phase. The entire area was one of high fertility. Agronomists have demonstrated that even in the bleak-looking and thin-soiled northeast, enough corn could be grown to support the average Maya family in 48 man-days of labor per year—ideal conditions for the development of higher culture.

Various parts of the peninsula developed distinctive cultural traditions at one time or another, and local area names (such as Puuc, Chenes) were unfortunately assigned to these often short-lived manifestations, which were again confused with periods of time. As our knowledge increases, we find an increasing homogeneity of culture over the entire area; and these deviant forms appear more strongly as variants within a single period than as geographic traditions with any extended validity. It will be noted that in our suggested taxonomy, we completely avoid geographic names. And our descriptions will be by periods rather than by areas.

The Problem of Early Man

The Paleo-Indian in Mesoamerica remains a thing apart from the advanced agriculturist who, appearing on the stage of history many thousand years after the disappearance of his hunting predecessors, laid the foundations for higher civilizations to follow.

No trace of preceramic culture has yet been identified in the Maya lowlands. This is strange. I feel it must reflect the lack of proper exploration in most of the area, for, in comparison to the barren and often cold plateau of central Mexico where Tepexpan man was found, this was indeed a Garden of Eden. The coastal portions, particularly, would have been little short of ideal habitat for people on the hunting and gathering stage. During two seasons' work on the Quintana Roo coast, a five-year-old child daily supplied our whole labor force with fish, rarely spending more than an hour with his bit of string and bent pin. The waters were crawling with edible crustaceans, notably lobster; edible mollusks, including the large and tasty conch, and the octopus were abundant. The forests were stocked with game: deer, peccary, monkey, and a variety of game birds. At many times of the year, fresh fruit was available in the trees. There is no reason to assume that nature would have been less bountiful 5,000 or 10,000 years ago; and it is hard to believe that this paradise could have been missed by the Paleo-Indian in his migrations.

The obvious thing to look for in a search for ancient man on the coast is shell heaps —for this rich source of food would almost certainly have been used—but shell heaps of such antiquity seem notably lacking. Here the geologists complicate our picture. One group informs us that during the many thousands of years involved the polar ice caps have melted sufficiently to raise the sea level as much as hundreds of feet, so that remains of coastal ancients of this period would now be under water far out to sea. Others tell us that the limestone shelf of Yucatan is slowing rising from the sea, pointing out, for example, that the northern coastal fringe of lagoons and marshy shore is almost surely of late quaternary formation. Therefore, Paleo-Indian sites must be sought farther inland, not on the present coast.

Inland, particularly on the flat northern plain, caves and cenotes, especially water caves, is a likely place to search for ancient man, but excavation and exploration of scores of caverns since the turn of the century have produced not a single indication of really early habitation. Archaeological investigations by divers in the Cenote Xlacah at Dzibilchaltun (Andrews, 1959; Marden, 1959) were carried beyond a point otherwise warranted in the faint hope of encountering some trace of early man at the base of the rich sediments there. Again, the result was completely negative.

A final approach, which has proved useful in the United States, is to enlist the aid of the amateur, informing him of the types of artifacts to be expected and situations where they might occur. Virtually all the larger estates in Yucatan have collections of antiquities, continuously added to as daily operations encounter the ever-present remains of the ancients. Unfortunately, however, the usual collector has been so spoiled by the abundant, showy, and often very beautiful artifacts of the later periods that he has not even saved items like bits of chipped flint or worked bone. It is doubtful that such collections not yet examined by specialists will contain relics of this primitive past epoch.

In short, it is difficult to believe that ancient man failed entirely to inhabit the Yucatan Peninsula, yet no relics have been found to indicate his existence there, and we may have to wait a long time until the first discoveries of this nature are made.

"FORMATIVE" CULTURES

The advanced agriculturalists mentioned above appeared on the Mesoamerican scene roughly 4,000 years ago, leaving behind them an enormous gap in cultural evolution. The fully documented transitions from hunter to agriculturalist, from paleolithic to neolithic industries, and from nomad to settled village-dweller are still to be found—and with them the origins of agriculture, of plastic arts whose products compare favorably with anything made later in the area, and of advanced social and political institutions necessary to accommodate the vastly increased interaction and interdependence among individuals.

The basic framework of these so-called "Formative" cultural developments was worked out in the southern lowlands and is described in more detail in other articles in this *Handbook*.[3] The ceramic remains were relatively scanty and in only one slightly questionable case (Str. E-VIIsub, Uaxactun) were they associated with architecture. On the Yucatan Peninsula, Formative remains were recognized only in more recent times. Brainerd (1951, 1958) defined three stages. "Early Formative" was defined by only a single form of jar from a single location (Mani Cenote "pattern burnished ware"), which he noted was similar to the very early Las Charcas level in the Guatemalan highlands. His "Middle Formative," only very briefly described before his death from collections at Santa Rosa Xtampak and Dzibilnocac in the Chenes, is not yet identified in the north. The "Late Formative" appeared at the bottom of the stratigraphic trenches at a large number of widely scattered sites in Yucatan and in the Chenes and Rio Bec areas of Campeche. Similar material was found by Sanders (1960a) at Tancah and Leona Vicario and

[3] Ed. note: See Willey, Ekholm, and Millon, Article 14, volume 1, for a discussion on Formative or Preclassic cultures.

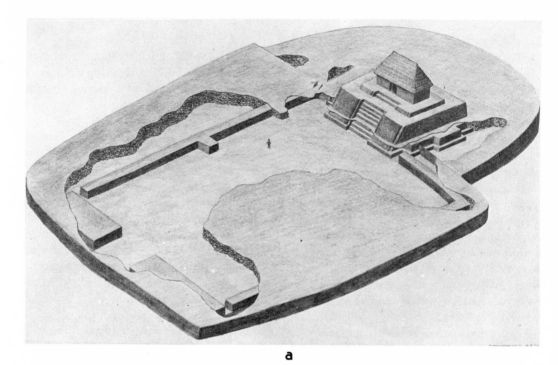

a

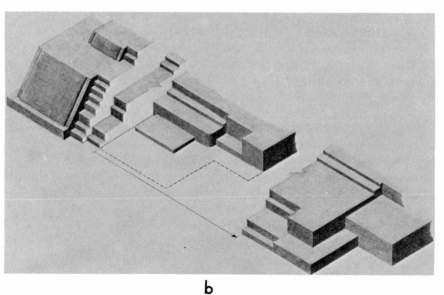

b

Fig. 1—STR. 450, DZIBILCHALTUN. *a,* Final construction stages probably date to last half of first millennium B.C. Reconstruction of thatch-roofed building atop is conjectural, based largely on better-preserved contemporaneous structures nearby. *b,* Cut-away drawing showing three directly superimposed structures which form the basis of this long Formative stratigraphy. Final structure (extreme left) is that which, with its flanking walls and courtyard, is shown buried beneath the larger last terrace in *a.* (Drawings by George E. Stuart.)

by me (*in* Proskouriakoff, 1957a) at Xcaret, Quintana Roo.[4] At most of these sites this early pottery occurs as refuse at the base of the stratigraphic trenches or pits. It was not found in pure samples and was not associated with architecture. Yaxuna, however, was an exception. Two of Brainerd's trenches in Str. 8, a very large mound, produced only "Late Formative" pottery, indicating that the mound itself was probably datable to that period. There is also evidence that inner portions of the large acropolis at Acanceh are of similar age (fig. 4).

The most abundant evidence regarding Formative culture in the Lowland Maya Area has been produced so recently that its analysis at present can be only extremely tentative. At Dzibilchaltun in northwestern Yucatan, a site frequently mentioned below, work was started during the 1959–60 field season on a large series of Formative structures which must have represented an impressive concentration of population. Identification of these early monuments was ironically facilitated by abundant cuts in the mounds made by stone robbers, who had been exploiting the area for many years. It was noted early in the work that a surprising number of these refuse-rich sections contained pure Formative pottery. Scores of structures were thus located, varying from simple house platforms through tall pyramid-temples to massive acropolis-like aggregations with buildings on several levels.

A preliminary excavation by John Feistel disclosed a house mound (Str. 226) built and added to three times during the Formative, then continuously occupied during the first and possibly into the second phase of the Early period. The base of this stratigraphy is secured by a radiocarbon determination of 310±80 B.C. Preliminary analysis of the 35,000 sherds produced indicates a mixture of Late Formative wares and forms which seem to be developmental of the traditions of the Early period to follow.

In another part of the site, Robert Funk excavated the small temple complex (Str. 450) illustrated in figure 1. A 4-m.-high platform had steep staircase and sloping, rounded balustrades on either side. An unvaulted stone-walled structure on the small secondary terrace was reached by two further stairs. Both platform and structure wall were of heavy block masonry, all blocks horizontally laid, so that the rounded edges and sloping face of the balustrades were achieved by modeling a very thick layer of stucco. The stucco bore no evidence of carved decoration. In front of the structure was a large courtyard, enclosed by very asymmetrical thick walls terminating in two masonry platforms, which probably supported structures of perishable material. The wall masonry was much like that in later Early period structures, but the retaining walls of some of the large terrace areas were of crude slabs of bedrock laid sidewise in mud mortar (fig. 2,*a,b*), different from anything built later at the site.

On excavation the temple illustrated turned out to be the third in a series of three completely superimposed structures. The entire courtyard and lower reaches of the third structure were finally buried under a greatly enlarged terrace (fig. 1,*b*). The four major structural periods contained 16 substantial ceramic components in firm sequence, each sealed by well-preserved plaster floors. This would seem to indicate a long history of occupation, but actually the 14 separate phases of construction may have been either very long or very short.

The group was abandoned before the end of the "Formative," as no later pottery appeared even on the surface. Preliminary analysis of the pottery and a C14 date of 240 B.C.±90 in association with the ninth structural phase indicate that this stratigraphy does, however, overlap the base of that at Str. 226. All Str. 450 ceramics

---

[4] Cf. also, R. E. Smith, 1955a; Smith and Gifford, 1959.

Fig. 2—LATE FORMATIVE MASONRY, STR. 450, DZIBILCHALTUN. *a (above),* Terrace wall. *b (below),* Building wall.

seem to fall roughly within the periods corresponding to Chicanel in the Peten and Chiapa de Corzo IV and V. But mixed in as refuse material in the lower reaches of the stratigraphy was an increasing body of distinctive (and finer) pottery much more closely resembling the Peten Mamom and Chiapa III, never in pure samples but abundantly.

At Str. 605, one of a group of about 25 ruined structures at the southwest corner of the site, William Moore carried stratigraphy back to include the earliest identified ceramic material. Five major construction stages emerged, divided into 15 substages in firm sequence, each accompanied by large ceramic samples. Stage I consisted of simple platforms with stuccoed mud walls, and small round houses with mud walls and thatched roofs. Associated with these was the early pottery mentioned above as mixed in the early Str. 450 refuse, and a C14 date of 975 B.C. ± 340.[4a] In Stage II, still during the prevalence of Mamom-like pottery, house construction changed to crudely cut and coursed stone block masonry, the platforms increased in size and were faced with masonry.

During Stage III at Str. 605, the stone dwelling units were either buried or removed, and the platform was enlarged and reoriented 180 degrees to face the south edge of a small paved plaza surrounded by tall platforms, in one case with a terraced façade. At this time, the group was obviously converted from a dwelling site to a ceremonial or administrative center. Generally, this early monumental architecture at the site, as at Strs. 605 and 450, is associated with pottery equivalent to the Chicanel phase in the Peten and to Chiapa IV and V.

[4a] LJ=505. The La Jolla dates, distinct from others, have 100 years added to the standard 1-sigma deviation "in order to include consideration of uncertainties in calibration, the drift in sensitivity of background, and other fluctuating factors" (Hobbs, Bien, and Suess, 1963, p. 254).

Fɪɢ. 3—"PRE-MAYA" (FORMATIVE PERIOD) SHELL MIDDEN, ISLA CANCUEN. Possibly a campsite where marine mollusks and turtles supplemented the diet of fish, birds, and local mammals. Tentative C14 dating on midden shells is 130 ʙ.ᴄ. ± 150. (Photo by E. W. Andrews.)

Many of the centers grew to striking size. Str. 500 began as a group of mounds resembling Str. 605 and surrounding separate units, which finally merged to form an acropolis of 70 by 110 m., with courts and plazas on different levels, some as much as 8 m. above ground.

Our knowledge of the antecedents of Maya civilization is still meager, but preliminary examination of the new Dzibilchaltun material has given some valuable clues. The first apparent horizon (Mamom–Chiapa III equivalent), starting roughly 800–1200 ʙ.ᴄ. and possibly earlier, is characterized by mud-walled houses and platforms, which later gave way to stone masonry. (Doubtless here, as in all later periods, many of the domestic structures were of completely perishable material.) Although large ceremonial construction has not been found, and the remains should

probably be assigned to what Wauchope (1950) refers to as "Village Formative" (Middle Formative in this volume), there was nothing primitive in the material culture of these people. The pottery was equal, if not superior, to anything produced later in this area. A second apparent horizon (Chicanel–Chiapa IV-V equivalent), which will probably be divided into two or more stages as analyses proceed, saw the development of massive architectural aggregations, which indicated a greatly increased complexity of social and (probably) religious organization. This culture had reached Wauchope's "Urban Formative" stage (Late Formative in this volume). The pottery of the horizon is distinctive, but inferior to that which came before. A final development began in the 3d century ʙ.ᴄ. The "Chicanel-like" pottery went through a marked coarsening and deterior-

295

ation of form and disappeared, while simultaneously there appeared new wares and shapes that seemed for the first time to be clearly ancestral to the Early period pottery which followed. These last developments may well have been accompanied by a similar decadence and disappearance of the earlier ceremonial architecture, as they have been associated only with simple house-platforms such as Strs. 225 and 226 at Dzibilchaltun.

More generally, we are left with the strong impression of the rise and fall of a distinctive earlier *non-Maya* culture in the first millennium before Christ, lacking any of the diagnostics of Maya culture and having radically different and apparently unrelated pottery. This earlier culture was much more widespread in Guatemala and southern Mexico than the Maya culture that followed. Some component sites such as Chiapa de Corzo are outside the area of later domination of Maya culture. Even within the Maya lowlands, the pottery of the area as a whole is much more homogeneous than that which came later when the area separated into the differing sub-areas of true Maya civilization. Only in the 3d century B.C., following an apparent decadence of this earlier culture, did traits appear which seem ancestral to the first truly Maya pottery—and this last phase should perhaps be regarded as a transition rather than a horizon of its own. Except for this last phase, there seems little apparent reason to call this earlier material Formative. A properly descriptive term, free of this unfortunate connotation, should be coined.

EARLY PERIOD

Sometime not long after the start of the Christian Era, two new ingredients were added to the previously generalized cultural remains of the Formative, to give rise to what we know as Maya civilization. The first of these, and the most striking, was the appearance of major sculpture in stone. Through its medium appeared the Maya hieroglyphic writing with its calendric, astronomic, and religious data, and through it we are suddenly introduced to the ceremonial and socio-political data reflected in the carvings. These had all existed before, surely, because they appear in advanced form and must have had a long developmental history. But previously, if recorded at all, such chronicles must have been on perishable materials such as fiber or wood. At roughly the same time, the characteristic corbeled vault of the Maya appeared, enabling the architects to make sudden and impressive advances in their ceremonial and civil construction.

After this explosive transition, probably much more sudden in the preserved remains than in the culture itself, there was a period of almost six centuries of orderly and essentially uninterrupted cultural progress which has been variously referred to as the "Old Empire," the "Classic period" (a name which, for reasons outlined below, it has become necessary to abandon), or the "Initial Series period." Perhaps the last

FIG. 4—ACROPOLIS, STRS. 1 AND 2, ACANCEH
a, Section through Strs. 1 and 2, scale 1:100. *b*, Plan, scale 1:200. *c*, Elevation, approx. scale 1:100. Limited excavation of an area atop this complex and very ruined acropolis in 1941 produced this architectural stratigraphy from an original Formative platform, through both phases of the Early period into Pure Florescent. Sherds found as apparent direct refuse in terrace corners of earliest platform shown were Late Formative. Str. 1, whose superior molding bears famous stucco façade, was built during first phase of Early period. Str. 2 (opposite), built in second phase of more evolved but basically similar masonry, was on a large addition to the earlier platform. Both structures were subsequently filled with rubble, as was court between. Over plaster floor covering this buried complex was built a later structure in typical carved stone veneer of the following Florescent period. (Drawing of stucco façade by Bates Littlehales, based on photos by Adela Breton in Peabody Museum, Harvard.)

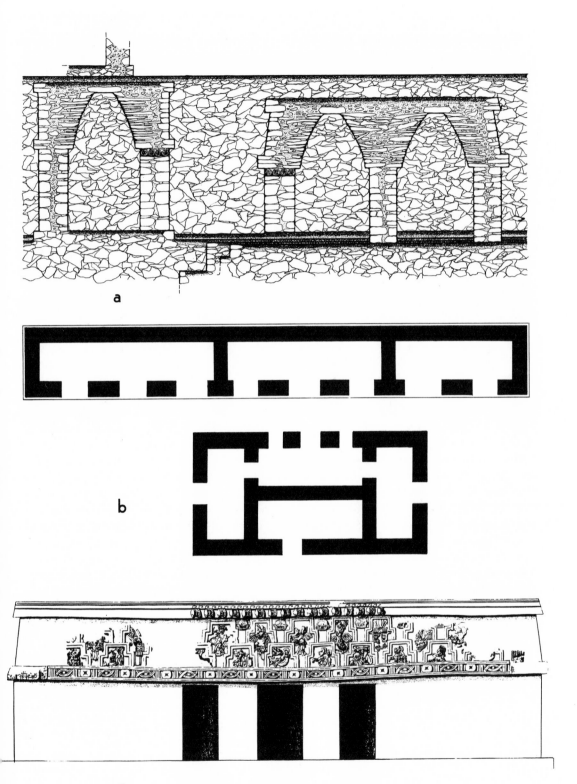

a

b

c

297

is the most apt term, as this is the known lifetime of the full, elaborate, and completely accurate Maya Long Count calendar which recorded dates precisely over millions of years in relative time—we say "relative time" because the calendar has not yet been decisively correlated with our own. Events in this period are datable with considerable certainty in the Maya calendar, thanks to the pioneer work at Uaxactun,[5] where careful excavation has associated the development of architecture and ceramics with the Long Count and enabled us to make exact cross-datings on the basis of abundant trade pottery in the northern lowlands, where the Initial Series mechanism was not as extensively used.

The Early period in the southern lowlands has been divided into two phases, largely on the basis of ceramics. In architecture, although A. L. Smith (1950) made a parallel division into Vault I and Vault II, the developmental sequence seems to have been an almost uninterrupted one.

In the old days, as we noted earlier, the northern peninsula was called the "New Empire" and was presumed to have been unoccupied until the break-up of the southern cities. Even as evidence accumulated that the area had long been inhabited, it was relegated to a position of secondary importance; but it has become increasingly clear in recent years that this attitude was most unjust. Starting back in the Formative, the north was densely populated. If Brainerd's surmise (1958) is correct, it has yielded the earliest material remains. The massive pre-Early period ceremonial constructions at Dzibilchaltun, and probably also Yaxuna and Acanceh, have no parallels elsewhere among the lowland Maya.[5a] Thus, the north has as good a claim as the

southern lowlands, if far from final proof, of having produced the seeds which led to lowland Maya civilization.

Throughout the six centuries of the Early period, the development of culture on the peninsula was a continuous one. As in the south, it was centered about complexes of ceremonial or civil architecture of greatly varying size, which served as nuclei of residential settlements of houses of perishable material, often on low platforms. To what extent these sites served as permanent homes for sizable populations, or merely as temporary ceremonial or civil gathering centers for a scattered population, remains to be proved. Although in the Early period the latter theory has been the fashionable interpretation, excavations at Dzibilchaltun have produced evidence of concentrated permanent population. At other than one-period sites, however, intensive exploratory excavation is essential to determine by artifact analysis which structures were inhabited at any one period. Such studies are in progress at Tikal, in British Honduras, and at Dzibilchaltun.

During the first phase of the Early period, starting approximately A.D. 20–280 and ending about 330–590 (note 6 explains the use of these hyphenated double dates in this and the following section, where cultural developments are anchored in the Maya rather than in the European calendar), there was a burst of architectural activity probably unparalleled in the area

[5] Cf. Ricketson and Ricketson, 1937; A. L. Smith, 1950; R. E. Smith, 1955b.
[5a] Similar massive complexes belonging in the Chicanel equivalent phase have recently been discovered at Tikal.

[6] Despite several generations of research, a definitive solution of the correlation of Maya and Christian calendars has not been achieved. Therefore, many events and activities during the Early period, dated accurately in the Maya calendar, may not yet be assigned a certain date in our own. The two most widely accepted solutions of this problem, each with a number of minor variants, place the Spanish conquest at roughly 12.9.0.0.0 and 11.16.0.0.0 in the Maya calendar, dates approximately 260 years apart. The hyphenated pairs of dates describing events during our discussion of the Early period give the Christian equivalents according to the *earlier* and the *later* of these clusters of correlations. They do *not* imply a date anywhere between the two figures.

Fig. 5—"PALACE GROUP," DZIBILCHALTUN. This double quadrangle of buildings, occupying approx. 21 acres around sacrificial cenote near center of archaeological zone, was built largely during second phase of Early period. However, buildings at right-hand side of right quadrangle show gradual transition from Early period to Florescent styles. Structures at top of right quadrangle were built in evolved Pure Florescent style. (Reconstruction drawing by George E. Stuart.)

Fig. 6—RECONSTRUCTION OF STRUCTURES ON TERRACE OF TEMPLE OF THE SEVEN DOLLS, DZIBILCHALTUN. This walled-in temple precinct is typical of late Early period architecture here. The group is connected with the central group by a sacbe, reminiscent of Early period sites in Quintana Roo and in El Peten, Guatemala. (Drawing by George E. Stuart.)

until the boom of ecclesiastical construction following the pacification of the area by the Spaniards in the 16th century. The two largest structures known to have been built by the Maya, the pyramids at Izamal and Dzilam, were probably erected at this time, although there is reason to believe that these, as did the massive Str. 8 at Yaxuna and the central part of the Acropolis at Acanceh, may have begun back in the Formative. At this time the famous Temple of the Stucco Façade (Str. 1) was built on the Acanceh Acropolis (fig. 4) as well as the complex pyramid some hundreds of meters north at the modern plaza.

Extensive architectural activity is dated at 9.2.0.0.0 (215–475) at Oxkintok at the western edge of the peninsula by its Initial Series lintel (see Shook, 1940). Parallel construction activity can be placed at this point in time on the East Coast at Tancah both by the distinctive Peten trade wares and by the 9.6.0.0.0 (294–554) date at Tulum, which was almost certainly removed from this nearby site. In central and southern Campeche and Quintana Roo, no stratigraphic archaeology has been undertaken (excepting the unpublished reconnaissance of Brainerd), and we are at a loss to specify cultural developments during

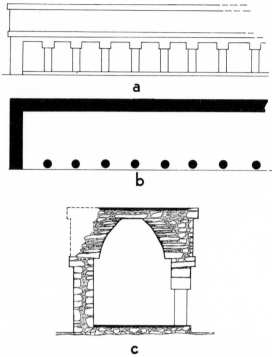

FIG. 7—STR. 1, SIHUNCHEN. *a*, Elevation, scale 1:200. *b*, Plan, scale 1:200. *c*, Section, scale 1:100. This relatively small structure, partially destroyed by stone robbers supplying the Merida-Uxmal highway, was discovered in 1942. Ceramic excavation was impossible, but architectural evidence indicates that the building was probably erected in first phase of Early period, despite round columns, which have been considered a trait of the much later Florescent.

this phase. The stela at Ichpaatun bearing the date 9.8.0.0.0 (333–593) probably antedates the major habitation of the site by at least five centuries. Carved from volcanic micaceous schist, it may have been brought as a relic from another site at some distance, as no such volcanic outcroppings have been found anywhere near the Chetumal area. Pottery of the first phase of the Early period is abundant at other sites in the northern peninsula, although unassociated with architecture—a negative notation, considering the lack of exploration in this area in terms of material of this age.

The second phase of the Early period in the Northern Maya Area was one of continued cultural development and refine-

ment in all the arts left us by the inclement climate of the area and the destructive tendencies of its later inhabitants. Most of the population centers mentioned in the preceding paragraph continued their development. History on the Caribbean coast seems to have been uninterrupted. The great city of Coba in northern Quintana Roo reached its greatest expansion in the early part of the second phase (where it appears to have been remarkably closely allied in the arts with sister cities in the south). Newer cities such as Yaxcopoil, Sihunchen, and Tzeme appeared, while older centers such as Yaxuna, Ake, Oxkintok, and Acanceh continued their growth. Str. 2 at the Acanceh site was built facing the Stucco Temple on an addition to the high acropolis (fig. 4). The largest known city during this phase was Dzibilchaltun, north of Merida. Over a zone of some 50 sq. km. there is a constant and dense distribution of human remains, usually concentrated in groups of one or more tall pyramid-temples surrounded by ranges of long rectangular rooms on lower platforms and by similar platforms which served as foundations for structures of perishable materials. Around these groups were heavy concentrations of stone-walled domestic houses and living platforms. In 1963–64 about 19 sq. km. of the zone was mapped in detail and found to contain 8526 structures, 224 of them vaulted. Some 700 were excavated or test-pitted, revealing that 90 per cent were in use at the end of the Early period and the start of the Florescent. Reconnaissance in the remainder of the approximately 50 sq. km. of archaeological zone showed a similar distribution of stone structures (totaling some 20,000). These figures do not include the houses of perishable material without platforms, for which we estimate roughly the same number. The picture is one of heavy urbanization and a population many times that which could be supported by available agricultural land (cf. Andrews, 1964). Figure 5 illustrates what

300

Fig. 8—EARLY PERIOD MASONRY. *a (left)*, Acanceh, Str. 2, room corner, showing lower wall, spring course, vault face, and masonry of dividing wall. Note that visible face of wall is composed largely of spalling, only the end of an occasional slab showing. All surfaces shown were covered with thick layer of stucco. *b (right)*, Sihunchen, Str. 1. Compare with cross-section in fig. 7.

seems to have been the central ceremonial complex at Dzibilchaltun.

Architecture of the Early period in the Northern Area was an orderly process of development of distinctive techniques, as was the case in the south, and is never confusable with that of another period or never sharply divisible into phases by sudden modifications of basic technique. It began with the introduction of the corbeled vault and ended with radical modifications of style and technics which distinguish it clearly from that which followed. Its definition is therefore almost as simple as the epigraphic, calendric, and artistic cults which were its concomitants in time. Based in the pre-existing Late Formative patterns of masonry substructures varying from low platforms to towering series of superimposed terraces (confusingly named "pyramids" after false prototypes in the Old World) and to even more complex acropolis-type foundations with structures built at many levels, the buildings themselves

show a startling uniformity in the entire Early period.

Walls were of true masonry, composed of structurally functional blocks of stone, often exceeding half the wall width, resting on one another to bear the weight of the structure above. At the start blocks were only very roughly surfaced; sometimes they were not reworked at all. Considerable spalling was needed to make proper stress contact, and the working into rectangular form was so crude that coursing was often highly irregular. The spring course and all other phases of the vault were of long, flat, completely unworked slabs, each weighted down at the rear by boulders and projecting slightly farther forward towards the center of the vaulted space until the two sides could be bridged by a larger flat slab. The principle was one of true corbeling. The rough inner and outer walls, and much more so the rough vault, were smoothed out by thick layers of stucco, which gave the surfaces their final contour. As the

301

FIG. 9—TEMPLE OF THE SEVEN DOLLS (STR. 1-SUB), DZIBILCHALTUN. View from northwest after construction. This structure was built at start of second phase of Early period. Two radiocarbon determinat date it at A.D. 483 ± 140. It was situated at center of a walled precinct surrounded by nine rectangular buiding low platforms, these mostly built into the wall. It was carefully buried under much larger pyramid later in s phase of Early period. Entire group was abandoned during Florescent. Much later, inhabitants of Decadent pe tunneled into original structure, removed much of the rubble with which it had been filled, and used inner roor subterranean shrine.

period progressed, wall blocks became more properly squared and the coursing consequently more regular. As cubing became more careful, spalling became less necessary and the blocks somewhat smaller, often leading to thicker concrete core between wall faces. Bonding of the walls at corners was never perfected, a frequent cause of structural failure throughout the period and wherever its traditions persisted later. The spring course of the corbeled vault which gave rise to Early period architecture became more pronounced and effective, becoming a much thicker and more

deeply tenoned slab to support the immense weight above. The vault slabs were more carefully ordered to produce the desired surface contour, the stucco facing becoming thinner as it became less and less responsible for the actual surface. But the structural principles of block-wall and slab-vault remained as characteristic of all architecture of the period.

Highly characteristic of these times were the *sacbeob* ("smooth ways" or "white ways" in Maya) or raised causeways, which not only connected the separate and often distant architectural groups of which the

Fɪɢ. 10—RESTORATION OF WEST FAÇADE, TEMPLE OF THE SEVEN DOLLS, DZIBILCHALTUN. West façade, which collapsed after this secondary use, was restored in the present painting by assembling still preserved elements on remaining three almost identical standing sides. Note unique functional windows at either side of central doorway. (Painting by Bates Littlehales, National Geographic Society.)

cities were composed, but sometimes crossed great distances in connecting the cities themselves. The principal sacbe at Dzibilchaltun, 20 m. wide and up to 2 m. tall, built of great blocks leveled with fine gravel and paved with plaster, ran for some 2.5 km. east-west to define the principal axis of the city. Seven other sacbeob lead from it to secondary centers. Yaxuna was connected to Coba by the longest sacbe yet found, which we suspect not only connected with Xcaret, the point of embarkation for Cozumel off the Caribbean coast, but also branched south to sites in the Tancah-Tulum area.

Sculptural art of the Early period, closely paralleling that of the south, was naturalistic, and as such certainly achieved its maximum and, in terms of our own concepts, optimum development. Sculpture was used for adornment of architecture and in the cult of stone monuments; and in these two quite different media it varied in composition and in quality from phase to phase and from site to site. Architectural ornamentation was essentially in carved and modeled stucco and normally succumbed first to the ravages of weather, vegetation, and the much more destructive human occupants of the area. It survived normally only when structures were completely abandoned or buried early in their life by others. Examples of such buried structures are the Stucco Temple at Acanceh (figs. 4, 12), and the Temple of the Seven Dolls at Dzibilchaltun (fig. 10). The colossal stucco heads and human figures from Izamal (fig. 13), belonging to this period, are illustrated by Stephens (1843, p. 434), Charnay (1887, pp. 307–15), and Holmes (1895–97, 1: 97–100).

Monumental art, expressed in the medium of stelae, altars, and massive architectural components such as lintels, was neither as extensively nor as highly developed in the northern as in the southern

303

FIG. 11—EARLY PERIOD ARCHITECTURE, DZIBILCHALTUN. Part of façade and masonry section of the "Standing Temple" (Str. 57), the only remaining standing masonry at the site at the time of its discovery. This structure, built at the end of the Early period, shares masonry traits with the latest architecture at Uaxactun and Tikal.

lowlands, but was nevertheless an important and diagnostic feature of the times. Monuments bearing Maya dates from 9.2.0.0.0 (A.D. 215–475) to 10.2.10.0.0 (619–879) are scattered across the northern area at Tulum, Coba, Chichen Itza, Dzibilchaltun, Xkalumkin, Oxkintok, and farther south at Xtampak and Etzna. Sculptural styles are closely allied to those of the southern area (Proskouriakoff, 1951). However, although occasional sculptures show a high degree of aesthetic merit (e.g., Stela 19 at Dzibilchaltun, fig. 14), the average compares most unfavorably with the splendid products of some southern sites as Copan or Piedras Negras.

In ceramics, the Northern Area seems to have developed divergent forms and techniques at a very early date in the Early period. The so-called slate wares which characterize so much of the later occupation of the area extend far back into the first phase of the Early period and, as we mentioned above, there is evidence that they may have developed directly from parent forms in the Late Formative. As is the case with architecture, there are as yet no decisive ceramic grounds to divide the Early period in the north. The six ceramic phases of the period worked out in the Peten have been of great use in tying the Yucatan stratigraphy into the Maya calendar and, indirectly, into absolute chronology. This has been particularly true at Dzibilchaltun, where literally thousands of Peten trade pieces pepper the Early period deposits. Where we have been able to show this material to R. E. Smith, he has been able to classify a gratifying portion down to exact subphase in the south. Apparently, although the Maya of the southern lowlands rarely condescended to import the monochrome or crudely "trickle"-decorated slate wares from the north (only six sherds of slate ware were identified at Uaxactun; see R. E. Smith, 1955b), the Yucatec were enthusiastic customers for the brightly col-

Fig. 12—EARLY PERIOD CARVED STUCCO FROM YUCATAN. Acanceh, Acropolis, Str. 1 ("Stucco Temple"), façade detail. For complete elevation of this building, cf. fig. 4. (Photo, Peabody Museum, Harvard University.)

ored and decorated polychromes of Guatemala.

FLORESCENT PERIOD
Pure Phase and Its Origins

The second great period of Maya civilization in the north is as distinctive as it is different from the preceding Early period or the following Decadent period. Were there not fairly clear evidence of an orderly period of transition both at the start and at the end of the Florescent, one would be inclined to suspect that the drastic changes in technology reflected sudden ethnic shifts in the area. As it is, much remains to be explained.

If the Early period was the era of the artist and the astronomer-priest, the Flores-

305

Fig. 13—"THE GREAT STUCCO FACE," IZAMAL. Part of a band of faces and entire human figures i
giant size forming a panel around face of one of substructure terraces, a trait found elsewhere at Izamal (se
text). (Drawing by Frederick Catherwood.)

cent would seem to have been that of the architect and some more secular form of ruler. Naturalistic art, in which the older Maya had excelled, practically vanished, and the artist became enslaved to the geometric requirements of the architect. The erstwhile supreme trinity of hieroglyphs, calendar, and astronomy (or, as Thompson chooses to put it, *astrology*), which appears to have dominated life and worship in the Early period, virtually disappeared from the scene, only to reappear later after the end of the Florescent. The elaborate Initial Series was lost forever at the death of the southern cities, where it had played such an important role in ceremonial life. Although the stela cult continued for a while, the art styles were different and apparently not, according to Proskouriakoff (1950), derived from Classic (Early period) tradition. Glyphic inscriptions also continued briefly, but soon the glyphs were neither familiar nor translatable, the forms strange, the bar-and-dot numerals in reverse order or at the wrong side of glyphs, more resembling those of continental Mexico. There is a strong impression of something foreign (fig. 17).

The architects of the Florescent reached a stage of perfection in their craft which was probably not attained anywhere else in the New World. The basic technics of this new tradition in building form were as different from those of the Early period as they were from those of the Decadent period which followed. Even in totally collapsed remains their products were unmistakable. The block-wall and slab-vault (corbeled) tradition of the Early period, surfaced and artistically decorated in carved and painted stucco, gave way to an utterly different type of construction consisting of durable concrete faced (but not walled) with a veneer of thin, beautifully dressed and perfectly squared blocks of stone whose function was purely decorative. Vault veneer stones, lacking the sup-

FIG. 14—STELA 19, DZIBILCHALTUN. This monument, stylistically dated about 9.11.0.0.0 (A.D. 392–652), was one of several broken up and re-used as building stone in Str. 36, at the northeast corner of the Great Plaza (fig. 5). Its glyphic text, although composed of familiar elements, is not legible. Stela 9, left standing in front of the structure, bears date 9.14.5.0.0 (A.D. 457–716), which gives close approximation of date of construction of Str. 36. (Drawing by George E. Stuart.)

307

FIG. 15—STELA 3, DZIBILCHALTUN. About 60 per cent of the monuments here were unsculptured, as in other ruins of the same era in El Peten, Guatemala. They probably depicted subjects similar to those of sculptured stelae, but in painted stucco.

FIG. 16—MODEL OF TEMPLE B, RIO BEC, QUINTANA ROO. (Model by Shoichi Ichikawa from photographs by Clarence L. Hay in 1912.)

a

Fig. 17—ARCHITECTURAL SCULPTURE FROM PURE PHASE OF FLORESCENT PERIOD AT DZIBILCHALTUN. *a (above)*, Hieroglyphic inscriptions from Str. 96, a final addition to the "Palace Group." These texts bear little resemblance to known forms of Maya writing, resembling more closely texts from this period in the Mexican highlands. *b (below)*, Panel of basal molding, Str. 99. Motif of alternating skulls and crossed human bones, which continued around entire basal molding, strongly resembles the highland Mexican *tzompantli* and was undoubtedly introduced from the north during this period. It is also found in the *cementerio* at Uxmal.

b

port of simple vertical superposition, were carefully beveled and preshaped with long tenons to hold them into the newly dominant concrete mass of the noncorbeled vault. Exterior façades, as in the Early period, were divided into an upper and a lower zone by three moldings. But whereas before these had been simple rectangular projections, they became complex multi-membered affairs in the Florescent, often with beveled courses producing members with triangular section at top or bottom. Figure 19,*b* shows a wall section at Uxmal illustrating this "new look" in building. There were equally basic changes in ornamental art. Whereas Early period buildings were decorated with panels of carved or painted stucco, Florescent façades were lavishly adorned with carved stone geometric mosaic. The corners and façade panels were most frequently decorated with

mosaic masks of the long-nosed god, often interspersed with areas of fretwork, lattice, and a variety of carved designs such as rosettes, spindles, and series of small columns. Sometimes small panels were left open for diminutive naturalistic sculptures of high quality, but even these were mere adjuncts to the basic geometric motifs. There is a remarkable uniformity in the relatively few individual mosaic elements which were used to make up the complex façade panels of the Florescent. Although their assemblage varied considerably from place to place, such items as rosettes, lattice fragments, or even the components such as earplugs, eyes, or noses of the ever-present masks are almost indistinguishable at sites as far apart as the Puuc, Dzibil-chaltun, and Chichen Itza. Indeed, it has been suggested that such individual components might well have been the product

309

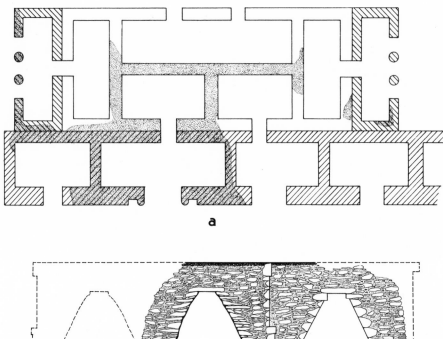

a

b

Fɪɢ. 18—YAXCOPOIL. Structure known as Aka'na. *a*, Plan, scale 1:200. *b*, Section, scale 1:100. Non-stippled portions of the plan are restored. The 5-room structure (outlined in white at center) was in late Early period style, with wall blocks pecked only to roughly rectangular form, unspecialized spring course and vault of rough slabs. Façade, where preserved behind the first addition, was of rough wall masonry covered with heavy layer of carved and painted stucco with some attached elements almost in full round. First long addition (shaded at lower right) was in finely faced veneer, with geometrically squared wall stones and façade stones, all vault stones both squared and beveled, and carved stone simple geometric motifs on façade. Two small end rooms (shaded at lower right) finally added were in pure Florescent style, with elaborate mosaic façade panels, round columns in doorways carved with warrior figures, and carved jambs. Construction of this building spans a gradual transition from late Early Period to Pure Florescent.

of different artists in different villages, who sold their particular components to architects at a number of sites.

The exact time when the Florescent Period began has been the subject of considerable speculation and controversy—and still is. Thompson (1937) suggested that the abbreviated inscriptions in Maya glyphs of familiar form at Chichen Itza all record dates in the last two decades of the Initial Series period, with two doubtful

exceptions on buildings of much later (Modified Florescent) style. The few legible glyphs on Florescent structures in the Puuc area seem to fall within the same pattern. This would seem to imply an overlay of about 20 years between the final gasp of Early period culture in the south and the beginnings of the Florescent in the north. But the material is so scanty as to make such a conclusion uncertain. The lack of architectural-ceramic stratigraphy, with

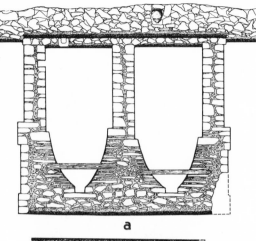

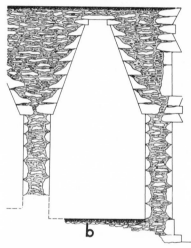

FIG. 19—SECTIONS SHOWING TYPICAL MA-SONRY TECHNIQUES OF EARLY PERIOD AND FLORESCENT PERIOD. *a (above)*, Str. 57, Dzibil-chaltun, late Early period, cross-datable by sealed pottery with late Tepeu 2 in the Peten. See photo in fig. 11. *b (below)*, Detail of House of the Turtles, Uxmal, typical Florescent construction. Scale 1:100.

date, not yet associated with the superb concrete and veneer construction characterizing the Florescent in the north. At Santa Rosa Xtampak two stelae dating about 9.17.0.0.0 (A.D. 511–771) may have been erected prior to the construction of buildings in the "Chenes" style. There is a single Initial Series date of 9.16.0.0.0 at Xkalumkin in Campeche on a structure again bearing traits of the Florescent. But Pollock (1940b) describes the buildings of this area as "distinctive in a sufficient number of details to justify their being set apart from the buildings of [the Puuc]." In sculpture, Proskouriakoff (1951, p. 111) places the arrival of her Quality X, "a group of traits presumably of separate local or foreign origin which cannot be derived from earlier classic style" (a striking parallel to our more general term Florescent), at 9.19.0.0.0 (A.D. 550–810) at Etzna and, presumably, other sites. Unfortunately, excepting the unpublished work of Brainerd, no stratigraphic excavation has been undertaken to place these cultural phenomena in the framework of the ceramic sequence.

The best evidence thus far as to the chronological placing of the Florescent is from Dzibilchaltun, the only site where the period lies inside a sealed stratigraphic sequence containing architecture, art, ceramics, and apparently valid cross-ties into the Maya Initial Series. We mentioned on page 305 the surprising wealth of Peten trade wares in the stratigraphy. The ceramic sequence at Strs. 13, 14, 15, at 38-sub and the later 38, and at 57-sub and 58 indicates beyond much question that the second phase of the Early period at Dzibilchaltun ended at roughly the same time as the Tepeu 2 phase in the Peten, which R. E. and A. L. Smith place at 10.0.0.0 (A.D. 570–830). Following the Early period at Dzibilchaltun, there is a clear architectural and artistic transition in the Palace group leading gradually into the distinctive styles of the Florescent. The evidence is that of a slow developmental sequence rather than

one exception, in the northern sites has made the problem a more difficult one, as the most easily recognizable changes marking the onset of the Florescent were in architecture. To the south and west of Yucatan in Campeche, certain aspects of Florescent may appear at an earlier date than they do in the Puuc and the north. In the so-called Chenes–Rio Bec area, the use of multiple mask panels and geometric façade elements may have appeared at an earlier

Fig. 20—MONJAS (NUNNERY) QUADRANGLE, UXMAL. Pure Florescent. Ball court in foreground.

Fig. 21—EAST RANGE, MONJAS (NUNNERY) QUADRANGLE, UXMAL. Pure Florescent. (Photo by Otto

one of diffusionary change, and this must have occupied a substantial period of time. It includes a gradual transition from block-wall and slab-vault masonry to pure con-crete-and-veneer construction, and from pure naturalistic stucco façade decoration through seminaturalistic motifs carved after construction on smooth blocks of stone to geometric assemblages of pre-carved stone elements. By the end of this transition, the abundance of late Tepeu trade pottery from the Peten had ceased, except for the diminishing carry-over of earlier refuse material re-used in construc-tion fill. This, paralleling the virtually total absence of Peten trade wares in the massive pottery collections from the pure Florescent sites in the Puuc, clearly bespeaks the prior abandonment of the southern cities.

This period of transition is clearly re-corded in the three construction phases of the Yaxcopoil structure (not far north of Uxmal) illustrated in figure 18. It may be significant that the two fragments of archi-tectural sculpture found in the final phase of the transitional structure were chosen by Proskouriakoff (1950) as illustrative of the newly arrived Quality X (mentioned above) representing a new sculptural tradi-tion in the area.

The alternative to assuming that the Pure Florescent period at Dzibilchaltun post-dated the abandonment of the southern cities (one which has been suggested by more than one colleague) is the assumption that this northernmost city was subjected in some way to a process of delayed diffu-sion, retaining its Early period culture long beyond the time when it had been aban-doned in favor of the Florescent tradition in the south. Much militates against this alternative, and this is positive rather than negative evidence. The ceramic cross-ties with the Peten sequence at Dzibilchaltun are unique in the Northern Area, and should be regarded as primary evidence. Cultural innovations (such as the traits defining the Florescent) might be subject

to delayed diffusion, but evolutionary se-quences such as those at Dzibilchaltun and Yaxcopoil are *not* susceptible to delayed diffusion, particularly between sites a few hours' walking distance apart such as Yax-copoil and Uxmal. Both Brainerd (1958) and Ruz (verbal information) emphasize the almost total absence of Peten trade sherds in the Puuc sites, which in itself should mark a lack of contemporaneity.

Actually, present indications are that evolved Florescent forms, after a long peri-od of organic evolution, were earlier on the northern plains than in the Puuc hills, where they probably achieved their opti-mum expression. Brainerd (1958) noted that the highly distinctive "Fine Gray" wares, so distinctive of pre-Florescent ce-ramics, were absent from the Puuc collec-tions, although present evidence indicates that they were imported from the southern mainland directly through the Puuc area. In the many burials unquestionably asso-ciated with the evolved Pure Florescent at Dzibilchaltun, Fine Gray vessels are sec-ond only to Medium Slate in occurrence. Similarly common is "Lustrous Streaky Brown Ware" (incorrectly labeled "red on thin gray" by Brainerd), which R. E. Smith (verbal information) associates closely with the Peten Gloss wares.

Modified Phase

Somewhere in the period A.D. 900–1100[7] there was a marked wave of influence from continental Mexico, very probably trace-able to the neighborhood of Tula in the state of Hidalgo. This was not the first of such periods of diffusion. Cultural inter-

[7] Two recently received radiocarbon determina-tions of clearly Modified Florescent deposits in the cave-sanctuary of Balankanche (Andrews, 1961a, pp. 28–40) date offerings at A.D. 870 ± 90–100 years. (La Jolla Laboratory, nos. 272, 273.)· Three new radiocarbon determinations (TBN=313=1, =2, =3) on unquestionably original beams from the Iglesia and the Chicchan-chob at Chichen Itza, both Pure Florescent struc-tures, have yielded dates of A.D. 600, 610, and 780, all ± 70.

313

Fig. 22—TEMPLE OF THE TURTLES, UXMAL. Note Pure Florescent concrete architecture. (Photo by
W. Andrews.)

314

Fɪɢ. 23—EAST WING OF THE MONJAS (NUNNERY), CHICHEN ITZA. Pure Florescent.

change had apparently been strong during the first phase of the Early period, diminishing during the second phase, then picking up again during the Pure Florescent. It has long been recognized that "Mexican" influences appeared at Puuc sites such as Kabah and Uxmal, which were abandoned before the start of the Modified Florescent (Proskouriakoff, 1950; Ruz, 1956, pp. 13, 43). Typical highland *tzompantlis* or skull racks appear at Uxmal and far back into Pure Florescent architecture at Dzibilchaltun (fig. 17,*b*). We noted in the last section the replacement of Maya glyphic writing by forms more reminiscent of the continental highlands (fig. 17,*a*). This diffusion of art forms was so strong as to lead Proskouriakoff to the interesting suggestion that, "It is possible that Toltec immigrants were in the country for some time before they established themselves as a dominant group of Chichen Itza, or that they were settled for a time in some peripheral location where they were in contact with the people of Yucatan" (1950, p. 170).

There is very little doubt that this non-Maya, probably Nahua-speaking, group established themselves at Chichen Itza, and from there exerted considerable control over the life of the northwestern part of the

315

FIG. 24—CARACOL, CHICHEN ITZA. In foreground is the Temple of the Wall Panels, a Modified Flore cent structure. The Caracol is presumed to be of the Transition to Modified Florescent. (Photo by Otto Done

Yucatan Peninsula. Before, or possibly as an immediate result of, this broad political control, the very numerous sites in the Puuc area were abandoned. Many of the cities on the flat northern plain, however, remained inhabited. This period of "Toltec" dominance, whose duration will remain poorly understood until a definitive solution of the correlation problem or added data from radiocarbon determinations or newer techniques of the physiochemists give us more accurate criteria, is described as the modified phase of the Florescent for reasons given below.

The nature of the origins of "Toltec"

power and the manner of its maintenance in Yucatan remain unknown. It may have been military, or religious, or secular in the sense that a few score Spaniards later dominated the same area by playing off one political group against another. On sculpture of the time, the warrior seems to have taken over from the priest or god as the focus of attention. But the group could not have been very numerous because they left no known imprint on the Maya as a race and little of their Nahua heritage on the Maya tongue. It has been suggested that they brought no women with them, which would explain

316

FIG. 25—CASA COLORADA, CHICHEN ITZA. Block masonry and stone mosaic façade typical of Florescent architecture elsewhere in Yucatan. (Photo by Otto Done.)

their failure to establish themselves as a permanent group, as well as their almost total absorption by their temporary subjects.

The "Toltecs" brought with them much that was new to Yucatan, including the first copper and gold; and they apparently enforced drastic modifications on the outward form of material culture there. In architecture radically new building forms appeared. The colonnade, known and used before, assumed vastly greater importance in planning. The basal molding of late Early period and Pure Florescent structures was replaced by a battered basal zone

pierced at outer floor level by the doorways. Forms of sculptural adornment were changed by innovations such as the carved serpent column and the reclining "chac mool" figures—relaxed bearers of the distinctive umbilical ashtrays. The emphasis in art (Proskouriakoff, 1950) shifted from the presentation of individual figures to group arrangements and portrayals of events. In pottery the famous and short-lived index fossil Tohil Plumbate from the Guatemala highlands makes its brief appearance, along with the imported "X-type Fine Orange" wares from Tabasco or southern Veracruz, the latter strongly influenc-

317

Fig. 26—CHICHEN ITZA. Lintel bearing date 10.2.9.1.9, the last Initial Series date known in Yucatan, was re-set on a structure of atlantean figures during final period at Chichen Itza at least three centuries later. (United Press Photo.)

ing the shapes and decorative elements of local wares. All these innovations are described elsewhere in this volume.

More important in this general description is the apparent fact that although the "Toltecs" brought with them and imposed a number of aesthetic changes clearly originating in their highland home, they brought few or no craftsmen and perforce grafted their innovations on the artisans of the Maya they dominated. As a result, although surface forms were altered, the basic technics of architecture, art, and ceramics remained unchanged from the first phase of the Florescent. In architecture the distinctive concrete construction with finely cut stone veneer and elaborate carved stone mosaic decoration persisted to

the end of the period. In pottery the identical slate wares with their relatively excellent texture and distinctively integrated slip continued to be manufactured. In art, although subject matter and emphasis changed, the basic technics persisted. All these basics were destined to disappear at the end of the period.

In most cultural taxonomies to date, the word "Classic" was applied to Maya culture up to the arrival of these Mexican migrants, everything thereafter being tagged as "Postclassic." I first pointed out two decades ago (1942, pp. 262–63) that this was an unfortunate division. A number of years of intensive excavation since the war have made it even more abundantly clear that what used to be called the "Puuc" or "Flo-

318

Fig. 27—EL CASTILLO, CHICHEN ITZA. Modified Florescent.

rescent" and the "Toltec" periods are manifestations of a single cultural tradition and that each of these components much more closely resembles the other than they do the major periods which preceded and followed. This will be more clear as we proceed to describe the changes to come in the final period of Maya culture. Meantime, the word "Classic" remains only as an attempt to force the realities of local culture into a Procrustean bed of preconceived patterns from foreign and unconnected areas, or a definition of local traditions in terms of waning and waxing external influences which we consider invalid criteria (Andrews, 1960, pp. 261–63). In the inevitable creation of the Florescent period, with its Pure and Modified phases, we have found it essential, in order to avoid confusion, to withdraw completely the word "Classic" from our descriptive taxonomy.

Monumental architecture of the Modified Florescent, which suffers little in comparison with any previous products of Maya civilization and in a number of ways marks a final triumph in design and utility, has thus far been identified only at Chichen Itza. The great if short-lived cities of the Puuc were abandoned by this time, following the fate of the cities of the southern area (and for equally unknown reasons). But many of the cities of the flat plains of northern Yucatan remained densely inhabited until modern times, yet this vital area has remained almost unexplored scientifically. At Dzibilchaltun, in the far northwest, where the cultural stratigraphy is uninterrupted from Formative times to the present day, no monumental remains have

319

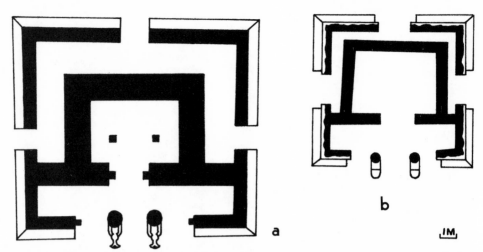

Fig. 28—GROUND PLANS OF CASTILLO, CHICHEN ITZA AND MAYAPAN. *a*, Chichen Itza (after Maudslay). The large vaulted structure is in Florescent veneered-concrete construction. *b*, Mayapan. Clearly copied from the still-standing structure at then abandoned Chichen, this building is smaller, capped by a beam-and-mortar roof over crude block masonry walls in the Decadent tradition. Several such clear-cut copies of probably semi-ruined Chichen structures are found at Mayapan. Scale 1:200.

yet been encountered in the Modified Florescent period, although the site has not yet been completely explored. During this period, however, the population must have been considerable; the ceramic remains form an impressive segment of the stratigraphy. The typical Florescent wares of the period are completely dominated by the innovations defined at Chichen Itza, indicating that, at least at this distance, the temporal sway of the foreigners was a firm one.

In Quintana Roo, and particularly on the Caribbean coast, neither the Pure nor the Modified phases of the Florescent seems to have established itself in any strength, a matter to which we shall return later.

DECADENT PERIOD

The third major period of Maya civilization was one of startling decay not only in all the material arts, but apparently in religious and socio-political institutions as well. The last 400 years before the Spanish conquest saw the Maya deteriorate from a great and integrated civilization to an aggregation of petty warring *cacicazgos*,

tribal units under warrior chiefs. Perhaps most striking is the complete disappearance of the highly distinctive technics in architecture, sculpture, and art which had so sharply distinguished the two phases of the Florescent, and the quite unmistakable reversion to the utterly different tradecraft of the Early period—almost as if an immense external wedge of culture had been removed.

Transitional Phase ("Black-on-Cream")

As was the case with the change from Early to Florescent traditions, the reversion to ancient norms at the end of the Florescent was not a sudden one, but a gradual transition which must have taken a considerable period of time. Vaillant (1927) was the first to recognize a distinctive pottery ware, called by him "Coarse-paste Slate," which occurred only on the surface as postoccupational pottery at Chichen Itza. Later it was found at the base of the stratigraphy defining the major occupation of Mayapan. Brainerd (1958) recognized its intermediate chronological position on the basis of concentrated deposits at Dzibilchaltun. R. E. Smith later suggested the much more satisfactory name "Black-on-Cream," a needed correction as, although aspects of Modified Florescent shape and decoration continue in the ware, the definitive slip and paste of Slate ware are no longer present, and the pottery is clearly closely related to that of the Decadent period.

The material arts changed so drastically between the end of the Modified Florescent Chichen Itza and the beginnings of Decadent Mayapan that I have long been inclined to postulate that this pottery, atop one and below the other stratigraphy, represented the interim predominance of some other site or group of sites. Positive confirmation was found in recent excavations at Dzibilchaltun. Sealed stratigraphies at two parts of the site started with pure samples of Modified Florescent Slate wares, continued with admixtures of Black-on-Cream, followed by pure sealed deposits, and then by an admixture of and finally predominance of the later red wares of the Decadent period. One of these stratigraphies (Strs. 36 and 39, excavated in 1959–60 by William E. Folan) included the construction of two buildings and repeated additions in changing architectural style in sealed association with Black-on-Cream ceramics (Andrews, 1961b). The architectural sequence supplied the missing (and gradual) transition between Modified Florescent and Decadent traditions. Sculpture of the period was not found, nor at this time are we able to evaluate chronologically the trade sherds in the large ceramic collections.

We can now be sure that there was a phase of incipient Decadent culture between the end of the Modified Florescent at Dzibilchaltun and Chichen Itza and the beginnings of true Decadent period culture at the former site and at Mayapan. The assemblage of pottery wares is complete in its catalogue of functional forms, utterly distinct from those that preceded or followed. The associated architecture is in clear transition from Florescent to Decadent forms. As to absolute chronology, we can now only note that allowance must be made for the passage of considerable extra time between the end of the Initial Series period and the

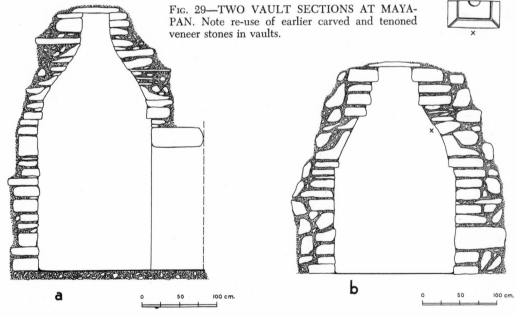

FIG. 29—TWO VAULT SECTIONS AT MAYAPAN. Note re-use of earlier carved and tenoned veneer stones in vaults.

a

b

0   50   100 cm.

0   50   100 cm.

FIG. 30—DECADENT PERIOD REOCCUPATION OF EARLY PERIOD STR. 1, DZIBILCHAL-TUN. After Str. 1 had been abandoned for some 500 years, Decadent period priests used it again, building a new stairway over the earlier ruined pyramid and tunneling into the buried temple.

beginnings of association with the Christian calendar during the history of Mayapan.

Early Phase (Mayapan)

Before disappearing completely as a civilization, the Maya made one last and relatively successful attempt at empire. Starting probably about A.D. 1200–1250, the tribe of Cocoms (the first time that we can speak with any certainty of either tribal units or individuals) built up, on the ruins of a much smaller earlier city at Mayapan, a political control over the entire northern plains—an empire closely paralleling that of the Aztecs, who arrived in the Valley of Mexico about the same time. Tyrannical domination was achieved over the entire northwest and north-central part of the peninsula, enforced, according to native chronicles (which only in this late era assume appearance of reflecting actual his-

tory), by holding members of the principal other ruling tribes as hostages in the capital city. This empire grew in power and influence until the doubtless excessively exploited tribes of the region flared into open rebellion, burned and destroyed Mayapan about 1440, and either killed or scattered the members of the ruling Cocom dynasty.

Vaillant, with his remarkable insight into cultural dynamics, referred to the Decadent period as a "Maya Renaissance"—paradoxically, a much more accurate definition than more recent references to periods of continued Mexican influence. In material culture the reversion to the basic technics of the Early period are as unmistakable as they were pitiable, for they were a far cry from the glories of the past. The old tradecraft looks almost as if it were sucked in from somewhere to fill a cultural vacuum.

In architecture the concrete construction

322

FIG. 31—EARLY PERIOD ARCHITECTURE AT XCARET, QUINTANA ROO.

Str. F-I: elevation, plan, and section. Note basal molding and complex three-member medial and superior moldings. Scale 1:100.

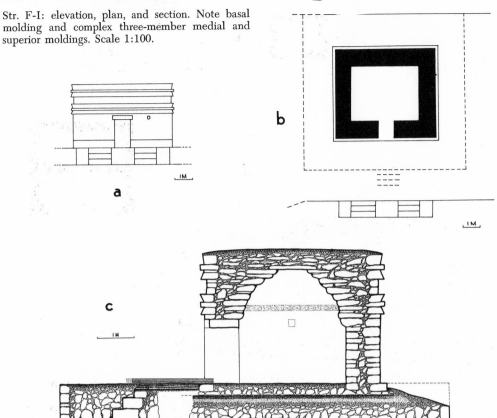

with its superb thin veneer of beautifully cut stone had vanished completely, giving way to the block-wall and slab-vault technique of the distant past. But the Decadent period architect seems to have failed to understand properly the new medium in which he was working. The stones of a handful of ruined Florescent buildings were re-used with frequently disastrous results. The thin, perfectly squared wall inlays, with virtually no functional bearing surface, were re-used as blocks; and the characteristic boot-shaped tenoned vault stones were re-used in corbeling (fig. 29). In either case, the stress of superior masonry, free of the tenacious earlier concrete, often pushed these misfits outward from their position, leading directly to collapse. Carved stone, other than these re-used fragments, disappeared from architecture, the

roughly pecked blocks of the walls more closely resembling those of the first phase of the Early period in quality. The elaborate carved mosaics of both phases of the Florescent vanished completely, to be replaced by the carved stucco of the Early period, although a crude echo of the past.

The change from purely hieratic to secular organization of the state, which we have seen probably began back in the Pure Florescent, is strongly reflected in two Decadent period innovations in city planning. Walled cities appeared for the first time in the lowlands,[8] and there was a sharply

[8] The city walls of Mayapan, Tulum, and Xcaret were of Decadent period construction. Certainly at Xcaret, probably at Mayapan, and possibly also at Tulum, they were of symbolic rather than tactical defensive nature. The wall at Chacchob (Pollock and Stromsvik, 1953) surrounded an area clearly occupied by vaulted structures of

323

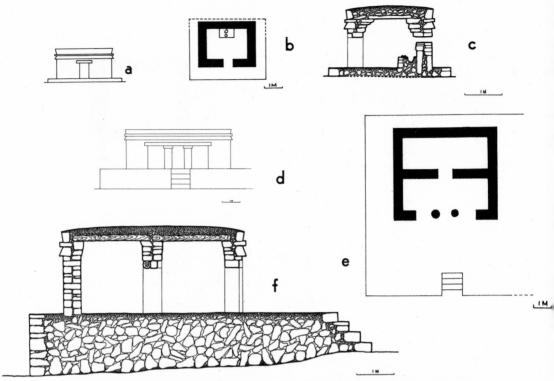

FIG. 32—DECADENT PERIOD ARCHITECTURE AT XCARET, QUINTANA ROO. *a-c,* Str. A-III, a diminutive vaulted shrine. *d-f,* Str. C-I, a two-roomed building with round doorway columns and beam-and-mortar roof. Note continuity of Early period architectural techniques, although basal and medial moldings are suppressed. Beam-and-mortar roof is common during Decadent period on East Coast, at Mayapan, and at Isla Cilvituk, Campeche (Andrews, 1934). It has antecedents at Uaxactun during the Early period, when it was also used for small shrines at Dzibilchaltun in Yucatan. Scale 1:100.

increasing emphasis on elegant (for the times) residential structures in or close to the temple precincts.[9]

The stela cult was revived, at least at Mayapan and Dzibilchaltun, but the sculpture is crude in the extreme; and, although the glyphs are once more in the style of the ancient Maya, many or sometimes all of the details of both glyphs and design were added in carved or painted stucco. Three inscriptions in Maya glyphs were

found on the altar added during the Decadent period re-use of the inner chamber of the Temple of the Seven Dolls at Dzibilchaltun, one possibly recording the katun endings at A.D. 1263, 1283, and 1303 (Andrews, 1960, p. 256, fig. 3). All are in Maya characters, after several centuries of use of unfamiliar forms since the end of the Initial Series period.

In pottery the slate wares so characteristic of Yucatan for over a thousand years vanish completely, to be replaced by much inferior products more closely resembling those of the distant past. Decadent pottery is of coarse, soft, gray to buff paste, slipped during the Transitional phase in thick cream, later in red. Ceremonial censers,

_____
Florescent age. This may be a parallel to the wall precinct centering about Str. 1 at Dzibilchaltun and including Strs. 2–9, all clearly of Early period date.

[9] Cf. J. E. S. Thompson, 1954b; D. E. Thompson and J. E. S. Thompson, 1955.

Fig. 33—XCARET, QUINTANA ROO, STR. H-I. Early period vaulted shrine. (Photo by E. W. Andrews.)

Fig. 34—XCARET, QUINTANA ROO, STR. J-I. Decadent period. This structure had a beam-and-mortar roof. Note simplified molding pattern. (Photo by E. W. Andrews.)

often in full anthropomorphic form, were made of coarse buff paste, unslipped but painted after firing in a variety of colors and garish designs.

Although the technics of the Decadent period mark an abrupt change, external forms in architecture, sculpture, and pottery often continue to imitate slavishly the products of the past. Buildings at Mayapan were often unmistakably copied from prototypes still standing at Chichen Itza (fig. 28); and J. E. S. Thompson (1957) has recently published clear evidence that at least some of the anthropomorphic censers were representations of Nahua deities from the Mexican highlands.

Remains of this period are not confined to the Yucatan plain. They have been found at Isla Cilvituk (Andrews, 1943) in southern Campeche, Santa Rita in British Honduras (Gann, 1900), Calderitas and Ichpaatun in the Chetumal area (Sanders, 1960a), and in unbroken and heavy sequence along the entire Caribbean coast of Quintana Roo. We shall have more to say of this latter occupation presently.

Late Phase (Postmonumental)

Although the first Spaniards appeared in Yucatan in 1511, it was 1541, a full century after the fall of Mayapan, before even the northern end of the peninsula was securely conquered. The archaeology of this phase is most poorly understood because of almost complete lack of excavation. Most of the principal archaeological sites were occupied. Chichen Itza, although its cenote still served as a place of pilgrimage and sacrifice, had probably not been the seat of a large population since the end of the Florescent. Mayapan was destroyed and abandoned as, of course, was long since the case with the Puuc cities. Dzibilchaltun, as so often, was an exception. There is evidence that both of the buried Early period structures (Strs. 1-sub and 38-sub), which were tunneled into in the Decadent and re-used as underground sanctuaries,

were in continued use well beyond the Monumental phase of the Decadent. Bits of glazed pottery in one, and iron in the other indicate, indeed, that these were used as places of worship after the arrival of the Spaniards. At the time of Spanish domination, the population at Dzibilchaltun was sufficient to warrant the construction of a colonial church almost in the center of the main ceremonial plaza.

The last century before the conquest must have been a hard one on the warlike tribes into which the Maya had degenerated. In 1464, according to the native chronicles, a hurricane devastated the area. In 1480 a plague brought even more serious consequences. And in 1514, three years after the first shipwrecked Spaniards had been thrown ashore (including Gerónimo de Aguilar, who later with Doña Marina served as Cortés' interpreter) but still three years before the formal discovery of the peninsula by Hernández de Córdoba, an epidemic of smallpox swept through Yucatan, with its usual catastrophic effects on a population innocent of earlier exposure.

Despite these vicissitudes, the Maya have survived the impact of European culture with almost unique success. They were dominated first by priest-kings and astronomers who took full advantage of nature's bounty in using the abundant free time of the populace in public works—doubtless under dire threats of drought and crop failure if they failed to obey the dictates read in the carefully observed movements of the heavenly bodies across the sacred precincts of time and the heavens. Under the later rulers of the Florescent they must have been equally exploited, as was certainly the case under the autocratic regime of the rulers of Mayapan. With this background, the demands of the Spanish *encomenderos*, which virtually exterminated the native population of the freedom-accustomed Antilles in a single generation, seem to have been merely the repetition of a familiar pattern to the conditioned Maya.

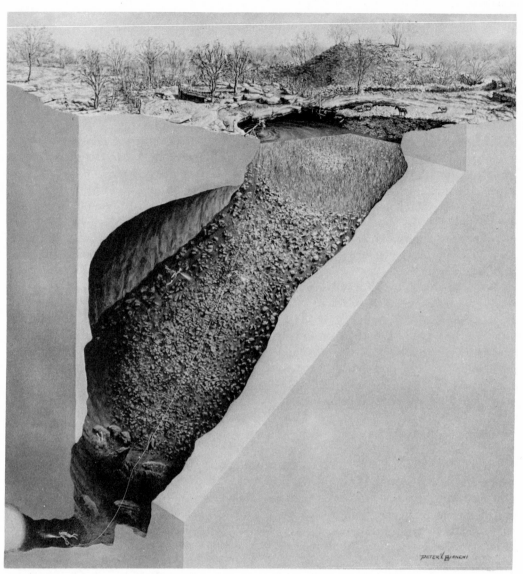

FIG. 35—CENOTE AT DZIBILCHALTUN. Cut-away drawing showing divers at various depths collecting archaeological specimens, of which the cenote yielded over 10,000, including objects of pottery, jade, carved shell, flint, obsidian, bone, and wood. (After painting by Peter V. Bianchi; copyright, National Geographic Society.)

Aside from several bloody outbreaks, ruthlessly suppressed by the newly arrived masters, the Maya farmer accepted his new yoke and retained a remarkable amount of his cultural and racial integrity into the day when his European masters unwittingly shared with him the fruits of revolutionary ventures, which are only in recent years radically changing his cultural heritage.

POSTSCRIPT: EAST COAST CULTURE AND THE PROBLEM OF THE FLORESCENT

We noted earlier that culture in the Northern Maya Area included a number of varying traditions which could be best regarded as horizons in time. With minor exceptions these variants, previously given potentially confusing geographic names such as "Rio Bec–Chenes," "Puuc," "Chichen," "Mayapan," were essentially short-lived manifestations which fitted most satisfactorily as horizontal components of the radically different tripartite vertical division we have postulated since 1942 for the totality of post-Formative Maya culture. We have listed two minor points of question: (a) the elaboration and repetition of façade motifs in the Rio Bec–Chenes area might have presaged the development of the Florescent tradition, which seems to have appeared through evolutionary processes well beyond the start of Cycle 10 in the north; (b) the Initial Series of Xkalumkin, although possibly presaging a later contemporaneous date or possibly moved from an earlier structure (as was the clear case with the Chichen Initial Series lintel in the doorway of an unquestioned Modified Florescent structure), antedates again the apparent northern origin of the associated architectural styles by a full century. Both of these seeming ambiguities must be clarified by scientific excavation in their respective areas.

We have thus far intentionally neglected specific mention of an architectural and artistic tradition on the Caribbean coast of Quintana Roo, which seems to have maintained its integrity from the first phase of the Early period until the arrival of the Spaniards, and whose isolation may be due to the abandonment of the jungle hinterlands from a time at least as early as and possibly two centuries earlier (to judge from the record at Coba) than the great southern sites. Lothrop at an early date (1924) postulated that the architecture at Tancah was of an earlier period than that of neighboring Tulum. Later explorations by Fernández (1945a,b), Escalona Ramos (1946), Lizardi Ramos (1939, 1940), and Sanders (1955), to mention only a few, gathered further data on the region. My excavations at Xcaret in 1955 and 1956 indicated a remarkable unity of architectural tradition in structures dated by associated pottery from the first phase of the Early period

through the Decadent period. Florescent tradition seems to have had virtually no impact on the architecture, which continued an orderly evolution of the earlier styles to the end (fig. 31; see also Proskouriakoff, 1957a, pp. 333–34). Sanders (1960a) confirmed this picture in his ceramic survey of the area from Laguna de Yalahau to Chetumal. Except at Xcaret and San Miguel de Cozumel, both on the pilgrimage route from the interior cities to the sacred island, even the Yucatan slate wares were almost completely absent—further strong evidence of the cultural isolation of this heavily populated littoral.

After the isolation during the Florescent, Decadent period architecture, art, and pottery of the East Coast and of the northern plain of Yucatan are virtually identical; their close relationship can scarcely be questioned. As the very traits which distinguished these manifestations were absent (or at least unknown) in Yucatan for the centuries of the Florescent, it would be logical to assume their sudden reintroduction around the 13th century from the East Coast, which is the only area in which they are known to have survived. This is probably the reason for the cultural renaissance, albeit a poor one, in Yucatan.[10]

The East Coast cities were among the last to be inhabited. Grijalva's expedition seems to have recorded the continued population of Tulum. Montejo's base for the conquest of Cozumel was Pole (Xcaret), where a colonial capilla was built among the still-standing temples of the considerable population (Proskouriakoff, 1957a).

SUMMARY: ARCHAEOLOGY OF THE NORTHERN MAYA AREA

The history on the peninsula we have given above differs considerably from descriptions currently in use. Actually, although of

[10] This hypothetical reconstruction involves probable continuation of Early period forms in ceramics as well as in architecture and/or a possibly earlier origin of "Decadent Red wares" on the East Coast.

necessity discarding certain descriptive terms as confusing geography with history, or foreign influences with the internal dynamics of local culture, it does no violence to existing concepts of history in the southern lowlands. It does give a much simpler picture of the longer history of the northern area in the light of considerable new factual evidence accumulated in recent years. After a Formative era, Maya civilization is divided into three clear periods:

Formative Era (approx. 1500–2000 B.C. to approx. A.D. zero).

Three stages are tentatively recognized, the last possibly formative of the advanced civilization to come. Perhaps earlier stages should be called "pre-Maya." Remains are found over the entire Maya lowlands, the earliest and most massive as well as the most abundant on the plain of northern Yucatan.

I. Early Period (approx. A.D. zero to 650–900)

Introduction of the corbeled vault and the cult of carved stone monuments gives rise to true Maya civilization. Theocratic rule, hieroglyphic writing, advanced calendar, astronomy give flavor to this period. Naturalistic art reached its highest development. This period saw the maximum extension of Maya culture. All cities except on Yucatan Peninsula were abandoned before the end of the period.

II. Florescent Period (A.D. 650–900 to 1200) Foreign or radically new local cultural innovations led Maya civilization to a second and drastically different upward development. New techniques brought architecture to its maximum perfection in New World, as naturalized art gave way to formalized and geometric expression. The cult of hieroglyphics-calendar-astronomy temporarily disappeared, probably accompanying a transition from theocratic to secular socio-political institutions. The great cities of the Puuc were abandoned at the end of the first phase of this period. During the second, monumental construction was limited to Chichen Itza on northern Yucatan plain.

III. Decadent Period (A.D. 1200–1450) The complete withdrawal or collapse of Florescent institutions and traditions created a cultural vacuum in Yucatan which drew in surviving traditions of Early period culture from the isolated Caribbean littoral of Quintana Roo. After the collapse of Chichen Itza, there was an interregnum of an as yet unknown center, followed by the development of an empire at Mayapan which controlled the entire northern plains area. Mayapan was destroyed in 1440. The following century, before Spanish conquest, was one of increasing disintegration into small, warring tribal groups.

REFERENCES

Andrews, 1942, 1943, 1959, 1960, 1961a, 1961b, 1964
Brainerd, 1951, 1958
Charnay, 1887
Escalona Ramos, 1946
Fernández, 1945a, 1945b, 1945c
Gann, 1900
Holmes, 1895–97
Hubbs, Bien, and Suess, 1963
Lizardi Ramos, 1939, 1940
Lothrop, 1924
Marden, 1959
Pollock, 1940b
—— and Stromsvik, 1953

Proskouriakoff, 1946, 1950, 1951, 1957a
Ricketson and Ricketson, 1937
Ruz L., 1956
Sanders, 1955, 1960a
Shook, 1940
Smith, A. L., 1950
Smith, R. E., 1955a, 1955b
—— and Gifford, 1959
Stephens, 1843
Thompson, D. E. and J. E. S., 1955
Thompson, J. E. S., 1937, 1954b, 1957
Vaillant, 1927
Wauchope, 1950

13. Archaeological Synthesis of the Southern Maya Lowlands

J. ERIC S. THOMPSON

THE REGION of the southern Maya lowlands, as here understood, is bounded on the north by a line running westward at approximately 18° 30′ from the northern tip of British Honduras to the southern shore of Laguna de Terminos but dipping to exclude the Rio Bec sites. On the east the boundary is the Bay of Honduras and a line slightly east of Los Higos and Copan, in Honduras; the south boundary extends from a short distance south of Copan westerly to the northern slope of the Sierra de Chama but with outposts extending up the Motagua and Panzos valleys. The line continues westward across the northern slopes of the Guatemala highlands and beyond the northern outposts of the Cuchumatanes across the plateau of Chiapas to include Comitan, thence northwestward to include the territory of the Tzotzil and Tzeltal,[1] Tila and Tortuguero and, with a jog, Comalcalco, the westernmost Maya

[1] Ed. note: Upland Chiapas may also be considered as "Maya highlands." See Lowe and Mason, Article 9, for a treatment of the archaeology of this region.

site, which lies only some 85 km. east of the great Olmec site of La Venta.

To the north were the Yucatec Maya; to the east, probably the Jicaque and Lenca; to the south, highland Maya and a scattering of Pipil settlements; to the southwest, unknown groups (some Nahuatl-speaking) in the central plateau of Chiapas, the Chiapanec, and Zoque; to the west Nahuatl-speaking peoples and the builders or inheritors of La Venta culture. This is based on present-day distribution and the situation in the colonial period; there probably has been little change in the past millennium except perhaps for the state of Tabasco.

Generally the region is only some 200 m. above sea level, but the Copan region (Copan approximately 650 m. high), the Maya mountains of British Honduras (up to 1200 m. high, but not favored by the Maya for settlement), and the Chiapan plateau (Comitan approximately 1650 m. high) present a different picture. They are included because linguistically and culturally they belong with the lowlands. Nevertheless, the cult of stelae with hieroglyph

331

Fɪɢ. 1—TEMPLE OF THE GIANT JAGUAR (TEMPLE I), TIKAL, GUATEMALA
Photo by George Holton; courtesy, University Museum, University of Pennsylvania.)

inscriptions and the employment of the corbeled vault had difficulty in effecting a lodgment in the Chiapan plateau.[2]

The most important waterway is the Usumacinta with its great tributaries, the Pasion (Xocmo), the Salinas (Xoy), the Lacantun, and far downstream the San Pedro Martir (Tachis). Farther north, the Candelaria and Belize rivers are important. The formation of the greater part of this area is limestone with overlying marl. Local variations have affected habitation, but except in areas of swamp or of poor soil, such as the Pine Ridge country of British Honduras and the savannas of the Peten, the land is generally suitable for slash-and-burn agriculture.

Rainfall throughout the region is very high. Punta Gorda, British Honduras, averages 3.60 m. annually; Villahermosa, Tabasco, recorded 2.50 m. for one year. There are wet and dry seasons, and the latitude (between 15° and 18° N.) together with the low altitude insure tropical conditions. Fauna and flora appear to have been the same in ancient times as today; unchanged pond levels, representations of the present-day fauna in art of the Classic period, evidence for chiclero's ulcer, and survivals of woods still typical of the area, such as zapote and *tzalam*,[3] argue against a climatic change.

At the present time practically all the low-lying area is covered with dense tropical rain forest. On the poorer savannas and "pine ridges" grasslands are interspersed with pine, *nance*, and *Crescentia cujete*, producer of the round gourds, which, sliced in half, served the Maya as cups. On the high ground of Chiapas live oak and pine predominate; the swamp lands at the deltas of the Usumacinta and Grijalva are for the most part of little value for crops.

The southern lowlands possess less natural wealth than do the highlands. There are no deposits of obsidian to supply the knife blades so essential to everyday life. The cores, from which were pressed off every one of the scores of thousands of obsidian blades strewn over every lowland site from the largest to those comprising a single mound, had to be imported. With the probable exception of the Maya Mountains in British Honduras, there were no local supplies of jade, although the Sierra de las Minas, the apparent source for much Maya jade, was not far beyond the southeastern limits of the area. The quetzal, so highly valued for its tail feathers, did not inhabit the lowlands. Except for small and unworked sources of gold near Copan and in the Maya mountains, there were no deposits of metal in the area. There were salt deposits in Chiapas (Mendizabal, 1928, pp. 163–67) and on the Chixoy River, but for the Peten–British Honduras area, local supplies did not suffice, and at the time of the Spanish conquest Yucatan exported salt to both the Tabasco and the Manche Chol areas. Salt was also obtained from boiling the ash of burned trunks of the guano (*Sabal*) palm, but that is hardly a source for a large population.[4]

The lowlands, however, had unlimited supplies of flint, and there is evidence of its export to the highlands of Guatemala.[5]

---

[2] All texts are late except Stela 10, Chinkultic. The ball-court marker with Initial Series 9.7.17.-12.14, usually attributed to Chinkultic, comes from Colonia La Esperanza, a few kilometers to the north, but in lower land (information of Don Xavier Mandujano S., whose father removed it). All European dates are according to the Goodman-Martínez-Thompson correlation.

[3] Chiclero's ulcer, which exists only in regions of tropical rain forests, is represented in Maya art. A piece of wood, identified by my Maya workers as *tzalam* (*Lyiloma bahamensis* Bentl.) was found by me at Chochkitam in 1931. It formed the ceiling of a cupboard in one of the rooms.

[4] López de Cogolludo (1867–68, bk. 12, ch. 7), and my personal observation in British Honduras.

[5] The trident-shaped eccentric flints in a cache at El Baul (Thompson, 1948, fig. 23) were certainly from the southern lowlands, and I suspect the accompanying blades had the same origin. I think it will be shown some day that many of the finest pieces of worked flint found in central Mexico had a similar origin.

FIG. 2—INTERIOR, PALACE OF FIVE STORIES, TIKAL, GUATEMALA
(Courtesy, University Museum, University of Pennsylvania.)

Some of the amber deposits in northern Chiapas were probably controlled by lowland Tzeltal and exported thence to distant parts of Mexico (Blom, 1959). There must, too, have been a steady export of skins and feathers, those of jaguars, parrots, toucans, humming birds, and alligators come readily to mind. Cacao plantations, particularly in Tabasco and the Belize Valley, must have financed many imports (Thompson, 1956). The ubiquitous limestone is an excellent building stone, and lime was probably exported to the highlands, for in Maya eyes it is the best lye for steeping shelled maize. Thus the southern lowlands could very likely maintain a balance of payment with their neighbors.

Limestone, as noted, supplied most of the area with excellent stone for building and for carving, but sandstone was used in some parts (Quirigua and Altar de Sacrificios), trachyte at Copan, slate in parts of British Honduras, and dolomite along the middle Usumacinta, whereas in the Usumacinta-Grijalva delta lack of stone forced the Maya to bake bricks or to utilize the huge accumulations of shells.

At the present time the great core of this region (the Peten and Usumacinta drainage) is largely uninhabited. The decline from the not very heavy settlement of the period of Spanish conquest to the present condition probably was largely caused by the spread of hookworm, malaria, and smallpox. On the other hand, the peripheries of this core, notably the Belize and Copan valleys, the delta of the Usumacinta and Grijalva rivers, and the uplands of Chiapas continue to support a fairly dense population, and a small recolonization of the Pasion-Sarstoon region has been undertaken haphazardly by highland Maya of Kekchi language moving north in the past 70–80 years from their homeland in the Alta Verapaz.

Nevertheless, the whole region, with the possible exception of the Chiapan plateau, was heavily populated during the Classic period and probably in the later part of the Preclassic period as well, despite the difficulties to be faced in bringing tropical rain forest under cultivation and the limited natural resources of much of the area. The density of house mounds and ceremonial centers in the area is remarkable (Ricketson and Ricketson, 1937, pp. 15–24; Willey, 1956a; Willey and Bullard, 1956; Bullard, 1960b).

LANGUAGES

On the basis of 16th–18th-century sources and present-day observation one may reasonably suppose that in the great belt which, extending from Comalcalco to Copan, bisects the southern lowlands the languages and dialects spoken proceeding from west to east, were Chontal, Palenque Chol, Manche Chol, and Chorti. All of these are closely related. In the northern Peten and adjacent British Honduras the language may have been Yucatec, but that does not differ strikingly from the other lowland languages and dialects. A Mopan, one of a small group living north of the Manche Chol, around San Luis and Dolores in southeastern Peten, could understand Yucatec without much difficulty, and in turn could understand Manche Chol.[6] In no case are these differences marked (Gates, 1932; Thompson, 1950, fig. 1). In the cold lands of Chiapas and spilling into the lower ground to the north are the Tzotzil, Tzeltal and Chaneabal (also called Tojolabal or Comiteco), all three of which fall in the lowland group but with evidence that they may have been longer separated from the true lowlanders (McQuown, 1956). Just on the edge of the area (south of the Tojolabales) was the now extinct Chicomuceltec which has strange affinities with Huaxtec and is

[6] In camp at Mountain Cow I had laborers drawn from both groups, and they conversed quite freely together. According to early sources, Mopan was a mixture (that is to say, lay between) Yucatec and Manche Chol, and Mopan and Manche Chol understood one another.

335

Fɪɢ. 3—HIEROGLYPHIC STAIRWAY, COPAN, HONDURAS. (Photo by Otto Done.)

quite out of place (Termer, 1930a). The absence of sharp breaks between adjacent languages and dialects—with the exception of the peripheral Chicomuceltec, they blend like the colors of the rainbow—seems good evidence that the geographical pattern of language distribution has changed only to a slight degree since the Classic period. There is fairly good evidence that the users of the Maya hieroglyphs spoke a language close to modern Yucatec (Thompson, 1958, p. 297).

Mᴀʏᴀ Rᴜɪɴs

In this southern lowland region there are approximately 80 sites with hieroglyphic inscriptions and perhaps three or four times

as many smaller sites which have either no stelae or only one or two plain stelae but which can be classified as primarily ceremonial in function. Nevertheless, the distribution is uneven. In some parts, notably the eastern half of the Peten, important ruins are close together; in others, particularly in the Calendaria, Mamantel, and San Pedro Martir drainages, important sites are rare. In one or two large areas the rarity of sites is probably due to lack of exploration; few were known to the south of the Usumacinta and Pasion valley until exploration in recent years produced a number of much importance. On the other hand, savanna and "pine ridge," with soils unsuited to maize cultivation, were

336

shunned by the Maya and account for some blanks on the map. The mountain area of central British Honduras and the swamps of the Usumacinta-Grijalva delta lack large Maya sites for the same reasons.[7]

Almost all Maya sites bear modern names, Spanish, English, Maya or pseudo-Maya. Copan, Tikal, Pusilha, and Quirigua conceivably might be original names, but probably no site in the southern lowlands retains its Classic period designation.

Maya ruins were first brought to the attention of the western world through the explorations of Spanish commissioners sent to Palenque in 1784–86, following an examination and report on the site by Canon Ramon de Ordoñez y Aguiar. The report of Antonio del Río, published in London in 1822, aroused the interest of John L. Stephens, who, with the artist Frederick Catherwood, described and illustrated such lowland sites as Copan, Quirigua, Palenque, and Uxmal, given to a keenly interested public in the former's *Incidents of travel in Central America, Chiapas, and Yucatan,* first published in 1841.

Serious archaeology in the southern lowlands started with the explorations of Alfred Maudslay and of Teobert Maler and with work at Copan by the Peabody Museum, Harvard University. The series of explorations in the Peten initiated in 1914 by Sylvanus G. Morley brought to light many new sites and monuments; they were largely successful because the Shufeldt chicle concession had opened the northern Peten to bush travel. Similarly, exploration for oil has led to the discovery of new sites in recent years.[8] Intensive excavation on a scale hitherto unknown is now being undertaken at Tikal by University Museum, Philadelphia, in collaboration with the Guatemalan government.

It was not until 1928 that the first ceramic sequence for the Maya area was formulated, and that stopped at the end of the Classic period. This fits into the framework of periods as used in this *Handbook,* as follows:

Middle Preclassic	Mamom
Late Preclassic	Chicanel
Protoclassic	Matzanel (Holmul I)
Early Classic	Tzakol
Late Classic	Tepeu
Terminal Classic	Tepeu 3
Postclassic[9]	

Outside the nuclear lowland area still earlier material has since been encountered. Because of its bearing on early occupation of the southern lowlands, one may note that from the cenote of Mani, Yucatan, Brainerd (1958, p. 24) recovered jars with burnished decoration underlying Middle Preclassic deposits. These he considered to be earlier than the local equivalents of Mamom which he had found in Campeche. Very recently, Altar de Sacrificios, on the Pasion River, has yielded pre-Mamom material which has its closest resemblances in the pottery of Chiapas 2. This last has produced three C14 dates of 900–800 B.C.

Coeval with, or earlier than, Mamom is the pottery recovered by G. B. Gordon from caves near Copan. Porter (1953, p. 54) has noted its close resemblance to that of Tlatilco–Middle Tlatilco, to judge by the subsequent study by Piña Chan (1958).

Mamom was first recognized at Uaxactun

---

[7] The map of the northern Peten displaying huge areas of swamp, perhaps former lakes, published by Bullard (1960b) is most revealing. Naturally, sites are not in low areas.

[8] For detailed accounts of early exploration in the Maya lowlands see Morley, 1937–38, 1: 76–102; Palacios, 1941; and Termer, 1952. For the impact of Stephens see Tozzer, 1941b. For notes on some early Mayanists see Thompson, 1950, pp. 28–34.

[9] Ceramic terms originate with Robert E. Smith (1955a), who refined the original sequence. [Ed. note: Some difference of opinion exists as to the placement of Maya ceramic phases in the general Mesoamerican framework of periods. Some authorities would place Mamom as Middle Preclassic. Chicanel may have beginning in Middle Preclassic but extends into Late Preclassic. Matzanel may be dated as Protoclassic, as in this *Handbook,* or be designated as Late Preclassic. See the chronological charts and discussions for Mesoamerica as a whole in Willey, Ekholm, and Millon, Article 14, volume 1.]

FIG. 4—UPPER PORTION OF STELA A, COPAN, HONDURAS. (Photo by B. T. Kurt.)

by Vaillant and Kidder under circumstances recorded by the latter (*in* A. L. Smith, 1950, pp. 3–4). The horizon is still identified only by pottery vessels and figurines and a few artifacts of stone and obsidian; as yet no structure is definitely assignable to it. Mamom material has been found at several sites in the Peten and British Honduras, and future investigation will probably show it to have been widespread. Brainerd (1958, p. 89) reported a local equivalent at two sites in the Chenes area of Campeche, and Andrews considers his earliest level at Dzibilchaltun, Yucatan,

338

to be a Yucatecan manifestation of Mamom. The horizon has produced a C14 date of 965 B.C. ± 200. The earliest material at Copan (Longyear, 1952, pp. 23–25) may be contemporaneous with Mamom.

The thesis that Mamom was a local manifestation of a Preclassic distribution extending from the Panuco to the Ulua Valley opens wide vistas (Drucker, 1943b, pp. 118–19; Ekholm, 1944, p. 503; Thompson, 1953, p. 448).

Late Preclassic, the Peten manifestation of which is Chicanel, was of considerable importance at Uaxactun and work now in progress at Tikal shows that the north terrace area and the Great Plaza were about as large in Chicanel times as at the height of the Classic period (there was also an earlier Mamom occupation). At Uaxactun Str. E-VIIsub and its associated plaza are assignable to Chicanel. This squat pyramid is of particular interest because of the giant stucco masks flanking its stairways, for they have given rise to much speculation on La Venta influences there (e.g. Covarrubias, 1957, pp. 223, 228–29; for the opposite view see Proskouriakoff, 1950, p. 102). Post holes in the flat summit of the pyramid indicated a structure of perishable materials. Something similar is now coming to light at Tikal, where painted stucco masks flanking the stairway of a partly demolished Chicanel pyramid or platform are in process of excavation.

Tikal has also yielded a rich Chicanel tomb roofed with a primitive corbeled vault (C14 date of about A.D. 1); the same primitive corbeled vaulting covered a Chicanel tomb at Altar de Sacrificios. Furniture in the Tikal tomb included a jade mask, about half natural size, with shell inlay of eyes and teeth, and Usulutan ware brought a great distance (Coe and McGinn, 1963). Clearly, building activities and rich tombs indicate a well-organized and stratified society. Late Preclassic is widespread over the whole Yucatan peninsula, confirmation of a large population.

Fig. 5—DOORWAY, COPAN, HONDURAS. West side, inner chamber of Temple 22. (After Maudslay.)

On the other hand, there is still a lack of sculpture assignable to this horizon in the lowlands. W. R. Coe (1962b) has suggested that the breaking up of obsolescent monuments might partly account for this, a view which finds confirmation in the fact that perhaps the only known Preclassic sculpture from the lowlands stands some distance above ground at the entrance to the cave of Loltun, Yucatan; reasons for discarding monuments in a ceremonial center would hardly apply to this rock carving. Proskouriakoff (1950, p. 155) sees its closest analogies on a stela at San Isidro Piedra

FIG. 6—STONE HEAD, CHAMELECON VALLEY, HONDURAS. (Courtesy, Middle American Research Institute, Tulane University.)

Parada, on the Pacific slope, a site which has produced other early sculpture, including a rock carving of Olmec type (Thompson, 1943c).

Present evidence indicates that Chicanel was approximately contemporaneous with the exuberant Miraflores horizon at Kaminaljuyu. A figurine cult is prominent in the Mamom horizon but its absence in Late Preclassic and Early Classic may indicate a shift in religious practices between Middle and Late Preclassic in the Maya lowlands. Whatever the situation may be with regard to Mamom times, one has the strong impression that the makers of Chicanel pottery were definitely Maya.

The Matzanel phase, formerly, as Holmul I, assigned to the start of the Classic period, is elevated to rank of its own as Protoclassic in this *Handbook*. It is of particular interest because through some of its traits, such as tetrapod bowls of specialized shapes, potstands, and "chocolate pots," once assigned to the enigmatic Q-complex, it is linked to phases outside the Maya area, notably Monte Alban II. Matzanel is scarcely represented at Uaxactun; the best evidence for it comes from Holmul in the Peten, and from Mountain Cow, Barton Ramie, and Douglas, British Honduras. It may have been of short duration.[10] In my opinion, it should be restored to Classic status, and if there is to be a Protoclassic horizon, Chicanel should be elevated to that rank. With hieroglyphic writing and corbeled vaulting already developed, its claim is good.

The Holmul I pottery was in two sealed ossuaries beneath rooms which were re-opened as needed, a custom which persisted till late Mayapan times (cf. Thompson and Thompson, 1955, p. 230). The important point is that the rooms above the Holmul ossuaries had corbeled vaulting, and one may reasonably accept Merwin's evidence that the cists had been used, if not constructed, after the building of free-standing and reasonably well-constructed vaulted rooms,[11] a distinct advance on Chicanel vaulted burial chambers beneath ground. A corbel-vaulted burial chamber with Matzanel pottery occurs at Mountain Cow (Thompson, 1931, p. 290). No sculpture has yet been identified as Late Preclassic or Protoclassic in the lowlands although it must surely exist.

[10] Merwin and Vaillant, 1932, pp. 54–55, 60–65; Anderson and Cook, 1944; Thompson, 1931, pls. 40–42, 44; Smith and Gifford, Article 19.

[11] Merwin and Vaillant, 1932, p. 20. Vaillant doubts Merwin's statement that the ossuary chambers were used after the vaulted rooms were erected, but Merwin's statement, besides being based on personal information (Vaillant never visited the site), is supported by archaeological data from elsewhere in the Maya area. Room 8, used in Matzanel times, continued in use in early Tzakol, a source of modern confusion.

Fɪɢ. 7—STELA D, QUIRIGUA, GUATEMALA. (After Maudslay.)

Fig. 8—MONOLITH ANIMAL B, QUIRIGUA, GUATEMALA. (After Maudslay.)

Trade, as in the earlier Preclassic horizons, was widespread. Apart from imports, such as jade and obsidian, conforming to earlier patterns, one might note a tetrapod dish with a fish painted on its base from a Matzanel burial at Mountain Cow, which is almost exactly duplicated by a vessel from Tzicuay, El Quiche (Thompson, 1931, pl. 42,*b*; Smith and Kidder, 1951, fig. 75*k*), and Usulatan decoration (perhaps imitation) on a tetrapod vessel from Douglas (Anderson and Cook, 1944, fig. 2,*l*) and as definite imitation at Mountain Cow (Thompson, 1931, pl. 41,*a*).

Assuming Merwin correctly assigned Str. B, Group II, Holmul, to Matzanel, we have some information on treatment of façades at that time. Whether from lack of experience or chance, the corbel-vaulted rooms are unusually narrow, the widest

342

reaching only 1.20 m. and the narrowest 55 cm.

TZAKOL (EARLY CLASSIC)

The Classic period, as the name implies, witnessed the florescence of Maya culture in the Southern Lowlands. It is divided into two ceramic phases, called Tzakol and Tepeu, each of which, in turn, has three subdivisions (R. E. Smith, 1955b); changes of masonry equate with the phases (A. L. Smith, 1950, pp. v, vi). The start of the Classic period is generally assigned to a position around 8.12.0.0.0 in the Maya calendar, corresponding to A.D. 278 according to the Goodman-Martínez-Thompson correlation, but a date perhaps two centuries earlier now seems more reasonable. The change from the Tzakol horizon to Tepeu has been correlated with the shift from

Vault I to Vault II type of architecture at Uaxactun, and this, on the assumption that dated monuments were not reset, equates with the Maya position 9.8.0.0.0 (A.D. 593). The custom of erecting dated monuments ceased at different times in different centers, but A.D. 900 is a reasonable date. By then, ceremonial activity on a large scale had come to an end in most centers; the two latest dated monuments appear to be one erected at La Muñeca probably in A.D. 899 and a second at the nearby center of San Lorenzo, which may carry a date equivalent to A.D. 928, 10.5.0.0.0 in the Maya calendar.

The transition from the end of the Preclassic period to full Classic does not seem to have been abrupt (Wauchope, 1950, p. 220). Indeed, one suspects it may have more substantiality for modern investigators than for those living at that time. Some Matzanel polychrome designs continue into early Tzakol, although changes in form are more perceptible. Lack of data leaves us uninformed on possible shifts in architecture, sculpture, and hieroglyphic texts, but one may suspect that the changes were evolutionary.

TEPEU (LATE CLASSIC)

Tepeu pottery is not a natural evolution from Tzakol. As Robert E. Smith (1955b, pp. 5, 6) has noted, plain kitchen wares changed radically. The representation of elaborate ceremonies in a highly realistic manner marks a break with the past, as does the constant use of bands of glyphs around rims, for on Tzakol pottery glyphs are rare and are not employed for decorative effects. Finally, pottery figurines, known in the Mamom phase but absent since then, return in the Late Classic period in great numbers and elaboration (they are moldmade whereas those of the Mamom period were handmade).

An apparent hiatus in Maya sculptural activity between 9.5.0.0.0 (A.D. 534) and 9.8.0.0.0 (A.D. 593) has been discussed by Proskouriakoff (1950, pp. 111–12). She points out that when sculpture reappears, it is in a changed style, and she notes the interesting possibility of coordinating this sculptural lacuna and the sequent new style with the replacement of Tzakol pottery by Tepeu and of the early masonry style by a later one.[12] So far as is at present known, the shift from Early to Late Classic did not involve any fundamental change in the Maya pattern of life revolving around the ceremonial center.

At the close of the Classic period intrusive ideas in sculpture (Proskouriakoff, 1950, pp. 150–53) and in pottery (Thompson, 1939a, pp. 231–32) are evident.

Work has been so concentrated in the area of northern Peten and British Honduras that the ceramic picture is out of balance. At Palenque there is nothing directly comparable to the Tzakol and Tepeu divisions and the monochrome aspect is far stronger, with apparent dependence on the Campeche-Tabasco coastal plain (Rands and Rands, 1957); even at Piedras Negras true Tzakol is rare and the later material, although it has much in common with Tepeu, is distinctive (Butler, 1935b). Copan also has its distinctive ceramic tradition, but with more than enough crossties with the Peten to manifest contemporaneity (Longyear, 1952). At present little is known of Maya ceramics in the Chiapan highlands during the Classic period;[13] much of the available material consists of incense burners and Late Classic or Postclassic material. Nevertheless, of a half-dozen sherds I examined at Tonina one was from a basal-flanged bowl of Tzakol type. Late Classic

---

[12] There are two or three dated monuments erected during this hiatus but they lack sculptured figures. The ball-court marker from Colonia La Esperanza falls in the period. The fact that katun 9.6.0.0.0 ended on the extremely unlucky month position 3 Uayeb, when no activity should take place, may account in part for the rarity of dated monuments at this time, but alone it does not explain the hiatus.

[13] Ed. note: See Lowe and Mason, Article 9.

Fig. 9—LINTEL, STR. 23, YAXCHILAN, CHIA-
PAS, MEXICO. Now in the British Museum.
(After Maudslay.)

is well represented in the Jonuta area (Berlin, 1953; 1956).

THE CLASSIC PERIOD "COLLAPSE"

The causes which led to the collapse of the
Classic period are not surely known. In
evaluating the explanations advanced one
must bear in mind that, to judge by the
dated inscriptions, the process was gradual
and seems to some extent to have been affected by the locations of sites. Some important ceremonial cities, notably Palenque, Piedras Negras, Quirigua, and Copan,
have no monuments dated later than A.D.

810 (9.19.0.0.0 in the Maya calendar), and
all except Piedras Negras lie close to the
southern border of the lowland Maya. One
or two isolated outposts—Sacchana (Quen
Santo) and Comitan—almost on the edge
of the Chiapas plateau, and sites on the
Pasion held out longer, as did two or three
sites in Yucatan, but the last redoubt of
dated monuments is in northern Peten and
adjacent parts of southern Campeche, comprising Tikal, Uaxactun, Flores, Xultun,
Ixlu, El Palmar, La Muñeca, Tzibanche
(dated jade bead), and San Lorenzo. It
may be significant that this area is most

Fig. 10—BACK OF DAIS OR ALTAR, PIEDRAS NEGRAS, GUATEMALA. Dragon monster with human figures looking out of eye sockets. (Courtesy, University Museum, University of Pennsylvania.)

distant from the borders of the Maya realm and supposed routes of navigation.

Morley (1946, p. 71), who believed that not only the ceremonial centers but the whole area, his "Old Empire," was evacuated at the close of the Classic period, felt that invasion of the agricultural land by grass, with which the Maya were unable to cope, forced emigration, but this opinion is very questionable (Thompson, 1954a, pp. 85–86). Exhaustion of the soil by the supposedly wasteful slash-and-burn system of agriculture has also been blamed for abandonment of the area, but Quirigua, surrounded by rich land annually renewed by flooding of the Motagua River, ceased to erect monuments long before centers situated in far poorer districts. Ursula Cowgill (1959) suggests that inadequate water reservoirs may account for the depopulation of much of the area. This is a variation on the thesis of Wythe Cooke (1931) that the present-day swamps of the Peten may have been lakes during the Classic period but are now silted. This might well account for the low population in the Peten in Postclassic times, but it can hardly account for the fall of sites on or near the banks of such rivers as the Usumacinta, Lacanha, Pusilha, Copan, and Motagua with their tributaries.

Epidemics of malaria, yellow fever, or hookworm have also been suggested as having caused depopulation of the southern lowlands, but it is reasonably certain that all three scourges were brought to Middle America by the white man or the slaves he imported.

The opinion that the Classic period may have been brought to an end by peasant revolts, which led to the extinction of a ruling class that had lost the confidence of the rank and file still seems as logical as any (Thompson, 1931, p. 230; 1954a, pp. 86–89). There is certainly evidence of purposeful destruction of symbols of the old hierarchy at Piedras Negras at the very end of the occupation of that center.

Evidence is accumulating that there was no general abandonment of the area at the close of the Classic period, although there may well have been a marked diminution in the population. The theory of liquidation of the theocracy carries with it the assumption that the peasant population continued their daily lives with little disturbance under minor headmen. There is growing evidence that for some time the people repaired to the ceremonial centers for the more important rites of their folk religion, far simpler than the rites of the old theocracy, but the untended buildings soon started to decay. Half-hearted attempts were

345

Fig. 11—THE PALACE, PALENQUE, CHIAPAS, MEXICO. Western court and tower, looking south. (After Maudslay.)

made to keep ceremonial centers in part use by blocking collapsed doorways. Burials with Postclassic pottery were made in Copan vaulted rooms and without pottery in abandoned rooms at Uaxactun.[14] Foundations of domestic dwellings of stone from Classic period buildings stand on the latest floors of courts at Uxmal, and something similar seems to have occurred at Tikal (W. R. Coe, 1962b), and perhaps Benque Viejo (MacKie, 1961, pp. 216–17).

Much evidence has been gathered on the resetting of stelae, whole or fragmentary and in some cases upside down, at Tikal,

and in some cases the evidence is conclusive that this happened after 10.2.0.0.0 (A.D. 869), the latest known date at that site (Satterthwaite, 1958a; W. R. Coe and Broman, 1958, p. 48; W. R. Coe, 1962b, pp. 484–87). The same resetting of stelae occurs elsewhere but without evidence as to when it happened. At Rio Bec the bottom half of Stela 5 had been reset upside down; at Calakmul the upper half of Stela 13 stood upside down about 3 m. from the lower half still *in situ*; at Naachtun Stela 23 had suffered a somewhat similar fate (Ruppert and Denison, 1943, pp. 102, 126, 135). Removal probably explains some cases of missing top halves of stelae.

One gets a picture of attempts to keep up a stela cult after the liquidation of the

[14] Summarized in Thompson, 1954a, pp. 88. Stromsvik in a letter (1960) remarks that several burials at Copan were in fallen debris, mainly around the ball court, but also in the east court.

346

hierarchy by peasants who were too ignorant to know whether a stela was right side up or not or who set pieces upside down because sacredness lay in the stone itself—folk memory of their importance in the past—not in the figures or hieroglyphic texts inscribed on it.[15]

Ceramic and other evidence for Postclassic use of ceremonial centers is accumulating: in some cases this was a real occupation continuing after the close of hierarchic activity; in other cases pilgrimages are indicated. It is not unlikely that Tepeu 3 was in part Postclassic; San Jose 5 certainly was. Recently MacKie (1961) has established that Benque Viejo IV (late Tepeu) is postoccupational in some parts at least of that site. Tripod bowls with "Turkish slipper" feet (Berlin, 1955a) may represent a carryover from the end of the Classic. This horizon is present also at Tikal (W. R. Coe, 1962b, p. 483).[16]

Metal, absent in the Classic period, occurred in the form of copper verdegris in a San Jose cache (Thompson, 1939a, p. 188). Metal finds at Copan comprise the feet of a pre-Columbian gold figure, fragments of brass casings of bullets, and a saucy bronze (?) lion. The first two were in an atypical cache beneath a stela[17] carrying a date corresponding without much doubt to A.D. 730 but probably dedicated somewhat later. I believe the cache to be, at least in part, intrusive. The metal lion (Gann, 1926, p. 198) was a recent offering presumably by the Chorti Maya living in the vicinity, and it is reasonable to suppose the metal objects in the stela cache have a similar origin.

Altar de Sacrificios witnessed a post-Tepeu 3 but pre-Tohil Plumbate occupation of short duration. Fine Orange of both Z and Y types occur together; there is much Fine Gray pottery together with the beginnings of grater bowls, and pottery figures rather like those Charnay found at Los Idolos, Tabasco, on jar lids. The material indicates influences from the Chontalapa, not surprising in view of Altar de Sacrificios' strategic position on merchant routes from the region to the Bay of Honduras and perhaps the Alta Verapaz (Willey and Smith, 1963).

Somewhat later in date is the appearance of Tohil pottery. A postoccupational burial at Copan yielded such vessels together with other trade pieces from Nicaragua and a tripod bowl with spherical feet shaped as human heads, a typical Postclassic feature. As noted, plumbate pottery, thought to be Tohil, occurs in presumed house mounds at Tikal. An effigy frog vessel from a cave near Benque Viejo is either Tohil Plumbate or a splendid copy. At Palenque polished flat stone heads and fragments of yokes (plain) on the floors of late rooms may date from the very close of the Classic there, but more probably are evidence of a Postclassic phase (Ruz, 1953, pp. 460–61). A stone yoke was also a surface find at Copan.

Present information seems against a heavy population in the early Postclassic, but it is worth bearing in mind that few or no traces have yet been identified of the fairly large population known to have occupied the Belize valley in the 17th century, although that territory has received a fair amount of archaeological attention. Moreover, a shift from pottery utensils to gourds and *jicaras* would make the village sites of

[15] Offerings to stelae and altars continue to the present day. Stromsvik (1947, p. 57) reports repeated offerings of copal and candles on an altar at Copan; at Tzendales, Tozzer (1907, p. 82) found five incense burners before a stela; at Benque Viejo a wooden cross has been placed on a fallen stela, and flowers and stones are left there as offerings (Gann, 1925a, p. 71); at La Honradez I found the pieces of a broken incense burner immediately in front of a stela.

[16] Ed. note: See Smith and Gifford, Article 19, for comments on Postclassic occupation at Barton Ramie, British Honduras.

[17] Stromsvik, 1942b, p. 71. Longyear (1952, p. 112), noting the atypical contents of the contents of the cache beneath Stela H, suggests it may have been deposited in the Postclassic period by visitors to the deserted ceremonial center. This seems the most reasonable explanation.

Fig. 12—SCULPTURED STONE SLAB, PALENQUE, CHIAPAS, MEXICO. West corridor of the Palace, House E. (After Maudslay.)

their users difficult to identify, particularly if huts were not set on platforms (cf. Bullard, 1960b, p. 359). Present-day Maya in parts of the lowlands use practically no pottery except large storage jars not easily broken, and even these are lacking among the Lacandon. The telltale obsidian flakes are also absent. When did they disappear? Mention of them by the friars is very rare.

Late Postclassic is most fully represented by the rich Cintla horizon of the Usuma-

cinta's lower reaches, which is surely contemporaneous with the Mayapan domination in Yucatan and is a post-plumbate horizon (Berlin, 1956). At the other extreme of the area, pottery figurines and other artifacts from Santa Rita, British Honduras, are almost indistinguishable from finds at Mayapan (Gann. 1900, pl. XXXVI; 1918, pl. 8). Indeed, there can be little doubt that the northern third of British Honduras was a part of the Province of

348

Chetumal at the close of the 15th century (Roys, 1957, pp. 159–65).

Topoxte, Peten (Bullard, 1960b, p. 370), and Indian Church, British Honduras (Castells, 1904; Gann, 1926, pp. 63–65), the former possibly and the latter probably, were within the limits of Chetumal. Both contain buildings with columns set in their portals in a style markedly reminiscent of Mexican-influenced buildings in Yucatan, as well as fragments of figure incense burners with strong Mayapan-Tulum affinities. On top of that, Indian Church yielded a feathered-serpent column with similar connections which had been re-used as a stuccoed stela (small stuccoed stelae occur also at Topoxte). The murals at Santa Rita (Gann, 1900) are overwhelmingly Mexican in style but they are set in the context of the Maya calendar (a sequence of tuns [360-day years] correctly labeled with their closing days). Topoxte, unlike the ceremonial centers of the Classic period, was almost certainly an urban center (Bullard, 1960b), as was Tayasal, last capital of the Itza (Thompson, 1951). Again in contrast to the centers of the Classic period, both had been sited on small islands clearly for defensive reasons. Cortés, in his fifth letter, describes towns fortified with palisades, moats, and watchtowers in the territory of the Cehaches, northwest of Tayasal.

Recent work on Temple 1, Tikal, revealed a pit penetrating 2 m. beneath the floor, and in this were human bones and fragments of late incense burners and pottery, evidence of resort, if only temporary, to Tikal in Late Postclassic times. There are also signs of this horizon along the middle Usumacinta (Satterthwaite, 1943b).

For the situation in the southern lowlands during the 16th–18th centuries there is a good deal of documentary, but not too much ethnological, information. Evidently, there was a fairly heavy concentration of population in the Usumacinta-Grijalva delta and that agrees with the archaeological data (the Cintla horizon). The plateau of Chiapas was well peopled, and from outposts, such as Tonina and Palenque, constant efforts were made to entice out of the forests the pagan Indians. The Prospero area seems to have been well settled (López de Cogolludo, 1867–68, bk. 12, ch. 7), although some, of Yucatec speech, may have been recent immigrants. Farther east, the Manche Chol and other groups were believed to be 30,000 strong in southeastern Peten and adjacent British Honduras. The great Dominican missionary, Francisco Moran, who had first-hand knowledge of the area, gave a figure of 100,000 for the whole area including the lower Chixoy and Lacandon territory. Even discounting that figure, as well as one estimate of 500,000 inhabitants for the same area, it is clear that there was a considerable population in the area (Thompson, 1938) and one sufficiently organized to maintain without break the old Maya calendar. The country around Tayasal was heavily populated as was that around Copan and the Golfo Dulce. Most of this information is from periods subsequent to the decimation of the population by smallpox.

CULTURAL FORMS AND INSTITUTIONS

Following this condensation of the historical succession in the southern lowlands, let us examine briefly the outstanding cultural manifestations, with the understanding that in the absence of special mention to the contrary, reference is to the Classic period.

The ceremonial center—or city, as it was termed early in this century[18]—one of the distinctive features of Maya culture, had its beginnings in the Preclassic and survives to this day in certain Maya towns, such as Chamula, in Chiapas, and Chichicastenango in the highlands of Guatemala. The term implies that the sites were not urban cen-

[18] The term "ceremonial center" has recently come under attack. As I seem to have originated the term (Thompson, 1928), I must bear the responsibility for it.

FIG. 13—TEMPLE OF THE SUN, PALENQUE, CHIAPAS, MEXICO. (After Maudslay.)

ters, but had either no permanent population at all or were inhabited continuously only by a small group of religious and perhaps civil functionaries, as in the present-day Tzotzil town of Chamula. The Franciscan Lizana (1893, ch. 2), writing of conditions immediately before the arrival of the Spaniards, definitely states that the Maya of Yucatan lived in their thatched huts in family settlements in the woods, and that the ceremonial centers served as temples and sanctuaries, and on top of each they had their gods. He adds that they were in such excellent condition and so new and white in appearance that they seemed to have been built not even 20 years ago. This description clearly applies not to an abandoned, but to a functioning, ceremonial center. From the other end of the Maya area we have a statement by Vásquez (1937–44, bk. 1, ch. 21) that the Indians would never have lived in towns had it not been for the friars. Furthermore, the Maya were forced to borrow a word from Nahua to describe an urban center (Thompson, 1943e, p. 23). Vásquez' statement is not strictly true, but it paints an Indian attitude which is supported by information from every corner of the Maya lowlands.

One can not speak of a standard ceremonial center in the lowlands. One thinks of it as having as its heart a great court or plaza compassed about with temples perched on high pyramids or with "palaces" low-sprawled on massive substructures and peppered with sculptured stelae. Yet Palenque, most perfect of Maya cities in sculpture and perhaps in its buildings, has no stelae and only a vestigial great court. Uaxactun was built on seven hills (an eighth, somewhat distant and so no disturber of the Roman simile, may have served as a center of communications with Tikal). The seven hills encircle a large water hole, which may have been larger, naturally or through man's effort, during the Classic period. There are two or three rather half-hearted causeways, but gener-

ally a pilgrim had to go uphill and down dale to get from one group to another (600 m. in direct line between the outskirts of Groups B and D).

Piedras Negras, built on what one might term a bluff on the north bank of the Usumacinta, is more compact but it is on different levels; the west end of the west group rises steeply to 80 m. above the river in contrast to the southeast end of the south group where the rise, of less than 30 m., is gentle. The use at Piedras Negras of masonry piers to produce in the "palace" buildings an almost colonnade effect is reminiscent of Palenque and had later echoes in Yucatan, but the stelae of Piedras Negras and, to a lesser extent, the courts in which they stand are not in the Palenque tradition. Those loggia-like structures at Palenque, Piedras Negras, and Yaxchilan are very different from the secretive, narrow-entranced buildings of the Peten. The subject matter of the sculptured monuments of those Usumacinta sites also differs from those prevalent in the Peten. These manifestations of nonconformity may hint that foreign impulses had led to religious and perhaps political attitudes which no longer demanded the seclusion of the small darkened temple.

Eastward from the confluence of the Pasion and the Salinas-Chixoy to the Bay of Honduras that glory of Maya architecture, the corbeled vault, largely disappears, and, indeed, important ceremonial centers completely lack stone buildings, so far as one can tell without excavation.[19] Lubaantun, in southern British Honduras, has substructures faced with magnificent cut and faced stone, but there are no stone superstructures.

The Pasion basin seems to have had a predilection for monumental stairways

[19] Altar de Sacrificios, now being excavated, has produced no corbeled vaulting and, as yet, no stone superstructure (Willey, Smith, Bullard, and Graham, 1960a, 1960b). Pusilha appears to have been similarly situated.

351

FIG. 14—SCULPTURED LID OF SARCOPHAGUS, PALENQUE, CHIAPAS, MEXICO. Tomb under the Temple of the Inscriptions. (Photo by Don Leonard.)

adorned with hieroglyphic texts and recumbent prisoners with bound arms and crossed legs, a fancy which recurs in the great hieroglyphic stairway at Copan.[20]

Copan itself is not set on hills, but rises from a flat plain on the verge of the Copan River, and perhaps for that reason it is compact. It comprises a great court, 235 m. north-south and almost half as wide, at the south end of which rises the great acropolis. A steep stairway, 24 m. high, ascends to Temple 11 forming the north edge of the acropolis. The view of this building, before its ruin, from the main court must have been, as was intended, awe-inspiring. Extraordinary impressive, too, must have been the vista from the acropolis of the Copan River far below. In scenic drama and in intermingled spiritual and temporal cares, a priest-ruler gazing down from the Copan acropolis had much in common with, say, a prince-archbishop of Salzburg contemplating the fast-flowing Salzach from his fortress-palace high above it.

The general homogeneity of Maya ceremonial centers is obvious, but in the study of the differences, particularly in types of buildings, may be the key to much knowledge. The function of buildings is a relatively new subject of inquiry; it was not until Blom (1930) opened our eyes to the obvious that ball courts have been recognized as a normal feature of Maya ceremonial centers of the Classic period. A suggestion that the loggia-style buildings may reflect different religious or political ideas has been made; the apparent distribution

[20] Jacobean monuments to men of the Fettiplace family in St. Mary, Swinbrook, Oxford (Betjeman, 1959, pl. 45) supply an entertaining parallel to this Maya motif. The recumbent effigies, resting on one elbow, with one leg bent, the other straight, and set one above the other, should be compared with the recumbent prisoners in the stairway of the newly discovered site of Tamarindito. Had these Fettiplace effigies been a millennium earlier and with an east Asian provenance, they would be cited as incontrovertible evidence of transpacific influences.

352

of sweat houses may have ethnological connotations. Archaeological investigation has revealed their presence so far only at Piedras Negras, Chichen Itza, and perhaps Palenque and Quirigua in the lowlands. The sweat house is not used by the present-day Maya of Yucatan or British Honduras, nor among the Chorti, and there is no report of its use among the Manche Chol or the Lacandon. It is common, however, among the Maya of the Guatemala highlands and of the Chiapan plateau and occurs among the Palencano Chol. It may be significant that there is some, although not complete, relationship between archaeological and ethnological distribution in the southern lowlands with a suggestion of a highland trait not too successful in establishing itself in the lowlands.[21] Whether the archaeological distribution of sweat houses in the lowlands has an ethnohistorical basis or not, there is obvious need for fuller identification of specialized structures.

Two specialized lowland assemblages should be noted. An arrangement of a single pyramid on the west side of a court facing three smaller structures, generally sharing a single platform, on the east side was first noted by Blom (Ricketson and Ricketson, 1937, pp. 105–109). This was subsequently found to be typical of many sites of northern Peten and adjacent regions (Ruppert, 1940). Blom and Ricketson believed the Uaxactun group to have been used for marking stations of the sun.

The second architectural feature, apparently confined to Tikal, is the twin-pyramid and stela-room complex noted by Shook (1957). This constitutes a pair of squat pyramids with stairways on all sides and with a low mound between them, on the south side of the group. Across a court, on the north side, lies a large room, presumed to have been thatched, which houses a stela. A line of plain stelae and altars is before the east pyramid. Five such complexes have been identified. They were erected in late Classic times to honor a succession of katun-markers.

In concluding this brief survey of the tangibles of lowland Classic, attention should be called to remarks by W. R. Coe (1962b, p. 506) that ritual shifts do not necessarily coincide with those of pottery; precise dating of architectural changes may show the same. At Tikal, he notes, a marked change in the stela cult occurs at or shortly before 9.14.0.0.0. There is a shift from pure limestone to a bedded and probably dolomitic limestone as primary material; stelae become taller and wider; rounded tops replace those of irregular shape; and altars become larger and heavier. At the same time the contents of votive caches associated with them change their character, and there is inconclusive evidence that the twin-pyramid complex may have come into use in 9.13.0.0.0. Such changes may have been more important to the Maya than shifts in pottery types, important as the latter seem to us.

Extremely little is known of the political and social organization of the southern lowlands during the Classic period. Probably hieroglyphic texts will throw some light on the subject (Thompson, 1958). "Emblem" glyphs (Berlin, 1958) may be the distinguishing characters of individual states, for these special glyphs, always with the same sets of affixes, seem to be confined to single important cities. That of Copan, for instance, is a bat glyph with Cauac infix; that of Yaxchilan, a certain sky sign; that of Palenque, the head of a death god or a plain bone. In some cases the same emblem glyph is shared by several cities not of the first rank. For example, the emblem glyph of Seibal, on the Pasion, is found also at La Amelia and at the recently discovered centers of Aguateca, Tamarandito, and Dos Pilas, all near Lake Petexbatun. The dis-

---

[21] The sweat house at Chichen Itza might have been a response to influences from the Mexican plateau, where the sweat house is very common. The discovery, since this article was in press, of a sweat house at Tikal weakens the above argument.

353

FIG. 15—PAGES 7 AND 8, DRESDEN CODEX

tance in direct line from Seibal to La Amelia is slightly over 60 km. At other sites in the immediate vicinity of La Amelia this glyph is not recognizable on surviving inscriptions. Here, then, we have a hint of several ceremonial centers, all important but not among the grandest sites, united by this glyph and possibly forming a politico-religious unit. An emblem glyph of Palenque, the bone sign already mentioned, appears with the requisite affixes in several small sites in the vicinity (Tortuguero, Jonuta, Miraflores), and this hints at a unit, not composed of several ceremonial centers of approximately equal importance, but one large site dominating several of lesser importance. Palenque, Tortuguero, and Jonuta form a roughly equilateral triangle, with sides of slightly over 60 km. Strangely, this bone emblem glyph with the correct affixes appears once at distant Copan (Stela A). Knowledge of why this glyph crops up at Copan would help enormously to our understanding of the intercity relationships.[22]

Both glyphs and details of sculpture or architecture make manifest Bonampak's dependence on Yaxchilan, Los Higos on Copan, El Cayo on Piedras Negras, and Caracol on Naranjo. Whether or not these involved political dependence it is more difficult to ascertain.

Very recently Proskouriakoff (1960) has offered a series of interpretations of inscriptions at Piedras Negras which relates them to the scenes depicted on groups of stelae on which they occur. These interpretations are of outstanding importance and open a completely new approach to the subject matter of the glyphic texts. She identifies the figures on the monuments as portraits of rulers and their families, and recognizes sets of monuments recording reigns (e.g. scenes depicting accession to power). She identifies birth dates or naming dates of the rulers followed by later ones which mark the accession to power. Name glyphs are also recognized. The revolutionary research holds out the splendid possibility of recovering complete dynasties—at least at some centers—during the Classic period.

We have not touched on the settlement pattern within the postulated city-state of the southern lowlands. Bullard (1960b) finds that in the Peten there is at a rough guess one minor ceremonial center (ordinarily a compact group with one or more pyramidal structures and lower buildings arranged around one or more courts, but commonly lacking stelae, altars, or ball court) for every 50–100 house mounds. Such minor ceremonial centers seem to have served these small zones, to use Bullard's term, more or less as the calpulli temples served the geographical divisions of Tenochtitlan. Seemingly, a number of these zones with their minor ceremonial centers, in turn, supported a large ceremonial center.

As we have noted, more than one large ceremonial center may have been in the same "state." In some cases—for example, La Amelia and El Caribe or Altar de Sacrificios and El Pabellon—only 3 or 4 km. separate two important centers. This situation is reminiscent of that found in the Valley of Mexico, where Tenochtitlan and Tlatelolco were even closer together and both were of first rank. The historical and political reasons which led to the development of those centers so close together are well known; it may well be that conditions of the same general nature gave rise to twin ceremonial centers in the Maya area.

On the possible existence of still larger politico-religious groupings one can only conjecture. Perhaps the use in much of Campeche and parts of Yucatan of a different set of year bearers to that current in the southern lowlands points to large regional groupings; similar shifts in other

[22] The Seibal emblem and the Palenque bone emblem are compounds of Glyphs 716 and 570 in my catalogue.

parts of Middle America in past and present times have had ethnical connotations. There is evidence of a short interlude of deviation at Yaxchilan at the height of the Classic period: the Campeche set of year bearers was adopted there, and Campeche and Yucatan influences in sculpture manifested themselves, but Yaxchilan sedately returned to conformity. One can only conjecture what caused that alien intrusion (Thompson, 1952a), but one is inclined to see in it the possibility of grouped city states.

The contents of the burial chamber beneath the Temple of the Inscriptions at Palenque (Ruz, 1952d) bear witness to the importance and wealth of the chiefs of lowland city states. Not only must the accumulation of capital in the form of jade buried with the chief have represented a surplus for many years favorable to the area he ruled vis-à-vis the controllers of the jade supplies, but on top of that, the huge pyramidal complex which was his shrine absorbed much more capital in the form of manual labor. This huge monument and its contents must have been a severe strain on the economy of the city-state of Palenque. Perhaps Palenque controlled some of the rich cacao-growing areas of Tabasco and adjacent Chiapas.

There were in the Palenque sarcophagus, excluding the 200 fragments of jade which formed the mask over the dead man's face, nearly 800 pieces of jade in the form of beads, rings, and earplugs. There was no weapon of any sort. The unceremonious treatment of the six persons, one or two of whom were female, whose jumbled remains were outside the entrance to the tomb, makes it almost certain that they were sacrificed attendants rather than members of the family of the occupant of the tomb. The nine figures in stucco on the walls of the chamber might have been portraits of fellow aristocrats, but there were also nine stucco figures on the walls of the tomb at

Comalcalco (Blom and LaFarge, 1926–27, pp. 117–30), so it is more probable that these represent the nine lords of the nights and the underworlds.

Such deductions as one can make from the above and other details concerning this burial point to a theocrat rather than a layman. This, of course, is in contrast to the situation which the Spaniards encountered some centuries later. The Chontal rulers of Acalan-Tixchel and the chiefs of Chetumal and Tayasal were secular chiefs, but they inherited the results of the rise of warfare in the Postclassic period.

The religious subjects depicted on the monuments and the fact that the name glyphs of gods are the same from one end of the region to the other (in some cases they correspond to nomenclature in colonial Yucatan) point to intellectual units in the lowlands. The hieroglyphic texts themselves confirm this unity. If a certain day in the 260-day sacred almanac was 7 Death at Copan, it was also 7 Death at Palenque and at Tikal. This can be proved because the Maya had the custom of recording the moon age corresponding to nearly all Initial Series, and all cities are in general agreement on the age of the moon at a given date. On the other hand, if 7 Death was celebrated on one day in one center and on another in another center, such lack of uniformity would show up in the lunar count. A priest from La Muñeca would have had no trouble in understanding a hieroglyphic text at Tortuguero.

All in all, a picture begins to emerge of a series of city-states, units in a larger cultural area, somewhat resembling the city-states of ancient Greece or mediaeval Italy, with some local variation in speech and customs but members of a single cultural unit.

The two greatest intellectual achievements of the Maya were their calculations as to the length of the synodical revolution of the planet Venus and their tables for predicting solar eclipses, although they had no means of knowing whether any predicted eclipse would be visible in the Maya area. The calculations and tables for both these astonishingly brilliant achievements appear in the Maya Dresden Codex, a late Yucatecan edition of an early hieroglyphic book now lost, but there are excellent grounds for supposing that these results had been achieved in the southern lowlands during the Classic period. Indeed, Teeple (1930, pp. 59–60) felt that there was evidence for the eclipse tables on monuments at Copan starting with Stela M erected in A.D. 756.

An achievement of a different nature was the development of the Maya philosophy of time which certainly had its roots in the southern lowlands of the Classic period (Thompson, 1954a, pp. 137–43).

Adequate coverage of those glories, Maya sculpture and architecture, is impossible in the few paragraphs available in this synthesis; to attempt it would be no compliment to reader or to the Maya artists and builders of long ago. Apart from papers in these volumes, the student of sculpture may refer to Spinden (1913), Kelemen (1943), and Proskouriakoff (1950); and the student of architecture, to Proskouriakoff (1946), Marquina (1951), and Kubler (1962).

Much information concerning the daily life, clothing, and weapons of the upper class may be obtained from the many pottery figurines of the Tepeu horizon found at such sites as Lubaantun (Joyce, 1933), Uaxactun (R. E. Smith, 1936), Palenque (Ruz, 1952c,d), and Piedras Negras (Butler, 1935b). Murals, notably those of Uaxactun (A. L. Smith, 1950, figs. 45, 46) and Bonampak (Ruppert, Thompson, and Proskouriakoff, 1955), and the wealth of figure-painted pottery of Tepeu 2 augment this source and yield much information on such subjects as music, dancing, ceremony, and warfare; but it must be remembered

that perhaps two centuries intervene between the execution of the Uaxactun mural and those of Bonampak, which date from the break-up of the Classic period.

A unique feature of our knowledge of Middle American cultures is that it derives from a blend of archaeology with ethnological observation from the 16th century onwards, and so one can often interpret archaeological data by observation of the living Maya. Illustrative of this are the designs on some pottery vessels of the Classic period representing legends and ceremonies. At least two polychrome (Thompson, 1939b, fig. 3; Lothrop, Foshag, and Mahler, 1957, pl. 81) and one moldmade vessel (Smith and Kidder, 1943, fig. 27,b) represent the incident in the legend of the sun and the moon in which the sun conceals himself in the deer's skin; a vessel from Huehuetenango (J. E. S. Thompson, 1961) shows several persons almost certainly engaged in the ceremony of drawing blood from the penis; and a carved or molded vessel from Copan (Longyear, 1952, fig. 117,a) shows the same rite of piercing the eye of a head held by the operator as appears on Codex Madrid, p. 99d.

These vessels not only provide a link between archaeology and ethnological records, they also inform us that myths and rites of the Classic period did not die with the close of that period. Similarly, scenes of human sacrifice and bloodletting rites, the presence of sting rays used for bloodletting in early tombs, and representations of deities such as the sun god and the long-nosed god, all in Classic period contexts but also reported by 16th-century sources, show, I think, that despite shifts in emphasis—from a theocratic to a secular organization—the continuity between Classic and Postclassic was not shattered to anywhere near the extent that was once thought to have been the case.

Agriculture, too, probably changed scarcely at all between, let us say, the 6th and 16th centuries, although, unfortunately, there are few representations of plants, except of maize and cacao, in the art of the Classic period. Hillside terracing against erosion occurred in the western part of central British Honduras (Gann, 1926, pp. 145, 156; Thompson, 1931, p. 229) and also around Aguacatenango on the Chiapas plateau (Guzman, 1958), in both areas almost surely during the Classic period. It would be interesting to know whether this practice continued in Postclassic times. One may reasonably assume that slash-and-burn milpa farming generally prevailed throughout the lowlands at all times.

Maya culture neither matured nor decayed in isolation; influences from outside the area surely affected the culture at all times starting with the undoubted relationships with outside the area in the Mamom period. Representations of Tlaloc on dated monuments reveal how those Mexican deities managed to insinuate themselves into Maya life at a quite early date and continued to do so again and again and in widely separated centers. They appear at Tikal on Stela 31 (A.D. 500 or earlier) and on Stela 16 (A.D. 711); at Copan on Stela 6 (A.D. 682) and the hieroglyphic stairway (ca. A.D. 750); at Piedras Negras on Stela 8 (A.D. 692); at La Mar on Stela 1 (A.D. 785); and on the murals of Bonampak (A.D. 790 or a little later). Whether these representations of the Mexican rain gods reflect an alien cult of the ruling caste and therefore witness to its inclination to outside ideas, or whether they denote repeated penetrations from outside, the conclusion to be drawn is the same, namely that the southern Maya lowlands did not dwell in splendid isolation. Toward the close of the Classic period exotic influences start to crowd in (Proskouriakoff, 1950, pp. 150–52).

The Classic period was not insulated from its neighbors, neither was its contact with the succeeding Postclassic period completely broken, as I have tried briefly to indicate. Our information, largely from Yucatan, is of a steady cultural degeneration in the Postclassic period, but the culture in the southern Maya lowlands, far less affected by Mexican influences, retained much of the basic culture of the Classic period. The frills disappeared with the end of the priest-ruler group, but one suspects that the pottery maker continued making the same water jars and simple wares and the flint knapper did not celebrate his freedom by blossoming forth with new tools. The Tlalocs, the feathered serpent, and the cult of the planet Venus were bundled out; the simple rites to the Chacs and gods of the soil and crops went on unchanged. So much stayed unaltered when the Spaniards took control; one may suppose that the same thing happened when their like-minded precursors lost control.

REFERENCES

Anderson and Cook, 1944
Berlin, 1953, 1955a, 1955b, 1956, 1958
Betjeman, 1959
Blom, 1930, 1959
—— and LaFarge, 1926–27
Brainerd, 1958
Bullard, 1960b
Butler, 1935b
Castells, 1904
Coe, W. R., 1962b
—— and Broman, 1958

—— and McGinn, 1963
Cooke, C. W., 1931
Covarrubias, 1957
Cowgill, G. L., 1959
Cowgill, U. M., 1959
Drucker, 1943b
Ekholm, 1944
Gann, 1900, 1918, 1925a, 1926, 1928b
Gates, 1932
Gordon and Mason, 1925–43
Guzman, 1958

Joyce, 1933
Kelemen, 1943
Lizana, 1893
Longyear, 1952
López de Cogolludo, 1867–68
Lothrop, Foshag, and Mahler, 1957
MacKie, 1961
McQuown, 1956
Marquina, 1951
Mendizabal, 1928
Merwin and Vaillant, 1932
Morley, 1937–38, 1946
Palacios, 1941
Piña Chan, 1958
Porter, 1953
Proskouriakoff, 1946, 1950, 1960
Rands and Rands, 1957
Ricketson and Ricketson, 1937
Roys, 1957
Ruppert, 1940
—— and Denison, 1943
——, Thompson, and Proskouriakoff, 1955

Ruz L., 1952c, 1952d, 1953, 1955a
Satterthwaite, 1943b, 1958a
Shook, 1957
Smith, A. L., 1950
—— and Kidder, 1943, 1951
Smith, R. E., 1936, 1955b
Spinden, 1913
Stromsvik, 1942b, 1947
Teeple, 1930
Termer, 1930a, 1952
Thompson, D. E. and J. E. S., 1955
Thompson, J. E. S., 1928, 1931, 1938, 1939a,
    1939b, 1943c, 1943d, 1948, 1950, 1951, 1952a,
    1953, 1954a, 1956, 1958, 1961
——, Pollock, and Charlot, 1932
Tozzer, 1907, 1941b
Vásquez, 1937–44
Wauchope, 1950
Willey, 1956a
—— and Bullard, 1956
—— and Smith, 1963
——, Smith, Bullard, and Graham, 1960a, 1960b

14. Prehistoric Settlement Patterns in the Maya Lowlands

GORDON R. WILLEY and
WILLIAM R. BULLARD, JR.

THE CIVILIZATION and social advancement of the old Maya of the lowlands are inferred from the architectural and artistic monuments these people left behind them. Such achievements would have been impossible without a depth of technological, aesthetic, and religious traditions and without a complex social and political organization through which to channel these traditions. As the tracing back into the past of monumental art and architecture is one kind of archaeological investigation which will help us understand how Maya civilization came into being, another line of inquiry asks questions about the components of Maya society. What, for example, were the relationships of political and religious leadership to an agricultural peasantry? To what extent were the Maya urbanized, and was there a "middle class" of artisans, bureaucrats, and merchants? These are difficult questions on a high level of inference, and in some of their aspects they will never be answered. But before any kind of a start can be made on them we need to know how the Maya distributed themselves on the land, how they were grouped and in what numbers. These data

of settlement pattern will not reveal all there is to know about ancient Maya social organization, but they provide the outer limits for inferences about it.

RECOGNITION OF MAYA HOUSE MOUNDS

It has always been a working assumption in Maya archaeology that the great ceremonial centers represented only one segment of former Maya society. These massive ruins of masonry-covered pyramids, platforms, temples, and palaces had been "capitals" for a theocratic leadership. They were heads without a body, and this body had been the peasant segment of society, represented archaeologically by modest ruin mounds of domestic houses. In a sense, then, the first studies of house mounds mark an interest in settlement patterns. The whole of the Maya social universe was now being considered rather than just a part of it.

For a good many years such investigations into the dwellings of the "common people" were rather casual and definitely secondary to the research in the ceremonial centers. Small, low artificial mounds in or near the centers were assumed to be the platforms on which simple, perishable domestic structures had been built. In 1890 E. H. Thompson (1892) referred to such small mounds near Labna, in Yucatan. A few years later Byron Gordon (1896, p. 26) noted similar mounds on the outskirts of the great center of Copan, Honduras; and E. L. Hewett (1913, pp. 242–43) excavated some of these house mounds near Quirigua, Guatemala. Little detailed information is available on these and other early investigations, but what there is, together with more recent findings, confirms that these small mounds were, indeed, common domestic dwelling locations.

More careful excavation and detailed reporting on such house mounds was initiated some years later with the work of Robert Wauchope at Uaxactun (Wauchope, 1934). Under Carnegie Institution auspices, he dug five presumed house mounds in the general vicinity of the Uaxactun ceremonial center. These mounds proved to be earth-and-rubble-filled platforms with masonry retaining walls. They ranged in size from about 6 to about 21 m. long and from about 4 to 9 m. wide, and up to 3 m. in height. They were found singly or in small "plazuela" groups of from two to five. Only one had the remains of a stone-vaulted superstructure comparable to those of the ceremonial buildings; the others sustained only low stone walls and appear to have supported pole-and-thatch superstructures differing not greatly from modern Maya bush houses. Wauchope's Uaxactun excavations led to his detailed and thorough study (1938) of modern Maya house-building techniques and their distribution. This study, undertaken for the purpose of collecting data to facilitate interpretation of ancient dwelling sites, demonstrated the continuity of many dwelling features from prehistoric times and strengthened the identification as house sites of small ruin mounds such as those at Uaxactun. In the course of this survey, Wauchope also examined 13 prehistoric

house ruins near Chichen Itza. These were low platforms, not exceeding 10 m. in length. They were usually grouped in small clusters of from two to four or more dwellings. Most had low wall bases, and Wauchope notes that some answered Bishop Landa's descriptions of conquest-period Yucatecan houses. Superstructures were, presumably, of poles and thatch.

Since Wauchope's study, others have made similar investigations in the Maya lowlands with comparable results. For example, at Barton Ramie in the Belize Valley of British Honduras, house mounds appear to consist of both platforms for single buildings and more complex "plazuela" units composed of two or more platforms arranged compactly around a central court. Upon excavation, the Barton Ramie mounds reveal platform fills of earth and stone, masonry retaining walls, and gravel and mortar floors. Evidences of interior benches are present in some mounds, and pole-and-thatch superstructures are indicated by occasional finds of post holes and burned wall material. Many mounds show the superimposed floors of rebuilding and continuous use over long periods of time. Manos and metates and other "everyday" utensils are found in great quantities. Although formalized fireplaces are lacking, a great deal of ash is found with other debris in fill between floors. Some Barton Ramie mounds had been used as burial places, but in these cases graves had been cut through prepared floors indicating that burial had not been the primary purpose of the mounds (Willey, Bullard, and Glass, 1955). Additional recent investigations of similar house-mound construction have been made at Mayapan (Smith and Ruppert, 1956), Tikal, and Altar de Sacrificios.[1]

In brief, the term "house mounds" as

---

[1] E. M. Shook (personal communication 1958–60) has described some of these excavations at Tikal. The Altar de Sacrificios work is under the direction of G. R. Willey and A. L. Smith.

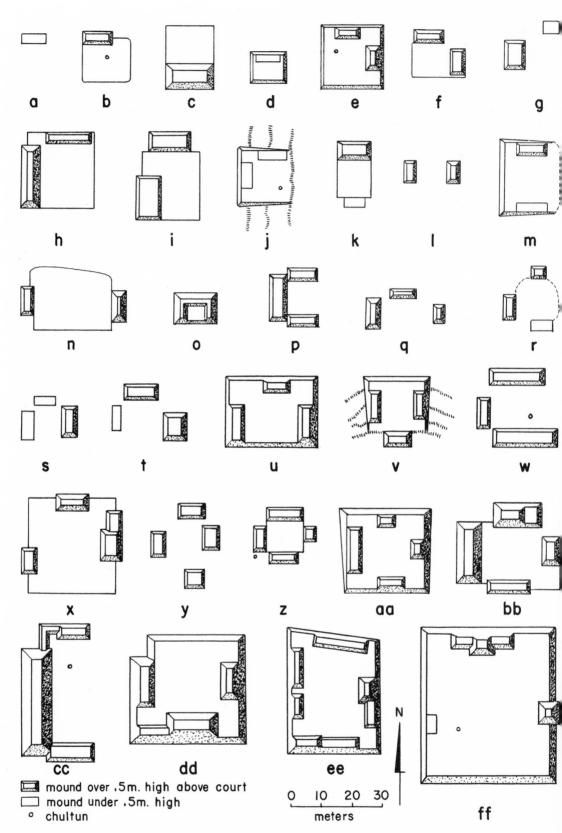

a b c d e f g

h i j k l m

n o p q r

s t u v w

x y z aa bb

cc dd ee ff

N

▨ mound over .5m. high above court
☐ mound under .5m. high
° chultun

0 10 20 30
meters

Fig. 1—HOUSE-MOUND PLANS FROM VICINITIES OF YAXHA AND DOS AGUADAS. *cc–ff*, Larger ruins prominent in cluster groupings. (After Bullard, 1960b, fig. 2.)

applied to the numerous small artificial platforms seems appropriate. There is little doubt that they mark Maya domestic house sites. The reasons for building raised platforms for dwellings may include the desire for proper drainage in a rain forest environment and the desire to cover old floors and detritus for new house construction, but more elusive cultural factors probably also played a part. Whether or not all ancient Maya house locations are indicated by such mounds is unknown and is a possible complicating factor in settlement study. Tests in the flats between mounds at Barton Ramie indicate that house sites with no visible surface mounding are rare.

It is evident from these investigations as well as from surface surveys that in all parts of the lowland area house mounds may occur singly, but commonly they are in small discrete units of two, three, four, or more grouped compactly in a "plazuela" arrangement around a court and often standing on a common substructure (fig. 1). Some investigators, especially those concerned with determination of structural details, have regarded each separate structure in such units as a separate "house." Others have tended to regard the entire unit, whether it be composed of one or of several separate mounds, as a "house." The units are strikingly similar in both arrangement and number of component structures to modern Maya household units in Yucatecan villages. The modern units may consist of one or more dwellings, but they also generally include separate structures for kitchens and storehouses which are similar architecturally to the dwellings. Since it is likely that the prehistoric and modern are functionally comparable, we believe it desirable in discussing settlement assemblages to refer to both isolated single mounds and the little "plazuela" type of units of two or more mounds as "households."

RECOGNITION OF SETTLEMENT ASSEMBLAGES

Although an interest in Maya settlement patterns begins with an interest in the domestic or house-mound ruins, this, in itself, does not constitute settlement study. A. M. Tozzer (1913, pp. 149–50) was one of the first to offer comment on numbers, density, and distribution of house mounds rather than on the mounds themselves. Riding through the Peten jungles on muleback, Tozzer observed that small mounds, singly or in groups of four or five arranged plaza-fashion, were located all along the jungle trails between such ceremonial centers as Tikal and Yaxha or Holmul and La Honradez. Tozzer also noted that the trails followed the high ground of the ridges among the *bajos* or swamps. Distances between these centers ranged from 25 to 60 km. His observations on the great numbers of mounds found at considerable distances from ceremonial centers were confirmed by P. W. Schufeldt (1950, p. 226), a chicle contractor of long experience in the Peten. Referring to a location near Laguna Perdida, Schufeldt states that innumerable small mounds were dotted over the land although the nearest large ruins (ceremonial centers) were some 30 km. distant.

Mountain Cow

J. E. S. Thompson was the first archaeologist to attempt to relate house mounds to ceremonial centers in a community assemblage. This assemblage of sites, known as Mountain Cow, is in the southern Cayo District of British Honduras. Here Thompson (1931, pp 238–48 ff.) located two ceremonial centers and two residential clusters all within an area 3.5 by 5.5 km. in extent. The small ceremonial centers, Hatzcap Ceel and Cahal Pichik, which are at opposite ends of the area, have pyramids, platforms, possible ball courts, and plain stelae. The two residential sites are at some distance

363

from the ceremonial centers and from each other. One is composed of 13 small terraces, each with from two to four house platforms; the other is a little smaller. The assemblage, as a whole, dates from the Late Preclassic through Late Classic periods. Thompson was of the opinion that by at least Late Classic times the community had functioned as a unit with both domestic and ceremonial components. It is possible, or even likely, that other residential units tributary to these same ceremonial centers lay farther out than Thompson explored and that a complete community assemblage was not isolated at Mountain Cow; however, for the first time we have the concept of the interrelated ceremonial and residential components of Maya settlement expressed in a single field and excavation report.

Uaxactun

A much more ambitious settlement project was carried out by O. G. Ricketson, Jr., of the Carnegie Institution, at the major ceremonial center of Uaxactun in the Peten (Ricketson and Ricketson, 1937, pp. 15–24). Ricketson's goal, however, was to determine, approximately, the number of house mounds (and persons) that had been tributary to the Uaxactun ceremonial center at any one time in the past. To do this he carefully surveyed a cruciform zone laid out with its four arms radiating from the Uaxactun center. Each arm of the cruciform was 1600 m. long and 365 m. wide so that a total of over 2,000,000 sq. m. of jungle terrain was searched for house mounds. Only 57 per cent of the survey zone was dry ground suitable for habitation and cultivation, the remainder being in swamps or *bajos*. Deducting from the habitable 57 per cent of the area the ceremonial center buildings and precincts, Ricketson was left with approximately 1,000,000 sq. m. or 1 sq. km. He discovered 78 house mounds in this sample. The mounds were not compactly arranged but

were situated in all parts of the cruciform without plan. High terrain appeared to be the only determining factor in their location. Multiplying the number of house mounds by the standard number of five persons, a figure of 390 persons per square kilometer of habitable land was obtained.[2] As a precaution, Ricketson quartered this figure, feeling that 25 per cent of the total mounds was a conservative estimate of those occupied at any given time. This reduces the estimate to 97 persons per square kilometer (271 persons per square mile). He could only guess at the radius of the Uaxactun-sustaining area and set this at 16 km. (10 miles). By applying his figures of houses, individuals, chances of simultaneous occupation, and habitable terrain to this larger geographic zone he emerged with an estimate of about 50,000 people as the population of the Uaxactun-sustaining area at any one time.

Belize Valley

Since Ricketson's work at Uaxactun a number of other studies have been concerned with the problem of the size and composition of community assemblages. One of these was conducted by G. R. Willey in the Belize River Valley of west-central British Honduras (Willey, Bullard, and Glass, 1955; Willey, 1956a,b). Maya settlement in the Belize Valley was found to be concentrated in the alluvial flats of the river in a continuous winding ribbon from the Guatemalan frontier almost to the seacoast. House mounds were dotted thickly over these river bottomlands. At Barton Ramie, about 5 km. downstream from Baking Pot (Ricketson, 1929), 265 mounds were mapped in an area of 2.5 sq. km. or at a ratio of 106 mounds per kilometer.

---

[2] Examination of Ricketson's house mound map (Ricketson and Ricketson, 1937, fig. 2) shows that he was counting individual platforms and disregarding the grouping of many of these into the little "plazuela" units which we are terming households. The number of household units represented appears to be about 40.

364

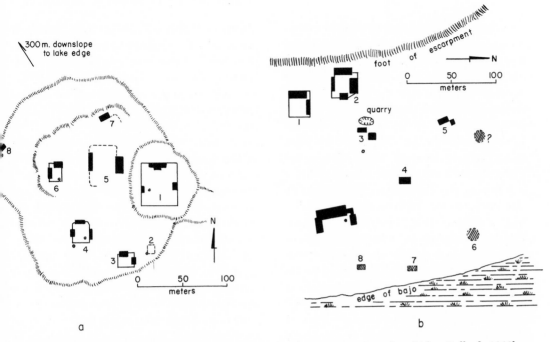

Fig. 2—HOUSE-MOUND CLUSTERS. *a,* Near Yaxha. *b,* Near Dos Aguadas. (After Bullard, 1960b, fig. 7.)

Sampling in other sections along the river indicated similar densities. The figures indicate a considerably higher concentration of settlement than Ricketson obtained for the vicinity of Uaxactun. Moreover, excavations in the larger Barton Ramie mounds have revealed a complex interior make-up, and each is probably more comparable to household units than to the individual structure platform on which Ricketson based his estimates. However, the greater degree of settlement concentration does not necessarily imply a greater population per square kilometer. Population figures should take into account the amount of agricultural land used to support the population. Ricketson apparently assumed that the land surrounding the houses was used for crops and that houses were evenly distributed over the countryside. Along the river flats of the Belize Valley, mounds are too closely spaced to have allowed room for much cultivation. The principal crops for the inhabitants of the house mounds

must have been grown elsewhere, presumably in the rolling hills which stretch back from the valley edges.

In order to date house building and mound use in the Belize Valley, 65 of the 265 Barton Ramie mounds were excavated. These test excavations for datable pottery showed a small but increasing Preclassic occupation, a sudden burst of house building in Protoclassic (Holmul I equivalent) times, a steady maintenance for the Early Classic and a slight increase for the earlier part of the Late Classic periods, and a tremendous increase in houses occupied in the full Late Classic (Tepeu 2-3 equivalent) period. House occupations fell off some, but remained appreciable, in a final Early Postclassic phase.[3]

[3] This contradicts earlier preliminary statements on the lack of a Postclassic occupation at Barton Ramie (Willey, 1956b). The detailed ceramic analyses of J. C. Gifford (personal communication 1960) have revealed a definite Postclassic horizon, although such diagnostic markers as Tohil Plumbate and X Fine Orange are lacking.

365

Delineation of community assemblages, or ceremonial-center–sustaining area units, was more difficult in the Belize Valley than the determination of period by period occupation of house mounds. The Belize Valley occupation stretches for about 60 km. by airline although much longer on the curving river course. Three major ceremonial centers—Benque Viejo (Thompson, 1940), Cahal Pech (Satterthwaite, 1951b), and Baking Pot (Ricketson, 1929)—are located towards the western end of the Valley and are about 10–15 km. apart. Benque Viejo and Cahal Pech are situated on heights overlooking the river valley; Baking Pot stands on the alluvial flats in the midst of the house-mound distribution. In addition to these major centers, minor ceremonial centers are scattered along the valley's entire length. One such minor center, marked by a small pyramid and associated lower mounds, lies within the Barton Ramie site area. Because no spatial breaks in house-mound distribution in the valley could be defined, the relationship of specific house mounds to specific minor ceremonial centers and aggregates of these to major ceremonial centers can only be speculated on; but since we know that most of these centers and probably most of the house mounds were in contemporaneous use in Late Classic times, it seems almost certain that they were integrated into some common social and political pattern.

Northeast Peten Survey

To pursue the question of the general distribution of settlement and of community assemblages, W. R. Bullard, Jr. (1960b) surveyed a large section of northeastern Peten, Guatemala, between Benque Viejo and the British Honduras border on the east, and the vicinity of Uaxactun and Tikal on the west. Much of this area suffers today from dry-season desiccation of surface-water sources and supports only a very small permanent population. Unlike west-central British Honduras, permanent

rivers are lacking. Lakes are few and small waterholes or *aguadas* are the most common present-day, and probably ancient, sources of water. Some of the *aguadas* are natural, others are artificial and of prehistoric construction. Despite the relative scarcity of permanent water supply, the area clearly supported large populations in the past. Not only does it include such major ceremonial centers as Yaxha, Holmul, Naranjo, and Nakum, but house mounds were seen with great frequency along trails in all parts of the area regardless of distance from major ceremonial centers. Careful examination indicated that mounds tended to concentrate in some places and not in others and that two terrain factors correlated with these concentrations. First, medium-high, well-drained, level ridgetops were preferred house locations with areas of steep slopes and *bajos,* low-lying tracts which become swampy in the wet season, left uninhabited. Second, house mounds tended to concentrate around the edges of lakes and *bajos* and near *aguadas*. These concentrations, however, were not as great or as clearly marked as the ribbon-like concentration of mounds along the Belize River in British Honduras.

Settlement pattern in northeast Peten was neither by isolated homestead nor by compact discrete units comparable to true towns or cities. Bullard was able to discern three levels of settlement assemblage which were applicable generally throughout the area. These are referred to as "clusters," "zones," and "districts" in ascending order of magnitude. *Clusters* are little groups of 5–12 houses found typically within an area some 200–300 m. square. The houses are arranged in no particular plan within this small area, and are located about 150–50 m. apart (fig. 2). Frequently, one cluster is separated from another by a terrain feature, such as a ravine; but in other instances there seems to be no such natural topographic division. Clusters may be separated by 200 m. or so of unoccupied ground, but

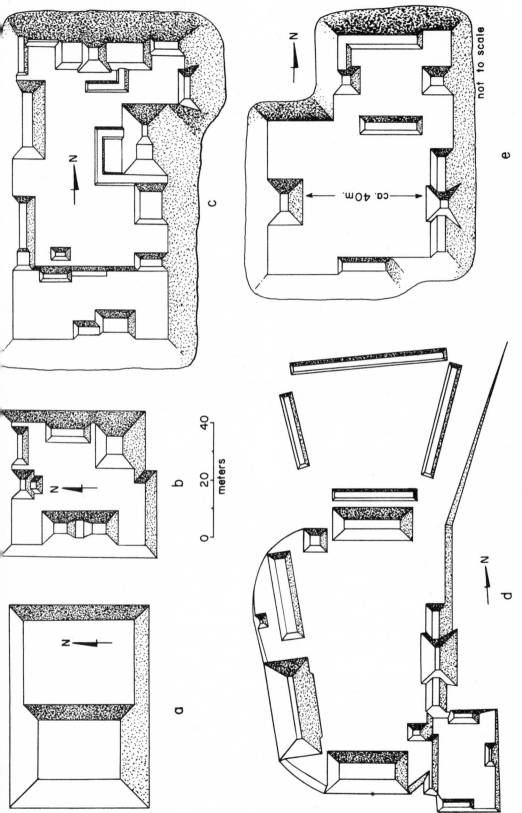

FIG. 3—MINOR CEREMONIAL CENTERS. *a*, La Flor. *b*, Dos Aguadas vicinity. *c*, Dos Aguadas vicinity. *d*, Yaxha Hill. *e*, El Venado. All from the Peten, Guatemala. (After Bullard, 1960b. fig. 3.)

there are examples where no easily recognizable spatial separation could be made out. In some areas explored, the tendency for the mounds to occur in these clusters could not be observed. The individual houses composing the cluster are what we have referred to as household units and are composed of one to four platforms placed so as to form a small "plazuela" unit (fig. 1). Sometimes, one ruin within the cluster will be larger and more elaborate than the others, suggesting a specialized building (see also Willey and Bullard, 1956).

The *zone* is made up of several clusters and comprises an estimated total of 50–100 houses. The average geographical extent of the zone is estimated at about 1 sq. km. although considerable variation in extent results from local topographical conditions. Zones sometimes are easily isolated geographically, being confined to a particular hill mass or to the vicinity of an *aguada,* but in other instances they may blend one with another. Each zone contains a minor ceremonial center. These centers have small pyramids and lower structures arranged around one, two, or three adjacent plazas (fig. 3). As a rule, minor centers are without stelae, altars, or ball courts. The minor center may be located at any point within the zone, and there is no tendency for houses or clusters to be grouped near the minor center. Presumably the minor centers were the religious and civic centers for the zones.

The term *districts* is applied to territories that were presumably the sustaining areas for major ceremonial centers. The size of the districts, as well as the placement of the zones within the districts, varies considerably according to the local geographical conditions; but the distribution of known major centers suggests that the average size is an area which encompasses about 100 sq. km. of arable and habitable land. The major ceremonial centers of the districts are aggregates of temples, palaces, and other structures and generally include ball

courts, stelae, and altars (fig. 4). Domestic settlement may or may not be heavy in the immediate vicinity of major centers, but such centers are often on hilltops at some distance from locations ideal for domestic settlement.

The northeast Peten survey was confined largely to settlements of the Classic period although these may be, to some extent, continuations of earlier Preclassic patterns. One important Postclassic settlement was included in the survey, but the nature of this settlement is such that it is more appropriately discussed in a following section.

Tikal

Tikal, in northeastern Peten, is the largest of Maya Classic major ceremonial centers. The maps of the University of Pennsylvania expedition show at least 3 sq. km. of large ceremonial construction with other ceremonial buildings found well out beyond this perimeter.[4] Small mounds, either single platforms or *plazuela* arrangements, are seen in all parts of the mapped area. Some are located near major ceremonial constructions, others are farther out from the central section of the site. In no location, however, does the map show them as closely packed concentrations. Instead, the density and spacing of household units in and about Tikal appear to be comparable to what was found at Uaxactun, along the Belize River, and in other parts of the Northeastern Peten.

Mayapan and Other Postclassic Sites

At Mayapan, in northern Yucatan, A. L. Smith and Karl Ruppert mapped over 4000 structures, including 2100 dwelling units or households, within the enclosing wall

[4] We are indebted to E. M. Shook, project director, and his associates for providing us with preliminary copies of sheets of the Tikal map (see also Shook, 1958) and for discussing with us the question of settlement around Tikal. Our interpretations of the maps and settlements, however, do not fully coincide with Shook's, who tends to see Tikal as more of an urban type of settlement than we do.

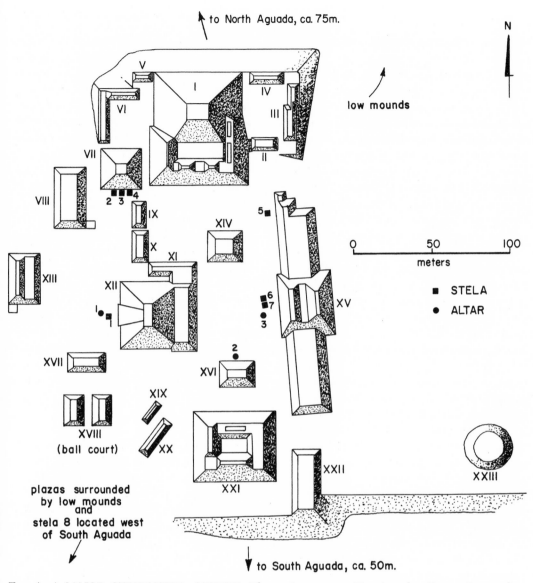

to North Aguada, ca. 75m.

N

low mounds

V

I

IV

VI

III

VII

II

VIII

IX

2 3 4

5

X

XI

XIV

0   50   100
meters

■ STELA
● ALTAR

XIII

XII

I

6
7
3

XV

2

XVII

XVI

XIX

XVIII
(ball court)

XX

plazas surrounded
by low mounds
and
stela 8 located west
of South Aguada

XXI

XXII

XXIII

to South Aguada, ca. 50m.

F<small>IG</small>. 4—A MAJOR CEREMONIAL CENTER. The main group at Dos Aguadas, Peten, Guatemala.
(After Bullard, 1960b, fig. 4.)

of that site. The Mayapan defense wall encircles an area of 4.2 sq. km. A relatively small ceremonial center lies at the heart of the site. Houses, found as single isolated platforms or in groups of two, three, or more arranged around little courtyards, are scattered at random throughout the area of the enclosure (Jones, 1952; Ruppert and A. L. Smith, 1952; A. L. Smith and Ruppert, 1956). The concentration and density of household units at Mayapan is far in excess of what was found in Peten or British Honduras Classic sites. Mayapan, of course, is the great Late Postclassic site of the northern lowlands, and its period of power is estimated to have been from about 1260 to 1460. During this time it had as many as 12,000 inhabitants (A. L. Smith, 1962). According to tradition, these inhabitants were petty town chiefs and village chiefs, together with their families and retainers, from the northern Yucatecan region. Quite probably merchants, artisans, and soldiers were also housed there. It seems unlikely that a large part of the population of the site could have been farmers. More probably, foodstuffs were brought to Mayapan from outlying hamlets beyond the walls (Ruppert and A. L. Smith, 1957). Postclassic Mayapan thus has the size and settlement characteristics of the large town or city as opposed to the more dispersed pattern of the Classic Peten sites.

Tulum, another Maya walled city of the Postclassic period, on the Quintana Roo coast, is also believed to have had a town type of settlement similar to that of Mayapan although smaller. Tulum has few house-mound platforms within its walls, but the area of the enclosure has extensive living refuse. This is in marked contrast to the nearby Classic site of Tancah. W. T. Sanders (1955, 1960a), who studied both, notes that Tancah is surrounded at distances of several kilometers by small clusters or hamlets of houses and that the ceremonial center itself lacks numerous house platforms or midden accumulations.

Postclassic concentrated towns are not entirely lacking in the southern lowlands. At Topoxte, in Lake Yaxha, some 80–100 house mounds are crowded on an island no more than 400 by 200 m. in extent in close proximity to a small ceremonial center. Two nearby islands have similar close-packed house platforms. The whole totals, perhaps, 200 household units, not a large city or town but certainly a different sort of settlement pattern than that observed at nearby Classic sites (Bullard, 1960a,b). Both the pottery and architecture of Topoxte imply a Postclassic date for the site, and its concentrated appearance recalls conquest period descriptions of the Itza capital of Tayasal, which was located on islands in Lake Peten.

The concentrated town pattern of Mayapan, Tulum, and Topoxte, with ceremonial centers immediately surrounded by close-packed households, is the kind of pattern which Landa described for 16th century Yucatan: ". . . the natives lived together in towns . . . in the middle of the town were their temples with beautiful plazas, and all around the temples stood the houses of the lords and the priests and then (those of) the most important people . . . and at the outskirts of the town were the houses of the lowest class" (Landa, 1941, p. 62). Both Morley (1946, pp. 312–13) and Thompson (1954a, pp. 66–67) were inclined to project this picture back to the earlier Classic Maya; Brainerd (1954, p. 70), on the other hand, felt that the concentrated dwelling town was a Postclassic phenomenon in the Maya lowlands, quite probably of Toltec-Mexican inspiration. With the archaeological survey evidence now at hand from the Classic sites of the south, we are inclined to agree with Brainerd.

Dzibilchaltun

A possible exception to the dispersed settlement pattern for the Classic period is Dzibilchaltun in far northern Yucatan. The site includes a ceremonial center, or series of relatively closely grouped ceremonial centers, surrounded by house ruins. E. W. Andrews, the excavator, gives the extent of the site as 50 sq. km. (1960). A survey now in progress indicates house-mound concentrations of extraordinary proportions within this zone. Estimates based on a 6.9-sq.-km. test area suggest a density as high as 1000 structures per square kilometer, or 50,000 for the zone as a whole. This estimate assumes that approximately one half of the total number of house structures were without substructure platforms and have left no surface trace. The house ruins are reported as being separated in heavy clusters, which are usually characterized by one or more larger vaulted or non-vaulted buildings, and often are connected to the central group by causeways.

Ceramic tests in 245 structures suggested that during the Formative period the population lived over the entire zone but tended to concentrate in the western part around massive ceremonial constructions. During the Late Formative and Early Period I (the latter equivalent to the Early Classic in the southern lowlands) there seems to have been no monumental architecture nor major concentration of settlement, although pottery and house mounds of the period occur. But during Early Period II and Florescent I (equivalent to Late Classic) Dzibilchaltun became the seat of a major ceremonial complex, and it is believed that the great majority of the estimated 50,000 structures at the site were occupied, if not continuously, at least at some point during this period of considerable length. Thereafter, through the Decadent period (Late Postclassic), density of settlement seems to have dwindled.

With concentrations of 1000 structures per square kilometer over a zone of 50 sq. km. Dzibilchaltun would be not only, as Andrews says, the largest urban concentration of its time in the New World, but also one of the very largest in the entire pre-industrial world. Since, as yet, only preliminary descriptions have appeared and the detailed maps have not been published, it is not now possible to appraise Dzibilchaltun's urban qualities or the degree to which its settlement pattern resembles or differs from other described sites in the Maya area. For example, we do not yet know the extent to which small structures at Dzibilchaltun are grouped into household units or the composition of these. The reported occurrence of heavy clusters of house ruins which also contain larger buildings suggests the *cluster* or *zone* pattern described from northeastern Peten. The tremendous increase in density of house structures during the period equivalent to the Late Classic seems to parallel the findings at Barton Ramie, although at Dzibilchaltun the population remained at a very

high level until somewhat after the decline of Classic civilization in the southern lowlands. The very high ruin densities during Early Period II and Florescent I (Late Classic) may reflect not so much an extraordinarily concentrated urban population as rapidly shifting hamlets and satellite communities similar to those which Sanders describes from Valladolid in present-day Yucatan (Sanders, 1960a, pp. 102–08). Other interpretations could also be advanced. The Dzibilchaltun settlement-pattern findings may have revolutionary implications, but it would be premature to attempt to assess them before the data are fully available.

SUMMARY OF MAYA LOWLAND SETTLEMENT FINDINGS

The ancient Maya built domestic structures on small, low, generally rectangular and oblong mounds. This conforms to historic and modern practices, and by further analogy with the living Maya it may be supposed that the houses that once stood on these mounds were of perishable pole, wattle, and thatch materials. On excavation the mounds have proved to be of earth and rock fill with masonry retaining walls and prepared floors. They contain household debris. Often they were used for burials, but this seems to have been a secondary purpose for the mounds. They occur singly or in discrete units of two, three, four, or more. When more than one mound is present, they are normally arranged around little courts, forming "plazuelas." Both the isolated single mounds and the little "plazuela" sets are similar and probably comparable in function to the household units of the modern Yucatecan Maya.

House mounds are found throughout the lowlands. They tend to occur in loose aggregates which correlate with well-drained terrain, water supply, and good farmlands. Ceremonial centers are within or near areas where there are house mounds. In northeastern Peten, the arrangements of house

371

mounds and ceremonial centers have been described in terms of territorial units. Small *clusters* of households, numbering from 5 to 12, occupy an area 200–300 m. in diameter. Several such clusters may be grouped into *zones*. These are territories of a square kilometer or so, each of which contains, in addition to the house mounds, a *minor ceremonial center* with small temple and palace mounds. Several zones are associated in a *district*. Districts contain on the average, perhaps, about 100 sq. km. of arable and habitable terrain, and each has a *major ceremonial center*. These major centers are the famed Maya great sites with the large pyramids, stone temples, palaces, ball courts, stelae, altars, and other monuments. The clusters, zones, and districts may be comparatively isolated from others of their respective categories, or settlement may be more or less continuous between them. In the Belize River Valley of British Honduras, house mounds are heavily concentrated in a strip along the river. Minor ceremonial centers are found quite frequently in or near the strip; major centers are less frequent and more widely spaced. It is quite possible that territorial units comparable to those in northeastern Peten existed in the Belize Valley, but the house-mound distribution along the river is so continuous that these units could not be observed.

Density of house mounds has been sampled in several places. At the Classic site of Uaxactun, 78 house platforms, combining into approximately 40 household units, were found in a cruciform area of 1 sq. km. of habitable land on the outskirts of the ceremonial precincts. At Barton Ramie in the Belize River Valley, about 100 mounds, each probably representing a household unit, are found to the square kilometer. Observations elsewhere in Peten suggest densities within these extremes for Classic settlement. It is clear, however, that the density of house mounds, as well as the size of the house-mound aggregates within

any particular square kilometer, will vary according to the topography, the nearness to water supply, and the relationship to agricultural land. Postclassic Mayapan represents a much greater density than any Classic site described to date, there being some 2100 households occurring at a density of about 500 to the square kilometer. This Postclassic settlement pattern differs significantly from the Classic pattern in that true town or city aggregates are present in the latter period.

A possible exception to the foregoing is Dzibilchaltun, where densities as high as 1000 structures per square kilometer for 50 sq. km. are suggested in recent preliminary notices. Nearly all these structures are believed to have been occupied during the Late Classic and Early Postclassic periods.[5]

INFERENCES

We conceive of two categories of inference about ancient Maya society and culture which derive as a whole or in part from settlement-pattern findings. The first is closer to the basic data than is the second. In it we consider land use and population density. The topics of the second category include some of the questions with which we introduced this article: the socio-political organization of the Maya and the relationships of leaders and peasantry; the nature of class distinctions; and the possible presence of a "middle class" of artisans, officials, and merchants.

Land Use

Concerning land use, there is no good evidence that the Maya ever placed primary reliance on anything but the *milpa* or "slash-and-burn" system of farming. Ricketson (Ricketson and Ricketson, 1937, pp. 10–13) has argued otherwise, maintaining

[5] Ed. note: These are, respectively, Andrews' "Late Early" and "Pure Florescent" periods and do not include his "Modified Florescent," during which, Andrews reports, there was very little construction at Dzibilchaltun.

that the prehistoric Maya practiced a more intensive, season-after-season cultivation of the same cleared plots; but today intensive cultivation in the Peten is impossible without artificial fertilizers, and it is very probable that the same conditions prevailed in the past. Ricketson's citing of the Cooke hypothesis of topsoil loss from intensive farming (as an explanation for the "collapse" of Maya civilization) to support his argument merely bolsters one hypothesis with another. In this connection it is of interest that the one type of soil which might seem to have been suitable for intensive maize cultivation, the alluvial bottomlands of the Belize River, were apparently not used for major crops. Houses were so thickly settled on the alluvial strip that there would have been no room to plant corn.[6]

Population Density

Population-size estimates have been a matter for considerable speculation (Ricketson and Ricketson, 1937, pp. 20–23; Morley, 1946, pp. 71–72, 137 ff.; Termer, 1951; Brainerd, 1954, pp. 75–79), and we shall not review all of them here. In general, estimates are of two kinds: those dealing with the Maya lowlands as a whole and those attempting to arrive at a figure for a particular site and its environs.

Efforts to arrive at population figures for large areas from inspections of small samples of mound distributions are open to a number of pitfalls. One of these involves appraisal of the population of individual households. It has been pointed out that individual house mounds frequently occur in units of two, three, four, or more and that these are comparable in size and layout to modern Yucatecan household units. The modern units may contain more than one family dwelling, but also often include architecturally similar kitchens and storehouses. Archaeological evidence is not yet

sufficient, nor may it ever be, to allow determination from surface remains as to which mounds in a unit were dwellings and which served other purposes. Nor, although it has been determined that modern Maya families average about five individuals, do we have adequate ethnographic data concerning the number of families occupying the modern household units to use as a basis of comparison.

A second problem is the number of household units occupied at any one time. Excavations and surveys in British Honduras and Peten have demonstrated that most areas of settlement were occupied from at least late Preclassic times until the end of the Classic period, a span of 1000 years or more, and that house structures were frequently modified and built over.

A third problem is the disposition of the settlement throughout the area under consideration and its relationship to agricultural land. Surveys have shown that house mounds tend to concentrate to a greater or lesser extent in some places and that other areas were uninhabited or only lightly settled. Thus, ruin counts within a particular square kilometer or two can only with hazard be projected to an area equivalent to the sustaining area of a major ceremonial center. Significant population counts should take into consideration not only the size of any particular aggregate of ruins, but also the amount of land used for the major crops which fed that population.

Ricketson estimated population for the Uaxactun environs on the basis of about 106 persons per square kilometer (ca. 271 per square mile), a figure determined by taking into account factors of habitable land, house-mound counts in a sample area, a reduction to one-quarter of the total mounds as occupied at one time, and a ration of five persons to each individual mound. He assumed that these figures included land used for agriculture. It is to be noted that Ricketson ignored the grouping of many of these mounds into house-

[6] The relatively small spaces between households on the alluvial flats might have been used for "garden crops" and cacao, however.

373

hold units, a complicating factor which would tend to reduce his figures further. On the other hand, his estimates of only one-quarter of the mounds occupied at once may be too low, at least for the Late Classic period. Ricketson regarded his figures as representative of the entire sustaining area of Uaxactun, which he supposed to be a circular area with an approximately 16-km. radius. He emerged with an estimate of 50,000 persons tributary to the ceremonial center. It seems highly unlikely that such a large area (over 800 sq. km.) would have pertained to Uaxactun. The mammoth ceremonial center of Tikal lies only 18 km. from Uaxactun. Perhaps an 8-km. radius would have been better for Uaxactun. This would bring the area down to about one-quarter and would give a total population of about 12,000 persons. Of course the same populations might have served both Uaxactun and Tikal on different levels of suzerainty, but this takes us even further into speculation.

For Barton Ramie we had approximately 100 mounds (presumably household units) per square kilometer of land. Moreover, there is evidence from numerous test samplings that all the mounds were probably occupied at one time, at least in the Late Classic period. Assuming that each mound had a minimum population of five persons, this would give a figure of 500 persons per square kilometer. To make these figures comparable to those at Uaxactun, however, we should have to take into account land used for agriculture, a factor which it is impossible to estimate since suitable *milpa* land stretches for many kilometers both north and south of the concentrated riverbank settlement.

The northeast Peten survey suggested that the sustaining area of a major ceremonial center, or *district*, comprised about 100 sq. km. of arable land on the average, an estimate based on the location of known major centers in that area. This theoretical figure may be used in conjunction with

population estimates made by studies of lowland Maya *milpa* agriculture in order to obtain an approximation of the average supporting population of a major center. Morley (1946, p. 151) concluded that in northern Yucatan it requires about 11.2 sq. miles to support 500 people. This reduces to a figure of 44.6 persons per square mile of arable land, and implies that for 100 sq. km. (38 sq. miles) the total population would be in the neighborhood of 1,695 persons. This figure seems much too low for the supporting populations of the large and magnificent major ceremonial centers of northeast Peten. Moreover, environmental conditions in Peten are different from those in northern Yucatan: the rainfall is higher and the soils are deeper. Ursula Cowgill (1960) on the basis of recent studies has suggested that in Peten 150–200 people can be supported by the *milpa* system per square mile of arable land. For 100 sq. km. (38 sq. miles), this estimate would result in a figure of 5700–7600 persons or a mean of about 6600 persons. These figures also seem somewhat low in relation to the size of the major centers, but may nevertheless be feasible.

The northeast Peten survey further suggested that the sustaining areas of major centers were divided into *zones* of 50–100 households, on the average, each of which supported a minor ceremonial center. If a household included only one family, this would give a supporting population of minor centers of 250–500 people and would, in conjunction with Cowgill's estimates, imply that a major ceremonial-center–sustaining area of 100 sq. km. contained 13–26 zones. If the average household held two families, there would be 500–1000 persons per minor center and 6–13 zones within a major center-sustaining area. This last estimate seems to fit better with observed conditions in northeastern Peten.

Regardless of the degree of validity of the above figures, we must caution against extending them, or any other figures based on studies within a specific region, blanket-wise over the whole of the Maya lowlands. Not only do different topographical and climatic conditions within the area imply specifically different ecological adjustments, but there are indications that house-mound density was not everywhere the same even within the same environmental region.

Socio-Political Organization

The Peten and Belize Valley surveys suggest the gross outlines of Maya lowland social and political organization. Surely, house-mound populations supported ceremonial centers, and ceremonial centers had some kind of an hierarchial ranking with reference to each other.

The *cluster* of house mounds appears as a reasonable equivalent to the sort of local social grouping usually known as a *hamlet.* Its inhabitants may have been kinsmen. The occasional larger mound in the cluster suggests a shrine.

The *zone* with its minor ceremonial center compares with the *village.* In this case the village settlement is extended rather than concentrated.

The *district* with its major center has no strict analogue in community terminology. In a sense it is a kind of city of a dispersed sort.

A political structure is implied by this ascending order of settlement units with minor leadership in the minor centers and greater power and authority residing in the major centers. It is also possible that on a still higher level several major ceremonial centers and their supporting populations owed allegiance to certain centers of great importance. This is more speculative and, until Maya hieroglypics are more fully translated, we have little to go on except relative size and magnificence of the centers. But if such paramount centers and large territorial states did exist, it seems likely that they exerted influence in the elevated spheres of religion, calendrics, luxury goods, and perhaps "foreign policy"

rather than on the more mundane levels of basic economics and the merchandising of foodstuff.

In considering such things as Maya leadership and peasant relations, social classes, and the refinements and particulars of the Maya social order, the archaeologist draws on a variety of data. For example, Maya leadership is thought to have been theocratic and priestly. This is an inference based on ethnohistoric information and on Maya art, architecture, and intellectual life. Similarly, when we try to understand priest and peasant relations we recall sculptures and paintings depicting these presumed priestly dignitaries in fine raiment and in poses of aristocratic hauteur, or we compare the contents of ceremonial-center tombs with the humbler house-mound graves of the villagers. These give us insights but so do settlement findings. One strong argument against an unbridgeable social rift between priest and peasant is the presence of the numerous minor ceremonial centers. If, as we believe, these were the centers sustained by small village-size populations, it is unlikely that they were permanently inhabited by an aristocracy remote from the populace (Willey, 1956b). Perhaps a pattern of rotating ceremonial offices was maintained, such as E. Z. Vogt (1959) has described for the modern highland Maya of Chiapas. And, quite possibly, candidates for higher priestly or government offices found their way up from the minor ceremonial-center level to that of the major centers. Yet the degree to which such a fluidity was feasible is open to debate. The intricaties of the calendar and the knowledge of the hieroglyphics, which must have been part of the learning of the high priests in the major centers, seem incompatible with a rotating, "rustic" priesthood.

It will be obvious that this is an important and complex question; depending on the way it is answered, other interpretations about the ancient Maya will take different turnings. From what is known now

375

we would guess that Maya society became more rigidly crystallized in the Late Classic period and that the gulf between peasant and priest tended to widen at that time. High offices in the great centers were probably retained as hereditary prerogatives. Proskouriakoff's (1960) recent analyses of Maya art and hieroglyphics strongly suggest this possibility of "royal lines."

The Question of Cities

The art, architecture, and fine crafts of the great ceremonial centers imply a class of full-time specialists. The size of the centers with their numerous temples and palaces offers a basis for inference about a host of minor priests and officials. Finally, the evidence of trade between Maya centers in prehistoric times and the known importance of markets for the historic Maya suggest merchant groups. Did such persons—artisans, minor officials, and merchants—compose a "middle class" distinct from either the priest leadership or the agricultural peasantry? The settlement evidence one might expect to find for such a class would be an urban town or condition.

The presence or absence of urban centers in the Maya lowlands and in other parts of pre-Columbian America have been much discussed in recent years. Argument has focused on two aspects of the problem. What are the criteria of urbanism or city life? And how are these to be recognized from archaeological remains? W. T. Sanders (1956) has proposed functional, economic criteria as the significant ones. In his opinion communities with substantial numbers of nonfarmers (75 per cent or more) and with population elements of heterogeneous functions and interests qualify as urban (see also Borhegyi, Article 2). He would place such criteria as size and monumental architecture as secondary. We agree in principle. The grouping of full-time artisans, officials, and merchants into a single center is another way of expressing this. The recognition of these elements and

this heterogeneity must come from the archaeological record, however; and to make such a recognition we must fall back upon criteria of form. Some of these criteria of form have been suggested by V. G. Childe (1950). Among them are large dwelling aggregates, monumentality in public building, great art styles, formalized religions with pantheons of deities and cadres of priests, interregional trade, social class divisions, writing, and the beginnings of true science. We have them all in Classic Maya society, either directly attested to or very immediately inferred, except what is probably the most diagnostic one, sheer size of dwelling aggregates. For this formal criterion, more than any other, would reflect the most essential characteristic of the city: large numbers of full-time specialists not engaged in primary food production.

Instead of being a densely settled, house-to-house and street-to-street aggregate of domestic dwellings, the Classic Maya ceremonial center is a temple, palace, and public-building complex surrounded at some distance by widely spaced households and hamlets which extend for many kilometers into the countryside. G. C. Vaillant (1940) believed the ceremonial center and scattered hamlet pattern of settlement to be a function of the necessities of *milpa* farming. It is certainly an expression of an agricultural way of life, of a society made up predominantly of farmers who lived relatively near their fields. With this rural settlement organization the Maya achieved much of what has been thought of as civilization—the great arts, building, writing, mathematics, and calendrics—but it was, as J. A. Wilson (1951) has said of ancient Egypt, a "civilization without cities."

How did this civilization come about? We must assume that it was through the coordination of the efforts of large though residentially dispersed populations. Maya sculpture and architecture are almost sure proof of some full-time artists and architects, and it is almost inconceivable that the great centers could have operated without corps of lesser officials. But, apparently, such personnel, at least in substantial numbers, continued to live at some distance from the centers in the old agricultural hamlet pattern. Interregional trade had an importance for the Classic lowland Maya. Obsidian from the highlands and sea shells from the coasts are found in tombs in the Peten. So merchants, too, were active. But for the development of a strong merchant class, on the order of the Aztec merchants of Tenochtitlan, a true city is a major prerequisite; and, from present evidence, it would appear that the Classic Maya never went as far in this direction as did the central Mexicans.

Yet the increase in size and number of ceremonial centers in the Late Classic period, and the house-mound evidence for a general population increase concomitant with this, suggests that the Maya may have been moving toward urbanism and toward a more heterogeneous society. In the Postclassic period we have a change in settlement pattern to a defensible concentrated town or small city. This change may be a measure of a "middle class" development, of an increase in the numbers and importance of artisans, governmental functionaries, and merchants. The fact that lowland Maya culture had been influenced by central Mexicans by this time is also a possible explanation for this change, but even if the concentrated town pattern were diffused by Toltecs or Aztecs, it would not necessarily negate the urban functions of that pattern. It is possible, of course, that the concentration of populations into towns in the Postclassic period was a response to conditions of warfare in the northern Maya lowlands.

REFERENCES

Andrews, 1960
Brainerd, 1954
Bullard, 1960b
Childe, 1950
Cowgill, 1960
Gordon, 1896
Hewett, 1913
Jones, 1952
Morley, 1946
Proskouriakoff, 1960
Ricketson, 1929
—— and Ricketson, 1937
Ruppert and Smith, 1952, 1957
Sanders, 1955, 1956, 1960a
Satterthwaite, 1951b

Schufeldt, 1950
Shook, 1958
Smith, A. L., 1962
—— and Ruppert, 1956
Termer, 1951
Thompson, E. H., 1892
Thompson, J. E. S., 1931, 1940, 1954a
Tozzer, 1913, 1941
Vaillant, 1940
Vogt, 1959
Wauchope, 1934, 1938
Willey, 1956a, 1956b
—— and Bullard, 1956
——, ——, and Glass, 1955
Wilson, 1951

15. Architecture of the Maya Lowlands

H. E. D. POLLOCK

I n 1940 I published an article concerned with the sources of our knowledge of Maya architecture. The subject was traced from the early 16th-century accounts of the conquistadors and Spanish historians to the field reports and other writings of present-day archaeologists. In the 20-odd years since that article a number of monographs and shorter papers dealing with the architecture of the lowland Maya have appeared. Many of these later works will be referred to in succeeding pages, and references to yet others will be found in the publications cited, giving the reader a quite comprehensive bibliography on the subject.[1]

The present article deals almost exclusively with the religious and civic, or ceremonial, architecture of the lowland Maya; domestic architecture, referred to in Article 14, receives only passing notice. The art of building, other than in the simplest forms, is never static over any length of time, and the formal architecture of the Maya was no exception. We shall try to trace development and change over the approximately two millennia of which we have

any record, and in doing this we shall refer to the major chronological divisions of Maya history. This chronology is discussed in Article 14, Volume 1, and in the opening articles of Volume 2. Here we shall use the terms Preclassic, Classic, and Postclassic for the major cultural periods, and shall subdivide each of these into Early and Late phases.

Not only did Maya architecture change with time but it developed differently in different areas. Some of these variations may be accounted for by environmental

[1] Among the many contributions to the study of lowland Maya architecture are Stephens (1841, 1843), Catherwood (1844), Maudslay (1889–1902), Holmes (1895–97), Maler (1901–03, pt. 2, 1911), Tozzer (1911, 1913, 1957), Spinden (1913), Lothrop (1924), Totten (1926), Morris, Charlot, and Morris (1931), Thompson, Pollock, and Charlot (1932), Ruppert (1935, 1943, 1952), Ricketson and Ricketson (1937), Morley (1937–38, vol. 5, pt. 2), J. E. S. Thompson (1939a), Ruppert and Denison (1943), Satterthwaite (1943–54), Ruz (1945b), Palacios (1945b), Proskouriakoff (1946), A. L. Smith (1950), Mariscal (1928), Marquina (1928, 1951), Ruppert, Thompson, and Proskouriakoff (1955), Kubler (1958, 1962), Robina (1959), Pollock, Roys, Proskouriakoff, and Smith (1962).

Fig. 1—MAP SHOWING AREAS OF PRINCIPAL ARCHITECTURAL STYLES OF THE LOWLAND MAYA

factors; others seem best explainable on cultural or historical grounds. The natural environment of the Maya lowlands is treated in Volume 1; and the opening articles of Volume 2 discuss cultural differences within the region. If we had anything like a complete record of Maya architecture over time and space, it is quite likely that we could identify a good many areas, each of which produced at one time or another an architecture sufficiently distinctive to set it apart from that of the others. Within the limits of our present knowledge, it seems practicable to establish 10 such areas, which are shown on the map (fig. 1). The extent and boundaries of the several

379

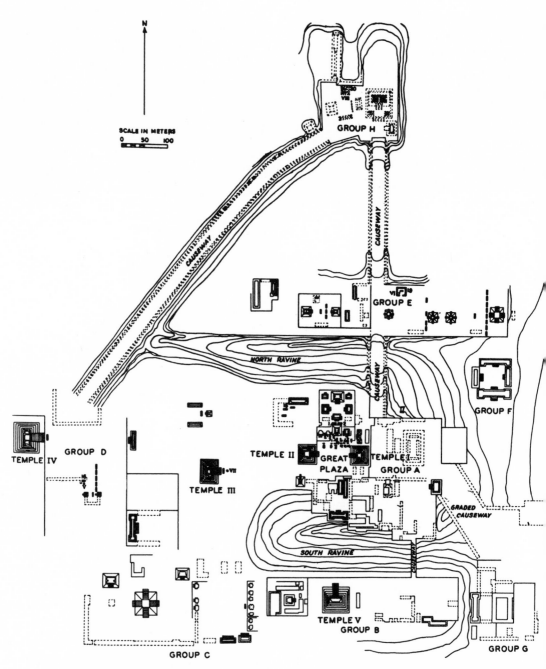

F<small>IG</small>. 2—MAP OF THE CENTRAL SECTION OF TIKAL. Central area. (After Morley.)

Central area. At center is the heart of the city: (from left to ;ht) Central Acropolis, Temples II and I with the Great Plaza between, and Northern Acropolis. (By Carlos ierra.)

areas are no more than approximations and should be considered highly tentative. Vacant spaces on the map do not imply that architectural remains are not present in those regions, but that our knowledge of the ruins is so scant, or the known remains are of such relatively minor character, that the architecture cannot be treated in this short article.[2]

Maya Cities

Nature

Although the settlement patterns of the ancient Maya are discussed in the preceding article in this volume, the subject is so intimately associated with our ideas concerning the nature of the so-called cities of the Maya that some mention of the matter must be made here. It is generally believed that these cities—and we have in mind at the moment the large architectural centers of the Classic period when Maya civilization reached an apogee—were not cities at all, in the sense of a concentrated urban

population, but were public centers, primarily ceremonial in nature. According to this view, the resident or semiresident population was small in comparison to what might be expected to surround a great public and ceremonial center under truly urban conditions.[3] The vast majority of the populace, it is thought, lived in small farming communities of a family or two, or in somewhat larger groups that might be termed hamlets, scattered through the countryside. The typical residence was almost surely the pole-and-thatch house in use today throughout the area, raised on a platform of earth or stone, and usually facing on a courtyard with one or more similar buildings on the other sides.

Although the conditions we have just suggested seem to have been true of Maya cities during the Classic, and very probably the Early Postclassic period, there appears to have been some change in Late Postclassic times. The ancient city of Mayapan is now known to have harbored an urban population of some 11,000–12,000 in an area of less than 5 sq. km. (Pollock, Roys,

[2] For reports on ruins in British Honduras, see J. E. S. Thompson, 1939a, pp. 278–82; for western Campeche, see Andrews, 1943; for lowland eastern Guatemala, see Shook and Smith, 1950, and A. L. Smith, 1955, pp. 58–60. The ruins west of Lake Izabal, although in a lowland region, are better compared to those of highland Guatemala (see A. L. Smith, Article 3).

[3] E. W. Andrews (unpublished MS) does not concur in this view. He believes that Dzibilchaltun, Yucatan, was a major urban settlement during the late Classic period as defined in the present article (Andrews' Pure Florescent). He further believes that a number of other Maya cities were urban at that time.

Proskouriakoff, and Smith, 1962, pt. 3). There is also a minor example of urbanism at Tulum (Sanders, 1960a, pp. 212–19). Writing about conditions in Yucatan before, presumably shortly before, the conquest, Landa clearly implies some degree of urbanism (Tozzer, 1941a, pp. 62–64). We know that by this time the native culture of Yucatan had been influenced strongly by peoples of Mexico, some of whom had developed a true urbanism. It is entirely possible, then, that late in their history the lowland Maya, stimulated by a foreign culture, were making occasional experiments in urbanism.

Landa's description of an aboriginal Maya town (*ibid.*) indicates a sort of concentric zoning, with the temples at the center, surrounded by the residences of the lords and priests, followed by the houses of important people, and finally, on the outskirts, those of the lower classes. This pattern is known, moreover, to have existed at Mayapan. We know rather little about the disposition of such residential structures as there were in cities of the Classic period. In so far as the cities seemingly represented a nonurban situation, conditions would hardly be comparable to those described by Landa.[4] There seems little question that the important religious structures occupied central positions in the plan of the city. There are also indications that pole-and-thatch buildings lay on the fringes of, and between, important architectural centers. What is mainly unknown is whether some of the large masonry structures were residences of dignitaries, or whether such people lived in structures of less permanent construction, and where those buildings were located. Until these questions are resolved, we can say little in regard to the residential pattern in Classic cities.

Size and Limits

In contrast to the modern practice of determining the size of a city by its population, Maya cities have generally been measured by the magnitude and extent of the architectural remains.[5] We have little knowledge of the size or character of the ancient populations within those cities, and it remains to be discovered how pertinent to the problem such figures will be when applied to the peculiar, nonurban conditions of the Maya centers.[6] Even by the seemingly straightforward criteria of the number, size, and extent of the civic and religious buildings, much remains to be learned about the specific and relative sizes of the ancient cities. Much of the mapping of sites that has been done is insufficient in extent and in detail, and the relatively few careful surveys that have been made almost invariably have shown the remains to be in greater number and more extensive than was previously believed. A most perplexing problem, and one that is yet to be solved, is the determination of the limits of many of the Maya cities. This problem is not present in the case of small, relatively isolated centers, but it is critical in areas with a heavy concentration of building remains, where groups of structures, varying in size and in distance from the heart of the city, continue outward in seemingly endless array. Under such conditions it is often impossible to say whether a certain group of buildings is part of the city or an independent entity.[7]

[4] Bullard (1960b, p. 369) finds no evidence in the ancient settlement pattern of northeastern Peten "for a concentric social gradation of this sort."

[5] Morley (1956, pp. 267–70), attempting the more subjective appraisal of importance rather than size, adds the number and excellence of the sculptured monuments to his criteria.

[6] See Sanders, 1960a, pp. 209–18, and Pollock, Roys, Proskouriakoff, and Smith, 1962, for estimates of the population of Maya cities, but note that Tulum and Mayapan represent urban conditions. The estimates of Termer (1951, pp. 105–106) are too general to be of use in determining the relative sizes of cities.

[7] Looking at the matter from a somewhat different point of view, Bullard (1960b, p. 369) has called attention to this problem.

We know nothing of the administrative organi-

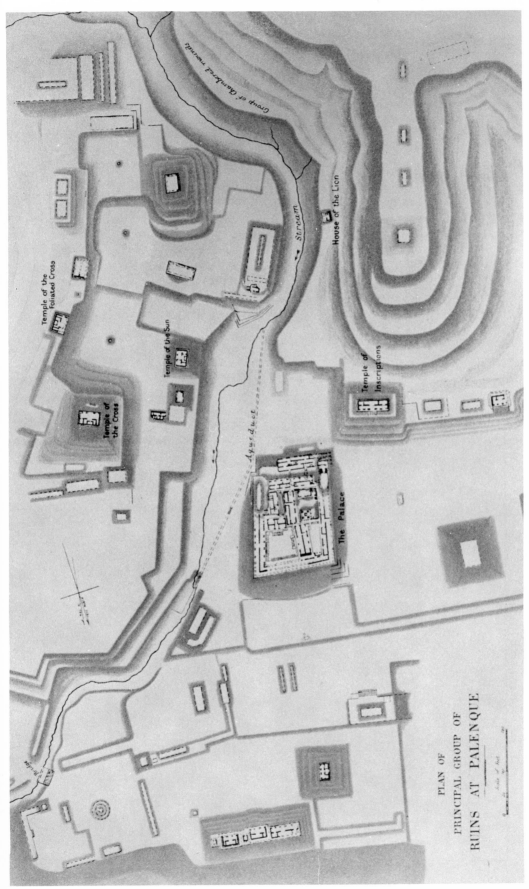

Group of Guaduced Temple

Stream

House of the Lion

Temple of the Foliated Cross

Temple of the Sun

Temple of Inscriptions

Temple of the Cross

Aqueduct

The Palace

Bridge

PLAN OF
PRINCIPAL GROUP OF
RUINS AT PALENQUE

Scale of Feet

Fig. 4—MAP OF PRINCIPAL CEREMONIAL CENTER AT PALENQUE. Western area. (After Maudslay.)

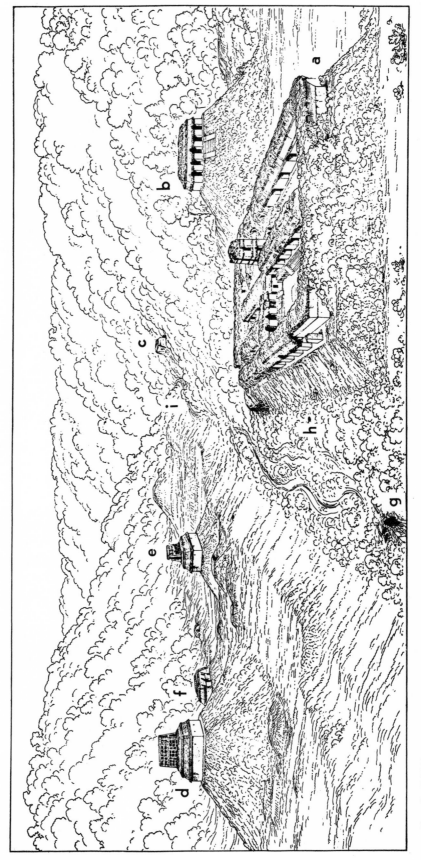

FIG. 5—PANORAMIC VIEW OF PALENQUE, LOOKING SOUTH. Western area. *a*, Palace. *b*, Temple of the Inscriptions. *c*, Temple of the Beau Relief. *d*, Temple of the Cross. *e*, Temple of the Sun. *f*, Temple of the Foliated Cross. *g*, Outlet of aqueduct. *h*, Break in aqueduct. *i*, Inlet of aqueduct. (After Holmes.)

In spite of the difficulties in this matter, one can make an appraisal, unfortunately more subjective than one would like, of the size of Maya cities. Tikal, in the heart of the Central area, has long been considered to be the largest known city. Recent mapping operations there have covered an area of 16 sq. km. and have discovered a profusion of building remains throughout the area and beyond (Carr and Hazard, 1961). As previously explained, we cannot be sure that all of this construction pertains to a single city, but the 100 or more buildings, some of them of huge proportions, three acropolises, and elaborate causeways that lie in the square kilometer at the heart of the city (figs. 2, 3) would alone mark Tikal as a great center. Other large cities in the Central area, not comparable to Tikal but covering an area of at least 1 km. by 0.5 km., and probably a good deal more, are Calakmul, Naachtun, Nakum, Naranjo, Uaxactun, and Yaxha.[8]

Copan, in the Southern area, with its huge acropolis that at one time covered an area of approximately 4 hectares (10 acres), rose at its highest point over 40 m. above the valley, and, with its wide courts and plazas, was a great center (fig. 7; and see Stromsvik, 1947, Map 3; Longyear, 1952, Map 1). So, too, were the Usumacinta River sites of Piedras Negras and Yaxchilan (Morley, 1937–38, pls. 201, 202; also see fig. 8). In the Western area the central group of buildings at Palenque, which is all that has been mapped in detail, covers an area of only about 0.6 by 0.4 km. (figs. 4, 5), but Blom and LaFarge (1926–27, p. 170 and Map 4) say that the ruins extend over an area of 16 sq. km., a concentration of remains that rivals that of Tikal.

The Puuc area exhibits a density of ruins comparable to the Central area.[9] Because of the dispersed pattern of building, it is a region in which it is particularly difficult to estimate the limits of a city. Mapping at Oxkintok (Shook, 1940), Kabah, and Sayil has disclosed a continuous pattern of ruins over areas of more than 1 sq. km.,[10] and the gigantic size of the buildings at Uxmal (figs. 41,b; 42,a), quite aside from the area of the site, shows it to be a great city (Morley, 1956, pl. 49; Blom, 1934, fig. 6). The map of Chichen Itza in the Northern Plain shows hundreds of buildings in an area of about 5 sq. km. and a huge ceremonial center at the northern end of the city (figs. 44, 9; and see Ruppert, 1952, fig. 151). Dzibilchaltun, once thought to be a minor site (Morley, 1956, Table 7), is now said to extend over an area of 50 sq. km., to present an immense concentration of remains, and possibly to be the largest known Maya city (Andrews, 1959, 1960, 1962, unpublished MS), a dramatic example of how our ideas can change with adequate mapping.[11]

The foregoing list of sites, which is by no means exhaustive, will give the reader some idea of what we think of as large Maya cities. From these larger concentrations of buildings Maya centers grade downward in all degree of size to those of no more

---

zation of the Classic Maya. Presumably this is reflected in the arrangement and distribution of the public buildings. We should like to suggest that the pattern we find might better be likened to modern ecclesiastical than to civil and political organization.

[8] See Marquina, 1951, pls. 278, 279, for comparative sizes of some well-known sites. And see note 22.

[9] The degree of concentration of building remains as presently known is probably to some extent a function of the amount of exploration, which has varied largely between areas.

[10] Detailed maps of Kabah and Sayil have not yet been published. See Brainerd, 1958, Maps 16, 17, for simplified and abbreviated versions.

[11] The detailed map of Dzibilchaltun has not yet been completed. We understand that the ruins of Xcanatun, once reported as a separate site (Shook, 1955a, p. 291), are now considered to be part of Dzibilchaltun. This points up another hazard in discussing the sizes of Maya centers. See Brainerd, 1958, Map 7, for a sketch-map of the central area of Dzibilchaltun.

than two or three buildings or even a single structure. It may be worthy of note that no large city is reported from the Pasion River,[12] the Rio Bec,[13] the Chenes, or the East Coast areas. The only large Postclassic[14] city known is Chichen Itza. Should Mayapan be judged as a ceremonial center rather than as an urban city, it would be small indeed.

ARCHITECTURE

Civic Planning

Before we discuss the plan of Maya cities, it may be well briefly to characterize the architecture. It was essentially monumental. From very early times the Maya builder made use of stone and mortar, thus allowing him to achieve architectural forms that would have been impossible had he been restricted to materials of less strength and permanence. The unit of planning was the rectangular court or plaza limited on one or more sides by buildings, and there was the tendency to place the civic and religious centers on natural rises which were leveled and terraced to accommodate the desired architectural arrangement.

As might be expected, civic planning developed through time and was influenced by local custom and environment. We know little about the planning of Preclassic centers, or about Preclassic architecture in

general. We do know that by Late Preclassic times the burning of limestone to make lime and the use of lime as a building material had been discovered. At Uaxactun in the Central area we find at Group E an example of a small rectangular plaza limited by buildings on three or four sides that was clearly ceremonial in nature and that is thought to be of this early date (fig. 6,a). Orientation of buildings was to the cardinal points. It has been mentioned that the characteristic dwelling of the Maya faced on a courtyard, often with buildings on other sides of the court. This arrangement may be presumed to have great antiquity, and one may hazard the guess that the courtyard, which is so basic to the ceremonial architecture, had its origin in domestic building.[15]

It has generally been thought that with the advent of the Early Classic period ceremonial architecture took a great step for-

---

[12] Reporting on recent exploration in the region of Lake Petexbatun, Vinson (1960) suggests a heavy concentration of ruins in an area some 15 km. in length. It is conceivable that adequate mapping might reveal a large site here.

[13] Some 10 groups of buildings in an area of possibly 50 or more square kilometers have been given the site name of Rio Bec. At present there is no reason to believe that these groups form a single site, but further exploration might disclose a continuous pattern of building remains over much of the area.

[14] Ed. note: To avoid confusion of terms, it should be noted here that on developmental grounds Andrews (Article 12) prefers, for Chichen Itza and the northern Maya lowlands, the term "Florescent," followed by "Decadent," for the periods chronologically equivalent to "Postclassic" in the southern Maya lowlands.

[15] Since the foregoing was written, new information has come to light concerning Preclassic building. Recent work at Tikal indicates that the Great Plaza and North Terrace covered much the same area in Late Preclassic times that they did in their final Classic stage, and that considerable building had gone on in the North Acropolis (Carr and Hazard, 1961, map; W. R. Coe, 1962b, p. 504; 1962a; Coe and McGinn, 1963). At Altar de Sacrificios on the Pasion River it is now known that in Late Preclassic times a complex of structures underlying Group B (Willey and Bullard, 1961, map) consisted of a small court surrounded on three sides by pyramid-temples and on the fourth by a building of unknown function (A. L. Smith, verbal information). There are, moreover, even earlier structures underlying these remains, indicating a ceremonial assemblage in Middle Preclassic times (see Willey and Smith, 1963, p. 86).

There has recently been uncovered at Dzibilchaltun in the Northern Plain a small temple and its rectangular courtyard enclosed along most of its perimeter by very narrow platforms or walls that are of Late Preclassic date (Andrews, 1961b, pp. 15–19 and fig. 1; 1962, pp. 158–60). This is of interest in lending weight to Kubler's (1958, pp. 526–27) deduction that fenced-in enclosures represent an early mode of space design in Middle America. There also has been found at Dzibilchaltun a huge acropolis-like complex of buildings of Late Preclassic date (see Andrews, Article 12, fig. 1). Andrews (1962, p. 164) goes on to say that this acropolis is by no means the largest of such early structures.

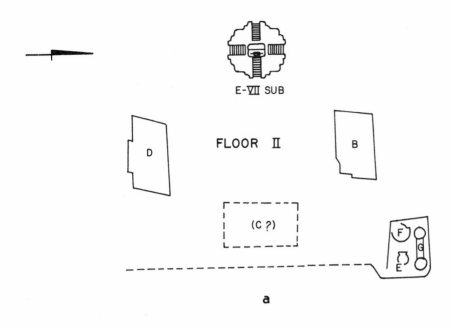

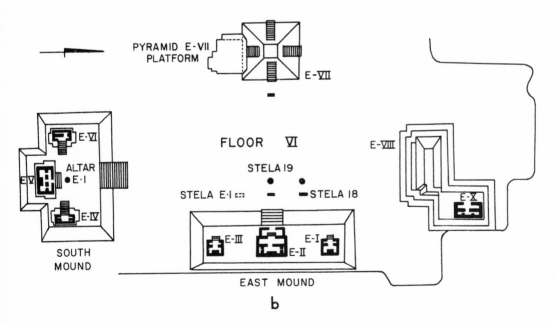

Fig. 6—PLANS OF CEREMONIAL CENTERS. Central area. *a*, Group E, Uaxactun, in Late Preclassic times (after Ricketson and Ricketson). *b*, Group E, Uaxactun, in Early Classic times (after *idem*).

Fig. 7.—RESTORATION DRAWING OF PRINCIPAL CEREMONIAL CENTER AT COPAN IN LATE CLASSIC TIMES, LOOKING SOUTHEAST Southern area. (After Proskouriakoff.)

ward not only in size and complexity of construction but in number of buildings erected (but see note 15). We nevertheless have meager knowledge of plans of cities. It is probable that all the groups which are thought to have formed the city of Uaxactun, our most carefully studied site, were occupied at this time (A. L. Smith, 1950, pp. 67–68), but only at Group E, where no later construction was carried on, is the architectural planning entirely clear. The basic plan there did not change from the preceding period, but structures became more elaborate, hieroglyphic monuments were introduced, and a geomantic arrangement of temples that may have been in existence even earlier was surely present at this time (fig. 6,b; and see Ricketson and Ricketson, 1937, pp. 105–109).[16] The grouping of three temples about a raised court is characteristic of this period at Uaxactun (see fig. 27) and may prove to be a more widespread trait of the times.[17] The early plans of Groups A and B, where there are many later buildings, are less clear than in Group E, but we know the two groups were already connected by a causeway and there is good indication that much of the final plan of the center had begun to take shape (A. L. Smith, 1950, fig. 142). At the nearby city of Tikal the great Northern Acropolis had nearly been completed (Shook, 1951c, p. 22),[18] the Great Plaza was in existence, and construction that led to the creation of the central Acropolis almost surely had be-

gun (figs. 2, 3). As in the preceding period, the orientation of buildings was to the cardinal directions.

There are several points that emerge from the meager knowledge we have about civic planning in Early Classic times. It appears that in the Central area, from where virtually all our information comes, the early plans of centers largely gave shape to what was to follow. The monumental character of the architecture had taken form and the design of architectural space through the location of buildings about courts and plazas had assumed a characteristic stamp.[19] Sculptured monolithic monuments in the form of stelae and altars were being used as adjuncts to the architecture. The fundamental principles of Maya civic planning and architectural effect had been developed. The following period witnessed the extension and elaboration of those principles.

A fact that has not commonly been brought out in discussions of civic planning, often referred to as "assemblage," is that they usually deal entirely with cities in their Late Classic or, more rarely, Postclassic stage. The majority of sites reached their maximum growth in Late Classic times, many earlier constructions having been submerged beneath later, and site maps quite naturally show the cities in that stage. Most of our information about civic planning consequently comes from the Late Classic centers.

As previously indicated, plans of cities were influenced not only by custom but by environment. The flood plains of Copan and Quirigua; the flat or gently sloping banks of the Pasion River; the steeply rising hills along the Usumacinta River; the mountainous shelf of Palenque and alluvial plain of Comalcalco; the low, wet, but often sharply broken terrain of the Peten; south-

---

[16] See Ruppert, 1940, and Ruppert and Denison, 1943, p. 5, for distribution of geomantic arrangement, all known examples of which are in the Central area. It is not unlikely that this is an Early Classic trait and marks an occupation of that date at sites where it occurs.

[17] Group B at Altar de Sacrificios (Willey and Bullard, 1961, map) with its temples on three sides of a court and a palace-like structure on the fourth side is now known to be of Early Classic date in its final phase of construction (A. L. Smith, verbal).

[18] Coe and McGinn (1963, pp. 25–26) now suggest that the North Acropolis had reached its final form by the end of the Early Classic period.

[19] Recent excavations indicate that these characteristics go back at least to Late Preclassic times (see note 15).

FIG. 8—RESTORATION DRAWING OF ACROPOLIS, PIEDRAS NEGRAS, LOOKING NORTH. Usumacinta area. Late Classic times. (After Proskouriakoff.)

ern Campeche; and southern Quintana Roo; the savannas, valleys, and hills of the Chenes and Puuc regions; and the flat northern Yucatan plain all offered different opportunities and challenges to the ancient builder. It is unfortunate that within the space of this article we cannot trace out in greater detail how the ancient builder adapted his architecture to the local environment, how he utilized and modified the terrain to stay within established forms, and where custom rather than environment seems to have been at play.

The Maya architect through most of his history was dealing with masses in the form of platforms, pyramids, and monumental buildings, and in his striving for pleasing and impressive effects it was quite natural that he should make use of varying levels of terraces and courts around which he grouped his structures. As the architecture was mainly religious, the product of a theocratic society, there was also the urge to create an esoteric atmosphere, one of remoteness from the everyday world, which was achieved by height and by sheltered areas. It is not surprising, then, to find on the plain of Copan in the Southern area a huge artificial acropolis supporting a closely knit system of courts, connecting areas, platforms, and pyramids crowned by temples, while from the foot of the acropolis stretch across the level plain the ample courts and great plaza that holds most of the hieroglyphic monuments (fig. 7). Orientation of buildings, which approximated the cardinal directions, on the other hand, was less exact than in the Central area, where the terrain actually offered more difficulties than at Copan. The extraordinary similarity of the plan of Quirigua (see Morley, 1937–38, pl. 214) to that of Copan, moreover, shows that custom was a factor as well as environment.

In marked contrast to these cities of the Southern area are those of the Usumacinta. There the terrain is so steep that any thought of a predetermined orientation of structures was out of the question, and height was achieved by the leveling and terracing of natural elevations (see Morley, 1937–38, pls. 201, 202; Satterthwaite, 1943–54, pt. 1, fig. 3). The towering mass of closely packed courts, broad stairways, and steep pyramids of the acropolis at Piedras Negras, for example, achieves its eminence above the rest of the city from the high hill upon which it rests (fig. 8). We know little of the plans of cities along the Pasion River, an affluent of the Usumacinta. Altar de Sacrificios, the one site that has been mapped adequately, shows a generally orderly arrangement of courts and plazas within groups, but the orientation of buildings is not so consistent as might be expected in the relatively level terrain (Willey and Bullard, 1961). It is not clear whether the acropolis was a feature or not.[20] A peculiarity of the site is the location of many of the stelae and altars on stairways and platforms of buildings rather than in courts and plazas (see Willey, Smith, Bullard, and Graham, 1960a, pp. 10–11; 1960b).

In the swamps and low hills of the Central area the Maya naturally sought the higher elevations for their important ceremonial centers. This at times gave a somewhat dispersed plan to the cities, dividing them into several distinct and separate architectural groups (e.g., see A. L. Smith, 1950, fig. 143; Carr and Hazard, 1961), but

the terrain was not so overpowering that it could not be modified to allow a consistent orientation of buildings, which was generally to the cardinal directions.[21] Possibly because of the limited area provided by hilltops and the long history of building at many of these sites, the typical group plan shows a compact arrangement of contiguous courts and plazas (see fig. 29). The acropolis is a frequent feature of these cities. Elevated causeways, important elements of the city plan, are known from a number of sites, and there are many examples of artificial reservoirs (see Bullard, 1960b, p. 363; Carr and Hazard, 1961, pp. 13–14). Hieroglyphic monuments occur most frequently in courts and plazas.[22]

The Western area differs from the others in that it includes two distinct environments, the alluvial plain of Tabasco and the foothills of the Chiapas mountains. We know little about the ruins on the plain. At Comalcalco there is a huge artificial platform, on which rest a number of buildings, and nearby systems of courts and plazas (Blom and LaFarge, 1926–27, fig. 84) that may be likened to Copan in the adaptation of the architecture to the environment. Orientation of buildings appears to be to the cardinal directions.[23] Palenque, the type site of the hill region, lies on a shelf bor-

---

[20] A. L. Smith (verbal) believes that Str. A-1, the greater part of which has been cut away by the river, was an acropolis. See Morley, 1937–38, pls. 196,b; 199,b; 200; vol. 2, figs. 41, 45, 49; Vinson, 1960, fig. 3, for sketch-maps of other Pasion River sites.

[21] There is some question in my mind if the strict orientation of structures to the cardinal directions shown on many site maps is not due to insufficiently accurate mapping. For example, compare the Tozzer (1911, pl. 29) map of Tikal with the more careful survey of the University Museum (Carr and Hazard, 1961), and note the true orientations of the five great temples (Tozzer, 1911, pp. 105–107). Also see the detailed map of Groups A and B at Uaxactun (A. L. Smith, 1950, fig. 142). See Carr and Hazard, 1961, pp. 7–15, for a discussion of orientation of buildings at Tikal and of other features of the site.

[22] A large collection of maps of sites in the Central area will be found in Morley, 1937–38, vol. 5, pt. 2. See also Ruppert and Denison, 1943.

[23] Our lack of knowledge of Comalcalco is soon to be remedied, it is hoped, by the publication of the results of recent work by G. F. Ekholm, of the American Museum of Natural History.

FIG. 9—RESTORATION DRAWING OF PRINCIPAL CEREMONIAL CENTER OF THE MAYA-TOLTEC AT CHICHEN ITZA, LOOKING SOUTH
Northern Plain area. Early Postclassic. (After Proskouriakoff.)

dered at the north by a precipitous escarpment and at the south by steeply rising hills. The sloping floor of the shelf is elaborately terraced, and, with the exception of a single great structure known as the Palace, which is a maze of interior courtyards and buildings, courts and plazas are mainly defined by terrace walls rather than by buildings (figs. 4, 5). The site thus has a more open appearance than others we have seen. Orientation of buildings seems at times to approximate the cardinal directions, at times to follow the contours of the terrain. Monolithic monuments are rare.

North of the Central area are the Rio Bec, Chenes, and Puuc areas. The most striking difference in the civic planning in these areas from that in the areas to the south is the lack of emphasis on the compact, integrated arrangement of closely contiguous courts and plazas.[24] There is nothing about the environment that dictated this change, unless perhaps the less rigorous terrain than in the Central and Usumacinta River areas, and it seems best explained as a matter of taste.[25] The acropolis, if present, is poorly defined, but systems of ascending courtyards and multistoried structures are not infrequent in the Puuc area and these may be in some respects comparable (see figs. 42,a; 41,a). Causeways are not uncommon in the Puuc area and in several instances they roughly follow the north-south axes of the cities,[26] but orientation of buildings seems to follow no consistent pattern in any of these northern areas. Hieroglyphic monuments are generally rare, and when present in the Puuc area seem usually to be grouped on separate platforms away from major courts or buildings.

It is strange that within the entire Maya lowlands we know of only one major city of the Early Postclassic period.[27] That is the great site of Chichen Itza in the Northern Plain. In Early Postclassic times[28] a people of mixed Maya-Toltec culture built a city here around and about an earlier Maya center of Late Classic date.[29] As will subsequently be seen, the Toltec architect was motivated by different traditions than was the Maya, and this is clearly seen in the plan of the main ceremonial center at Chichen Itza (fig. 44).[30] There is a spaciousness of planning here that is quite unlike what we have seen (fig. 9). The principal temple rests near the center rather than at one side of the tremendous plaza, and series of well defined, contiguous courts are absent. The arrangement of structures is axial in space, a Mexican highland trait. Orientation of buildings is quite consistent, approximating 17° east of north, which is common to the cities of central Mexico, as pointed out by Marquina (1951, p. 14).

By Late Postclassic times[31] the Maya had

[24] Maps of Rio Bec area sites are found in Ruppert and Denison, 1943; of Chenes area sites in Seler, 1916, fig. 11, and Robina, 1956, pls. 5, 9; of Puuc area sites in Marquina, 1928, facing p. 66, following p. 68; Marquina, 1951, pl. 232; Morley, 1956, pl. 49; Brainerd, 1958, Maps 14–17.

[25] According to present thought, the period of intensive occupation of these sites was shorter than in the cities of the Central area. This might to some extent account for the less crowded architecture.

[26] See Brainerd, 1958, Maps 14, 16, 17. The Late Classic plan of the site of Chichen Itza also shows this pattern (Ruppert, 1952, fig. 151, Sacbe No. 7).

[27] This strikes me as so strange that I cannot but wonder if our historical and chronological reconstructions for northern Yucatan are correct (see Pollock, 1952, pp. 238–39).

[28] Ed. note: Andrews' "Modified Florescent" (see Andrews, Article 12); His "Pure Florescent" precedes it at Chichen Itza.

[29] The Northern Plain was inhabited from Preclassic times to the conquest, but we know little about Preclassic or Classic settlements (but see note 15). A Late Postclassic city will be mentioned shortly. See Ruppert, 1952, fig. 151, for map of Chichen Itza.

[30] Kubler (1961; 1962, pp. 174–88) believes that the Maya-Toltec architecture of Chichen Itza is highly eclectic and not derived directly from the Toltec builders of Tula, Hidalgo (but see Ruz, 1962a).

[31] Ed. note: In the northern Maya lowlands this is Andrews' Decadent (see Andrews, Article 12).

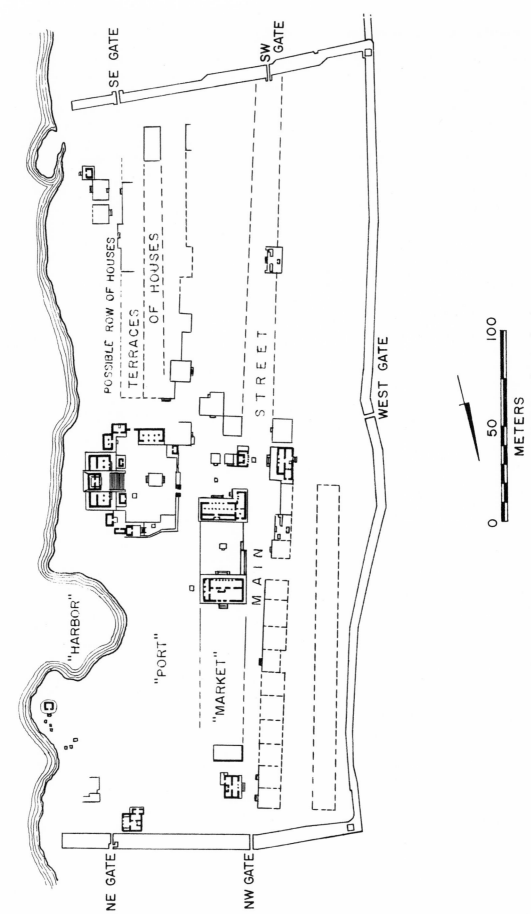

Fig. 10—MAP OF TULUM. East Coast area. Ceremonial center is at top center. (After Sanders.)

begun, apparently under foreign stimulus, experiments in urbanism (but see note 3). The largest of these was the walled city of Mayapan.[32] The main ceremonial center at that site seems to have started as a miniature copy of the great Maya-Toltec center at Chichen Itza, with the principal temple centrally located (Pollock, Roys, Proskouriakoff, and Smith, 1962, pt. 2). As later construction proceeded, however, the center developed into the earlier system of closed courtyards, in this case crowded and cluttered and with little of the fine proportions of the Classic architecture (see fig. 48). Orientation of buildings was fairly consistent, approximating the cardinal directions, and the long-abandoned stela cult was revived.

Sanders (1960a, pp. 218–19) finds five types of settlement in the East Coast area, some of the sites going back to Preclassic times but the majority of them being of Late Postclassic date. Although it represents a rare type of settlement, the most carefully studied and in some respects the most interesting site is the little walled city of Tulum, which Sanders (ibid., pp. 212–18) believes to have been urban in character. The town was laid out along the axis of a main street, oriented approximately 17° east of north, with residential structures on each side and running back from the street (fig. 10). The ceremonial center was a walled enclosure, on the far side of which the principal temple looked down the transverse axis of the city. The plan is reminiscent of highland Mexican cities, and there is little about it to compare to the earlier Maya centers.

Building Plans and Building Instruments

We know virtually nothing of the planning that preceded the erection of a Maya building. We do not know if any working drawings were made or, if so, in what detail they were prepared. No one has yet been able to point to any unit of measurement. Some of the buildings attained a

complexity of structural design and an intricacy of ornamentation, however, that make it difficult to believe the builders had no previously perfected guide to go by.[33] It is also hard to think of them working without some unit of measure, not necessarily standardized and in general use, but that leastwise would be held to during the construction of a single building. Over the centuries from Preclassic to Late Classic times Maya builders clearly attained an increasing mastery of the art of building, and this at least would indicate an architectural lore, whether codified and reduced to record or not, that was handed down from generation to generation.

In the matter of instruments, there is nothing to suggest that the Maya had any better means of obtaining a level than the unaided eye. Horizontal lines are rarely level and slopes are often inconsistent. There is also no indication that they had any means for turning a right angle. Corners of buildings are almost never true in this respect. The plumb bob the Maya seem to have known, and they surely had

[32] City walls are found at Mayapan (Shook, 1952c), Chacchob (Pollock and Stromsvik, 1953; Ruppert and Smith, 1957), Tulum (Lothrop, 1924; Sanders, 1960a), Xelha (Lothrop, 1924), Ichpaatun (Sanders, 1960a), and possibly at Xcaret (G. Mason, 1927, pp. 228–29). All examples of this feature, apparently inspired by late foreign influences in the Maya region, seem to be of Late Postclassic date, although the time of construction of the wall at Chacchob is open to question.

An instance of the presumed fortification of a Late Classic city is Becan, which is reputedly surrounded by a "moat" (Ruppert and Denison, 1943, pp. 54–55). I am extremely sceptical of this ditch ever being intended to hold water or to serve the functions of a moat. I think it more likely it is a great borrow pit from which the city was built.

[33] There is an example of the walls of a building having first been outlined on the plastered floor of the platform on which it rested (A. L. Smith, 1950, p. 24). We know from mural paintings and codices that the Maya were quite proficient in drawing, and one can easily imagine architectural sketches.

FIG. 11—RESTORATION DRAWING OF STR. K-5 3D, PIEDRAS NEGRAS. Usumacinta area. Early Class (After Proskouriakoff.)

the line. Walls are often precisely vertical and straight for their full length.

Building Materials

Although stone and lime mortar are the characteristic materials of the monumental architecture of the Maya, other materials came into play. Pole-and-thatch houses rested on masonry platforms or pyramids (see Ricketson and Ricketson, 1937, pp. 72–74; Satterthwaite, 1943–54), and buildings with stone walls carried thatched roofs (Satterthwaite, *ibid.*, and see our fig. 11). Wood was also used with masonry construction to bind fill (A. L. Smith, 1950, p. 69), as lintels over doorways and niches, beams across vaults, architraves between columns, and joists to support flat masonry roofs (figs. 16, 14, 18). Dirt and clay, usually mixed with stone, and sascab, a weathered and disintegrated limestone (Littmann, 1958), were employed as fill and at times between stones in place of mortar (Trik, 1939, pp. 95–96). Clay was daubed on pole

walls. In Tabasco, where there were no ready sources of stone, fired brick and shell were used as building materials (Charnay, 1887, p. 188 and chap. 12; Blom and La-Farge, 1926–27, pp. 105–114; Berlin, 1956, pp. 102–109; and see note 39).

By far the most common stone for building was the ubiquitous limestone of the lowland area. Other stones employed locally were tuff, sandstone, slate, and dolomite.[34] Lime was obtained by burning limestone (see Morris, Charlot, and Morris, 1931, 1: 220–23) or shell. Sand was relatively scarce over much of the area and it was for the most part replaced by sascab as a binding material for mortar. By mixing mortar and rock a lime concrete was obtained and was used extensively as a structural material. Plaster and stucco of pure

[34] Tuff was used at Copan, sandstone at Quirigua, Pusilha, Tonina, and at times at Palenque and Altar de Sacrificios, slate occasionally in British Honduras, dolomite occasionally in the Pasion and Usumacinta River areas.

396

lime or with admixtures of sascab were also used extensively.

Quarrying, Stonecutting, and Transportation

A number of quarries have been found in or near the ancient cities, and there is probably material available for more careful studies of quarrying techniques than have yet been made.[35] Large blocks seem to have been obtained by cutting away the native rock from around the piece to be removed, then undercutting, and finally prying loose with poles or perhaps wedges of hardwood (see Morley, 1956, p. 332). Natural fissures and cleavage planes must have been utilized when present (Morley, 1935, p. 28), and advantage taken of the pockets of softer rock or sascab that in many places underlie the hard surface cap (see Morris, Charlot, and Morris, 1931, 1: 215; A. L. Smith, 1950, p. 69). Smaller stones were undoubtedly derived both from quarrying and from collecting loose surface rock.

Although we have a fair repertoire of the tools used for stoneworking, we know rather little of the precise process. It seems to have been a matter of fracturing with heavy weights of stone or wood, of prying, of splitting with wedges, of pecking, chipping, flaking, abrading, and occasionally sawing (Holmes, 1895–97, p. 198; Morris, Charlot, and Morris, 1931, 1: 217). Some of the softer stones were undoubtedly cut with knifelike implements. The most common material for tools was the native flint, but hard nodules of limestone and imported stones, such as diorite and obsidian,

were also used. Known tools include pick-like implements and hammerstones both hand-held and hafted, celts used as hatchet or adz, chisels, and a considerable number of smaller flaked tools for graving or incising. In spite of this array of implements, it remains unclear, at least in my mind, precisely what the techniques were that produced the vast quantities of well-shaped, dressed, and fitted stone that went into Maya building.[36]

The transportation of materials to the building site was strictly a matter of manpower. The ancient Maya had no beasts of burden and they seemingly did not know the wheel-and-axle as a mechanical aid, so that carts, pulleys, or block-and-tackle were not available to move the heavy timbers and even heavier blocks of stone that at times were needed. We can imagine earth, lime, and sascab carried in wood, bark, or basketry containers. Mortar was probably handled in pottery or wooden vessels. The Maya unquestionably had ropes and probably knew the use of rollers. It is conceivable they utilized some form of sledge. They may have employed the inclined plane, and it is likely they knew the advantage of running a rope over a horizontal beam to raise great weights (see Morley, 1956, pls. 64, 65). With these simple aids, transportation seems to have been a matter of harnessing sufficient manpower to the object to be moved.

Construction and Masonry

The terraces, platforms, and truncated pyramids generally supported other constructions, and in this capacity they are known as substructures. They consisted essentially of masonry retaining walls that held inside a rough fill of rubble.[37] The

[35] For locations of quarries see Morley, 1920, p. 6 and pl. 3; Morley, 1937–38, pls. 197, 201, 210,b; Ruppert and Denison, 1943, p. 23 and pl. 61; A. L. Smith, 1950, fig. 143; Vinson, 1960; and see Carr and Hazard, 1961, p. 12, for quarries at Tikal. Our most informative study (Holmes, 1895–97, pp. 279–85) of quarrying techniques deals with Oaxaca, but there is no reason to believe they differed greatly from those in use in the Maya area. Also see Outwater, 1957, for quarrying and stonecutting in highland Mexico.

[36] Coe, Shook, and Satterthwaite (1961, pp. 42–45) discuss the shaping and carving of wooden lintels at Tikal.

[37] There are exceptions to this generalization, as, for example, a tight fill of stone and mortar, where the entire structure is of solid masonry, and dirt

FIG. 12—RESTORATION DRAWING OF TEMPLE II, TIKAL. Central area. Late Classic. (After Proskouriakoff.)

character of the fill, of the retaining walls, and the manner in which the structure was built vary greatly. Dirt, mud, stone, sascab, mortar, debris of habitation were the standard materials for fill, and these were mixed, combined, and laid in endless ways. Shell was also used. At times there were rough walls within the fill, rough work levels, and especially prepared footings for the building that was to rest on top (fig. 16,f), measures designed to give added support to what was thought to be an unstable mass. The extremely common practice of building over earlier construction often led to the same result of lending stability to the fill of the later substructure.[38]

The outer retaining walls, the masonry of which varied widely both in time and in locality, may be divided, broadly speaking, into two classes: those that were sufficiently stable in themselves to retain the fill, and those that needed additional support from inner walls, or some such device, to resist the lateral thrust of the fill. The former were built of large, deeply set stones, the face of the wall often being raised with an inward slope further to resist the outward pressures. Such construction is found in most areas and at nearly all times. An example of the other class of construction is the shallow, tilelike facing stones, known as veneer masonry, that were laid against a tight stable fill or a rough inner wall which was the true retaining wall (fig. 16,f). This construction is diagnostic of Late Classic substructures in the Central area, of Early Postclassic at Chichen Itza, and is occasionally used elsewhere in Late Classic times. An intermediate form consisted of fairly deep facing stones backed by a tight fill which in turn retained a loose fill. These are but examples, and there is great variety in the manner in which substructural walls were built.[39] There is also an infinite variety in the quality of stonecutting. It is probable that the great majority of substructural walls were covered with plaster.

Most Maya substructures were of sufficient height to require stairways. These

_____

fill encased in plaster or stucco (Berlin, 1956, pp. 102, 110), where the plaster can hardly be thought of as a true masonry retaining wall.

[38] Morris, Charlot, and Morris (1931, 1: 146–

48) give an extraordinarily detailed description of the activities of overseer and masons in constructing the fill of a pyramid at Chichen Itza. Also see *ibid.*, 1: 204–206, for an account of the preparation of the building site before construction began and of the subsequent activities of the masons.

[39] A hitherto unreported form of construction has recently been found in structures of Late Preclassic and even earlier date at Altar de Sacrificios. According to A. L. Smith, of the Peabody Museum, Harvard University, to whom I am indebted for this information, the substructural walls are formed of bivalve shells, still joined, laid much in the manner of cobblestones in dirt or mud mortar. See also Willey and Bullard, 1961, p. 84; Willey and Smith, 1963, p. 86 and fig. 4.

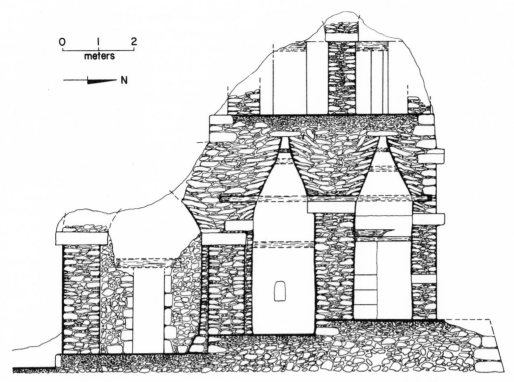

FIG. 13—SECOND-STORY CONSTRUCTION. Central area. Str. A-XVIII, Uaxactun. (After A. L. Smith.)

were at times inset (fig. 26), but more often projected from the side of the substructure (fig. 12). Most frequently the stairway rose in a single steep flight, but there are many examples of two or more flights with intervening landings. When the stairway projected it was built either as an integral part of the substructure, so that the fill of each merged, or as a separate unit laid against the substructural wall or a rough retaining wall made especially to receive the staircase (see Ruppert, 1935, p. 43). The masonry of the side walls of the stairway, which were at times topped by ramplike slopes (fig. 41,a), unfortunately known as balustrades in the terminology of Maya architecture, and the character of the fill were similar to, and as varied as, those of substructures. This same variety in construction was true of the steps, where each riser might be made of a single course of large stones that also

formed the tread, or be made of shallow stones backed by lime concrete to complete the tread, or be built up of several courses of stone. Stairways seem almost invariably to have been covered by plaster, numerous coats often being present.

Once the substructure was raised to the desired height, the upper surface was leveled and was then capped by a rough work floor or by the final finished floor. The choice was dictated both by local custom and by what construction was to follow. There is some indication that at times, and particularly in early times, floors were built of tamped earth, clay, or sascab (see A. L. Smith, 1950, p. 76), but the characteristic plaster floor of the Maya is known to have been employed in the Late Preclassic period and to have been constructed in much the same fashion from then on. Such construction consisted of a lower layer of

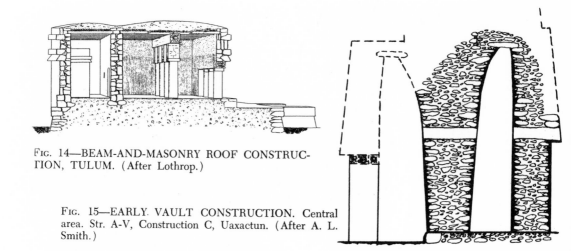

Fig. 14—BEAM-AND-MASONRY ROOF CONSTRUC-
TION, TULUM. (After Lothrop.)

Fig. 15—EARLY VAULT CONSTRUCTION. Central
area. Str. A-V, Construction C, Uaxactun. (After A. L.
Smith.)

debris to fill the chinks and even off the rough fill below, when that was necessary, upon which debris was laid a stratum of concrete of small stone and mortar, and lastly a layer of relatively pure lime plaster, at times colored and often highly polished (fig. 16,*f*; and see Morris, Charlot, and Morris, 1931, 1: 224).

The building that crowned the substructure usually did not rest directly on it but on an intermediate construction known as a building platform (see fig. 12). There were exceptions to this practice, particularly by the Early Postclassic (Andrews' Modified Florescent) Maya-Toltec builders of the Northern Plain, but during most of Maya history the building platform was in general use. These constructions normally were only slightly larger in plan than the building above, and they followed the outline of the walls of the latter, an indication that the building was planned in advance. Building platforms varied in height from a single course of stones to several meters, and they frequently required stairways. In method of construction they were essentially similar to substructures, but the upper surfaces were sometimes built on two or more levels to provide higher floors in the rear chambers of the buildings they supported (fig. 13).

The structure that stood on the building platform, or at times directly on the sub-structure, is commonly referred to as the superstructure. These buildings invariably contained interior space.[40] There is some reason to believe that the earliest superstructures were built of wood and thatch (A. L. Smith, 1950, pp. 70, 72), and it is probable that this form of construction was used to some extent throughout the history of Maya building. There are also indications of masonry walls having been roofed with pole-and-thatch (fig. 11, and see Satterthwaite, 1939),[41] and examples of beam-and-masonry roofs, very common in the late history of the Maya, are known to have occurred in relatively early times (A. L. Smith, 1950, p. 80). The latter were built of wooden beams that spanned the width of the room, on which were placed at right angles small poles laid side by side, and the whole was capped by a concrete slab with an upper surface of plaster (see fig. 14). By far the most characteristic way of roofing ceremonial buildings, however, was the so-called Maya vault, which involved the slop-

[40] There are a few rare examples of buildings that might be thought of as superstructures, or similar to superstructures, such as the false temples of the Rio Bec area (fig. 38) and the towers of the Chenes area (fig. 40), that are solid. To all intents and purposes, however, the superstructure by definition involves interior space.

[41] This type of construction has been reported as occurring on buildings of Late Preclassic date at Dzibilchaltun. See Andrews, 1961b, fig. 1; 1962, fig. 7.

400

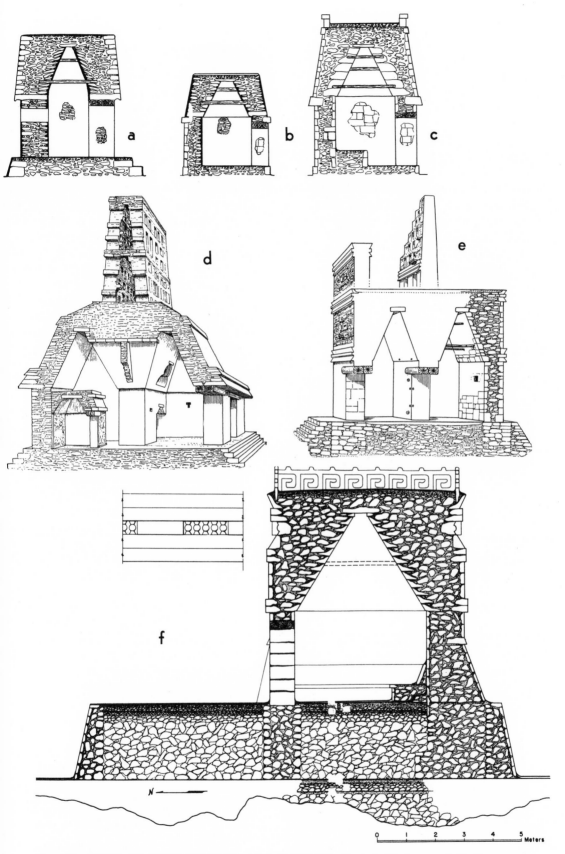

Fig. 16—TYPES OF CONSTRUCTION AND MASONRY. Central, Western, and Northern Plain areas. *a*, Early Classic, Uaxactun (after A. L. Smith). *b*, Transitional Late Classic, Uaxactun (after A. L. Smith). *c*, Late Classic, Uaxactun (after A. L. Smith). *d*, Temple of the Cross, Palenque (after Holmes). *e*, Red House, Chichen Itza (after Holmes). *f*, Mercado, Chichen Itza (after Ruppert).

ing upward and inward of two masonry walls until they touched or, more frequently, could be bridged at the top by capstones.[42]

Once the Maya builder began the construction of hollow, masonry buildings, and hit upon the vault as a means of roofing them, he was faced with new and untried problems. Such problems involved not only the strength and behavior of his materials under stress, but the uncertain stability of an imperfectly balanced mass.[43] That the Maya approached these problems tentatively and with caution is seen in the heavy walls and narrow rooms of some early construction where the inward slope begins at the foot of the wall and continues all the way to the peak of the vault (fig. 15). Most of the slope, moreover, was on each face of the medial wall, which was a balanced mass. Later, the Maya built proportionately thinner walls and raised them vertically to about half the height of the room, at which point the spring of the vault occurred, thus necessitating a more pronounced overhang at a more critical angle and providing badly unbalanced blocks of masonry above the outer walls of the building (figs. 16, 17). A fear on the part of the builders of this unbalanced property of the vault is apparently seen in the almost universal use of wooden beams that bridged the vault and were set deeply into the masonry at each side.

There were two common forms of construction, involving different types of masonry, that were used by the Maya in building their superstructures. The first was the use of deeply set stones, at times penetrating the entire thickness of the walls and well into the vault faces, so that the stones were an essential part of the construction and a major factor in bearing the super-

imposed load (figs. 16,a; 13; 15). This construction was used in Early Classic times and persisted in some areas throughout the history of building.[44] The second, which is known as veneer masonry, was the use of relatively shallow, tilelike stones backed by a hearting of mortar and rough stone (figs. 16,f; 17,c). In this case the facing stones supplied almost no support, and it was the lime concrete hearting, which set into a monolithic mass, that was the primary structural factor.[45] Although these two methods of construction sometimes were both used in a single building, the walls being of veneer, the vault of slab masonry, and at times reached an intermediate stage, so that both the facing stones and the concrete fill were important factors in the support of the structure, at their two extremes they were highly distinctive. Veneer masonry was used in, and seems to be diagnostic of, Late Classic superstructures in the Central, Rio Bec, Chenes, and Puuc areas, and is typical of the Early Postclassic architecture of the Northern Plain.

An aberrant form of construction was employed at Copan and Quirigua where wall and vault stones, and for that matter the retaining walls of substructures, were set in mud mortar rather than the usual lime mortar, and where the hearting was of mud and stone (Trik, 1939, pp. 94–99). As the mud had no adhesive strength, it was the simple weight of the stones that kept the masonry in place, a weakness that was intensified by an almost complete disregard of the breaking of joints between courses except at salient corners where a

[42] See A. L. Smith, 1940, for a discussion of the origin, development, and distribution of the vault in Middle America. Also see notes 61 and 72.

[43] The engineering principles of the Maya vault have been analyzed by L. Roys (1934).

[44] A possible exception is seen at Oxkintok where a crude veneer wall masonry is found on buildings that appear to be of Early Classic date (Shook, 1940, p. 168, fig. 3).

[45] Where this construction was employed, buildings were normally erected in three stages: (1) the lower walls, (2) the vault, (3) the upper façade and roof cap. Each stage was presumably allowed to rest, and the mortar to set, before going further, thus indicating that the Maya by this time had learned much about the properties of lime mortar.

402

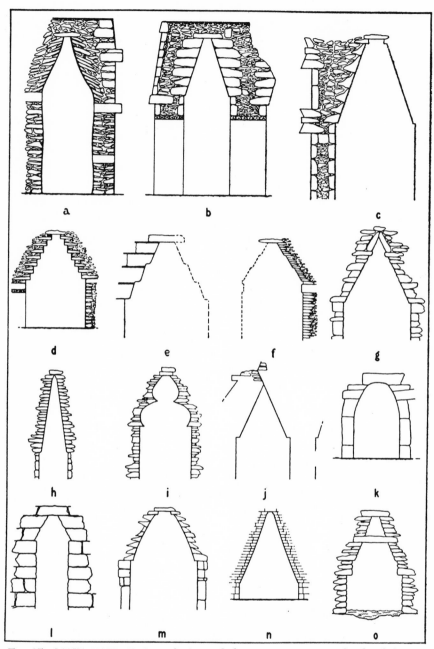

FIG. 17—MAYA VAULTS. Several areas. *a,b,d,* Uaxactun. *c,n,* Uxmal. *e,l,* Tikal. *f,i,o,* Palenque. *g,h,k,* Chichen Itza. *j,* Comalcalco. *m,* Labna. (After A. L. Smith.)

FIG. 18—RESTORATION DRAWING OF INTERIOR OF NORTH COLONNADE, CHICHEN ITZA. Northern Plain area. Early Postclassic. (After Proskouriakoff.)

sort of bonding was at times employed (see *ibid.*, p. 95).[46] It has already been mentioned that baked brick was used in place of stone in Tabasco. Walls and vaults of buildings seem to have been made solidly of brick laid in lime mortar (Blom and La-Farge, 1926–27, fig. 89).[47] So far as we know, the exterior wall surfaces and interior wall and vault faces of Maya buildings were invariably coated with lime plaster. This was true even at Copan and Quirigua where, as we have just seen, lime mortar was not used in the masonry, although it was employed extensively for floors (Trik, 1939, p. 96) and presumably for the roof caps of buildings.[48]

Doorways for the most part offered no particular problem to the Maya builder. Jambs were usually constructed of masonry similar to that of the walls (fig. 16,*a-c*), but in the Puuc area in Late Classic times they were built of large stones that ran the full width of each jamb. The majority

of lintels were wooden beams, but stone was frequently used, particularly over narrow entrances, and stone lintels were characteristic in the Puuc and in much of the Usumacinta architecture, the lintel often resting on a corbel at the top of each jamb (fig. 41,*a*). Interior doorways, normally narrower than outer, occasionally were bridged by vaults (figs. 16,*d*; 17,*i*), but on the whole this was rare.

In Late Classic times rectangular masonry piers were used to attain closely spaced, multiple entrances (fig. 8) and round and

[46] Mud mortar is also reported from Dzibilchaltun in the Northern Plain (Andrews, 1962, fig. 2). The lack of breaking of joints and of bonding, except at salient corners (see Satterthwaite, 1943–54, pt. 1, p. 16), were weaknesses common to virtually all Maya masonry.

[47] In this region where limestone was lacking, lime was obtained by burning shell.

[48] The roof cap was a slab of lime concrete with an upper surface of plaster, identical to floors in construction but built with a camber to provide drainage (see fig. 16,*f*).

404

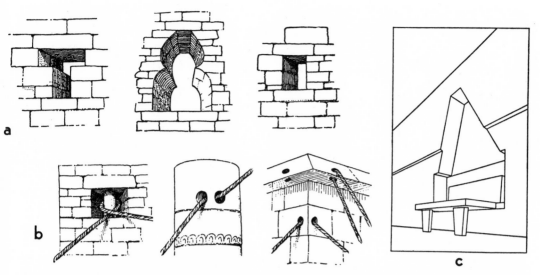

FIG. 19—MISCELLANEOUS ARCHITECTURAL FEATURES. *a,* Wall openings (after Holmes). Left and center, Palenque; right, general. *b,* Cordholders (after Holmes). *c,* Throne in palace, Piedras Negras (after Morley).

square columns to create wider doorways than had previously been feasible. Columns were built of stone blocks, drums, and shafts, and rarely of small stone masonry. Often topped by square capitals and occasionally by round ones, columns were particularly favored at this time in the Puuc area (fig. 41,*a*) and were employed sparingly in the Rio Bec area.[49] In the Postclassic period columns were used in the Northern Plain and East Coast areas not only in entrances but as primary supports for roofs (fig. 14), and in the vaulted colonnades of Chichen Itza, built during the early part of that period, we find the most daring construction attempted by the ancient builders, the ultimate stage in the long progression from heavy walls and narrow rooms to great, wide vaults supported on rows of slender columns (figs. 18, 45;

and see Morris, Charlot, and Morris, 1931, 1: 207–208).[50]

Small wall openings, such as drains at floor level and ventilators often placed immediately below the spring of the vault, were common (fig. 19,*a*, right). They rarely exceed 30 cm. in width and were simply capped by stones of the necessary length. Openings of a size to be called windows were rare (fig. 16,*a*; and see Tozzer, 1911, p. 99; A. L. Smith, 1950, pp. 21, 77; Andrews, 1959, pp. 105–107). They carried wooden or stone lintels.[51] At Palenque some quite large wall openings between rooms are spanned by masonry that may be likened to the Maya vault (figs. 16,*d*; 19,*a*, center). Wall depressions, such as niches and cupboard-like forms, of which there were many, were roofed by wood or stone lintels. Cordholders, which were placed mainly on inner wall surfaces at each side of entrances, were made in many forms

[49] Interesting examples of lintel supports that are borderline between piers and columns are found in the Lacanja region of the Usumacinta River area (Healey, 1950). The only known instance in this area of round piers or columns also occurs in that region (*ibid.,* p. 14). This architecture is presumably of the Late Classic period. The writer knows of but one example of columns, apparently of post-Classic date, in the Central area (Maler, 1908a, fig. 11; Bullard, 1960a, p. 552).

[50] It will subsequently be seen that the colonnade was introduced to the Maya by a foreign culture. See Acosta, 1959, pp. 507–13, on the evolution of columnar supports.

[51] At Comalcalco there seems to have been a window with a huge brick as a lintel (Blom and LaFarge, 1926–27, p. 109).

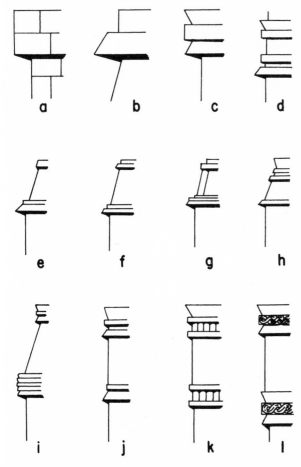

FIG. 20—MOLDINGS. *a,* Southern area. *b,* Usumacinta River area. *c,d,h–j,* Chichen Itza. *c,k,l,* Puuc area. *e–g,* Palenque. (After Spinden.)

but essentially were holes or depressions with a crosspiece of stone or bone (fig. 19,*b.*) Rodholders, hemispherical depressions in the faces of doorjambs, were common in the Puuc area and probably were widely used (see A. L. Smith, 1950, p. 78).

Benches and altars, frequent features inside of buildings, were usually solid constructions built against one or more walls of a room (figs. 16,*c;* 18; 45) The upper surfaces were floored with plaster and the exposed walls of the bench or altar not infrequently were indented with niches. At Piedras Negras there were table-like constructions of large stone slabs, supported

by legs, that appear to have served as thrones (fig. 19,*c;* and see Satterthwaite, 1937), and at Chichen Itza the Maya-Toltec built some of their altars of slabs resting on small atlantean figures (Morris, Charlot, and Morris, 1931, 1: 16–20).

Interior stairways were not a common feature of Maya architecture but were by no means rare. As interior space in buildings was almost invariably cramped, stairways that rose to any appreciable height, such as to second stories, normally were winding.[52] Once the plan of the stairway had been laid out, a task that in some situations must have been fairly exacting, the construction of the steps should have offered little difficulty, but the roof of the stair passage, often built of successively higher vaults, must have called for considerable ingenuity.

A great many Maya buildings carried masonry constructions above the roof line that are known as roof structures. At times these attained huge proportions, assuming a bulk equal to the building beneath and being considerably higher (fig. 12). When they were placed over the rear or medial wall of a building, they are known as roof combs, when over the front wall, as flying façades (fig. 16,*e*). Although there was great variety in the design of roof combs, they may be divided into two general forms: those that were hollow, approximating the shape of an A or inverted V in cross-section (fig. 16,*d*), and those that were solid in section (fig. 16,*e*). Both kinds were frequently perforated with window-like openings (fig. 42,*b*). Flying façades, which were much more rare, were invariably of the single-wall, solid type and were also perforated. The hollow roof comb was mainly restricted to the Central, Usumacinta River, and Western areas; the solid was

[52] For examples see Maudslay, 1889–1902, vol. 4, pls. 39, 46; Spinden, 1913, fig. 142; A. L. Smith, 1950, figs. 85, 86,*a;* Ruz, 1955a, fig. 1. A spiral stairway is described and illustrated by Ruppert (1935, pp. 225–32).

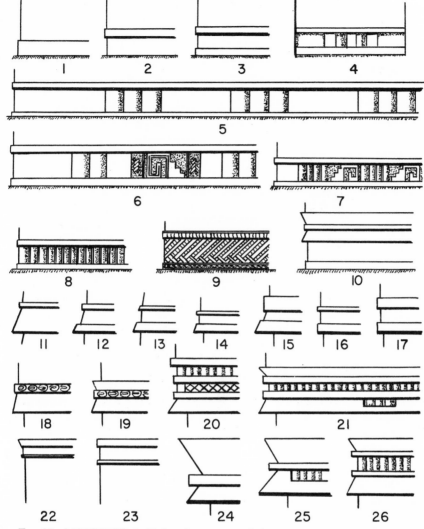

Fig. 21—MOLDINGS. 1–10, basal; 11–21, medial; 22–26, cornice. 1, 7, 8, 14, 16, 18–25, Puuc area. 2, 3, Central area. 4–6, 9, 11–13, Rio Bec area. 10, 15, 17, 26, Chenes-Puuc transitional. (After Ruz.)

used in all other areas except the Southern and Pasion River, where no roof combs have so far been found. Flying façades seem to have been restricted to the Chenes, Puuc, and Northern Plain areas. Besides roof structures there were small decorative elements of stone or stucco on the edges of roofs that are known as roof crests (fig. 16,f). They are known to have been used at Uaxactun in the Late Classic period and at Chichen Itza and in the East Coast centers in Postclassic times. Low parapets have

also been found at Uaxactun (figs. 16,c; 30).

Second and third stories on Maya buildings were not uncommon, there being at least one example of a structure of four stories.[53] Very rarely did the builder risk

[53] This is the so-called Palace of Five Stories, or Str. 10, at Tikal (Maler, 1911, pp. 15–20; Tozzer, 1911, pp. 111–13). I am of the opinion that the supposed fifth story was in fact a roof comb. Str. 5 at Chacmultun might also be thought of as a building of four stories (E. H. Thompson, 1904, fig. 11).

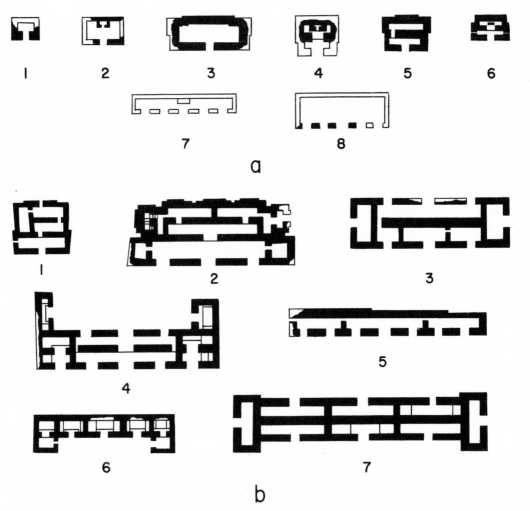

FIG. 22–PLANS OF BUILDINGS AT UAXACTUN. Central area. *a*, Temple types: 1–6, Early Classic; 7, 8, Late Classic. *b*, Palace types: 1, 2, Early Classic; 3–7, Late Classic. (After A. L. Smith.)

footing a wall of an upper story over a vault below. Such walls were placed either over the walls of lower stories (fig. 13) or, more frequently, over solid fill. The latter arrangement was particularly favored in the Puuc area in Late Classic times (see fig. 41,*a*).

Extremely few Maya buildings were without some ornamentation. Horizontal moldings halfway up the façade, where they are known as medial moldings, and at roof line, where they are known as cornice moldings, were all but universal except on the heavy, sloped upper façades of the early architecture of the Central area. There also

were often moldings on substructures and building platforms. Moldings took many designs and comprised from one to as many as six members (figs. 20, 21). The lowest member of the medial molding was formed of deeply set stones (figs. 16,*a-d*) that were major elements in the support of the often overhanging masonry of the upper façade. Aside from moldings, roof structures and upper façades of buildings usually carried elaborate decoration worked out in stucco or stone. Generally speaking, stucco was favored in the Central, Usumacinta, Western, and Rio Bec areas, but with some stone in use in the last. In the Chenes area stone and stucco were equally employed for decoration. Stone was favored in the Southern and Puuc areas, and in the Northern Plaint in Late Classic and Early Postclassic (Andrews' Florescent) times. In Late Postclassic (Decadent) times in the Northern Plain in Late Classic and Early Postclassic came into vogue. Painting, both on exteriors and interiors of buildings, was undoubtedly common, although most of it has disappeared. Pigments were mostly of inorganic substances (Morris, Charlot, and Morris, 1931, 1: 355–56; Ruppert, Thompson, and Proskouriakoff, 1955, p. 67; Pollock, Roys, Proskouriakoff, and Smith, 1962, pt. 2).

Types and Functions of Buildings

Although our knowledge of the function of Maya buildings has increased over the years, it is still woefully inadequate. That the vast majority of structures served a religious purpose seems highly probable (see Holmes, 1895–97, pp. 22–23), but within most classes of buildings presently defined there is great variety of design and undoubtedly a wide range of precise functions.[54] *Temples* and *shrines* in their most typical forms (figs. 22,*a*,1-6; 24,*a*), because of the restricted interior arrangements and exalted locations of the former (fig. 12), and the diminutive sizes of the latter (fig. 48), seem fairly surely to have housed the esoteric rites of a select priesthood, in the first instance, and to have a place for offerings and prayer in the second. We know, however, that there were several types of shrines (fig. 48; see Pollock, Roys, Proskouriakoff, and Smith, 1962), that in size and design they grade into what might be

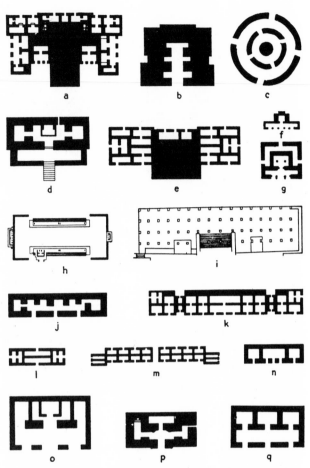

FIG. 23—PLANS OF BUILDINGS. Various areas. *a*, Palace, Santa Rosa Xtampak. *b*, Temple IV, Tikal. *c*, Caracol, Chichen Itza. *d*, Temple E-II, Uaxactun. *e*, Akabtzib, Chichen Itza. *f*, Sweat House No. 2, Chichen Itza. *g*, Castillo, Chichen Itza. *h*, Great Ball Court, Chichen Itza. *i*, Northwest Colonnade, Chichen Itza. *j*, Str. 33, Yaxchilan. *k*, Governor's Palace, Uxmal. *l*, House of the Turtles, Uxmal. *m*, House of the Pigeons, Uxmal. *n*, Str. 21, Yaxchilan. *o*, Temple of the Sun, Palenque. *p*, Temple 22, Copan. *q*, Red House, Chichen Itza. (After Morley.)

considered to be small temples (fig. 22,*a*,6), and that temple and palace types, although distinct at their two extremes, grade into each other (figs. 22, 23).[55]

[54] Kubler (1958, pp. 528, 530) has called attention to the "poorly differentiated functional building types" of Maya architecture. Morley's (1956, Table 8) "Classification of Maya buildings and other constructions according to their probable uses" is misleading in that it is actually a listing of structures according to types, the functions of some of which are known, of others are questionable, and of yet others are unknown.

[55] A. L. Smith (1950, p. 73) has pointed out the difficulty of distinguishing between temples and palaces at Uaxactun. He also notes that the functions of some buildings changed with time. M. D. Coe (1956) has suggested that temples and palaces were erected as "funerary temples" and makes no distinction between them in that function.

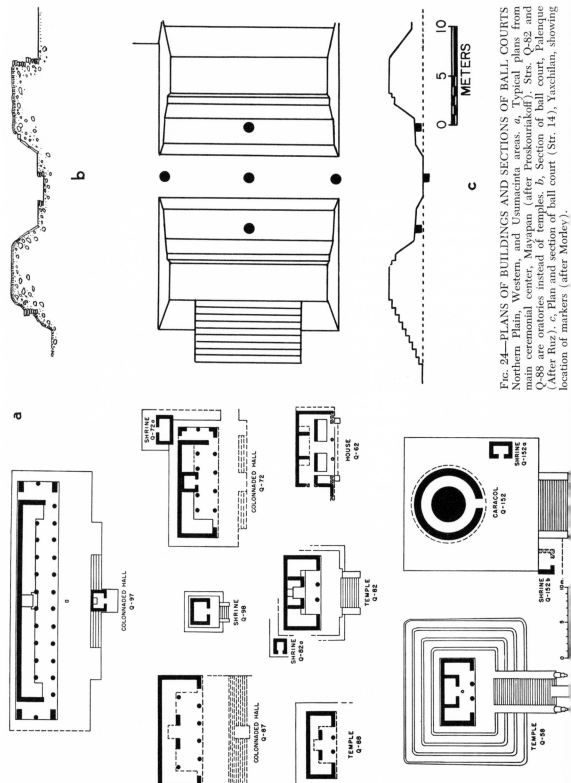

Fig. 24—PLANS OF BUILDINGS AND SECTIONS OF BALL COURTS Northern Plain, Western, and Usumacinta areas. *a,* Typical plans from main ceremonial center, Mayapan (after Proskouriakoff). Strs. Q-82 and Q-88 are oratories instead of temples. *b,* Section of ball court, Palenque (After Ruz). *c,* Plan and section of ball court (Str. 14), Yaxchilan, showing location of markers (after Morley).

The least satisfactory class of buildings, both from the point of view of type and of function, is the so-called *palace*. This term is used primarily for multiroomed structures that most often rest on relatively low sub-structures (figs. 22,*b*; 23,*a,e,k,m*; 41), but it has tended to be a catch-all designation for buildings that fit into no other class. To add to the confusion, we know little about the function of palaces. The name was first applied in the belief that such structures were residences of the priests and nobility, and excavations at Uaxactun have indicated that they did indeed have a domiciliary as well as a religious function (A. L. Smith, 1950, p. 72). At Piedras Negras, on the other hand, findings suggest that some palaces were places of meeting and audi-ence and not residences (Satterthwaite, 1937). Other functions attributed to pal-aces, but with little direct proof, are that they served as "men's houses," for noviti-ates in training, or possibly to house people performing periodic rites.[56] The great va-riety of size and of interior arrangement of palaces surely indicates they served many purposes, but beyond the general one of religion we can say little.

Two types of structures that seem clear

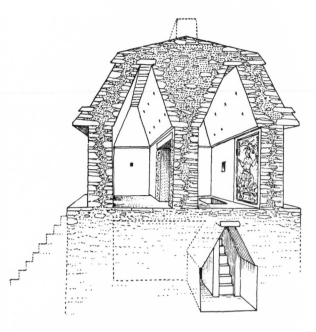

FIG. 25—TEMPLE OF THE BEAU RELIEF, PA-LENQUE, SHOWING SUBTERRANEAN TOMB. (After Holmes.)

as to function are *ball courts* (figs. 23,*h*; 24,*b,c*; 32) and *sweat houses* (figs. 23,*f*; 36), both of which provided for activities of a ceremonial and religious nature.[57] The des-ignation of certain flat-topped constructions that carried no superstructures as *cere-monial platforms* (figs. 26, 46) unquestion-ably has some validity, but the term is gen-eral and diffuse in meaning, and the type covers a wide range of buildings (see A. L. Smith, 1950, p. 72). *Mortuary structures*, containing chambers to receive the dead (fig. 25), clearly performed the mausoleum function, but they were built in the form of temples, shrines, and platforms and seem to have served other uses besides burial (see note 55). In Late Postclassic times at Mayapan the *oratory* appears to be a de-finable type of building in which ancestor worship took place (figs. 24,*a*; 48,*a*; and see Thompson and Thompson, 1955, pp. 232–42; Pollock, Roys, Proskouriakoff, and

[56] Recent work at the Late Postclassic urban towns of Mayapan and Tulum has identified true palaces, i.e. residences of important people, that are set somewhat apart from the ceremonial cen-ters (J. E. S. Thompson, 1954b; Thompson and Thompson, 1955; Proskouriakoff and Temple, 1955; Pollock, Roys, Proskouriakoff, and Smith, 1962, pt. 3; Sanders, 1960a, pp. 212–13. At Mayapan colonnaded halls (figs. 24,*a*; 48) which may have been the equivalent of so-called palaces in Classic sites, seem surely to have had dormitory functions, probably the housing of people for limited lengths of time, while on religious duty or in training, rather than having been primary residences (Pollock, Roys, Proskouriakoff, and Smith, 1962, pt. 2). Although we must be cau-tious in drawing comparisons between conditions in these urban centers, heavily influenced by foreign cultures, and in the Classic cities, the find-ings are nevertheless of interest in our search for the functions of palaces. Also see note 55 above. Recent work at Tikal has identified small palace-like structures at some distance from the cere-monial center (W. R. Coe, 1962b, p. 502).

[57] See Stern, 1950, pp. 34–35, for ball courts; Satterthwaite, 1943–54, pt. 5, for sweat houses.

Smith, 1962). A class of buildings set apart by some authors, but which I consider to include structures of several functions, is the *tower* (figs. 5; 23,*c*; 24,*a*; 40; 43).[58] Lastly, we might mention the *portal vault*, which most frequently is a passage through a building (see figs. 41,*b*; 42,*a,b*), but at times stands alone as an independent structure (Smith and Ruppert, 1954a; Ruz, 1955b, p. 13). It probably served the same function in either situation, namely, to mark and to formalize the entrance to a precinct.

The *city walls* of Late Postclassic times have been referred to earlier (see note 32). The purpose of these walls has commonly been thought of as one of defense, but it is open to question, and particularly in the case of Mayapan, where the wall offered no great deterrent to attack, if they were not to delimit precincts. The roads, or *causeways*, that form approaches to ceremonial centers, run between groups of structures within centers (figs. 2, 29), and connect one city with another (Thompson, Pollock, and Charlot, 1932, pp. 128–29; Villa, 1934; Saville, 1935; Carr and Hazard, 1961), appear to pertain more to civic planning, the design and ordering of space, than to transportation, although the latter was undoubtedly a secondary function (see Kubler, 1958, pp. 515–17). Another kind of construction that had to do with civic planning was the vaulted passage, a sort of *aqueduct*, that channeled a stream underground through the ceremonial center at Palenque (figs. 4; 5; 17,*o*; and see Ruz, 1952b, pp. 33–34).[59] *Bridges* across streams occur at that site (Holmes, 1895–97, pp. 203–206)

and at Pusilha (Gann, 1928a, pp. 216–18; Gruning, 1930, fig. 1) and are reported to cross a chasm at Aguateca (Vinson, 1960, fig. 3).

A number of constructions of a practical nature had to do with water supply. In the Central area, and very probably in the Puuc area, there were artificial *reservoirs* (A. L. Smith, 1950, pp. 61, 84; Shook, 1958, p. 18; Bullard, 1960b, p. 363; Carr and Hazard, 1961, pp. 13–14; Stephens, 1843, 1: 248–50, 2: 208–14, 224–28; Erosa, 1948, pp. 6–7). Bottle-shaped underground cisterns, known as *chultuns*, are found in great numbers in the Puuc area and undoubtedly were an important source of water supply (E. H. Thompson, 1897b). Chultuns also occur in the Central area, but they were not for water storage, and their use is unknown (A. L. Smith, 1950, pp. 48, 84–85; Carr and Hazard, 1961, p. 11). The ancient Maya seem occasionally to have dug shallow *wells*. A single example is known from the Peten (Bullard, 1960b, p. 363), another from the Southern area (Ricketson, 1935), and a well at the bottom of a deep natural sink at Chichen Itza is thought to be of aboriginal origin (Brainerd, 1958, p. 38).

Architectural Style

PRECLASSIC PERIOD. We do not know very much about the architecture of the lowland Maya in the Preclassic period. Our best recorded example is a small pyramid at Uaxactun, known as E-VIIsub (fig. 26), that is generally thought to be of Late Preclassic date (A. L. Smith, 1950, p. 63). Pyramids A and B of Str. A-I complex at the same site and of the same period were also sufficiently preserved to give us some idea of the character of the architecture of this time in the Central area (R. E. Smith, 1937, pp. 218–23). Fragmentary and largely unstudied remains are known from the Northern Plain (Shook, 1955a, pp. 290–92). The work of the University of Pennsylvania Museum at Tikal is exposing buildings of this period, an example of which is referred

---

[58] The round towers of Chichen Itza (Ruppert, 1935) and of Mayapan (Pollock, 1936, pp. 109–113) are probably temples. The towers of the Chenes area (Maler, 1895, pp. 281–82; Case, 1911, facing p. 184) suggest places for offerings and prayer, and might be thought of as shrines. The tower at Palenque is unique (Holmes, 1895–97, pp. 179–86; Ruz, 1958, pp. 71–74); its function is unknown.

[59] See Blom and LaFarge, 1926–27, pp. 184–85, for another aqueduct near Palenque.

Fig. 26—RESTORATION DRAWING OF STR. E-VIISUB AT UXACTUN. Central area. Late Preclassic. (After Proskouriakoff.)

to below, and the efforts of Tulane University at Dzibilchaltun in the Northern Plain (see note 15) and of the Peabody Museum of Harvard University at Altar de Sacrificios in the Pasion River area (see note 39) are providing additional examples, but at present these still remain largely undescribed.

A glance at the illustration will show Str. E-VIIsub to be a low, stepped pyramid, rather squat compared to later pyramids of the Maya, with an inset stairway flanked by grotesque masks and by smaller stairways, an arrangement that is repeated, with the exception of the flight of stairs and masks on the building platform, on all four sides of the pyramid (Ricketson and Ricketson, 1937, pp. 73–78). The whole structure is heavily coated with stucco. In the heavy apron moldings overhanging narrow clear zones, a band molding, and basal moldings on the terraces we see features of Maya architecture that occur commonly in the Central area, and to some extent in other areas, throughout the following Classic period. A rise in level from front to rear of the upper surface of the building platform, not seen in the illustration, is also characteristic of later times. The use of four main stairways, except on ceremonial platforms, and small subsidiary stairways are not such common traits, and the flanking of stairways by masks is relatively rare.[60] The heavy stucco coating gives this pyramid an over-all modeled effect not usually associated with Maya architecture, but it is possible that many other structures in their original state may have had more of the softly rounded quality seen in E-VIIsub than is apparent in their present weathered condition.

[60] Masks flanking stairways of Late Preclassic date have recently been uncovered at Tikal (Coe and McGinn, 1963, pp. 26, 29, 32). This trait may prove to be characteristic of early architecture in the Central area.

413

FIG. 27—RESTORATION DRAWING OF STR. A-V, STAGE 1, UAXACTUN. Central area. Early Classic. (After Proskouriakoff.)

FIG. 28—RESTORATION DRAWING OF STR. A-V, STAGE 4, UAXACTUN. Central area. End of Early Classic. (After Proskouriakoff.)

By and large we see much that is characteristic of Maya substructures already in existence at this early date. Str. E-VIIsub has been classified as a ceremonial platform (A. L. Smith, 1950, p. 72), as it carried no superstructure. There were indications, however, that at an earlier time it supported a building of perishable materials, and it may once have been a pyramid-temple. Until very recently it was thought that masonry superstructures did not exist in Preclassic times. An example has recently been found at Tikal (W. R. Coe, 1962b, p. 501; Coe and McGinn, 1963, pp. 26–32). I have little knowledge of this building. It is presently unknown whether or not the structure was vaulted, but the evidence apparently is clear that superstructures with masonry walls were being constructed in Late Preclassic times (see note 41).

CLASSIC PERIOD. By the end of the Preclassic period the Maya of the Central area were well along in evolving a distinctive style for their platforms and pyramids, and they had begun to experiment with hollow masonry buildings. We do not know if the vault had come into use on buildings at that early date.[61] The earliest examples yet discovered are from Early Classic times, and from then on the vault seems to have been the most generally accepting form of roofing masonry buildings. Kubler (1958) has pointed out the monumental character of the formal architecture of the Maya and how little concerned the early builders were with the enclosing of interior space. The high, narrow, Maya vault was well suited to an architecture of this sort, and its wide-

spread acceptance strongly influenced the design and evolution of hollow masonry buildings.

There is unquestionably a good deal of Early Classic architecture available for study, but much of it remains buried and many of the visible buildings cannot yet be identified with certainty as being of this time. Our largest body of well-documented material comes from Uaxactun, where five of the six varieties of ceremonial structures defined by A. L. Smith (1950, pp. 72–74) were already in use. Only the ball court was absent. The ceremonial platform, with its four stairways and unencumbered upper surface, continued in much the same form as in the preceding period but without indications of the elaborate decoration seen on Str. E-VIIIsub. This is a type of construction, sometimes with four stairways, sometimes with one, two, or three, that was used throughout the history of Maya building. It is for the most part not particularly interesting from the architectural point of view and will mainly be disregarded in future pages.

Figure 27 shows three temples, collectively known as Str. A-V, built near the beginning of the Classic period. Each temple encloses two narrow, parallel chambers not much wider than the thickness of the walls that surround them (fig. 22,a,5). It will be seen that the upper zone of the façades is in effect a broad apron molding that overhangs a clear zone formed by the vertical lower walls of the buildings. This is essentially a duplication of the design of the substructural platform and building platforms, the only change being in the proportionate width of the clear zone. It is an indication of how the architect was thinking of the design of solid masses. The roof combs give height to what otherwise would be very squat monuments, and the paneled arrangement at the rear of each temple and the break in the line of the wall at each end of the building add vertical lines to enhance the effect of height and to break the monotony of a preponderance of horizontal lines.

[61] In Late Preclassic times tombs are known to have been roofed by capstones resting on corbels (Merwin and Vaillant, 1932, pp. 20, 37–39, 40), possibly the forerunner of the vault, and there is one questionable instance of construction that may more closely have approached the true Maya vault (A. L. Smith, 1950, pp. 71, 101). Also see A. L. Smith, 1940, pp. 203–05. Since the above was written, a clear-cut example of a Late Preclassic tomb roofed by a vault has been discovered at Tikal (W. R. Coe, 1962a, no. 8, p. 45; Coe and McGinn, 1963, pp. 30–32).

FIG. 29—RESTORATION DRAWING OF GROUPS A AND B, UAXACTUN, IN LATE CLASSIC TIMES, LOOKING NORTHWEST. Central area. (After Proskouriakoff.)

In the use of the upper façades and the roof combs for embellishment we see a practice that was adhered to throughout most of Maya architecture. Besides these temples grouped around a raised courtyard, the pyramid-temple, an example of which is seen in the left center foreground of figure 29, was being built at this time, and undoubtedly had its progenitor in even earlier times. It remained one of the important architectural forms throughout Maya history.

In figure 28 we see the same complex of three temples near the end of the Early Classic period (see Proskouriakoff, 1946, pls. 28–31). Three shrines have been placed across the open side of the court, thus shielding it from view and providing an esoteric character to that precinct. These shrines are in effect small temples, with floor plans similar to the larger temples, the major difference being a door at one end, or both ends, of each front room (fig. 22,a,6). Other kinds of shrines are little chambers against the back walls of rear rooms of temples (fig. 22,a,4) and tiny box-like constructions, large enough only to hold an idol, placed at the centers of stairways.

A palace, in this case of two stories, built near the end of Early Classic times is shown at the right in figure 30. This particular example is somewhat unusual in resting on a relatively high substructure. The rather complicated floor plan with its numerous, poorly lighted rooms and the winding stairway to the upper story is seen in figure 22,b,2. The breaking of horizontal lines at the rear and ends of the building is here carried even further than in the case of the temples.

Mortuary structures, as defined by A. L. Smith (1950, p. 73), are buildings erected primarily to receive human burials. In Early Classic times at Uaxactun there was a simple platform containing a burial vault, and a pyramid-temple, beneath the floor of which was a shaft leading to a burial chamber in the pyramid below (*ibid.*, pp. 51–52). Other than the presence of burial chambers, these structures are a typical platform and a temple and need not detain us.[62]

Little is known of the Early Classic architecture of the Southern, Pasion, and Usumacinta River areas. At Copan there is a ball court thought to be of this time (Stromsvik, 1952, pp. 197–98), and as such it is unique, all other examples being of later date. An Early Classic structure has recently been uncovered at Altar de Sacrificios (Willey and Bullard, 1961, pp. 83–84). The pyramid rose in nine or ten terraces with nearly vertical walls and no signs of moldings. An elaborate stairway of four flights with stelae and altars on the intervening landings led to a summit platform that is believed to have supported a building mainly of perishable materials.[63] To judge from our fragmentary data, this structure represents quite a different architectural tradition than that of the Central area. Although there are early hieroglyphic inscriptions at Yaxchilan, some of them on lintels, there is doubt that they accurately date the buildings (e.g. see Morley, 1937–38, 2: 365–67), and it will take further study to distinguish the early structures from the later in the rather uniform architectural style of this site. At Piedras Negras, where the vault seems to have been employed only in later times, an Early Classic temple, shown in figure 11, carried a roof of perishable materials. The wide doorways separated by piers, the relative lightness of the walls, and the width of the room are made possible by the light roof construction and are in marked contrast to the heavy vaulted temples of the Central area. So too is the severe simplicity of the building platform. The substructure, on the other hand, with

---

[62] For other examples of Early Classic architecture in the Central area, see Merwin and Vaillant, 1932, figs. 12–16; Shook, 1951c, figs. 27, 29–36.

[63] I am indebted to G. R. Willey and A. L. Smith, of Peabody Museum, Harvard University, for this information. See also note 17.

Fɪɢ. 30—RESTORATION DRAWING OF STR. A-V, STAGE 8, UAXACTUN. Central area. End of Late Classic. Str. A-XVIII, an Early Classic palace, in background. (After Proskouriakoff.)

its apron moldings at the corners and projecting blocks on the sides is reminiscent of the early architecture of the other area.

We know of no building remains in the Western, Rio Bec, or Chenes areas that are clearly of Early Classic date. In the western region of the Puuc area and in the Northern Plain there are several sites where architecture that seems to be of this period has been found. On the basis of epigraphic and ceramic evidence (Shook, 1940; Brainerd, 1958, pp. 13–15), the earlier buildings at Oxkintok, which is a site that exhibits two styles of architecture, were constructed late in Early Classic times.[64] Broadly speaking, the style has much in common with that of the Central area, there being instances of sloped upper façade zones and apron moldings, but in the vertical upper façade, moldings of more than one member, the flying façade, and a crude form of veneer wall masonry (Shook, 1940, fig. 3), we see traits that foreshadow later developments, particularly in the Puuc area. There are remains of pyramid-temples at Oxkintok, but in too ruinous condition to determine their

[64] Ed. note: This is Andrews' Early period in the Northern Lowlands (see Andrews, Article 12).

418

character. To judge by stylistic similarity, this early architecture is also found at Bakna in the same area. Sites in the Northern Plain with architectural remains thought to be of Early Classic date are Acanceh, where there is a pyramid quite similar to the Late Preclassic Str. E-VIIsub at Uaxactun and a building made famous by the beautifully preserved stucco decoration on its façade (Marquina, 1951, pls. 242–44), Izamal (*ibid.*, fig. 29 and pl. 245), and Ake, remarkable for a huge, crudely built colonnade (Charnay, 1887, pp. 297–99), a feature that does not appear elsewhere until Postclassic times.[65]

In the Late Classic period, called by some writers the Florescent period, Maya

[65] See Andrews, 1942, pp. 257–59, and Brainerd, 1958, pp. 18–21, for the dating of these remains. The stucco relief on the façade at Acanceh (see Andrews, Article 12, fig. 3) has been likened to the art of central Mexico (Spinden, 1913, p. 213), and the colonnade at Ake further suggests influences from that direction. There are apparently examples of Early Classic (Andrews' Early period) architecture at Dzibilchaltun (Andrews, 1962, pp. 168–70), but they have not been sufficiently described to be commented on here. See Sanders, 1955, p. 184, and Andrews, Article 12, fig. 16, for a minor example of Early Classic architecture in the East Coast area.

cities reached their greatest size, having expanded around earlier centers, built in open plazas, converted existing structures to new uses, and with great frequency having submerged earlier buildings beneath later construction. Figure 29 is a restoration drawing of Groups A and B at Uaxactun. The pyramid-temple and the high palace-type building in the middle foreground are Early Classic structures. The great palace complex beyond the pyramid-temple is the Late Classic outgrowth of the three temples we examined earlier (figs. 27, 28). The causeway connecting the two groups is a later version of an Early Classic road. There are a number of other early buildings that are less well defined in the illustration, but the majority are of Late Classic date. This view is probably fairly typical of a Late Classic center of the Central area. I suspect that if it is in any way atypical, it is in the presence of a greater proportion of Early Classic structures than would normally be preserved and in use at this time.

Turning to figure 30, we see Str. A-V at Uaxactun at the end of the Late Classic period (see Proskouriakoff, 1946, pls. 28–35). What started as a group of three temples about a court (fig. 27) has now become a large complex of buildings of the palace type, an excellent example of a change in function with the passage of time. Only one of the temples remains intact; the three shrines (fig. 28) have been incorporated into a single structure; all other early construction is submerged. The architecture remains massive but with notable changes in execution. The heavy apron moldings of the early period are less popular. Terrace walls are often severely plain, and moldings on superstructures are narrow bands that frame the decoration on the upper façade, a treatment that was hesitatingly suggested in Early Classic times. Although multiple entrances were used before, they are now more common and relieve what would otherwise be the rather stark façades of the blocklike buildings. In place of the tower-

Fig. 31—RESTORATION DRAWING OF HIERO-GLYPHIC STAIRWAY, COPAN. Southern area. Late Classic. (After Proskouriakoff.)

ing roof combs there are small roof crests, or the roof is edged by low parapets, and height is attained by second and third stories. These changing tastes find their ultimate expression in a temple in which the five doorways are separated by narrow masonry piers and the lightly constructed walls and wide room indicate that the long popular vault had been replaced by a beam-and-masonry or a thatched roof (fig. 22,a,8, and fig. 29, just beyond left corner of Str. A-V). There was also introduced at this time a new type of building, the ball court (A. L. Smith, 1950, fig. 98), a type to be described presently.

Late Classic architecture varies not only between areas but between cities. At Tikal, only a few kilometers away, there seems to have been in some respects a greater

Fig. 32—RESTORATION DRAWING OF BALL COURT III, COPAN. Southern area. Late Classic. (After Proskouriakoff.)

Fig. 33—RESTORATION DRAWING OF JAGUAR STAIRWAY AND TEMPLE 22, COPAN. Southern area. Late Classic. (After Proskouriakoff.)

420

conservatism than at Uaxactun. The great pyramid-temples, which are generally considered to be of Late Classic date, are extraordinarily similar in design to the earlier temples at Uaxactun (fig. 12). The battered upper façade, that is in effect a heavy apron molding, is more common than narrow band moldings. Engineering practices, on the other hand, can be quite daring in the size and height of building and in the willingness to superimpose one story on another (see Maler, 1911, figs. 3, 6; Tozzer, 1911, figs. 21, 24).[66] Not at all conservative, and possibly reflecting outside influences, is the Palace of the Façades with Vertical Grooves (Maler, 1911, fig. 1), which in simulating split columns in the lower wall zone and in elaboration of moldings is reminiscent of the Late Classic architecture of the Puuc area. An innovation, seemingly unique to Tikal, is the "twin-pyramid complex," consisting of two flat-topped pyramids, or ceremonial platforms, each with four stairways, that face each other on the east and west sides of a court, while a long low masonry building occupies the south side, and a walled enclosure with a stela and altar inside is on the north. These complexes apparently were "katun-markers" (Shook, 1958, pp. 9–10; W. R. Coe, 1962b, pp. 479, 502).[67]

Our best examples of architecture in the Southern area are at Copan. The entire ceremonial center of the city as we see it today, and as it is shown restored in figure 7, seems to be of Late Classic date. The center was made up predominantly of temples, there being no structure that one can point to as clearly being of palace design. Both the pyramid-temple (fig. 31) and the temple on a relatively low platform (fig. 33) were present. Also present were ceremonial platforms and a ball court (fig. 32). The latter is the uppermost of three superimposed courts (Stromsvik, 1952). Maya ball courts may differ in profile, character of end zones, and superstructures, but the Copan example, which is type B of the

Acosta and Moedano (1946) classification, is on the whole typical of the majority of Late Classic courts.[68] The parrot-head sculptures on the benches are unusual, but occur at the nearby site of La Union (Stromsvik, 1952, pp. 199–201), and may be a trait of this area. The markers on the floor of the court are known from a number of lowland sites.

It will be seen from the illustrations that the heavy apron moldings that were in use in the Early Classic period in the Central area, and persisted into Late Classic times at Tikal, were not in vogue at Copan. Terrace walls and walls of superstructures tended to be vertical and to carry band moldings that were essentially rectangular in section (fig. 20,a), although there may have been coping courses with an overhanging bevel (Trik, 1939, fig. 3). Medial moldings at times rose over doorways (fig. 32). Ornament was for the most part restricted to the upper façade of buildings but might extend to the lower walls at corners and around entrances and was used on stairways. Of particular interest are the doorways framed by serpent mouths in profile (fig. 33), a distinctive feature that finds its most common expression, as will shortly be seen, in the architecture of the Rio Bec and Chenes areas. In marked contrast to the Central area, where architectural decoration was mainly in stucco, Copan is notable for the vast amounts of sculptured stone.[69]

---

[66] I believe that Str. 10, the Palace of Five Stories, at Tikal is actually four stories, the topmost construction being a roof comb.

[67] Morley, 1937–38, has an excellent bibliography for the Central area. Also see Totten, 1926, pp. 52–63; J. E. S. Thompson, 1939a; Ruppert and Denison, 1943; Marquina, 1951, pp. 518–76.

[68] See A. L. Smith, 1950, fig. 98, and Shook, 1951c, fig. 25, for examples of such courts at Uaxactun and Tikal.

[69] The best bibliography for the Southern area is in Morley, 1920. See also Totten, 1926, pp. 38–51, 66–69; Marquina, 1928, pp. 60–61, and 1951, pp. 576–607; Morley, 1935; Yde, 1938, pp. 40–58; Proskouriakoff, 1946, pls. 8–12; Stromsvik, 1947.

Fig. 34—RESTORATION DRAWING OF STR. K-5 1ST, PIEDRAS NEGRAS. Usumacinta area. Late Classic. (After Proskouriakoff.)

Fig. 35—MODEL OF STR. 33, YAXCHILAN. Usumacinta area. Late Classic.

We know too little of the remains of the Pasion River area properly to speak of architectural style. Up to the present no building roofed with the elsewhere common vault has been identified, and the absence of that feature alone would set the architecture apart from that of other areas.[70] The predominant characteristic of the remains as they are presently known is substructural mounds with little indication of masonry superstructures (Willey, Smith, Bullard, and Graham, 1960a, pp. 10–11; 1960b; Willey and Bullard, 1961; Willey and Smith, 1963, p. 87). A Late Classic ball court at Altar de Sacrificios is of the same type as the one at Copan (Smith and Willey, 1962, p. 320), but without masonry superstructures, and there is the possibility that a ball court exists at Cancuen (Morley, 1937–38, 2: 240). The relatively frequent employment of low-relief sculpture on stairways (*ibid.*, pp. 253–60; Vinson, 1960, fig. 5) and the general accenting of stairways as an architectural feature may be characteristic of the area as well as the already mentioned tendency to place stelae and altars on stairways and upper platforms of substructures rather than in the more usual position in front of buildings at court level.[71]

Turning to the area of the Usumacinta River, we find at the site of Piedras Negras (figs. 8, 34) an architecture distinct from that of the Central area but that at the same time has clearly been influenced by it(Satterthwaite, 1941). The heavy apron moldings and projecting blocks on substructural terraces are features we have seen in Early and Late Classic times in the other area. So too are the break in the line of the end

walls of superstructures, the sloped and decorated upper façade zones, and the roof comb at the rear of the building. The medial molding of a rectangular and an apron member (fig. 20,*b*), a standard form in the Usumacinta area, is, on the other hand, rare in the Central area. The masks at each side of the stairway in figure 34 are a form of decoration we have seen before but are, so far as we know, a rare feature at any time (but see note 60).

Palace architecture is not unlike that of the Late Classic period at Uaxactun but shows more standardization than in the Central area, two rows of longitudinal rooms with transverse rooms at each end of the building being the most common plan at Piedras Negras. Numerous entrances to palaces are the rule, and beam- and masonry roof construction, in contrast to the vault, was at all times popular.[72] In general, the architecture has a lightness not associated with that of the Central and Southern areas, and there is the implication that the builders had some interest in the design of interior space, although the forms were still massive and essentially monumental.

A somewhat different expression of the Usumacinta River style, and a more common one, is seen at Yaxchilan on the Chiapas side of the river, where are most of the known sites of this area. The pyramid-temple does not seem to be at all common. Building types are notably undifferentiated as to function. The multiple-entrance building, three being the most common number of doorways, is prevalent, and piers between entrances often are relatively narrow as at Piedras Negras (fig. 23,*j,n*). Upper façade zones are sloped, and the two-member medial molding seen at the other site is typical. The vault, so far as we know, is more common here than at Piedras

[70] Since writing the above, I have been informed by A. L. Smith that there is at least one example of the vault at Seibal. It is of interest to note that the ruins in the vicinity of Poptun (Shook and Smith, 1950) and the recently discovered site of Xutilha (Satterthwaite, 1961), which are near the headwaters of eastern tributaries of the Pasion River, are reported to exhibit no vaulted buildings.

[71] Besides the references cited for the Pasion River area, see Maler, 1908a.

[72] An interesting compromise between the vaulted and flat, beam-and-mortar ceiling is seen in fig. 36. Also see Satterthwaite, 1943–54, pt. 5, pp. 73–75.

FIG. 36—RESTORATION DRAWING OF STR. P-7, A SWEAT HOUSE, PIEDRAS NEGRAS. Usumacinta area. Late Classic. (After Proskouriakoff.)

Negras and construction tends to be heavier. Roof combs, which are normally over the center of the building, on the other hand, show considerable delicacy of design, almost invariably being perforated (fig. 35). Decoration, mainly in stucco in this area, was largely confined to the roof comb and upper façade with the exception of sculptured stone lintels. This last feature is much more prominent at Yaxchilan than at Piedras Negras, where stelae seem to have been more in vogue as a medium for recording hieroglyphic texts and other sculpture.

There are two ball courts at Yaxchilan, one of which has a different profile than we have previously seen (fig. 24,c) and is type A of the Acosta and Moedano (1946) classification. There are also two ball courts at Piedras Negras (Satterthwaite, 1943–54,

pt. 4), one of which is of type A, the other of type B. Another type of building of which the function is clearly distinguishable is the sweat house (fig. 36). There are eight known examples at Piedras Negras and a questionable example at El Chile (Satterthwaite, 1943–54, pt. 5).[73]

At Palenque, the type site of the Western area, the pyramid-temple is a popular building type (figs. 4, 5). Particularly characteristic of the Palenque temple is the interior shrine with its own separate roof (figs. 16,d; 37), and several of the temples have been found to harbor elaborate tombs in their substructures (fig. 25; and see Ruz, 1955a). Centrally placed in the ceremonial center

[73] Morley, 1937–38, has a good bibliography for the Usumacinta River area. Also see Marquina, 1951, pp. 667–716; Ruppert, Thompson, and Proskouriakoff, 1955.

424

FIG. 37—RESTORATION DRAWING OF SHRINE IN TEMPLE OF THE CROSS, PALEN-
QUE. Western area. Late Classic. (After Proskouriakoff.)

Fig. 38—RESTORATION DRAWING OF STR. 1, XPUHIL. Rio Bec area. Late Classic. (After Proskouria-koff.)

is a huge aggregation of courts, patios, and galleries, known as the Palace, that rest on a great platform, near the center of which rises a tower four stories in height (fig. 5).

Terrace walls of substructures character-istically are built on a slight batter, but may at times be vertical, and carry band moldings at top and bottom, the face of the molding paralleling the slope of the wall. Walls of superstructures tend to be light in relation to vault span (fig. 23,o), and upper façades are typically more sloped, as opposed to the vertical, than in the archi-tecture of the Central and Usumacinta River area, the outer face sometimes almost paralleling the soffit of the vault (fig. 16,d). Moldings are acutely beveled, in keeping with the sloped upper façades, and are strongly projecting (fig. 20,e-g). Roof

combs, which are common, are lightly con-structed with many perforations. Stucco decoration covers both roof comb and up-per façade, the latter in the form of a panel created by moldings and a slightly raised border at each corner of the building (fig. 20,g). This paneling of the upper zone of the façade is found in other areas but is virtually standard here. Sculpture, both in stone and stucco, is prevalent inside of buildings (fig. 37) and is found at each side of stairways to building platforms in the Palace group.

The square tower at Palenque, with its solid base and three upper stories con-nected by a winding stairway, is unique in Maya architecture (see note 58). A ball court at the site is somewhat different in profile from those we have seen previously

426

(fig. 24,*b*). It seems to fall into Acosta and Moedano's (1946) type A category. Quite recently a sweat house has been found in the Palace group (Ruz, 1952c, p. 56), as well as constructions that are thought to be toilets (*ibid.*, and Ruz, 1958, pp. 118–23). The aqueduct and bridge at the site have been mentioned earlier. All in all, there is much that is unusual here, and one may look upon the builders of Palenque as innovators.

That the ruins of the Tabasco plain with their vastly different environment and unusual brick construction should be included in the same area as Palenque and other centers in the hills to the south is debatable. We know very little about the architecture of the plain, Comalcalco being the only city that has received much attention and much of that work remaining to be published (see note 23). Such information as we have shows definite similarities to the architecture and art of Palenque. The profile of buildings, both in shape of molding and of upper façade, is a case in point (see Charnay, 1887, p. 199; Blom and LaFarge, 1926–27, fig. 92). The temple with interior, roofed shrine (Proskouriakoff, 1957b, p. 218) and subterranean tomb (*ibid.*, and Blom and LaFarge, 1926–27, figs. 87, 88) is another. There is also the magnificent stucco modeling at Comalcalco (*ibid.*, figs. 97, 100–103, 105–110), which is strikingly like that of Palenque. It is for these reasons that the Tabasco plain is tentatively linked with the hill region to the south as areas exhibiting the same style of architecture in Late Classic times.[74]

The Rio Bec area takes its name from the type site where a well-preserved building of the style peculiar to the area was first discovered (Périgny, 1908). This style is quite different from what we have seen to the south and is more closely allied to the architecture of the several areas that make up the northern half of the lowland Maya territory. Indeed, if one were to divide all lowland architecture of Late Classic times into only two styles, a northern and a southern, the dividing line between their areas of typical occurrence would be the border of the Rio Bec and Central areas. The compact, orderly arrangement of buildings, already referred to in the southern cities, was generally absent in the north. The acropolis, quite prevalent in the south, is not a clearly definable architectural form in the north. The profile of superstructures shows the vertical upper zone of the façade to have been preferred in the north, while a sloped upper façade, with the apparent exception of the buildings of the Southern area, was favored in the south. Veneer masonry in walls of superstructures was standard in Late Classic times in the north, whereas it was in use only in the Central area in the south. Lastly, a most noticeable difference was the widespread employment of hieroglyphic monuments, many of them recording Initial Series dates, in the south, whereas this trait, and the use of Initial Series dates in general, was relatively rare in the north (and see Foncerrada, 1962, p. 232).

Figure 38 shows a building that is typical of the architecture of the Rio Bec area. Whether this structure is to be considered a temple or a palace I am uncertain. In that it contains twelve chambers (Ruppert and Denison, 1943, fig. 108) it is more closely allied to the palaces we have seen elsewhere. The design of the building, on the other hand, and the fact that clear-cut examples of temples are rare in this area, leave one wondering as to its classification. It is quite possible that certain structures combined the functions of temple and palace.

Extremely characteristic of the Rio Bec style of architecture are the towers that simulate pyramid-temples, with stairways too steep to be functional and superstruc-

[74] Saville's (1928) bibliography on Palenque covers most sources for the Western area. Beside references previously cited, see Marquina, 1951, pp. 607–63; Séjourné, 1952a; Ruz, 1958, Sáenz, 1956.

Fig. 39—MODEL OF STR. 2, HOCHOB. Chenes area. Late Classic. (Brooklyn Museum Coll.)

tures with false doorways and without interior rooms. Equally characteristic are the division of the façade into what appears to be three distinct buildings, the serpent mouths in profile at each side of the false doorways, a trait we have met before only at Copan, and the masks with large fangs over doorways. Moldings on superstructures are more complex than those seen previously (fig. 21,4–6,9,11–13), usually being of three members, the lowest an apron, the middle member often carrying groups of colonnettes or other decoration (Ruppert and Denison, 1943, figs. 32, 102). Decoration in the form of masks, geometric designs, or split columns, often arranged in panels, is common on lower façades (e.g. *ibid.*, figs. 45,a; 96; 102; 112; 114), and there is the occasional use of supporting columns in doorways (*ibid.*, figs. 77–79, 117, 119), a feature not previously observed (but see note 49). Roof combs, which are placed over the rear or medial walls of superstructures, are of the solid, single-wall type and generally are perforated.

The pyramid-temple seems to be rare in the Rio Bec area. Palace structures of a number of rooms and of more conventional design than the building illustrated are known (*ibid.*, figs. 34, 76, 95) and not infrequently consist of two stories, the upper story placed over solid fill rather than over the walls of lower rooms. Ball courts have been found at several sites, the two ex-

amples of which the profile is known (*ibid.*, p. 6) being of type B of the Acosta and Moedano (1946) classification.[75]

The Chenes area is named after a geographical region that derives its name from the Maya word for "well" (*chen*), because of the numerous wells in those parts. We know much less about the remains of this region than about those of the Rio Bec area. The Chenes architecture seems to be transitional between the latter and the Puuc architecture to the north, being much closer in style to the Rio Bec remains.[76] We find at the site of Dzibilnocac, for example, a structure with three towers, the central one of which supports a simulated temple building with false doorways of the serpent-mouth type, quite in the tradition of the Rio Bec style. The one end tower that remains standing is crowned by a superstructure of two chambers approached by stairways on opposite sides of the tower. On each of the other sides of the building is a false doorway, and all doorways are of the serpent-mouth variety (Seler, 1916, figs. 45, 55, pl. 9).

At Hochob, the best studied of all Chenes

[75] Besides references cited here, see list of references in Ruppert and Denison, 1943, for the Rio Bec area. Also see Merwin, 1913; Marquina, 1951, pp. 716–21.

[76] In contrast to my point of view, Marquina (1951, pp. 721–25) groups the Chenes remains with those of the Puuc area.

428

sites, there is a long structure that once supported three buildings, each apparently of two rooms approached from opposite sides by extraordinarily steep, but functional, stairways (Robina, 1956, pl. 5, V-VII). On the other sides of the buildings are false doorways, but none of the entrances, false or real, is of the serpent-mouth variety (*ibid.*, pl. 2, left; pl. 3, right). Two buildings on the same plaza, however, have typical serpent-mouth entrances (fig. 39; and see *ibid.*, pls. 3, 4). As in the case of such buildings in the Rio Bec area, the façades are made to give the impression of three separate structures. A form of architecture we have not previously seen, and of which only three examples are known, is the solid tower, standing apart and resembling a narrow and attenuated roof comb (fig. 40; and see Maler, 1895, figs. 10, 17; Case, 1911, facing p. 184).

All these forms, with the possible exception of the last, are directly related to the architecture of the Rio Bec area. The execution was different, but the Chenes architect must have been guided by purposes and objectives similar to those that directed his southern counterpart. The major differences seem to have come out of influences from the adjoining Puuc area. Masonry techniques in the Chenes architecture are more like those of the Puuc than of the Rio Bec buildings. Whereas architectural decoration in the latter area was mainly of stucco, the Chenes builders used a considerable amount of cut stone, often heavily overlaid with stucco, and the classic Puuc style employed only finely cut stone finished by a thin layer of plaster. In the Chenes remains, moreover, we see the flying façade (fig. 39), a northern trait not found south of this area.[77]

The Puuc area derives its name from the Maya word for "range of hills," a prominent topographic feature along the northeastern

[77] In addition to references cited for the Chenes area, see bibliography in Ruz, 1945b. Also see Stephens, 1843; E. H. Thompson, 1898.

Fig. 40—TOWER AT NOCUCHICH. Chenes area. Late Classic. (Courtesy, Peabody Museum, Harvard University.)

and western borders of the region. There are a tremendous number of relatively well preserved remains in the area, the majority of them built of well-cut, veneer masonry (fig. 17,*c*) and further characterized by the excellently carved stone ornamentation. This mode of building represents what may be called the Puuc classic style. Besides the architecture of this style, we find remains

FIG. 41—RESTORATION DRAWINGS OF BUILDINGS AT SAYIL AND UXMAL. Puuc area. *a (above),* Palace, Sayil. Late Classic. *b (below),* Monjas Quadrangle, Uxmal. Late Classic. (After Proskouriakoff.)

that on stylistic grounds, and on a few scraps of stratigraphic evidence, appear to be earlier, although still presumably of Late Classic date. There are, for example, buildings with veneer wall masonry but with vaults of rough slabs. This construction is more prevalent in the western part of the area and could well be an outgrowth of the Early Classic architecture of Oxkintok. Another type of building is the temple, often a pyramid-temple, that carries a simple rectangular medial molding and a roof structure that employs stucco as a decorative medium (Maler, 1895, figs. 1, 2; Mariscal, 1928, fig. 44; Marquina, 1951, fig. 368). The rectangular medial molding, which generally rises in level over doorways, is often associated with buildings in which the doorway columns, jambs, or lintels carry hieroglyphic inscriptions or human figures carved in low relief (Marquina, 1951, figs. 340–42). All these characteristics seem to be early in relation to the Puuc classic style, but we cannot be certain of this until better architectural stratigraphy has been developed.[78]

Figures 41 and 42 show examples of the Puuc classic style of architecture. Virtually all important types of buildings are shown with the exception of the ball court, which is of Acosta and Moedano's (1946) type B. Less stressed than might be in the illustrations is the small structure of two, three, or four rooms which occurs in great quantities, singly or in twos or threes facing on a court, among large structures within a city, at the edges of the cities, or in isolated groups. (Marquina, 1951, figs. 343, 348–51). Their function is not clear; they may have served as temples or in some other capacity.

Standard forms of architecture, such as the multistoried palace of many rooms, the palace that has grown by accretion and somewhat haphazardly, the portal vault, the closed quadrangle, the pyramid-temple, and the system of closed courts ascending to a temple are well shown (also see fig. 23,k-m).

One's first impression of this architecture might be to notice a sharpness of line, a crisp quality, that for the most part we have not seen elsewhere. This is true not only of the simple lines of the substructural terraces, of the sharply relieved moldings and generally level roof lines, but of much of the decoration which is executed in precisely carved stone covered by only a thin coat of plaster. The vertical upper zone of the façade is the generally accepted form, thus giving a strongly rectangular quality to the architecture. This is at times relieved by façade decoration that projects above the roof (fig. 41,b) and by serrated roof combs (fig. 42,a), but on the whole such features are rare and the simple horizontal roof line is much the most frequent. Supporting columns in doorways, seen sparingly in the Rio Bec area, are here extremely common (fig. 41,a). Moldings are most often of three members, but there is great variety (figs. 20,c,k,l; 21,1,7–8,14,16,18–25). One member often carries decoration of colonnettes or some geometric design. Moldings with as many as six members are known (fig. 21,20). Although the upper zone of the façade was the favorite area for decoration, split columns, frets, and masks being the most common forms, lower façade zones also frequently carried ornament. Roof structures, usually perforated, are of the solid, single-wall type and are placed over the centers of buildings or as flying façades above front walls.[79]

[78] The temple shown in Marquina, 1951, fig. 368, is early in relation to the pyramid at the right which carries the remains of a superstructure of Puuc classic style. The lowest story to the left of the stairway in our fig. 41,a, which was originally a separate building, shows an example of the simple medial molding. Another example is seen at the lower left of fig. 42,c.

[79] Many sources for the Puuc area will be found in Saville, 1921. See also E. H. Thompson, 1897b, 1898, 1904; Maler, 1902; Totten, 1926, pp. 160–69, 173–217; Marquina, 1928, pp. 61–70; Palacios,

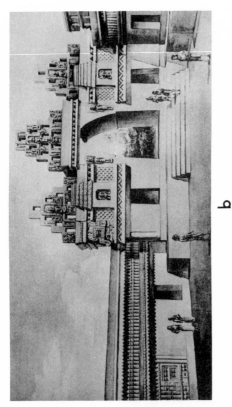

b

c

a

FIG. 42—RESTORATION DRAWINGS OF BUILDINGS AT UXMAL AND LABNA. Puuc area. *a,* Palomas Group, Uxmal. Late Classic. *b,* Portal Vault, Labna. Late Classic. *c,* Palace, Labna. Late Classic. (After Proskouriakoff.)

G. 43—RESTORATION DRAWING OF RED HOUSE, CHICHEN ITZA. Northern Plain area. Late Classic. The round tower in the distance, the Caracol, is presumably Postclassic. (After Proskouriakoff.)

Scattered examples of Puuc style architecture have been found on the Northern Plain as far east as Chichen Itza (figs. 16,e; 43) and Yaxuna.[80] Unfortunately, the ruins of this area have suffered greater devastation than in any other lowland region. It is quite possible that the Puuc style of architecture extended over virtually all of the modern state of Yucatan, but there is so little left standing that only extensive excavation can decide the matter. There is no reason to believe, in any event, that the heartland of the style was not the Puuc area. With the end of Late Classic times, building activity on any sizable scale seems to have ceased throughout the lowland Maya region with the exception of the Northern Plain and East Coast areas.

POSTCLASSIC PERIOD. Chichen Itza in the

Northern Plain is the only site where architecture of the Early Postclassic (Andrews' Modified Florescent) period is known to exist in any quantity. Remains that appear to be similar to those at Chichen Itza have been found at the cursorily explored site of Huaymil (Shook, 1955a, pp. 293–94), and there may be buildings, as yet unidentified, at a number of places on the Northern Plain and East Coast where pottery of the period is known to occur, but we presently can point to virtually no architecture of this time outside of Chichen Itza and its environs.

The building remains at Chichen Itza show two clearly distinguishable styles of architecture that represent different periods. The earlier is Late Classic (Andrews' Pure Florescent) in date and is closely allied to the style of the Puuc area. The later, which is the one that concerns us here, is Early Postclassic (Andrews' Modified Florescent) and represents a blending of Maya and foreign traditions. The Maya tradition stems from the Puuc architectural style; the foreign is that of the Toltec of Tula in central Mexico (but see note 30). As might be expected of Maya workmen

1928b, and 1945a, pp. 405–64; Reygadas, 1928; Hissink, 1934; Ruz, 1945b, pp. 42–61, and 1955b, 1955c, 1956; Proskouriakoff, 1946, pls. 14–20; Foncerrada, 1962.

[80] Landa's description of the ancient buildings at Tihoo, now the city of Merida, leaves little doubt that the Puuc architectural tradition was followed there (Tozzer, 1941a, pp. 174–76). Andrews (1960; 1962, pp. 154, 174) reports building remains of Puuc style at Dzibilchaltun. He assigns them to his "Pure Florescent" period.

433

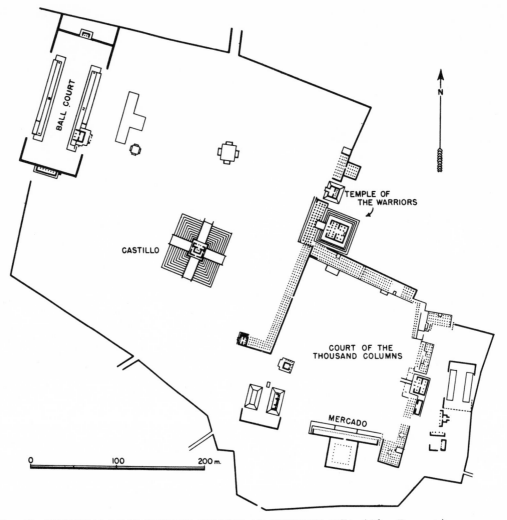

Fɪɢ. 44—PRINCIPAL MAYA-TOLTEC CENTER AT CHICHEN ITZA. (After Ruppert.)

under foreign overlords, masonry techniques changed very little (fig. 16,*f*). The Toltec, moreover, accepted the Maya vault in place of their own beam-and-masonry roofs for many buildings, and made plentiful use of typical Maya moldings. They also employed the Maya mask as a decorative element. Aside from these compromises with local tradition, the new architecture was radically different from what we have seen.

The early Maya builder, it will be remembered, was intent on monumental forms, the use of masses balanced against one another, the arrangement of them on different levels, the outlining of precincts and areas. He had little care for space within buildings. As time went on, he built with thinner walls and wider rooms, and his structures became more finely delineated, but he still viewed his work primarily as the designing of exterior space. The Toltec architect was differently motivated. He, too, was using monumental forms, and he was concerned with the arrangement of exterior space, although in a somewhat different manner than the Maya, but he was also interested in the utilization of interior space, and this interest led him to the use of the column, not merely in doorways, as we

434

have seen elsewhere, but as a primary support for the roof. The replacement of walls by rows of columns created large, open spaces inside of buildings and brought drastic changes in design, most readily seen in the new and different plans of superstructures (fig. 44).

Figure 9 gives an excellent impression of the spaciousness of the great ceremonial center at Chichen Itza (and see p. 393). Examples of Maya-Toltec architecture are shown in more detail in figures 18, 45, and 46. The plan of the principal temple, the Castillo (fig. 23,*g*), is quite different from anything we have previously seen. So too is that of the Temple of the Warriors (fig. 44), which is strikingly like the plan of the principal temple at Tula (see Tozzer, 1957, figs. 49, 51). The gallery-patio type of structure is new to us (fig. 44, Mercado; and see Ruppert, 1943, 1950), as are the many colonnades (figs. 44; 23,*i*; 18, 45), and the

round tower (figs. 23,*c*; 43). These are but samples of the wide range of building types that are strikingly unlike the earlier Maya forms.[81]

Types of buildings we have seen before, but executed differently, are the temple with interior shrine, the ceremonial platform (fig. 46), the portal vault, the sweat house (fig. 23,*f*), and the ball court (figs. 44; 23,*h*; 9, right). The Great Ball Court is unique among all known courts in matter of size. It is of Acosta and Moedano's (1946) type C, known elsewhere in the Maya lowlands only at Etzna (Ruz, 1945b, fig. 3,*21,22*), with one other questionable example at Chichen Itza. Besides the Great Ball Court there are eight other courts at Chichen Itza, the greatest concentration at any site in Middle America. They are of

[81] An exhaustive study of the Maya-Toltec architecture of Chichen Itza will be found in Tozzer, 1957.

435

FIG. 46—RESTORATION DRAWING OF PLATFORM OF THE EAGLES AND JAGUARS (LEFT) AND PLATFORM OF THE SKULL (RIGHT), CHICHEN ITZA. Northern Plain area. Early Postclasssic. (After Proskouriakoff.)

normal size and are generally of type B, but with some questionable examples of type A (Ruppert, 1952, figs. 16, 33, 39, 49, 112, 114, 116).

Details of architectural design that differ from earlier practices are the battered lower wall and paneled upper zone of substructural terraces (fig. 46), the lack of building platforms, and the battered basal zones of walls of superstructures (fig. 16,f). These features are characteristically Toltec. Roof combs and flying façades are replaced by roof crests (fig. 16,f), a trait we have seen at Uaxactun in the Central area. A number of new forms of ornament were introduced, mainly dealing with the worship of the god Kukulcan and with certain warrior cults, the most striking of which were doorways with columns in the form of feathered serpents (fig. 47), stairway balustrades also simulating serpents (fig. 43, center) and bas-relief motifs of eagles and jaguars (fig. 46). Other sculptural forms were the so-called chac mool figure (fig. 18) and the sacrificial stone, the latter a truncated pyramidal block some 50 or 60 cm. in height. Hieroglyphic monuments did not exist, and glyphic inscriptions in any form were rare.

Although the Maya-Toltec architecture of Early Postclassic times lacked the finesse of the Puuc classic style, it was robust, daring, and executed on a grand scale. It marked the end of the great architecture of the lowland Maya. In it we see a final burst of vigor, possibly brought about by cultural hybridization, but at all events the last bloom of a long and fine tradition.[82]

Architectural remains of the Late Postclassic period have been found in Tabasco, southwestern Campeche, eastern Guatemala, central Peten, northern British Honduras, Quintana Roo, and Yucatan.[83] Only along the coast of Quintana Roo and at

[82] Besides the references cited, see Tozzer, 1957, for a bibliography of Chichen Itza and the Northern Plain. Also see note 83.

[83] See Berlin, 1956; Andrews, 1943; A. L. Smith, 1955, pp. 58–60 (and see note 2, above); Maler, 1908b, pp. 55–60; Bullard, 1960a; 1960b; pp. 370–71; Gann, 1900, 1918; Lothrop, 1924 (and see bibliography); G. Mason, 1927; Marquina, 1928, pp. 70–71, and 1951, pp. 808–31; Thompson, Pollock, and Charlot, 1932; Yde, 1932; Lizardi, 1939, and 1940; Fernández, 1941, 1945a, 1945b, 1945c; Fernández, Lizardi, and Rozo, 1945; Palacios, 1945a, pp. 542–54; Escalona, 1946; Sanders, 1960a; Carnegie Institution, 1952–57; Pollock, Roys, Proskouriakoff, and Smith, 1962; Andrews, 1960; 1961b; 1962, pp. 156–57; 176–77.

Mayapan in the Northern Plain are the remains in sufficient number, sufficiently well preserved, or sufficiently well recorded to provide us with a definitive architectural style. All the buildings at Mayapan and the vast preponderance of them in the East Coast area are built in this Late Postclassic style. It is the typical architecture of both places.

The Late Postclassic period witnessed a pronounced degradation of culture in northern Yucatan, and the building art was no exception to the trend. Ceremonial centers were less extensive in area (fig. 10), civic and religious buildings were smaller, the quality of workmanship was far inferior to that of preceding periods. Stonecutting was a poorly developed art, and the architects relied on thick coats of plaster to cover the rough masonry of buildings. The vault, so long the standard form of roofing, was largely replaced by the beam-and-masonry roof (fig. 14). Decorative elements were mainly executed in stucco, and there was extensive use of mural painting.

Late Postclassic architecture was the poorly integrated product of several styles. It incorporated some earlier Maya practices, it drew on the Maya-Toltec architecture of Chichen-Itza, and it was affected by foreign influences, possibly from the Gulf Coast areas to the west. The closed court and plaza, an arrangement little featured by the Toltec, was revived (fig. 48). At Mayapan, but not in the East Coast area, the stela cult also was revived. Certain temples at Mayapan, on the other hand, clearly were built in imitation of the Maya-Toltec style. The principal temple is almost a replica on a smaller scale of the principal temple at Chichen Itza (fig. 48,a). Several smaller pyramid-temples exhibit the basal batter on superstructural walls, the serpent-column entrance (fig. 48,b), and the serpent balustrades (fig. 24,a) so characteristic of the Maya-Toltec style. Serpent columns are also found in the East Coast area. Architectural decoration featured the diving

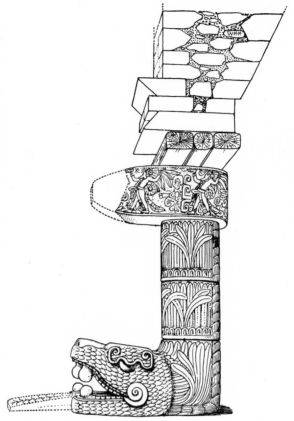

FIG. 47—SERPENT COLUMN IN DOORWAY, CHICHEN ITZA. (After Holmes.)

god (see Lothrop, 1924, p. 47), probably not a Maya motif, and anthropomorphic columns (fig. 48,b), some of the figures possibly in an atlantean position. Such crude stone sculpture as there was mainly portrayed non-Maya forms.

The colonnaded hall, somewhat differently planned than at Chichen Itza, was a common building type (figs. 24,a; 48). It seems to have taken the place of the earlier multiroomed palace (see note 56). A type of building we have seen before and that now appears in great numbers is the shrine. It is found isolated (Sanders, 1960a, p. 218), set somewhat apart, as an adjunct to other structures, on stairways of colonnaded halls, and inside of those halls (figs. 24,a; 48; and see Pollock, Roys, Proskouriakoff, and

437

FIG. 48—RESTORATION DRAWINGS OF MAIN CEREMONIAL CENTER, MAYAPAN. Northern Plain area. *a (above)*, Principal temple (Str. Q-162) with colonnaded hall (Str. Q-151) at right, large shrine (Str. Q-148) at left, and oratory (Str. Q-153) and small shrine facing viewer, looking west. Late Postclassic. *b (below)*, Temple (Str. Q-143) at left, small shrine (Str. Q-146) at center, large shrine (Str. Q-149) at right, and colonnaded hall (Str. Q-145) in background, looking south. Late Postclassic. (After Proskouria-koff.)

Smith, 1962, pt. 2). The shrine also is found associated with domestic architecture. So too is the oratory, a type of building found both in residential groups and in the ceremonial center of Mayapan (figs. 24,a; 48,a). Mortuary structures, if that is the proper term, involving mass burial occur in the form of temples and shrines. There are a number of examples of round buildings, presumably a foreign trait (fig. 24,a). Surprisingly, the ball court does not occur in the lowlands at this time, although it is common in the Maya highlands. The sweat house also has not been identified.

It will be recalled that building on any sizable scale seems to have ended throughout the greater part of the lowland Maya area with the close of the Classic period. In the intervening centuries between Late Classic and Late Postclassic times there had been a final florescence of the building art under the stimulus of Maya-Toltec people who created a hybridized style in many respects more foreign than Maya. The Late Postclassic builders were, then, to a great extent cut off from the great traditions of the past, and the architecture they created clearly shows this lack. The style was eclectic, borrowing ideas and customs from here and there, but never able successfully to amalgamate the various elements or to create a worthwhile tradition of its own (see Pollock, Roys, Proskouriakoff, and Smith, 1962, pt. 2).

REFERENCES

Acosta, 1959
—— and Moedano, 1946
Andrews, 1942, 1943, 1959, 1960, 1961b, 1962
Berlin, 1956
Blom, 1934
—— and LaFarge, 1926–27
Brainerd, 1958
Bullard, 1960a, 1960b
Carnegie Inst., 1952–57
Carr and Hazard, 1961
Case, 1911
Catherwood, 1844
Charnay, 1887
Coe, M. D., 1956
Coe, W. R., 1962a, 1962b
—— and McGinn, 1963
——, Shook, and Satterthwaite, 1961
Enciclopedia Yucatanense, 1944–47
Erosa, 1948
Escalona, 1946
Estado Actual, 1928
Fernández, 1941, 1945a, 1945b, 1945c
——, Lizardi R., and Rozo, 1945
Foncerrada de Molina, 1962
For the Dean, 1950
Gann, 1900, 1918, 1928a
Gruning, 1930
Healey, 1950
Hissink, 1934
Holmes, 1895–97
Kubler, 1958, 1961, 1962
Littmann, 1958

Lizardi R., 1939, 1940, 1941
Longyear, 1952
Lothrop, 1924
Maler, 1895, 1901–03, 1908a, 1908b, 1911
Mariscal, 1928
Marquina, 1928, 1951
Mason, G., 1927
Maudslay, 1889–1902
Maya and their Neighbors, 1940
Merwin, 1913
—— and Vaillant, 1932
Morley, 1920, 1935, 1937–38, 1956
Morris, Charlot, and Morris, 1931
Outwater, 1957
Palacios, 1928b, 1945a, 1945b
Périgny, 1908
Pollock, 1936, 1940a, 1952
——, Roys, Proskouriakoff, and Smith, 1962
—— and Stromsvik, 1953
Proskouriakoff, 1946, 1957b
—— and Temple, 1955
Reygadas, 1928
Ricketson, 1935
—— and Ricketson, 1937
Robina, 1956, 1959
Roys, L., 1934
Ruppert, 1935, 1940, 1943, 1950, 1952
—— and Denison, 1943
—— and Smith, 1957
——, Thompson, and Proskouriakoff, 1955
Ruz L., 1945b, 1952b, 1952c, 1955a, 1955b, 1955c, 1956, 1958, 1962a

439

Sáenz, 1956
Sanders, 1955, 1960a
Satterthwaite, 1937, 1939, 1941, 1943–54, 1961
Saville, 1921, 1928, 1935
Séjourné, 1952a
Seler, 1916
Shook, 1940, 1951c, 1952c, 1955a, 1958
—— and Smith, 1950
Smith, A. L., 1937, 1940, 1950, 1955
—— and Ruppert, 1954a
—— and Willey, 1962
Smith, R. E., 1937
Spinden, 1913
Stephens, 1841, 1843
Stern, 1950
Stromsvik, 1947, 1952

Tax, 1951
Termer, 1951
Thompson, D. E. and J. E. S., 1955
Thompson, E. H., 1897b, 1898, 1904
Thompson, J. E. S., 1939a, 1954b
——, Pollock, and Charlot, 1932
Totten, 1926
Tozzer, 1911, 1913, 1941a, 1957
Trik, 1939
Villa, 1934
Vinson, 1960
Vivó, 1946a
Willey and Bullard, 1961
—— and Smith, 1963
——, Smith, Bullard, and Graham, 1960a, 1960b
Yde, 1932, 1938

16. Tombs and Funerary Practices in the Maya Lowlands

ALBERTO RUZ L.

IN THIS SURVEY we follow the definitions given elsewhere in this volume for the Maya lowlands (see also Thompson, 1954a, p. 18). In general, this region (fig. 1) corresponds to the historic distribution of the Maya lowland languages and to the distribution of archaeological sites with Maya hieroglyphic inscriptions and corbeled-vault architecture. We have also included the valley of the middle Motagua River, which was Pipil country in late prehistoric and early historic times but was occupied by the Maya at an earlier period (Smith and Kidder, 1943, p. 111).

Our presentation of funerary practices follows the geographical subdivisions of Peten–British Honduras, Copan-Motagua, Usumacinta-Grijalva, and northern Yucatan Peninsula.

Terminology defining burial types is similar to that of A. L. Smith's (1950, p. 88) at Uaxactun except that instead of "crypt" the word "grave" here designates a more or less well built tomb, which has low walls, a slab cover, sometimes a stucco floor, and which, because of its low height, is not really a chamber. Our conception of "crypt" implies a larger and more important construction than those referred to under this name by Smith, which are, in effect, no more than masonry coffins for one or more bodies. Neither has Smith's denomination of chamber "a" or "b" been used. We have tried to determine whether a chamber was intended especially for funerary use or was previously part of a civil or ceremonial construction.

Types of burials may be: (1) *simple*, merely holes in the ground or in the fill of a building without special features; (2) *in caves or chultuns*, funerary use of natural caves and hollows or cisterns dug in the ground; (3) *in cists*, better-defined burials than simple ones, with crudely constructed walls or stones to outline or mark them, without lids, and generally smaller than an extended body; (4) *in graves*, types of coffins constructed of masonry or slabs, with a cover, with or without stucco floor, and large enough for at least one extended body; and (5) *in chambers*, rooms of varying size, of at least a man's stature in height, with well-constructed masonry walls and vaulted roofs. They may have been built as

441

Fig. 1—MAP OF MAYA LOWLANDS SHOWING SITES MENTIONED IN TEXT

funerary chambers or may be civil or ceremonial structures later used as tombs.

From data taken from 60 archaeological sites containing about 1000 burials we have tried to determine the location of the burial, its primary or secondary character, age, sex, position and bearing of the body, presence and kind of offerings, and the period to which it may be assigned. This by no means exhausts the number of Maya lowland sites containing burials, but most of the important ones are included.

PETEN–BRITISH HONDURAS

Uaxactun, Guatemala

The burials at Uaxactun (simple, in cists, graves, or chambers) are under plazas, patios, platforms, residential rooms, or temples; in the core of pyramids or within benches or altars; and in construction refuse or rubble. Burials in chultuns are special cases (Wauchope, 1934, pp. 141–42; Ricketson and Ricketson, 1937, pp. 139–49; A. L. Smith, 1937, pp. 17–18; 1950, pp. 88–102).

All burials are primary except three; one third are of children or infants; and most of the others are males. Flexed burials are more numerous than the extended. The orientation of the body varied during the early periods, but later tended to become fixed with the head nearly always toward the north.

Burials in ceremonial buildings are nearly always of males, but in the residential structures they are indiscriminately of men and women. The secondary and multiple burials are all of women and children. Some children's crania placed between bowls suggest sacrifices as does the burial of a headless woman.

Most of the well-preserved crania showed artificial deformation. Only adults exhibited dental mutilations, and dental inlays of pyrite or jade were found only in male crania.

One cranium cut laterally and lacking the facial portion suggests evidence of

Landa's information regarding the treatment given to the heads of Cocom lords which were cut and artificially restored (Landa, 1938, pp. 139–40; 1941, p. 131).

In several important burials in funeral chambers the bones were covered with red paint, probably cinnabar. Apparently, this had settled from a shroud with which the corpse had been covered, or perhaps the body had been painted before burial.

The heads of several skeletons were covered by a plate or a bowl, and in one instance by a large conch. Other skeletons had pieces of charcoal over the pelvis, and sometimes ray spines. In two instances a plate had been placed face down over the pelvic area.

The presence of burned ropes and textile markings in several tombs reveals the practice of tying or shrouding the flexed corpse. Two child burials contained an adult phalanx, probably a woman's; in two others jade beads had been placed in the children's mouths.

During the Early Developmental period[1] the burials are simple and of adults. The flexed and extended positions occur without any fixed orientation for the head. Offerings are scarce, poor, and lacking in pottery. Only five burials from this period are known.

During the Late Developmental period (Chicanel phase) simple burials continue, but burials in cists begin to appear. In both types about half are adults (of both sexes), and the other half are children or infants. The flexed position predominates over extended, and orientation of the head is to the north. In addition to jade and shell offerings ceramics also begin to appear in the burials. Charcoal is frequently found. Fifteen burials belong to this period.

---

[1] Ed. note: The term "Developmental period" corresponds to Preclassic period or Formative period. The Early Developmental period at Uaxactun to which the author refers is represented by the Mamom phase. Other authorities are inclined to place the Mamom phase in the Mesoamerican-wide Middle Preclassic period.

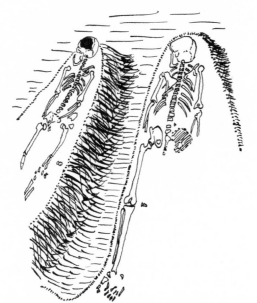

FIG. 2—SIMPLE EXTENDED BURIALS IN MOUNDS, BAKING POT, BRITISH HONDURAS. (After Ricketson, 1929, fig. 3,c.)

The Early Classic period (Tzakol phase) is characterized by the almost total disappearance of simple burials, the increase of burials in cists, and the construction of graves and funeral chambers. A third of the burials are children or infants. The funeral chambers contain only males, except one in which the skeleton of a woman with a foetus was accompanied by another woman and a baby.

The tendency toward flexed burials increases, but the more important burials in chambers are generally extended, head to the east. Almost all burials are associated with offerings, and those in chambers are particularly rich in ceramics, jade, shells, and other materials. Twenty-eight burials belong to this period.

Almost all burials of the Late Classic period (Tepeu phase) are associated with graves and cists although there are a few simple ones and one in a chamber (non-funerary). The proportion of children and infants (about a third) is the same as in the preceding period, and the occurrences of adult men and women are about the

444

same. The flexed position has become nearly invariable; burials in house mounds are all flexed. Although the head may still lie in any direction, orientations to the north predominate. Offerings are less rich and less abundant than in the preceding period. There are 61 burials positively associated with this period.

There is little to say about the Postclassic period. The few burials from this period (seven) were in the rubble of buildings not in use. All are simple, except one in a cist on the bench of a room. Excepting this one (a child with a jade bead in his mouth), they lack offerings. These Postclassic burials were in such very bad condition that little can be deduced about the orientation and position of the bodies.

Tikal, Guatemala

The scarcity of published data from the explorations of Tikal started a few years ago (W. R. Coe and Broman, 1958, pp. 41–44; Life Magazine, Oct. 26, 1959, pp. 93–96; Life en Español, Nov. 16, 1959, pp. 84–87) makes it difficult to present adequate information. So far, only 24 burials have been uncovered, said to be similar to those of Uaxactun (E. M. Shook, personal communication). Of these the publications mention three simple ones under the floors or at the foot of structures, one in a grave under a platform, and three in funeral chambers under a pyramid. All seem to be adults, mainly males where sex could be determined. The extended position predominates as does the northward orientation. The offerings in one of the funeral chambers (Burial 10) was particularly rich in ceramics and included a rich jade mosaic together with shell and quartz. This burial belongs to the Early Classic period; the others about which there is information pertain to the Late Classic.

Holmul, Guatemala

Information on this site reveals only 22 burials (Merwin and Vaillant, 1932, pp.

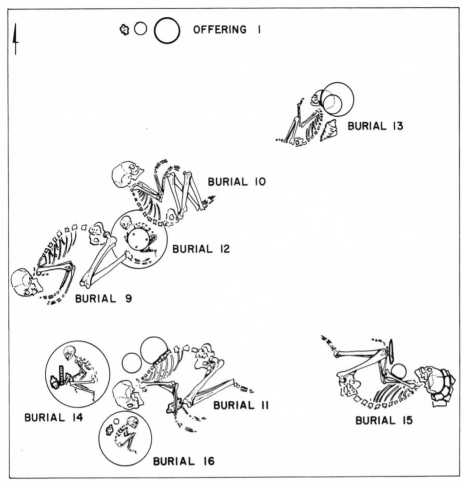

Fig. 3—SIMPLE FLEXED BURIALS ON THE FLOOR, JAINA, CAMPECHE, MEXICO. (After Piña Chan, 1948, pit 5.)

13–16, 29–40, 43–45, 50–52), which include the main types known: simple within platforms of pyramids; in cists, crudely constructed under temples; in funeral chambers, inside pyramids; and in rooms of buildings used for burials and then sealed and covered by other structures.

The different types of burials are as common in the Early Classic as in the Late Classic period. Those skeletons sufficiently preserved were identified as adults. The flexed position is as frequent as the extended, the head may lie in any direction. The Early Classic period is characterized by richer offerings and by greater use of chambers for successive burials in structures which were then abandoned.

Hormiguero, Campeche

Although this site is not in the Peten proper, it was included in this geographical division. The only feature of interest to us is a vaulted chamber in Str. 6, which possibly was constructed for funerary purposes. A stairway from one of the rooms descends into it. An opening in the floor of the chamber leads to a small chultun in which lay only a fragment of a metate, but which could have served a funeral function (Ruppert and Denison, 1943, p. 41).

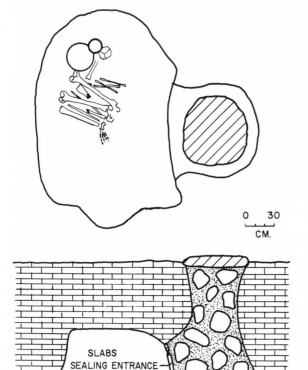

0   30
CM.

FIG. 4—CHULTUN BURIAL, UAXACTUN, GUATE-MALA. (After Wauchope, 1934, fig. 12.)

SLABS
SEALING ENTRANCE

San Jose, British Honduras

The wealth of information regarding this site includes data on 72 burials (Thompson, 1939a, pp. 193–220). With the exception of two secondary burials, one in a cist and another in an urn, all are simple and most are under the floors of rooms in ceremonial structures. Some, however, are in pyramidal mounds lacking superstructures. As at Uaxactun, a third of the burials are of children or infants, frequently grouped in the same place or in a similar location, as, for example, under the thresholds of the different entrances of a building.

In the middle phases of San Jose (II–III) the occurrence of extended or flexed posi-

tions is equal, but later only the latter occurs, except for one extended burial and another of probably seated position. With very few exceptions the head is always oriented toward the south. Some crania were protected by flat earthen bowls.

The offerings are rather poor, perhaps because of the secondary importance of the site; many of the burials lack them entirely. Burials of children in phase IV are generally accompanied by clay figurines.

Baking Pot, British Honduras

All the burials (15) uncovered in this site (Ricketson, 1929, pp. 8–24) were in a mound, within the mound nucleus or in the mound base. With the exception of one in a masonry grave, the others are simple. Also, with the exception of one child, all are adult burials, males and females. The position of nearly all the bodies is extended, face down, head to the south. Most burials lacked offerings; others had very few and poor offerings. The richest burial in this regard was in a grave in the center of the mound.

Benque Viejo, British Honduras

The few data pertaining to this site all relate to the same structure (Thompson, 1940, pp. 27–28). The three burials are simple ones, under the bench or floor of one building. One is of a child, flexed; all three had heads oriented to the south. No offerings, or very poor ones, existed.

Southern Cayo District, British Honduras

The data refer to three sites: Tzimin Kax, Cahal Cunil, and Hatzcap Ceel (Thompson, 1931, pp. 254–56, 284–94, 313–22). The first has 12 burials, all simple in chultuns, cists, and funeral chambers; the second has four burials, simple ones in cists and funeral chambers; the third records only a single funeral chamber.

There is no preferred orientation. Many of the burials are secondary; some are multiple. Several phalanges, possibly a wom-

446

an's, were in clay vessels in the grave of a young man whose skeleton was in a sitting position. The burials of the equivalent of Holmul I[2] are in chultuns and are probably all secondary; those of Holmul V[3] are in cists (secondary) or in funeral chambers under plazas or mounds. Offerings are lacking or unimportant.

Corozal District, British Honduras

This includes areas explored principally by Gann; they are, among others, Santa Rita, Noh Mul, Corozal, Rio Hondo (several sites in British Honduras and one in Quintana Roo, Mexico, on the banks of the river), Santa Elena, Pueblo Nuevo, Honey Camp, and Progreso.

Most data come from Santa Rita. The burials (11) are usually simple and lie in the nuclei of masonry and dirt of mounds or under mounds which appear to have been constructed for funeral purposes. These structures belong to Postclassic times, and, obviously, the burials contained in the mounds belong to the same period. Those under the mounds belong, generally, to the Early Classic period although some are contemporaneous with the mounds. Burial positions may be extended, flexed, or massed without order in trenches. No standard orientation was observed. Multiple burials include as many as 30 individuals. Offerings are poor. Aside from these simple burials there are some in rather rough cists excavated from the rock under the mounds or included in the nuclei of mounds. These may be primary or secondary burials, and they have few offerings (Gann, 1918, pp. 59–66).

In Noh Mul, near Santa Rita, four burials were discovered in cists and funeral chambers in mounds. Among the poor offerings with them was a toy metate associated with an infant burial (T. and M. Gann, 1939, pp. 1–6; Anderson and Cook, 1944, pp. 83–85).

[3] Ed. note: Late Classic equivalent.
[2] Ed. note: Late Preclassic or Protoclassic.

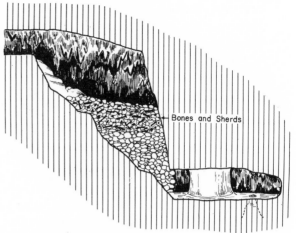

FIG. 5—SECONDARY MULTIPLE BURIALS IN CENOTE CAVE, MAYAPAN, YUCATAN, MEXICO. (After R. E. Smith, 1953, fig. 2,c.)

From Corozal we have information regarding 28 simple burials in mounds and six cists excavated in the ground under other mounds. The state of the skeletal remains yielded no significant data, nor are the offerings of importance (Gann, 1914–16, p. 38; 1918, pp. 99, 125–26).

Funerary mounds were found near Rio Hondo. One of them, in an undetermined exact location on the upper course of the river, contained 40 adult crania in an orderly alignment. This form of secondary burial may indicate a collective sacrifice. The skulls were accompanied by objects of bone and stone (Gann, 1918, pp. 86–90). At the mouth of the same river in British Honduras was a mound with a funeral chamber (ibid., pp. 104–05); and on the northern side of the river, in Quintana Roo, burials were discovered in cists and in funeral chambers (ibid., pp. 105–12). In one case the remains in a cist were those of a secondary burial in an urn. These burials either lacked offerings or had only very poor ones, and did not yield any data on position or orientation.

In the same district of Corozal, in Honey Camp (Gann, 1928b, p. 51) and Pueblo Nuevo (Gann, 1918, pp. 112–13, 136–37), simple burials lay under or over floors of

447

houses covered by mounds. Two were extended; one of these had a plate over its head. In Progreso, an infant burial was found in a cist in the nucleus of a mound. It was accompanied by a vase which contained a terminal phalanx, probably a woman's (Gann, 1914–16, p. 38; 1918, p. 132).

Southern British Honduras

Although we have no information regarding the skeletal remains, for these were found in decomposed condition, we know of simple burials in mounds or pyramids at Lubaantun (Gann, 1928b, p. 242) and on Wild Cane Bay (Gann, 1918, pp. 135–36). Also graves and funeral chambers are reported from mounds at Kendal (Gann, 1918, pp. 92–97) and Pomona (Kidder and Ekholm, 1951, pp. 126–27). The burials in the latter site correspond to the Early Classic period; those of Wild Cane Bay must be Postclassic or, perhaps, Protohistoric.

COPAN–MOTAGUA

Copan, Honduras

This important ceremonial center exhibits different types of burials: simple, in caves, cists, and funeral chambers. The highest number yet discovered, about 75, belong to the first group, which occur generally in the ground, sometimes in zones which suggest a cemetery or a tendency towards group burial. There are also some simple burials in mounds, under or close to house foundations, or under patio floors. All those belonging to the Early Classic period are extended, generally on their back, although one lay on its face with head to the west. However, all those associated with house foundations are flexed. In so far as we have data on Copan Late Classic burials, these were flexed and tended to be oriented to the east. Some were seated; in one case the head was protected by a stone slab. The offerings were quite varied (Peabody Museum, 1896, pp. 26–28; Stromsvik, 1941, p. 295; 1942; Longyear, 1952, pp. 37–40).

448

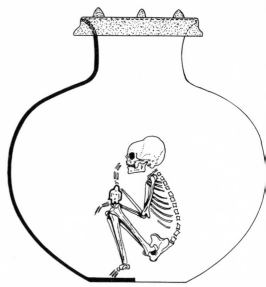

Fɪɢ. 6—INFANT BURIALS IN JAR, JAINA, CAMPECHE, MEXICO. (After Piña Chan, 1948, fig. 2.)

Of the three burials in caves, one was secondary and multiple, another extended, and a third seated. Offerings were poor or absent (Gordon, 1898, pp. 7–9).

About 25 burials should be considered cist burials although most of them are mentioned as funeral chambers (Stromsvik, 1942a; Longyear, 1952, pp. 43–47). They are regarded here as cists in view of their reduced dimensions, although they are better constructed than the usual cists. They are found under or near rooms, in the ground, under patios, and in or under mounds. A few of these burials, all extended, belong to the later Preclassic and Early Classic periods. All those of the Early Classic are flexed except one which is seated. There does not seem to have been a fixed norm for the orientation of the bodies. About half of the offerings consist of jade objects.

A dozen true funeral chambers were also found in Copan; these were in mounds, under structures, or simply below ground (Peabody Museum, 1896, pp. 29–32; Longyear, 1952, pp. 40–45). Of these the burials belonging to the Late Classic were extend-

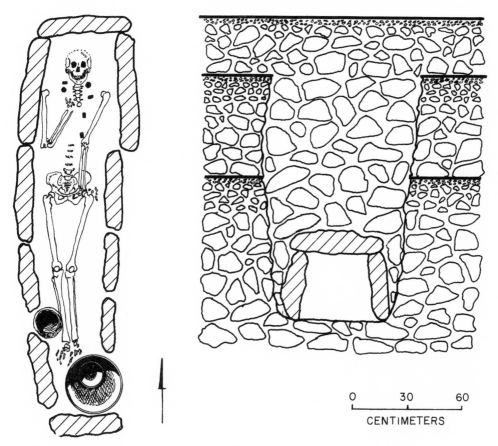

F<small>IG</small>. 7—CIST BURIAL, UAXACTUN, GUATEMALA. (After A. L. Smith, 1950, fig. 133,*e,f.*)

ed with the head to the south, whereas those of Postclassic times were flexed without definite orientation. Except for a very few cases, the remains were too decomposed to yield any data regarding sex or age. The offerings were quite rich in the Late Classic burials but poor in the following period.

Motagua, Guatemala

This information refers to San Agustin Acasaguastlan and Guaytan (Espinoza, 1934–35, pp. 55–58; Kidder, 1935, pp. 109–17; Smith and Kidder, 1943, pp. 55, 58, 122–29).

Excepting one simple burial, the other six burials in Acasaguastlan were in funeral chambers. In Guaytan three were simple burials, five in graves, and only two in

funeral chambers. All seem to belong to a late epoch (the end of the Late Classic).

Most of the funeral chambers of both places are provided with corridors which open on the south side of the mound in which they are found. There is one exception which opens to the north. They are roofed with rough vaults of overlapping stone slabs, and slabs are also used as doors. Generally, the burials are multiple. Although many skeletons apparently were removed to make room for more bodies, they were generally placed head to the north and in an extended position. The tombs of Guaytan contain rich offerings, which include red pigment in receptacles or covering the bones of the dead.

The graves were in the earth or under structures older than the mounds which

449

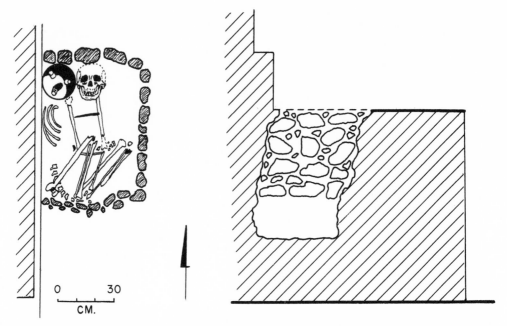

FIG. 8—GRAVE BURIAL, UAXACTUN, GUATEMALA. (After A. L. Smith, 1950, fig. 129a,b.)

covered them. The skeletons were always extended, with the head to east or north. They belonged to adults of both sexes and to children. In some cases these were successive burials. Offerings were poor.

The simple burials could have been associated with the tombs. They were in the ground at the front of tomb entrances or in structures connected to the mounds. The extended position seems to be the usual one, but data are insufficient regarding the orientation of the bodies.

USUMACINTA–GRIJALVA

Most of the sites in this territory are between the lower and middle Usumacinta and Grijalva rivers. We have grouped the sites geographically into three sections, from mountains to coast.

Mountainous Sites

These include Hun Chabin, Huxjal, Lago Lacandon, Moxiuil, San Felipe, Zapaluta, San Nicolas, Santa Catarina, Najos, Santo Domingo, Metzazok, Floresta, Colonia Vi-

torico Grajales, Chiptic, Cieneguilla, Rosario Trabajo, and Tzajalob (Blom and LaFarge, 1927, p. 416; Blom, 1954). All are in Chiapas.

Most of the burials from these sites were secondary and lay in caves. Generally they were large piles of bones and crania, sometimes accompanied by pottery. Almost all were of a late period, probably Postclassic. In some cases human ashes had been deposited in vessels placed inside the caves. A special case is Tzajalob, in which pots with ashes and carbonized bones lay in a subterranean cross-shaped masonry tomb roofed with slabs. Other simple, secondary, or multiple burials of crania and bones were found in Moxiuil in undescribed funeral chambers.

Intermediate Sites

Palenque, Yoxiha, San Antonio, and Yaxchilan represent this region of intermediate elevation.

At Palenque six simple burials are reported. Four others were in crudely con-

450

structed cists. But most of the Palenque burials (20) were found in graves or funeral chambers (18). All belong to the Late Classic period.

The Palenque simple burials occur under floors of buildings or terraces. The cists have been found only in the patios of Group 4, next to graves so crude that they differ but little from cists (B. C. and R. L. Rands, 1959). The typical Palenque graves —coffins made of slabs with a horizontal slab as cover—are generally under the temple floors. In some cases these have lateral niches. Floors may be of stucco or stone slabs (Blom and LaFarge, 1926, p. 111; Ruz, 1952a, p. 55; 1952b, p. 34; 1958a, pp. 135, 153–81; 1958b, pp. 199, 204, 208; 1958c, pp. 260–63). The sepulcher discovered in Temple 21 constitutes a type intermediate between a grave and a chamber. It is small but has the chamber feature of a stairway (Ruz, 1958b, pp. 212–16).

There exist numerous chambers in terraces, mounds, platforms, and pyramids at Palenque, generally constructed for funeral purposes (E. H. Thompson, 1895, pp. 418–421; Blom and LaFarge, 1926, pp. 177–88). At least in one case an enclosed stairway was used as a funeral chamber (Blom and LaFarge, 1926, p. 180; Ruz, 1952a, p. 54). The chambers may be entered by a corridor and antechamber, or from above by a stairway; but these means of access may also be lacking. Most chambers contained a sarcophagus (Blom and LaFarge, 1926, p. 177); one chamber contained four sarcophagi (Blom and LaFarge, 1926, p. 182; Ruz, 1952a, pp. 54–55). In the Temple of the Inscriptions the famous sarcophagus is monolithic rather than constructed of slabs. The tombs in this temple, as well as in Temple 18-A, are connected to a sanctuary by a narrow masonry tunnel that may have served as a magic conduit. In both tombs the walls were decorated with stucco: bas relief in the Temple of the Inscriptions, paintings in Temple 18-A. Also, in both cases multiple primary burials of five or six

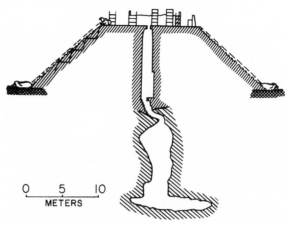

FIG. 9—SECONDARY BURIAL IN WELL AND CAVE, CHICHEN ITZA, YUCATAN, MEXICO. (After J. C. Harrington, in E. H. Thompson, 1938, fig. 2.)

skeletons of young men were at the entrance of the tomb, precisely at the base of the slab which served as a door (Ruz, 1955a, pp. 83–110; 1962b, p. 73).

Except for one instance mentioned by Edward Thompson (1895, pp. 419–21), all Palenque burials for which we have information regarding orientation were placed with the head to the north and were extended on their backs. Where there is no exact information but where the north-south orientation of the tomb is known, it is quite probable that the head was to the north. Some burials were flexed, such as the multiple burials before the tombs in the Temple of the Inscriptions and Temple 18-A, apparently because of limited space. A skeleton of a young woman was seated in a corner in the funeral chamber of Temple 18-A (Ruz, 1962b, p. 70).

Group 4 burials at Palenque (B. C. and R. L. Rands, 1959) lacked offerings or were associated only with pottery fragments; but with the other burials pottery, jade, conch shell, and obsidian were found. Offerings in the sepulchers under the temples were generally richer. Those in the tomb of the Temple of the Inscriptions were particularly valuable since the individual had been buried with his jewels and a jade mosaic mask (Ruz, 1955a, pp. 83–110).

451

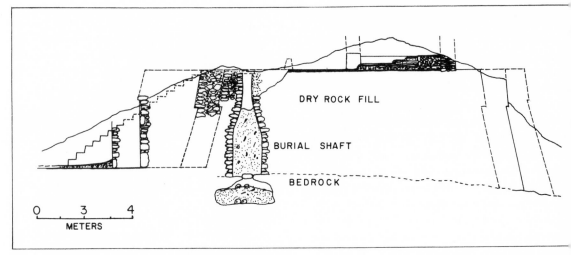

F<small>IG</small>. 10—BURIALS IN WELL AND CHULTUN, MAYAPAN, YUCATAN, MEXICO. (After Shook, 1954a, fig. 4

Several, if not all, of the graves under the floors of the temples were undoubtedly constructed at the same time as the temples, prior to the laying down of the stucco floors and before the interior walls separating sanctuaries from tomb entrances were erected. The tomb in the Temple of the Inscriptions as well as that in Temple 18-A were constructed before their respective enclosing pyramids or platforms (Ruz, 1955a, pp. 83–110; 1962b). Probably this is also the case with the Temple of Bello Relieve or Casa de León with its stairway which descends from the sanctuary to a small subterranean chamber (Holmes, 1895–97, pp. 188–91).

At Yoxiha and San Antonio, both in Chiapas and not far south of Palenque, we have data regarding funeral chambers in mounds. In Yoxiha these are two superimposed chambers corresponding to different times. The bottom one had no skeletons and is possibly an antechamber of a tomb not yet discovered. The one above had a skeleton whose head was oriented to the north. Both chambers contained ceramics which link them with Palenque (Blom and La-Farge, 1926, pp. 226–33). Of San Antonio we only know that the chamber was provided with an entrance corridor (Blom and LaFarge, 1927, pp. 322–23).

We have very little information regarding

Yaxchilan in Chiapas. Maudslay (1889–1902, 2: 45) mentions one chamber in Building H which may have had funeral functions. However, since he describes two corridors with stairs that join the chamber with the outside, we may suppose it to be the lower gallery in Str. 19, or Maler's "labyrinth" (Maler, 1901–03, pp. 137–39). In this case it would not seem to have had a funerary character. Maler (1903, pp. 168–69) also speaks of "sepulchral pyramids" at Yaxchilan, but these were not explored. This designation is not yet justified, but it is not impossible that pyramids may have enclosed sepulchers.

Finally, in referring to highlands in the region of the Usumacinta, without more precise location, Cogolludo (1955, bk. 12, ch. 7, p. 347) mentions flexed burials seated in round holes in the ground, together with food for the dead man and for the animals he ate during life.

Coastal Sites

Sepulchers of different types were found in Tabasco at varying distances from the coast. Some were simple burials in the ground under the floor of a plaza in Bellote (Berlin, 1953, p. 109). Others were in the cave of El Zopo (Blom and LaFarge, 1926, pp. 156–57). Still others were in funeral chambers built in mounds or in ceremonial buildings. From Bellote we know that such sepulchers existed in oyster-shell mounds recently destroyed (Mexico en la Cultura, no. 592, July 17, 1960). In El Encanto the supposedly funerary chambers (there are no data or skeletons) were constructed with bricks as were the ones from Comalcalco (Berlin, 1953, p. 112).

From Comalcalco, Tabasco, we know of a tomb whose walls were decorated with stucco relief and which must have contained a sarcophagus that rested on four small pillars. (The sarcophagus was not found but the pillars were.) The tomb had been sacked before archaeological discovery, and only a few pieces of bone were found on the floor (Blom and LaFarge, 1926, pp. 115–30). Chambers under Comalcalco Temples 1 and 2, which had an entrance over the façade between a double stairway which led to the sanctuary, may also have had sepulchral functions (Blom and LaFarge, 1926, pp. 107–08).

Information about burial offerings is scarce: pottery was found with burials at El Zopo, Bellote, and El Encanto; shell pectorals and vestiges of red pigment are reported from the sacked tomb of Comalcalco. In spite of such scanty data it is believed that the burials of this region belong to the Late Classic period.

NORTHERN YUCATAN

Of about 400 burials that we know of in northern Yucatan approximately 300 are from Jaina and Mayapan. The rest are distributed among a dozen other sites: Chichen Itza, Kabah, Dzibilchaltun, Xkichmook, Tulum, Labna, Kul, and cave sites in the Puuc region.

In addition to archaeological information there are some data from historical sources regarding funeral practices in Yucatan. Landa (1938, p. 139; 1941, p. 130) mentions simple burials in or behind houses which were abandoned after the burial. In these instances stones and corn had been put in the mouth of the corpse. He also re-

fers to the practice of cremation of important individuals and later placing their ashes in urns fashioned as hollow clay or wooden statues (1938, p. 139; 1941, pp. 130–31). He mentions the special case at Izamal of a secondary burial (ashes and long-bones) which had been placed in a pottery jar accompanied by jade beads (1938, pp. 70–210; 1941, pp. 19, 171–72). Landa also tells of what happened to the skulls of the Cocom lords after their decapitation. Facial features were drawn on them with a "certain dye," and they were kept in the houses (1938, pp. 139–40; 1941, p. 131). According to Tozzer (Landa, 1941, note 545, pp. 119–20), relative to a work by Scholes and Adams, in Sotuta and Homun, shortly after the Spanish conquest, the bodies of the sacrificial victims were thrown into dry wells or into caves. Or, sometimes, they were buried or abandoned in the wilderness or in churches. It is possible that in Sotuta they were thrown into a cenote.

Jaina, Campeche

The numerous burials in this site (about 225) justify it being considered a necropolis (Moedano, 1946, pp. 217–42; Piña Chan, 1948, pp. 13–30). These burials may be (1) simple and placed directly in the ground, or (2) in pottery vessels covered with a bowl or plate and buried in the ground. In both cases they occurred outside of buildings. Nearly all are primary although some secondary ones are found in the vessels.

Among the simple burials adults (of both sexes) predominate although there are quite a few children. All burials in pottery jars are infants. Except for two extended burials, all others are in a flexed position. There is no definite norm for orienting the bodies. In most cases the head is protected by a pottery plate or bowl. Frequently, the bones are covered with red pigment. Cranial deformation and dental mutilation are rare. Offerings, which occur with nearly all the burials, are varied and, in some

453

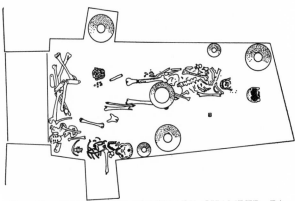

Fig. 11—BURIALS IN FUNERARY CHAMBER, PA-
LENQUE, CHIAPAS, MEXICO. (Ruz, 1959, pl. 3.)

cases, quite rich. A pottery figurine between
the arms of the body is almost a rule. All
burials of Jaina belong to the Late Classic
period.[4]

Mayapan, Yucatan

The systematic explorations carried out by
the Carnegie Institution of Washington for
several years afford much detailed information regarding some 70 burials. The types of
burials found in other parts of the Maya
area also exist in Mayapan: simple, in pottery vessels, in cists, graves, funeral chambers, and chultuns, as well as cremations.

Simple burials are in the ground under
or over the floors of plazas, patios, house
platforms, and civil or ceremonial buildings (R. M. Adams, 1953, pp. 145, 160;
A. L. Smith and Ruppert, 1953, pp. 185,
188, 193–94; 1956, pp. 483–94, 501, 503, 508;
Shook, 1954a, p. 258; 1954b, pp. 19–20;
1954c, pp. 91–92; R. E. Smith, 1954a, p. 57;
J. E. S. Thompson, 1954b, p. 77; Proskouriakoff and Temple, 1955, p. 315; Shook and
Irving, 1955, pp. 146, 152–54; Chowning
and Thompson, 1956, pp. 427, 435). One
fourth of the simple burials are infants, and
among the adults there are more males than
females. Most simple adult burials are primary, in a flexed position, and with the
head indistinctly oriented. Sometimes skulls

[4] Ed. note: Andrews' Pure Florescent.

454

are found by themselves (A. L. Smith and
Ruppert, 1953, p. 185; Shook and Irving,
1955, p. 154). In some cases it is supposed
that the head was separated from the body
and the skeleton disarticulated before
burial (Shook, 1954a, p. 258; Shook and
Irving, 1955, pp. 146, 152–53). A secondary
burial of more than 10 individuals was discovered in a natural cave in the walls of a
cenote (R. E. Smith, 1953, pp. 71–72). In
one case the cranium was protected by a
bowl (R. E. Smith, 1954a, p. 57). Offerings
with these burials are not rich and may be
totally lacking in some instances.

A few secondary burials in pottery vessels were found in Mayapan. Two were of
children (R. E. Smith, 1954a, p. 55), and
two others were mostly ashes and fragments
of bone (Thompson and Thompson, 1955,
pp. 234–36; Chowning and Thompson,
1956, p. 436). They were on a platform inside an altar and in a chultun under the
room of a building.

Burials in cists are associated with structures, domestic as well as civil buildings
and temples. They occur under floors,
benches, or altars or in the nuclei of platforms (R. M. Adams, 1953, pp. 151–57,
160–64; Shook, 1953, p. 209; 1954a, pp.
254–262; Ruppert and Smith, 1954, pp. 32,
37–41; Thompson and Thompson, 1955, pp.
234–35; Proskouriakoff and Temple, 1955,
pp. 306–07, 326–27; Chowning and Thompson, 1956, pp. 434–37; A. L. Smith and Ruppert, 1956, pp. 478–81, 487–98, 504–07).
One-fifth are infants. Males predominate
among the adult burials. The flexed position is nearly an absolute rule; the head
tends to lie to the east. Most of them are
of primary type, but many were not placed
contemporaneously in the same cists (R.
M. Adams, 1953, pp. 151, 153, 163; Shook,
1954a, p. 259; Thompson and Thompson,
1955, pp. 234–35). In one secondary burial
some of the bones were charred (Adams,
1953, p. 160).

The burials in graves are in similar locations as those in cists, that is to say, under

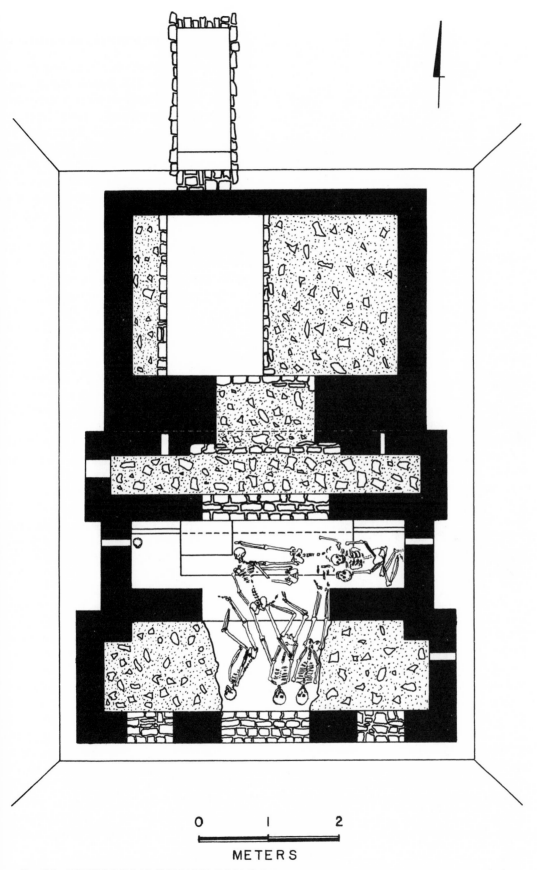

O   I   2

METERS

FIG. 12—BURIALS IN ABANDONED ROOMS OF TEMPLE, HOLMUL, GUATEMALA. (After Merwin and Vaillant, 1932, fig. 12.)

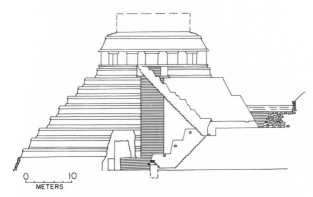

0   10
METERS

FIG. 13—FUNERARY CHAMBER UNDER PYRAMID, PALENQUE, CHIAPAS, MEXICO. Cross section of Temple of the Inscriptions, showing vaulted stairway descending to funerary chamber. (After Ruz.)

floors of rooms, corridors, benches and plazas (A. L. Smith and Ruppert, 1953, pp. 190–91; 1956, pp. 475–77, 491–506; Ruppert and Smith, 1954, pp. 30, 35, 39–40; R. E. Smith, 1954a, p. 55; Chowning, 1956, pp. 446–47). They are mainly primary, and the proportion of adults (90 per cent) is greater than in the types of burials previously mentioned. The flexed position predominates, but there is no definite orientation. A multiple burial of 15 individuals represents successive inhumations, and most of the skeletons had the head separated from the body (Chowning, 1956, pp. 446–47).

Funeral chambers are not as frequent in Mayapan as are cists and graves. They show up under house benches or under floors of platforms (Ruppert and Smith, 1952, pp. 46–51; 1954, pp. 29, 32–33; A. L. Smith and Ruppert, 1953, pp. 190–95; Thompson and Thompson, 1955, pp. 228, 229–38). One chamber believed to have had a funerary purpose, but which had been sacked, is provided with an antechamber which is reached by a stairway from the portico (Smith and Ruppert, 1953, pp. 181–83). We have few data on sex, age, or position as the condition of these burials was very bad; however, most of the crania were oriented to the east. All the burials had relatively poor offerings, as is usual at Mayapan.

456

Extraordinary cases were two burials in bottle-shaped pits, constructed inside of pyramids, one directly above bedrock (Shook, 1954a, pp. 254–56) and the other over a funerary chultun (*ibid.*, pp. 259–71). One of these pits contained more than 40 skeletons of adults and children of both sexes, together with animal remains. The presence of a sacrificial stone near the mouth of the bottle-shaped pit, on the platform of Str. Q-95, confirms the belief that these skeletons represent sacrificial victims which had been thrown into the pit (*ibid.*, p. 271). Objects which probably had been considered as offerings were found with the remains.

We have mentioned a chultun under one of these pits. It was covered by a slab and also contained human remains. Of these, an adult male, a female, and two children were identified. The last three exhibit cranial deformation. Several burial objects were associated (Shook, 1954a, p. 269). In another chultun, under the room of a building, were several skeletons, all flexed and without offerings (Chowning and Thompson, 1956, pp. 435–36).

Of all the crania examined at Mayapan only 16 were artificially deformed, and of more than 1000 teeth studied, only three were filed (Fry, 1956, pp. 552–63).

Chichen Itza, Yucatan

From this important site in which groups of buildings were carefully explored, we have burial data only for the Templo del Osario, or Tomb of the High Priest, and the Caracol.

Seven burials were in the Osario in a pit which descends from the temple to a natural cave under the floor. The human remains were so badly destroyed that it is impossible to tell whether they are primary or secondary burials. Nor are there data on age, sex, or position. Other bones, calcined and mixed with ashes, were in the corridor and in the stairway which leads from the pit to the cave. Finally, of the numerous bones in the cave, many were calcined or charred. Objects thrown or deposited as offerings were with all burials (E. H. Thompson, 1938, pp. 20–27, 45–53).

Most of the burials discovered in the nuclei of the platforms during exploration of the Caracol were of the simple form (Ruppert, 1935, pp. 30–36, 140). Two were found in pots. All were secondary.

The simple burials are all multiple. One of these included up to a dozen individuals, nearly all children. Another consisted of 24 crania of adults and children arranged in rows and placed apart from the rest of the bones (Ruppert, 1935, pp. 120–24). Objects deposited as offerings accompanied the human remains.

The skeletal remains recovered from the Cenote of Sacrifice and, according to tradition, belonging to the victims thrown into the well, number 13 adult males, 8 females and 21 children (Tozzer, 1957, p. 205). The many objects recovered, some of much value, must have been thrown in with the victims as offerings.

Kabah, Yucatan

Of the few burials known from this site, all are from funeral chambers. One was constructed in the natural ground, and two others were built in an artificial terrace. Two of these three were oriented north-south, the other east-west. They had been sacked except for one which contained two vessels and, possibly, ashes mixed with dirt. This chamber communicated with a small grave, possibly an infant's tomb. Another chamber had rings attached to the corbeled vault which suggests that the corpse had rested on a litter suspended from the vault (Ruz, 1948).

Dzibilchaltun, Yucatan

Several burials in graves were under the floors of buildings belonging to the Classic period.[5] These consisted of skeletons of

adults, extended and accompanied by offerings (Andrews, 1959, p. 99). An infant burial in a jar lay under a floor of a plaza. Human bones and many other objects, principally pottery, were recovered from the cenote Xlach in the same site (Marden, 1959, pp. 115–16).

Xkichmook, Yucatan

About 15 burials were described by Edward Thompson (1898, pp. 218–24). They include simple burials, burials in cists and in graves. All were under the floors of rooms in several buildings except for some much destroyed graves and cists encountered in the nuclei of two mounds. In all these burials bones were scarce and badly preserved, and we have no data on sex, age, or position. Several burials seem to be secondary; in three cases crania were protected by plates or flat bowls. The burials belong to the Late Classic period (see note 4).

Tulum, Quintana Roo

Five graves were in platforms. Four of these were oriented north-south; the other, of cruciform shape, was oriented east-west. Data on the remains are lacking or insufficient to determine age, sex, or position (Lothrop, 1924, pp. 91, 97, 102). These burials belong to the Postclassic period.

Caves and Chultuns

In several areas of northern Yucatan, especially in the Puuc region, burials were in natural caves. These are generally secondary and may or may not have offerings. Such burials are mentioned in Actun Coyoc and Xhambak (Mercer, 1896, pp. 35, 131); Loltun (E. H. Thompson, 1897a, pp. 19–20); Oxkutzcab, where some burials are found in "haltuns"—small natural openings in the rocks (E. H. Thompson, 1904, pp. 5–6); and Mani (Landa, 1938, p. 226; 1941, p. 188).

All the data at our disposal regarding burials in chultuns refer to Labná (E. H. Thompson, 1897b, pp. 10–12, 15–17) except

[5] Ed. note: Andrews' Early.

457

for one in Xul (E. H. Thompson, 1904, p. 8). Excepting two primary flexed burials with heads to the north and northwest, the rest are secondary and reduced to a few bones and teeth. Some objects of pottery, stone, shell, and obsidian were discovered with these burials. They probably all belong to the Late Classic period (see note 4).

CONCLUSIONS

Even with all the foregoing data it is impossible to draw a complete picture of funeral practices in the Maya lowlands for several reasons: (1) large territories, although partially surveyed, have not been thoroughly explored; (2) only a few of the explored sites were studied intensively and extensively; (3) the data presented by many investigators are inadequate. Nevertheless, the situation has improved since Ricketson (1925, p. 381) emphasized the meagerness and inconsistency of burial data from the Maya region. This has been due largely to the systematic work carried out principally at Uaxactun, Holmul, San Jose, Jaina, Palenque, and Mayapan.

We can say that the Maya employed almost every known way to dispose of their dead: cremation, simple inhumation (in the ground or in buildings), burials in caves and chultuns, in urns, in specific construction (cists, graves, and funeral chambers), and in rooms of buildings originally designed for worship or habitation. But these different modes were not universally used in all sites of the Maya area; nor can we assign them a categoric geographical distribution. We can say, however, that important sites generally exhibit all of these burial modes and that minor centers show one or few types of burials.

Certain types of burials, for example those in chultuns and caves, are determined by geological conditions. It is also possible that the lack of humus and alluvial sediments in northern Yucatan, with bedrock close to the surface and burial difficult, may have contributed to the preference for cre-

mation over inhumation; but these geologic factors do not explain why this practice was reserved for what appear to have been the members of the aristocracy. The relatively few burials in the Yucatecan ceremonial centers, such as Uxmal and Chichen Itza, seem to confirm what Landa said with regard to cremation among the higher classes. Mayapan is excepted, for it is not only a ceremonial center but a true city, and we also know from Landa that it was a custom among the common people to bury their dead in or close to the houses, as the investigations have revealed. The scarcity of deformed skulls and of mutilated teeth from Mayapan is probably a consequence of the urban character of this site with its dense plebeian population even though dental mutilation may not be exclusively associated with the higher social classes (Romero, 1958, p. 227).

The existence of a true cemetery in Jaina, and probably at other sites on the west coast of the Yucatan peninsula, may have been by way of compensation for the difficult natural conditions for ground burial in certain parts of Yucatan. These necropoli served as burial places for many other centers more or less distant. On the Tabascan coast the absence of stone explains the use of bricks for the construction of chambers and larger structures, and of shells for burial mounds.

Several characteristics may be observed in the burials of the Maya area that have universal value among peoples that have reached a high cultural level. The most important one is the tendency to protect the corpse. Even simple burials in the ground, without a structure to protect them, nevertheless exhibit partial protection, mainly by a plate, shallow bowl, shell, or rock slab to cover the head. In other cases it does not seem to have been the head which needed protection but the sex organs. On the other hand, the protection of the body is proportional to the resources available in each case, and this may imply a marked differ-

458

ence in the social class or hierarchial position of the deceased. It seems evident that between the simple burials with few or no offerings and without a specific funeral structure and such a funeral crypt as that in the Temple of the Inscriptions at Palenque, there is a progressive scale which reflects the class divisions and the different civil and religious ranks to which individuals belonged. The more or less rough cists, the graves of varying construction, the funeral chambers of different sizes, the rooms in buildings employed as tombs, and the quality of the offerings all suggest different class and rank categories in the funeral practices of the ancient Maya.

Another universal characteristic is that of placing with the corpse not only food and drink but objects which belonged to him and which characterize his office or rank and, sometimes, his sex and age. Such practices bespeak a belief in an afterlife in which people had the same necessities and occupations as in their earthly existence. For example, when the deceased was a great personage, perhaps a prince or a high priest, it was supposed that he would need wives and servants in the other world. Such is implied in burial by the presence of associated human sacrifices.

Another custom involving human sacrifice was that of burying victims at the inauguration, or termination of the construction, of a civil or ceremonial building. Many of the burials in Maya monuments, mainly of children or of skulls alone, show indications of being foundation or dedication sacrifices.

The presence of red pigment or cinnabar powder over bones and offerings is not an exclusively Maya practice, for it is known in Oaxaca and in other places. Possibly the color red, associated with the east where the sun is reborn every morning, may also have been a symbol of resurrection for men. The finding of a jade bead in the mouth, in Maya burials as well as Zapotec and Mixtec, confirms the writings

of the chroniclers of the Spanish conquest when they refer to the belief of the Mayas and the Mexicans that jade was the currency to obtain foodstuffs and to facilitate one's entrance into the next world. The occurrence of female phalanges with infant burials probably indicates the desire that something of the mother remain with the dead child. In this connection it should be remembered that the middle finger of the left hand of a mother who died in childbirth was revered and carried into battle by Aztec warriors in their shields as a magical protection (Sahagún, 1946, bk. 6, ch. 29). The presence of carbon and ray spines over the pelvis of the dead relates to rites or beliefs whose meaning we do not know. The discovery of fabric and rope vestiges in some tombs probably indicates that the flexed burials were wrapped and tied to form funeral bundles of the sort mentioned in Spanish chronicles and Mexican codices. The masonry tubes found in two tombs in Palenque have not been reported elsewhere in the Maya area, but canals discovered in Zapotecan tombs may have had the same function—presumably that of a magical link between the sepulcher and the temple or between the subterranean world and the world of the living (Caso, 1932d, p. 497).

Aside from general patterns and traits which pertain to the Maya area and to wide Mesoamerican spheres, some regional and local characteristics are noted which are also susceptible to chronological examination. In the Peten, for example, funeral practices begin as simple burials without definite position or orientation. They then become more elaborate in the Late Classic period, when they include such features as chambers and tend to follow stricter norms as to position, orientation, and the type of burial found in the different contexts.

In British Honduras burials are mostly simple ones in mounds or buildings. Those of the Motagua Valley are in funeral chambers in mounds utilized for successive buri-

459

als. In Palenque they are generally in sarcophagi, which form graves when they are included in the nuclei of structures, or they may be in specialized mortuary receptacles within chambers. Those of Tabasco are in baked-brick chambers in mounds. Those of Jaina are simple burials in the earth or infant burials in pottery jars. In northern Yucatan the scarcity of burials in the ceremonial centers is a characteristic, except for urban Mayapan and for the cemetery of Jaina.

There exists no general norm with regard to body orientation for the whole area; neither can we establish any definite geographical patterning. However, it seems that in the Peten, the valley of the Motagua, and the drainage of the Usumacinta-Grijalva the head-to-north orientation predominates. In British Honduras the head of the deceased was usually placed to the south.

The diversity of funeral patterns in the Maya area parallels what is revealed by artistic styles. This may reflect divisions into entities with a certain degree of political and cultural autonomy. At the same time burial differences undoubtedly correspond to differences of function, social status, and natural environment in the various centers. The changes undergone by certain burial norms in the few sites in which these have been studied chronologically also may result from external influences which are difficult or impossible to appraise until we have a more complete picture of the entire Maya lowland area and the surrounding areas with their corresponding regional and local sequences. The occurrences of similar funeral practices throughout the Maya area, as well as in other Mesoamerican cultures, indicate the fundamental unity which unites the Maya and these other cultures in spite of their divergent development.

REFERENCES

Adams, R. M., 1953
Anderson and Cook, 1944
Andrews, 1959
Berlin, 1953
Blom, 1954
—— and LaFarge, 1926–27
Breton, 1908
Caso, 1932d
Chowning, 1956
—— and Thompson, 1956
Coe, M. D., 1956
Coe, W. R., and Broman, 1958
Cogolludo, 1955
Espinoza, 1934–35
Fry, 1956
Gann, 1914–16, 1918, 1928b
—— and Gann, 1939
Gordon, 1898
Holmes, 1895–97
Kidder, 1935
—— and Ekholm, 1951
Landa, 1938, 1941
Life Magazine, 1959

Life en Español, 1959
Longyear, 1952
Lothrop, 1924
Maler, 1901–03
Marden, 1959
Maudslay, 1889–1902
Mercer, 1896
Merwin, 1909–10
—— and Vaillant, 1932
Moedano K., 1946
Peabody Museum, 1896
Piña Chan, 1948
Price, 1899
Proskouriakoff and Temple, 1955
Rands, 1959
Ricketson, 1925, 1929, 1937
Romero, 1958
Ruppert, 1935
—— and Denison, 1943
—— and Smith, 1952, 1954
Ruz L., 1948, 1952a, 1952b, 1955a, 1958, 1962b
Sahagún, 1946
Shook, 1953, 1954a, 1954b, 1954c

——and Irving, 1955
Smith, A. L., 1937, 1950
—— and Kidder, 1943
—— and Ruppert, 1953, 1956
Smith, R. E., 1937, 1953, 1954a
Stromsvik, 1941, 1942a
Suarez, 1960
Thompson, D. E. and J. E. S., 1955

Thompson, E. H., 1895, 1897a, 1897b, 1898, 1904, 1938
Thompson, J. E. S., 1930, 1931, 1939a, 1940, 1954a, 1954b
Tozzer, 1957
Waldeck, 1866
Wauchope, 1934
Zavala, 1949

17. Caches and Offertory Practices of the Maya Lowlands

WILLIAM R. COE

THE TERM "cache," prefaced by "dedicatory" or "votive," customarily designates a limited but significant variety of offerings found apart from human interments though not necessarily devoid of human skeletal remains.

The bulk of lowland Maya offerings were intentionally hidden in some manner. The content and location of such appropriately designated caches were in practically all known cases ceremonial. Ritual content, location, and purpose distinguished lowland offerings from the utilitarian storage and ageing caches commonly encountered in the literature on North American archaeology. It is gradually becoming apparent, however, that not all lowland offerings were secreted, and that the primary heading must be "offerings," under which "cache" may be applied to a particular and major offertory pattern.

Hidden offerings (truly cached) are preponderantly from concentrations of usually exotic ritual objects in the fills of structures, often but not always on the central front-rear axes. Their objective was presumably related to that of the construction itself—

to a deity, a personage, an event, a chronological cycle, or other purpose.

Less well represented is a type of offering which might be designated "terminal." This offering appears to have been reflective, that is, oriented to an obsolete structure on the verge of being buried by a new one. Such offering may have been simply left in a whole or fragmentary state on the surface of the obsolete structure or superficially intruded into it. Concealment by new construction nevertheless might be considered as incidental and such offerings cannot be classified properly as "caches."

Offerings were also placed beneath occupation surfaces during their use. These intrusive offerings, concealed by floor patching or tamped fill, may have functioned in conjunction with important ceremonies, for instance, in the 260-day cycle. Situations arise, however, in excavation which are uncertain: was the offering made during occupation, or at the close of it with subsequent architectural addition? If the latter, interpretation as a "terminal offering" is conceivably appropriate.

Although many caches are connected

462

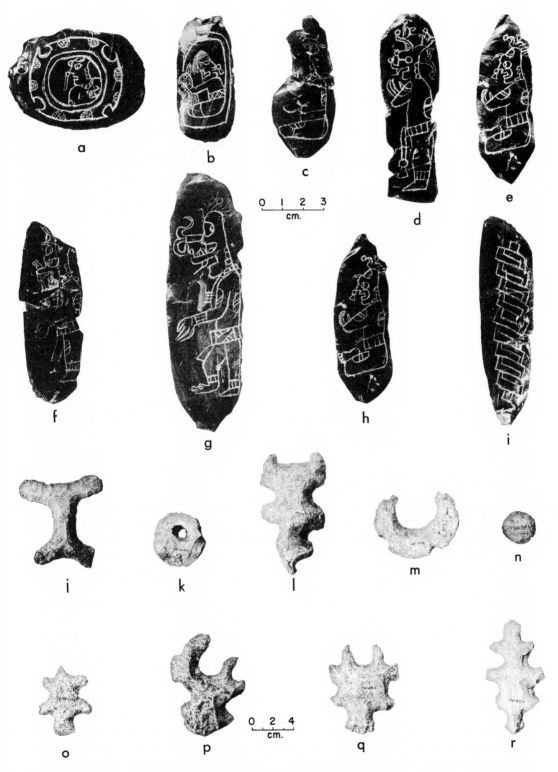

FIG. 1—TYPICAL LATE CLASSIC MONUMENT-ASSOCIATED CACHE, TIKAL, GUATEMA-
LA. Cache 42, with Stela P20, stone portion only. *a–i,* Incised obsidians. *j–r,* Eccentric flints (half
scale of obsidians). (Courtesy, University Museum, University of Pennsylvania.)

with structures, a considerable number have been set with monuments during their installation. Some evidence exists for redeposition of monument-associated caches, but no conclusive evidence is known for intruding an offering following the placement of the associated monument. Monument offerings possibly had the same temporal, commemorative function of the monument itself. This presumption bears on the question of whether or not "plain" stelae had painted or stucco figures and texts. There is to date no evident distinction between caches set with carved monuments and those with now plain ones.

Hidden structure- and monument-associated offerings are to be contrasted with "exposed offerings." Occasionally in excavation a concentration, say, of pottery is encountered on the latest occupation surface but beneath humus and accumulated debris, perhaps a sacrifice towards some end involving pottery vessels. Although the evidence may have been buried with time, there are no signs that the remains were purposely concealed. This category, which is one of situation, may be interpreted as "terminal offering."

Other far less archaeologically tangible "exposed offerings" would be those of incense, blood, animals, humans, etc. Such offerings are well documented by Bishop Landa and can be verified in various art media for earlier times, at least as early as the Late Classic period.

The classification or even recognition of lowland offerings is by no means hard and fast. At times it is not easy to distinguish a cache from a burial. A lip-to-lip set of bowls may contain a human skull, quite unconnected with what is clearly a burial, as, for instance, at Uaxactun (A. L. Smith, 1950, p. 93). Perhaps the only reliable diagnostic here (apart from the fact that the whole arrangement was in a "cache" situation) is one's estimate of whether the skull was an *object* or a *person* in the minds of those responsible for its curious interment.

If the former, the entire disposition constitutes a hidden offering; if the latter, a burial, regardless of incompleteness. Our nomenclature, conditioned by our own beliefs and concepts, may be misleading in attempts to explain ancient Maya behavior.

PRECLASSIC OFFERINGS

Very little is known of lowland offerings in the Preclassic or Formative period, partly due to lack of stone monuments. One Preclassic (Chicanel) offering was encountered at Uaxactun (R. E. Smith, 1937, fig. 17,*g*; A. L. Smith, 1950, Table 8, Cache A16); no cache at all was found in E-VII-sub although this structure was partially trenched on the front-rear axis. The single Uaxactun cache of this era consisted of a lidded jar containing a small jade bead, set in a repository cut through the floor associated with Pyramid A of the A-I Complex. Two pot bases were located above the floor but seemingly in relation to the cache. This situation suggests either a terminal offering made with respect to the obsolete Pyramid A (the earliest) or an offering dedicated to the new Pyramid B but intruded into the floor fronting the older building. In either case, the offering would seem to belong to the Preclassic period. (cf. R. E. Smith, 1955b, Table 3, Pyramid B).

Excavations in the Tikal Preclassic (Chicanel-affiliated) period have disclosed a single sure offering which comprised a large vessel containing a nested plate, the base of a large vessel, and an intact lancet-type obsidian flake-blade. This offering (Cache 24; W. R. Coe, n.d.) appears to have been dedicatory, beneath the earliest floor, and off the apparent central axis of construction.

At San Jose in British Honduras, an offering of two pottery vessels pertains to Period I, apparently Late Preclassic (Thompson, 1939a, pp. 187–188).

Obviously little interpretive weight can be given to these three examples. The absence of typical Classic items (eccentrics, flints, and obsidians, etc.; see below) may or may not be coincidental.

CLASSIC OFFERINGS

Offerings of objects pertaining to this era are abundantly represented at Uaxactun (A. L. Smith, 1950), Piedras Negras (W. R. Coe, 1959), Tikal (W. R. Coe, n.d.), and in lesser quantities at San Jose (Thompson, 1939a), Copan (Longyear, 1952), Quirigua (Stromsvik, 1942b), and at the Mountain Cow sites (Thompson, 1931). Reports on Palenque, Uxmal, as well as various British Honduras sites (Benque Viejo, Nohmul, Baking Pot, etc.) contain additional data on caches of this period (summarized by W. R. Coe, 1959, p. 108 ff.).

A long-standing problem has been to determine whether or not cache contents are of cross-dating value within and among lowland centers (cf. Thompson, 1931, p. 336). Analysis of 56 caches from Tikal (W. R. Coe, n.d.) and examination of subsequently excavated offerings show fairly distinct and profound shifts in content with time, providing a general and occasionally a specific predictability. By and large, the two other large series of caches (at Uaxactun and Piedras Negras) fail in their own different ways to show a significant or at least useful change of composition.

Caches from Monuments

Many stelae were originally erected at Tikal with offerings around their bases and particularly under them. When a monument was reset, caches, possibly salvaged, were conventionally placed with them. Resetting of monuments is a serious handicap in judging chronology but normal, primary associations as well as cache seriation indicate the following sequence:

Early monument-associated caches, consisting of eccentric flints (crude workmanship, essentially unifacial with little retouching, in the form of tridents, laurel-leaf blades, alternate-opposite notched blades, discs, etc., often in large quantities), eccentric obsidians (simple notched blade-cores with many definite patterns of notching), masses of obsidian flake-blade fragments and flakes along with flint flakes, shells (preponderantly Atlantic species, such as *Arca* and *Cardium*), occasional small human figurines of shell, shell beads, human teeth and bone scraps, and pottery vessels.

Transitional monument-associated caches, comprising eccentric flints (frequently of fine workmanship in a variety of forms not previously produced; far smaller quantities than in early caches), eccentric obsidians (generally made from flakes rather than blade-cores and in a considerable range of forms), occasional incised obsidians (generally silhouetted so that, had incision been omitted, classification as eccentric would be justified; incised designs, though evidently patterned, differ from those in late monument caches), marine shells (same general range as early caches), occasional jade bit or bead, and human skeletal scraps (another carry-over from early times).

Late monument-associated caches (9.14.-0.0.0 to 10.2.0.0.0, with possibly earlier beginnings), with eccentric flints (nine as a rule; majority of distinct forms occur from cache to cache; workmanship and size variable), incised obsidians (ideally nine in number with the same nine deities and symbols in each cached series or set; four stylistic groups recognizable and of chronological value), often pottery vessels (one to four; specialized cache ware frequently with rectangular form; stone material generally outside vessel) and rarely a scrap or bead of jadeite. A single cache was at times divided among contemporaneously erected stelae.

In brief, the trends apparent in Tikal monument caches were from early (probably first part of Early Classic times) quantity with strong standardization of form, to transitional lesser quantity in content but with perhaps greater freedom of forms to-

465

gether with the appearance of incised obsidian, and finally to the statically constituted late monument offering of nine flint, nine incised obsidians and a total absence of eccentric obsidians. Given a conventionally set carved or plain late stela, its cache can be reasonably predicted. A typical Late Classic monument offering is shown in figure 1.

At Uaxactun, the situation regarding monument-associated caches is less certain due to incomplete excavation of stela contexts. Thirteen stelae yielded caches ranging in time from about 8.18.0.0.0 to 9.19.-0.0.0 or slightly afterwards. The limited Uaxactun series provides the following conclusions: (1) eccentric flints were common items throughout the latter part of the Early Classic period but may have been omitted from stela offerings during or following the Tepeu 1 ceramic phase (beginning of Late Classic period); (2) eccentric obsidians in the form of notched blade-cores occurred relatively early (Cache D3) but were absent in the later Caches A19 and A25 though reappearing in the contemporary early Late Classic Caches A38 and A39; (3) obsidian flake-blades and/or chips were sporadically placed in stela caches throughout the known sequence; (4) the Early Classic caches are generally comparable in content to those characterized as early in the Tikal series (Uaxactun Caches D1 and D2 are aberrant in this respect); (5) no Tikal transitional and late caches are represented in the Uaxactun collection of monument caches. Seen from Tikal, Uaxactun stela caches are on the whole of the early type but with numerous important differences. Despite the proximity of Tikal and Uaxactun, marked distinctions occur in this component.

A. L. Smith (1950) fully tabulates content and provenience of Uaxactun monument caches. I have attempted (n.d.) to assess development of these caches and Tikal-Uaxactun discrepancies.

At Piedras Negras cached offerings appeared in the course of monument investigation (W. R. Coe, 1959, p. 99). Certain monuments clustering around 9.12.0.0.0 to 9.14.0.0.0 produced rich caches of eccentric flints and obsidians, objects of shell and jadeite. Other monuments, somewhat later, lacked such items, their offerings being composed in one instance of a pottery censer, in others of portable altars. A peculiarity of Piedras Negras was the column altar; a considerable number of temple structures investigated showed lines of these evident focal points of ceremony, set along the central axes. Many of these altars had been set in position with caches beneath them. The pairing of altars and caches continued over a long period. The offerings were frequently composed of a specialized cache vessel, of a form seemingly unique to Piedras Negras, the interior of which was smeared with a lime paste. Within the lidded vessel were a fairly typical complement of eccentric flints and obsidians, sometimes engraved pieces of jadeite and shell. Piedras Negras caches show no significant change in time or in composition (so marked at Tikal) between offerings placed with monuments or with structures.

There is excellent but not full correlation between stelae and offerings set at their base. By and large, when a stela, either plain or carved (at Tikal plain stelae were apparently always plain) was erected, an offering was placed with it. When a group of stelae were erected simultaneously, at least one stela was set with a cache; this appears to have been the rule at Tikal, as if one offering applied to the group. In other groups, an offering might be divided, flints and obsidians apportioned to one stela, pottery vessels to another; evidence for this has also been encountered at Tikal. At Piedras Negras and Caracol (British Honduras) altars occasionally had separate offerings. No altar cache, however, has come to light at Tikal or Uaxactun; the

466

frequent formal pairing of stela and altar at these sites would suggest that the stela cache pertained to the "stela-altar unit." The correlation of monuments and caches with eccentric components is perhaps verified at Palenque where no eccentric items have come to light and no monuments fall clearly in the stela category. The correlation is weakest at Quirigua and Copan, both peripheral to the Peten.

On the whole, monument-associated caches have not proved particularly useful for dating purposes. At Tikal, the one exception, caches may merely confirm epigraphic and stylistic traits of carved stelae and the form, stone type, and stratigraphic position of plain stelae. Even here caches are nevertheless of considerable use in evaluating or detecting transitional situations and may also be excellent clues to the resetting of either or both stela and cache.

Caches from Structures

Structure-associated offerings have been reported from practically all Classic sites where ceremonial architecture has been excavated. Taken as a whole, these offerings are baffling in the diversity of their contents, but at certain centers they show important traces of regularity.

At Tikal considerable standardization of Late Classic structure offerings has been noted (W. R. Coe, n.d.). These caches are obviously in contrast to those set with contemporaneous stelae (i.e., late monument offerings). Late structure offerings did include eccentric obsidians, a traditional component but one markedly absent in current stela caches. While both cache types possess incised obsidians, those that were set in structure offerings were not numerically standardized or of the same designs as that set with stelae. The same is largely true of the accompanying eccentric flints. Unworked shells and other exotic marine material were used also at times in late structure offerings but never in the co-eval stela caches.

Structure caches contemporary with Tikal early monument caches appear to have been closely related, particularly in lithic components. We have far stronger grounds in recognizing change in monument caches than in structure offerings, but as excavation increases the latter we shall learn how these changes occurred.

At Piedras Negras a large proportion of structure-associated caches appeared with column altars, ritual accessories of the temple structures to which they belonged (W. R. Coe, 1959). No fundamental differences between these offerings and the ones unconnected with column altars or set beneath floors and the like, are detectable. This is on the whole true for both dedicatory and intrusive offerings. The picture of column altar caches and structure caches is one of essential stability throughout some two centuries (W. R. Coe, 1959, p. 98 ff). As noted, Tikal caches evolved with a decided split between those with monuments and those with structures. Too little is known of Piedras Negras monument caches, but when structure and column altar caches are considered together, Piedras Negras differs from Tikal in offertory practices, despite a common production of eccentrics, predilection for marine material, and so forth. The relationship between these two sites in this regard remains problematic (see Satterthwaite, 1941, for architectural parallelism). One can point out the Tikal incised obsidians and the Piedras Negras incised jadeites (with cognate subject matter), but even on this relatively minor level no adequate explanation comes to mind.

At Uaxactun, Early and Late Classic structure caches are hard to place in any developmental perspective. Eccentrics seem to have been restricted to Early Classic offerings placed in structures. One can only hope that further discoveries of structure caches at Tikal will reveal distinct trends in such offertory practices as at Uaxactun. An interesting discrepancy occurred in a Late Classic structure at Uaxactun in Cache

A26 (A. L. Smith, 1950; Kidder, 1947), which in addition to pottery vessels and shells contained nine incised obsidians forming a complete set and essentially identical to sets recently found at Tikal in late monument caches. There is every reason to see the Uaxactun set as having been manufactured at Tikal; but at Tikal this full set would have entered a monument offering (if found in a structure setting, one would suspect disturbance and re-use). Despite proximity of the two sites, this set of obsidians was seemingly misunderstood at Uaxactun as to their proper offertory use.

POSTCLASSIC OFFERINGS

Cached offerings found with structures during this era are on record in some quantity at Chichen Itza and Mayapan. In content, these offerings, both dedicatory and intrusive, at best can be said to be only reminiscent of ideal Classic period offerings in the region to the south. Eccentric stone objects are practically nonexistent. On the whole, exotic items continued to comprise offerings (for summary, see W. R. Coe, 1959, p. 110). It is noteworthy that the custom of making caches of ritual objects not only survived whatever factors contributed to the dissolution of Classic Maya culture but also persisted after the collapse of Toltec dominance in northern Yucatan. Unfortunately, too little beyond architecture and ceramics is known of the Classic period in this part of the peninsula. Possibly current excavations at Dzibilchaltun may settle the question of whether Chichen Itza and subsequent Mayapan cached offerings were or were not manifestations of a distinct regional tradition with northern Classic period roots.

For Mayapan, Proskouriakoff (1962b) has noted the practice of setting a small pottery effigy bowl or tripod cup in a shallow cist in the floor in front of the common masonry altar or within the altar itself. The vessel often contained a few shell or jade beads and infrequently animal bones and ashes. Other offerings consisted of obsidian flake-blades and stingray spines, both items used in bloodletting sacrifices. Some gold, jade pebbles, and pieces of rock crystal entered still other offerings. Offerings were salvaged during rebuilding. The eventual collapse of the center saw extensive looting of offerings (a feature for which there is growing evidence at Tikal).

Numerous types of offerings in the context of "sacrifice" are described or indicated by Landa (Tozzer, 1941a)—individuals, blood, food—certain of which are clearly depicted in Classic media (e.g., the drawing of lingual blood at Yaxchilan).

REFERENCES

Coe, W. R., n.d., 1959
Kidder, 1947
Longyear, 1952
Proskouriakoff, 1962b
Satterthwaite, 1941

Smith, A. L., 1950
Smith, R. E., 1937
Stromsvik, 1942b
Thompson, J. E. S., 1931, 1939a
Tozzer, 1941a

18. Sculpture and Major Arts of the Maya Lowlands

TATIANA PROSKOURIAKOFF

COMPREHENSIVE HISTORY of art for this area has yet to be written and probably will not appear for some time, for though there are copious data for such a history, adequate records have not been assembled, and the erosion and fragmentary condition of most of the sculptures limit illustrative material to the better-preserved pieces, most of which come from a few well-known sites. Photographs of sculptures are scattered through many archaeological reports, but detail is often poorly discernible in them. The most comprehensive series of illustrations, with much valuable background material presented in the text, is to be found in Pijoán, 1946. Many other authors have presented selected samples from various sites, among them: Spinden, 1913; Kelemen, 1943, 1956; Toscano, 1944; Morley, 1946; Médioni, 1950; Proskouriakoff, 1950; J. E. S. Thompson, 1954a; Covarrubias, 1957; Cook de Leonard, 1959a. Specific major sites are best covered in Maudslay, 1889–1902, and in Maler, 1901–03, 1908a, and 1908b, but no single volume contains a balanced representation of all the many artistic schools

that flourished in the area in the millennium and a half before the Spanish conquest.

The outstanding style that we call the Classic Maya style represents a stage of pre-industrial, one might even say premercantile, civilization, in which art was closely allied with ritual activities and was predominantly monumental. The large upright slabs of stone called stelae were set firmly in floors of plazas or on terraces near prominent temples, and their carving usually featured a single human figure in ceremonial regalia, accompanied by hieroglyphic inscriptions. Close to a thousand such monuments are known, the majority from the region south of a line connecting the Laguna de Terminos with the Bay of Chetumal. Most of the monuments in the south are inscribed with Initial Series, a type of calendrical notation which permits us to date them in the Maya count with considerable confidence and to arrange them in a chronological sequence. The resulting series, including associated altars, architectural sculptures and the few examples of wood-carving, stucco, and painting that survive, is stylistically coherent and shows a

469

consistent artistic development reflecting various facets of the changing historical scene. It is here presented in sequent arrangement, using arbitrary time divisions of quarter-cycles in the Maya count, which correspond roughly to our centuries. The beginning of the sequence in the middle of Cycle 8 is equated to A.D. 292 by the Goodman-Martínez-Thompson correlation, and to A.D. 32 by Spinden. The last known stela sculptured with a human figure and a legible inscription was erected in either A.D. 889 or A.D. 629 according to these correlations, though a few stelae without inscriptions may be somewhat later. Thus the development and decline of the Classic monumental style covered a period of at least six centuries.

In the north, stelae continued to be erected until about a century before the foundation of Merida in 1541, but few of the ancient monuments can be dated precisely, and the archaeological sequences are not well enough known to permit a chronological arrangement. Separate sections, therefore, treat with the various local styles that probably preceded the conquest of Yucatan by the Toltec, with the new style of carving introduced by the conquerors at Chichen Itza, with the subsequent decadent period when Mayapan was the capital city, and with the few pieces that may be attributable to the period of social disorganization and conflict which immediately preceded the coming of the Spaniards. I have been able to touch only in the most cursory fashion on these lesser provincial, eclectic, and decadent styles, though I believe that a study of such divergent phenomena may provide more enlightenment on the role that the arts played in Maya culture than a concentration on the masterpieces of the Classic age. I have also thought worthy of mention the changing relations between the monumental arts and the minor crafts, for apart from their intrinsic interest, they probably reflect important changes in social organization.

470

Of formal and aesthetic qualities I have had little to say, in part because I do not think myself qualified as a critic, but also because I believe that aesthetic effects are incidental to the communicative function of art, and that emphasis on them reveals the bias of the present age far more than it clarifies the intentions of the past. Instead, I have tried to draw attention to the symbolic content of Classic sculptures, the interpretation of which may prove to be even more difficult than hieroglyphic decipherment, but may contribute more in the long run to aesthetic appreciation than any degree of formal analysis.

CLASSIC STYLE: GENERAL CONSIDERATIONS

At its climax, the Classic style of the Maya lowlands is comparable to the great styles of antiquity in the eastern hemisphere, but its mode of expression is unlike that of any other art, and may mislead the casual observer who interprets it in the light of modes more familiar to him. The uniqueness of the Maya style lies in a keen interest in natural forms where it concerns the representation of human and animal figures, combined with a remarkably systematic grotesque symbolism used to convey the theme and its ritual significance. In European arts, when elements are abstracted from nature and recombined in grotesque forms, such forms are either whimsical products of individual fantasy or representations of specific mythological creatures. One cannot fully explain Maya grotesques in this way. Their serious intent is inherent in their use in monumental sculpture, but the elements of which they are composed do not form stable associations but are recombined in such a protean manner that they cannot be conceived as describing definite entities. We are of necessity led to believe that they are not pictorial forms but compositions of ideograms, capable of expressing very complex conceptions and differing from hieroglyphic writing only in their lack of serial arrangement and adherence to syntax. Grotesques sometimes substitute for formal characters in hieroglyphic writing, and when they do they frequently express abstractions such as numbers or periods of time. This intimate relation between writing and art symbolism has been implicitly accepted by many epigraphers as evidence of the strongly ideographic nature of the script, but its converse implications in regard to the use of grotesques in art have not been considered with the attention they deserve.

Spinden (1913, pp. 49–76) followed the conventional approach of attempting to identify various grotesques as deities, but although his success was limited and he found only two or three forms that correspond to pictures of gods in the codices, he offered no adequate explanation of the variability of forms that repeatedly frustrated his efforts. Although his work remains the best and the most comprehensive study of the problem published so far, its failure to clarify principles governing the composition of grotesque forms leaves us with a formidable obstacle to a full appreciation of Maya art. Rands has since made detailed studies of individual elements, namely, the water-symbol (1955) and the water-lily motif (1953), refuting successfully the alleged Asiatic origin of the latter, but such studies do not touch upon the problems posed by larger compositions, which continue to elude interpretation.

Even in regard to the very natural human figures on stelae, there is wide divergence of opinion. The view that Maya stelae were time-markers concerned almost exclusively with prognostics for the katuns has given rise to the notion that the human figures are portraits of gods or of anonymous priests engaged in worship, though currently this idea is losing ground to more realistic interpretations. A series of records at Piedras Negras resembles archives of successive reigns (Proskouriakoff, 1960) and suggests the possibility of identifying the figures on monuments with historical personages named in the inscriptions. Berlin's recent work on Palenque (as yet unpublished) holds similar promise of clarifying specific themes in temple texts. A clearer understanding of the subject matter and of the modes of its symbolic expression may vitally affect future aesthetic evaluations of the style. Current criticism, based almost entirely on formal considerations, is likely to ignore the effect of understanding on visual perception. The feeling, frequently expressed, that Maya sculpture is overelaborate, and the common tendency to style it as "baroque" is probably due to an inability to grasp its forms readily and to appreciate the scheme of their relations. The ideographic composition was an integral part of every work of art and evidently served to convey aspects of reality that could not be pictorially presented. Any aesthetic critique that ignores this function of grotesque forms is bound to see them as mere elaborations and to judge them superfluous. Nevertheless, even its harshest critics agree that Classic Maya art was the most complex and sophisticated art of the American continent, and Miguel Covarrubias, who frankly professed a preference for less exuberant styles, credits it with "an aristocratic refinement and elegance, a delicacy of concept and technical achievement, comparable only to that of its contemporary arts of the Far East" (Covarrubias, 1957, p. 227).

Classic Style: Historical Review
Note on Origins

We are still handicapped today by lack of information that bears on the origins and early history of the Classic style. The hypothesis, once entertained by Morley (1946, pp. 38–49), and others, that the art of monumental carving arose spontaneously in the Peten while the culture of neighboring peoples was still in a primitive agricultural stage is no longer tenable. On the other hand, attempts to trace the origin of the

471

FIG. 1—STELA 29, TIKAL. The earliest known
monument in the Peten. (Courtesy, University Museum,
University of Pennsylvania.)

art of the Peten to the Gulf coast of Mexico or to highland Guatemala are somewhat premature, for the oldest remains of the great Peten sites have not yet been so well explored that one can judge how deeply the Classic style is rooted in its own locality.

At present we have only the assemblage of stucco masks on Pyramid E-VIIsub at Uaxactun to represent the sculpture associated with remains of the Chicanel phase, the period of the first known ceremonial constructions in the major lowland sites. Observers have noted a strong resemblance in these masks to the earlier style of La Venta, Tabasco, which no doubt connotes a real though perhaps very indirect connection between the two styles. The stucco mask as a sculptural form is typical in Classic Maya architecture, and the general arrangement of the masks—a bird-form at the top, anthropomorphic masks in the middle, and the serpent at the base—has parallels in later Classic reliefs showing birds above the central motif and a two-headed dragon below. If the masks of E-VIIsub are typical of the Preclassic period, then monumental art in the Peten probably has a longer history than is indicated by known dates on stelae. At present we may be seeing only the peak of its development, which now appears to have been one of a series of such waves of creative activity that arose and subsided at different times in the several regions of Mesoamerica.

Earliest Classic Stelae:
Second Half of Cycle 8

The earliest known historical date on a monument from the Maya lowlands is 8.12.14.8.15 13 Men 3 Zip, on the recently discovered Stela 29 at Tikal (fig. 1). This stela is fairly typical of monuments carved in Cycle 8, which occur, so far as we know, only in a circumscribed area in northeastern Peten. Stelae of this period are large limestone slabs, some as high as 3 m., poorly shaped and planed, and carved in low relief that rides over declivities in the stone.

Small round altars are often placed in front of them. A single masculine figure is depicted on the front, and the hieroglyphic inscription appears on the back or, more rarely in this period, on the sides. Typically, the early figure stands with its shoulders in front view and with the head and the lower part of the body in profile. The feet are placed one behind the other, the mass of the body evenly balanced upon them. Hands are often drawn in clasped position, the forefinger curled around the thumb, and one arm is sharply bent, with an object resting in the crook of the elbow. When an object is held in an extended hand it does not rest on the palm, since the hand is usually turned into the plane of the carving.

This manner of presenting objects in their most characteristic form rather than in their normal position is applied to ornaments as well as to the figure itself. Huge earplugs attached to the headdress, which is fastened under the chin and completely encircles the face, are strikingly characteristic at this time, and a heavy chain usually suspends from the belt a grotesque ornament that hangs behind the legs of the figure.

Stelae carved in Cycle 8 often retain traits of great antiquity which they share with monuments of other styles of Mesoamerica. The motif above the figure on Stela 29, for instance, recalls the downgazing gods of Zapotecan art, and the faces seen in cloud motifs above figures on early monuments from the Pacific slope of Guatemala. On Stela 1 from Uolantun (Morley, 1938, vol. 5, pl. 66,*b*), the upflung arm of the figure resembles the pose of figures from Santa Lucia Cotzumalhuapa (J. E. S. Thompson, 1948, fig. 2,*e-g*), while the simple flowing outline of the body and the small feet are reminiscent of figures from La Venta. Ultimately, however, it is the elaborately dressed figure holding a two-headed serpent bar that emerges as the typical figure of the Maya lowland style, and it is such figures that first appear

473

Fɪɢ. 2—ALTAR 12, TIKAL. Early Classic period. (Courtesy, University Museum, University of Pennsylvania.)

in peripheral sites such as Yaxchilan in the west, Copan in the southeast, and eventually at Coba, far to the north.

Period of Expansion:
First Quarter of Cycle 9

The distribution of Early Classic monuments suggests rapid diffusion of the Classic tradition on trade routes following the major waterways—westward along the drainage of the Usumacinta, eastward along the Belize River and the Rio Hondo, and finally on coastal routes to northern Yucatan and to Honduras. In the interior of Campeche, just north of the Peten, the practice of erecting stelae for some reason never took root. The standing remains of this

region are late, and it is not known whether this area was sparsely occupied in Early Classic times or if, on the contrary, a well-established local tradition formed a barrier to cultural diffusion in this direction.

The style of the first quarter of Cycle 9 remains remarkably uniform, considering its territorial spread and the variety of new sculptural forms it encompasses. Carved, round altars, such as Altar 12 from Tikal (fig. 2), continue to be used with stelae in the Peten, but most early altars from Copan are rectangular (Morley, 1920, pl. 8). In the west, carved stone lintels appear, and the first two stelae erected at Yaxchilan, Stelae 14 and 27 (Morley, 1938, vol. 5, pl. 103), are designed as rectangular panels.

474

Before 9.3.0.0.0 there is already a carved hieroglyphic lintel at Oxkintok in northern Yucatan (Shook, 1940, fig. 1), and at least one stela that can be ascribed to this period. In all these forms the characteristics of the early Peten style are clearly discernible.

The spread of monumental carving is sometimes attributed to the colonization of new areas by people from the Peten. It can be equally well, and perhaps in some cases better, explained by the adoption of the practice of carving monuments in towns already established and growing prosperous through trade with the central area. There seems to have been at this time a stable system of trade routes extending over most of Mesoamerica, probably maintained by the military might of Teotihuacan, a city in the Valley of Mexico whose influence was very widespread. In spite of distance and intervening cultures, the Classic style of the Maya and that of Teotihuacan met in outlying regions of the Maya area. At Kaminaljuyu, in the Guatemala highlands, carved altars in the Maya style were used in association with constructions built in the style of Teotihuacan (Kidder, Jennings, and Shook, 1946, p. 35). Both styles are also reflected in stuccoed and painted vessels found in the tombs. At the other extreme of the Maya area, the stucco decoration on a building at Acanceh, Yucatan, has features alien to the Maya style that once were attributed to late influence from Mexico, but that are now recognized as related to Teotihuacan mural painting (Seler, 1902–23, vol. 5, no. 4, pls. 2–9). In the central region of the Maya area, influences from the highlands of Mexico are less evident, but on the newly discovered Stela 31 of Tikal, with a date of 9.0.10.0.0, such traits as the atlatl, and the Tlaloc form with its characteristic feather headdress, clearly reflect highland origin. The later copious use of featherwork in the design of Maya headdresses doubtless began in this early period of highland contact.

Nevertheless, there is remarkably little blending between the two styles, possibly because Maya art was already embarked on its course of development toward a more naturalistic view of life and an interest in mundane events. In this respect, painting was always in advance of sculpture, and the mural on the wall of Str. B-XIII at Uaxactun (A. L. Smith, 1950, fig. 46), like the later and more famous mural at Bonampak, depicts a historic scene in which a troupe of mimes and musicians takes part. On both murals, a linear arrangement of figures in two tiers is dominant, though attention is drawn to some groups by their more studied composition. The figures are drawn with a delicate black line, colors are applied without shading, and there is almost no background, so that the silhouettes are strongly stressed. The colors of the Uaxactun mural are limited to tones of ochers and reds, with the addition of a gray. No samples were subjected to laboratory analysis, but the presumption is that mineral pigments were used, mixed in an aqueous medium and applied to dry plaster. The Bonampak mural uses a larger range of hues, with considerable mixture of pigments, and is more dramatic in its conception and more expressive of the emotional tone of its scenes. Its greater sensitivity of line and more minute observation of significant details is an instance of the growing interest in the beauty of natural forms that is so characteristic of the Late Classic development.

Period of Transition:
Second Quarter of Cycle 9

This interval saw radical changes in the monumental style of the lowlands, but there are too few stelae at this time to show how these changes came about. Two monuments, Stela 1 at Tulum, carved in 9.7.0.0.0 (Lothrop, 1924, pl. 1,A,B), and Stela 1 at Ichpaatun, 9.8.0.0.0 (Gann, 1926, pp. 48, 49), intimate that trade was now carried on along the east coast as well as through Tabasco. Trade between the Maya and

475

Fig. 3—ARCHITECTURAL SCULPTURE. *a (left)*, Stucco head from northwest patio of palace, Palenque (photo by Alberto Ruz Lhuillier; courtesy, Instituto Nacional de Antropología e Historia). *b (right)*, Stucco head from beneath sarcophagus in tomb of Temple of the Inscriptions, Palenque (photo by Irmgard Groth-Kimball; courtesy, Instituto Nacional de Antropología e Historia).

peoples of Mexico seems to have declined, and some sort of disturbance in the central area is indicated by a hiatus in the sequences of known monuments that at some sites lasts into the next quarter-cycle. Many stelae apparently were broken up or mutilated, since an abnormally large proportion of them are fragments. Possibly the explanation lies in the fall of the great city of Teotihuacan, or in the waning of its influence, which exposed the Maya to conflict with their neighbors. On the other hand, the conflict may have been internal, arising from the rivalry of the western cities that had grown prosperous on foreign trade, or from competition of secular authorities with the religious hierarchy. Whatever the

cause, the style of the Peten now lost its dominance, and when the monumental sequence picks up again after 9.9.0.0.0, each regional center of art has its own distinctive style.

Late Classic traits first appear at the end of the previous quarter-cycle at Tikal, in a group of monuments completely different from those that preceded them. This new group, comprising Stelae 10, 12, 14 (?), 23, and 25 (Satterthwaite, 1958a), presents figures in high relief, and for the first time includes figures that apparently represent women. The figures wear feathered headdresses, and though the head is sometimes rendered in profile, the body of the main figure is in full-front view and the feet

Fig. 4—CENTRAL SLAB OF THE TABLET FROM THE INNER SHRINE OF THE TEMPLE OF THE CROSS, PALENQUE. (Courtesy, British Museum.)

point outward, a position that is typical of Late Classic times. All the monuments had been mutilated, but it is difficult to tell whether the damage is recent or old. Stela 23 was reset as a fragment, and the base of Stela 25 was reshaped, so there is no doubt that these monuments were broken before building activity ceased at Tikal, though circumstances indicate that the resetting was done in a very late period (Coe and Broman, 1958). After this group, there is a long hiatus in the monumental sequence, which the undated Stelae 17 and 26 can only partially fill (Satterthwaite, 1958b). There is a similar gap at Uaxactun, and at no site can we follow the transition from Early to Late Classic times in an uninterrupted sequence, except possibly at Caracol, British Honduras, where, however, early traits seem to survive much longer than in the central sites. On Stela 1 erected in 9.8.0.0.0 the figure still stands in the Early Classic pose with its feet both pointing in the same direction. Complex designs above the figure, apparently elaborations of the sky-god motif such as that on Stela 29 at Tikal, survive at least until 9.9.0.0.0, as does the diagonal position of the serpent bar, which is also found at Coba in northern Quintana Roo, where a sequence of stelae begins at about this time. Sequences of monuments spring up almost simultaneously in other outlying regions, each region exhibiting its own highly individual mannerisms.

Period of Reintegration: Third Quarter of Cycle 9

After 9.9.0.0.0 the incidence of known stelae rises rapidly, and one may infer that conditions had stabilized and a period of unprecedented prosperity began in the Maya area. Gradually, regional distinctions fade, and when the Period of Uniformity of the lunar count begins about 9.12.15.0.0, the area is once more united by a homogeneous artistic style, though preferences for certain techniques and arrangements

478

continue to characterize its several regions. Haberland (1953) distinguished four major and three minor provinces and three intermediate regions by the types of ornaments worn by Maya figures, but the major division at this time is between the north and the south roughly on a line connecting Laguna de Terminos with the Bay of Chetumal. This distinction grows sharper with the consolidation of the southern area.

It is not at all improbable that the southern provinces were led to form some sort of affiliation in reaction to continuing border hostilities, especially in the west, where carved stone panels at Piedras Negras frequently feature warriors and portray martial scenes. Stylistically, the period is one of progressive elaboration and refinement of forms, and of expanding variability in motifs, with increasing secular and humanistic concern. Many of the innovations seem to stem from Palenque or from the lower Usumacinta, where lintels and wall panels supplement the conventional stela form.

All the most notable sculpture at Palenque is executed either in very low relief on stone tablets or in stucco on walls and roof combs of buildings. Palenque art is ideographic and pictorial rather than monumental. The figures show very clearly the standard of physical beauty that prevailed among the Maya people. It is a calm, aristocratic beauty without marked sexual features. Musculature is never stressed in the male body, and the characteristics of the female body are modestly concealed. All outlines are fluid and continuous. The face is narrow, with high cheekbones and a prominent curved nose, accentuated by a strong cranial deformation that narrows and slopes the forehead back from lightly indicated brow ridges. The mouth is small, and the chin often recedes and is softly rounded. Eyes have a tendency to slant very slightly, and the upper line is almost straight, whereas the lower curves to meet it at a sharp outer corner. In later times, these traits are variously modified by the requirements of realistic portraiture, and we see harsh, angular features, with creases about the mouth that give the countenance character and asperity (fig. 3,*a*), but at first the aim was to depict an ideal type, serene and without personal idiosyncrasy (figs. 3,*b*; 4).

The deceptive simplicity of Palenque sculptures appeals to the modern taste, and many critics judge it to be the finest sculpture in the Maya area. The composition of symbolic forms in an independent ensemble allowed the artist to concentrate on the portrayal of the human figure without the usual encumbrances of elaborate symbolic accoutrement. The natural lines of the figure are carefully studied and stressed. The symbolic compositions, however, are very complex, and though they reflect a single over-all plan they vary greatly in the detail that gives them specific significance.

On the panel of the Temple of the Cross (fig. 4) and on the lid of the sarcophagus in the tomb beneath the Temple of the Inscriptions (Ruz, 1952d, fig. 10) the central element is a cross that is thought to represent a mythical tree springing from the rear head of a two-headed earth dragon, identified by its fleshless jaw and the three-part symbol above its forehead. The front head of this dragon is a serpentine head and is shown in two profiles enclosing the lower half of the panel and the recumbent human figure on the sarcophagus lid. This suggests that elsewhere human heads in serpent jaws may depict dead heroes. On the cross in both compositions hangs a two-headed serpent, and above is a bird with a grotesque head and with serpent heads on its wings. The designs also include a sky band in which we recognize signs for the sun, the moon, and some of the planets. One gets the impression that the structure of the

FIG. 5—STELA 11, PIEDRAS NEGRAS. Date 9.15.0.0.0. (Courtesy, Peabody Museum, Harvard University.)

479

FIG. 6—STELA P, COPAN, Date 9.9.10.0.0.
(Courtesy, Peabody Museum, Harvard University.)

cosmos is here made to bear upon the mundane scene through the use and manipulation of these symbols.

The two-headed serpent bar is represented at Palenque by the serpent hanging on the tree, but is never shown in the hands of the figures. The object most frequently held is a manikin, sometimes as a small figure seated on a cushion, once as a baby in arms, and in other cases as a short staff or axe, with a mask head at one end, and a snake head on the other. The manikin scepter, which later seems to replace the serpent bar at many sites, probably originates in these earlier Palenque forms.

A close parallel to the Palenque panel compositions occurs on the so-called "niche" stelae of Piedras Negras. Here the principal figure sits in an elevated doorway represented by a niche in the monument, which permits the figure to be shown in high relief (fig. 5). The doorway is draped by raised curtains and a ladder marked with footprints leads up to where the figure is sitting. Over the doorway is a stylized form of the Palenque bird holding a snake in its mouth. Sometimes the head is that of an owl, but more often it is a conventional mask. Surrounding the niche is the sky band of astronomical signs, and below is the two-headed dragon. Human sacrifice is represented in at least two of these compositions. Stelae with the niche motif were always the first of a group to be set up, and I have suggested (1960) that they may celebrate the accession of a new ruler, whose portraits appear on subsequent monuments of the group that show the ruler as a warrior, or scattering grains for planting or for divination, or seated upon a throne in the presence of other figures. Some of the additional figures appear to be women, youths, and children.

Piedras Negras sculpture is notable for its pleasing combination of high and low relief, and for its meticulous rendering of textures and of textile designs. Before 9.12.15.0.0, when the first stela of the group

Fig. 7—STELA 22, TIKAL. Date 9.17.0.0.0, Great period. (Courtesy, University Museum, University of Pennsylvania.)

in front of Str. J-4 was set up, red seems to have been the only pigment used for painting the monuments, and occasionally there are holes for the insertion of elements made of other materials, doubtless to provide accents of contrasting color. After 9.12.15.0.0 this practice was discontinued and stelae were painted in full polychrome. The variety of compositions on stelae at Piedras Negras makes them as a group more expressive than the rigidly designed monuments of the Peten. The relaxation of the pose of the principal figure, however, which later gives them grace and elegance was achieved gradually. Even the sculptured panels that are less formal, as a rule, than stelae, at first depict only static arrays of warriors. It is interesting to observe that

481

FIG. 8—ARCHITECTURAL SCULPTURE. *a*, Part of wooden Lintel 3, Temple I, Tikal. *b*, Stone Lintel 25, Str. 23, Yaxchilan. (Courtesy British Museum.)

such martial motifs become less frequent at Piedras Negras as their incidence rises at Yaxchilan. The later opulence of the city of Yaxchilan, therefore, may be at least partially due to its military enterprises.

Yaxchilan very early developed a typical stela composition. Of its two earliest monuments (Morley, 1938, vol. 5, pl. 103), one, Stela 14, is carved after the manner of the Peten, with the figure holding a serpent bar; but the other, Stela 27, presents a figure that Maler (1901–03, p. 126) called "the benevolent god," pouring from his hands "the good things of life," a form that Rands (1955, figs. 18, 19) later identified with the symbol for water. This type of figure becomes standard at Yaxchilan, and is often associated with portraits enclosed in cartouches above it and with the representation of a two-headed sky serpent (Maler, 1901–03, pls. 69–71). A comparison of the latter form with the earth dragons of Palenque and Piedras Negras gives a good illustration of the sort of structural variation to which Maya grotesques are subject. The serpent heads and the planetary band are here disassociated from the rear head of the dragon and are combined with symbols for the planet Venus and the sun.

Group compositions of figures on stelae are not infrequent at Yaxchilan, and the figure of a warrior is a favorite motif. The elaboration of scenes on lintels, however, probably began after 9.14.0.0.0, and most of the known lintels are considerably later. Morley suggests dates that give the lintels a longer chronological spread, but his earlier dates are unreliable, and many are stylistically improbable. In the early part of the Late Classic period, Yaxchilan was not yet the powerful city it later became, and this we may gather from the fact that its style exerts no great influence in the region between the Jatate River and the Usumacinta, where later it is strongly reflected in the monuments of Bonampak. The early carvings from Bonampak (Rup-

pert, Thompson, and Proskouriakoff, 1955, fig. 16) and Stela 7 at Lacanha (Lizardi Ramos, 1949, fig. 9) show more resemblance to sculptures from Piedras Negras than to those of Yaxchilan.

South of the Jatate, the Classic tradition is found in the foothills of the Chiapas highland, and in the high valley at Chinkultic and Comitan. At Tonina there are a number of statues in full round in addition to the stela form. Such statues are extremely rare in the lowland Maya area, and I know of only two examples, one at Palenque (Ruz, 1958, pl. 51), and another at Yaxchilan (Morley, 1938, pl. 107,a). The technique of carving in full round is here doubtless an influence from styles of western Tabasco or of southern Veracruz.

On the other hand, sculpture in high relief but not altogether in full round is widely distributed along the foothills of the highlands from Palenque to Copan. An early sculptured head from Palenque (Ruz, 1958, fig. 9), a carving from Salinas de los Nueve Cerros, reported by Seler (1902–23, vol. 3, no. 3, pl. 1), and the early stelae of Copan all show a generic similarity. The first stelae of Copan, however, preserve a flatness of relief and an essentially graphic quality (fig. 6) that disappears only when in 9.12.10.0.0, with the erection of Stela 6, new elements of dress that have precedents in the Usumacinta region were introduced into the style. Afterward, Copan rapidly rose to artistic eminence with the design of complex forms freely oriented in space. That the new techniques developed here never spread northward into the central region is probably due to the difficulty of obtaining material of sufficiently good quality in the limestone region. Copan was fortunate in having a local stone, a greenish fine-grained trachyte, that was evidently easily worked in the round.

Group compositions were never attempted on stelae at Copan, but at least one monument, Stela H, appears to represent a woman. It has no Initial Series inscription

a

b

Fig. 9—DETAILS FROM THE MURAL
IN ROOM 2, STR. 1, BONAMPAK.
(Photos by Giles G. Healey; courtesy,
Peabody Museum, Harvard University.)

of its own, but repeats a date on Stela A, and Morley's placement of it one Calendar Round (52 years) later is unjustified, since the two monuments form a pair.

The practice of thus pairing stelae with male and female figures, instead of depicting both on one monument, is illustrated in the Peten by Naranjo Stelae 22 and 24, 30 and 29, 28 and 31, and by Calakmul Stelae 28 and 29. Peten designs continue to be somewhat conservative, but influences from the Lower Usumacinta region are increasingly felt; and after 9.14.0.0.0, when Tikal began to set up a series of stelae placed in enclosures (Satterthwaite, 1956a), we can perceive a gathering momentum in artistic invention.

Classic Style in Northern Yucatan

Northern Yucatan recedes at this time from the main stream of the Late Classic development. Once established, the style of Coba continued for some time with its rigid, somewhat archaic conventions—the diagonal position of the serpent bar, and the stiff pose of the main figure, which stands with small bound prisoners at its feet. Some of the figures are dressed in skirts and may represent women, but other details of their dress and accoutrement are so exactly like those of the men that Charlot fails to distinguish the sexes (Thompson, Pollock, and Charlot, 1932, p. 185). A prevalent feature of dress here is a large, low-hanging pendant suspended from the neck of the figure. This pendant later appears in other regions of Yucatan where some of the qualities of the Classic style persist.

Various local developments in the north interfered with the formation of vigorous regional monumental styles. There is a sufficient scattering of Classic stelae of the third quarter of Cycle 9 in western sites such as Dzibilchaltun, Jaina, and Etzna, to suggest that the Classic style was still dominant, but there are many undated carvings of diverse schools that probably should also be placed in this period. It is very likely that the distinctive styles of architecture in the Puuc and the Chenes regions were just beginning to take form, and the adaptation of figure sculpture to architectural uses produced stylistic changes that we cannot at present date with any degree of accuracy.

Climax: Last Quarter of Cycle 9

The date 9.15.0.0.0 was celebrated on more monuments in the Maya area than any other Period Ending. It marks a climax of a gradual but irregular development that led to what is often called "The Great Period" of Classic lowland art. To be sure, not all the sculpture produced in this period is of equal quality, but the masterpieces far exceed in number those of earlier periods, and many of them come from small sites that are otherwise undistinguished. The best art of this period achieved its expressive power by the relaxation of the pose of the stela figure and by the lively effects of sinuous lines used in the composition of grotesque designs. The trend toward greater freedom in composition undoubtedly originated at Palenque and in the lower Usumacinta area, but influences apparently flowed in both directions. Thus, the motif of the jaguar on a wooden lintel in Temple I of Tikal (fig. 8,a) is duplicated on Stela 10 at Piedras Negras (Morley, 1938, vol. 5, pl. 130,c; Maler, 1901–03, pl. 19), and on Lintel 3 of Tikal's Temple IV (Maudslay, 1889–1902, vol. 3, pl. 77) there is the serpent-winged bird and the two-headed dragon motif that is so characteristic of the western sites. At Palenque we see the influence of more ornate and exuberant schools on such carvings as the two fragments found just southwest of the palace tower (Palacios, 1937, figs. 21, 22).

Experiments in scenic composition are represented by such monuments as Stela 12, Piedras Negras, which depicts a warrior and his prisoners (Maler, 1901–03, pl. 21), and by Lintel 3 (Morley, 1938, vol. 5, pl. 146), on which is presented an audience

485

ticularly for the mural paintings in its Str. 1 (fig. 9). In the context of other Meso-american arts, these paintings are unique in their descriptive power, which uses facial expression and gesture to an unprecedented degree in portraying the scene and bringing out the personal characteristics of even its minor characters. The draftsmanship is superbly sure and free of overpreoccupation with realistic aspects of forms. Unlike the earlier mural of Uaxactun, the Bonampak painting is in full polychrome, and the background of one of the scenes is the vivid "Maya blue," a mysterious pigment no longer in use today. The composition of this pigment has been studied recently by Dr. Rutherford J. Gettens, formerly of the Fogg Museum of Art at Harvard, and by Miss Anna O. Shepard of the Carnegie Institution of Washington, but the results of their investigations have not been fully published and the source of this pigment to this day remains unknown.

At Copan, the stela form retained its somewhat rigid design, and attention was lavished on ornamental detail. After 9.16.-10.0.0 stelae were no longer erected, but architectural sculpture reached a new apex of excellence in the famous "singing girls" or maize gods that once decorated the upper façade of Str. 22 (fig. 10). The inner door of this temple displays the two-headed dragon motif (Trik, 1939, pls. 12, 13), and the outer doorway simulates the open mouth of a huge serpent, which is a treatment typical in the Chenes and Rio Bec regions. At Copan all the designs are rendered in stone, including the masks at the corners of the building. The carving was evidently done *in situ*, but the sculpture must have been roughly blocked out before the pieces were set into the masonry. This technique seems to have been peculiar to Copan, where stucco was little used.

At Quirigua, on the other hand, stucco was the more common medium, and its destruction has left the architecture undistinguished. The sequence of stelae begins

FIG. 10—HEAD OF SEATED STONE FIGURE FROM THE UPPER FAÇADE OF TEMPLE 22, COPAN. (Courtesy, Peabody Museum, Harvard University.)

before the enthroned figure of a chief. The relief on this panel, which is not a true lintel, was actually undercut, so that parts of the figures were in full round; the composition, though badly damaged, still shows the informal grouping and the natural treatment of figures that characterize the masterpieces of this period.

The artists of Yaxchilan had achieved almost equal craftsmanship in carvings prior to 9.15.0.0.0 (fig. 8,*b*), but probably as a result of the city's great military preoccupations its later lintels show a marked decline in originality and technique. As the period progresses there appears also a certain straining after dramatic effects, as, for example, in the enormous size (2.70 by 5.06 m.) of Stela 1 at Bonampak (Ruppert, Thompson, and Proskouriakoff, 1955, fig. 18) and in the exaggerated features of the face of the figure with its deeply undercut pupil or iris of the eye.

Bonampak is a small site and famous par-

here about fifteen years before that at Copan breaks off. Stela H, erected in 9.16.-0.0.0, is in many ways similar to the monuments of Copan, and shows the figure holding a ceremonial bar. Later, the manikin scepter is featured, and some figures are shown in dancing pose, a motif that becomes common at this time in the Peten as well. Perhaps because of the hardness of the native sandstone, round relief was replaced in Quirigua by deep but flat relief combined with fully modeled rendering of the human face and sometimes of the arms and legs, a technique similar to that of Piedras Negras and providing a very effective contrast of forms. The stelae of Quirigua are massive; the largest, Stela E, stands 8.07 m. high and must weigh close to 65 tons. For a time, from 9.17.10.0.0 to 9.18.-5.0.0, huge zoomorphs take the place of stelae. These look like large boulders shaped into various monsters of uncertain genus, sometimes with human figures in their jaws. Some have long inscriptions; with Zoomorphs O and P, there are flat, irregularly shaped carved altars (Maudslay, 1889–1902, pls. 52–57; Morley, 1938, vols. 3, 4, frontispieces). These monuments illustrate the intricacy of Maya symbolic composition at its highest peak, and so far their intent remains problematical.

The almost simultaneous interruption of stela sequences in Copan and Quirigua, and the substitution of grotesque forms, raises the question of a possible influence from the Rio Bec style, which may have been spreading southward into territory that was once part of the Peten. The archaeology of the Rio Bec region and of the Chenes region to the northwest, which has a very similar architecture, is only sketchily known. Enough exploration has been made, however, to indicate that stelae were not part of the cultural complex, and that the distinguishing feature here is the so-called "Quetzalcoatl" façade of buildings, which Thompson has shown to have been misnamed and which he believes sym-

FIG. 11—STELA 10, XULTUN
Date 10.3.0.0.0, Decadent period. (Courtesy, Peabody Museum, Harvard University.)

bolizes the entrance to the underworld by the open jaws of the earth dragon (Thompson, 1942). The sculpture of such façades in the Chenes–Rio Bec region is executed only in part in stone, and is finished with stucco, which carries most of the detail. It

487

is intricate, and striking effects are produced by deep shadows of projecting and receding elements of the stone framework, but its overconcentrated design and its obsession with a single motif precludes variety and originality in its design. While the Rio Bec style seems to have moved southward, the Chenes style encroached upon northern Yucatan, where it became somewhat modified in adapting itself to the technique of building prevalent in the Puuc region. The chronology of these events, however, is obscure since there has been virtually no excavation in Chenes and Rio Bec sites.

Eclipse: First Quarter of Cycle 10

The disappearance of Classic Maya culture has always seemed to observers inexplicably and mysteriously sudden. In the west, at Palenque, at Piedras Negras, and at Yaxchilan, there is no indication of a decline in the arts. The monumental sequences simply stop, when art is at the very peak of its development. At Piedras Negras, signs of violence and destruction may be interpreted as evidence of revolution or conquest, but nowhere are there indications of a later occupation, unless it is in the few fragments of yokes and hachas found in a late deposit at Palenque (Ruz, 1953). At Copan and at Quirigua, at the other extreme of the area, we find exactly the same condition. Only in the central area, along the upper drainage of the Usumacinta and in the highlands of Chiapas, do we find monuments still being erected after 9.19.0.0.0, and even here they are drastically reduced in number. Monuments that can be attributed to the Katun 10.0.0.-0.0–10.1.0.0.0 are so few that the later stelae appear to represent a resumption of the practice of erecting them after a temporary interruption.

Stelae erected immediately after 10.1.-0.0 still follow the Classic tradition, showing, however, a rather restless, flamboyant treatment of forms. After 10.2.0.0.0 there is a definite decline in draftsmanship, and in some cases a relapse into archaic mannerisms or an adoption of exotic traits. The first of these changes is well illustrated by Stelae 3 and 10 at Xultun (10.1.10.0.0, 10.3.0.0.0). The detail on the latter monument is rendered by simple grooves, with virtually no modeling (fig. 11). Stela 50 at Calakmul (Ruppert and Denison, 1943, pl. 50,b) is a very extreme example of the end result of this process of degeneration. The other type of change took place on the periphery of the much reduced Classic area. At Seibal, for example, a comparison of Stela 11, erected in 10.1.0.0.0, with Stela 1, erected in 10.2.0.0.0 (Maler, 1908a, pls. 9, 3) shows a return to the early position of the Maya figure, and to the use of an early type of sandal, apparently due to the influences of a ruder, retarded culture. Stela 3, of unknown date, shows a mixture of traits—the paneled arrangement popular in northern Yucatan, rectangular glyphs containing the cipactli motif used by the Toltec, and Tlaloc and Ehecatl masks that suggest other highland sources (fig. 12,a). On Stela 4 at Ucanal (10.1.0.0.0), a figure in the sky carries darts and an atlatl, a weapon used principally by the Toltec (Morley, 1938, vol. 5, pl. 94,a). At Flores, on the lake where the Itza took their final stand, the serpent motif is stressed on a monument, and the human figure is greatly reduced (Morley, 1938, vol. 5, pl. 157,e). Since no Toltec sites are found anywhere in the vicinity, one is inclined to attribute the exotic traits on late stelae to the intrusion of peoples from highland Guatemala who had long been separated from the main stream of Classic Maya culture.

NORTHERN YUCATAN BEFORE THE TOLTEC CONQUEST

Northern Yucatan, although it had no share in the climactic development of the south, had its own somewhat later period of "Florescence," when a style of architecture originating in the Puuc region, together with a distinct ceramic complex spread over

FIG. 12—SCULPTURES SHOWING VARYING DEGREES OF DIVERGENCE FROM CLASSIC TRADITION. *a*, Stela 3, Seibal. *b*, Stela 21, Oxkintok. *c*, Stela 5, Sayil. *d*, Column of Str. 4B1, Sayil. (Courtesy, Peabody Museum, Harvard University.)

most of the area. This architecture is characterized by finely cut stone which forms a veneer on walls constructed mostly of rubble and concrete. Its decoration consists of presculptured interchangeable elements assembled into masks and geometric forms, occasionally interspersed with organic motifs apparently sculptured *in situ.* The technique is often referred to as "mosaic sculpture," and although it is excellent in craftsmanship, its scope of design is limited. No single monumental style is associated with the Puuc Florescence, though there is reason to think that stelae were being erected at that time in at least some of the sites. They were not placed near the principal temples, however, but were usually collocated on platforms apart from the main architectural groups, and we do not know the character of their association with other remains. It seems likely that the practice of erecting stelae was confined to certain ethnic groups or cults that continued to follow ancient traditions. The monuments that are found in Florescent Puuc sites are generally crudely sculptured and seldom have legible inscriptions (fig. 12,*c*). Some follow fairly closely the standard Classic arrangement of a single figure on the face of the stela; others diverge from it in many different ways. One of the new designs features a paneled arrangement of the field, often with scenes containing two or more figures. It is particularly well represented at the site of Oxkintok, where we also see radical changes in costume. The warrior pictured on Stela 21, for example (fig. 12,*b*), carries a long rectangular shield, wears a bar noseplug, and has vertically arranged plumes on his headdress. These are traits by which Tozzer identifies the Maya in Toltec-dominated Chichen Itza (Tozzer, 1930), a people whose costumes and no doubt also manners and customs were very different from those of the south.

In some sites of the Puuc region, and in others just west of the hills, we find build-ings that lack mosaic sculpture and feature sculptured jambs and columns. In one such building at Xcalumkin there is recorded an Initial Series, reading 9.15.12.6.9 7 Muluc 1 Kankin. The figures carved on the jambs of this building wear the long bar necklace that derives from the earlier Classic figures of Coba, and carry on many features of the Classic tradition. Other figures carved on columns and jambs show varying degrees of relationship to the Classic style (Proskouriakoff, 1950, figs. 94–105). Those at Xculoc and Sayil are similar in their rendering to late decadent monuments and feature a sunken disc worn on the chest of the figure (fig. 12,*d*). The shield carried by warriors is round and very much like that of the Xcalumkin figure. The lack of any traits that would link these sculptures with those of Chichen Itza, and the fact that they remain localized when buildings with mosaic sculpture appear in other regions of northern Yucatan, suggest that sculptured columns were a feature of an earlier phase of development. On the other hand, the high-relief figures that occur on columns at Oxkintok, Dzecilna, Xcochkax, and Dzitbalche may have served as a prototype for the stucco figures that later adorned the colonnades of Mayapan, and they are so unMaya in physical type that one is tempted to attribute them to a very late period when the ethnic composition of peoples in this area was rapidly changing. The chronology of the northern remains, however, is so uncertain and local conditions so diverse that no general scheme of development can be drawn to which one can refer the many contrasting styles that are represented.

Although our inability to draw a consistent picture of art development in northern Yucatan can be blamed in part on the lack of chronological data, it is clear that there was no single standard, no concerted direction to artistic endeavor. Whether the multiplicity of styles which prevented such a spectacular rise as occurred in the south

490

a   b

FIG. 13—MURALS FROM THE NORTHERN REGION. *a,* Restoration by Ann Axtell Morris of a mural from the Temple of the Warriors, Chichen Itza (courtesy, Peabody Museum, Harvard University). *b,* Painting on jamb of inner door of a structure in ruins of Tohcok, Campeche (copy by T. Proskouriakoff).

is also a sign of adaptability that saved the cultures of the north from utter extinction is a question that may well be pondered. When we have enough information to bridge the gaps between the decadence of the Classic style in Yucatan, the emergence of such sculptures as the paneled stelae of Oxkintok or the jambs of Str. 2C6 (the Codz Poop) of Kabah, and the foundation of Toltec Chichen Itza, we may have a history that will enlighten us on the relation of the arts to other aspects of culture, which now we can only vaguely envisage.

PERIOD OF TOLTEC DOMINANCE

The Toltec style when it appears at Chichen Itza is unmistakable. With few exceptions it duplicates in every particular the motifs, the technique, and the arrangement of figures found at Tula, Hidalgo, and it is often assumed that the Toltec brought this style with them into Yucatan. However, it is difficult to account for its origin in the Valley of Mexico where there was no precedent for such low-relief carving. Nor could the source be Veracruz, for the Tol-

tec did not use the ornamental devices that characterize the coastal arts. I strongly suspect that the Toltec may have learned the art of carving from the Maya, either from immigrant artists fleeing from whatever disaster was overtaking their homeland, or perhaps through their conquests in Yucatan. The style of the reliefs on the Pyramid of Xochicalco suggests an intimate blend of Toltec and Maya forms. Moreover, one of the typical motifs of Toltec art, a recumbent figure, could be easily derived from the traditional recumbent figure of the Maya, such, for example, as that on Lintel 39 at Yaxchilan (Maler, 1901–03, pl. 65) or similar molded figures on hemispherical Fine Orange bowls that we find in late ceramic collections from Classic Maya sites. The Late Classic Maya position of the figure and the Maya scroll, although not very common, both occur in Toltec art. What the Toltec themselves contributed was a vigor inherent in their single-minded endeavor to perpetuate the memory of their military and political exploits, carried on under the aegis of the Feathered Serpent.

491

These exploits were group enterprises and the focus of attention is on the group rather than on individuals, who are designated only by name or title. The carving was done on square and round pillars of buildings, on altars interrupting the long benches of colonnades, on the benches of ball courts, on wooden lintels, and on interior walls. Monotonous files of warriors, groups of bound prisoners, and symbols of death and human sacrifice are repeated again and again with little variation (fig. 14,a). Religious symbolism is focused on the feathered serpent and simple animal figures that indicate the military orders, though the serpent-bird and the mask were incorporated in the designs without apparent incongruity. The most successful examples of Toltec art are the murals which present realistic scenes of combat and conquest (fig. 13,a), and the gold discs worked in repoussé which celebrate Toltec victories over the Maya (Lothrop, 1952, figs. 10, 30–37, 40–45).

A curious anomaly among the martial scenes is the composition of the panels on the Temple of the Wall Panels (Ruppert, 1931), which presents a legendary or mythical theme with monkeys and other animals as the protagonists. This composition was undoubtedly derived from the Teotihuacan tradition and is entirely alien to the Maya culture.

Among functional forms introduced by the Toltec were the great serpent columns of the big temples, the chac mool figures reclining with their heads sharply turned to one side and apparently used as repositories for offerings (fig. 14,d) standard bearers designed to hold some sort of emblematic device (fig. 14,b), and the "atlantean" figures, both in the form of interior columns of small temples and as supports for large table altars (fig. 14,c). In Tozzer (1957) one can find a comprehensive discussion of all these Toltec forms.

The promise of a really dramatic art concerned with the realistic presentation of his-

torical events, which was originally inherent in the innovations brought into the Maya area by the Toltec, apparently did not have an opportunity to mature. In the later productions of Chichen Itza there is a noticeable falling off in the quality of the carving, with increasing reliance on paint to conceal its defects and on various devices such as space-fillers to round out imperfect compositions. The destruction of the city finally put a stop to all ambitious projects, and neither sculpture nor painting ever rose again in the Maya area to the level of a fine art.

MAYAPAN

The sculpture and the painting of this last great city are purely religious and symbolic, making no attempt at a descriptive treatment of reality. The murals that survive in the east coast cities of Quintana Roo (fig. 15) and at Santa Rita in British Honduras (Gann, 1900, pl. 30) are very much like pictures in Maya codices and deal largely with anthropomorphic divinities, which probably originate in Mexico or in the Mixtec area. A similar style was used on stelae at Mayapan, to judge from the one surviving example preserved in the hacienda at Xcanchakan. Morley (1920, fig. 90) has pointed out its close resemblance to a page of the Paris Codex. The small figures and the paneled arrangement are no doubt derived from earlier monuments such as those of Oxkintok, but the scenes no longer pertain to human activities. The relief is completely flat, detail being shown with incising or grooving, and the glyphs are merely blocked out to be painted in the squares above the figures. Anthropomorphic gods are portrayed at Mayapan also as full-round figures in stone and stucco, apparently the "idols" that it was said were introduced by the founder of the city, a Mexican called Kukulcan (the Feathered Serpent). Sometimes these sculptures were constructed in parts, doweled together or tenoned into masonry. The crude joints

Fig. 14—SCULPTURES FROM CHICHEN ITZA. *a*, Toltec warrior from Column 3, Temple of the Warriors, Chichen Itza. *b*, Standard bearer, Temple of the Warriors. *c*, Atlantean altar support, Temple of the Warriors. *d*, Chac mool statue from the Platform of the Eagles, Chichen Itza. (Courtesy, Peabody Museum, Harvard University.)

FIG. 15—DETAIL OF MURAL FROM TEMPLE OF THE DIVING GOD, TULUM, QUINTANA ROO. (Courtesy, Peabody Museum, Harvard University.)

receptacle in its back (fig. 16). The turtle often has the head of an old man, tentatively identified with God D of the Maya codices, and the interesting feature of these sculptures is that the semblance of an animal form is retained even when the figure is fully anthropomorphic, for the old man is often shown crouching under a mantle that simulates the form of a carapace. Such imposition of an animal form on a human subject is characteristic of earlier arts in Veracruz.

One can get a better idea of the art of Mayapan from the numerous pottery incense burners with attached figures than from the badly weathered sculptures, which are essentially in the same style. Thompson (1957) finds that Mexican and Maya gods occur in almost equal numbers. The gods can be recognized by the symbols they wear, by their body paint, and by occasional grotesque facial features. Otherwise, they are all designed after a set pattern that leaves very little to artistic choice. The style was widespread at this time, and similar incense burners have been found on the east coast of Yucatan, in surface deposits as Chichen Itza, and in sporadic surface finds at many other northern sites.

THE CENTURY BEFORE THE CONQUEST

Uninteresting as is the art of Mayapan, after the destruction of the city in the middle of the 15th century, it seems to have deteriorated still further. Andrews (1939) has reported some sculptures from Telantunich, in central Quintana Roo, that he believes were made in this period. The technique of these sculptures is an ancient one observed in the highlands of Guatemala and named "silhouetted relief" by Kidder (Kidder, Jennings, and Shook, 1946, pp. 102, 103), the form being blocked out by perforations cut through a slab of stone. There is no apparent stylistic relation, however, between the early carvings of Guatemala and those found at Telantunich. The

were smoothed out with plaster, and the statues were then painted. High-relief modeled figures of stucco were applied to columns, and though they can hardly be regarded as works of art, the few fragments that remain show somewhat greater artistry than do the stone cult objects.

Grotesque symbolism survives at Mayapan in the form of the serpent column, which is changed into a monster with forefeet, seeming to combine an earlier Maya conception of the earth dragon with that of the Toltec serpent. A small figure astride the serpent head is an innovation of unknown origin (see Proskouriakoff, 1962b).

A type of portable sculpture closely associated with worship in small shrines takes the form of a turtle, sometimes with a small

phallic motif is strong in these sculptures, and Andrews (1943) also describes similarly worked phallic figures still used today as idols at Pustunich in southwestern Campeche.

His reports raise an interesting question concerning sporadic occurrences of phallic symbolism in earlier times. Such symbolism is not normally associated with any of the major styles on the peninsula, but we find some evidences of it with both Puuc and Toltec remains. The Phallic Group at Chichen Itza takes its name from the association of phallic forms with a building built in the Puuc tradition, and Tozzer (1957, pp. 110, 111) mentions six sites in the Puuc region, where phallic symbols have been found. In late Toltec times, figures with exposed genitals occur in the Mercado and in the Temple of the Little Heads. These manifestations are entirely foreign to the spirit of Classic Maya art, and seem to be associated with its decadence, perhaps connoting the presence of popular cults suppressed by state religions but emerging repeatedly in periods of stress and decline. The impossibility of dating closely such aberrant sculptures, however, leaves the significance of their occurrence problematical.

FIG. 16—STONE TURTLE FROM MAYAPAN. (Courtesy, Peabody Museum, Harvard University.)

MONUMENTAL ART AND THE MINOR CRAFTS

Many pieces of jade, shell, pottery, and bone that are found in lowland Maya sites exhibit as much artistry as the finest of Maya sculptures. The relations between the craft styles and the prevalent monumental style, however, are not always the same and reflect changes in the status and organization of various artisans.

Pottery from the earliest deposits of the major sites, though excellently made, is decorated in very simple and primitive fashion, and it is probably safe to assume that Classic Maya art developed first in other media. Many of the angular designs on very early Peten gloss wares bear no relation to the style of the major arts.

Others, on tetrapod vessels found in early Holmul tombs, already show the qualities that distinguish the Classic Maya style: scroll arrangements based on the structure of the serpent grotesque, a decided preference for rectangularity, and a line of rhythmically varying curvature that avoids both circular and angular forms. This style is firmly established in Tzakol 2 and 3 polychromes, and shows advanced specialization in its adaptation of human figures and other complex motifs to the restricted field provided by the conventional vessel forms. In jade relief carving of the early period, the human figure is likewise simplified by specific conventions peculiar to the craft, and the serpent head is a common grotesque, having essentially the same structure as in monumental art. The purely hieratic and naturalistic modes proper to monuments and painting never appear in relief on jade. Such designs are merely incised, as on the well-known Leyden Plate, which presents a typical stela figure. When similar figures appear on pottery, the vessel is first coated with stucco and then painted. This suggests that the artists were not trained in craft techniques and argues a considerable degree of specialization and organization within the orbit of a single artistic tradition.

The use of hieroglyphs in ceramic decoration is rare in the Early Classic period, but increases enormously in the Tepeu 1 phase. This might be explained by the growing literacy of Maya communities, but it seems more likely that there was developing a distinct group of trained artisans, who later began to specialize in the art of prefired figure painting on simple cylindrical vessels. These artisans were painters of the first rank, and their art, less hampered by hieratic conventions, often surpasses that of the sculptors. The principal centers of figure painting appear to have been located in the eastern half of the Peten and in Alta Verapaz. In the west, plastic techniques were more highly developed, and the figurines of Jonuta and Jaina are prized for their often informal and very realistic representations. The majority of the ceramic craftsmen of the Late Classic period, however, reverted to much simpler designs based on repetitive patterns, and the regional differences that developed seem to bear no relationship to the prevalent sculptural styles. Thus, for example, at Copan, where sculpture was in the purest Maya tradition, figure-painted pottery is strongly influenced by styles of Salvador. Palenque, so expressive in its sculpture, produced virtually no decorated pottery, but Alta Verapaz, where no Maya sculpture, stelae or masonry vaults are known, is famous for pottery vessels painted with human and animal figures in the lowland Maya style.

The stylistic diversity of local crafts, at a time when the integrity of the monumental style was at its peak, suggests cosmopolitan communities, possibly with considerable ethnic diversity in their composition, united chiefly by the common tradition of a socially superior class. It argues a high development of formal institutions that tend to isolate and preserve a dominant tradition against many competing influences.

Toward the end of the Classic period there is a sharp decline in the ceramic arts. Occasional pieces were impressed by molds with monumental motifs, but the situation was probably very much like that in northern Yucatan in the period that is usually designated as "Florescent," when, with the exception of rare pieces of carved Slate Ware, most vessels are decorated with a very simple trickle technique, or with incised designs crudely copied from imported wares. This indicates a more dispersed and less specialized craft, and it is probably for this reason that it was little affected by the Toltec conquest.

The Toltec imposed their martial motifs and the feathered-serpent theme on designs in jade, and probably stimulated the craft of jade carving by the importation of jades of fine quality from Mexico, but we do not know whether any of their designs were made locally in Yucatan or by Maya craftsmen. It is suggestive, however, that though the technique of gold repoussé work was undoubtedly a Toltec importation, and though the discs recovered from the Sacrificial Cenote of Chichen Itza repeatedly show the Toltec victorious over the Maya, the use of hieroglyphs and Maya grotesques indicate that the craftsmen were almost certainly Maya and not the conquerors themselves.

After the fall of Chichen Itza, all arts and crafts deteriorated sharply and reverted to a primitive equivalence, so that the dominant style is expressed best in pottery incense burners rather than in monumental sculpture. This condition probably connotes a very low order of specialization and organization of craftsmen and no distinction of art as an independent pursuit.

The varying situations are, to be sure, much more complex in fact than they appear in these summary statements, and our knowledge of the distribution of the minor crafts is as yet insufficient to lead to definite conclusions. Nevertheless, the rich potential for inference on social organization inherent in the relations of the arts and

496

crafts is increasingly being drawn upon in archaeological reports, and we are probably approaching a time when such material can be put to use in attempts at historical reconstruction of the changing social conditions that are implied by successive archaeological phases.

SUMMARY

The dramatic development of the Classic Maya style in the southern lowlands had a climax and denouement worthy of a noble tragedy. It documents the rise and fall of a civilization to which it is so intimately related that the two can be identified without equivocation. The situation in the north seems to have been very different. Here the arts rose but to moderate competence. There were many styles, but only one, the style of the conquering Toltec, that we can identify with a coherent tradition. For the historian of culture as well as for the historian of art, the contrast between the north and the south should present some points of unusual interest. The unique symbolism represented in Classic Maya grotesques merits more detailed study than it has so far received. It might be pertinent to inquire why such symbolism did not spread to the north, and why naturalism stopped short of comparable development there. Possibly the variety of styles in the northern region was in itself a factor that prevented a single direction in artistic development, or there may have been social conditions that inhibited the emergence of unusual talent. There is yet much basic work to be done in the northern area before the art historian has sufficient chronological and cultural data to attack these questions. What is more, the function of the arts in incipient civilizations and their effect on other aspects of culture are not at present well enough understood to guide us in the selection of the qualities in art that are of greatest evolutionary significance. We can only rely on the general observation that the arts of the Maya people living in the southern lowlands possessed an eloquence that has been able to overcome to an extraordinary degree the formidable barriers of time and cultural contrast that stand between us and the Maya and to make their life vivid if not altogether comprehensible to us. This surely is one of the more striking results of cultural evolution that in many other respects has gradually broadened and intensified man's awareness not only of the universe that surrounds him but also of his own past.

REFERENCES

Andrews, 1939, 1943
Berlin, n.d.
Coe, W. R., and Broman, 1958
Cook de Leonard, 1959a
Covarrubias, 1957
Gann, 1900, 1926
Haberland, 1953
Kelemen, 1956
Kidder, Jennings, and Shook, 1946
Lizardi R., 1949
Lothrop, 1924, 1952
Maler, 1901–03, 1908a, 1908b
Maudslay, 1889–1902
Médioni, 1950
Morley, 1920, 1937–38, 1946
Palacios, 1937
Pijoán, 1946

Proskouriakoff, 1950, 1960, 1962a
Rands, 1953, 1955
Ruppert, 1931
—— and Denison, 1943
——, Thompson, and Proskouriakoff, 1955
Ruz L., 1952d, 1953, 1958
Satterthwaite, 1956a, 1958a, 1958b
Seler, n.d., 1902–23
Shook, 1940
Smith, A. L., 1950
Smith, R. E., 1955b
Spinden, 1913
Thompson, J. E. S., 1942, 1948, 1954a, 1957
——, Pollock, and Charlot, 1932
Toscano, 1944
Tozzer, 1930, 1957
Trik, 1939

19. Pottery of the Maya Lowlands

ROBERT E. SMITH and
JAMES C. GIFFORD

THIS EXAMINATION of pottery recovered archaeologically from the Maya Lowland Region will review the subject geographically and chronologically. The availability of source material, together with limitations concerning the data and nature of the evidence at hand from the subregions and periods, will be indicated. The information that has been derived from excavations and survey for the Maya lowlands is quite uneven, however, particularly as it pertains to ceramics. In some locales sites have been intensively excavated, in others they have only been sampled by minor excavations, and in still others they have been viewed merely in rapid survey.[1] Ceramic evidence from the domestic and ceremonial contexts of Maya sites and settlements is not comparable in kind. In general, ceremonial centers have received more attention; and in some of these, because of dating possibilities by means of calendrical inscriptions on monuments, pottery has been neglected as a way to chronology. Recently, with a shift in interest to smaller, presumably domestic or rural sites that are devoid of monuments or great architec-

tural endeavors, ceramics have assumed a more important role as indicators of time.

Maya pottery changed profoundly and diversely through time. When these ceramic changes cluster at demonstrable points in a chronology, the pottery comes to form a substantial portion of the evidence used by the archaeologist to mark off major

---

[1] *Sites intensively excavated*—Southern Subregion: San Jose, Benque Viejo, Barton Ramie, Uaxactun, and Copan. Northern Subregion: Chichen Itza, Santa Cruz, and Mayapan. *Sites sampled by comparatively less intensive or minor excavations*—Southern Subregion: Holmul and Guaytan. Western Subregion: Palenque. *Sites investigated as part of archaeological surveys*—Northern Subregion: Acanceh, Yaxuna, Mani, Coba, sites in the Puuc Sector (Brainerd), Dzibilnocac, and Santa Rosa Xtampak (Brainerd collections in Merida Museum), Tancah, Tulum, and Ichpaatun (Sanders), Xicalango, and Jaina (Ruz). Western Subregion: Atasta, Jonuta, and Tecolpan (Berlin, 1956) and Tiradero (Berlin, 1953). A number of sites have received archaeological attention, sometimes of rather impressive proportions, such as Dzibilchaltun, Altar de Sacrificios, and Tikal; but where detailed ceramic data have as yet not been published, they are not listed. For important lowland Maya ceramic relationships with sites in Chiapas, Mexico (an area outside the scope of this article), see various papers of the New World Archaeological Foundation and the work of Bruce W. Warren.

periods and phases. For chronological purposes midden or refuse dumps are the best deposits. Unfortunately, these are rare in Maya sites. Much of the Maya lowlands is a porous limestone, scantily covered with soil. Such a lack of soil made it necessary for the prehistoric populations to salvage refuse dumps and use these deposits for structural pack between floors, as cores for mounds, or in fill for plazas. Those middens which remain and which have been found are, for the most part, of two categories: those of a single phase, with or without minor chronological change, and the extremely scarce multiple-phase deeply stratified deposits. Examples of the former are the accumulations found in inside corners at the base of terraces at Uaxactun (R. E. Smith, 1955b, pp. 15–16), Kabah, Uxmal,[21] Chichen Itza,[2j] and Mayapan.[2r] Instances of the latter include the deep subplaza

---

[2] Bibliographic site references are indicated by the footnote number 2 plus a lowercase letter (such as [2a]). Sites about which we have important ceramic information are listed alphabetically by subregion. Seldom are more than two authors responsible for published or "to be published" pottery analytical data concerning any one site.

Southern Subregion:
[2a] Barton Ramie: Two reports are in preparation concerning recently completed excavations at this site: *Prehistoric Maya Settlements in the Belize Valley* by Gordon R. Willey, William R. Bullard, John B. Glass, and James C. Gifford; and *Maya Pottery from Barton Ramie in the Belize Valley* by James C. Gifford. Both monographs are to appear as Papers of the Peabody Museum, Harvard University.
[2b] Benque Viejo: J. E. S. Thompson, 1940.
[2c] Copan: Longyear, 1952.
[2d] Guaytan: A. L. Smith and Kidder, 1943.
[2e] Holmul: Merwin and Vaillant, 1932.
[2f] Piedras Negras: Butler, 1935b. Robert L. Rands has recently studied those collections of pottery from this site that are in the University Museum at the University of Pennsylvania; his report concerning this material is in preparation.
[2g] San Jose: J. E. S. Thompson, 1939a.
[2h] Uaxactun: Ricketson and Ricketson, 1937; R. E. Smith, 1955b.

Northern Subregion:
[2i] Acanceh: Brainerd, 1958.
[2j] Chichen Itza: Brainerd, 1958; R. E. Smith, in preparation.
[2k] Coba: Brainerd, 1958.

refuse at Uaxactun (R. E. Smith, 1955b, pp. 13–15, Pits E4 and A2), the Santa Cruz site (R. E. Smith, 1954a, pp. 53–56, Platform A), and the Barton Ramie, British Honduras, house mounds.[2a]

Differences in Maya pottery can also be indicative of functional contexts, and the kinds of pottery represented may provide clues as to the ceremonial or nonceremonial use of a site or building. Our present limited knowledge of the relationships between

---

[21] Kabah and Uxmal: Brainerd, 1958; R. E. Smith, in preparation.
[2m] Dzibilchaltun: Brainerd, 1958; Andrews, 1959, 1960. Further reports concerning recent excavations at this site are in preparation by Andrews (1960).
[2n] Dzibilnocac: Merida Museum Collections, Brainerd.
[2o] Ichpaatun: Sanders, 1960a.
[2p] Jaina: Ruz, 1945a.
[2q] Mani: Brainerd, 1958.
[2r] Mayapan: Brainerd, 1958; R. E. Smith, in preparation.
[2s] Santa Cruz: R. E. Smith, 1954a, 1955a.
[2t] Santa Rosa Xtampak: Merida Museum Collections, Brainerd.
[2u] Tancah: Sanders, 1960a.
[2v] Tulum: Sanders, 1960a.
[2w] Xicalango: Ruz, 1945a.
[2x] Xpuhil: Brainerd, 1958.
[2y] Yaxuna: Brainerd, 1958.

Western Subregion:
[2z] Atasta: Berlin, 1956.
[2aa] Comalcalco: Collections of pottery from this site are under study by Gordon F. Ekholm at the American Museum of Natural History in New York and by others, principally Ramón Piña Chan at the Instituto Nacional de Antropología e Historia in Mexico.
[2bb] Jonuta: Berlin, 1956.
[2cc] Palenque: Rands and Rands, 1957, 1959. Other studies by the Rands are in preparation. See also B. C. Rands, 1954; Ruz, 1958.
[2dd] Tecolpan: Berlin, 1956.
[2ee] Tiradero: Berlin, 1953.

There are also several significant general and special studies dealing with lowland Maya pottery such as Vaillant, 1927; J. E. S. Thompson, 1945; Wauchope, 1950; and R. E. Smith, 1958. Archaeological excavations now in progress at Altar de Sacrificios under the direction of Gordon R. Willey and A. L. Smith and at Tikal under the direction of Edwin M. Shook and William R. Coe should disclose valuable ceramic information that will constitute forthcoming pottery reports. For Altar de Sacrificios see R. E. W. Adams, 1962, 1963; for Tikal, reports in preparation by T. P. Culbert.

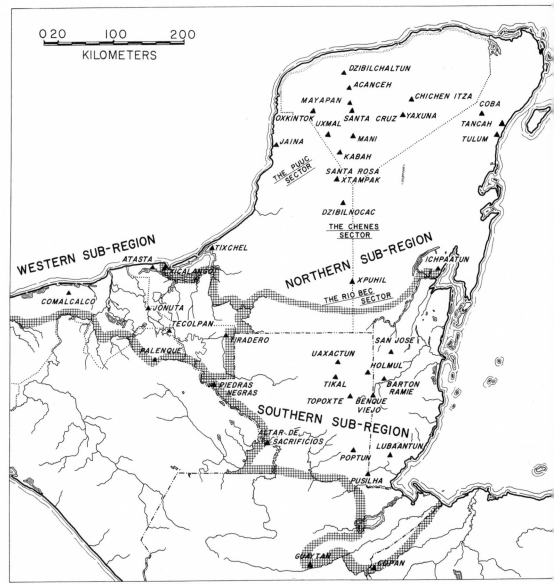

Fig. 1—MAP OF THE LOWLAND MAYA REGION SHOWING SUBREGIONS AND SITES ABOUT WHICH IMPORTANT EVIDENCE IS KNOWN OF THE POTTERY

ceramics and settlement or architectural types, however, seldom permits us to make such judgments on the basis of pottery types alone.

Both chronological and functional aspects of a situation are frequently represented in the same deposit. Being often of foreign manufacture or purposely commissioned for a special occasion, burial or cache pottery tells something of the mortuary or religious customs and also provides

important associations of a chronological and cross-cultural sort that help the archaeologist link related time periods and postulate trade between regions. Mayapan furnishes excellent examples of the different physical situations in which pottery is found in Maya ruins. Here, debris at the base of a ceremonial pyramid is overwhelmingly stocked with effigy censers; a midden associated with the kitchen of a residential structure is filled with cooking

500

and storage vessel fragments; a collection from a cenote contains abundant water-jar pieces; and a normal house-mound fill deposit includes a little of everything in the way of ceramic detritus.

In a broader frame of reference certain intrinsic changes in pottery, indicative not only of chronology but disparities in context suggestive of function, may allow for hypotheses concerning the general development of Maya civilization. For example, Early Classic Maya pottery appears to be relatively uniform from Piedras Negras[2f] in the west, through Uaxactun[2h] and Tikal in the central Peten, to Barton Ramie[2a] in British Honduras in the east. With respect to these sites this ceramic uniformity links ceremonial centers as well as rural house-mound groups. Despite local frequency differences in types, the same excellent decorated and monochrome pottery types seem to extend all along this line. Although attribute and mode differences do exist from one site to another, they are *within types* and these differences may be easily encompassed on a *variety* basis. This contrasts with pottery of the succeeding Late Classic period when new types set off British Honduras and the central Peten and even the western Peten from one another. Where differences had been of a varietal magnitude, they are now between types, and the former close ceramic affinities no longer obtain either geographically or between ceremonial centers and rural domestic communities.

Such observations are extremely tentative, but we offer them as a working hypothesis and submit that over-all considerations of this kind are a key to further study bearing on both chronological and functional relationships within Maya pottery as a whole.

Subregional Review

In this review we refer to ceramic types, varieties, modes, groups, complexes, and wares (defined in note 3) by specific names.

Each name stands for a body of descriptive data. This systematic organization of Maya ceramics has been made in the belief that pottery analysis will yield greater return for

[3] A *pottery type* is a recognizably distinct ceramic unit that represents an aggregate of explicit ceramic attributes, also objectified within one or several varieties, that, when taken as a whole, are indicative of a particular class of pottery produced during a specific time interval within a specific region. A type is always the sum total of its established variety plus all other varieties within its sphere.

The *ceramic variety* is viewed as the basic unit of analysis, which in due course, consequent on an increase in depth of total ceramic knowledge, becomes synonymous with either the type (as in the case of a single-variety type) or one of a number of varieties within a type.

A *pottery mode* is an attribute or, far more often, a cluster of attributes that, as a discrete vessel segment, displays significance in its own right. We feel it is best to study modes separately in order to ascertain their individual behavior in cross-cutting varieties and types through time and space. (Phillips and Gifford, 1959; Smith, Willey, and Gifford, 1960.)

A *ceramic group* is a set of closely related and very similar pottery types that demonstrate a distinctive homogeneity in range of variation concerning form, base color, technological and other allied attributes. Types included within any one ceramic group are always of the same pottery ware. A ceramic group is in a sense more or less a "super-type." (Smith and Gifford, 1959, revised edition as explained in note 4.) In the analysis of Maya pottery recovered from Barton Ramie in British Honduras (Willey, Bullard, Glass, and Gifford, 1965), the problem of naming individual ceramic groups was resolved in the following way. Since in any single ceramic group there are represented a number of type-classes (red, incised, black-on-red, composite), the name of the ceramic group does not include any type-class term. If a type-class term is included, the inference is unavoidable that all the types involved are of that type-class. This could be true in some cases, but more often it is not. Following this observation, the Barton Ramie studies dropped the type-class term; for example, the Palmar Polychrome Group became the Palmar Ceramic Group. This was instigated by Albert H. Norweb, who made the points outlined above after reading a copy of the present manuscript. Because we felt this change to be of importance to the entire approach, the ceramic group nomenclature in this text has been altered to reflect the deletion of type-class terms from ceramic group titles. In order to cause the minimum word deletion in the proofs, type-class terms have been transposed from within the ceramic group title to preceding the title. We intend that the

501

cultural study if it is founded on a basic corpus of comparable ceramic units that have been defined in detail.[4]

Geographically, we have divided the Maya Lowland Region into Southern, Northern, and Western subregions (fig. 1). The Southern Subregion takes in the eastern part of southern Campeche in Mexico, the Peten and lower Motagua Valley in Guatemala, British Honduras, and the extreme western fringe of Honduras; the Northern Subregion, entirely within the Peninsula of Yucatan, includes Yucatan, Quintana Roo, and northern Campeche; the Western Subregion, also in Mexico, comprises southwestern Campeche, Tabas-

co, and northeastern Chiapas. We shall briefly recapitulate the ceramic development in the three subregions and then give somewhat closer scrutiny to their ceramic content period by period. Four of the more prominent local phase sequences are correlated in figure 2.

Southern Subregion

Here the key sites are: Uaxactun and Holmul in the Peten; San Jose, Benque Viejo, and Barton Ramie in central western British Honduras; Guaytan in the Motagua Valley of Guatemala; and Copan in western Honduras.[2a-h] Uaxactun, Holmul, San Jose, Benque Viejo, and Barton Ramie, all in the heavily forested greater Peten, have much in common environmentally as well as culturally.

During the Middle Preclassic period (earliest period represented in this part of the Maya lowlands), at sites where they occur, Mamom-like ceramic complexes present themselves from the start as well-developed pottery configurations. In the Late Preclassic, sequent Chicanel-like ceramic complexes manifest a special versatility with respect to forms and the selective addition of certain dichrome decorative techniques.

Ceramic complexes follow which cover a Late Preclassic to Early Classic Transitional interval. These are Protoclassic complexes (Wauchope, 1950, pp. 220–21), called Matzanel at Uaxactun where it was barely present, Holmul I at Holmul, and Floral Park at Barton Ramie (Willey and Gifford, 1961). The major Protoclassic representation is at the latter two sites and at Poptun, where the complex was never named. A decidedly eastern geographical orientation is suggested which ranges through British Honduras, and just over the border this colony shares with Guatemala. These complexes include a number of types and modes new and easily distinguished from the pottery that had been prevalent before. Among the most impor-

words transposed (red, orange, polychrome, and others) be regarded simply as adjectives. For example, Palmar Polychrome Group becomes polychrome Palmar Group. Ultimate usage, however, we feel should be Palmar Ceramic Group. These changes could not be made in the charts (figs. 4, 5); in the captions to figures 6–16 the color adjective refers to the group and does not necessarily describe the exact color of the specific vessel depicted.

A *ceramic complex* is the sum total of modes and varieties (types) that comprises the full pottery content of an archaeological unit; usually that unit is a phase. The content of any one ceramic complex is accordingly all that is known of the pottery in a culture of a region, subregion, or locality during a specified interval of time (Phillips and Gifford, 1959). Subcomplexes may also exist that are specially oriented toward religious, ceremonial, or other patterns within any given phase of a culture.

A *pottery ware* is composed of types that are similar technologically, displaying a close consistency in range of variation with regard to attributes of surface finish and paste composition (excepting temper). Member types of a ware usually show sundry techniques of decoration, surface manipulation, shape and other nontechnological attributes.

[4] See Phillips and Gifford, 1959, and the following papers, which discuss the reasons and desirability for pottery analysis oriented toward cultural inference as well as description: Smith, Willey, and Gifford, 1960; Gifford, 1960; Rands, 1961a,b; Smith and Gifford, 1959. The last refers to a limited mimeographed edition of "A check list of prehistoric Maya pottery types and varieties," originally circulated by the authors as a preliminary working draft. Now obsolete, it will be replaced by a revised edition (Smith and Gifford, in press).

TIME	YUCATAN	UAXACTUN	BARTON RAMIE	SAN JOSE
1500	CHAUACA			
	CHIKINCHEL			
1400	TASES			
1300				
1200	HOCABA		(ABANDONMENT ?)	
1100	SOTUTA	(ABANDONMENT ?)	NEW TOWN	(ABANDONMENT ?)
1000				
900	CEHPECH	TEPEU 3	SPANISH	SAN JOSE V
800		TEPEU 2	LOOKOUT	SAN JOSE IV
700	MOTUL	TEPEU 1	TIGER RUN	SAN JOSE III
600				
500		TZAKOL 3		
400	COCHUAH	TZAKOL 2		SAN JOSE II
300			HERMITAGE	
200		TZAKOL 1		
100	CHAKAN	MATZANEL	FLORAL PARK	
A.D./B.C.				
100			MOUNT	
200			HOPE	
300				
400	TIHOSUCO	CHICANEL	BARTON CREEK	SAN JOSE I
500				
600			JENNEY CREEK	
700				
800				
900	CUPUL	MAMOM		
1000				
	? ↓ ? ECAB	↓ ?	↓ ?	

FIG. 2—CORRELATION OF LOCAL PHASE SEQUENCES REPRESENTED IN YUCATAN,[2j,r] AT UAXACTUN,[2h] BARTON RAMIE[2a] (PROVISIONAL), AND SAN JOSE.[2g] The most recent revision of the local phase sequences represented here, together with the time intervals now thought most appropriate to them, may be found in Willey, Bullard, Glass, and Gifford, in press, fig. 3.

tant form modes are mammiform tetrapodal supports on vases or bowls with outcurving sides angling to a convex base and spouted jars. It is in this set of Protoclassic ceramic complexes that polychrome painted pottery first makes its appearance in Maya lowlands, thus heralding the advent of the Classic Maya polychrome ceramic sequences that spread over the entire Lowland Region to hold sway in Maya pottery for hundreds of years to come.

Commencing in the Early Classic period, the focal points of Maya pottery are in the greater Peten. Here the ceramics of such complexes as Tzakol 1 through Tepeu 2 at Uaxactun,[2h] San Jose II–IV,[2g] and Hermit-

age through Spanish Lookout at Barton Ramie[2a] reveal the development of the pottery-making standards of Classic Maya. As do the Protoclassic complexes, Tepeu 3–like ceramic complexes suggest another period of pottery transition, this time from Late Classic Tepeu 2–like materials to an Early Postclassic which is contemporaneous at least in part with the Cehpech ceramic complex[21] to the north.

At many of the sites examined in the lowlands there is definite ceramic evidence of Postclassic occupation both in rural communities and in the environs of, if not in, ceremonial centers themselves. The decorated and red pottery types involved seem

503

An indication by period of the ceramic evidence for occupation in the Maya Lowlands at 27 sites and the Puuc Sector

		EARLY PRECLASSIC	MIDDLE PRECLASSIC	LATE PRECLASSIC	PROTOCLASSIC	EARLY CLASSIC	LATE CLASSIC	LATE CLASSIC – EARLY POSTCLASSIC TRANSITION	EARLY POSTCLASSIC	MIDDLE POSTCLASSIC	LATE POSTCLASSIC	PROTOHISTORIC	COLONIAL
SOUTHERN · SUB-REGION	Barton Ramie		X	X	▲	▲	▲	X	▲				
	Benque Viejo		●	●		●	▲	X	●				
	Copan		●	X		▲	▲	X	●				
	Guaytan		O	●		X	▲	●	O				
	Holmul				X	▲	X						
	San Jose		O	X		▲	▲	X	O				
	Uaxactun		▲	▲	●	▲	▲	▲	O				
NORTHERN · SUB-REGION	Acanceh			X		●	X	●	●	●	●		
	Chichen Itza			X	O	X	●	X	▲	▲	X		
	Coba					X	▲	●	O	O	●		
	Dzibilnocac		●	X	O	X	X	▲					
	Ichpaatun									X	▲		
	Jaina					●	X	X	●	O	●		●
	Mani	▲	X	X	O	X	●	X	●	X	X	●	▲
	Mayapan		●	●	O	X	X	X	X	▲	▲	O	X
	Santa Cruz		●	X	O	●	X	●	X	X			
	Santa Rosa Xtampak		X	X	O	X	X	▲					
	Tancah			X	O	X	X	X	●	X	●	O	
	Tulum									X	▲	O	O
	Xicalango		●	X	●	●	●		●	●	X		
	Xpuhil		●	X	O	X	X	▲					
	Yaxuna		●	X		X	X	▲	X	●	●		
	Puuc Sector		O	●		●	●	▲	●				
WESTERN · SUB-REGION	Atasta					●	●	●			▲	X	
	Jonuta					X	▲	●					
	Palenque		●	●		●	▲	●	●				
	Tecolpan					X	▲	●					
	Tiradero		●	X		●	●	●					

KEY: Ceramic evidence for occupation at a site during a given period may be questionable (O); present, but rare, or not enough is known of the pottery to enable further assessment (●); moderate to well represented (X); or abundant (▲).

FIG. 3—EVALUATION BY PERIOD OF THE CERAMIC EVIDENCE FOR OCCUPATION AT CERTAIN MAYA LOWLAND SITES. In some instances evaluations will be more heavily graded than are type representations for equivalent periods in fig. 4. When this happens, it means pottery type occurrences have been taken into account that are not listed in fig. 4.

to exhibit northern influences that tend to relate them to fine orange Silho Group specimens and to a few others assignable to the Sotuta Ceramic Complex of the Early Postclassic period in the Northern Subregion. Quite recently excavations at Flores and inspection of other miscellaneous collections from sites around Lake Peten (George L. Cowgill,[5] personal communications, 1960), in house mounds and elsewhere at Tikal (R. E. W. Adams and Trik, 1961; E. M. Shook, personal communications, 1960–61), and at Barton Ramie[2a] have unearthed Early Postclassic ceramic material that suggests a considerable pottery and population distribution for this period.

From Barton Ramie house mounds the Early Postclassic pottery has been called the New Town Ceramic Complex.[2a] It is of particular interest for at least two reasons: (a) there is a complete shift in the nature of the pottery involved which is marked by a demonstrable change in and near collapse of pottery-production standards, and (b) the ratio of decorated and red types to unslipped or rough surfaced types falls dramatically.

At Topoxte William R. Bullard, Jr., discovered in the course of a settlement pattern survey (1960b) and in subsequent test excavations during the 1960 season at the island site itself (personal communications, 1960–61) that there is present what may be considered a Late Postclassic phase. Thus far Topoxte is the only known site where such a Late Postclassic complex is represented in the Southern Subregion.

Guaytan,[2d] in the middle Motagua Valley, seems to have a distinctive subpattern of its own, differing in some respects rather strikingly from that of the Peten. Only

---

[5] Cowgill has also found Early Postclassic pottery types such as Ixpop Polychrome, Paxcaman Red, or Augustine Red in collections from the following sites: Poptun, Nohoch Ek, Itsimte?, Paso Caballos?, and Wild Cane Cay off the coast of British Honduras.

slight evidence exists of Preclassic pottery although with more intensive digging a sizable sample might possibly be exposed. The principal period of occupation was from about 9.0.0.0.0 to 10.8.0.0.0 in the Maya calendar and coincided, therefore, with a time when the Maya were enjoying the full measure of their florescence. Yet during this essentially Classic Maya period, with outstanding Classic architecture and sculpture at Quirigua to the north and Copan to the east, Guaytan maintained its own distinctive art, architecture and ceramics, all strongly flavored by highland Guatemala influences.

The ruins of Copan,[2c] in the valley of the Copan River, in the extreme western part of Honduras, are typical of the best in Classic Maya architecture and sculpture. Nevertheless, its ceramic traditions are derived from areas to the east such as eastern El Salvador and the Ulua and Comayagua valleys in Honduras. This appears to have been true from the Late Preclassic period on up through Early Postclassic times in spite of the occurrence of a few trade pieces from the Peten and Guatemala highlands.

Northern Subregion

Here the most thoroughly examined sites are those in the Puuc Sector, especially Uxmal and Kabah,[21] and the 15 sites listed for this subregion in figure 3. Sites in the Puuc Sector constitute a very closely knit cultural entity. The Cehpech Ceramic Complex occurs at such sites as Uxmal, Kabah, Sayil, and Labna, and seems to be underlain by Preclassic and earlier Classic sherd material at Oxkintok on the northern fringe of this sector. The longer sequence of occupation at Oxkintok is further extended at still more northerly Dzibilchaltun.[2m] Currently under intensive and extensive excavation by E. Wyllys Andrews, Dzibilchaltun is expected to yield a complete representation from Ecab phase through Chauaca phase that should omit little concerning cultural development in Yucatan. Acanceh,[2i] a site about halfway between Merida and Mayapan, is ceramically, perhaps, most closely associated with Dzibilchaltun. The occupation there is slightly shorter, however, ranging only from Late Preclassic through Late Postclassic.

Yaxuna,[2y] in south central Yucatan, and Coba,[2k] in northwestern Quintana Roo, are linked not only by a causeway but by a mutual participation in strong southern Maya Classic influence. This influence at Coba is evident not only in the pottery but also in the principal architectural assemblage whereas at Yaxuna the evidence is purely ceramic, the standing architecture being similar to that found in Puuc sites where the Cehpech Ceramic Complex predominates. Yet the abundant Yaxuna Classic pottery, both the Peten-like and that of clearly local inspiration, is stratigraphically earlier than the Cehpech pottery. Furthermore, the ceramic history at Yaxuna indicates a much longer and more continuous occupation than seems to have been the situation at Coba (fig. 3). At Coba there seems to be a special emphasis on the early Tepeu 1–like portion of the Motul Ceramic Complex.

Chichen Itza appears to have had a long uninterrupted occupation (fig. 3). During the Early Mexican period (Toltec),[6] the site rose to its greatest achievements architecturally, artistically, and ceramically; thereafter the ceremonial part of the city appears to have been largely abandoned, except as a shrine for pilgrims. At both Mayapan[2r] (and its suburb, Santa Cruz[2s]) and Mani[2q] even longer ceramic histories have been disclosed, but in each case the emphasis differs (fig. 3).

Santa Rosa Xtampak[2t] and Dzibilnocac[2n] of the Chenes Sector, and Xpuhil[2x] of the Rio Bec Sector, located on a north-south axis in central Campeche, may be grouped together by ceramic content. All these sites have a continuous ceramic history dating from the Middle Preclassic period through the Late Classic–Early Postclassic Transition period. Peten-like Classic pottery diminishes notably through these sites from south to north. On the other hand, Puuc Slate Ware, often represented by types and varieties different from those found in the Puuc Sector itself, is abundant at each site. It is also true that in both the Chenes and Rio Bec sectors, Puuc Slate Ware appears to have its earliest roots in the Classic period. If more extensive excavation is carried out at sites farther north such as Dzibilchaltun, Oxkintok, Mani, and even Kabah and Uxmal in the Puuc Sector, a Late Classic[7] association for Puuc Slate Ware is probable.

In northern Campeche, as described by Ruz (1945b), the ceramic range at Jaina spans the Early Classic[8] to Late Classic–Early Postclassic Transition periods plus a few Early Postclassic, Late Postclassic, and Colonial sherds found on the surface. To supplement evidence produced at Jaina, Xicalango[2w] provided an excellent sample of Late Preclassic and Late Postclassic pottery, the intervening ceramic complexes being conspicuous by the scarcity of sherds assignable to them.[9] Along the east coast of the Yucatan peninsula in Quintana Roo, three sites were chosen as most representative of that district. Tancah[2u] has an almost continuous ceramic record from Late Preclassic through Late Postclassic, whereas both Tulum[2v] and Ichpaatun[2o] are Middle and Late Postclassic sites that include an excellent representation of both Hocaba and Tases-like Ceramic Complex pottery with new (as yet undefined and unnamed) types and varieties.

[6] Ed. note: This is Andrews' Modified Florescent (Article 12).

[7] Ed. note: This is Andrews' Pure Florescent (Article 12).

[8] Ed. note: This is Andrews' Early period.

[9] Other west coast Campeche sites touched on by Ruz are Champoton, Tixchel, Los Guariches, and (inland) Edzna.

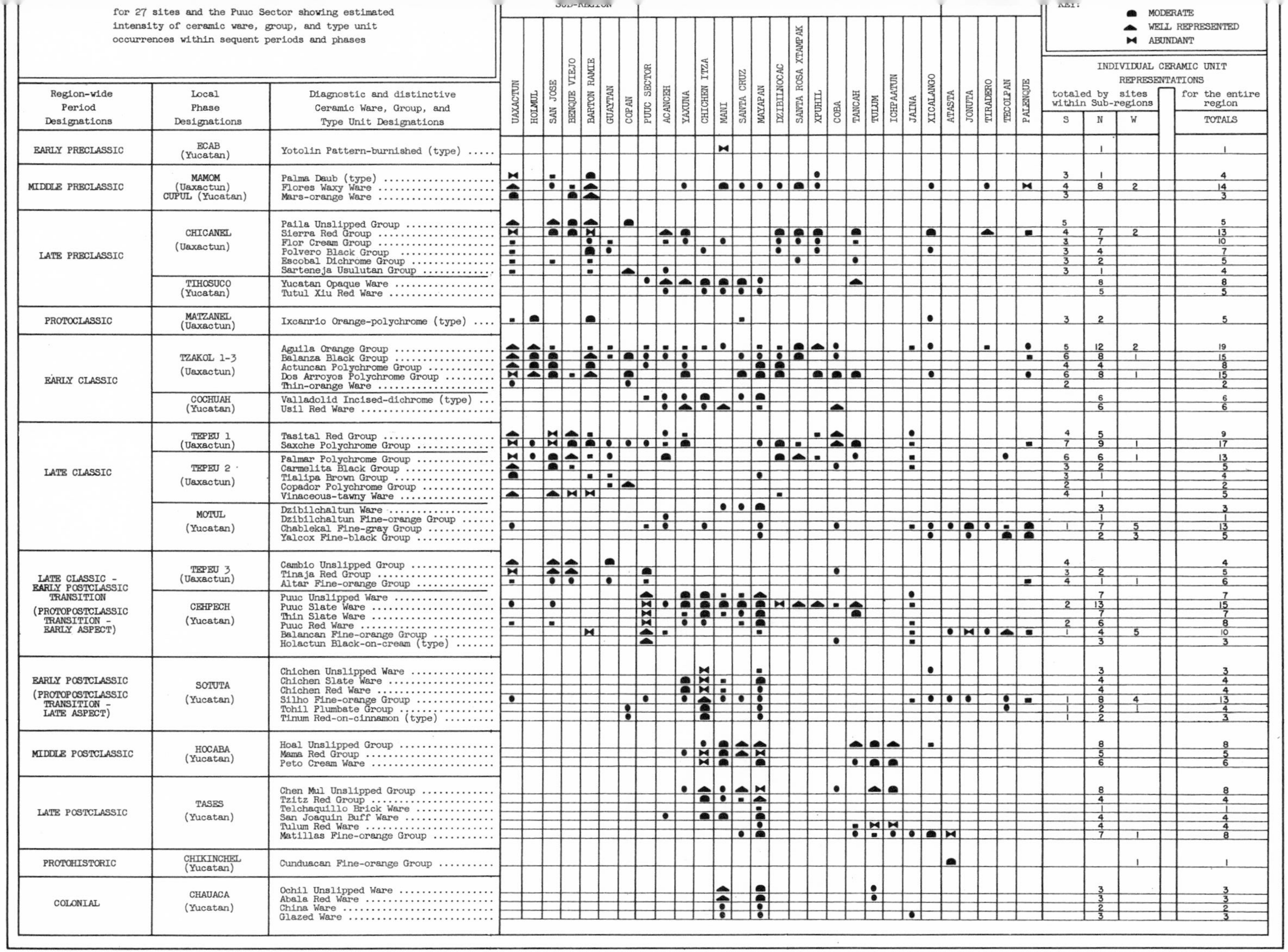

FIG. 4—MAYA LOWLAND POTTERY DISTRIBUTION CHART

Western Subregion

This subregion does not compare favorably with either the Northern or Southern as far as ceramic coverage is concerned. With the exception of Palenque[2cc] and Comalcalco[2aa] where fairly intensive excavations have been carried out, the subregion has merely been surveyed. Pottery from Palenque is under study by the Rands (Rands and Rands, 1957, 1959, 1960; R. L. Rands, 1961a), but on the basis of preliminary findings, it may be said that a few sherds are Preclassic, a few are Early Classic, and the large mass is Late Classic. Specific affiliations with Piedras Negras occur rarely, as do some late ties with the Tabasco plains and perhaps the Alta Verapaz of Guatemala. The Protoclassic period does not seem to be represented. Palenque pottery shows an unusual degree of technological variation, with vessel walls characteristically thin, polychrome decoration comparatively unimportant, and shapes differing from other lowland Maya norms. Most important, nevertheless, is cognizance of the strong sense of ceramic isolation which pervades the Palenque material.

Tecolpan[2dd] and Jonuta[2bb] include a small sample of early Late Classic (Tepeu 1–like) polychrome types and a large collection of Late Classic Fine Gray Ware and Fine Black Ware. Nevertheless, the principal period represented is the Late Classic–Early Postclassic Transition with its fine orange Balancan Group. An Early Postclassic period is suspected at Tecolpan in particular since a few sherds of both the fine orange Silho Group and Plumbate Ware have been found. Atasta,[2z] like Xicalango, is primarily a Late Postclassic site, but there are a few examples of earlier wares such as Fine Gray and early Fine Orange. There is also present a fair quantity of Protohistoric pottery, especially of the fine orange Cunduacan Group. Tiradero, on the other hand, is more closely linked with the Peten and has produced

pottery from the Middle Preclassic through the Late Classic periods.

PERIOD REVIEW

Various ceramic complexes and wares have been mentioned frequently. A more precise account of their constituents now follows period by period. Whether or not and to what extent a type, ceramic group, or ware has been found at any of 27 leading sites or in the Puuc Sector has been collated in figure 4. Decorative techniques have also been correlated by ware, ceramic group, and type units in figure 5. Information in either of these categories is therefore generally not repeated in the text. Detailed cross-references by type to illustrations in such basic ceramic reports as Smith, 1955b, and Brainerd, 1958 (and other similar volumes), are also here held to a minimum because they have been fully catalogued elsewhere (see note 4).

Preclassic Period

When considered as a whole, the earliest pottery known from the Maya lowlands is of excellent quality. It is far in advance of anything that could possibly be thought of as the beginnings of pottery making in any region. The lowland Preclassic period may perhaps extend into antiquity in excess of 1000 to 2000 years B.C. from approximately A.D. 100 to 100 B.C., depending on the presence or absence of a Protoclassic manifestation. No absolute time values have been arrived at for the earliest archaeological evidence, however.[10]

In the Southern Subregion two ceramic complexes have been recognized and have received detailed descriptive treatment at Uaxactun:[2h] Mamom, the earlier, and Chicanel, the later. These have counterparts

[10] Ed. note: 2000 B.C. would be a somewhat earlier estimate for the beginning of the Preclassic period than is given elsewhere in this *Handbook*. A 100 B.C. upper end of the Preclassic range is favored here. This does not, as in other papers in the *Handbook*, include the Protoclassic period, which has been grouped here with the Classic.

MAYA LOWLAND POTTERY DECORATIVE TECHNIQUES
correlated with ceramic ware, group and type units within sequent periods and phases

Region-wide Period Designations	Local Phase Designations	Diagnostic and distinctive Ceramic Ware, Group, and Type Unit Designations	PATTERN-BURNISHING	DAUB-PAINTING IN RED	FIRE INCISING	INCISING	GROOVED-INCISING	CHAMFERING	FLUTING	IMPRESSING	PAINTING IN RED	STRIATION	PUNCTATING	APPLIQUÉ	PAINTING IN NEGATIVE RESIST	POLYCHROME PAINTING	MODELING	GOUGED-INCISED CARVING	PLANO-RELIEF CARVING	PAINTING IN BLACK	GADROONING	MODELED-CARVING	COMPOSITE DECORATION	POST-FIRE PAINTING	INCISED-POLYCHROME	MONOCHROME ONLY
EARLY PRECLASSIC	ECAB (Yucatan)	Yotolin Pattern-burnished (type)	●																							
MIDDLE PRECLASSIC	MAMOM (Uaxactun) / CUPUL (Yucatan)	Palma Daub (type)		●																						
		Flores Waxy Ware			●	●	●	●	●		●			●												
		Mars-orange Ware			●	●																				●
LATE PRECLASSIC	CHICANEL (Uaxactun)	Paila Unslipped Group				●	●																			
		Sierra Red Group				●	●				●	●	●													
		Flor Cream Group				●	●				●															
		Polvero Black Group				●	●				●															
		Escobal Dichrome Group												●												
		Sarteneja Usulutan Group																								
	TIHOSUCO (Yucatan)	Yucatan Opaque Ware				●	●																			
		Tutul Xiu Red Ware																								
PROTOCLASSIC	MATZANEL (Uaxactun)	Ixcanrio Orange-polychrome (type)																				●				
EARLY CLASSIC	TZAKOL 1-3 (Uaxactun)	Aguila Orange Group				●					●															
		Balanza Black Group				●												●	●	●						
		Actuncan Polychrome Group														●										
		Dos Arroyos Polychrome Group														●										
		Thin-orange Ware				●																				
	COCHUAH (Yucatan)	Valladolid Incised-dichrome (type)				●					●									●						
		Usil Red Ware				●					●															
LATE CLASSIC	TEPEU 1 (Uaxactun)	Tasital Red Group				●					●															
		Saxche Polychrome Group														●										
	TEPEU 2 (Uaxactun)	Palmar Polychrome Group				●										●							●			
		Carmelita Black Group				●			●										●	●						
		Tialipa Brown Group									●															
		Copador Polychrome Group														●										
		Vinaceous-tawny Ware									●									●						
	MOTUL (Yucatan)	Dzibilchaltun Ware				●																				
		Dzibilchaltun Fine-orange Group				●					●															
		Chablekal Fine-gray Group																		●						
		Yalcox Fine-black Group																		●						
LATE CLASSIC – EARLY POSTCLASSIC TRANSITION (PROTOPOSTCLASSIC TRANSITION – EARLY ASPECT)	TEPEU 3 (Uaxactun)	Cambio Unslipped Group								●	●	●	●	●												
		Tinaja Red Group									●	●		●												
		Achote Black Group									●							●	●							
		Altar Fine-orange Group									●									●		●	●			
	CEHPECH (Yucatan)	Puuc Unslipped Ware								●	●	●		●												
		Puuc Slate Ware								●	●							●	●	●						
		Thin Slate Ware									●							●	●	●					●	
		Puuc Red Ware									●									●			●		●	
		Balancan Fine-orange Group																		●		●			●	
		Holactun Black-on-cream (type)																		●			●			
EARLY POSTCLASSIC (PROTOPOSTCLASSIC TRANSITION – LATE ASPECT)	SOTUTA (Yucatan)	Chichen Unslipped Ware									●			●												
		Chichen Slate Ware									●							●		●						
		Chichen Red Ware									●									●						
		Silho Fine-orange Group																●		●		●	●	●		
		Tohil Plumbate Group															●					●	●	●		
		Tinum Red-on-cinnamon (type)																		●						
MIDDLE POSTCLASSIC	HOCABA (Yucatan)	Hoal Unslipped Group									●	●		●												
		Mama Red Group									●									●						
		Peto Cream Ware																				●				
LATE POSTCLASSIC	TASES (Yucatan)	Chen Mul Unslipped Group									●	●		●									●		●	
		Tzitz Red Group									●									●			●			
		Telchaquillo Brick Ware									●															
		San Joaquin Buff Ware									●											●				
		Tulum Red Ware									●									●		●				
		Matillas Fine-orange Group																		●		●			●	
PROTOHISTORIC	CHIKINCHEL (Yucatan)	Cuduacan Fine-orange Group																●								●
COLONIAL	CHAUACA (Yucatan)	Ochil Unslipped Ware																					●			
		Abala Red Ware									●															
		China Ware																								
		Glazed Ware																								

FIG. 5—CORRELATION OF MAYA LOWLAND POTTERY DECORATIVE TECHNIQUES WITH CERAMIC UNITS

at other sites, such as Barton Ramie, that bear out and in fact subdivide the original Uaxactun findings (fig. 2). In the Northern Subregion Brainerd (1958, pp. 89–90) separates the Preclassic period into Early, Middle, and Late. R. E. Smith (in preparation) has recognized three ceramic complexes (Ecab, Cupul, and Tihosuco, respectively) that seem to coincide with Brainerd's divisions. No pottery units or complexes have as yet been clearly identified for this time interval in the Western Subregion. Consequently where pottery must be spoken of, we are forced to extend the Southern nomenclature into this subregion while discussing the Preclassic and Classic periods and then project the Northern terminology into it during the Postclassic and Protohistoric periods.

SOUTHERN SUBREGION. Mamom pottery is well represented in the Peten and northwestern British Honduras, but it is absent in the Motagua Valley and at Copan.[11]

Palma Daub (fig. 6,*a*), originally termed Daub Ware (R. E. Smith, 1955b, pp. 26, 111, 112; fig. 15,*c*), is the most diagnostic Mamom type in Uaxactun Unslipped Ware. It displays coarse-textured paste; decoration is by way of daubing crude red swirls and vertical or horizontal bands on the vessel body; solid red paint generally covers the neck exterior to just below the lip on the interior surface; Palma Daub is restricted to jar forms.

Flores Waxy Ware (fig. 6,*b,c*) includes at least 12 types that together usually comprise a major portion of any Mamom pottery deposit. This ware displays a surface finish that is slipped and burnished to produce a unique "waxy" feel. Otherwise Flores Waxy Ware includes, among its attributes, a thin, soft slip; crazing, rootlet-marking, and fire-clouding; colors of red (most common), black, variegated, orange, cream, buff, brown, and gray. Paste is medium-coarse textured with sherd temper predominating; decorative combinations involve chevrons, dash lines, diamonds, guilloches, rectangles, reverse curves or S-shapes, and triangles (often hatched) in various design patterns; most common forms are plates with flaring sides and flat base, pseudo-cuspidor-shaped bowls, and globular wide-mouthed jars with low to medium-high necks. Muxanal Red-on-cream is an important type in this ware because although vessels are presumably entirely cream-slipped, a secondary red slip is added to either the exterior or interior of plates or round-sided bowls, thereby pro-

ducing the only form of Mamom painted decoration except for very rare instances where red dots occur.

With the possible exception of Palma Daub, Mars Orange Ware is the most widely known Mamom pottery. Although among the oldest pottery in the Maya lowlands, it is technically beyond much that follows. This pottery is perhaps not slipped (a slipped variety is found at Barton Ramie[2a]); surfaces are usually the color of the paste, sometimes ranging to brown, are well smoothed and polished, leaving a pleasing finish that never attains to gloss; paste is conspicuously fine textured, usually ash tempered, and uniformly Mars Orange (Ridgway, 1912) in color; incising, grooving, and fine-incising are decorative techniques often used to embellish exterior vessel walls with horizontal or oblique lines; rim interiors are sometimes grooved horizontally; forms include deep or cuspidor-shape bowls, plates with flaring sides and direct or wide-everted rims, and round-sided dishes.

Future work at other sites will probably result in two or possibly even three ceramic complexes that equate with what at Uaxactun was included in a single complex, Chicanel. Chicanel pottery deposits are massive and occur widely throughout the Southern Subregion and elsewhere. Often used as base fill beneath great plazas and buildings of later origin, Chicanel sherds underlie other depositions in quantity so regularly and so often as to make one ponder just how large a pottery-making population might have been required to produce the millions upon millions of Chicanel sherds that must lie beneath the surface of the Maya lowlands.

The unslipped Paila Group (within Uaxactun Unslipped Ware) is an important Chicanel component. Surfaces of this pottery are generally indifferently smoothed or show striations; globular, wide-mouth jars with medium-high to low, flaring or outcurving necks are the most common ves-

---

[11] The only other collections where Palma Daub has thus far been recognized are now in Peabody Museum, Harvard University. They are from Playa de los Muertos and Yarumela, both in Honduras.

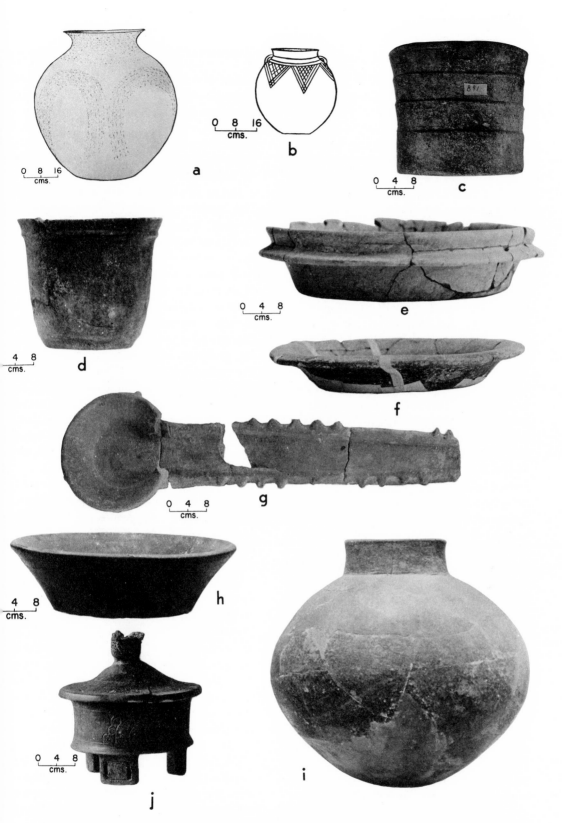

F<small>IG.</small> 6—SELECTED EXAMPLES OF POTTERY FROM THE MAMOM, CHICANEL, AND
TZAKOL CERAMIC COMPLEXES. *a–c* (Mamom): *a*, Palma Daub (type) jar; *b*, black
Chunhinta Group jar; *c*, black Chunhinta Group bowl. *d–f* (Chicanel): *d*, red Sierra Group
bowl; *e*, cream Flor Group dish; *f*, black Polvero Group dish. *g–i* (Tzakol 1–3): *g*, unslipped
Quintal Group ladle censer; *h,i*, orange Aguila Group bowl (*h*), jar (*i*). *j* (Tzakol 3), black
Balanza Group tripod bowl and cover. All examples from Uaxactun.

sel form (with no handles at Uaxactun; with strap handles at San Jose, Benque Viejo, and Copan).

Paso Caballo Waxy Ware is the real hallmark of Chicanel.[12] It embraces a number of significant ceramic groups such as the red Sierra Group, cream Flor Group (figs. 6,e; 7,c), black Polvero Group (figs. 6,f; 7,b), dichrome Escobal Group, and Usulutan Sarteneja Group. One of the outstanding attributes associated with the ware as a whole is a thin, soft, uniform slip that is burnished and fashioned to produce a diagnostic "waxy" feel (these attributes are shared with Flores Waxy Ware and might better be thought of as the lead attributes that set these two Preclassic waxy wares apart from all other Middle American pottery). Crazing is a distinctive Chicanel feature; paste is medium-coarse textured, predominantly sherd tempered in the central Peten, ranging to calcite with some sherd and on to pure calcite tempering in British Honduras. A greater diversity of vessel shapes compared to those of Mamom is usual in Paso Caballo Waxy Ware: the wide-everted or thickened-rim plate is the dominant form mode, followed in relative consequence by wide-mouth jars, bowls with flaring or recurved sides, and bowls with an incurved rim. Red Sierra Group types (figs. 6,d;7,a) usually form a clear majority in any Chicanel collection; a plain red surface finish is the general rule but frequently other decorative techniques (in addition to those shown in fig. 5) or embellishments are brought into play on this pottery, such as modeled ridges (fig. 6,d), rim or flange protuberances or bulges and, at Uaxactun, modeled heads.

At Barton Ramie the red Sierra Group is supplemented by an impressive collection of similar but simpler forms that entirely lack the red Sierra Group decorative features; vessel walls are also consistently

[12] There may possibly be a connection between these early Waxy Wares and Slate Ware of much later periods.

much thinner. This, the red Hillbank Group, may have a more restricted and perhaps somewhat later (Late Preclassic) time value and be peculiar to British Honduras. Although its differing character is clearly discernible, its exact chronological place and affiliation are not entirely explained or indicated by the Barton Ramie stratigraphic data or pottery evidence.[2a]

A plain burnished red pottery, having some of the form (wide-everted and thickened rim) and decorative (modeled rim protuberances or bulges and bird heads) modes of the red Sierra Group, is described and illustrated from Copan by Longyear (1952, p. 24; figs. 3,d; 49,b-e). However, other attributes, particularly those of vessel form, associate these vessels more closely with the early pottery of Yarumela, Playa de los Muertos, and Santa Rita of the Comayagua and Ulua valleys. Also from Copan there exists a sizable vessel collection decorated in a negative-painted style using a resist technique. Part of this collection may be of the Usulutan Sarteneja Group, but most of it is undoubtedly of a ware or wares as yet undescribed in detail and not named. The two major negative-painted resist types of the Chicanel Usulutan Sarteneja Group are best known from Uaxactun. At Barton Ramie nice pieces of one of these, Savannah Bank Usulutan, occur. This type appears to range through Late Chicanel. The other type, Sarteneja Usulutan, was represented by a few sherds. A single Chicanel specimen from Guaytan, apparently unique there, is of the cream Flor Group (A. L. Smith and Kidder, 1943, fig. 23,c). It is a tetrapod bowl with a shape usually associated with Usulutan types but having groove-incised arcs on the rim.

The dichrome Escobal Group, although as a ceramic group it encompasses various color combinations, is widely represented by Escobal Red-on-buff (type). Decoration may simply involve a change of color from exterior to interior, or be more complex

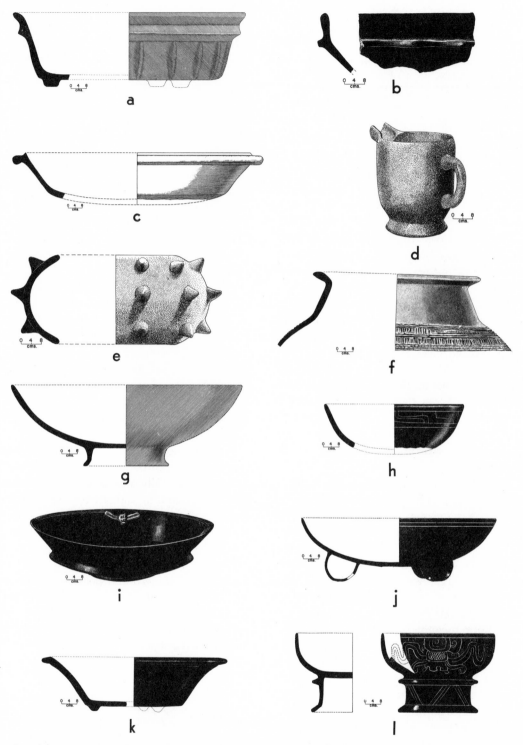

Fig. 7—SELECTED EXAMPLES OF POTTERY FROM THE CHICANEL AND TZAKOL CERAMIC COMPLEXES. *a–c*, (Chicanel): *a*, red Sierra Group tripod lateral-flange dish; *b*, black Polvero Group lateral-flange bowl; *c*, cream Flor Group rim flange dish. *e–g* (Tzakol 2–3): *e,f*, unslipped Quintal Group pot stand *(e)*, jar *(f)*; *g*, orange Aguila Group ring-stand bowl. *d,h–l* (Tzakol 3): black Balanza Group pitcher *(d)*, round-sided bowl *(h)*, basal-flange bowl *(i)*, tripod round-sided dish *(j)*, tripod bowl *(k)*, pedestal-base bowl *(l)*. All examples from Uaxactun.

involving red parallel vertical stripes (J. E. S. Thompson, 1939a, p. 85, fig. 35) and dots or bands of dots. Specimens of any of the types in this group have not been found abundantly at any special site.

NORTHERN SUBREGION. Contrary to previous beliefs, Preclassic pottery is as abundant in the Northern Subregion as in the Southern, if not more so. Brainerd's (1958, pp. 24, 48, 89; fig. 30,c, 1–35) Early Preclassic, however, is based only on evidence from Mani. One ware, Homun Unslipped, and a single bottle form with a distinctive narrow, exteriorly thickened neck go with other attributes to provide what is known of the only pottery type involved, Yotolin Pattern-burnished.

Flores Waxy Ware has been found at many sites throughout the subregion. Although usually present in relatively small quantities, it outweighs other kinds of pottery in Middle Preclassic deposits and therefore is diagnostic for this period even though it is clear that future analysis will show other wares and types are present to give the Northern Subregion at least some ceramic units that are peculiar to this subregion alone.

During the Late Preclassic two distinct ceramic complexes clearly manifest themselves: a Chicanel complex of Southern origin and the Tihosuco Ceramic Complex of local manufacture. The Chicanel Ceramic Complex is primarily composed of Paso Caballo Waxy Ware and includes elements of the same ceramic groups as described for the Peten. It is interesting, and no doubt meaningful, that pottery influences extend and pervade from the Southern up through the Northern Subregion during Preclassic times. These ceramic influences are not reciprocal, and there seems to be little or nothing in the way of a north-to-south pottery flow either of ceramic ideas or whole vessels.

Of the indigenous Tihosuco Ceramic Complex, Yucatan Opaque Ware[13] displays a well-smoothed, slipped and polished sur-face finish that is opaque red or orange-red with gray or yellowish splotches; this color may also range to cream or black. Most common shapes are flat-bottomed bowls with flaring sides and slip-covered bases, hemispherical bowls, cuspidors, and jars. Customary decorative techniques are pre-slip incising and grooving and, rarely, post-slip incising. At sites throughout the Puuc Sector the distribution of Yucatan Opaque Ware is quite widespread but with only rare (Brainerd, 1958, fig. 60,a) accumulations within trenches, such as at Kabah. Certain incised examples from Santa Cruz are illustrated by R. E. Smith (1955a, fig. 1,l,m).

Tutul Xiu Red Ware (called Formative Red Slip over Striated by Brainerd) includes but one type at present: Tipikal Red-on-striated. Jar forms are the only ones represented; exteriors are slipped (strong red in color) over finely striated and lightly polished surfaces; paste color ranges from cinnamon through buff to gray. This type has thus far been recorded from only five sites, all in Yucatan.

WESTERN SUBREGION. Here Preclassic pottery is poorly represented. We do not know if this is culturally significant or primarily due to limited investigation in this subregion. A few questionable Mamom-like sherds have been found at Tiradero and Palenque.

For the Late Preclassic period there is material at Tiradero and possibly at Palenque. The Tiradero[2ee] collection is excellent Chicanel. Paso Caballo Waxy Ware is especially abundant, as exemplified by the red Sierra Group with its full complement of vessel forms, including many of the diag-

---

[13] This ware is perhaps an overly inclusive unit that has been recognized and described in an attempt to draw together the early monochrome non-waxy and opaque materials called Formative Monochrome and Flaky Red by Brainerd (1958, pp. 48–49). Almost all the sherds in the north which do show a waxy finish and consequently are not included in Brainerd's Formative Monochrome are Paso Caballo Waxy Ware.

nostic wide-everted and grooved-rim bowls. At Palenque,[2cc] on the other hand, a few red Sierra Group sherds may be present but their weathered condition leaves an element of doubt.

Classic (and Protoclassic) Periods

Knowledge regarding Maya lowland pottery during the Classic period is largely confined to information drawn from sites in the Southern Subregion. What little is known from adjoining subregions derives in great measure from pieces traded from the south. This does not mean, however, that the Northern and Western subregions were unoccupied or produced no pottery throughout times contemporary with Peten Classic. Quite the contrary is probably true, but information about this occupancy is extremely vague.

In the greater Peten, dated stelae have indicated a Classic time range extending from approximately A.D. 300 to 900. (Due to the virtual absence of a Protoclassic period at Uaxactun, this time interval is extended to meet the Late Preclassic termination at about A.D. 100.)

An interval between Late Preclassic and Early Classic has been observed with special emphasis in the east toward British Honduras. It is usually referred to as a Protoclassic period[14] (Wauchope, 1950, pp. 220–221; Willey and Gifford, 1961) extending from possibly as early as 100 B.C. to A.D. 300 in the east, with the time involved diminishing upward the farther west one proceeds until it is perhaps not even present at Piedras Negras[2f] or Palenque.[2cc] The Protoclassic ceramics have many Classic features, and it seems logical to consider them in a role introductory to the fully Classic Maya pottery despite their more restricted geographical distribution.

SOUTHERN SUBREGION. An indication of what is regarded as Protoclassic was pro-

[14] Ed. note: The Protoclassic period has been included in the Late Preclassic by Willey, Ekholm, and Millon, Article 14, volume 1.

vided in the section "Subregional Review" and need not be repeated here. The questions of the sources for the modes and types involved in the Protoclassic complexes is of high interest, however, because most of these features and ceramic units are new to the Maya Lowland Region. R. E. Smith feels that some of the new traits are present in older Mamom or Chicanel contexts in the Peten, and that, with two exceptions, those traits which cannot be derived from these sources can be traced directly to Preclassic ceramic complexes in the highlands of Guatemala where they were of Maya inspiration. The two exceptions are the orange gloss pottery embodied by the orange Aguacate Ceramic Group[2a] and the polychrome decoration primarily involved in Ixcanrio Orange-polychrome. Smith believes we need not even go outside the lowlands in search of origins concerning these two features. His view sees the types involved as firmly planted in eastern Peten (Holmul to Poptun) and adjacent western British Honduras (Barton Ramie to Mountain Cow), and considers that there is no evidence of an earlier source for these elements to the south or southwest of the eastern Peten–British Honduras sector. He believes that they arose either here or somewhat to the north in northern British Honduras and southern Quintana Roo. Supporting data are lacking, however, as the latter geographical zone is all but unknown archaeologically. Gifford favors an origin to the south in northern and western Central America or, as a second choice, in the central or eastern Guatemala highlands (Willey and Gifford, 1961). Links through the unusual and strikingly large bulbous mammiform foot mode and other traits to Honduras (Strong, Kidder, and Paul, 1938; Wauchope, 1950, fig. 3 and p. 242; Canby, 1951) and through such manifestations as Gualacho phase pottery into El Salvador (Haberland, 1960, p. 26) favor a southern origin. According to Haberland, the Gualacho Ceramic Complex is "nearly 80 per

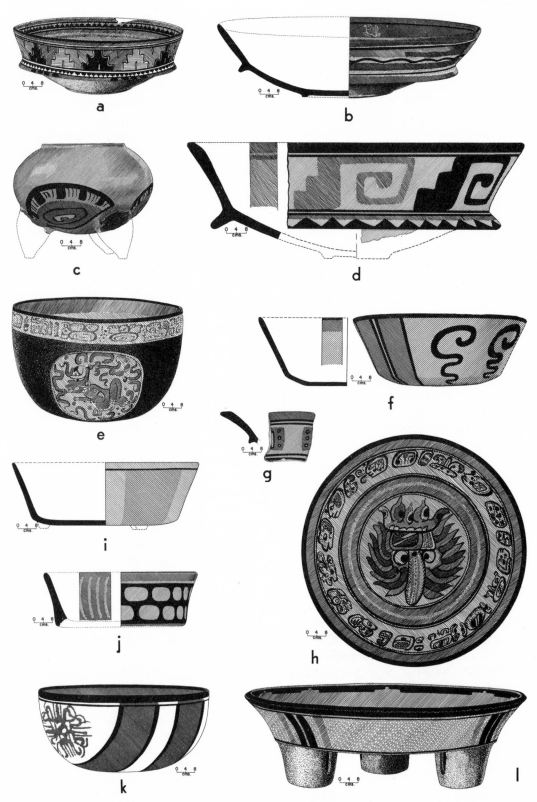

Fig. 8—SELECTED EXAMPLES OF POTTERY FROM THE TZAKOL, TEPEU 1, 2, AND 3 CERAMIC COMPLEXES. *a–d* (Tzakol 2–3): polychrome Dos Arroyos Group basal-flange bowls (*a,b,d*), tripod bowl (*c*). *e–h* (Tepeu 1): polychrome Saxche Group, round-sided bowl (*e*), flaring-sided bowl (*f*), basal-ridge tripod plates (*g,h*). *i–k* (Tepeu 2): *i*, Vinaceous Tawny Ware tripod bowl; *j,k*, polychrome Palmar Group bowls. *l* (Tepeu 3): polychrome Danta Group tripod dish. All examples from Uaxactun.

cent an orange ware" where vessel shapes "include rounded open-mouthed vessels with wide outflaring rims" and along with globular jars, "bowls with either outflaring or nearly straight walls and four big mammiform legs." Gualacho is placed at 1000 B.C. (*ibid.*, fig. 2) or earlier.

The most important thing about the Protoclassic pottery complexes is that they include new modes, and these innovations suggest new and, with reference to the Peten, outside influences such as might have to do with a migration or influx of people. These influences did not destroy existing patterns but impinged upon and eventually changed them as the innovations were gradually absorbed. A new era opened up with these changes and their spread to the west: the Classic Maya period. In the Classic pottery, the large mammiform feet and spouted vessel forms are discarded, but other vessel forms, a definite style of polychrome decoration, and the more generalized Peten Gloss Ware continued on, to be both adopted and adapted by Classic Maya potters.

Uaxactun[2h] provides the most thoroughly studied and published collection of Classic ceramics. Based on work at Uaxactun, the period was divided into Early Classic and Late Classic. These were subdivided into Tzakol 1, 2, and 3 and Tepeu 1 and 2 respectively; here Early Classic pottery will be taken up as a single Tzakol Ceramic Complex. Although types of the unslipped Quintal Group (figs. 6,*g*; 7,*e,f*) are always well represented, nothing overshadows the importance of Peten Gloss Ware in this complex. Within it four ceramic groups, the orange Aguila Group (figs. 6,*h,i*; 7,*g*), the black Balanza Group (figs. 6,*j*; 7,*d,h-l*), the polychrome Actuncan Group, and the polychrome Dos Arroyos Group (fig. 8,*a-d*) are particularly distinctive.

Peten Gloss Ware displays a diagnostically glossy surface finish that has been carefully smoothed, slipped, and highly polished in perhaps special ways or even treated to achieve the unique velvet gloss that is present on finest specimens. Slip color is diverse, ranging from orange to variegated, red, black, brown, buff, gray, and cream; polychrome and dichrome painting was effected on an orange, buff, gray, or cream base slip; negative painting also is practiced in a resist technique to produce such types at Japon Resist. The most common forms are jars (fig. 6,*i*), basal-flange bowls (figs. 7,*i*; 8,*a,b,d*), basal-Z-angle and basal-rounded-Z-angle bowls, cylinder tripods, round-sided bowls with flat base (fig. 7,*h*), with tripod base, with ring base or ring stand (fig. 7,*g*) or with pedestal base (fig. 7,*l*), restricted-orifice tripod bowls (fig. 8,*c*), flaring-sided bowls with flat base, everted-rim tripod bowls (fig. 7,*k*), and pitchers (fig. 7,*d*). The best representation of most of the attributes listed above for Uaxactun is in contemporaneous complexes at Holmul[2e] and San Jose.[2g] Peten Gloss Ware types that appear at Guaytan[2d] and Copan[2c] are the result of trade.

Thin Orange Ware occasionally appears in the southern Maya lowlands. Since it is a highland Guatemala product that may actually have originated in Puebla, Mexico, only the forms found at Uaxactun need be mentioned. These include a round-sided bowl with ring-stand base, and an everted-rim bowl (R. E. Smith, 1955b, fig. 23,*a*, 12) that sports an incised horizontal guilloche band. Longyear reports the one other lowland find from Copan (1952, p. 28).

The Early Classic ceramic design style is conveyed by either of three artistic media: abstract designs that are generally geometric; conventional designs that are ordinarily standardizations of such natural phenomena as toads and birds—these are transformed into limited line replicas (R. E. Smith, 1955b, pp. 69, 71); and symbolic designs having to do entirely with serpents and involving complicated intermeshings of

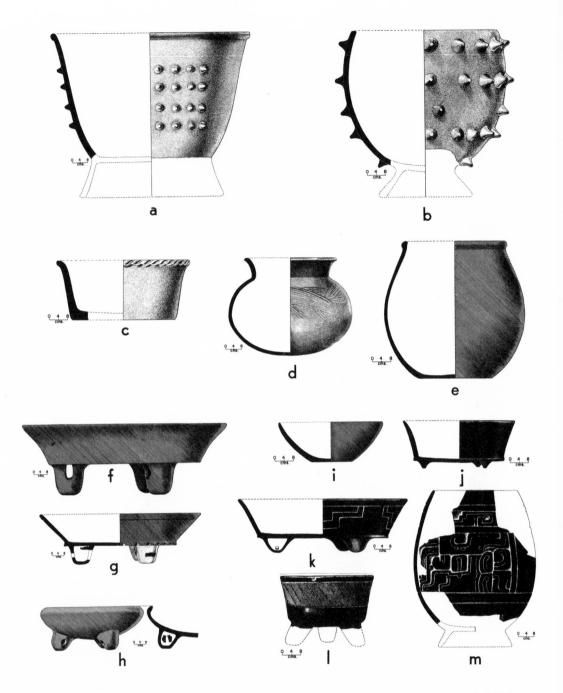

Fig. 9—SELECTED EXAMPLES OF POTTERY FROM THE TEPEU 3 CERAMIC COM-
PLEX. *a–d*, unslipped Cambio Group vessels. *e–i*, red Tinaja Group jar (*e*), tripod dishes
(*f,g*), tripod bowl (*h*), round-sided bowl (*i*). *j–m*, black Achote Group tripod dishes (*j–l*), and
barrel-shape vase with ring-stand base (*m*). All examples from Uaxactun.

scrolls, a ∪-shape element, a double yoke
design, and numerous other elements
(*ibid.*, pp. 70–71).

Pottery of the Late Classic period is in-

troduced by a new set of types that are
most easily recognized through the differing (from those of Early Classic) set of
forms involved. The transition from Tzakol

518

3 to Tepeu 1 may be characterized as blended and easy but swift by comparison to a longer interval of transition at Barton Ramie[2a] and elsewhere away from the central Peten. The Tepeu 1 ceramic groups most frequently encountered are the red Tasital Group and the polychrome Saxche Group (fig. 8,*e-h*). In the former incising and impressing decorate the principal forms: water and storage jars, and basins with restricted orifice.

In the polychrome Saxche Group designs in a variety of beautiful colors are painted on an orange, cream, or red background base slip. Any of the following styles of design may occur among these types: geometric (fig. 8,*f*), glyph banding (fig. 8,*e,g,h*), sky-band signs, figure painting (fig. 8,*h*), and reserve-space circle motifs. The use of a reserve-space technique is quite common in connection with details of positive-painted motifs, especially in figure painting. The design style of Tepeu 1 painted types is a continuation of the usually geometric abstract media that is so much a part of Tzakol painted expression, together with a development of and far greater emphasis on the naturalistic representations of figure painting and glyph banding. These aspects were touched on during Tzakol 3, but it is in Tepeu 1 that they come to form a basic part of Maya artistic representations on pottery. The most familiar forms associated with Tepeu I Peten Gloss Ware are restricted-orifice bowls, barrel-shape vases, hemispherical bowls, flaring-sided bowls rounding to the base (fig. 8,*f*), cylindrical vases, and basal-ridge tripod plates (fig. 8,*g,h*).

The late Late Classic Tepeu 2 Ceramic Complex is the end product of the long Maya Classic pottery continuum at Uaxactun. Peten Gloss Ware types still predominate but they are now accompanied in quantity by types of a new Vinaceous Tawny Ware having its centers of maximum frequency in the Belize Valley of British Honduras. Uaxactun probably acquired examples of this ware by trade from the east.

Of particular importance within the Peten Gloss Ware of Tepeu 2 are three ceramic groups. The black Infierno Group and the brown Tialipa Group display such vessel forms as flaring-sided flat-bottomed bowls, flaring-sided bowls with lateral angle, flaring-sided tripod plates and dishes, and cylindrical vases. The polychrome Palmar Group (fig. 8,*j,k*) incorporates four background colors—orange, cream, buff, and red—on which is set forth a remarkable display of extremely consistent design combinations best appreciated by referring directly to the fine series of original illustrations (R. E. Smith, 1955b, figs. 53–64). Tepeu 2 polychromes are *the* types where pure design patterns flower in Maya pottery. The forms on which these abstract geometric, naturalistic, or glyphic polychrome designs are reproduced are flaring-sided tripod plates, slightly flaring-sided flat-bottomed bowls (fig. 8,*j*), basal-flanged (-notched or -stepped) tripod plates, cylindrical vases, jars, and round-sided bowls (fig. 8,*k*). The polychrome Copador Group of Copan[2c] is considered a gloss ware but it is probably a separate ware apart from Peten Gloss Ware. Major differences that make the group distinctive are the constant use of specular hematite red as a decorative component and design patterns that make use of glyph-like figures, representations of human beings, and birds executed in a Copador style never quite duplicated in other types. Vessel forms are (most important) round-sided bowls (fig. 10,*k,l*), cylindrical vases, recurving-sided bowls, and small jars.

Vinaceous Tawny Ware is consistently volcanic ash tempered (an outstanding criterion). Surfaces are slipped and lightly polished, leaving a semi-matte finish; slip color is consistently Ridgway's (1912) Vinaceous Tawny ranging in rare instances to Cinnamon. The usual decorations are simple geometric patterns in black and red, less frequently in red or black alone; there is a

Fig. 10—SELECTED EXAMPLES OF POTTERY FROM THE MOTUL, TEPEU 3, CEH-PECH, SOTUTA, AND COPAN LATE CLASSIC CERAMIC COMPLEXES. *a–f* (Motul): *a–e*, Fine Gray Ware vessels (*a–c,e*, Merida Museum; *d*, Regil Coll., Merida). *f*, fine orange Komchen Group bowl (Marquez Coll., Merida). *g* (Tepeu 3), fine orange Altar Group vase (Uaxactun). *h* (Cehpech), fine orange Balancan Group vase (Temax). *i,j* (Sotuta), fine orange Silho Group vessels (*i*, Marquez Coll., Merida; *j*, Chichen Itza). *k,l* (Copan, Late Classic), polychrome Copador Group bowls (Copan).

plain undecorated type as well as one (Anonal Polychrome) employing the polychrome style on a cream or buff exterior surfacing. Forms have a narrow range of variation that include (most commonly) flaring-sided tripod dishes (fig. 8,*i*), slightly flaring-sided bowls, jars, and barrel-shaped vases.

NORTHERN SUBREGION. Of the more outstanding Protoclassic types, there is record of examples of Ixcanrio Orange-polychrome only from the Yucatan Peninsula sites of Santa Cruz[2s] and Xicalango.[2w] These are trade pieces. All through the Classic interval Southern Subregion pottery (especially that of the central Peten) finds its way through trade channels to sites in the Northern Subregion. These occurrences are noted for both Early and Late Classic and an idea of the intensity of the ceramic groups represented is given in figure 4. It has been observed that trade increases both in volume and geographical extent as Tzakol 2–3 is approached, evidently leveling off thereafter during Late Classic phases.

The Cochuah Ceramic Complex includes most of the known pottery in Yucatan during the Early Classic period there (see note 8). Within this complex two types are diagnostic: (a) Xanaba Red (Usil Red Ware) absorbs all of Brainerd's (1958, pp. 49–50) Flaky Redware (that may be assumed, because of form and other attributes, to belong in his Early Regional Stage) and some of his Regional Redware; and (b) Batres Red (Yucatan Gloss Ware) probably corresponds to what Brainerd (1958, pp. 50–51) has called Oxkintok Coarse and Oxkintok Thin Monochrome. Usil Red Ware also closely resembles Peten Gloss Ware except that there is not an exact duplication of vessel shape.

Valladolid Incised-dichrome is another marker for the period. It is a gloss ware type that displays an unusual decorative technique embodying large painted designs outlined by incising which is also combined with punctation to fill painted sections (Flaky Dichrome, Brainerd, 1958, p. 50, fig. 6). There are in addition distinctively deep interior striations in the jar form.

The Late Classic period in the Northern Subregion (see note 7) is probably the most difficult to pin down. The Motul Ceramic Complex (fig. 10,*a-f*) represents the time span involved and is contemporaneous with Uaxactun Tepeu 1 and 2. This local complex includes Dzibilchaltun Ware, which displays an irregular surface covered by a red to cinnamon buff matte or polished slip. The only forms noted are medium-size jars and flaring-sided tripod (usually slab footed) dishes (see Brainerd's Red on Thin Grayware).

The fine orange Komchen Group differs quite noticeably from other fine orange groups in attributes of vessel form, decorative techniques, and style of design. Principal forms are flaring-sided flat-bottomed bowls, outcurving low beakers, barrel-shaped vessels, and rarely hemispherical bowls; the first two forms are ordinarily decorated with patterns rather crudely incised through a slip that is often white; black painted lines and designs are also sometimes present; incised decorative motifs include human figures, scrolls, zigzag lines, dotted circles, and, in one instance, an ahau (fig. 10,*f*). The fine gray Chablekal Group (Brainerd's Fine Grayware) displays a fine-textured, untempered, gray paste; surface finish does not differ from the paste and is merely smoothed to a matte appearance. Most common vessel forms include low beakers with a flat (fig. 10,*b*) or double bottom (fig. 10,*e*), lateral-angle bowls (fig. 10,*d*), cylindrical vases (fig. 10,*a*) and rarely wide-mouth jars (fig. 10,*c*).

WESTERN SUBREGION. So little is known of Classic period archaeology in this subregion that the pottery cannot be intelligently discussed beyond noting the occurrences given in figure 4. Motul Complex types are more plentiful than are those from the Peten. At

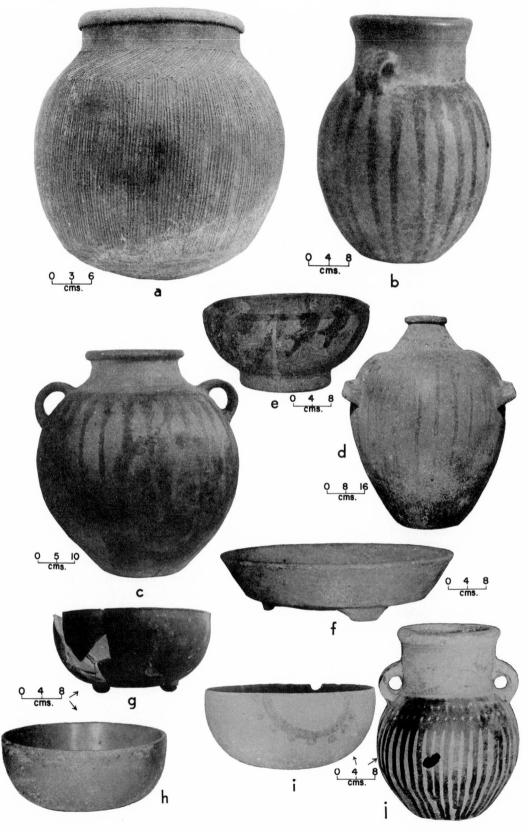

Fig. 11—SELECTED EXAMPLES OF POTTERY FROM THE CEHPECH CERAMIC COMPLEX.
a, Puuc Unslipped Ware jar. *b–d*, Puuc Slate Ware jars. *e,f*, Puuc Slate Ware ring-stand bowl and
tripod dish. *g–i*, Puuc Red Ware bowls. *j*, Holactun Black-on-cream (type). (*a*, Chichen Itza;
b–f,j, Regil Coll., Merida; *g,i*, Uxmal; *h*, Merida Museum.)

Palenque[2cc] and Tecolpan[2dd] in addition to the fine gray Chablekal Group, the fine black Yalcox Group is important; sherds of this group tend to be fine textured, untempered, and undecorated.

Late Classic – Early Postclassic Transition Period

Good information concerning the pottery of what might be called a "Protopostclassic" period is available from the Southern and Northern subregions. In the Western Subregion only fine orange Balancan Group occurrences have been recorded. There are strong reasons for regarding this as a Transition period. Basic and fundamental changes in the pottery traditions took place and include: a nearly complete return to monochrome types; a sharp reduction of ash and sherd tempering in favor of calcite; and (in major centers) the introduction of use patterns requiring incense burners in quantity (censers were rarely and selectively used before this time).

This period came to an abrupt end in the Southern Subregion before it had a chance to develop into anything that resembles the Northern Postclassic. Evidence at Barton Ramie and elsewhere, which at first glance seems contradictory to the previous statement, indicates that a substantial Postclassic population continued living in the Southern Subregion for an undetermined length of time (perhaps even into the 12th century). Their pottery (and general material setting), however, *differs radically* and *profoundly* from complexes such as Uaxactun Tepeu 3 or San Jose IV–V, which is the pottery we consider "Transitional."

By contrast to this greater Peten situation an examination of the Northern Subregion disclosed a long interval, now usually called the Early Postclassic period, that is ceramically transitional from Late Classic materials to those which predominate in the true Postclassic period (presently termed Middle and Late Postclassic). During this Transition period interval (involving the Cehpech and Sotuta Ceramic Complexes) three pottery phenomena gradually become paramount, in a developmental sense, and eventually become the principal traits of Northern Middle and Late Postclassic ceramic complexes. Monochrome red becomes the most common and very abundant nonceremonial pottery, and in these red types calcite is uniformly utilized for tempering purposes. Incense burners become a major part of, and must have been of great ceremonial significance within, the ceramic pattern. The use and manufacture of incense burners seem to increase constantly with time on through the Tases phase.

Such a Transition period is also further marked by the appearance in the North of two sequent Slate wares, a kind of pottery without any direct counterpart elsewhere. It comes to dominate completely the ceramic picture in the Northern Subregion during this era. A waxy or soapy surface finish sets the Slate wares apart just as an unusually high gloss distinguishes Peten Gloss Ware. It is possible that the waxy-like Slate finish in some way reaches back to the Preclassic waxy wares for its origin, but demonstrably immediate beginnings appear in the latter part of the Late Classic period.

SOUTHERN SUBREGION. The Tepeu 3 Ceramic Complex,[2h] the San Jose IV and V Complexes at San Jose,[2g] and the Late Facet pottery of Spanish Lookout phase at Barton Ramie[2a] are all of this period. Since these three are similar in most respects, only the Tepeu 3 Complex will be detailed.

Apart from unslipped Cambio Group types (fig. 9,*a-d*), most typical of Tepeu 3 pottery are the red Tinaja Group and the black Achote Group (both Peten Gloss Ware). Vessel forms include flaring-sided tripod plates (fig. 9,*f,g,k*), round-sided bowls (fig. 9,*i*), and barrel-shape bowls with ring-stand base (fig. 9,*m*). Forms exclusive to the red Tinaja Group are jars (fig. 9,*e*), restricted-orifice bowls, basins with incurved rim, restricted-bead-orifice barrel-shape bowls with flat base, and in-

523

FIG. 12—SELECTED EXAMPLES OF POTTERY FROM THE CEHPECH AND SOTUTA
CERAMIC COMPLEXES. *a–c* (Cehpech), Thin Slate Ware vessels. *d–j* (Sotuta): *d,* Tinum
Red-on-cinnamon (type) ladle censer; *e,* Chichen Slate Ware jar; *f,* Chichen Red Ware bowl;
g–i, plumbate Tohil Group vessels; *j,* Chichen Unslipped Ware ladle censer. (*a,c,d,g–i,* Regil
Coll., Merida; *b,e,* Merida Museum; *f,j,* Chichen Itza.)

curved-rim tripod bowls (fig. 9,*h*); forms exclusive to the black Achote Group are flaring-sided tripod bowls (fig. 9,*j,l*), and cylindrical vases. Within the polychrome Danta Group are the major types displaying painted decoration (fig. 8,*l*). These types probably derive from the Tepeu 2 polychrome Palmar Group but they are never present in quantity.

Although a vital element of the Tepeu 3 Ceramic Complex, the fine orange Altar Group does not extend eastward into British Honduras in any quantity. Its strength is to the west, more in the vicinity of Altar de Sacrificios. This pottery displays orange or reddish brown, very fine-textured, untempered paste; surfaces well smoothed, slipped, and highly polished; the slip possibly running a shade darker than the paste. Vessel forms (R. E. Smith, 1958, fig. 2) include round-sided bowls, barrel-shape with ring-stand base (fig. 10,*g*), and barrel-shape with flat base.

NORTHERN SUBREGION. The Cehpech Ceramic Complex represents the Late Classic – Early Postclassic Transition period in the north. It is at least partly (if not entirely) contemporaneous with the southern Tepeu 3 Ceramic Complex. The Cehpech Ceramic Complex might in the future more properly be designated an "Early Aspect" of what to us is a much larger, more valid and inclusive "Protopostclassic" period that would subsume the Sotuta Ceramic Complex as a "Late Aspect."

Puuc Unslipped Ware is significant because it includes most jars (fig. 11,*a*) and censers of the Cehpech Ceramic Complex. Puuc Slate Ware displays medium-to-fine-textured paste tempered with calcite, ash, clay lumps, or potsherds. Surface and paste are similar in color ranging through gray to brown; surface finish is smoothed, slipped, and polished to provide a modest luster and produce a waxy feel; surface imperfections include fire-clouding, crazing, and purple or white dendritic markings. Vessel forms include jars (fig. 11,*b-d*),

basins, flaring-sided tripod dishes (fig. 11,*f*), and incurved-rim ring-stand bowls (fig. 11,*e*).

Thin Slate Ware resembles Puuc Slate Ware in waxy surface feel and a few forms, but otherwise the wares are quite distinct. Thin Slate Ware displays fine-textured paste uniformly tempered with saccharoidal calcite; surface and paste are alike in color ranging from pearl gray to cream; surface finish is extremely well smoothed, slipped, polished, and generally free of blemishes. The ware is normally thin walled and its forms include hemispherical bowls with flat bottom (fig. 12,*b*) or ring-stand, cylindrical vases (fig. 12,*a*), and low beakers (fig. 12,*c*). Puuc Red Ware shares many of these forms and is also a thin pottery with a similar waxy feel to surfaces that otherwise are uniformly the same red color as the paste. Vessel forms are hemispherical bowls (fig. 11,*h,i*), tripod bead-lip bowls (fig. 11,*g*), basins, flaring-sided tripod dishes, and cylindrical vases.

The fine orange Balancan Group may in reality have its origins in eastern Tabasco or southwestern Campeche but it becomes an outstanding element of the Cehpech Ceramic Complex. It varies from other fine orange groups in its decorative techniques and vessel forms: an orange, white, or rarely a black slip may be employed; vessel forms (R. E. Smith, 1958, fig. 1) include flaring-sided bowls rounding to flat base, hemispherical bowls with ring-stand base, and cylindrical vases (fig. 10,*h*).

Holactun Black-on-cream is a type that displays a coarse-textured paste usually sherd tempered which in its pinkish to cinnamon color contrasts with the cream slip. Vessel surfaces have been smoothed and polished but are often lumpy; the cream slip has a tendency to peel off; the only decoration is painted in black, usually in parallel vertical lines that present a "trickle" effect. Vessel forms include jars (fig. 11,*j*) and basins, both often having T-shaped rims.

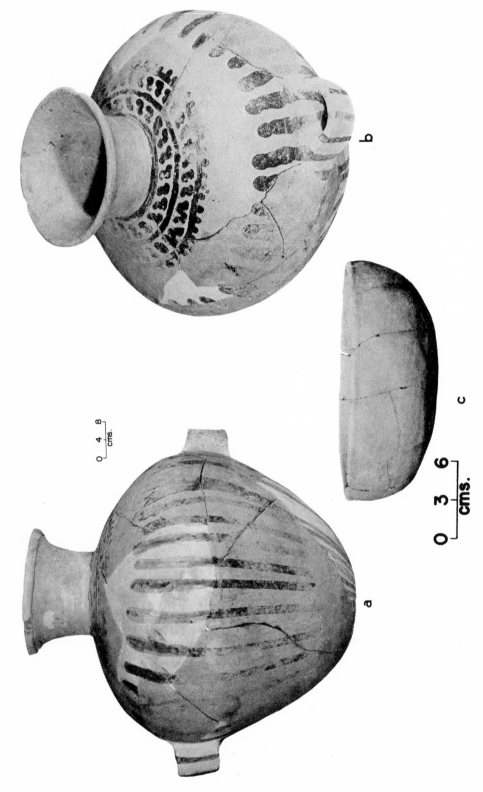

FIG. 13—SELECTED EXAMPLES OF POTTERY FROM THE HOCABA CERAMIC COMPLEX. *a–c*, Peto Cream Ware jars (*a,b*), bowl (*c*). All examples from Mayapan.

WESTERN SUBREGION. There has been nothing as yet discovered in this subregion to give any firm indications that a full ceramic complex existed comparable to Tepeu 3 of the south or Cehpech of the north. Even Palenque[2cc] appears to offer little in the way of a solid occupation that produced pottery dating later than a Tepeu 2 equivalent. The fine orange Balancan Group, however, is known from Western Subregion sites as are examples of Fine Gray Ware. Berlin's Jonuta Horizon (1956, pp. 129–34) also suggests pottery that would be of this period so that the Cehpech Ceramic Complex or one resembling it may be present.

Early Postclassic Period

It is only in the Northern Subregion that a ceramic complex (Sotuta) has been recognized that clearly represents pottery of what may be considered an Early Postclassic period or a "Late Aspect" of the Transition period just examined (see note 7). A few sherds of the Sotuta Ceramic Complex have been found at sites in the Southern and Western subregions testifying not only to the fact that these types reached the south and west well after the ceremonial centers were abandoned but that people must have been living there to receive and carry on such trade. Phases such as New Town at Barton Ramie[2a] seem surely to have been at least partially contemporary with the Sotuta phase, possibly even continuing on to overlap the later Hocaba phase as well. Our "Subregional Review" covering the greater Peten occupation believed to have occurred during Early Postclassic times cannot be elaborated in the present state of our knowledge.

NORTHERN SUBREGION. The Sotuta Ceramic Complex is composed of three locally manufactured wares: two groups obtained in Yucatan through trade, and an additional type. All of these must at least be mentioned if we are to give even a superficial understanding of pottery of this period.

Chichen Unslipped Ware is important because of its jar and censer forms; among the latter are ladle censers (fig. 12,*j*), handled hourglass censers, and pedestal-base vase censers. Some vessels show a white calcareous coating; decorative techniques include appliqué and postfire painting or a combination of the two; surfaces are normally otherwise well smoothed but not polished and are often covered with coarse striations.

Chichen Slate Ware (Brainerd's Mexican Medium Slateware) differs little from Puuc Slate Ware except in the following significant attributes: a strong contrast between a usually gray slip and a reddish brown or red paste; decorative techniques that contribute to distinctive Chichen Slate Ware design styles executed on jars (fig. 12,*e*), basins, bowls, grater bowls, ladle censers, and potlids. Chichen Red Ware (Brainerd's Mexican Medium Redware) is much the same as Puuc Red Ware except that it displays more blemishes, different forms, techniques of decoration, and styles of design. The surfaces of Chichen Red Ware are often fire-clouded and may carry a secondary cream slip on vessel exteriors. Vessel forms include jars, pyriform vessels, cylindrical vases with pedestal base, flaring-sided tripod dishes, and round-sided bowls (fig. 12,*f*).

The fine orange Silho Group is familiar to most persons interested in Middle American pottery because handsome vessels appear in many collections. It is amazing pottery in the way singular shapes and differing decorative techniques are so artfully combined. The group is thoroughly described by R. E. Smith (1957; 1958, pp. 153–55) and needs no further description here aside from an illustration (fig. 10,*j*).

Similarly, the famous plumbate Tohil Group need not be redescribed except to illustrate two of the most common forms (fig. 12,*g,h,i*). Those interested in details concerning Tohil Plumbate types are referred to Shepard's monograph (1948).

527

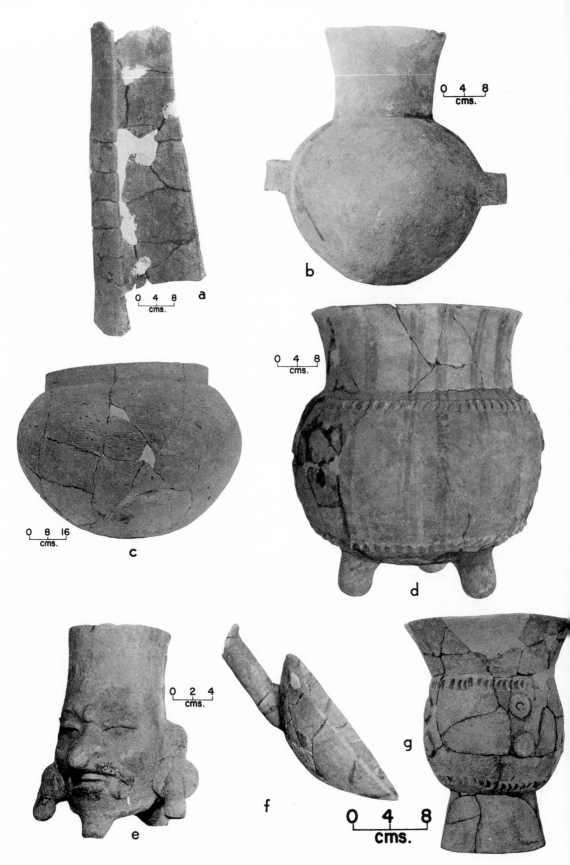

FIG. 14—SELECTED EXAMPLES OF POTTERY FROM THE HOCABA AND TASES CERAMIC COMPLEXES. *a,b,e* (Tases): *a*, Telchaquillo Brick Ware (light-shield?); *b*, San Joaquin Buff Ware jar; *e*, unslipped Chen Mul Group effigy cup. *c,d,f,g* (Hocaba): Hoal Unslipped Ware jar (*c*), tripod jar (*d*), ladle censer (*f*), pedestal-base vase censer (*g*). All examples from Mayapan.

Tinum Red-on-cinnamon is a type included by Brainerd under Early Mexican Unslipped Ware as a special form, perforated "Mixtec type" ladle-handled censers. Actually this is the only form recognized. An example (fig. 12,*d*) is reproduced from the Regil collection in Merida. This type may have been traded to the Northern Subregion but instances of copying by local potters are suspected.

Middle Postclassic Period

This period has been observed only in the Northern Subregion and even here it is not easy to define. Andrews (1960, p. 256) seems to view the interval as a transitional one much as we feel about the previous period. If we are both correct, our "Transition period" might eventually be extended upward in time to also include both the Early Postclassic and this Middle Postclassic period. Andrews' thoughts appear to be inspired in part by his observations concerning a black-on-cream ware which we call Peto Cream Ware. This ware derives many attributes of form and decoration from Chichen Slate Ware; others it takes from the fine orange Silho Group; technologically its paste composition is identical to that of Mayapan Red Ware. The precise time position of Peto Cream Ware is in question. We do not know if it was already a minority pottery in the latest portion of the Sotuta Complex that became more important as time elapsed, or if the pure samples of it found by Brainerd and Andrews at Dzibilchaltun indicate a single ware complex existing between the Sotuta and Hocaba complexes. Our own preference is to think of this ware as merely one (perhaps early) element of the Hocaba Ceramic Complex. It is accordingly identified with the unslipped Hoal Group and the red Mama Group in a complex (Hocaba) that follows the Toltec era of Chichen Itza.

Peto Cream Ware displays lumpy surfaces although smoothed, slipped, and lightly polished; the slip is opaque usually in a cream range on a gray to cinnamon paste ground. Decorations are painted in black but the technique of application is unusual and peculiar to this ware; because the paint could evidently not properly withstand oxidation in the original firing, the black carbon paint must have been applied as a distinct layer after firing and carbonized in such a way as not to discolor the underlying clay. Vessel forms include jars (fig. 13,*a,b*), round-sided bowls (fig. 13,*c*), tripod bowls, grater bowls, and various vase forms.

The unslipped Hoal Group displays vessel surfaces that are roughly to fairly evenly smoothed but never polished; some vessels have a fine sandpaper-like finish ranging to the coarseness of a wood rasp, others are striated. Vessel forms include jars (fig. 14,*c*), ladle censers (fig. 14,*f*), tripod jar censers (fig. 14,*d*), and pedestal-base vase censers (fig. 14,*g*). Mayapan Red Ware is divided into an early group (red Mama – Hocaba Complex) and a late group (red Tzitz – Tases Complex). The red Mama Group displays surfaces that are indifferently smoothed, slipped, and polished but that tend to show a luminous luster; slip color varies from red to other shades on a pink to pale red paste ground. Vessel forms include jars, grater bowls, flaring-sided and round-sided tripod bowls that are slipped all over.

Late Postclassic Period

In the Southern Subregion there are few ceramic data for this period. However, Bullard (1960b, pp. 370–71; and personal communications, 1960–61, regarding pottery taken from 1960 tests) calls attention to a probable Late Postclassic settlement at the Lake Yaxcha island of Topoxte where architectural features and pottery traits combine to give rather definite support to his assumption. The ceramic traits include Mayapan-like censers of effigy and other forms, a distinct ceramic group of cream-

529

Fɪɢ. 15—SELECTED EXAMPLES OF POTTERY FROM THE TASES CERAMIC COM-
PLEX. a, Chen Mul Unslipped effigy censer. b–e, Mayapan Red Ware tripod jars (b,c), jar
(d), pedestal-base plate (e). All examples from Mayapan.

based pottery units displaying decoration in red (in some instances with orange and/or black) most reminiscent of Pele Polychrome (type) at Mayapan, and certain vessel foot form modes which resemble those found in late sites on the east coast of the Yucatan peninsula. In the Northern Subregion ceramic achievements of this period are fairly well contained within the Tases Ceramic Complex. Berlin (1956) has identified the Cintla Horizon and associated pottery as of this period in the Western Subregion.

NORTHERN SUBREGION. The Tases Ceramic Complex – unslipped Chen Mul Group (figs. 14,*e*; 15,*a*) displays the following vessel forms: jars, including an especially huge storage jar (Proskouriakoff and Temple, 1955, fig. 12,*g,h*), censers (same forms as are present in the Hocaba Ceramic Complex), effigy vessels, and bowls of various shapes.

The red Tzitz Group differs from its earlier counterpart, the red Mama Group, in the development of a number of additional or new attributes and modes. These include a tendency to prefer a darker red slip color, four new decorative techniques (fig. 5), and some among the vessel forms shown in figures 15,*b-e*, and 16,*a-k*. The fine orange Matillas Group (fig. 16,*l*) was formerly called V Fine Orange and is described by R. E. Smith (1958, p. 157) and Berlin (1956, pp. 135–36). Although an important pottery element of the Tases Ceramic Complex, it is nevertheless a trade pottery from Tabasco, where it occurs in large percentages.

Telchaquillo Brick Ware displays a coarse friable red paste containing gray to black particles that are probably vitrified bits of sherd temper; surfaces that are vertically smoothed, slipped red, and lightly polished; and interior surfaces that are often crazed and fire-blackened. A few sherds show exterior incised geometric designs. The only form known (fig. 14,*a*) is a sort of split tube, thicker and wider at the bottom, that might conceivably have been used as a light-shield. San Joaquin Buff Ware is largely the same as Mayapan Red Ware except for base color and painted decorations; slip and paste are alike ranging from buff to cinnamon. A jar form is shown in figure 14,*b*.

The distribution of Tulum Red Ware centers on the east coast. It displays fine-to-medium-textured pale orange paste with calcite-quartz temper; surfaces are very well smoothed, slipped red, and lightly polished; vessel forms include jars, flaring-sided tripod bowls, basal-flange bowls, hemispherical bowls, and grater bowls.

WESTERN SUBREGION. Berlin's (1956, pp. 135–41) Cintla Horizon "older stage" pottery provides the few data available for this period in the west. The fine orange Matillas Group is heavily involved and at some as yet unspecified site or sites between the lagoon systems north of Comalcalco and those of the Laguna de Terminos, these types probably originated, enjoyed their greatest popularity, and were manufactured in quantity to be traded elsewhere. The three principal sites at present known to have very high fine orange Matillas Group representations are Tamulte de las Sabanas, Juarez, and Atasta. Berlin notes other unnamed pottery associated with the group at these sites. This material includes modeled pottery portraying objects such as litters, altars, platforms displaying figures, human and animal effigies, and miniature temples; two kinds of censers are also present in a different ware, an hourglass form and the ladle form. Any pottery later than the Sotuta Ceramic Complex is conspicuous by its absence at other western sites such as Jonuta, Tecolpan, Huimango, Tiradero, or Palenque.

Protohistoric Period

There is nothing to report for this period from the Southern and Northern subregions. In the Western Subregion the fine orange Cunduacan Group stands out to

531

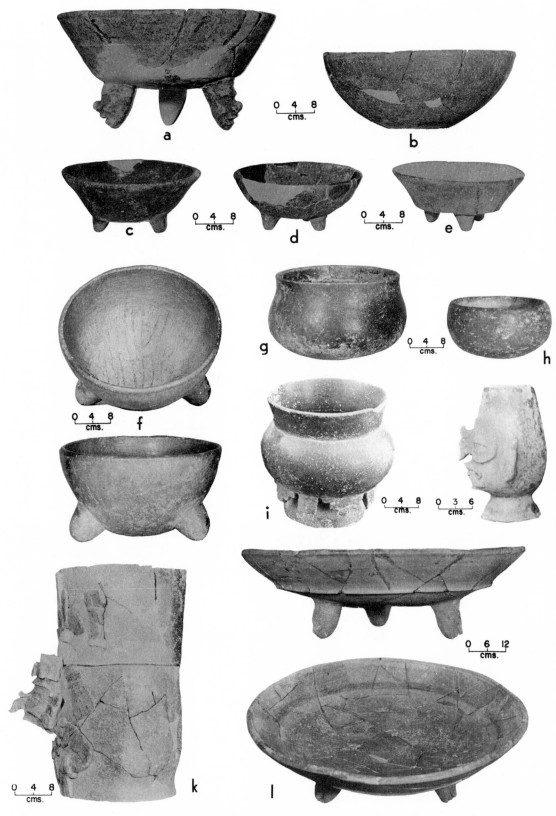

FIG. 16—SELECTED EXAMPLES OF POTTERY FROM THE TASES CERAMIC COM-
PLEX. *a–k*, Mayapan Red Ware: tripod bowls (*a,c–e*), round-sided bowl (*b*), grater bowl (*f*),
deep bowls (*g–i*), effigy vessels (*j,k*). *l*, fine orange Matillas Group tripod plate. All examples
from Mayapan.

proclaim the existence of pottery producers there during the interval between A.D. 1460 (estimated date for the fall of Mayapan) and the conquest. In so far as it is known, Berlin fully discusses and describes the fine orange Cunduacan Group as U Fine Orange (1956, pp. 136–38; see also R. E. Smith, 1958). A complete lack of decoration and the appearance of modeled censers are especially significant features distinguishing it from other earlier fine orange groups. It must be assumed that other ceramic units mentioned in Berlin's report (1956, pp. 138–41) in connection with the fine orange Cunduacan Group, coarse ware, tempered orange, and medium-textured gray, form another part of a Western Protohistoric Chikinchel-like Ceramic Complex.

Colonial Period

It is highly probable that Colonial period pottery was present at a number of lowland Maya sites that have been investigated archaeologically, but for one reason or another these evidences remain unrecorded in the literature. The only record available is from Mani and Mayapan[2r] in the Northern Subregion, where the Colonial period Chauaca Ceramic Complex has been recognized. Principal elements in this complex include: Ochil Unslipped Ware, Abala Red Ware, China Ware, and Glazed Ware. A brief published review of these wares appears in figure 33 and its caption of Brainerd's 1958 report.

"Modern Yucatecan Maya Pottery Making" (R. H. Thompson, 1958) is a monograph set in an archaeological framework that provides an unusually comprehensive coverage of contemporary (1951) ceramic manufacture at eight towns in Campeche and Yucatan.

SUMMARY AND COMMENT

Maya lowland pottery does not comprise as homogeneous an aggregate as one might imagine. The three subregions tend more and more, as their patterns develop, to follow divergent trends in the making and decorating of pottery types. Only during the Preclassic period is there a strong impression of widespread ceramic homogeneity over the entire lowland region. Beginning with the Protoclassic and continuing into the Early Classic in the Southern Subregion, is a trend toward the massive production and extensive distribution of Peten Gloss Ware monochrome and polychrome types. As the Late Classic period develops, this leads with cumulative swiftness to ever-widening separations between pottery of one subregion and that of another. In addition, important ceramic differences are also manifest between geographical units within the Southern Subregion.

In the north there may be a small amount of gloss ware produced locally in Classic times (see note 8), but the greater proportion comes from southern centers of manufacture. The bulk of the indigenous Northern Subregion Classic wares is medium-lustered monochrome of genuinely different character. Actually northern potters hit their stride and take their place as the equals of any during the great "Slate Ware Interval" (Cehpech and Sotuta Ceramic Complexes) of the Transition and Early Postclassic periods (Andrews' Florescent) when slate pottery types appeared in strength. Meanwhile contemporary potters in the Southern Subregion return to an emphasis on the making of monochrome types. Thus, during the comparatively brief Transition period (Uaxactun Tepeu 3 phase) in the south there seems to be a kind of ceramic rapprochement with the north.

Little is known archaeologically of the Western Subregion during the Early Classic, but in the Late Classic period fine-textured wares such as Fine Orange, Fine Gray, and Fine Black (sometimes Thin Black) come to play an important role, as they do to a lesser extent over the Northern Subregion. By the Late Classic – Early Postclassic Transition period, fine-textured

533

pottery dominates the ceramic scene except for the presence of a well-established un-slipped coarse ware. Once into the Late Postclassic period, the fine orange Matillas Group constitutes almost the total pottery picture in the Western Subregion.

Although this same fine orange Matillas Group is also present in the Northern Subregion, it is as trade merchandise from the west; and Mayapan and Tulum Red Wares, in company with abundantly represented coarse unslipped wares, govern the situation here. During the Late Postclassic period in the Southern Subregion such pottery influences as appear seem to have originated in the Northern Subregion, particularly in the environs of the east coast.

Thus in two of these subregions a distinctive ceramic tradition is ultimately attained: the west becomes known for its untempered fine wares, such as the fine orange Matillas and Cunduacan Groups, and the north for calcite-tempered, red-slipped pottery such as the Mayapan and Tulum Red Wares. In the south, on the other hand, the great Peten Gloss Ware ceramic tradition has spent itself and terminated long before the pottery spoken of above appeared; the subregion now suffers a decline in its own pottery-making standards so serious as to lead to almost complete dependence on northern potters for monochrome and decorated pottery ideas and trade pieces. The local southern unslipped wares become unparalleled in the inferior character of their technical aspects.

It would be most gratifying and profitable if the sources of, and the influences involved in, the creation of such extremely divergent ceramic results were better known and understood, but they are not. One may hypothesize that the fine ware trend in the western Maya lowlands was conceived in the state of Veracruz and that the late red wares of the Northern Subregion developed somewhere in southern Quintana Roo and possibly northern British Honduras, but these are only suspicions. At present and in the near future what is needed to resolve these problems and others is more intensive digging throughout the entire Western Subregion as well as in parts of the Northern Subregion, with urgent attention directed toward southern Quintana Roo and northern British Honduras.

REFERENCES

Adams, R. E. W., 1962, 1963
—— and Trik, 1961
Andrews, 1959, 1960
Berlin, 1953, 1956
Brainerd, 1958
Bullard, 1960b
Butler, 1935b
Canby, 1951
Gifford, 1960
Haberland, 1960
Longyear, 1952
Merwin and Vaillant, 1932
Phillips and Gifford, 1959
Proskouriakoff and Temple, 1955
Rands, B. C., 1954
Rands, R. L., 1961a, 1961b
—— and Rands, 1957, 1959, 1960

Ricketson and Ricketson, 1937
Ridgway, 1912
Ruz L., 1945a, 1958
Sanders, 1960a
Shepard, 1948
Smith, A. L., and Kidder, 1943
Smith, R. E., 1954a, 1955a, 1955b, 1957, 1958
—— and Gifford, 1959, in press
——, Willey, and Gifford, 1960
Strong, Kidder, and Paul, 1938
Thompson, J. E. S., 1939a, 1940, 1945
Thompson, R. H., 1958
Vaillant, 1927
Wauchope, 1950
Willey and Gifford, 1961
——, Bullard, Glass, and Gifford, in press

20. Pottery Figurines of the Maya Lowlands

ROBERT L. RANDS and
BARBARA C. RANDS

THROUGHOUT the Lowland Maya Area, as elsewhere in Mesoamerica, quantities of small fired clay figurines were produced.[1] Mainly representing humans and animals, they often took the form of whistles. Rattle effigies were more restricted, both in time and space, and seem to comprise a tangential development or introduction from outside the Maya lowlands. Still other figurines are pottery statuettes, capable of no musical production. Although precise functions are uncertain, figurines may at various times have been associated with sympathetic magic, religious ceremonies, or more purely secular activities. At least in certain periods, the figurines were probably made by craft specialists, for considerable skill in modeling and in the preparation of molds is demonstrated. A number of the effigies are notable expressions of Maya art. While size varies, the majority are less than 20 cm. in height. Specimens found archaeologically are rarely complete except when present in graves and occasional caches, but even fragments are useful in tracing temporal and spatial relationships and can provide information about aspects of ancient Maya life and costume. The figurine tradition was from earliest times spasmodic, reaching its height of elaboration in the Late Classic period. Preclassic, Classic, and many Postclassic examples differ fundamentally in method of manufacture, subject matter, and artistic treatment.[2]

In spite of strong generic connections, figurines known from the Maya lowlands and Mexico offer many striking contrasts. Preclassic figurines of the Lowland Maya Area show an almost monotonous uniformity as compared to the diversity of figurine types in the Valley of Mexico. Comparative-

[1] This article has profited from suggestions by William R. Coe, Gordon F. Ekholm, and Robert E. Smith.

[2] Although numerous figurines have been illustrated as art objects or have received cursory descriptive treatment, comprehensive studies are few. In addition to citations in the text, short but useful discussions of lowland Maya figurines include Spinden, 1913; Brainerd, 1954; Morley, 1956. Unpublished or incompletely published studies of major figurine collections are being made or are to be made by R. E. Smith (Uaxactun), Haviland (Tikal), Cook de Leonard (Jaina), Willey (Altar de Sacrificios), Rands (Piedras Negras, Palenque), and Ekholm (Comalcalco).

535

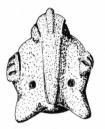

FIG. 1—UAXACTUN, PRECLASSIC. Height 4 cm. (After Ricketson and Ricketson, 1937, fig. 140,*d',d".*)

ly rare in the Maya Preclassic are such characteristic Mexican traits as coffee-bean eyes, body paint, accentuated wasp waists, and prominent turbans. Action and jauntiness are largely lacking. In Classic times, however, the situation was reversed, for locally, at least, this period witnessed the Maya climax in imaginative treatment as well as sophistication and aesthetic refinement. Postclassic figurines, by comparison, were dull in both areas.

PRECLASSIC

In the Maya lowlands, Preclassic figurines are best known from the Mamom deposits at Uaxactun (Ricketson and Ricketson, 1937; R. E. Smith, 1936, 1955b). Examples are not found in the later Chicanel materials, and their absence during the latter part of the Preclassic period in other parts of the southern lowlands is generally accepted. Figurines are extremely rare or absent in any Preclassic materials from Yucatan.

Forms and Technique

Preclassic figurines were hand modeled. Solid human miniatures are the most common form. Hollow whistles representing birds, animals, or human heads also occur, and hollow human effigies which did not serve as whistles are known. The tail comprises the mouthpiece on bird whistles, one to three stops opening from the sounding chamber formed by the body (fig. 1). The mouthpiece occurs at the top in human-

head whistles. Holes for suspension, usually behind the head, appear on most whistles and many of the human figures. At Uaxactun the human torso was apparently made prior to the head, which was sometimes formed around a projecting stump rising, necklike, from the body. Vents appear on hollow limbs and bodies. Projecting elements such as nose, lips, earplugs, and headdress, and occasionally eyes, were appliquéd. Solid circular punches in the center of the elliptical eyes and at earplugs, breasts, and navel formed another diagnostic technique. Punctation or simple incising indicated the hair, incising also showing eyebrows, fingers, and toes. Similar methods were employed in manufacturing the bird whistles, eyes usually being grooved and centrally punched, wings appliquéd, and feathers incised. Whistles and other fig-

FIG. 2—CAYO DISTRICT, BRITISH HONDURAS, PRECLASSIC. Height 7.5 cm. (Courtesy, University Museum, University of Pennsylvania.)

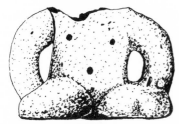

FIG. 3—UAXACTUN, PRECLASSIC. Height 5.7 cm. (After Ricketson and Ricketson, 1937, pl. 70,g.)

FIG. 4—UAXACTUN, PRECLASSIC. Height 6.3 cm. (After Ricketson and Ricketson, 1937, pl. 70,c.)

FIG. 5—UAXACTUN, PRECLASSIC. Height 7 cm. (Courtesy, Peabody Museum, Harvard University.)

urines were generally slipped, often with red, but not painted.

Subjects

Human figurines are standing or seated (figs. 2, 3). Females appear frequently, identifiable by punctate nipples and occasionally well-rounded breasts (figs. 3, 4). Pregnancy, fronto-occipital head deformation, scarification, and filed teeth are sometimes suggested (Porter, 1953, p. 55; J. E. S. Thompson, 1946, p. 25). Costume is simple, normally being restricted to small caps or turbanlike headdresses and round earplugs (figs. 5–9). Although the body is usually nude, skirtlike garments and necklaces are not completely unknown. A specialized subject consists of puffed-cheek human-head whistles, with cheeks distended as if the figure were blowing or whistling.

Styles

Most Preclassic figurines are direct in execution, basic techniques of manufacture being subject to little secondary refinement or elaboration. The resulting style is vigorous but unsophisticated. Heads tend to be disproportionately large (fig. 2) and set directly on broad, heavy shoulders. Limbs sometimes terminate without hands or feet; when present, these appendages often taper into reduced stubby or concave elements. Fine detail is nevertheless known in the representation of fingers and toes. Calves of the leg are occasionally exaggerated. Bodily details are largely unstressed except for heavily punctate nipples and navel. The face is often rounded. A boldly projecting, wedge-shaped nose is characteristic, being cut off sharply at the line of the nostrils

537

Fig. 6—UAXACTUN, PRECLASSIC. Height 7 cm. (Courtesy, Peabody Museum, Harvard University.)

ico (M. D. Coe, 1957a). Variations, however, may be noted within the lowland Maya zone. Especially close relationships to the nearby Ulua Valley are evidenced in handmade figurines at Copan (Longyear, 1952, p. 104). Heads from Coban, Alta Verapaz, are distinguished by punctate nostrils and closely spaced appliquéd elements which frame the head, like a braid, from ear to ear (fig. 8). A similar treatment of hair or headdress occurs at Topoxte (Lake Yaxha) (Bullard, personal communication, 1960). Exceptionally crude figurines are known from British Honduras (fig. 2). At Uaxactun itself, variation exists between flat, crudely appliquéd heads and those realistically modeled (figs. 5, 6). Of no little interest is the occurrence of the baby-face figurine, strongly Olmec in characteristics, at Tierra Blanca, Tabasco, on the lower Usumacinta (fig. 9).

(figs. 5–7). The oblique axes of the large, grooved eyes are frequently emphasized by incised eyebrows which arch upward from the nose, paralleling the lines of the eyes (figs. 6, 7). The center of the eye is further marked by deep punctation. In contrast to the emphasis accorded the eye and other facial features, scant attention was normally given to details of hair or headdress.

Although the figurines as described are particularly characteristic of Uaxactun, similar forms extend beyond the central Peten. Close agreement with Uaxactun norms is found on the lower Usumacinta at Trinidad, Tabasco (figs. 6, 7). Relationships exist in Preclassic horizons outside the lowland Maya area at Kaminaljuyu (Kidder, Article 5), Tres Zapotes–La Venta (Drucker, 1952a), and Panuco (MacNeish, 1954); general correspondences appear in Type A figurines from central Mexico

Fig. 7—TRINDAD, TABASCO, PRECLASSIC. Height 6.5 cm. (Courtesy, University Museum, University of Pennsylvania.)

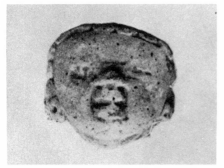

FIG. 8—COBAN, ALTA VERAPAZ, PRECLAS-SIC. Height 3 cm. (After Ricketson and Ricketson, 1937, pl. 74,*a*,2.)

CLASSIC

Lowland Maya figurines of the Classic period display an elaboration and sophistication absent in the Preclassic. Most are attributable to the Late Classic, being assigned to Tepeu deposits at Uaxactun (R. E. Smith, 1936), Full Classic at Copan (Longyear, 1952), San Jose 4 in British Honduras (J. E. S. Thompson, 1939a), Chama 3–4 in the Alta Verapaz (Butler, 1940), Jonuta horizon in Tabasco (Berlin, 1956), and Florescent in the Puuc (Brainerd, 1958). The importance of figurines late in the Classic sequence is also indicated by incompletely studied collections from Piedras Negras, Palenque, and Tikal. The new artistic and technical concepts possibly made their appearance in the Early Classic, and an extension into Postclassic times may also have occurred. A human effigy whistle (fig. 10) is reported from an Early Classic burial at Nebaj; head and headdress are moldmade, the body being modeled by hand (A. L. Smith and Kidder, 1951, p. 76). Ruz (1945b, pp. 71–72) ascribes the elaborately modeled figurines in Jaina style to a Tzakol–early Tepeu horizon, prior to the rise of moldmade figurines, which are in turn believed to precede the Mexican period. Confirmation of this suggested sequence of figurines in coastal Campeche has not, however, been published.

FIG. 9—TIERRA BLANCA (BETWEEN EMILIANO ZAPATA AND BALANCAN, TABASCO), PRECLASSIC. Height 10 cm.

Forms and Technique

Among developments in figurine manufacture, the use of molds had special importance. Molds, many with intricate detail, were made of fired clay, examples occasionally being found in Classic deposits. Plastic clay was pressed into molds to form the front of moldmade figurines; the base and back, usually plain, were added by hand. Detail might be heightened by appliquéing additional elements or retouching with a tool. Other figurines were partially moldmade or entirely handmodeled. A well-known specimen (fig. 37) is distinctive in manufacture, being constructed from a series of separately formed elements. Finishing techniques often differed from the Preclassic. Although a white wash appears on examples from Jaina, and Puuc figurines were often slipped, some tendency

539

FIG. 10—NEBAJ, CLASSIC. Height 16.7 cm.
(After A. L. Smith and Kidder, 1951, fig. 87,*a*.)

exists for Classic specimens to be well
smoothed but unslipped. On the other
hand, there was considerable use of blue
and red paint, yellow also being a popular
color at Jaina.

Notable for its high artistic development,
one class of effigies consists of free-limbed
humans, with modeled arms and legs
welded to the torso (fig. 11). The head was
sometimes made in a mold (compare fig.
12) and tenoned by a modeled neck to the
body (fig. 13). The torso might be hollow,
with an aperture at the neck into which
the tenon could be inserted, or solid. A
number of these figurines were apparently
modeled entirely by hand. Referred to as
"freestanding," the class also includes seated
persons. Certain small, free-limbed figures
are distinctive for their comparative crude-
ness. Uncommon, free-limbed human figure
whistles form a related group (figs. 10, 14).

540

FIG. 11—JAINA, CLASSIC. Height ca. 18 cm.
(After Rubín de la Borbolla, 1953, pl. 175.)

Mold-pressed human-figure whistles differ fundamentally, the front of the figurine
—head, limbs, and torso—being made from
one mold in a single operation (figs. 15–17).
The separately modeled whistle mouthpiece was usually added to the back, often
in a basal position, but was occasionally
placed at head, shoulder, knee, or other location. Frequently the mouthpiece pro-
truded downward from the base, serving
with two stubby modeled feet to form a

FIG. 12—LABNA, CLASSIC. Height 6 cm. (After Brainerd, 1958, fig. 56,*t*.)

FIG. 13—PALENQUE, CLASSIC. Height 5.5 cm.

FIG. 14—JAINA STYLE, CLASSIC. Height 16 cm. (After Kelemen, 1943, pl. 133,*a*.)

FIG. 15—PALENQUE, CLASSIC. (Courtesy, Instituto Nacional de Antropología e Historia, Mexico.)

FIG. 17—TIKAL, CLASSIC. Height 10.2 cm. (Courtesy, University Museum, University of Pennsylvania.)

FIG. 16—NEBAJ, CLASSIC. Height 21 cm. (Courtesy, University Museum, University of Pennsylvania.)

tripod support, allowing the human effigy to stand erect. A flat base with mouthpiece projecting from the back on the same level is also common. Holes for suspension are sometimes present. Mold-pressed whistles are hollow, the sound chamber often extending upward from the mouthpiece into the head. Stops, when occurring, usually are located in the back. The presence of stops permits the production of additional notes, thereby technically differentiating the ocarina from the simple, one-pitched

whistle, although the term "whistle" is commonly used to include single- and multi-note varieties (Joyce, 1933, p. xv; Martí, 1955, p. 63; Brainerd, 1958, p. 218).

Most of the additional figurine forms correspond in basic method of manufacture to the mold-pressed human effigy whistles. Differences may be simply that of subject (birds, animals, figures on thrones). Double figures, formed of two-headed beings or comprising persons or birds placed side by side on the same figurine, constitute another special class (fig. 18). Pellets, placed in human-figure rattles before front and back were joined, sometimes substituted for the usual whistle structure (fig. 19). Effigy flutes or flageolets frequently bear moldmade faces (fig. 20). "Whistle-boxes" consist of thronelike pedestals onto the

542

G. 18—PIEDRAS NEGRAS, CLASSIC. Height 9.5 cm.
Courtesy, University Museum, University of Pennsyl-
nia.)

FIG. 19—CAMPECHE COAST STYLE, CLASSIC
OR EARLY POSTCLASSIC. (After Fuhrmann,
1923, pl. 59.)

top of which small human figures were
welded (fig. 21). Movable arms and legs
characterize the rare jointed figurines (fig.
22). Exotic modeled pieces are known,
their range in form and subject being uncertain because of difficulty in establishing
the authenticity of many specimens. A human head emerging from a flower (fig. 23)
and group scenes exemplify this heterogeneous lot.

Subjects

Only a sample of the diverse human,
animal, anthropomorphic, and grotesque
subjects appearing in Classic Maya figurines can be mentioned. Female figures, although not ubiquitous as in the Preclassic,
had considerable popularity. Identified by
rounded breasts, women wear skirts, *huipil*-
like garments, elaborate turbans, and wide-

brimmed conical hats (figs. 24–27). Long
hair is sometimes parted in the center (figs.
28, 29). With rare exceptions, children,
daily life, and eroticism received little attention. Male figures are recognizable by
the presence of a loincloth or, very rarely,
a beard. Supplementary items of costume
occasionally make further identification
possible. Ball-game players (fig. 30) are
distinguished by large protective belt,
knee-pad, ball, and perhaps glove (J. E. S.
Thompson, 1943b). Masked figures from
Lubaantun, wearing close-fitting, visor-like
helmets, are also identified by Joyce (1933)
as ball-game players (fig. 31). Warriors
form a large group. Diagnostics include
macuahuitl (war club inset with stone

543

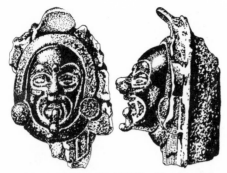

Fig. 20—LABNA, CLASSIC. Height 8.4 cm. (After Brainerd, 1958, fig. 56,*j*.)

a

Fig. 22—CAMPECHE COAST STYLE, CLASSIC OR EARLY POSTCLASSIC. Height 33 cm. (Courtesy, University Museum, University of Pennsylvania.)

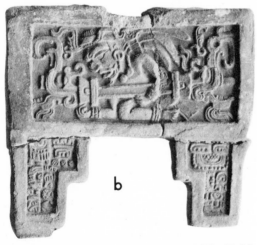

b

Fig. 21—CHAJCAR, ALTA VERAPAZ, CLASSIC. (*a*, after Dieseldorff, 1926–33, vol. 1, fig. 18; *b*, courtesy, Peabody Museum, Harvard University.)

Fig. 24—ZONA SALA, CHIAPAS, CLASSIC.
Height 16.5 cm. (Courtesy, University Museum,
University of Pennsylvania.)

Fig. 23—JAINA STYLE, CLASSIC. Height 20 cm.
(Courtesy, University Museum, University of Pennsylvania.)

FIG. 25—JAINA, CLASSIC. Height ca. 18 cm. (After Rubín de la Borbolla, 1953, pl. 177.)

blades) and shield (figs. 32, 33). A large bird or animal helmet, which would provide protection against blows directed toward head and neck, sometimes encases the face (fig. 34). The puffy-cheeked, pot-bellied "Fat God" normally wears a union-suitlike garment, apparently the *ichcahuipilli* or quilted cotton armor of the Aztecs (fig. 35). A fan is usually held instead of an offensive weapon, although a few heavy-paunched individuals are shown with shield, war club, or less closely fitting forms of body armor (fig. 32). Portraying unusual action, figure 36 may represent a

FIG. 26—JAINA, CLASSIC. (After Linné, 1956, p. 123.)

warrior about to decapitate a captive whom he holds by the hair; and probable trophy heads, suspended in inverted position on the chest, appear on other figurines (fig. 37). Dancing males, with foot upraised, sometimes hold vegetal produce such as maize or cacao in the hand, an association consistent with an identification of the figures as participants in agricultural ceremonies (fig. 38). Musicians with rattles also occur (fig. 16). Other figures, seated in a litter (Joyce, 1933, pl. 6,5) or on a throne (fig. 39), are clearly of high rank or status.

In contrast, the great majority of male or female figurines are standing or seated impassively, without costume or other characteristics which relate them obviously to a particular social role. To be sure, J. E. S. Thompson (1946, p. 24) has suggested that one of the widely distributed figurine traits,

FIG. 27—UAXACTUN, CLASSIC. Height 8 cm. (Courtesy, Peabody Museum, Harvard University.)

FIG. 28—ALTA VERAPAZ, CLASSIC. Height 15 cm. (Courtesy, Peabody Museum, Harvard University.)

FIG. 29—"PALENQUE" (JONUTA STYLE), CLASSIC. Height 7 cm. (Courtesy, Museum of the American Indian, Heye Foundation.)

FIG. 30—TECOLPAN, CHIAPAS, CLASSIC. Height 12.5 cm. (Courtesy, American Museum of Natural History.)

a row of raised circles above the nose, may denote rank, group, or status (figs. 13, 34). This has also been interpreted as a device to induce crossed eyes (Lothrop, Foshag, and Mahler, 1957, pp. 253–55). An extension of the nose onto the forehead sometimes appears immediately below the circles or takes their place (figs. 36, 39, 40). Beads, ornaments stuck on the skin, or scarification may be depicted. Facial tattooing or scarification is, in any case, clearly shown on a number of figurines, and artificial head deformation is often pronounced (figs. 41, 13).

Nonhuman and anthropomorphic figurines portray a wide range of subjects. Owls and other birds, monkeys, jaguars, and dogs are shown in naturalistic fashion, although human articles of attire, such as necklaces or earplugs, were sometimes added (figs. 42, 43). Other figurines, combining manlike bodies with bird or animal heads, could represent either supernatural beings or masked humans. Several instances occur of an anthropomorphic jaguar that towers above one or more apparently adult humans (Spinden, 1913, pl. 17,*10*; J. E. S. Thompson, 1939a, pl. 23,*a,c*). Appearing close to the jaguar's legs, the humans are dwarfed by this powerful but seemingly protecting anthropomorphic figure. The scene strongly recalls Stela 10, Piedras Negras (9.15.10.0.0), Lintel 3 of Temple I,

FIG. 32—PALENQUE, CLASSIC. (Courtesy, Peabody Museum, Harvard University.)

FIG. 33—PALENQUE, CLASSIC. (Courtesy, Peabody Museum, Harvard University.)

548

FIG. 34—CHAMA, CLASSIC. Height 16.5 cm. (Courtesy, University Museum, University of Pennsylvania.)

FIG. 35—JAINA, CLASSIC. (After Linné, 1956, p. 121.)

Tikal (ca. 9.13.0.0.0), and Lintel 2 of Temple IV, Tikal (ca. 9.16.0.0.0) (Maler, 1901–03, pl. 19; W. R. Coe, Shook, and Satterthwaite, 1961, p. 39, figs. 13, 22). In some figurines having grotesque faces, an attempt appears to have been made to depart from reality in the representation of supernatural beings or god-impersonators (fig. 44). In other grotesques, human features may merely have been caricatured or grossly exaggerated to achieve artistic impact (fig. 33).

Although methods of figurine classification are not standardized, the subjects portrayed have generally served as a major criterion for establishing types. Butler (1935a) recognizes almost 20 types of persons or characteristic poses in lowland Maya figurines of the Classic period. Among those not mentioned above are the hunchback, woman with adult child (fig. 24), owl man, nude fat man, woman-at-metate, seated woman, cross-legged figure with hands on knees (fig. 25), woman with hands at sides (fig. 29), figure with hands raised, figure with hands down (fig. 17),

FIG. 38—ALTA VERAPAZ, GUATEMALA, CLASSIC Height 23 cm. (Courtesy, University Museum, University of Pennsylvania.)

FIG. 36—CHIPAL, ALTA VERAPAZ, CLASSIC. Height 16 cm. (Courtesy, University Museum, University of Pennsylvania.)

FIG. 37—PUEBLO COPANAHUASTA (BETWEEN LA LIBERTAD AND COMITAN, CHIAPAS), CLASSIC. Height 16 cm. (Courtesy, American Museum of Natural History.)

FIG. 39—JAINA STYLE, CLASSIC. (Courtesy Peabody Museum, Harvard University.)

FIG. 40—PALENQUE, CLASSIC. Height 5 cm. (Courtesy, University Museum, University of Pennsylvania.)

FIG. 41—USUMACINTA RIVER, SOUTHERN MEXICO, CLASSIC. Height 5 cm. (Courtesy, American Museum of Natural History.)

standing woman with hands resting at waist, and standing woman with hands turned out. Berlin's classification of Jonuta figurines emphasizes details of the head to a greater degree but is similar in the weight given to subjects or isolated motifs: dot decorated, bar decorated, hat bearer, baby-buffoon, old animal man, the Maya Horus, broad-faced woman, and throne figurines (Berlin, 1956, pp. 125–26). A satisfactory approach to figurine classification is admittedly difficult, especially when one must work with fragmentary materials. It would seem more rewarding, nevertheless, to establish types on the basis of combinations of attributes which include style, technology, and form. Much of the subject matter and many decorative elements, which cross-cut these basic categories, could then be analyzed as modes.

Styles

Realism, elegance, and refinement are pronounced in Classic as compared to Preclassic figurines. Except in the portrayal of grotesques, facial features are shown with minimal stylization, and proportions of head and body are generally lifelike. Unlike the Preclassic treatment, attention is often directed from the figurine's face and body to headdress and clothing, which catch the eye because of their consummate detail. The characteristic passive features and lack of musculature facilitate this subordination of the person to his accoutrements. Contrast with the Preclassic, observable in various features, is nowhere more apparent than in the eyes, where lidded, almond-shaped forms replace the grooved-and-punctate.

551

Fig. 42—PETEN, CLASSIC
Height 5.5 cm. (After R. E.
Smith, 1954b, fig. 3,m.)

Stylistic diversity nonetheless exists. An
attempt to systematize these differences
has been made by Butler (1935a), who
recognizes two general styles (X, Y) and
three basic headforms (A, B, C). Style X,
a "realistic, finely executed" rendering of
the human body, is contrasted with the
"crude, bold treatment" of Style Y. Headforms A, B, and C refer, respectively, to
oval face with slanting forehead and sloping chin, square face with upright to
bulging forehead, and wide face with
slanting forehead and projecting chin (fig.
45). Style X and Headform A have the
greatest incidence, appearing on both mold-
pressed and free-limbed figurines. A
stepped or terraced hair arrangement is
frequently associated with this style and
form of head (figs. 14, 24–26, 40).

Certain stylistic differences correlate with
manufacturing techniques. This may be due
to the direct influence of methods of manufacture on style but could also result from
the fortuitous co-existence of the particular
technical and stylistic approaches. Whatever the causal factors, figurines made from
complete-figure molds tend to be flat in
front, the back and sides showing less
natural rounding than on modeled specimens. The head is not separated from the
torso by a well-defined neck as in free-
limbed humans (figs. 11, 14). Rather, the
chin appears at the level of the shoulders
or is set against the chest, and the face may
be flanked by hair or costume (figs. 17, 28).
Such devices minimize the discrete nature
of head and torso, giving an essentially
rectangular unity to the figurine and its
mold. Again in contrast to the freestanding
figurines, which frequently attain balance
through the use of a wide stance, the legs

552

Fig. 43—JAINA STYLE, CLASSIC. Height 13.5
cm. (Courtesy, University Museum, University of
Pennsylvania.)

often are united by a long skirt, a wide low-
hanging loincloth apron, or a seated pos-
ture (figs. 26, 16, 15). Arms rest against
the body, and one of the hands may hold
a fan or other object, which appears in low
relief. The moldmade figurine whistles, accordingly, exploit detail rather than basic
shape to achieve effect, for there has been
an essential union of head, body, limbs, and
costume.

Temporal distinctions among the Classic
figurines are poorly understood. A sequence
from free-limbed to mold-impressed human figurines has often been assumed
(Brainerd, 1958, p. 219). Supporting this
are: the general Mesoamerican tendency
for hand-modeled figurines to precede

FIG. 44—PALENQUE, CLASSIC. Height approx. 16 cm. (Courtesy, Peabody Museum, Harvard University.)

moldmade; stylistic differences between free-limbed and moldmade figures at Jaina, suggesting that the two were not contemporaneous; the strong tendency for mold-pressed forms at Jaina to be made from fine-paste orange clay—an indication of lateness, consistent with the temporal position of Fine Orange pottery; and the clear temporal priority of a free-limbed figurine over a mold-pressed specimen from Nebaj tombs (figs. 10, 16). Moreover, the stylistic simplicity of many moldmade figurines at Jaina could suggest an early Postclassic degeneration from Classic norms. At Palenque, however, abundant figurine materials indicate the increasing popularity of the free-limbed form at the end of the occupation in terminal Classic times.

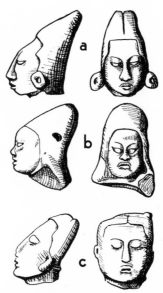

FIG. 45—CLASSIC HEAD FORMS, PIEDRAS NEGRAS. *a*, Head form A. *b*, Head form B. *c*, Head form C. (After Butler, 1935a, fig. 1,*a–c*.)

Figurine heads which constitute a variant of Butler's Style Y occur in stratigraphically early contexts at Piedras Negras and Palenque (figs. 46, 47; Butler, 1935b, p. 46). Heads are broad, fairly flat, and solid, with a squared headdress that frames the face, extending down to prominent circular earplugs. Heads of this type are rare at each site, a single specimen being known from Palenque, and contrast sharply in style with the abundant later figurines. Associated pottery at Piedras Negras indicates an Early Classic dating.

Regional Styles and Relationships

Although participating in a common tradition, Classic figurines of the Lowland Maya Area exhibit significant regional variations. Boundaries of stylistic subareas cannot be satisfactorily defined, for sizable collections have been made at only a few sites. The extent of trade in figurines from their place of manufacture is undetermined. Molds were not found in the extensive excavations at Uaxactun, which suggests that the figurines were imported, but occur with

553

FIG. 46—PIEDRAS NEGRAS, CLASSIC. Height 6.4 cm. (Courtesy, University Museum, University of Pennsylvania.)

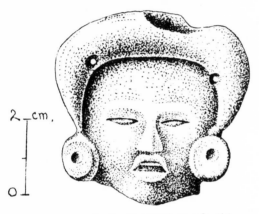

FIG. 47—PALENQUE, CLASSIC. Height 5.6 cm. (Courtesy, Instituto Nacional de Antropología e Historia, Mexico.)

FIG. 48—PUUC STYLE, CLASSIC. Height 8.8 cm. (After Brainerd, 1958, fig. 55,*aa.*)

figurines at nearby Tikal. At Palenque, where considerable technological diversity exists in the ceramics, both figurines and molds occur in the same paste as apparently indigenous pottery, indicating a place of manufacture at or near the site (Rands and Rands, 1959, p. 225). On the other hand, large numbers of burials containing figurines have been found at Jaina, leading to the suggestion that effigies made over a considerable area may have been brought there to be deposited with the dead (Shook and Proskouriakoff, 1951; Brainerd, 1958, p. 219).

We consider eight subareas.

PUUC (E. H. Thompson, 1897b; Brainerd, 1958). To a degree unusual in Maya figurines, effigy representation is supplemental to the essential form of the musical instrument. Effigy flutes and whistles with solid, moldmade heads but simplified bodies are characteristic. Often arms are vestigial and legs nonexistent, as the whistle terminates in a flat base, into which the mouthpiece opens directly from the bottom (fig. 48). Brainerd notes resemblances to Uaxactun figurines of the Tepeu 3 subphase and calls attention to the surprising absence of Jaina examples in collections from the Puuc.

JAINA-CAMPECHE COAST (Hamy, 1897; Maler, 1912; Ruz Lhuillier, 1945b; Toscano, 1945; Moedano Köer, 1946; Piña Chan, 1948; Shook and Proskouriakoff, 1951; Lothrop, Foshag, and Mahler, 1957; Spinden, 1957a; Brainerd, 1958; Cook de Leonard, 1959b). Beyond the unusually large number of complete specimens recovered from burials, the fame of Jaina's figurines rests on the deft realism and imaginative range in solid, free-limbed, frequently hand-modeled human forms (figs. 11, 23). Moldmade figurines, in contrast, are usually highly stylized, with extreme dorsoventral flattening, broad faces, and shallow decorative detail. Females appear frequently, and traits such as jointed figurines, rattles, and figures with hands upraised—of limited occurrence elsewhere—are likewise characteristic in the mold-impressed group. (See figs. 19, 22, "Campeche Coast" style.) In modeled examples, males with arms crossed on the chest (fig. 14) and bare-shouldered, seated female figures with spindly arms and legs (fig. 25) are frequently found. Costume tends to be fairly simple except for large, ornately appliquéd caps and turbans. Feathers and masks are uncommon in the headdress, in contrast to portions of the southern Maya lowlands and the Alta Verapaz. Nevertheless, the free-limbed figurines have strong affiliations with the Usumacinta, whereas mold-impressed examples show correspondences to forms in Veracruz (Butler, 1935a; Peterson, 1952; Medellín Zenil and Peterson, 1954; Brainerd, 1958, p. 219).

JONUTA-LOWER USUMACINTA (Rickards, 1910; Maler, 1912; Blom and LaFarge, 1926–27, vol. 1; Berlin, 1956). The numerous Jonuta figurines are frequently untempered, corresponding in paste to Fine Orange pottery (R. E. Smith, 1958, p. 157), a feature shared with moldmade figurines at Jaina to the northeast and Altar de Sacrificios, in the upper Usumacinta drainage, to the south. This distribution, as well as stylistic considerations, indicates that the Lower Usumacinta probably played an important role in the dissemination of figurine traits. Additional features occurring with unusual frequency at Jonuta and Jaina include facial tattooing or scarification, elaborate turbans, thrones, and rattles. Figurines from the Lower Usumacinta show considerable diversity. In addition to the typical realistic heads, broad-faced women appear with long hair parted in the center (fig. 29, purportedly from Palenque, is representative of this Jonuta type.) Hooded figures, whose hands are brought together over the chest with fingers pointing upward, occur sporadically (fig. 49); although the terraced hair is a Classic trait, the cape markings and position of the hands provide close correspondences to an insecurely dated stone sculpture from San Simon, Yucatan

FIG. 49—MONTECRISTO (EMILIANO ZAPATA), TABASCO, CLASSIC. Height 12 cm. (Courtesy, Smithsonian Institution.)

(Proskouriakoff, 1951, fig. 6,b). Whistles with stops in the forehead constitute another local form (fig. 41). Certain of these divergent types may prove to be of Postclassic origin.

PALENQUE (Ruz Lhuillier, 1952a, 1952c, 1962b; B. C. Rands, 1954). Hierarchal aspects are pronounced in Palenque figurines. The numerous grotesque faces resemble those modeled in stucco and on probable pottery incense burners at the site. Superimposed mask headdresses framed by feathers (fig. 44) closely resemble stelae from Quirigua and Tonina. An apparently quilted textile hanging from the neck, perhaps a form of flexible armor (fig. 33), also appears on Jaina figurines and on stone sculptures from Yaxchilan, being virtually unknown elsewhere.[3] Further correspondences between Palenque and Jaina figurines include the abundance of free-limbed humans, high nose passing onto the forehead, and row of circles above the nose. Human heads from the two sites often agree closely in style, correspondences extending to a vertical slot above the forehead in which decorations might be placed (figs. 25, 40). Yet turbans are rare at Palenque. A distinctive feature of Palenque figurines is the large number of grotesque and animal-headed warriors (figs. 32, 33). Whistles at Palenque, in contrast to many Maya sites, are predominantly of the single-note variety, and the figurines as a whole tend to be unusually small.

MIDDLE AND UPPER USUMACINTA (Butler, 1935b; Willey, Smith, Bullard, and Graham, 1960b). A strong if comparatively unspectacular figurine development is indicated on the basis of fragmentary materials excavated at Piedras Negras and Altar de Sacrificios, as well as occasional finds from other localities. Fine Orange figurines, common at Altar, are unknown at Piedras Negras yet occur at both Jaina and Jonuta; temporal factors may help to explain this apparently interrupted distribution. Human faces at Altar tend to be slightly wider than at Piedras Negras, suggesting an affiliation with Alta Verapaz figurines a short distance to the south, whereas specimens from Piedras Negras, mostly of Butler's Headform A, correspond more closely in this

regard to typical lowland Maya norms. At the present time a distinctive, over-all regional style cannot be formulated.

ALTA VERAPAZ – NEBAJ (Seler, 1902–23, 3: 670–87; Dieseldorff, 1926–33, vol. 1; Butler, 1940; A. L. Smith and Kidder, 1951; R. E. Smith, 1952; A. Kidder and Samayoa Chinchilla, 1959). A rich development of moldmade figurines occurred, especially in the Coban district. Although the style is regionally distinctive, basic affiliations are toward the Maya lowlands. Effigies have marked dorsoventral flattening. The resulting side flanges, unlike Jaina examples, serve as a background on which a wealth of accoutrements, sometimes ceremonial in nature, appear in low relief (fig. 38). Elaborate feather headdresses are frequently shown on the flanges, being characterized by openwork and length of plumage (fig. 16). Turbans and tattooing, traits of a more northerly distribution, are rare. The face, broad but realistic, generally lacks a row of dots or a high nose extending onto the forehead. Considerable animation is shown, dancing figures being characteristic and portrayals of everyday life having a vivid naturalism (figs. 38, 28). Contributing to this realism is a departure from the rigid bilateral symmetry which typifies many Maya figurines. Whistle pedestals for figurines are thronelike but in addition to glyphs bear unusually elaborate low-relief designs, which attain the quality of stone sculptures from the Maya lowlands. This is well seen in figure 21,b, a semireclining figure holding a ceremonial bar, which closely resembles the compositions on Lintels 38–40, Yaxchilan (ca. 9.17.0.0.0) (Maler, 1901–03, pl. 65).

PETEN (R. E. Smith, 1936, 1954b). Figurine development was along general lines, with comparatively little local elaboration. As elsewhere, mold-pressed whistles with tail mouthpiece constituted the basic form. Seated figures with mask headdresses and feather panaches are abundant at Tikal (fig. 17). Like the Fat God, aged humans,

[3] Hierarchal features on modeled ceramics at Palenque and their correspondences in stone sculpture are discussed by Rands and Rands (1959). The distinctive, low-hanging neckpiece was popular on figurines from Palenque and Jaina (figs. 33, 39) and on Yaxchilan monuments (Stelae 18, 20, Lintels 4, 12, 16, 26, 45, 46) (ca. 9.13.0.0.0 – 10.0.10.0.0). Comparable objects, usually shown hanging from the wrist, appear frequently at Bonampak (ca. 9.18.0.0.0) (Ruppert, Thompson, and Proskouriakoff, 1955, figs. 17,b; 28).

owls, and wide-brimmed conical hats, they are closely duplicated outside the Peten, although some of these traits may prove to have a greater concentration in this area. Flageolets sometimes strongly resemble Puuc types.

LUBAANTUN (Gann, 1925a, 1928a; Joyce, 1926, 1933; Joyce, Clark, and Thompson, 1927). In contrast to adjacent areas, Lubaantun was the locale of a spectacular development of moldmade whistle figurines. Other features important at Lubaantun (dots above the nose, turbans, thrones decorated with pseudoglyphs) are known primarily from Campeche and the Lower Usumacinta. The presence of figurines showing daily life is reminiscent of the Alta Verapaz. On the other hand, masked figures, wearing curious helmets, are strongly localized (fig. 31).

Classic figurines are poorly represented in other portions of the Maya lowlands, such as Copan, the lower Motagua, and the eastern part of the Yucatan Peninsula. In the far west, toward Comalcalco, figurines are apparently more abundant, but the nature of relationships with the Jonuta zone is not clear. It is possible to group the lowland Maya figurines into different geographic units than those just presented. Thus a broad area embracing Jaina, Jonuta, and Palenque may be recognized as one of two climax zones of the Maya figurine tradition, the other centering in the Alta Verapaz.

POSTCLASSIC

In the Postclassic period, the lowland Maya figurine tradition suffered a partial eclipse. The decline may have been under way by the close of the Classic sequence, as seen at Uaxactun, where crudely modeled and appliquéd figurines are found on the surface; in Holmul 5 and San Jose 5 materials from British Honduras (J. E. S. Thompson, 1931, p. 256; 1939a, pl. 22,1,2); and at Jaina, where the apparently terminal Classic or beginning Postclassic moldmade figurines

FIG. 50—JUAREZ, TABASCO, POSTCLASSIC. Width 49.5 cm. (After Berlin, 1956, fig. 6,*ii.*)

FIG. 51—SANTA RITA, BRITISH HONDURAS, POSTCLASSIC. Height 14 cm. (After Gann, 1918, fig. 16.)

suggest a stylistic retrogression. Figurines are virtually unknown from the Mexican period in Yucatan, although small, figurine-like vessels were modeled in animal form (Brainerd, 1958, p. 218). Though still sparse and stylistically simple, figurines were more numerous on a late Postclassic horizon. A degeneration in technique from Classic times is indicated. Several late examples from Mayapan and British Honduras are described as unfired (Gann, 1918, p. 61), and the use of molds appears to have lost much of its importance. Emphasis

557

turned from manufacture of figurines to the modeling of elaborate effigy censers.

Postclassic figurines are best known from Mayapan and contemporaneous sites in the Yucatan Peninsula (A. L. Smith and Ruppert, 1954b, 1956; Sanders, 1960a), Santa Rita (Gann, 1900, 1918), and Tabasco (Berlin, 1956). Forms include bird and animal whistles, male and female effigies, occasionally in the form of whistles, and jointed human figures. While throne-based figurines of Classic type are unknown, the Cintla horizon in Tabasco reveals one-piece platforms, supported by caryatids, upon which a principal figure stands; strongly Mexicanized motifs occur (fig. 50). Modeled temple miniatures are also found. A popular subject at Santa Rita and elsewhere consists of warriors armed with lances. Stylistically, Postclassic figurines as known at the present time are typified by the simplification of the human figure, rather than by an integrated body of traits. Features which may prove to characterize one or more Postclassic styles include flat-topped heads, thickset forearms with large hands, flaccid arms and legs that seem almost jointless, round appliquéd earplugs which project prominently from the sides of the head, and the extensive use of small round fillets to indicate diadems, labrets, or other ornaments (fig. 51). Some of these features are shared with effigy censers. Absent are the Classic diagnostics of finely delineated heads, attention to details of costume, and realistic anatomical proportions.

PRESUMED FUNCTIONS

Many figurines—Preclassic, Classic, and Postclassic—were whistles. Holes for suspension are especially common on Preclassic whistles, and those objects may sometimes have been worn around the neck, where they could be readily used. It has been suggested that whistles were employed thus in hunting, their notes simulating the call of the bird or animal represented (Ricketson and Ricketson, 1937, p. 217). Whistles could also have been worn by participants in religious ceremonies, or carried by some other means in the many cases where suspension holes are absent. Effigy rattles were possibly used as an accompaniment to singing or dancing but may have provided idle entertainment, in the manner of cascabel feet on pottery vessels. Multiple functions as musical instruments seem probable.

Effigy whistles and rattles, as well as figurines without music-making properties, presumably derived some significance from the type of object which was represented. Preclassic female figurines are commonly thought to be associated with principles of growth and fertility. Use of figurines as household gods or amulets is possible, although portrayals are mostly naturalistic, lacking the grotesque features generally found on deities in codices or monumental art. While religious symbolism is difficult to pin down with certainty, it appears to be unusually strong in the figurines of Palenque and the Alta Verapaz. A religio-ceremonial significance may be indicated by the rare occurrence of cached figurines.[4] Figurines are abundant in close proximity to temples and other major structures at Palenque but at Tikal have been found predominantly in small domestic structures. Borhegyi (1956b) has related figurines of the Guatemala highlands to a folk cult, more or less independent of the priestly hierarchy. In addition to ceremonial functions on hierarchal or lay levels, figurines may have served as ritual objects for more purely individual purposes, or even as tokens of secular status. Warrior

[4] Buried deposits of figurines are known at Palenque (Ruz 1952c, pls. 14, 35–40) and Santa Rita (Gann, 1900, pp. 680–85; 1918, pp. 59–60). Pottery figurines, however, do not form part of the basic cache pattern of the lowland Maya (W. R. Coe, Article 17).

and throne-based figurines come to mind in the latter connection. Figurines are known from burials,[5] and it has been claimed that female interments at Lubaantun were accompanied by female figurines, male effigies being placed with burials of the masculine sex (Gann and Gann, 1939, p. 18). Finally, one cannot rule out occasional use of the clay figures as toys.

CONCLUSIONS

Figurine traits underwent differing degrees of change in the Maya lowlands. Although the basic approach to the manufacture and decoration of human effigies contrasted fundamentally in Preclassic and Late Classic periods, many of the bird whistles are quite similar (figs. 1, 42). Certain Postclassic figurines are unelaborated versions of Classic norms, yet others more closely resemble the crude simplicity of the Preclassic. Most Classic figurine heads are realistically proportioned, but others are exceptionally wide faced. Figure 46 is representative of a rarely encountered, flat, wide-faced type which apparently occurred in Early Classic deposits at Piedras Negras. Head and headdress resemble moldmade examples at Jaina, which are commonly thought to date from the end of the Classic or early Postclassic (fig. 19). Such correspondences can be attributed to faulty dating, to the existence of a long-lived wide-faced tradition after the appearance of the characteristic Late Classic head form, or to a recombination of traits leading to the semi-independent development of partially analogous forms.

[5] In addition to the many occurrences at Jaina, figurines are more or less securely associated with burials at Nebaj (A. L. Smith and Kidder, 1951), Chama (Butler, 1940), Zona Sala (Blom and LaFarge, 1926–27, vol. 1), Palenque (Holmes, 1895–97, pt. 2), Hatzcap Ceel (J. E. S. Thompson, 1931), San Jose (J. E. S. Thompson, 1939a), Nohmul (Gann and Gann, 1939), and Mayapan (A. L. Smith and Ruppert, 1954b). All these occurrences are on a Classic or Postclassic level.

Temporal distribution of figurines in the Maya lowlands is curious in other ways. Important in the Mamom phase, figurines were apparently no longer made in the Chicanel and at best were of limited occurrence in the Early Classic period. The Late Classic resurgence, which witnessed the flowering of the figurine tradition, was followed by a marked Postclassic decline. This fluctuation contrasts with the unbroken tradition of figurine making in large portions of southern and central Mexico. Figurine manufacture may, therefore, have been reintroduced to the lowland Maya from outside sources.

On the other hand, the Maya interest in modeling, apparently kept alive by effigy adornment on pottery vessels, could eventually have contributed to the rise of figurine production. Modeled incensario-like objects occur as early as the Tzakol phase (Ricketson and Ricketson, 1937, fig. 191), and during Tzakol times human and animal effigies frequently formed handles on scutate covers. The greatest development of incensario modeling, however, apparently occurred late in the Classic period, more or less synchronously with the figurine climax and at a time when polychrome pottery had begun to wane. It is possible that the importance of ceramic modeling in general, including figurines and their molds, was in inverse ratio to the popularity of polychrome decoration. Along the same lines, Maya figurines attained some of their greatest development in places, such as Jaina and Palenque, which were peripheral to the Peten-centered polychrome tradition.

In Classic times, the area of most intensive figurine elaboration stretched in an arc along the western edge of the Maya lowlands, from Campeche to Tabasco and Chiapas, the Usumacinta River, and its headwaters in the Alta Verapaz. With the exception of Lubaantun, the eastern and central lowlands saw only a moderate de-

559

velopment of figurines. The importance of figurines in the west is consistent with the hypothesis that influences from Mexico brought about the reintroduction of figurines into the lowland Maya, or at least helped to revitalize the local tradition.

REFERENCES

Berlin, 1956
Blom and LaFarge, 1926–27
Borhegyi, 1956b
Brainerd, 1954, 1958
Butler, 1935a, 1935b, 1940
Coe, M. D., 1957a
Coe, W. R., Shook, and Satterthwaite, 1961
Cook de Leonard, 1959b
Danzel and Fuhrmann, 1923
Dieseldorff, 1926–33
Drucker, 1952a
Gann, 1900, 1918, 1925a, 1928a
—— and Gann, 1939
Hamy, 1897
Hay, 1940
Holmes, 1895–97
Joyce, 1926, 1933
——, Clark, and Thompson, 1927
Kelemen, 1943
Kidder, A., and Samayoa Chinchilla, 1959
Linné, 1956
Longyear, 1952
Lothrop, Foshag, and Mahler, 1957
MacNeish, 1954
Maler, 1901–03, 1912
Martí, 1955
Maudslay, 1889–1902

Medellín Zenil and Peterson, 1954
Moedano K., 1946
Morley, 1956
Peterson, 1952
Piña Chan, 1948
Porter, 1953
Proskouriakoff, 1951
Rands, B. C., 1954
Rands and Rands, 1959
Rickards, 1910
Ricketson and Ricketson, 1937
Rubín de la Borbolla, 1953
Ruppert, Thompson, and Proskouriakoff, 1955
Ruz L., 1945b, 1952a, 1952c, 1962b
Sanders, 1960a
Seler, 1902–23
Shook and Proskouriakoff, 1951
Smith, A. L., and Kidder, 1951
—— and Ruppert, 1954b, 1956
Smith, R. E., 1936, 1952, 1954b, 1955b, 1958
Spinden, 1913, 1957a
Thompson, E. H., 1897b
Thompson, J. E. S., 1931, 1939a, 1943b, 1946, 1954b
Toscano, 1945
Willey, Smith, Bullard, and Graham, 1960b